McGoldrick

Retail Marketing

Peter J. McGoldrick

Manchester School of Management, *UMIST*

The McGraw-Hill Companies

London • New York • St Louis • San Francisco • Auckland
Bogotá • Caracas • Lisbon • Madrid • Mexico • Milan
Montreal • New Delhi • Panama • Paris • San Juan • São Paulo
Singapore • Sydney • Tokyo • Toronto

Retail Marketing

Peter J. McGoldrick

ISBN 0077092503

Published by McGraw-Hill Education
Shoppenhangers Road
Maidenhead
Berkshire
SL6 2QL
Telephone: 44 (0) 1628 502 500
Fax: 44 (0) 1628 770 224
Website: www.mcgraw-hill.co.uk

British Library Cataloguing in Publication Data

A catalogue record for this book is available from the British Library

Library of Congress Cataloguing in Publication Data

The Library of Congress data for this book has been applied for

Acquisitions Editor: Tracey Alcock
Senior Development Editor: Caroline Howell
Senior Marketing Manager: Petra Skytte
Senior Production Manager: Max Elvey
New Media Developer: Douglas Greenwood

Produced for McGraw-Hill by Gecko Limited
Text design by Gecko Limited
Cover design by Gecko Limited
Printed and bound in Great Britain by Bell and Bain Ltd, Glasgow

Acknowledgements

The publishers would like to thank the many individuals, institutions and companies for permission to reproduce images in this book. Every effort has been made to trace ownership of copyright. The publishers would be happy to make arrangements with any copyright holder whom it has not been possible to contact.

Contents

PART THREE
THE RETAILING SANS FRONTIÈRES

14   International Retailing

15   E-tail marketing

Acknowledgements

I would like to thank all the people who have helped to maintain my enthusiasm for retail marketing. The encouragement of Martin Christopher, John Dawson and Bert Robenbloom was extremely important when the first edition was conceived, and since. Over recent years I have been grateful to the many reviewers, lecturers and readers who have encouraged the production of this second edition.

It is not possible to acknowledge individually all the retail managers who have helped me in my research and course development: their influence on this book has however been considerable. I would especially like to thank Sir Terry Leahy, Tesco CEO and Visiting Professor at UMIST, for his many inspirational lectures and for his continued support in our research initiatives. I would also like to thank the executives at Experian and David Wood for their excellent contributions to our courses.

Members of the Manchester Retail Research Forum have provided continuous support, guidance, initiatives and reality checks over the last four years. I am grateful to Sarah Charles and Peter Shotter, who have chaired this Forum, and to the members from Asda-WalMart, BAA, BhS, Boots, BT, Coca-Cola, Colgate-Palmolive, Exel, GfK, Kingfisher, KPMG, Marks & Spencer, A. C. Nielsen, Safeway, J. Sainsbury, Somerfield, Tesco and W.H. Smith.

Keeping track of a vast literature base requires the extensive help and co-operation of some top class libraries. I would like to thank John French, Rita Olive and their colleagues in the UMIST Library Service, as well as the librarians of Manchester Business School, the Institute of Grocery Distribution and the British Library at St Pancras. I am particularly grateful to the editor of Retail Review, Bob Hilton, and his colleague Linda Walkden at the Co-operative Group Library and Information Service.

The material in this book is drawn from many sources which, whenever possible, are individually acknowledged within the text. I am grateful to all the publishers and authors who gave their permission, usually freely, to quote extracts and exhibits. The book has also been influenced by many colleagues and doctoral students with whom I have worked at UMIST and elsewhere. I am especially grateful to Kathy Keeling and Linda Macaulay, for their e-commerce insights, and to David Lennard and Peter Barton, for their work for the Retail Forum.

In meeting the deadlines for publication, I am grateful for the timely contributions of Steve Burt, Director of the Institute for Retail Studies in Stirling, and Jonathan Reynolds, Director of The Oxford Institute of Retail Management. By taking over the major tasks of producing chapters 14 and 15 respectively, they have brought their additional perspectives and special expertise to the project.

At McGraw-Hill, I must thank Melissa Rosati, European Editorial Director, for her continuously positive approach to the project. I am also grateful for the fast yet fastidious work of the editorial team, notably Caroline Howell and Carol Lucas. At UMIST, I am especially appreciative of the help of Debbie Lee and Janet Denny, who converted most of this manuscript to electronic form.

Thank you all.

Preface

Many parts of the world have now seen a dramatic metamorphosis within the retailing industry, as retailers have ceased to play the subordinate role in the marketing of consumer goods. The power and influence of many major retailers now greatly exceeds that of their manufacturer-suppliers. This change has intensified the need for a rigorous and systematic approach to retail marketing. It has also created more exciting career opportunities within the industry, as retailers go out to recruit, develop and motivate this new and sophisticated breed of retail managers.

This book has been written for all serious students of retailing, whether they be practising managers or members of undergraduate/postgraduate programmes in universities. The focus is upon the functions and challenges of retail marketing management, but the subject matter is also relevant to those in related areas, such as manufacturers sales, shopping centre development, consumer research, consultancy, advertising and Internet services. Most of the examples and cases quoted relate to major, often international, retail companies, but many of the concepts and strategies explored within this text could also be exploited by smaller retail businesses.

Any illusion that retail marketing is a less rigorous or demanding discipline than product marketing should be quickly dispelled. In addition to the problems faced by any marketer, most retailers must also manage a very large product assortment, deal with the complexities and risks of selecting new locations, and successfully manage a constant and direct interface with their customers. To the manager, student or researcher, the challenges of retail marketing are both formidable and stimulating.

A scientific approach to the strategies and functions of retail marketing is advocated, while acknowledging the vital role of creativity and flair. Current and emerging techniques are analysed but it is not the intention to provide universal prescriptions. One company's winning formula can prove to be another's recipe for disaster. The approach is therefore to develop frameworks and guidelines for the effective analysis of management problems. Available theory is presented, when considered relevant, but certainly not exalted. Every effort has been made to present the material, at times complex, in a style that is clear and free of excessive jargon.

The content of this text has been derived form a very wide range of sources and evolved through the years of teaching retail marketing to undergraduates, postgraduates and management courses. Insights have been provided by numerous retail managers with whom I have worked, through research, consultancy, teaching and the Retail Research Forum. The research base of the text has been derived mainly from the retailing and marketing literature, but contributions from many other disciplines are also presented.

Having introduced the function of retail marketing in Chapter 1, Part One of the book follows a progression through the logical stages in planning retail strategy. Chapter 2 examines the changing environment and structure of retailing, making many international comparisons. In Chapter 3, the importance of correctly identifying consumer needs and wants is emphasized, both in building patronage and in maintaining customer loyalty. Chapter 4 presents some of the planning frameworks that can assist in strategic analysis, establishing strategic direction, achieving growth and positioning the retail offering. Chapters 5 and 6 are concerned with evaluating retailing performance, the former in terms of store image and brand equity, the latter in terms of productivity and profitability measures.

Part Two examines seven major elements of the retail marketing mix, Chapter 7 focusing upon store location decisions and techniques. Chapter 8 looks at the retail buying function, including developments in category management and the supply chain. Chapter 9 examines developments in retailer's own brands, including strategies of differentiation and supply. The many dimensions of retail pricing are the focus of Chapter 10, while Chapter 11 looks at the trends and major decision areas in advertising and promotion. Chapter 12 considers the in-store selling environment, from its overall design and atmosphere, through to the detailed management of space. Several key elements of retail service are the subject of Chapter 13, including techniques for measuring customer satisfaction with service quality.

Part Three, 'Retailing Sans Frontières', reviews two ways in which retailers have sought to expand beyond the boundaries of their domestic, store-based operations. Chapter 14 examines the ways in which retailing has internationalized, and the strategic options for development outside home markets. Business-to-consumer (B2C) e-commerce has been the subject of intense interest over recent years: Chapter 15 looks at developments, strategies and prospects for B2C.

It is recognized that some elements of retail marketing have now developed a massive research base that cannot be acknowledged fully within a wide-ranging text. However, in each chapter extensive references are provided to facilitate further study in depth. Review questions are also provided, as the basis for group discussion and to help individual readers apply the concepts encountered within each chapter. Further supplementery resources for lecturers and students can be found at the Online Learning Centre at www.mcgraw-hill.co.uk/textbooks/mcgoldrick.

One

Introduction to Retail Marketing

Retailing is an activity of enormous economic significance to most developed nations. In Britain, 2.5 million people are employed in retailing, comprising 10.5 per cent of all employees (National Statistics, 2001a). In the European Union as a whole, over 14 million people are employed in retail, around 20 million in the USA (Euromonitor, 2000). Retail sales in Britain exceed £200 billion, representing 36 per cent of total expenditure by consumers (Nielsen, 2001). Retailing is also a very visible form of economic activity, which exerts a major influence upon the lives of consumers.

In spite of its scale and importance, the retailing industry was not initially at the forefront in embracing the marketing concept. Manufacturers of fast-moving consumer goods (fmcg) were in the vanguard of marketing development, companies such as Procter & Gamble and Unilever often being regarded as 'universities of marketing' (Corstjens and Corstjens, 1995). As retailing became more concentrated, the major retailers started to wield their new-found power through aggressive buying, high-budget advertising and elaborate store designs. The use of marketing weapons, however, did not always indicate that the marketing concept was being applied. It is only within the last two decades that many retailers have taken an enlightened and integrative view of their marketing activities.

The marketing concept may be expressed simply, as the identification and satisfaction of customer needs and wants, at a profit. The application of this concept is not a simple matter, nor is it a problem that can be solved just by appointing a marketing department. It involves the development of a philosophy that must pervade all sections of the organization, from chief executive to the most junior member of the store staff. Systems must be established for monitoring consumers' perceptions and motivations, and for assessing changes in the marketing environment. Internally, an integrative structure must be developed which delivers a co-ordinated response to these opportunities and challenges, at a suitable rate of return. This is the scope of retail marketing and the subject matter of this text.

1.1 Evolution of Retail Marketing

This section examines the development and characteristics of the retail marketing function. Retailers are no longer subordinate components of manufacturers' marketing channels: major retailers now dominate marketing channels, having increased their power vis-à-vis that of wholesalers and manufacturers. Progressively, they have taken greater or complete control over each element of the marketing mix. Accordingly, the marketing function has progressively acquired a pivotal role within most major retail organizations.

1.1.1 The Development of Retailer Power

Traditionally, marketing texts have depicted retailing as a relatively passive link within the channel of distribution from manufacturers to retailers. Over the years, a vast volume of literature contributed to this view of 'downstream resellers' (Spriggs, 1994) within manufacturers' channels. However, this manufacturer-centred view of channels has seriously understated the power, scope and importance of retail marketing. Now it is equally, if not more, realistic to talk of 'channels of supply' within a retailer-centred view of the marketing process.

The dangers of regarding distribution channels as passive and orderly adjuncts to the manufacturer's marketing activities were recognized at an early stage by McVey (1960):

> *The middleman is not a hired link in a chain forged by a manufacturer but rather an independent market, the focus of a large group of customers for whom he buys.*

> *As he grows and builds a following, he may find that his prestige in his market is greater than that of the suppliers whose goods he sells.*

These early insights proved to be highly accurate: ironically, the USA was not the first country to experience the full effects of retailer power. Pommerening (1979) depicted a major shift in channel power by the 1970s in several European countries:

- 1950s: 'Manufacturer is king—post-war shortages and a fragmented distribution system place the primary emphasis upon manufacturing and supply.
- 1960s: 'Consumer is king'—increasing competition brought more emphasis upon marketing and the development of manufacturer brands.
- 1970s: 'Trade is king'—the more concentrated and powerful retailing industry increasingly took over the functions of marketing.

This movement certainly did not slow down after the 1970s, as major multiples continued to consolidate their positions. Their share of the UK grocery market, for example, was 61 per cent in 1980 but over 85 per cent by 2000 (Nielsen, 2001). A number of factors have been linked to this shift in power, including:

1 The abolition of resale price maintenance (RPM), from 1964 in the UK in most product sectors, left the retailer free of manufacturer stipulation of shelf prices. Now able to deploy fully the powerful weapon of price, the strong soon started to become stronger.
2 The development of retailer brands, both in terms of retailer branded products and the retailers' names as brands (Chapter 9), eventually started to overshadow manufacturer brands (KPMG, 2000b).
3 Concentration of retail trade, a trend not confined to Western Europe and North America. In Australia, the top five retailers command 43 per cent of retail trade, the top five in New Zealand 45 per cent (Euromonitor, 2000).
4 Terms of trade: horizontal market power, relative to other retailers, interacts with vertical market power, relative to suppliers (Clarke, 2000). If a large multiple can obtain major branded items for nearly 9 per cent less than a small multiple, this fuels further growth, concentration and buying power (Competition Commission, 2000).
5 Information: retailers no longer depend upon better informed manufacturers, they have their own scanner data (Farris and Ailawadi, 1992). This has also increased the control of retailers over supply chains, as their information drives the logistical and manufacturing functions (Dawson, 2000).

Table 1.1 illustrates the level of dependence of large suppliers now upon their top five retail customers. On average, these five customers handle 86.2 per cent of the UK sales of these suppliers, the top customer alone accounting for 38.4 per cent. This illustrates the relative weakness of the manufacturers in negotiations with these customers, who have the power to curtail a major proportion of their brands' distribution.

Table 1.1 Dependence of suppliers on major retailers

Source: Competition Commission (2000).

Major grocery retailers	Average % of suppliers' sales	% of UK retail sales
Top 1	38.4	32.2
Top 2	56.9	46.8
Top 3	69.7	56.4
Top 4	79.1	63.3
Top 5	86.2	68.5

The impact of this shift in power was not restricted to manufacturers: wholesalers found that they had been largely sidestepped by the major multiple retailers (Foord et al., 1996). The decline of traditional wholesaling occurred in part because 'they neither have the "store equity" nor the "brand equity" to differentiate themselves' (Ailawadi et al., 1995). Figure 1.1 illustrates how the role of the wholesaler within a 'conventional channel' has been largely bypassed within modern 'vertical marketing systems' (Dawson, 1995). To achieve co-ordinated marketing flows from points of production to points of ultimate use, some manufacturers have bought their way into retailing. Others, such as Benetton, have achieved similar results through franchising (Key Note, 1998).

On the other side of the coin, major retailers have increasingly subsumed the wholesaling role and many have also taken over the tasks of physical distribution. Alternatively, transportation and warehousing may be subcontracted to specialist companies, such as Exel Logistics (McKinnon, 1996). The manufacturer's exclusive hold over the design and production functions has also been eroded. Although few retailers have chosen to acquire manufacturing facilities directly, they can be closely involved in product design, raw material acquisition, performance specification and quality control. Marks & Spencer was the first retailer to be dubbed 'manufacturer without factories': others have now followed its lead.

In response to these pressures, there has been much regrouping and rationalization within the wholesaling sector. Following the decline of traditional wholesaling, some of the more aggressive cash and carry operators, such as Booker and Landmark, have filled the void (Nielsen, 2001), deploying buying, pricing and promotional techniques more akin to those of large-scale retailing. Another response has been the development of wholesaler-led voluntary groups (see Sec. 2.2).

Figure 1.1 Changes in the marketing channel

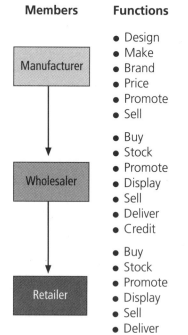

| **Conventional channels** | | **Vertical marketing systems** | |
Members	Functions	Members	Functions
Manufacturer	• Design • Make • Brand • Price • Promote • Sell	Manufacturer / Wholesaler / Retailer	• Design • Make • Brand • Price • Promote • Buy • Stock • Display • Sell • Deliver • Credit
Wholesaler	• Buy • Stock • Promote • Display • Sell • Deliver • Credit		
Retailer	• Buy • Stock • Promote • Display • Sell • Deliver • Credit		

Just as the manufacturers and many wholesalers lost power, so too did the majority of smaller retailers (Ailawadi et al., 1995). Consequently, there have been pressures within many countries to restrict the power of major retailers through legislation, akin to the Robinson–Patman Act in the USA. This sought to limit the power of large retailers to demand superior terms, regardless of whether these terms could be justified by scale economies (Ingene and Parry, 2000). In practice, through the development of retailer brands and other measures, large US retailers have been able to obtain superior terms.

In the UK, the issues arising from retailer power were referred to the (then) Monopolies and Mergers Commission (1981), then to the Office of Fair Trading (1985). In both cases, the status quo was broadly endorsed, largely on the ground that government interference could be against the interests of the consumer. It was held that regulation could raise prices, reduce service, restrict the development of efficient retailing and maybe lead to more importing, if discounts could not be obtained from home suppliers. These two reports provided regulatory conditions supportive of the emergence of a 'golden age' in UK food retailing (Wrigley, 1994).

Since then, concerns about major retailers' horizontal and vertical power has prompted various restrictions and remedies in Europe, (see Table 8.12), and investigations by the European Commission (McCarthy, 1999). The UK Competition Commission (2000) proposed a binding Code of Practice to place relations between supermarkets and their suppliers on a clearer and more predictable basis. It also drew attention to issues of local competition, where local markets were dominated by one or two major players. Overall, however, the Competition Commission (2000) recognized the benefits to consumers of most aspects of the status quo: as the Trade and Industry Secretary commented:

> *A competitive market is the best way of securing a good deal for the customer. The enquiry has found that the industry is currently broadly competitive and, as a result, I have accepted the Competition Commission's recommendations (DTI, 2000).*

1.1.2 Control of the Retail Marketing Mix

The concept of the retail mix developed alongside that of the marketing mix, although the degree of control that retailers could exert has been a function of the manufacturer–retailer power balance. In one of the first treatments of the topic, Lazer and Kelley (1961) defined the retail mix as:

> – *the total package of goods and services that a store offers for sale to the public.*
> – *the composite of all effort which was programmed by management and which embodies the adjustment of the retail store to its market environment.*

This early definition rightly emphasized that retailing is not just about offering products for sale, but a complex product/service proposition. It also stressed the importance of co-ordinating the mix with a programmed effort, focused upon the needs and opportunities within the market.

While manufacturers could exert extensive control over pricing and other elements of the mix, the scope for producing a co-ordinated and carefully attuned retail mix was rather limited. The shift of power, however, has given retailers far more scope to utilize the full range of marketing elements in pursuit of their strategic objectives. This has not only had a profound influence upon the effectiveness of retail marketing, it has also changed the very nature of consumer goods marketing.

Figure 1.2 illustrates the extent to which the control of key elements of marketing have shifted from manufacturers to retailers. This shift was observed in many European countries by Pommerening (1979) and has continued since then. While the extent and pace of shift has varied between retail sectors and countries, the overall trends are clear.

1 *Product design:* where retailers previously selected from among goods designed by manufacturers, retailers now specify, sometimes to the point of designing, their product requirements far more closely. In developing retailer brand ranges, clothing retailers employ fashion designers, while the supermarket retailers employ food scientists (Temperley and Kirkup, 2000).
2 *Shelf price:* following the abolition of resale price maintenance in most sectors and countries, this element experienced a drastic shift of control. After intensive lobbying by some retailers (Harrison, 2000), the last of RPM, on over-the-counter medicines, was removed in the UK (Retail Review, 2001a). Paradoxically, the adoption of category management (see Chapter 8) has recently increased the influence, if not control, of major manufacturers' over shelf prices within some categories (Competition Commission, 2000).

Figure 1.2 Control of marketing elements

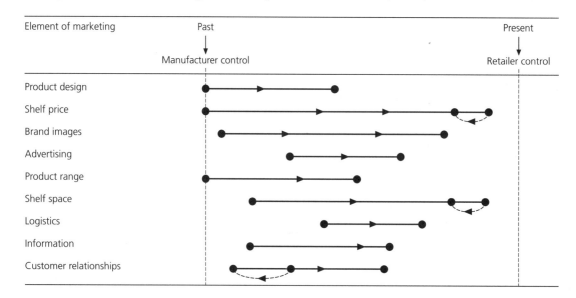

3 *Brand images:* the brand equity of major retailers now exceeds that of even leading suppliers. Brands such as Coca-Cola and Persil are powerful but restricted to narrow categories. The Tesco brand, on the other hand, is reinforced by their stores, staff, loyalty programme and Tesco branded products, including many financial services. Retailers have progressed from being just merchants to retail brand managers (Kumar, 1997).

4 *Advertising:* major retailers are now outspending most manufacturers, assisted by advertising allowances from manufacturers (Nielsen, 2001). They have also become more sophisticated in their multi-channel communication strategies, including broadcast media, published media, direct mail and Internet (Hamil and Kitchen, 1999).

5 *Product range:* retailers have become adept at assembling a product mix oriented towards their target markets, using diverse, sources both national and international (Liu and McGoldrick 1996). They are less concerned about stocking a manufacturer's full range, unless the incentives to do so are large (Smith et al., 1995).

6 *Shelf space:* although store sizes have increased, the demands upon selling space have increased even faster. Retailers now use sophisticated models to maximize the effectiveness of space allocations. However, where category management is deployed, the manufacturer(s) involved have regained some influence over category space management (Management Horizons, 1999).

7 *Logistics:* retailers have taken a firm grip on inventory management and the supply chain, using their own vehicles and distribution centres, or those of a third party contactor. The adoption of efficient customer response (ECR: Chapter 8) has extended the retailer's influence even further back up the supply chain (Accenture, 2000).

8 *Information:* prior to the advent of point-of-sale scanning, the balance of information-power was firmly in favour of manufacturers. With their vast funds of data on product movements, promotional elasticities, customer spending, etc., retailer are now in a position to sell this information, or to share it on a selective basis (Competition Commission, 2000).

9 *Customer relationships:* in the early days of chain store retailing, stores were often impersonal: customer relationships suffered, as large manufacturers spoke more directly with consumers. Retailers are now focusing far more on customer relationship management, through loyalty schemes and other means, shifting the balance of loyalty from brands to stores (Messinger and Narasimhan, 1995).

The renaissance of relationship marketing has prompted many to question the 'law-like generalizations' of marketing (e.g. Chenet and Johansen, 1999; Sheth and Sisodia, 1999). Indeed, the concept of 'the mix' has come under scrutiny, not least as it can create a fixation upon functions rather than focus. McGoldrick and Andre (1997) observed distinct waves of emphasis over three decades, as retailers collectively

Figure 1.3 Waves of retail marketing emphasis

Source: McGoldrick and Andre (1997).

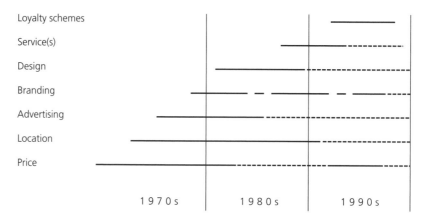

became obsessed with a particular element of the mix. As Fig. 1.3 illustrates, retailers' expenditures on advertising soared in the 1970s, design dominated the 1980s and loyalty schemes filled the pages of trade magazines in the 1990s.

Clearly, if many retailers focus upon one element of the mix, differentiation becomes less and other elements of performance are likely to suffer. However, it is difficult for retail strategists to ignore the hype that typically surrounds the arrival, or more often revival, of a marketing solution. From a study of low and high performance retailers, Berry concludes that there are no 'silver bullets' to solve retailing woes:

> *Today's shoppers want the total customer experience: superior solutions to their needs, respect, an emotional connection, fair prices and convenience. Offering four out of the five pillars isn't enough; a retailer must offer them all (Berry, 2001).*

1.1.3 The Retail Marketing Function

Having gained power and control over the retail marketing mix, this was not invariably translated into a truly co-ordinated marketing function. Many retailers have used the weapons of marketing without necessarily adopting an integrative and strategic approach to their marketing activities. To a large extent, this arose through the lack of a strong marketing function within the organization. While J. Sainsbury, for example, has had a large and wide-ranging marketing function for many years (MacNeary, 1981), the majority of marketing departments in retail companies were established in the 1980s (Piercy, 1987; Piercy and Alexander 1988). A comparative study by Greenley and Shipley (1992) found more established marketing functions in supermarket chains, whereas department stores still tended to be more sales oriented.

As the retail marketing function has grown and evolved, the external environment has become ever more challenging (Keh and Park, 1997). Over the last decade, retailers have had to cope with the threats and opportunities presented by tighter restrictions on stores formats, intensified competition, internationalization, new supply chain systems, e-commerce and much more. Managerial skills and competences are therefore critical determinants of a retailer's ability to operate successfully in a highly turbulent environment (Dawson, 1995). This has created the need for a new breed of retailing professionals:

> *The retail sector has some of the most innovative and successful companies in the world, yet it is only recently that retailing has become recognised as a true profession (Jennison, 1997).*

The impact of effective leadership in retailing has also become very apparent:

> *Good leaders are missionary they take their people a few steps further than they would go on their own accord. It would be out of character if they did not have a mission to become the biggest, the best, or the most profitable. But they are wise enough to achieve their mission in stages (Collins, 1992).*

Noticeably, the top three supermarket chains in the UK have appointed previous marketing directors to their posts of chief executive over the last 10 years. This is indicative of the focal position now given to the marketing function within highly successful retailing organizations. While there is still a culture of short-termism in some retail companies (Hogarth-Scott and Parkinson, 1993), others take a longer-term perspective and look to the marketing function to help pull together the many strands of retail strategy and operations (McDonald and Tideman, 1993).

Achieving an integrated marketing function does not necessarily involve drawing more and more responsibilities into the marketing department (Davies and Liu, 1995). Indeed, as the scope of marketing extends from the core of retail strategy to the extremities of operations, it is clear that the marketing function must both influence and interact with many specialist areas. Figure 1.4 depicts several core activities of the marketing function, and some of the other areas and activities that it must seek to integrate. Each of these is addressed in more detail in subsequent chapters.

Given the necessary ubiquity of marketing in all parts of a retail business, some have suggested that, within retailing and other service companies, everyone is in effect a marketer (Berry et al., 1990). However, it is equally clear that a company must pursue a coherent mission, while encouraging some empowerment and initiative in achieving it. One solution to this apparent dilemma is the concept of the balanced scorecard, which translates strategic visions into specific, measurable goals (Kaplan and Norton, 1996). These goals typically relate to financial objectives, customer satisfaction, business processes and the capacity of the organization for innovation, learning and growth. As the goals can be communicated to, and applied at, every level in the organization, the balanced scorecard has provided a valuable tool for linking and co-ordinating within retail companies. The scorecard is considered in more detail in Chapter 4, in the context of retail strategy and planning.

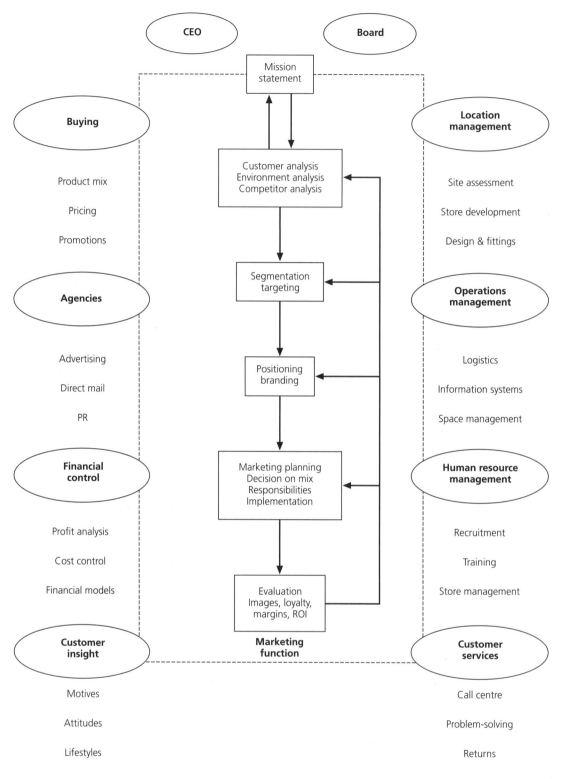

Figure 1.4 Integrated marketing function

1.2 IT and Retail Marketing

Few would dispute that decision-making in retail marketing, or indeed in any other form of business, can only be as good as the information upon which the decisions are based. The rapid progress in the development and applications of information technology (IT) is therefore highly pertinent to the evolution of retail marketing. Compared with some areas of manufacturing, the retail industry was initially cautious in its adoption of IT into management processes (Dawson, 1994). This was, in part, related to disillusionment with the failure of some early systems to deliver on promises (Hogarth-Scott and Parkinson, 1994).

By the end of the last millennium, however, the influence of IT had spread across the whole of the retail value chain (Al-Sudairy and Tang, 2000). No longer was IT the preserve of logistics and operations management, it was enabling and informing new strategies, increasingly influencing the very structure of the industry. Figure 1.5 illustrates how two areas of innovation, electronic point of sale (EpoS) and the Internet, have impacted upon operations, strategy and retail structure.

The Internet pervades every area of strategy, as well as enabling new forms of business-to-business (B2B) and business-to-consumer (B2C) e-commerce. Electronic point of sale, which started life as primarily an operational tool, now supplies the 'data warehouses' that underpin customer loyalty programmes, the basis of many relationship marketing strategies. The capabilities of EPoS to monitor demand and optimize stock have also enabled the development of scaled-down superstores and a new generation of convenience stores, offering wider, locally tailored assortments within relatively small outlets.

Figure 1.5 Examples of multi-level impacts

Level	Technology	Enables	Consequences
Structure	EPoS	Wider assortments in smaller outlets	Increased competition in city centres, market towns, etc.
	Internet	B2C e-commerce	Increased competition, especially for music, books, software, etc.
Strategy	EPoS	Loyalty programmes	Relationship marketing activities
	Internet	Retailers' websites	Price transparency Product information 'Clicks and mortar'
Operations	EPoS	Scanning and self-scanning	Faster service Better stock control Lower costs
	Internet	B2B e-commerce	Efficient consumer response Internet auctions Lower supply prices

This has intensified competition in areas not previously regarded as viable by the major retailers. Although falling costs make IT more accessible to small retailers (Cameron-Waller, 1995), it is the larger companies that have gained the most. Paradoxically, a major benefit of IT to larger retailers is the ability to overcome the problems of their size, enabling local responsiveness while harnessing the full power of a national or international organization.

This section takes a brief overview of three areas of technological development, each of which is examined in more detail in later chapters. First, supply-side IT is considered, from electronic data interchanges (EDI) to Internet-based links with suppliers. These technologies are increasingly interlinked, through sales-based ordering, with the 'front-end' EPoS systems; there are also many more technological developments at store level. Finally, home-based technologies are considered, as the opportunities and threats of e-tailing become increasingly salient.

1.2.1 Supply-Side IT

Before the arrival of electronic data interchange between retailers and major suppliers, the ordering process was characterized by voluminous paperwork, needless delays, incompatible systems and many errors. The adoption of EDI from the 1980s necessarily ran alongside the development of common codes and standards for the exchange of electronic data. EDI is defined as:

> *The digital exchange of information between the computer systems of different companies. In this context, it can be viewed as the replacement of paper-based transactions (orders, schedules, invoices and advice notes) with a computer-readable format, communicated via electronic media (Hendry, 1995).*

Electronic data interchange facilitates information flows not only between retailers and their suppliers, it also links their distribution centres, regional offices, stores, transport companies (if used) and, if appropriate, customs and other external agencies. As the transmission of orders and invoices has become almost instantaneous, so too have the links with banks moved from paper to electronic systems. Figure 1.6 illustrates some of the many information and product flows within the supply chain cycle.

Within the supply chain, the communication function has been described as the *glue that holds together a channel of distribution* (Mollenkopf et al., 2001). While there is some evidence of smaller suppliers and even some retailers being coerced by trading partners into adopting EDI, overall it has been found to improve relationships within the channel (Vijayasarathy and Tyler, 1997). The timely flow of information and the reduction of errors have assisted scheduling by suppliers and effective inventory management by retailers. Electronic data interchange systems have had a doubly beneficial impact upon retailers margins, both through cost reductions and sales enhancement, as Table 1.2 illustrates.

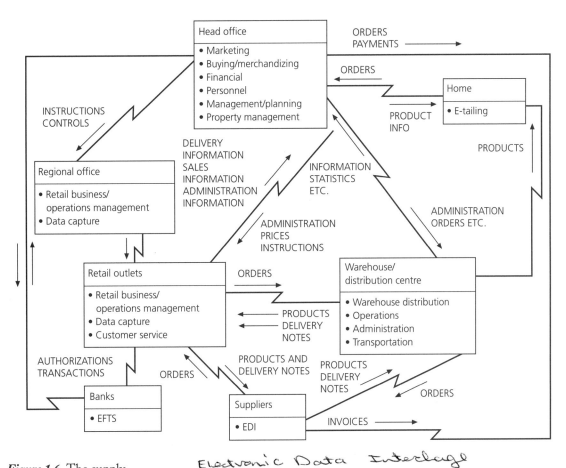

Figure 1.6 The supply chain cycle

Source: Adapted from Dawson (1995).

Electronic Data Interchage

While EDI systems transformed retailer–supplier communications over the last 20 years, the Internet is now playing a leading role in B2B e-commerce. Some question whether there is a continued role now for 'old style' EDI (e.g. Sawabini, 2001), in that the costs of entry to such private networks is higher than the Internet. However, in that major retailers and suppliers have invested heavily in their EDI links, the Boston Consulting Group forecasts coexistence of the two systems (Cross, 2000). The Internet's role is however expanding very rapidly:

> *The 'one-to-one' nature of EDI has been amplified by the 'one-to-many' capabilities of the Internet—the Internet allows many trading partners, or potential trading partners, to exchange knowledge simultaneously (Cross, 2000).*

Table 1.2 EDI and retail margins

Cost reduction →	Improved margins ← Sales enhancement
Less administration	Increased assortment
Lower stockholding	Reduced out-of-stock
Fewer buying errors	Improved customer service
Fewer markdowns	Swift seasonal adjustments
Better stockturn	Quick response to trends

Some of the capabilities of the Internet in the B2B context have already been demonstrated through the development of international exchanges. Sears Roebuck and Kroger in the USA, Coles Myer in Australia, Carrefour in France, Metro in Germany and J. Sainsbury in the the UK participate in the GlobalNetExchange:

> *Retailers input details of their needs and the system automatically aggregates the orders and invites tenders from suppliers. It also forecasts likely demand and could eventually also be involved in planning and distribution (Retail Intelligence, 2000).*

The WorldWide Retail Exchange (WWRE) boasts a strong membership of over 55 retailers, including Tesco, Kingfisher, Boots, Dixons and John Lewis (IGD, 2001). This exchange too expands the opportunities for global sourcing and 'reverse auctions', whereby potential suppliers bid for a large order notified through the Internet exchange . One member of the WWRE, Ahold of The Netherlands, believes that it may be drawing 30–50 per cent of its requirements through the exchange by 2010 (Retail Review, 2001b). The impacts upon retail buying of efficient consumer response (ECR), the Internet and other technological developments are considered further in Chapter 8.

1.2.2 Store-Based IT

A conspicuous manifestation of IT in many stores is the scanning of bar codes by EPoS systems. A prerequisite of these systems was the development of internationally agreed standards for bar codes, and their widespread inclusion by manufacturers on the labels of fast-moving consumer goods (Bol and Speh, 1986). The system in widespread use throughout Europe and elsewhere includes 13 digits, two for the country of origin, five for the supplier, five for the product and one check digit to minimize scanner errors.

By the mid-1990s, three-quarters of volume in food stores were scanned by EPoS systems in Belgium, Denmark, the UK and France (Leeflang and van Raaij, 1995). By the start of the current decade, this proportion had grown to 91.4 per cent of grocery volumes in the UK (Nielsen, 2001). Among most of the major multiples, including some convenience store multiples, non-scanning stores had become a thing of the past. The falling costs of EPoS make the technology accessible to independent stores too, although only 9 per cent of independent grocery stores are EPoS equipped (Nielsen, 2001).

Table 1.3 summarizes the many potential benefits of EPoS systems, in terms of logistics, productivity, buying, customer service and marketing strategies. Over the years of EPoS development and adoption, the emphasis had shifted from logistical/productivity gains to the benefits to customer service and marketing. In part, this reflected the early problems encountered by retailers in dealing with a vast glut of EPoS data (Little, 1987). To illustrate the problem for a supermarket chain:

$$
\begin{array}{rl}
600 & \text{stores} \\
25\,000 & \text{coded items} \\
10 & \text{measures per item} \\
5 & \text{bytes/measure} \\
\end{array}
$$

= 750 million bytes/week

While some of the analytical problems could be outsourced to agencies (Penford, 1994), the fuller realization of marketing benefits has

Table 1.3 Benefits of EPoS systems

Logistical

- Immediate recording of sales and rapid flow of information
- Stockholding can be reduced as less need for 'safety stock'
- Orders to suppliers can be automatically suggested or triggered (sales-based ordering: SBO)
- Deliveries can be better scheduled to reduce loading area congestion

Costs/productivity

- Faster checkouts, therefore lower labour costs
- Knowledge of transaction flows facilitates tighter labour scheduling
- Staff performance, at least in quantitative terms, is monitored
- Cost management is facilitated
- No item price-marking required (in most countries/states)
- Better stock control leads to more productive use of space for selling

Buying

- Buyers' records constantly updated, showing trends by product and by store
- Less reliance on external data sources
- Data can be sold to or shared with manufacturers or other parties
- Forecasts can be based on detailed knowledge of seasonal and local trends

Customer service

- Bigger assortment, due to better stockturn, and less out-of-stocks
- Reduced queues at checkouts
- Itemized receipts
- Fewer checkout errors (usually)
- Additional time-saving if used with EFTPoS payment systems or on-line authorization of credit

Marketing strategy

- Immediate feedback after adjustments in prices, product mix, displays, advertising or promotions
- Experiments and product trials can be conducted and monitored quickly
- Purchase patterns can be analysed to improve store layouts and inform category management decisions
- Analyses by time of day can advise decisions on opening hours and service levels
- Loyalty cards extend the scope of recording and analysis, providing further scope for relationship marketing

required the development of sophisticated, analytical skills within major retail organizations. These have given retailers deeper insights into the effects of price or display changes, using advanced forms of regression analysis (Rossi et al., 2000) and neural networks (Ainscough and Aronson, 1999).

Adding to their data warehouses, many major retailers operate loyalty programmes, enabling transactions to be linked to a specific customer. As discussed in Chapter 3, these function at varying levels of sophistication but the more advanced ones provide unparalleled insights into the buying behaviour of regular customers. Of course, customers must be incentivized to produce their 'loyalty card' at the checkout, with discounts of 1 per cent at least, over 5 per cent in a few cases (Mintel, 1999). While non-cash incentives can sometimes be subsidized or provided by a third party, the overall costs of loyalty programmes can consume around half of the marketing expenditure of major retailers (Deloitte & Touche, 1999). However, some consider this to be money well spent, given the extra scope for relationship marketing activities (Chenet and Johansen, 1999).

Alongside the development of EPoS has been the widespread adoption of electronic funds transfer at the point of sale (EFTPoS). Having become well accustomed to using credit cards in retail outlets, many consumers readily accepted the option of using debit cards (Antonides et al., 1999: see also Chapter 13). Although this means that the money transfers from consumer to retailer fairly rapidly, many shoppers appreciate the convenience of obtaining cash-back at the checkout. An EFTPoS system with on-line authorization also completes the transaction in about a third of the time taken to write and accept a cheque.

Information technology developments have not been confined to the checkout, with several retailers trialling mobile self-scanning systems, including Safeway, Tesco and Waitrose (Retail Review, 1996a; SuperMarketing, 1997). With these systems, registered customers take a hand-held scanner around the store, scanning items as they are put in the trolley. Although some must be re-scanned for security reasons, in theory this eliminates the need to unload then reload goods at the checkout. Mobile scanners have also been deployed in the hands of store staff, offering scan and pay service anywhere in the store or, for bulky goods, even in the car park (Retail Automation, 1996).

Electronic point of sale systems are not, however, error-free, usually because of staff failures to update shelf-edge price records in line with the price data on the in-store computers. Discrepancies in two to 10 per cent of scans have been noted in studies in the USA (Clodfelter, 1998) and in New Zealand (Garland, 1992), although sometimes the undercharging more than compensates for the overcharging. The latter are most likely to occur when the data file has not been adjusted for promotional offers (Goodstein, 1994). A solution may be found in another piece of technology, the electronic shelf-edge label (ESEL). These have been trialled in Connecticut by Shaws, a J. Sainsbury subsidiary, with 100 per cent at-the-shelf pricing accuracy (Retail Review, 2000). At $5–$10 per ESEL, they are still expensive but, with falling costs, are becoming viable in terms of labour savings and customer satisfaction (Retail Review, 2000).

While bar codes provide scannable product identification, other forms of tagging also provide security against theft. These are commonly used by clothing retailers but new technologies are being explored to make tagging feasible with lower prices. These include tiny tags that can be built into packs or bottles, so that items can be detected and recorded, without being placed on the checkout belt. For food products, there are envisaged: *'Minute, edible carbon-based 'tags', allowing any food item at all to be coded—at least until the customer eats the evidence'* (Mandeville, 1996). These technologies have the potential both to help customers, and to stop them from helping themselves. Theft of trolleys can also be deterred by the use of chip-equipped trolleys, detectable if leaving the car park area (Retail Review, 1996b). Another application for trolley tagging is the tracking of customers' progress through the store. This information can inform layout and display systems (Chapter 12), as well as providing faster service by predicting demands upon the checkouts at any point in time (Chapter 13).

In-store technology is also manifest in the use of kiosks, many of which now use touchscreen technology, offering a variety of functions (Keeling et al., 2001). Shoppers can acquire information about product locations and promotions: used in conjunction with loyalty cards, they can also print 'tailor-made' coupons for the shopper. Possibly the most extreme form of in-store technology is that which eliminates the need for staff, other than to replenish stocks. Robot shops, more common in Japan, are now appearing in Europe, including the Shop24 stores in Paris, carrying a small assortment of 200 food and drink convenience needs (Aubrée, 2001).

1.2.3 Home-Based IT   While the humble telephone has provided an electronic link for home shopping for many decades, it was the Internet that made home-based technologies a major focus of retail strategies. By 2000, 31 per cent of adults in the UK had a personal computer (PC) at home and many others used PCs at work, college or another person's home to access the Internet (Advertising Association, 2001). In addition, interactive television (iTV) services have developed which provide, arguably, more user-friendly access to home shopping, as well as banking and many other services. As Internet services improve their speed and quality, and as iTV expands its scope, the distinctions between them become increasingly blurred (PriceWaterhouseCoopers, 2000).

Table 1.4 illustrates that 14.3 per cent of households had used the Internet to make a purchase by 2000, with a somewhat smaller percentage using one of the interactive television services for this purpose. However, with over 50 per cent of UK households passed by broadband cables, 27 per cent of which are connected, there is clearly much scope for growth in these cable, satellite and other iTV services (Advertising Association, 2001). Overall, some 17.3 per cent of UK households had bought on line, compared with 10.4 per cent in Europe as a whole, 33.5 per cent in the USA (IGD, 2001).

Not surprisingly, on-line purchasing is strongly concentrated among the more wealthy, younger households, in line with Internet access and

Table 1.4 Purchasing via Internet or iTV

Sources: Advertising Association (2001) based on A C Nielsen Homescan data.

Ever purchased anything via Internet or interactive television	Internet %	iTV %
All households	14.3	3.2
Social grade: ABC1	22.9	2.4
C2DE	6.5	3.9
Life stage: pre-family	31.2	1.9
new family	15.8	5.5
maturing family	17.1	5.5
older couples	7.2	2.1

usage. Sixty-six per cent of ABs have used the Internet in the last 12 months, compared with only 20 per cent of DEs. The age bias is equally pronounced, 68 per cent of 18–24 year-olds having been on-line, compared with 25 per cent in the 55–64 age group (Advertising Association, 2001). The earlier Internet adopters have been profiled as innovators, impulsive, variety seekers and less risk aversive, characteristics that are common to early adopters of most technologies (Donthu and Garcia, 1999). As the Internet and iTV cease to be regarded as 'new technology' and enter the mainstream of household communications, annual growth rates of 21 per cent are forecast in Western Europe (Morgan Stanley Dean Witter, 2001).

Home shopping has not been the primary reason for most connections to, and use of, the Internet. The main reasons tend to be e-mail (34 per cent) and information on goods or services (22 per cent) (National Statistics, 2001b). However, this is indicative of the complementary role of the Internet as consumers search for information on goods, compare prices, etc. Those who do use it for shopping are motivated mainly by convenience and time-saving (Morganosky and Cude, 2000). Not everyone however agrees that the Internet shopping services currently available are quicker or easier than going to the shop (Advertising Association, 2001). Others are deterred by fears about security and/or the inconvenience of delivery timings (Dunnhumby Associates, 2000).

Chapter 15 examines the extremely variable forecasts for e-tailing's market share: one source predicts that over 17 per cent of books but barely 3 per cent of clothing will be sold this way in 2004 (Verdict, 2000a). Another suggests that 10 per cent of all European groceries will be bought on line (in value terms) by 2010 (The Grocer, 2001). However, these figures underestimate the overall impact of the Internet on retail marketing. Increasingly, retailers will adopt multi-channel strategies, as stores and Internet develop complementary roles within consumers' buying behaviour (KPMG, 2000a).

1.3 Theories of Retail Change

As a further perspective upon the development of retail marketing, this section examines briefly some of the theories that have attempted to explain changes over time in retail institutions, companies and stores. A detailed review of these was provided by Brown (1987), who observed: 'theory is a rather generous term for what have been described as little more than inductively derived generalizations'. There is merit, however, in trying to derive lessons from history, an area in which the retailing discipline has not been especially active (Alexander, 1997). Alexander and Akehurst (1999) call for a 'greater volume of traffic' between the disciplines of retailing and history. As in retail management itself, there has been a tendency in retail research to concentrate upon what is new, or just around the next corner, ignoring the insights to be derived from historical analysis. As Hollander (1986) commented:

> *longer-range, deeper and more macroscopic analysis can illuminate many important retailing issues. The past is prologue, not prototype, so while history may not repeat itself, it will suggest both questions and useful answers.*

In spite of their well-documented limitations, cyclical theories have attracted a large volume of literature, providing some insights into change in retail institutions. The most widely quoted are the 'wheel of retailing' and the 'retail life cycle'. A further generalization, the 'retail accordion' is discussed in Chapter 4, being especially germane to retailers' choices between strategies of diversification and generalization (Hart, 1999). In essence, the accordion theory holds that retailing, over time, tends to alternate between wider, general assortments and narrower, more specialized ranges.

The regularities suggested by these theories may not appear to sit well with the 'postmodern condition', which subscribes to the view that history is discontinuous, fragmented, contingent, context and locality dependent, uncertain, unpredictable and, above all, shapeless (Brown, 1995). However, if regarded as common strategic ailments, rather than as universal laws, then the early detection of cyclical symptoms can assist in effecting a timely cure. Indeed, in spite of an abiding suspicion of 'academic theory' among many practising managers, cyclical theories often resonate with their own insights and experiences in retail organizations. The two most widely quoted cyclical theories are therefore now examined, namely, the 'wheel of retailing' and the 'retail life cycle'. Other, non-cyclical frameworks are then considered, focusing upon the ways in which retail organizations and formats have adapted to changes in their economic, political, legal, technological and competitive environments.

1.3.1 The Wheel of Retailing

This concept was suggested by McNair (1958) and subsequently analysed by Hollander (1960):

> *This hypothesis holds that new types of retailers usually enter the market as low-status, low-margin, low-price operators. Gradually they acquire more elaborate establishments and facilities, with both increased investments and higher operating costs. Finally, they mature as higher-cost, high-price merchants, vulnerable to newer types who, in turn, go through the same pattern.*

Figure 1.7 illustrates the phases of the 'wheel', with the marketing mix and characteristics that could be associated with each of these phases. History reveals a number of conforming examples. Department stores, which started mainly as low-cost competitors to the smaller retailers, elaborated their style, eventually being severely undercut by supermarkets and discount warehouses (McNair, 1958). In due course, the supermarkets themselves started to trade up, unable to compete with each other on price alone (Bucklin, 1972). Similar tendencies have been observed among clothing stores, leisure outlets and other specialist stores, with the trading-up process tending to quicken (McNair and May, 1978). More recently, the concept has been applied, in adapted form, to the evolution of the retail warehouse (Brown, 1990) and to signs of trading-up by warehouse membership clubs in the USA (Sampson and Tigert, 1994).

Several possible causes of the wheel pattern have been hypothesized: the following list is adapted from Hollander (1960) and Brown (1991).

Figure 1.7 The wheel of retailing
Source: Brown (1988).

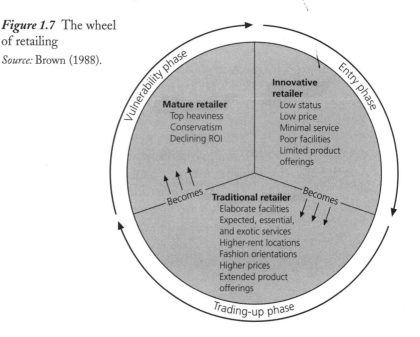

1 *Management personality:* becomes less cost-conscious and aggressive as the original entrepreneurs either grow older or hand over control to less dynamic successors.

2 *Personal preferences:* decision-makers are sometime prone to create environments and add services that they would expect themselves, in spite of most of their customers being considerably less affluent than they are.

3 *Misguidance:* examples are cited elsewhere in this book of retailers being urged by suppliers to invest in expensive design refits, advertising campaigns, extra services, etc.

4 *Imperfect competition:* fearful of retaliation, retailers avoid direct price competition, preferring to compete on services. This creates a ratchet-like process of cost and margin increases.

5 *Excess capacity:* as a format expands, the available business is spread more thinly. Price-cutting therefore becomes suicidal, so retailers opt for non-price competition.

6 *Rising expectations:* increasing overall living standards, especially in times of economic boom, persuade retailers to upgrade their offerings in line with consumers' rising expectations.

7 *Illusion:* the addition of higher margin lines may give a spurious impression of trading up, even though margins on the original product range may be unaltered.

Many writers have warned of the dangers of generalizing the 'wheel' hypothesis too widely. Kaynak (1979) observed that 'imported' retail formats are often copied from those already developed elsewhere: they may therefore start with an upmarket trading position, then subsequently trade down. Following a longitudinal study of electrical goods discounter Comet, Savitt (1984) complained that: 'the "wheel of retailing" pervades the marketing literature as if it were a law rather than an untested hypothesis'.

It is also unrealistic to assume that a company cannot turn back 'the wheel', although some would argue that this is simply a company reinventing itself at the start of the cycle. In a world where images are constantly tracked and positioning decisions are far more explicit, a company is now more likely to detect 'wheel-like' symptoms. In its celebrated 'operation checkout', Tesco regained the focus on price that had become blurred in the 1970s. More recently, Asda used the 'Rollback' promotion as a way to announce a return to an earlier price position (Verdict, 2000b).

1.3.2 The Retail Life Cycle

The retail life cycle, expounded by Davidson et al. (1976), attempted to overcome two of the most distinct limitations of the 'wheel'. First, the emphasis upon changing costs and margins does little to explain the evolution of retail forms that enter the market at a high margin position. Second, the rate, diversity and direction of retail innovation was becoming increasingly difficult to explain within the 'wheel' framework.

The product life cycle, from which the retail life cycle was derived, is a concept very familiar to marketing practitioners and scholars (e.g. Levitt, 1965). The idea that the retail institutions themselves, like the products they sell, have a life cycle was formalized somewhat later. The life cycle may be divided broadly into four phases: introduction, growth, maturity and decline.

Organizations at the introduction (innovation) stage are characterized as having few competitors, rapid sales growth and low to moderate profitability. As growth accelerates, profitability is usually rising, so competition starts to increase. At the maturity stage, there will be many direct and some indirect competitors, so profitability would typically start to moderate. As more, innovatory, indirect competitors develop, sales and profits will fall, placing the institution or format clearly in the decline phase.

Figure 1.8 illustrates these four phases, with examples of formats generally regarded as being at each stage. This also demonstrates the hazards of such generalizations, as there are many exceptions and international differences. Eurostat (1993), for example, illustrated that large grocery stores are at the introduction/early growth stages in southern Europe but well into the maturity stage in the UK and France. Neither can it be assumed that city centre department stores are all in decline, as the proprietor of Harrods would no doubt agree!

In so far as life cycles can be observed, these are becoming much shorter. Davidson et al. (1976) estimated that the city centre department store took 80 years to reach its peak share, in 1940 in the USA. It then took 45 years for the variety store to peak in 1955, and 20 years for the discount department store to peak in 1970. More recent evidence points to ever shortening life cycles, for example, among warehouse clubs

Figure 1.8 The retail life cycle

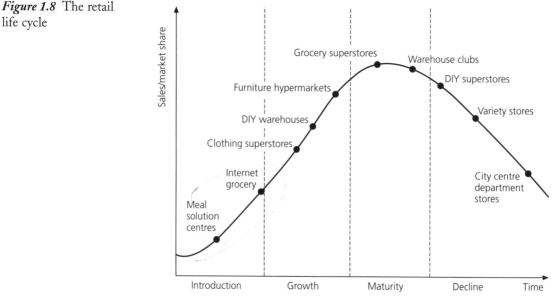

(Retail Review, 1996c). Burns et al. (1997) estimated that concepts born in the 1970s averaged 16 years until earnings began to stagnate, but the fall-off was coming after just eight years for some more recently introduced concepts. Shortening life cycles have a number of implications for retail strategists.

1 Long-term investments in expensive property assets must be viewed with caution.
2 A satisfactory return on investment needs to be achieved in a shorter timescale.
3 A retailer may utilize portfolio analysis (see Chapter 4) to assess the position of its various assets vis-à-vis the life-cycle stage of each, to protect itself from overall decline (Davidson and Johnson, 1981).
4 Sometimes a format should be superseded before it enters sharp decline, especially if this facilitates the sale of existing stores or sites. For example, B & Q replaced many of its superstores with 'category killer' do-it-yourself (DIY) warehouses.
5 It can take many years, if ever, to recover from an earnings collapse: renewal should precede this, even if it involves difficult changes within the organization (Burns et al., 1997).

1.3.3 Non-Cyclical Frameworks

All the cyclical theories suffer from the weaknesses of being deterministic and inflexible, focusing upon patterns rather than processes. In their simplest form, they ignore the influences of the economic environment and management tends to be portrayed as powerless to resist the cycle (Brown, 1991). Environmental and conflict theories, on the other hand, are more flexible, emphasizing the ways that organizations/institutions adapt to changes in the environment and in the competitive arena respectively.

The *environmental approach* holds that new or evolved forms of retailing are manifestations of changes in the economic, social, demographic, political, legal and/or technological environments (Meloche et al., 1988). Given the popularity of PEST, SWOT and other frameworks for auditing the business environment, it is entirely plausible the strategies should be formed that react to major changes. As these strategic audit tools are considered in more detail in Chapter 4, here it is appropriate to provide just a few examples.

1 Earlier in this chapter, the political changes outlawing resale price maintenance were seen to have a profound effect, not just upon suppliers but upon weaker retailers, previously protected by the maintained prices.
2 Similarly, the decision to legalize Sunday trading was opposed by many small retailers, who would lose some of their convenience advantage.
3 Economic downturns tend to provide fertile breeding grounds for discount formats, while exposing the weaknesses of less efficient, middle-ground retailers.

4 Technology, as discussed in Sec. 1.2, has influenced retailing in many ways. Over the years, the widespread adoption of the motor car, refrigerator and freezers have profoundly influenced how often, and where, we shop for food.

5 The fragmentation of consumer tastes and needs have left vulnerable the retailers that retain a mass market orientation.

6 Retailers that cannot refocus and refresh their appeal to new and expanding need segments are likely to perish with their dwindling customer base.

Some proponents of the environmental perspective suggest that a form of economic ecology or 'natural selection' occurs, with only the fittest retailing species likely to survive in the long term (Etgar, 1984). While Davies (1998) warns against the dangers of overplaying the ecological analogies, he adds:

> *It is common to see references to the 'survival of the fittest', 'natural dominance', 'natural selection', 'triumph of the best', etc., and to read about the march of retail progress supplanting more 'primitive' retail forms.*

The main strengths of the environmental frameworks are their flexibility, focus upon the 'uncontrollables' and their applicability in a wide variety of contexts. The historical analysis of Gowings of Sydney, by Miller and Merilees (2000), illustrates how this 134 year-old retailer adapted through wars, depression and many societal changes to achieve its great longevity. Quoting from Clark (1992), the authors observe: 'The story of the past should have the same effect as all great stories— It should turn the mind of the reader to the things that matter.'

Conflict theories, for their part, tend to ignore the wider environmental context, explaining retail change in terms of the rivalry between new and established retail institutions Within Gist's (1968) dialectical theory, retail evolution follows a pattern of thesis, antithesis and resulting synthesis (Pioch and Schmidt, 2000). In other words, when an existing institution is challenged by a new one with a differential advantage, it will adopt strategies and tactics in the direction of that advantage, thereby negating some of the newcomer's advantage. The newcomer may then adapt its strategy to maintain its competitive advantage. These mutual adaptations gradually move the retailers together in terms of merchandise offerings, service and price.

Retailers offering discounted prices and/or larger assortments have often provided a challenge to existing formats. In their early days of trading, Asda and Morrison used many old mill locations to provide spacious, certainly not luxurious, low-cost retailing environments. This challenged the current orthodoxy that discounting was associated with narrow assortments. The high street supermarkets, such as Tesco and Sainsbury, moved into larger, superstore locations to compete more effectively. Asda and Morrisons also developed modern superstores, causing convergence of formats.

At a later stage, the superstores responded to the perceived challenge of the warehouse clubs by introducing ranges of bulk packs, particularly in the larger outlets. The warehouse clubs have responded to diminished competitive advantage by adopting some of the trappings of superstores, such as additional services and improved shopping environments (Sampson and Tigert, 1994).

The crisis-response model provides an elaboration upon how retailers typically respond to the conflict situation. It suggests four stages in their response: shock, defensive retreat, acknowledgement and assessment, and adaptation (Dawson, 1979). The shock stages are often well documented within the pages of trade journals, with innumerable column metres devoted to the 'warehouse club threat' in the early 1990s, the 'Wal-Mart threat' in the late 1990s. If a threat proves to be too great to be countered by normal defensive measures, retailers are then forced to reassess their fundamental business models, including margin expectations, payback periods on stores, etc.

In common with all theories of retailing change, conflict theories have attracted criticism. Pioch and Schmidt (2000) observe that, along with the cyclical theories, they largely ignore the sociocultural and economic context. The limitations of retailing change theories have prompted two types of response:

1 The creation of combination models, incorporating elements of cyclical, environmental and conflict theories (e.g. Agergaard et al., 1970; Brown, 1991; Sampson and Tigert, 1994).

2 The suggestion that researchers should focus more upon the evolution of individual retailing institutions, increasing understanding of both the internal and external causes of retail change (Brown, 1991).

Indeed, these two approaches are not entirely incompatible. It is important to recognize that strategic planning in retailing has moved on somewhat since these theories were initially conceived. Major retailers are now more proactive in their environmental monitoring and strategic positioning, giving them more power to forge their own destinies. However, while incomplete and imperfect in many ways, the generalizations and theories of retail change still contain some powerful warnings from history. These may at least help strategists to identify forces and tendencies that contribute to the decline of institutions, formats and individual organizations.

SUMMARY

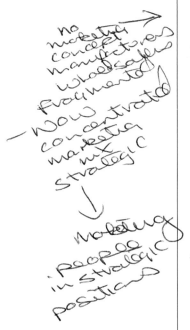

In spite of its enormous scale and economic significance, the retailing industry in general did not adopt the marketing concept at an early stage. For many years there was a tendency to regard retailers as subordinate, even passive, elements of manufacturer-led marketing channels. The rapid shift of power from manufacturers to retailers has forced a change in this view. From being a highly fragmented industry, retailing is now highly concentrated in many sectors, with some major retailers having grown larger than their largest suppliers. The use of legislation to limit the buying power of large retailers has been explored in several countries.

The more powerful retailers have taken an increasing degree of control over the elements of the retail marketing mix. With the abolition of resale price maintenance, the shift of control was most rapid in the case of retail pricing, but every other element of the mix has also become increasingly retailer led. Initially there was a tendency for retailers to wield their marketing power at the tactical, rather than the strategic, level. The last 20 years have seen the development of more co-ordinated marketing functions within many retail companies, although in others the role of marketing is still mainly at the operational level.

Well-informed and appropriate retail marketing decisions require the availability of comprehensive, timely and accurate information. The influence of information technology now pervades retailing at the operational, strategic and structural levels. Electronic point of sale (EPoS) systems, for example, provide many operational benefits in terms of stock control, automatic reordering, lower checkout cost and better customer service. Linked now with information from loyalty or other store cards, they provide the data to underpin retailers' increased emphasis upon relationship marketing strategies.

The Internet is proving even more pervasive, providing an alternative to existing electronic data interchange (EDI) systems between retailers and suppliers. This has opened up more flexibility in product sourcing, though on-line reverse auctions. For consumers, the Internet provides an additional channel through which to gain information about retailers, their products and their prices. With the parallel developments in cable and other forms of 'interactive' television, consumers' choices of home shopping options are also increasing.

Retailing is clearly a dynamic industry, subject to constant change brought about by economic, demographic, legislative, technological and competitive forces. Some writers have observed cyclical tendencies in the lives and trading styles of retail companies and institutions. The 'wheel of retailing' hypothesis suggests that retail innovators tend to trade up, leaving themselves eventually vulnerable to new innovators. The concept of the life cycle has also been applied to retail institutions, and retail life-cycles are getting much shorter. The 'retail accordion' holds that retail assortments tend, over time, to alternate between narrow/specialized and wide/generalized.

The rigidity of these cyclical theories have led some to prefer environmental frameworks, which see retailing forms as manifestations of changes in the economic, social, demographic, political, legal and technological environments. Some draw upon ecological analogies, holding that only the fittest retailing species survive the changes. Conflict theories, on the other hand, focus upon reactions to the arrival of a new competitive threat.

While all these generalizations have been subject of criticisms, they do summarize important lessons from history, underlining the need for positive, long-term marketing planning.

REVIEW QUESTIONS

1 'The middleman is not a hired link in a chain forged by a manufacturer.' Discuss.

2 How do you explain the shift of power from manufacturers to retailers in many countries?

3 Do you believe that the power of retailers will continue to grow? Justify your answer.

4 Focusing upon a retail sector of your choice, illustrate how the control of the marketing mix elements has shifted from manufacturers to retailers.

5 To pull together the many strands of retail strategy and operations, the retail marketing function must influence and interact with many specialist areas, both in and around the organization. Taking a retail company of your choice, illustrate the nature and diversity of these interactions.

6 Show how the information provided by electronic point of sale (EPoS) systems can assist in the development and refinement of retail marketing strategy.

7 The provision of mobile scanners for use by customers requires considerable investment in electronic hardware. Your director has asked you to draft a cost-benefit analysis of the introduction of self-scanning, including 'hard' and 'soft' costs/benefits. What factors would you include in the analysis?

8 Illustrate the ways in which the Internet now influences retail operations, strategy and structure.

9 Explain McNair's 'wheel of retailing' hypothesis, giving examples of retail companies or institutions that have (a) complied, and (b) not complied with this hypothesis.

10 Why are retail life cycles becoming shorter? Discuss the implications of this for retail marketing strategy.

11 Consider any situation in which an established retail format is facing new competition from an innovative retail format. How would conflict theory suggest that these rivals may react over the years to come?

12 'History is discontinuous, fragmented, contingent, context and locality dependent, uncertain and, above all, shapeless'. Discuss this viewpoint and its implications for theories of retail change.

REFERENCES

Accenture (2000) ECR2000—*Day-to-day Category Management Study*, Accenture, London.

Advertising Association (2001) *Lifestyle Pocket Book 2001*, NTC Publications, Henley-on-Thames.

Agergaard, E., P.A. Olsen and J. Allpass (1970) 'The interaction between retailing and the urban centre structure: a theory of spiral movement', *Environment and Planning*, 21 (1), 55–71.

Ailawadi, K.L., N. Borin and P.W. Farris (1995) 'Market power and performance: a cross-industry analysis of manufacturers and retailers', *Journal of Retailing*, 71 (3), 211-248.

Ainscough, T.L. and J.E. Aronson (1999) 'An empirical investigation and comparison of neural networks and regression for scanner data analysis', *Journal of Retailing and Consumer Services*, 6 (4), 205–217.

Al-Sudairy, M.A. and N.K.H. Tang (2000) 'Information technology in Saudi Arabia's supermarket chains', *International Journal of Retail & Distribution Management*, 28 (8), 341–356.

Alexander, N. (1997) 'Objects in the rearview mirror may appear closer than they are', *International Review of Retail, Distribution and Consumer Research*, 7 (4), 383–403.

Alexander, N. and G. Akehurst (1999) *The Emergence of Modern Retailing* 1750–1950, Frank Cass, London.

Antonides, G., H.B. Amesz and I.C. Hulscher (1999) 'Adoption of payment systems in ten countries—a case study of diffusion of innovations', *European Journal of Marketing*, 33 (11/12), 1123–1135.

Aubrée, H. (2001) 'Enter the robotshop', *The Grocer*, 10 February, 42.

Berry, L.L. (2001) 'The old pillars of new retailing', *Harvard Business Review*, 79 (4), 131–137.

Berry, L.L., L.G. Gresham and N.L. Millikin (1990) 'Marketing in retailing: a research agenda', *International Review of Retail, Distribution and Consumer Research*, 1 (1), 5–16.

Bol, J.P.W. and T.W. Speh (1986) 'How retailers can profit from scanners—an investigation into the uses of scanner data', in *Retail Strategies for Profit and Growth*, ESOMAR (ed.), ESOMAR, Amsterdam, pp. 225–245.

Brown, S. (1987) 'Institutional change in retailing: a review and synthesis', *European Journal of Marketing*, 21 (6), 5–36.

Brown, S. (1988) 'The wheel of the wheel of retailing', *International Journal of Retailing*, 3 (1), 16–37.

Brown, S. (1990) 'Innovation and evolution in UK retailing: the retail warehouse', *European Journal of Marketing*, 24 (9), 39–54.

Brown, S. (1991) 'Variations on a marketing enigma: the wheel of retailing theory', *Journal of Marketing Management*, 7, 131–155.

Brown, S. (1995) 'Postmodernism, the wheel of retailing and the will to power', *International Review of Retail, Distribution and Consumer Research*, 5 (3), 387–414.

Bucklin, L.P. (1972) *Competition and Evolution in the Distributive Trades*, Prentice-Hall, Englewood Cliffs, NJ.

Burns, K.B., H. Enright, J.F. Hayes, K. McLaughlin and C. Shi (1997) 'The art and science of renewal', *McKinsey Quarterly*, 2, 100–113.

Cameron-Waller, M. (1995) *Small Retailers and Technology*, Centre for Exploitation of Science and Technology, London.

Chenet, P. and J.I. Johansen (1999) *Beyond Loyalty: The Next Generation of Strategic Customer Relationship Marketing*, Oak Trees Press, Dublin.

Clark, M. (1992) *A Historian's Apprenticeship*, Melbourne University Press, Melbourne.

Clarke, I. (2000) 'Retail power, competition and local consumer choice in the UK grocery sector', *European Journal of Marketing*, 34 (8), 975–1002.

Clodfelter, G.R. (1998) 'Pricing accuracy at grocery stores and other retail stores using scanners', *International Journal of Retail & Distribution Management*, 26 (11), 412–420.

Collins, A. (1992) *Competitive Retail Marketing*, McGraw-Hill, Maidenhead.

Competition Commission (2000) *Supermarkets: A Report on the Supply of Groceries from Multiple Stores in the United Kingdom*, The Stationery Office, London.

Corstjens, J. and M. Corstjens (1995) *Store Wars: The Battle for Mindspace and Shelfspace*, Wiley, Chicester.

Cross, G.J. (2000) 'How e-business is transforming supply chain management', *Journal of Business Strategy*, 21 (2), 36–39.

Davidson, W.R., A.D. Bates and S.J. Bass (1976) 'The retail life cycle', *Harvard Business Review*, 54 (6), 89–96.

Davidson, W.R. and N.E. Johnson (1981) 'Portfolio theory and the retailing life cycle', in *Theory in Retailing: Traditional and Non-Traditional Sources*, R.W. Stampfl and E.C. Hirschman (eds), American Marketing Association, Chicago, pp. 51–63.

Davies, G. and H. Liu (1995) 'The retailer's marketing mix and commercial performance', *International Review of Retail, Distribution and Consumer Research*, 5 (2), 147–166.

Davies, K. (1998) 'Applying evolutionary models to the retail sector', *International Review of Retail, Distribution and Consumer Research*, 8 (2), 165–181.

Dawson, J.A. (1979) *The Marketing Environment*, Croom Helm, London.

Dawson, J.A. (1994) 'Applications of information management in European retailing', *International Review of Retail, Distribution and Consumer Research*, 4 (2), 219–238.

Dawson, J.A. (1995) 'Retail change in the European Community', in *Retail Planning Policies in Western Europe*, R.L. Davies (ed.), Routledge, London, pp. 1–30.

Dawson, J.A. (2000) 'Viewpoint: retailer power, manufacturer power, competition and some questions of economic analysis', *International Journal of Retail & Distribution Management*, 28 (1), 5–8.

Deloitte & Touche (1999) *Retail Benchmarking Study*, Deloitte & Touche, London.

Donthu, N. and A. Garcia (1999) 'The Internet shopper', *Journal of Advertising Research*, 39 (3), 52–58.

DTI (2000) 'Byers publishes Competition Commission report on supermarkets', *News Release*, 10 October, Department of Trade and Industry, London.

Dunnhumby Associates (2000) *The Millennium Shopper*, Dunnhumby Associates, London.

Etgar, M. (1984) 'The retail ecology model: a comprehensive model of retail change', in *Research in Marketing, Volume 7*, J. Sheth (ed.), JAI Press, Greenwich, CT, pp. 41–62.

Euromonitor (2000) *Retail Trade International*, Euromonitor, London.

Eurostat (1993) *Retailing in the European Single Market*, Statistical Office of the European Communities, Brussels.

Farris, P.W. and K.L. Ailawadi (1992) 'Retail power: monster or mouse?', *Journal of Retailing*, 68 (4), 351–369.

Foord, J., S. Bowlby and C. Tillsley (1996) 'The changing place of retailer-supplier relations in British retailing', in *Retailing, Consumption and Capital: Towards the New Retail Geography*, N. Wrigley and M. Lowe (eds), Longman, Harlow, pp. 68–89.

Garland, R. (1992) 'Pricing errors in the supermarket: who pays?', *International Journal of Retail & Distribution Management*, **20** (1), 25–30.

Gist, R.R. (1968) *Retailing: Concepts and Decisions*, Wiley, New York.

Goodstein, R.C. (1994) 'UPC scanner pricing systems: are they accurate?', *Journal of Marketing*, **58** (2), 20–30.

Greenley, G.E. and D. Shipley (1992) 'A comparative study of operational marketing practices among British department stores and supermarkets', *European Journal of Marketing*, **26** (5), 22–35.

Hamil, J. and P. Kitchen (1999) 'The Internet: international context', in *Marketing Communications: Principles and Practice*, P. J. Kitchen (ed.), Thomson Business Press, London, pp. 381–402.

Harrison, S. (2000) 'Shouts and whispers: the lobbying campaigns for and against resale price maintenance', *European Journal of Marketing*, **34** (1/2), 207–222.

Hart, C. (1999) 'The retail accordion and assortment strategies: an exploratory study', *International Review of Retail, Distribution and Consumer Research*, **9** (2), 111–126.

Hendry, M. (1995) *Improving Retail Efficiency through EDI*, FT/Pearson, London.

Hogarth-Scott, S. and S.T. Parkinson (1993) 'Who does the marketing in retailing?', *European Journal of Marketing*, **27** (3), 51–62.

Hogarth-Scott, S. and S.T. Parkinson (1994) 'Barriers and stimuli to the use of information technology in retailing', *International Review of Retail, Distribution and Consumer Research*, **4** (3), 257–275.

Hollander, S. (1986) 'A rearview mirror might help us drive forward: a call for more historical studies in retailing', *Journal of Retailing*, **62** (1), 7–10.

Hollander, S.C. (1960) 'The wheel of retailing', *Journal of Marketing*, **24** (3), 37–42.

IGD (2001) *European Grocery Retailing*, Institute of Grocery Distribution, Watford.

Ingene, C.A. and M.E. Parry (2000) 'Is channel co-ordination all it is cracked up to be?', *Journal of Retailing*, **76** (4), 511–547.

Jennison, P. (1997) 'The new professionalism in retailing', *European Retail Digest*, **14** (Spring), 11–13.

Kaplan, R.S. and D.P. Norton (1996) 'Using the balanced scorecard as a strategic management system', *Harvard Business Review*, **74** (1), 75–85.

Kaynak, E. (1979) 'A refined approach to the wheel of retailing', *European Journal of Marketing*, **13** (7), 237–245.

Keeling, K.J., L. Macaulay, D. Fowler, P.J. McGoldrick and G. Vassilopoulou (2001) 'Electronic kiosk provision of public information: toward understanding and quantifying facilitators and barriers to use', *Proceedings of HCI Ninth International Conference*, New Orleans.

Keh, H.T. and S.Y. Park (1997) To market, to market: the changing face of grocery retailing', *Long Range Planning*, **30** (6), 836–846.

Key Note (1998) *Franchising*, Key Note, London.

KPMG (2000a) *The Quiet Revolution*, KPMG, London.

KPMG (2000b) *Customer Loyalty & Private Label Products*, KPMG, London.

Kumar, N. (1997) 'The revolution in retailing: from market driven to market driving', *Long Range Planning*, **30** (6), 830–835.

Lazer, W. and E.J. Kelley (1961) 'The retailing mix: planning and management', *Journal of Retailing*, **37** (1), 34–41.

Leeflang, P.S.H. and W.F. van Raaij (1995) 'The changing consumer in the European Union: a meta-analysis', *International Journal of Research in Marketing*, **12**, 373–387.

Levitt, T. (1965) 'Exploit the product life cycle', *Harvard Business Review*, **43** (6), 81–94.

Little, J.D.C. (1987) 'Information technology in marketing', *Working Paper 1860–87*, MIT, Cambridge, MA.

Liu, H. and P.J. McGoldrick (1996) 'International retail sourcing: trends, nature, and processs', *Journal of International Marketing*, **4** (4), 9–33.

MacNeary, A. (1981) *J. Sainsbury: an Investment Review*, Capel-Cure Myers, London.

Maltz, E. and R.K. Srivastava (1997) 'Managing retailer-supplier partnerships with EDI: evaluation and implementation', *Long Range Planning*, **30** (6), 862–876.

Management Horizons (1999) *Profit from Category Management*, Management Horizons, London.

Mandeville, E. (1996) 'Tagging along', *Retail Automation*, **16** (2), 13–14.

McCarthy, N. (1999) 'An analysis of the European Commission's decision on the Rewe-Meinl merger', *European Retail Digest*, **21** (March), 71–72.

McDonald, M.H.B. and C.C.S. Tideman (1993) *Retail Marketing Plans*, Butterworth-Heinemann, Oxford.

McGoldrick, P.J. and E. Andre (1997) 'Consumer misbehaviour: promiscuity or loyalty in grocery shopping', *Journal of Retailing and Grocery Services*, **4** (2), 73–81.

McKinnon, A. (1996) *The Development of Retail Logistics in the UK*, Technology Foresight: Retail & Distribution Panel, Office of Science and Technology, London.

McNair, M.P. (1958) 'Significant trends and developments in the post war period', in *Competitive Distribution in a Free High Level Economy and its Implications for the University*, A.B. Smith (ed.), University of Pittsburgh Press, Pittsburgh, PA, pp. 1–25.

McNair, M.P. and E.G. May (1978) 'The next revolution of the retailing wheel', *Harvard Business Review*, **56** (5), 89–91.

McVey, P. (1960) 'Are channels of distribution what the text books say?', *Journal of Marketing*, **24** (3), 61–65.

Meloche, M.S., C.A. di Benedetto and J.E. Yudelson (1988) 'A framework for the analysis of the growth and development of retail institutions', in *Retailing: Its Present and Future*, R.L. King (ed.), American Collegiate Retailing Association, Charleston, IL, pp. 6–11.

Messinger, P.R. and C. Narasimhan (1995) 'Has power shifted in the grocery channel?', *Marketing Science*, **14** (2), 189–223.

Miller, D. and B. Merrilees (2000) '"Gone to Gowings"—an analysis of success factors in retail longevity: Gowings of Sydney', *Service Industries Journal*, **20** (1), 61–85.

Mintel (1999) *Customer Loyalty in Retailing*, Mintel, London.

Mollenkopf, D., M. White and A. Zwart (2001) 'EDI adoption in New Zealand firms: understanding proactive versus reactive adoption behaviour', *Journal of Marketing Channels*, **8** (1/2), 33–63.

Monopolies and Mergers Commission (1981) *Discounts to Retailers*, HMSO, London.

Morgan Stanley Dean Witter (2001) *Internet: New Media & eCommerce & PC Software*, MSDW, London.

Morganosky, M.A. and B.J. Cude (2000) 'Consumer response to online grocery shopping', *International Journal of Retail & Distribution Management*, **28** (1), 17–26.

National Statistics (2001a) 'Labour market data', *Labour Market Trends*, **109** (4), 528–529.

National Statistics (2001b) *Social Trends*, The Stationery Office, London.

Nielsen (2001) *Retail Pocket Book 2001*, NTC Publications, Henley-on-Thames.

Penford, M. (1994) 'Continuous research: Art Nielsen to AD 2000', *Journal of the Market Research Society*, **36** (1), 19–28.

Piercy, N. (1987) 'Marketing in UK retailing', *Retail & Distribution Management*, pt1, **15** (2), 52–55; pt 2, **15** (3), 58–60.

Piercy, N. and N. Alexander (1988) 'The status quo of the marketing organisation in UK retailing: a neglected phenomenon', *Service Industries Journal*, **8** (2), 155–175.

Pioch, E.A. and R.A. Schmidt (2000) 'Consumption and the retail change process: a comparative analysis of toy retailing in Italy and France', *International Review of Retail, Distribution and Consumer Research*, **10** (2), 183–203.

Pommerening, D.J. (1979) 'Brand marketing: fresh thinking needed', *Marketing Trends*, **1**, 7–9.

PriceWaterhouseCoopers (2000) *Consumers or Content? The Digital Dilemma*, PWC, London.

Retail Automation (1996) 'Going portable at point-of-sale', *Retail Automation*, **16** (1), 6–8.

Retail Intelligence (2000) 'Expanding the trading exchange', *UK Retail Report*, 111 (June), 94–95.

Retail Review (1996a) 'Safeway goes national with self-scanning', *Retail Review*, **222** (May), 10–11.

Retail Review (1996b) 'Beefing up the technology—instore and out', *Retail Review*, **219** (February), 7.

Retail Review (1996c) 'Warehouse clubs peaking on home ground', *Retail Review*, **219** (February), 6–7.

Retail Review (2000) 'ESEL—a concept still ahead of its time', *Retail Review*, **266** (October), 6.

Retail Review (2001a) 'RPM lifted from OTC medicines', *Retail Review*, **271** (May/June), 11–13.

Retail Review (2001b) 'Tesco tuned in to non-food challenge, aided by B2B exchanges', *Retail Review*, **269** (March), 6–7.

Rossi, P., P. DeLurgio and D. Kantor (2000) 'Making sense of scanner data', *Harvard Business Review*, **78** (2), 24.

Sampson, S.D. and D.J. Tigert (1994) 'The impact of warehouse membership clubs: the wheel of retailing turns one more time', *International Review of Retail, Distribution and Consumer Research*, **4** (1), 33–59.

Savitt, R. (1984) 'The "wheel of retailing" and retail product management', *European Journal of Marketing*, **18** (6/7), 43–54.

Sawabini, S. (2001) 'EDI and the Internet: can two generations of e-commerce co-exist?', *Journal of Business Strategy*, **22** (1), 41–43.

Sheth, J.N. and R.S. Sidosia (1999) 'Revisiting marketing's lawlike generalizations', *Journal of the Academy of Marketing Science*, **27** (1), 71–87.

Smith, G.E., M.P. Venkatraman and L.H. Wortzel (1995) 'Strategic marketing fit in manufacturer–retailer relationships: price leader versus merchandise differentiators', *Journal of Retailing*, **71** (3), 297–315.

Spriggs, M.T. (1994) 'A framework for more valid measures of channel member performance', *Journal of Retailing*, **70** (4), 327–343.

SuperMarketing (1997) 'Tesco self-scan pilot', *SuperMarketing*, 24 January, 5.

Temperley, J. and M. Kirkup (2000) 'CWS Retail: responsible product development', in *Contemporary Cases in Retail Operations Management*, B.M. Oldfield, R.A. Schmidt, I. Clarke, C. Hart and M.H. Kirkup (eds), Macmillan, Basingstoke, pp. 210–224.

The Grocer (2001) 'Net about relationships and loyalty—not money', *The Grocer*, 3 March, 13.

Verdict (2000a) *Verdict Forecasts Electronic Shopping 2000*, Verdict Research, London.

Verdict (2000b) *Verdict on Grocers and Supermarkets*, Verdict Research, London.

Vijayasarathy, L.R. and M.L. Tyler (1997) 'Adoption factors and electronic data interchange use: a survey of retail companies', *International Journal of Retail & Distribution Management*, **25** (9), 286–292.

Wrigley, N. (1994) 'After the stores wars', *Journal of Retailing and Consumer Services*, **1** (1), 5–20.

PART ONE
RETAIL MARKETING STRATEGY

Two
The Competitive Environment

INTRODUCTION

A prerequisite for successful strategic planning is a clear understanding of the major elements and trends within the environment of retail marketing. Without this, major opportunities are likely to be missed and threats to the company may well go undetected, until its position has already been undermined. For many years the retail environment has been subject to major changes in terms of competition and store types. Now the changes are becoming more rapid and more diverse, with increasingly demanding consumers and with growing competition between retail formats and between different retailing channels. A full review of these changes would be beyond the scope of this chapter and, indeed, would become rapidly outdated. The purpose of this chapter is to draw attention to some of the most salient elements and to identify major sources of current information on these trends.

The first section considers changes in consumers' expenditure and shopping patterns, examining some of the underlying influences upon these changes and prospects for the years ahead. Attention then turns to the structure of the retailing industry, starting with an overview of the main types of retailing organization, i.e., multiples, independents, co-operative societies, symbol groups and franchises. Changes in the number of types of retail formats are then considered, including small stores, convenience stores, department stores, superstores, hypermarkets, various types of shopping centre and some non-store formats. The development of, and prospects for, e-shopping are considered in more detail in Chapter 15.

2.1 Consumption and Shopping Patterns

This section offers a very brief overview of some key indicators of economic, demographic and behavioural change within the retailing environment. The analysis of expenditure patterns shows significant shifting between categories, with many of the projected growth areas being outside the current scope of mainstream retailers. Attention then turns to the changing consumer, starting with basic demographic trends in population, age and household structures. Less tangible but equally important trends in lifestyles and values are also considered. Finally, indications for shopping patterns are evaluated, notably the mobility of shoppers and shopping frequencies for basic commodities.

2.1.1 Expenditure Trends

The total value of consumer expenditure grew by 27.7 per cent through the 1990s in the UK (Nielsen, 2001), with continued growth also in the other countries of Europe (Advertising Association, 2001). On the face of it, this growth would seem to provide an 'economic cushion' to protect less efficient retailers, while more dynamic ones expand. However, this is not the case, as the share of consumer expenditure through retailer outlets has continued to decline, in spite of retailers' diversifications into non-traditional goods and services.

Table 2.1 illustrates the spending trends in four major categories. Each lost share, in the case of food from 12.5 to 9.8 per cent. As this decline reflects zero growth in food expenditure, the grocery retailers have been strongly motivated to search for growth in other expenditure categories, including health and beauty products, clothing and financial services. Their success is reflected in the fact that 'predominantly food stores' held their 16 per cent share of consumer expenditure, despite the falling share of spending on food. Clothing and footwear suffered a smaller decline in share, as category expenditure grew by 20 per cent. However, textile, clothing and footwear retailers were less successful than the grocers at defending their expenditure shares, which fell by 21 per cent.

Table 2.1 Expenditure through retailers

Source: Nielsen (2001), based on 'Consumer Trends' and 'Business Monitor', both National Statistics publications.

Expenditures	**1990 £bn**	**1999 £bn**
Total (1999 prices)	441	563
Food	55	55
(% of total)	(12.5)	(9.8)
Alcohol and tobacco	39	45
(% of total)	(8.8)	(8.0)
Clothing and footwear	28	34
(% of total)	(6.3)	(6.0)
Durable goods	3.5	55
(% of total)	(10.2)	(9.8)
% through retail outlets	**%**	**%**
All retailers	38.6	35.6
Predominantly food stores	16.0	16.0
Textile, clothing, footwear	6.4	5.3
Household goods	4.8	4.6

These data illustrate that consumers' spending on basic products does not continue to grow in pace with increases in gross domestic product (GDP) and overall spending. A far broader view of spending patterns is therefore needed to explore categories that have demonstrated stronger growth. Table 2.2 examines some of the categories with the greatest increases and decreases over the 10 years to the year 2000. Much of the strongest growth was outside the traditional domains of retailing, in leisure, financial services, holidays and medical areas. This explains the strong interest of the superstore retailers and others in financial services, and the continued advances of Boots the Chemists into optical and medical services (Retail Review, 2000a).

Among categories with the greatest decreases, some staple food products are conspicuous. However, it should not be assumed that all food categories are in decline, by any means. Although spending on butter and oils has declined sharply, reflecting increased diet consciousness (Mintel, 1997), margarine expenditure grew by 50 per cent over the 10 years to 2000 (Advertising Association, 2001). This reflects the success of high value-added, low-fat and cholesterol-reducing products. Ready-to-eat meals have increased in sales by 134 per cent, responding to the quest for convenience and, in some cases, healthier options (Mintel, 2001). Other food categories that have demonstrated real growth include pasta, rice, cereals, pizzas and fruit juices.

There are many problems involved in the forecasting of consumer expenditure, especially in the longer term. However, retailers do require such forecasts as a basis for their medium- and long-term planning. Significant changes in economic conditions or fiscal policy can exert major influences upon the use of credit, the savings ratio and overall spending. In times of recession, spending on basics tend to be fairly resilient, while non-essential purchases tend to be postponed. When times are better, household goods, clothing and footwear sales have traditionally prospered, although there is now much competition for increased disposable incomes. The relative prosperity of the late 1990s saw increased expenditure on housing, health, leisure, education and personal pensions (Morgan Stanley Dean Witter, 1999).

Table 2.2 Changes in household expenditures, 1990–2000

Note: based on constant 2000 prices.

Source: Advertising Association (2001), based on 'Consumer Trends', National Statistics.

Greatest increases	% change	Greatest decreases	% change
Stockbrokers' charges	191	Newspapers	−10
Cinema	157	Meat and bacon	−10
Self-drive hire	156	Television and video	−11
Novelties, souvenirs	120	Electricity	−11
Photographic and optical	117	Household soaps	−12
Spectacles, contact lenses	102	Milk, cheese, eggs	−16
Education	101	Bread	−20
Sports goods and toys	98	Gas	−24
Other financial services	83	Travel goods	−25
Medication	82	Tobacco products	−27
Other services	78	Tea, coffee, cocoa	−27
Accident insurance	77	Oil and fats	−28
Vehicles	74	Other fuels	−29
Cider and perry	74	Engine oil	−50
Air fares	72	Driving lessons	−51
Furniture, pictures, etc.	70	Sugar	−55
Betting and gaming	67	Shoe repairs	−68
Wine	65	Repairs	−72

Table 2.3 offers growth forecasts for 30 categories, based on Cambridge Econometrics data. The growth in audio-visual, information and communications equipment is expected to continue, as existing formats are rapidly superseded by new technologies. The projected high growth in expenditure abroad may appear a difficult target for retailers, yet involvement in travel services and in airport retailing, at home and abroad, can capture some of that share (Freathy and O'Connell, 1999).

These projections point to strong growth in the 'experiential' products and services, including holidays, recreation and electronic media (Schmitt, 1999). The home is expected to be part of the desired experience, with increased spending anticipated on furnishings and maintenance products. Such forecasts can provide valuable pointers for retailers, yet their evaluations must probe deeper than these broad category indications. They must also consider congruence with their brands, positioning and existing competences. Examples of successful and not so successful diversifications are considered in Chapter 4.

Table 2.3 Growth forecasts for selected items

Source: Advertising Association (2001), based upon Cambridge Econometrics data.

Category	2010 indexed on 1995 spending
Audio-visual, photo. and info. equipment	442
Communications	351
Expenditure abroad	327
Other recreational equipment	312
Medical products and equipment	390
Household appliances	250
Other durables	232
Household textiles	213
Maintenance of housing	204
Financial services	190
Package holidays	181
Furniture and carpets	180
Catering services	175
Tools and equipment	172
Other travel	169
Personal effects	168
Tableware and household utensils	166
Other services	164
Clothing	155
Purchase of vehicles	155
Household goods maintenance	148
Rail travel	147
Accommodation services	147
Footwear	139
Wine, cider and perry	138
Out-patient services	134
Recreational and cultured services	137
Insurance	136
Non-alcoholic drinks	134
Educational services	134

2.1.2 The Changing Consumer

Retail sales and expenditure data provide essential indicators of market sizes and trends, but they do little to explain why these changes occur. They do even less to pick out consumer needs and desires that currently are not being fulfilled. For this purpose, a close understanding of the consumer is required, and ways of achieving this are the subject of the next chapter. Here we will look briefly at some of the most significant aspects of consumer change affecting retailers. An extensive collection of relevant data, updated annually, is available in the affordable *Lifestyle Pocket Book* (Advertising Association, 2001). For those with bigger budgets, a wide-ranging review of changing consumer trends is published annually by Mintel (2001).

Significant changes are occurring within the demographic structure of the marketplace, which include trends in population, age and household sizes. The population of the UK has reached 60 million and is projected to grow by around 3 per cent, over each of the next two decades. This is largely the result of increasing life expectancy, rather than a rising number of births. As Table 2.4 illustrates, the population under 15 years of age is projected to fall over the next 10 years, from around 12.0 million to 11.3 million. Retailers targeting the teens therefore face not only increasing competition but also a market which, in demographic terms at least, is shrinking. By the year 2008, the number of pensioners will exceed the number of children for the first time (Retail Review, 1999a).

Table 2.4 Population projections: age bands

Source: derived from National Statistics (2000a).

Age brand	2001 %	2011 %	2021 %	2031 %
0–14	20.1	18.3	17.8	17.4
15–29	17.7	18.1	16.9	16.0
30–44	23.1	20.2	19.0	19.0
45–59	18.8	20.6	20.8	18.0
60–74	12.9	15.1	16.7	18.8
75+	7.4	7.7	8.7	10.7
Total (millions)	**59.9**	**61.7**	**63.6**	**64.8**

A tendency to defer childbirth also influences spending patterns within the various age cohorts. In 1990, only 30.7 per cent of births were to mothers over 30, which had risen to 45.4 per cent by 1999 (National Statistics, 2001a). Consequently, the number of childless twentysomethings has increased significantly, with implications for the spending power and patterns of that cohort. These young singles tend to spend more, treat themselves to quality products and go shopping more frequently (Smails, 1996). Subsequently, those having children later are likely to have more spending power to direct at their children: the net result is less under 15s but more spending per child (Mintel, 2001).

In 1961, the proportion of the population aged 60 or over was 16.6 per cent, which had grown to 20.3 per cent by 2001. By 2031, nearly 30 per cent of people in the UK are expected to be 60 or over, with clear indications for investments in pensions and other financial services.

As less and less of these older consumers will be dependent on state provision in the future, they present opportunities which many retailers have been slow to recognize (Burt and Gabbott, 1995). This age cohort will include far more healthy, affluent and discerning consumers than are portrayed by most stereotypes of 'older people' (Scase, 1999). As Harrison (1994) commented:

> *Forget disparaging terms like 'wrinklies' and 'empty nesters', which imply lonely, feeble souls. This new breed will be fitter and healthier than ever before. They will travel abroad and will enjoy experimenting with food.*

The ageing population is certainly a feature of most European markets (Leeflang and van Raaij, 1995). In terms of those over 64 years old, the UK is close to the European average of 16 per cent, Italy having the highest proportion at 17.6 per cent (National Statistics, 2001b). By 2020, it is anticipated that 43 per cent of the Irish population will be over 45, compared with 50 and 55 per cent in Spain and Finland respectively (Reynolds, 1996). These demographic shifts have implications not only for marketing but also for retailers' recruitment of personnel, with many now targeting more actively the over 45s.

The size and composition of households has also been the subject of substantial change throughout Europe (Leeflang and van Raaij, 1995). As Table 2.5 illustrates, nearly two-thirds of all UK households now comprise one or two people: the traditional two adult, two children household, so long the focus of television commercials, has now shrunk to 13 per cent. The fastest growth has been in the one-person households, attributed to rising divorce rates, more people remaining single and more choosing to live alone. This has implications for the number and types of household goods required, and for the sale of single portion convenience foods.

Even within many traditional units, there is now the 'cellular household', in which the ownership of duplicate televisions, audio equipment and other durables allows different members of the household to pursue their own lifestyles as and when they chose. Mintel (2001) observes that there are now more televisions than people in the UK, a third of households owning three or more sets. This fragmentation of household activities is also reflected in eating habits, with more snacking and differential eating times within households (Scase, 1999).

Table 2.5 Size of households

Source: derived from Advertising Association (2001); National Statistics (2000b).

Persons	1985 %	1995 %	2000 %
1	24	28	31
2	33	35	33
3	17	16	16
4	17	15	13
5+	8	7	6
Average size	**2.56**	**2.40**	**2.31**

Brown (1995) refers to 'plurivalence' as an aspect of postmodern popular culture, symbolized by expressions such as:

▶ 'There is no fashion only fashions.'
▶ 'There are no rules, only choices.'
▶ 'Anything goes.'
▶ 'Do your own thing.'

As changes in consumer habits and tastes cannot be explained in terms of demographics alone, researchers and practitioners have been developing more intricate ways of defining lifestyles. For example, the PRIZM system, widely used by marketers in the USA, defines 40 categories, based upon demographic, lifestyle and consumption data (Englis and Soloman, 1995). However, such classifications do not always transfer readily across national boundaries. Brunso and Grunert (1998) also observe that lifestyles can be category specific, for example, a food lifestyle, housing lifestyle or transport lifestyle.

Measures of attitudes and values provide insights into sociocultural trends, and can produce comparisons between countries and over time. For example, the Research Institute on Social Change (RISC) undertook surveys in more than 40 countries, providing an understanding of changing values and priorities. Concern for the environment, for example, was manifest at the earliest stage in Sweden, then spreading to Germany, then France, then Spain (Solomon et al., 1999). Through the early-mid 1990s, the British were seen to shift in the direction of greater stability/security, more interest in ethics and community, and towards a more globally oriented view.

Figure 2.1 Social value trends map

Source: based upon information supplied by Experian, developed in collaboration with Insight Marketing.

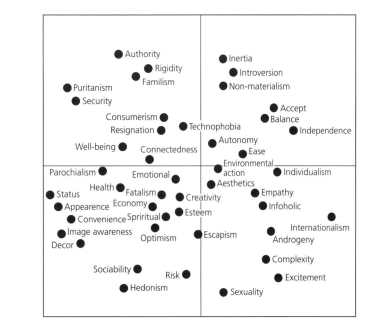

Figure 2.1 depicts 46 of the values trends that have been monitored by the UK consultancies Insight Marketing and Experian for over 20 years. The positions on this trends map illustrate the correlations between the various values: these measures enabled the companies to develop social value groups for segmentation purposes. While most of the trend labels in Fig. 2.1 are self-evident, a few are explained further.

- *Androgeny*: a blurring between feminine and masculine roles, i.e. a view that qualities like gentleness, sensitivity, independence and strength are not the preserves of one sex or the other.
- *Balance*: believe that drive and ambition are not crucial to success.
- *Connectedness*: every individual action, no matter how small, has wider repercussions.
- *Complexity*: important to see the possibilities in a situation rather than adjusting to 'facts' as they are.
- *Familism*: tend to be attracted to 'traditional values', such as family ties.
- *Hedonism*: believe that the pursuit of pleasure is what life is about.
- *Infoholic*: read anything that comes their way and are excited by new ideas in science and technology.
- *Resignation*: belief that there is no point in trying because it will make no difference.
- *Spirituality*: not necessarily religious in the conventional sense but believe energy can be channelled from the spiritual world.

The logic underpinning the detailed analysis of values is that a person's values or beliefs change only slowly over time, underpinning almost everything that they do. Attitudes and lifestyles, on the other hand, do change in the medium term, becoming manifest as behaviour patterns in the short term (Insight Marketing, 2001). Values may be seen therefore to provide a more stable map of longer-term change, and bases for market segmentation.

Some of the traditional and more intricate segmentation systems are considered further in Chapter 3. Many of the traditional segmentation systems have, however, found it difficult to cope with the trends towards individualism, social dissolution and fragmentation, often identified as elements of the 'postmodern condition' (e.g. Solomon et al., 1999). Cova (1996) expresses how the breaking down of conventional groupings has been followed by the emergence of new communities or 'tribes':

> *Modern society was conceived as an ensemble of social groups: socio-professional categories, social classes, and so on. Postmodern society, in contrast, resembles a network of societal micro-groups in which people share strong emotional links, a common subculture, a vision of life.*
>
> *[They] develop their own complexes of meanings and symbols, and form more or less stable tribes that are invisible to the categories of modern sociology.*

2.1.3 Shopping Patterns

Concern for the environment is widespread among European consumers (Leeflang and van Raaij, 1995) and retailers for their part are keen to establish their 'green' credentials (Knight, 2000). However, attacks on the motor car by the environmentally minded have had little impact upon car ownership or usage. According to Mintel (2000a), 59 per cent of men and 48 per cent of women regard their cars as important to their current lifestyles. So, in spite of environmental pressures and some of the most expensive fuel in Europe, car ownership continues to grow in Britain.

Table 2.6 shows how the proportion of 'no car' households continued to decline during the 1990s. While this decline was slower than in the 1980s, the increase in multi-car households gained pace. Bearing in mind that households are also getting smaller, this represents a major growth in access to a motor vehicle.

The growth in car usage has been largely explained by an increase in women drivers. While the male/female percentages with driving licences were 80/49 respectively in 1990, this ratio had changed to 82/59 by the end of the decade (Advertising Association, 2001). However, there are major differences in the rates of car ownership and usage in different types of area. Due to congestion, parking problems, other expenses and a wider choice of public transport, some 38 per cent of households in London and other Metropolitan areas do not have a car. This has clear implications for the role of convenience stores and the potential of e-tailing in these conurbations.

In most areas however cars are the most frequently used mode of transport for reaching shops and other services (National Statistics, 2001b). This has widened the competitive arena from immediate localities to much larger geographical areas. The impact of this upon retail marketing has been considerable: as shoppers became willing and able to select from retail outlets over a wide area, there have been two main effects:

1 Less attractive outlets, no longer enjoying a spatial monopoly, are forced either to compete more vigorously or to go out of business.
2 Large outlets can pursue greater economies of scale by drawing trade from a very wide catchment area, if their retail mix is sufficiently attractive to shoppers.

Increased shopper mobility had an early impact upon the retail grocery trade but now all sectors have been affected, to a greater or lesser extent, by this change. Schiller (1987) and Fernie (1998) have referred to 'waves' of out-of-town development, as more and more goods tend to be sold in out-of-town locations.

Table 2.6 Car ownership in Britain

Source: Nielsen (2001), based on Target Group Index.

Households with:	1980	1990	1999
No car	39	29	24
One car	44	46	41
Two or more cars	17	25	35

Increasing environmental concerns and government restrictions are now slowing this trend (Ibrahim and McGoldrick, 2002), although not before shopping patterns have been profoundly altered. A combination of strong assortments, less crowds (in some cases) and easy, free parking have provided strong attractions to the out-of-town formats (Stimson, 1994). However, congestion is no longer limited to city areas, the loading of motorways having more than doubled between 1981 and 2000 (National Statistics, 2001b). Dour forecasts of increased suburban and inter-urban congestion suggest that, while car availability will grow, real accessibility will decline sharply.

The impact of the shift towards longer distance, primarily car-borne shopping is manifest in a relatively low frequency shopping pattern, by European standards. Table 2.7 compares the frequency with which shoppers patronize their primary grocery stores in 16 European countries. The contrasts become even more striking if extended to Eastern European countries, where a third of people shopped daily (Mueller and Broderick, 1995). However, shopping patterns there are changing rapidly, with increased car ownership and the arrival of many international retailers, including Tesco (see Chapter 14).

The UK frequency is far lower if the analysis is confined to the major superstore retailers, to which weekly visits are the norm. The frequency of shopping at Co-op stores actually increased significantly after 1996, reflecting that organization's switch of emphasis from superstores to high street and convenience store retailing (Neilsen, 2001). The arrival of the Aldi and Netto discount stores also increased the overall number of shopping visits among those who patronized both superstores, for choice, and discounters, for low prices (Schmidt et al., 1994).

For the majority, however, less frequent shopping for basic commodities is a desirable objective, being a logical response to 'time poverty', real or perceived. With over 90 per cent of households now owning a freezer (Advertising Association, 2001), most could extend the shopping cycle further, subject to the constraints of storage space and product shelf-lives. However, Barton and McGoldrick (2001) identified surprisingly high levels of domestic out-of-stock, suggesting that

Table 2.7 Visits per week to primary grocery store

Source: Bell (1999), based on Nielsen data.

Country	Visits per week	Country	Visits per week
Greece	4.37	Italy	2.27
Norway	2.89	Ireland	2.04
Finland	2.85	Germany	2.01
Austria	2.50	Portugal	1.89
Denmark	2.50	UK	1.81
Spain	2.47	Belgium	1.76
The Netherlands	2.39	Luxembourg	1.73
Sweden	2.32	France	1.67
		Total Europe	2.14

consumers' inventory management systems had not fully adapted to longer shopping cycles. This suggests a continued role for convenience, 'top-up' shops, as well as opportunities for electronic, in-home inventory management systems.

2.2 Types of Retailing Organization

This section now looks at one important element of the competitive environment of retailing, namely, the main types of retailing organization. As noted in Chapter 1, the increased power of retailers within the marketing channel would not have come about without the rapid growth of the larger retailers. The shift of trade between independents and multiples is considered first, with the position of the largest multiples in the UK compared with those elsewhere in the world. Attention is then given to co-operative societies and symbol groups, both of which have retained a significant presence, especially in the grocery sector. Finally, the growth of franchising, both nationally and internationally, is considered.

2.2.1 Multiples v. Independents

One of the most significant features of retail industry structure has been the increasing proportion of trade taken by multiples, at the expense of other types of organization. Multiples are usually referred to as 'corporate chains' in the USA. In Europe, different sources have variously defined a multiple as a retailer with at least two, five or ten outlets, so caution is advised when comparing data.

The growth of retailer power, already discussed in Chapter 1, has been driven by the growth of the major multiple organizations. Figure 2.2 summarizes a 'virtuous circle' of growth and power, as each unit of growth can create improved buying power and economies of scale. The most obvious manifestation of buying power is in the terms obtained in the supply of goods (Competition Commission, 2000; see also Chapter 8). However, the powerful retailer also has advantages in recruiting staff, in acquisitions and in the services that it buys from outside suppliers, such as advertising agencies, accounting, legal services, etc.

Economies of scale naturally flow from the ability to develop products, store formats, advertising messages and a brand image that can be rolled out over a larger number of locations. The appropriate calibre of management expertise is also a valuable asset, the shortage of which can represent a major entry barrier to prospective competitors (Gable et al., 1995). The supply chain is another area in which major retailers have sought to maximize their scale advantages:

> *A business like Tesco will, every year, work hard to improve buying terms and supply-chain efficiency.*
>
> *According to Tesco, since the mid 1990s, it has been unlocking around 0.2% of margin gain every year through this route in the UK alone (Fowler et al., 1999).*

These margin gains enable a retailer to offer more customer value in a number of different ways, through more competitive pricing and/or

Figure 2.2 Multiples'
growth cycle

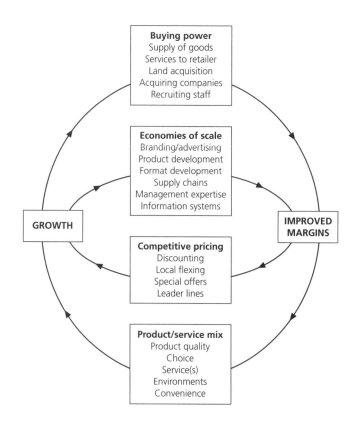

improvements in its product/service mix. This is the crucial stage of converting past growth into future growth, by focusing margin gains upon benefits of maximum relevance to the target clientele. However, if growth is bought at too great a cost, buying power may increase but overall profits will decline, restricting options for further growth.

Indeed, if the arrows in Fig. 2.2 are reversed, and the captions adapted accordingly, this would summarize the vicious circle in which many independents and weaker multiples have found themselves. A weak buying position and an absence of scale economies depletes margins, making it necessary to raise prices and/or economize on products and services. This leads to decline and further weakening of the organization's position.

This cycle of growth or decline helps to explain why multiples cannot be content simply to maintain their shares, if the industry or sector overall is becoming more highly concentrated. This process of concentration has been traced back to the start of the last century but gathered pace in the latter half (Nielsen, 2001). Grocery multiples held around 20 per cent of sector share in 1950, but commanded around 84 per cent by the year 2000.

Table 2.8 illustrates the concentration levels in five sectors of UK retailing, although the estimates of these vary between data sources. Mintel (2000b), for example, credits the top three grocery retailers with a combined share of 47.1 per cent, whereas the Institute of Grocery Distribution (IGD) data place their combined share at 36.3 per cent

Sector / Company	Share %	
Womenswear	**1995**	**1999**
Marks & Spencer	16.3	13.5
Arcadia	7.6	11.3
Next	3.2	4.7
Debenhams	4.6	4.6
New Look	1.6	3.0
BhS	2.5	2.4
C&A	2.8	2.1
Asda	1.0	2.1
House of Fraser	2.0	2.1
Littlewoods	2.2	1.7
John Lewis	1.1	1.3
River Island	1.4	1.2
Etam	1.5	1.2
Matalan	0.7	1.1
Tesco	0.7	1.0
Menswear	**1996**	**2000**
Marks & Spencer	13.6	11.4
Arcadia	7.6	6.8
Next	4.0	5.7
Debenhams	4.0	3.9
C&A	2.4	2.4
Matalan	1.0	2.5
Moss Bros	2.1	2.4
Asda	1.6	2.2
House of Fraser	1.9	2.0
River Island	2.1	1.8
Gap	1.0	1.5
Ciro Citterio	0.8	1.3
John Lewis	1.1	1.2
Littlewoods	1.6	1.1
Tesco	0.5	0.7

Sector / Company	Share %	
Grocery	**1993**	**1999**
Tesco	10.4	15.6
Sainsbury	12.1	11.8
Asda	6.5	8.9
Safeway	7.5	7.4
Somerfield	4.3	6.2
Kwik Save		4.1
Morrisons	1.9	3.0
Marks & Spencer	3.0	2.9
Waitrose	1.6	1.9
Iceland	1.6	1.9
Furniture/floor coverings	**1995**	**1999**
MFI	11.6	7.5
GUS/Argos	4.8	4.9
IKEA	2.2	4.2
DFS	2.8	4.1
Harveys	1.4	2.6
Courts	1.9	2.6
John Lewis	2.2	2.3
HomeMark	2.0	2.0
Littlewoods	1.5	1.9
Marks & Spencer	1.8	1.7
Magnet	1.1	1.7
Electricals	**1995**	**1998**
Dixon Group	20.5	27.0
including: Dixons		6.7
Currys		12.0
PC World		6.6
Comet	6.4	8.1
Scottish Power	2.7	2.5
Powerhouse	1.0	1.3

Table 2.8 Sector shares of leading multiples

Source: compiled from various issues of Retail Review, based on estimates from Verdict Research and the Institute of Grocery Distribution.

(Retail Review, 2000b). These contrasts arise from different definitions of what comprise 'groceries' and 'grocers'. The Competition Commission (2000) restricted its comparisons to: 'The market for one stop grocery shopping, carried out in stores of 1,400 sq. metres or more.' Using this definition, the top three grocers were attributed with a considerably higher share of 58.7 per cent. While these different data-sets reveal the same competitive trends between companies and over time, the different definitions make comparisons between data sources more hazardous. It is clearly important to recognize the bases upon which market share data have been calculated, as they can lead to very different conclusions.

Even the more conservative estimates of the IGD show continued concentration of share in the grocery sector, largely through the growth of Tesco and Asda. However, the same is not true of the menswear sector, where the two leading players, Marks & Spencer and the Arcadia group, both lost share between 1996 and 2000. Clearly, buying power and economies of scale drive continued growth only if those advantages are focused upon satisfying customer needs more effectively than the competition.

Noticeable in the menswear sector is the growth of discounter Matalan, increased clothing sales in supermarkets, especially Asda, and the progress of Next's more fashionable ranges. Similar trends may be detected in the womenswear sector, although here Arcadia achieved more progress through its various formats (see Chapter 4). The importance of a strong statement on fashion, quality and/or price is becoming clear in the clothing sectors, as middle-ground generalists find life more difficult. Indeed, the analysis of these trends underpinned the decision by C&A to exit the UK market in 2001. The problems of some market leaders can open up more opportunities for successful independents, although in practice other, well-focused multiples are the main beneficiaries.

While expenditures on furnishings grew rapidly through the 1990s (Advertising Association, 2001), the market leadership of MFI became increasingly challenged by IKEA and DFS, with the combined GUS/Argos also holding nearly 5 per cent. Again, the leader's loss of share has been attributed to a lapse in customer focus (Retail Review, 2000c). In the electricals sector, the Dixons Group has gained very clear leadership, only two other specialists having shares of over 2 per cent. However, Argos also claims nearly 5 per cent of this sector (Retail Review, 1999b). In the DIY sector, there is now a very high degree of concentration, the top three companies accounting for nearly 74 per cent of trade since the merging of Focus, Do It All, Wickes and Great Mills (Retail Review, 2000d):

- B & Q 32.6 per cent
- Focus 22.6 per cent
- Homebase 18.5 per cent

In judging the impact of industry concentration upon consumer choice, it is important to examine market shares at local level (Clarke et al., 1994). The Competition Commission (2000) concluded that most consumers travel no more than 15 minutes for their regular grocery shopping, although of course they may travel much further to find the furniture or clothes of their choice. Table 2.9 illustrates marked contrasts between the leading grocers' market shares in six regions of the UK. In Northern Ireland, Tesco holds almost double its national share of one-stop grocery shopping, whereas Asda is not represented there. On the other hand, Asda holds a larger share than Tesco in northern Britain.

The high levels of local concentration have led analysts to conclude that there is now limited scope for further mergers within certain retail

Region	Tesco	Sainsbury	Asda
N. Ireland	46.5	17.4	0.0
Scotland	19.1	6.3	19.3
North East	5.7	9.8	24.0
North West	18.8	14.1	24.8
Yorkshire	16.2	13.7	19.1
Wales	31.5	1.1	15.7
West Midlands	18.5	22.6	13.9
East Midlands	18.4	18.3	14.2
South West	28.8	21.0	10.0
South East	31.5	27.2	8.9
London	23.6	35.9	6.0
East Anglia	36.8	25.0	8.1

Table 2.9 Regional shares of three major grocers

Note: based upon the Commission's definition of market shares, which are not comparable with those in Table 2.8.

Source: Competition Commission (2000).

Table 2.10 Concentration of retail trade

Source: derived from Euromonitor (2000a).

sectors (Morgan Stanley Dean Witter, 2000). However, the levels of overall retail concentration in the UK are no longer exceptionally high, by international standards. Table 2.10 shows that the top five retailers in The Netherlands hold 63.5 per cent of retail trade, Royal Ahold alone having over 30 per cent. This compares with Tesco's 7.2 per cent in the UK, when expressed as a proportion of total retail trade (Euromonitor, 2000a). Paradoxically, this in effect gives UK retailers more scope to expand into other sectors, rather than to expand further within their own areas of specialism.

Concentration is also high in Australia (Treadgold, 1996), where Coles Myer and Woolworth hold 19.0 and 15.5 per cent respectively of retail trade. In New Zealand, the Foodstuffs Group and Progressive Enterprises hold shares of 19.1 and 10.7 per cent respectively.

Country	% Trade by top		Country	% Trade by top	
	Five	**Ten**		**Five**	**Ten**
Australia	43.1	49.3	Indonesia	4.7	6.4
Argentina	9.0	11.9	Japan	5.1	7.6
Belgium	24.2	28.8	Ireland	36.2	46.7
Brazil	8.5	11.8	Italy	10.0	15.7
Canada	23.9	38.3	Malaysia	8.2	11.8
Czech Rep.	8.1	10.7	Mexico	13.5	16.4
China	0.4	0.8	The Netherlands	63.5	77.5
Denmark	31.1	36.7	New Zealand	45.0	53.4
Finland	43.2	49.8	Portugal	24.3	26.5
France	28.4	41.6	Spain	18.9	27.4
Germany	25.9	34.8	Sweden	51.0	63.5
Greece	9.4	13.2	Switzerland	35.2	40.2
Hungary	19.2	26.7	UK	23.5	33.3
India	0.6	0.8	USA	17.2	25.0

The Canadian and US retail sectors have also seen rapid growth of chain store shares (Management Horizons, 2000; Rinehart and Zizzo, 1995). In Western Europe, several countries, including Ireland (Cullen and Whelan, 1997) now have higher industry concentration than the UK. In Eastern Europe, concentration is increasing rapidly, largely powered by internationalization (see Chapter 14). In the Czech Republic, all of the top five retailers, which include Tesco, are international. Detailed reviews of retail industry structures around the world can be found in the volumes of Retail Trade International by Mintel (2000a).

2.2.2 Co-operative Societies

Most retail co-operative societies are multiples, in so far as they are organizations with ten or more branches. However, they are usually analysed as a separate type of organization, being quite distinctive in both history and constitution (Eliot, 1994). The current co-operative movement was founded over 150 years ago, the first retail shop being opened by the Rochdale Pioneers in 1844:

> *The harsh living conditions of Victorian England inspired the start of a new approach to the supply of goods and the provision of social and educational facilities for ordinary working people (Swindley, 1993).*

As a response to exploitation at the time by shop owners and manufacturers, the movement spread rapidly and provoked some retaliations for its challenges to the status quo (Davies, 2000). As goods and services were withheld from co-operators, the movement spread into manufacturing, farming and insurance. By the 1930s, the 'Co-ops' were the largest single force in British retailing, which was dominated at the time by relatively inefficient independents. The Co-ops were therefore enjoying the buying power and economies of scale characteristic of the growth cycle (Fig. 2.2). The special principles of the co-operative movement held a particular appeal then, and remain in force today:

1 *Voluntary and open membership*: anyone can join, regardless of race, religion or political affiliation.
2 *Democratic control*: the ultimate control of societies lies with the members: one member one vote.
3 *Share capital* should receive only a limited rate of interest.
4 *Surplus (profits)* should be distributed to members in proportion to their purchases: the members dividend (or 'divi') (Eliot, 1996).

Over their long history, the co-operatives have been credited with many innovations. In 1876, the movement expanded internationally, starting in New York, then Canada and Western Europe (Swindley, 1993). Through its manufacturing divisions, it was a leader in own-brand products and, more recently, in international purchasing alliances and bar-code scanning. Paradoxically, it also pioneered the membership concept, which has now been vigorously reinvented in the loyalty programmes of its major rivals (McGoldrick and Andre, 1997).

The co-operative societies collectively remained the largest retailer in the UK until the late 1980s. However, that share was split between numerous regional societies, so control was fragmented. Societies were reluctant to merge until unable to continue alone, so their gradual amalgamation was not building upon positions of strength. Even the two largest societies, the Co-operative Wholesale Society (CWS) and Co-operative Retail Services (CRS) resisted merger until 2000, when it eventually went ahead (Retail Review, 2000e), to form the Co-operative Group (CWS) Ltd (Retail Review, 2001a). This was spurred on by an attempted takeover of the CWS in 1997, which sought to break up the mutual organization and return cash to its members.

As Table 2.11 illustrates, although the Co-operative Group has now over 1000 outlets, the remaining Co-op stores are still split between many regional societies. However, there is now more co-ordination than this analysis would suggest. The Co-operative Retail Trading Group (CRTG) co-ordinates the buying of 27 co-operative societies, representing nearly 2000 shops (Retail Review, 2000f). The CRTG is therefore able to harness around 75 per cent of the Co-op's buying power, offering suppliers co-ordinated distribution, pricing and promotions. The Co-op has been described as: 'A multi-faced giant, which has had to learn to balance Co-operative principles with hard-headed commercialism' (SuperMarketing, 1996).

Table 2.11 Co-operative societies and outlets

Sources: Nielsen (2001); Co-operative Union data.

Major societies	Outlets	Major societies	Outlets
Co-operative Group (CWS)	1059	Southern Co-operatives	94
United Norwest	546	Anglia	93
Shoefayre	366	Plymouth & S. Devon	84
Midlands	264	Heart of England	80
Co-op Chemists	274	West Midlands	76
Scottish Midland	192	Colchester & Essex	72
Yorkshire	183	Lothian & Borders	68
Lincoln	133	Sheffield	48
Ipswich & Norwich	102	Leeds	42
Oxford, Swindon & Gloucester	98		

Outlet types	
Superstores and large supermarkets	274
Supermarkets and convenience stores	2065
Non-food	1193
(including: 85 department stores,	
369 shoe shops	
532 pharmacies	
69 opticians)	
Services	975
(including: 521 hairdressing salons	
98 restaurants/snack bars	
198 garages/filling stations	
144 Co-operative Banks	

Alas, these changes occurred too late to defend the 15 per cent share of the grocery trade that the Co-ops enjoyed in 1970. This had fallen to 4.5 per cent by 1998, and was forecast to drop to 4 per cent by 2003 (Euromonitor, 2000a). However, with more power centralized in the Co-operative Group and CRTG, some see a brighter future for the Co-op. It is now focusing upon its convenience stores and medium-sized supermarkets, reflecting the problems of competing in an increasingly saturated superstore sector. The Co-operative Bank, wholly owned by the Co-operative Group, has demonstrated how the ethical stance can compete in the modern world, the bank adding £97 million to trading profits in 2000 (Retail Review, 2001a). It has also developed 171 Handy Banks, mini-banks often in stores, and the successful Internet service 'Smile'.

The co-operatives have also been under severe pressure in Europe, Japan and elsewhere (Le Blanc and Nguyen, 2001). By the end of the 1980s, they had all but disappeared in The Netherlands, as in Belgium (Euromonitor, 1989). This is not however the case in Switzerland, where one co-operative, Migros, alone holds 15.8 per cent of all retail trade, or in Denmark, where FDB is the leading retailer with 16.6 per cent (Euromonitor, 2000a). Co-operatives also retain around 20 per cent of the food trade in Finland and Sweden (European Retail, 1999a). Table 2.12 illustrates the marked contrasts between the strength of co-operatives in eight countries of Europe. In Switzerland, the Co-ops collectively hold more than half of the grocery market. In Italy, Co-op Italia is the country's leading food and non-food retailer, yet holds only 2.7 per cent of total retail trade. Some of this international strength is harnessed through international alliances, including NAF International and Intergroup, but scope exists to develop this further (IGD, 2000).

2.2.3 Franchising

Franchising, in various forms, has a long history in both the UK and the USA (Fulop, 1996a). Only from the 1980s, however, has it emerged as a major element of retail structure in the UK. The number of franchised outlets grew from around 2600 in 1980 to 38 000 in 1998, with forecasts of a further, threefold increase by 2002 (Key Note, 2000a). France has proved especially conducive to the spread of franchised retailing: some 40

Table 2.12 Co-ops: international comparison

Note: (f) = forecast, here and in subsequent tables.

Source: derived from Euromonitor (2000a).

Country	Share of food trade	
	1998 %	2003(f) %
Switzerland	59.2	57.2
Denmark	21.5	21.5
Sweden	19.7	20.4
Hungary	16.6	6.0
Poland	13.5	11.7
Norway	9.5	9.4
Italy	6.2	8.4
UK	4.5	4.3

per cent of Europe's franchise businesses are in France, 57 per cent of these being retailers. In the USA, there were estimated to be nearly half a million franchised businesses by 1998, capturing between one-third and two-thirds of sales in many retail and service sectors (Michael, 1999).

The term 'franchising' has been used to describe various types of trading arrangements and opinions differ as to what truly comprises a franchise. Stern and Stanworth (1988) took a broad view of the concept and identified four main contexts within which the term has been applied:

1 *The manufacturer–dealer franchise*: within this arrangement, the manufacturer is the franchisor and the franchisee sells direct to the public. Many such franchises are found in the retailing of cars and petrol.
2 *The manufacture–wholesaler franchise*: the most notable examples are Coca-Cola and Pepsi-Cola, who franchise the independent bottlers/canners who, in turn, sell to retail outlets.
3 *The wholesaler–retailer franchise*: symbol groups such as Spar, discussed below, could be described as this type of franchise.
4 *The business format franchise:* the franchisor grants permission for the franchisee to sell the former's products or services. The franchisor also provides a proven method of trading, plus support and advice in setting up and operating the business.

Mendelsohn (1992) takes the view that only the last of these categories is truly franchising and that the term has been misapplied elsewhere. Most of the phenomenal growth in recent years has indeed been from within this category. Around 18 per cent of business format franchising is in retailing, other major categories being industrial services, catering and building services (Fulop, 1996a). Franchising has proved especially advantageous to niche retailers, such as Body Shop, who required rapid expansion as a key component of their strategy (Roddick, 1991). It has also become a widely used entry strategy into international retailing (Foreward and Fulop, 1996): this context is considered further in Chapter 14.

Figure 2.3 summarizes the main advantages of franchising to both parties in the agreement, along with some potential pitfalls. As well as a relatively low cost, rapid route to expansion, the franchisor gains the energy and enthusiasm of a network of owner-franchisees. Consequently, the franchisor should incur lower costs in monitoring those aspects of outlet operation that IT systems alone cannot monitor, such as store cleanliness, staff attitudes, etc. (Sen, 2001). If gaps remain or occur in the network, the franchisor also has the choice to introduce some directly managed outlets (Cliquet, 2000a; Pilling et al., 1995). Indeed, it has been suggested that franchisors may wish to increase the extent of direct control, once the retail markets have been developed and when more resources are available to invest in the retail network (Dant et al., 1996; Oxenfeldt and Kelly, 1968).

Franchisor	Advantages	Franchisee
Rapid growth is possible	Retains some independence	
Less capital required	Rewards proportional to success achieved	
Franchisees make highly motivated owner-managers	Less start-up risk	
Lower monitoring costs	Loans more readily available	
Chain can include some directly managed outlets	Support and advice in setting up and operating	
Scope for internationalization	Use of well-known brand name	
Low-risk way to test/develop a market	National/international marketing activity	

Franchisor	Potential problems	Franchisee
Less control over day-to-day operations	Turnover and income may not meet expectations	
Reputation may be damaged by some franchisees	May start to resent restrictions	
Franchisee motivation may wane over time	Less scope for initiative and localization	
Some franchisees take short-term view, e.g. on IT or new format investment	Cheaper supplies may be available from other sources	
A franchisee may become too powerful: chains within chains	Still paying fees for marketing, even when a loyal customer base is established	
Restricts use of other channels if exclusive geographical area agreed	As turnover increases, so typically does the fee	

Figure 2.3 Franchising: advantages and problems

Source: based upon several sources, notably Fulop (1996b).

While the franchisor maintains the right to monitor the operation of franchisees (Agrawal and Lal, 1995), this does not equate to full control over day-to-day operations. Consequently, it may be necessary to withdraw the franchise in cases where underperformance threatens the image of the overall brand. It has also been found that, when some franchisees reach the 'comfort zone' of having fulfilled their financial aspirations, they become less motivated or willing to invest in new systems (Fulop, 1996b). Many franchisors allow franchisees to develop more than one outlet, and these 'chains within chains' often outperform individual outlets (Bradach, 1995). However, this can start to threaten the power of the franchisor. Another problem for franchisors is that agreements on exclusive territories can limit their ability to intensify the network or to develop new channels (Stassen and Mittelstaedt, 1995).

From the viewpoint of the franchisee, a major advantage is the ability to start a small business with relatively low risk of failure (Fulop, 1996a). Consequently, banks are likely to lend to franchisees more readily than to completely independent start-ups (Fulop, 1996b). The franchisee gains access to professional management expertise more typical of a large, multiple organization, with advice on site selection, layouts, training, financial and legal matters. Rather than having to build a reputation from scratch, the franchisee also has the immediate benefit of national/international brand recognition, supported by marketing activities well beyond the scope of an independent retailer.

While the vast majority of franchises are profitable (Key Note, 1998), some franchisees find that profits fall short of expectations. This can lead to a growing resentment of the fees paid to the franchisor for advertising and other services (Michael, 1999; Sen, 1995). In particular, this is an issue if the franchisee, now with an established customer base, sees diminishing benefits from the advertising and other support services (Fulop, 1996b). As the franchisee grows in confidence as a retailer, he or she may also resent the restrictions imposed by the franchisor (Vignali et al., 1993).

In theory, and often in practice too, franchising achieves the best of both worlds in business, combining the power and sophistication of a large organization with the energy and commitment of the independent owner-manager. With good communications and the appropriate psychological climate, the franchisor–franchisee relationship can be highly cohesive and effective in achieving its aims (Strutton et al., 1995). However, there is always the hazard that, over time, the franchisor may reduce its marketing efforts, or the franchisee its service, relying on the efforts of the other parties to maintain a reasonable volume of trade (Rao and Srinivasan, 2001). In the USA, many of Burger King's franchisees demanded greater control over the running of the franchise, complaining of sluggish sales yet growing franchise fees (Key Note, 2000a).

2.2.4 Symbol Groups

A response by wholesalers and independent retailers to the growth of the multiples has been the formation of 'symbol', 'voluntary' or 'affiliation' groups. Within this form of contractual chain, a group name is utilized and the retailers normally are required to obtain a specified proportion of their goods from the group wholesalers. The basis of the contract is that the retailer sacrifices some freedom of action for the sake of big retailer disciplines that the sponsoring wholesaler seeks to provide (Retail Review, 2000g). Member retailers normally pay a levy towards the costs of the services that the group provides, obtaining several advantages in return:

1 Loans and financial support to develop or to extend/refurbish units.
2 Group buying power normally leads to better prices than an independent could obtain.
3 Benefits are gained through own-brand products and the group image.
4 Turnover is increased through lower prices, group marketing expertise, promotions, etc.
5 Selling costs as a percentage of turnover are therefore reduced.
6 Labour productivity is improved through higher turnover and better administrative systems.
7 Space productivity improves through advice on space allocations, merchandising and display.
8 Profitability and return on capital is improved.

In the UK, symbol groups are most conspicuous in the grocery and chemists sectors. Groups do operate in other areas, such as the Euronics group in the electrical sector, with nearly 800 affiliated members (Nielsen, 2001) and 1500 outlets. In some cases, the distinctions between symbol groups and buying groups (see Chapter 8) become blurred, with few signs of the group brand being apparent to the consumers.

Table 2.13 shows the number of outlets affiliated to the main grocery and chemists groups. In the late 1980s, both Numark and Vantange had over 2000 chemists shops within their chains, which had dropped by more than a quarter by the start of this millennium (Euromonitor, 1988; Nielsen, 2001). This reflects some weeding out of non-compliant members but also a shift of trade to pharmacies within superstores. The abolition of resale price maintenance on over-the-counter medicines is likely to increase pressure on the symbol and independent chemists (Harrison, 2000; Retail Review, 2001b).

Table 2.13 Some symbol groups

Source: based upon Nielsen (2001) estimates.

Sector	Group	No. of outlets
Grocery	Spar Convenience Stores	2800
	Happy Shopper	2000
	Londis	1800
	Lifestyle (Scandia)	1350
	Family Choice	1150
	Costcutter	790
	Mace Marketing Services	550
	Best-in (Bestway)	500
Chemists	Vantage	1500
	Newmark	1385
Florists	Interflora	2400
Electrical	Euronics	1500
Sports goods	Intersport	350

In the grocery sector, the Spar brand is the largest of the symbol groups, but the Nisa/Today's buying group actually serves more outlets, 3500 in all. Although some stores now carry the 'Nisa' name, scope to develop a fully branded group is limited by the fact that Nisa buys for other groups and small multiples, including Budgens, Booths, Jacksons, Londis and Costcutter (Retail Review, 1999c).

Spar (UK) was formed in 1957 and soon developed to include 30 wholesalers and 4000 small retailers (Competition Commission, 2000). Owing to consolidation in the wholesale sector, it now has just six wholesalers. Each wholesaler works a defined territory, called a Guild. All Spar retailers are members of the local Guild and the National Guild of Spar, with representatives on the national committees (IGD, 1999). The number of outlets had dropped to 2350 by 1995 (Retail Review, 1995). In part, this reflected the application of stricter membership criteria and outlet numbers rose again to nearly 2800 by 2001 (Nielsen, 2001).

The original Spar group was founded in The Netherlands in the 1930s, emulating voluntary group practices then observed in the USA. It has grown to become a truly international brand, being represented across five continents, with 19 000 stores in 28 countries (Retail Review, 2000g). Spar International is not a monolithic operation, rather a loose federation of wholesaler-led national associates that exchange ideas and jointly purchase selected products, including some Spar own brands. It operates in a range of formats, from superstores to convenience stores, the latter being its focus in the UK. However, that sector is becoming increasingly crowded, with competition from other symbol groups, the Co-ops and the multiples.

While symbol groups command only a modest share of UK retail trade, they are of major influence in the Scandinavian countries and in Germany. Many of the shops are wholesaler owned, rather than being operated by affiliated independents. The two main grocery groups in Germany, Rewe and Edeka, have sales on a par with those of Tesco in the UK, being listed among the top six retailers in Western Europe (Nielsen, 2001). However, this has involved much streamlining and consolidation within the groups, the majority of their stores now being directly controlled by regional wholesalers or the central organizations (Zanderighi and Zaninotto, 1994).

In Canada, symbol groups including A & P (the Great Atlantic and Pacific Company) hold around 30 per cent of the food trade, but this is declining due to strong competition from Wal-Mart and Price Costco (Euromonitor, 2000). In Australia, where around 80 per cent of grocery sales are controlled by the top three multiples (Woolworths, Coles Myer and Franklins), most of the independents are affiliated to, or franchised by, large wholesaling groups, such as Davids and FAL (Foodland Associated Limited).

2.3 Major Retail Formats

Retailing lacks a single, firm basis upon which to classify retail formats (Brown, 1986). While definitions have been developed to specify characteristics of some formats, such as superstores or department stores, these definitions often vary between sources. The boundaries between formats are also becoming increasingly blurred; Wal-Mart, for example, has been variously described as operating discount stores, hypermarkets, department stores, power centres, etc. The fact is that a Wal-Mart store typically has elements of each of these formats: like many of today's retailers, they have sought value-creating opportunities outside the existing conventions.

With increasing competitive intensity, different stores formats are in a continuous process of innovation, as they compete for a more heterogeneous and demanding market (González-Benito, 2001). Morganosky (1997) refers to:

Cross-channel retail wars, resulting in consumers having an abundance of retail choices.

Consumers are continually seeking new outlets and demanding more from those retailers they choose to patronize.

Rather than a neat set of relatively discrete format types, we now have a spectrum of retail operations that differ on several dimensions. These include assortment width, service levels, customer demography (Arnold, 2000), size, institutional factors, location, form of organization, sales philosophy (Brown, 1986), groupings of outlets and drawing power of outlets (Wileman, 1993). A format may therefore be positioned and defined on a number of different dimensions including:

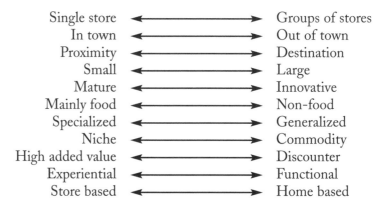

Single store	Groups of stores
In town	Out of town
Proximity	Destination
Small	Large
Mature	Innovative
Mainly food	Non-food
Specialized	Generalized
Niche	Commodity
High added value	Discounter
Experiential	Functional
Store based	Home based

These and other dimensions suggest numerous growth vectors for the expanding retailer, a topic to which we will return in Chapter 4. In this sector, some of the main retail formats are considered, in each case looking at how that format has adapted through increased, inter-type competition (Miller et al., 1999).

2.3.1 Retail Outlet Density

A strong indicator of the shift from smaller to larger retail formats is the long-term decline in shop numbers. In the UK, this was most rapid in the 1970s, when numbers dropped from 509 818 in 1971 to 362 500 in 1980. This represented a loss of over 16 000 outlets a year, around 45 per day, during those years. Since then, the decline in numbers has continued, albeit at a slower rate, down to 260 819 outlets by 1999 (Euromonitor, 2000b). This still represented a loss rate of over 5000 outlets per year, or around 14 a day, during the 1980s and 1990s.

This has left the UK with a relatively low number of outlets per unit of population, but not uniquely low. Table 2.14 compares outlet densities around Europe and elsewhere, revealing some striking contrasts. Greece has nearly four times more shops than the UK, relative to population, the Czech Republic nearly six times more. These contrasts arise from differences in planning regimes, stages in the development of larger formats and the continued appeal of small, neighbourhood stores in some contexts.

At the other extreme, Russia has one of the lowest store densities, and this actually fell during the 1990s (Euromonitor, 2000a). This reflects the underprovision of stores in this country and the cramped conditions in many existing ones. The very low density in Vietnam reflects the large rural areas with little formal retail provision: there are considerably more shops within the major cities than this ratio implies. The urban store densities in India and in the Philippines are also much higher than those of the rural areas. While it is clearly beyond the scope of this section to discuss all the reasons behind these structural differences, detailed analyses can be found within Euromonitor (2000a).

It would be incorrect to imply that store numbers are falling in all countries. Table 2.15 analyses the changes in the latter half of the 1990s in 16 European countries. Overall, store numbers fell by nine per cent between 1994 and 1999, the greatest decreases being in Italy, Spain and the UK. In each case, these changes largely reflect the continued effects of large store openings in previous years.

Table 2.14 Outlets per 1000 population

Source: derived from Euromonitor (2000a).

Country	Density	Country	Density
Austria	4.0	Australia	5.6
Belgium	12.1	Argentina	9.0
Bulgaria	10.1	Brazil	6.5
Czech Republic	25.9	Canada	6.5
Denmark	9.1	Chile	10.0
Finland	5.1	China	12.6
France	5.4	Colombia	7.7
Germany	5.7	Egypt	7.8
Greece	17.8	Hong Kong	6.6
Hungary	21.0	India	5.4
Ireland	8.8	Indonesia	7.2
Italy	7.9	Israel	7.2
Luxembourg	10.4	Japan	11.2
The Netherlands	11.0	Malaysia	8.5
Norway	9.0	Mexico	12.2
Poland	11.7	Morocco	9.3
Portugal	16.2	New Zealand	5.9
Romania	20.9	Philippines	1.9
Russia	1.2	Singapore	6.6
Slovak Republic	14.0	Africa	2.5
Spain	15.0	South Korea	17.1
Sweden	4.3	Taiwan	21.3
Switzerland	7.8	Thailand	16.6
Turkey	8.1	USA	3.4
Ukraine	2.4	Venezuela	5.8
UK	4.5	Vietnam	0.8

On the other hand, outlet numbers increased by 34 per cent in Portugal, representing the rapid addition of new formats over that period and increases in retail provision in areas previously underserved. Some countries saw only modest changes, including France, which had experienced a 45 per cent fall in outlet numbers of the previous seven-year period (Euromonitor, 1989; 2000b). This dramatic change in trend

Table 2.15 Retail outlets in Europe

Source: derived from Euromonitor (2000b).

Country	1994 (000)	1999 (000)	% change
Italy	627	439	–30.0
Spain	629	531	–15.6
UK	307	261	–14.9
Finland	29	28	–5.7
The Netherlands	179	169	–5.6
Germany	481	466	–3.2
France	324	318	–1.9
Austria	39	38	–0.8
Denmark	49	49	0.0
Switzerland	55	55	+0.9
Sweden	38	38	+1.0
Ireland	32	32	+1.5
Greece	194	201	+3.6
Belgium	113	124	+9.9
Norway	36	41	+15.3
Portugal	119	160	+34.2
Total	3250	2950	–9.2

reflects tighter regulations on new large store openings, as in a number of other European countries (Cliquet, 2000b). These regulations slow the decline of independent small outlets, while also increasing the appeal and viability of smaller formats for major retailers. Of these legal and planning rules, Corporate Intelligence Group complained:

> *Too often they are the result of successful lobbying either by manufacturers or representatives of small retailers, the latter representing those retailers that consumers have chosen not to shop with. In Belgium and France, it is virtually impossible to open a new hypermarket (Retail Review, 1999d).*

2.3.2 Small-Store Formats

The decline in shop numbers in Britain and many other countries has been most strongly reflected in the thinning out of traditional small stores, many of which were independent, family firms. It is more difficult for a small shop to achieve the economies of scale in buying, management expertise and labour that can be achieved by larger chains. Referring to the 'ousting of smallness', Nooteboom et al. (1986) detail some of the economic forces that have tended to press small, independent stores out of many European markets. Noticeably, periodic downturns in national economies, causing general pressure on retail margins, have had an especially seriously effect upon these stores.

Because of the adverse implications of this trend, especially in terms of the welfare of more isolated, poorer and/or less mobile consumers, a number of studies have examined its causes in some detail (e.g. Dawson, 1983; Kirby and Law, 1981; Smith and Sparks, 2000). Major reasons for the decline of small, independent retailers were summarized by Smith and Sparks (2000):

▶ Inadequacies in the trading environment
  – economic and social change
  – competition from multiple retailers
  – locational difficulties.

▶ Inadequacies in the retail form
  – operating costs
  – investment capital availability
  – supply problems.

▶ Inadequacies in management
  – expertise and techniques
  – entrepreneur's age.

By their very nature, small independent stores are extremely variable in their quality, some doing an admirable job in serving local needs. However, Verdict (2000) paints a gloomy picture of many traditional, neighbourhood stores:

> *High pricing, poor quality perishables, indifferent customer service, and untidy stores are pushing shoppers into travelling to bigger stores to fulfil their needs – and this at the very moment when many of these larger operations should be losing some of their appeal for top-up purposes, as they extend their ranges into non-foods and their store sizes to accommodate them.*

If small stores lose their appeal, they suffer a form of 'triple jeopardy', with fewer customers, who visit them less often, and spend less per visit (Bhat and Fox, 1996). Their problems in obtaining the required (small) quantities of supplies at reasonable prices also reflect a vicious circle, whereby the decline of the independents has contributed to a decline in the delivered wholesale trade, and an increase in the minimum sizes of delivered orders. Unaffiliated independents have therefore been obliged to make more use of cash-and-carry wholesalers, thereby further lengthening their working days and increasing an already very high workload.

A factor that slowed the decline of small shops in many urban areas was the influence of ethnic groups in retailing (Ward, 1987). They proved to be more resilient to the pressures upon small retailers, and the survival rates of their stores have tended to be higher (McEvoy and Aldrich, 1986). In part, this was achieved by lowering the financial barriers to entry and to survival, in particular, by attributing low labour costs. Many also proved adept at assembling a product and service mix well attuned to their local communities.

Clearly, there is a future for small shops, provided they fulfil a role complementary to that of the larger stores, which dominate in most sectors. Many of the reasons for small-store closures relate to problems of management expertise and supply chains, not to their smallness per se. The opportunities for small stores have now been enhanced by two main factors:

1 The inconvenience of most large stores for top-up shopping (Verdict, 2000).
2 Government restrictions on large store developments in many countries (Retail Review, 1999d).

The convenience store, or c-store, is an expression of this new role for smaller outlets, and the concept has been adopted extensively in several sectors. Some of the independents, arguably, pioneered elements of the c-store concept, notably long opening hours and assortments geared to high frequency and top-up shopping needs. Extensive c-store developments, however, have now been made by the voluntary groups, co-operatives, franchises and, more recently, the major multiples.

Like most retail formats, c-stores have been variously defined (e.g. Nielsen, 2001). The following was offered by Key Note (2001a):

> *A convenience store is defined as a small grocer, confectioner, tobacconist and newsagent (CTN), off-licence or petrol forecourt shop, with between 500 and 3,000 square feet of selling space; trading for 7 days a week, including public holidays; open continuously from 8am to 11pm or for 24 hours a day; located within or close to a local community, for whom it offers a friendly and nearby source for regular daily purchases, top-up and emergency items, and a range of services, such as photo-processing, dry cleaning, video rental and games hire.*

The convenience store format is long established in the USA, the Southland Corporation having initiated the 7-Eleven format in 1946 (Sparks, 1994). In due course, this concept and name was licensed and franchised around the world, including Japan from 1973. In 1991, the Southland Corporation was effectively taken over by its Japanese subsidiary. There are now over 7000 7-Eleven stores in Japan and nearly 3000 in the USA and Canada (Ebeltoft Group, 1998). Somewhat unusually, c-stores held a 70 per cent share of the grocery market in Japan, although this is now being eroded by the development of larger units. Table 2.16 suggests the contrasting market shares held by c-stores in 12 countries.

Unaffiliated independents still operate about half of c-stores in the UK but, as Table 2.17 illustrates, these produce only 36 per cent of c-store sector sales. Each of the other organization types produces more sales per outlet, notably the multiples, co-operatives and symbol groups. Among the 'convenience multiples' are T & S Stores, trading as 'One Stop', and T.M. Retail, trading as McColls, Martins and Forbuoys (Retail Review, 2000h). The major multiples are now adding to the c-store fray, including Tesco, Sainsbury and Safeway (see Chapter 4).

With so much renewed attention being given to the sector, c-store formats are set to evolve rapidly. They are already being used as pick-up points for customers using e-tailers; for some people, this is more convenient than waiting at home for the delivery to arrive (Retail

Table 2.16 C-stores' share of grocery trade

Source: Ebeltoft Group (1998).

	1997 %	**2002(f) %**
Australia	2.3	2.1
Canada	7.3	8.4
Denmark	47.0	40.0
France	4.4	5.5
Germany	10.0	15.6
Italy	38.0	29.0
Japan	70.0	58.0
The Netherlands	2.0	4.0
Spain	1.0	2.0
Switzerland	3.5	7.0
UK	19.0	25.0
USA	20.2	19.7

Review, 2001c). Another variation upon the c-store theme, albeit of more variable sizes, is the 'meal solution centre', described as being:

> *Located in the high street and near offices, railway stations and road junctions. The focus will be on quality, freshness and convenience, a cross between McDonald's and Fortnum & Mason. With a mix of ready-to-eat and easy to prepare meals, they will eliminate the need to plan ahead (IGD, 2000).*

These reflect the fragmentation of consumer lifestyles, discussed earlier. With culinary skills in decline, increasing numbers of women in employment and the range of leisure activities continuing to broaden, many shoppers will pay more for time saved. Informal eating practices are becoming the norm, including such variations as: 'Snacking, snatching, cheating-in, special-in, dining down and dining-up' (IGD, 2001). Meal solution centres will cater for the less predictable, more spontaneous eating practices, both at home and at work.

2.3.3 Large-Store Formats

At the other end of the retailing spectrum, the number of large stores has increased dramatically over the last 30 years. While supermarkets were the large food stores of the 1950s and 1960s, from the 1970s two larger formats spread rapidly: the superstore and the hypermarket. Like so

Table 2.17 Convenience store types

Source: Key Note (2001a).

Organization type (UK)	Outlets	% outlets	(£bn) sales	% sales
Unaffiliated independents	22 000	50.5	6.21	36.3
Forecourt stores	10 606	24.3	4.08	23.8
Symbol groups	6810	15.6	3.86	22.5
Co-operatives	1241	2.8	0.80	4.7
Off-licence c-stores	200	0.5	0.18	1.1
Convenience multiples	2519	5.8	1.77	10.3
Major multiples	216	0.5	0.23	1.3

many terms in retailing, these are all subject to various definitions, the following being adapted from Key Note (2001b):

- **Small supermarkets**: self service grocery stores of between 3000 and 12 000 square feet, which sell food, beverages and other goods.
- **Large supermarkets**: those between 12 000 and 25 000 square feet.
- **Superstores**: outlets specializing in grocery sales (although not exclusively selling food) with a floor space of between 25 000 and 50 000 square feet, usually on one level with car parking provision.
- **Hypermarkets**: with over 50 000 square feet, usually located in edge-of-town and out-of-town locations, with extensive car parks.

While US and UK definitions tend to specify space in terms of square feet, elsewhere square metres are the unit of measurement. Some sources use a multiplier of 10 to convert metric definitions to square feet, although that in itself creates inconsistencies, as 10.76 is more accurate (Watson, 1996). To add to the problems of comparisons, in Europe superstores are often referred to as small hypermarkets and in Germany, different size thresholds apply (Euromonitor, 2000a). In the USA, the terms 'hypermarket' and 'supercentre' are often regarded as synonymous (e.g. Arnold and Luthra, 2000).

In the UK, the terms 'superstore' and 'hypermarket' are frequently used interchangeably. Some multiples have avoided using the term 'hypermarket', in that the prospect of a new 'superstore' may be less intimidating to local residents and more acceptable to planning authorities. The exclusive prerogative of the grocery trade to the terms has also been thoroughly eroded, as more non-food retailers have sought to escape the confines of traditional town centres and high street locations. 'Superstore' is therefore commonly used to describe large outlets in the electrical, furniture, DIY, clothing, footwear and other sectors.

Grocery superstores/hypermarkets originated in France in 1963, where there are now more than 1100 (Cliquet, 2000b). The first openings in the UK started in 1967, with the concept spreading rapidly over the next three decades, even during recessions (Hallsworth and McClatchey, 1994). Some evidence suggests that large stores have, on average, 10 per cent lower costs per unit than small stores, most of this being passed on through lower prices (Aalto-Setälä, 2000). By the year 2000, there were 1177 grocery superstores/hypermarkets in the UK (Nielsen, 2001).

Consumers worldwide have proved responsive to the combination of large assortments and lower prices that larger stores can offer (Seiders and Tigert, 2000). Table 2.18 provides an indication of the penetration achieved by superstores/hypermarkets in various countries, subject to the usual caveats regarding data and definition compatibility. In spite of the high level of retail concentration in The Netherlands, strict regulations result in superstore penetration being very low. In contrast, Portugal saw very rapid development of these large formats from the late 1980s, until slowed down by new regulations in the mid-1990s (Farhangmehr et al.,

Table 2.18 Superstore and hypermarket share of food market

Notes: [1] Based upon different data sources.

[2] Different size criterion (> 15,000m^2).

Sources: derived from Euromonitor (2000a); Farhangmehr et al. (2001); Merrilees and Miller (1997); Nielsen (2000).

Country	1998 %	2003 (f) %
Australia[1]	40.0	–
Austria	3.7	4.2
Belgium	11.0	12.2
Denmark	17.47	17.4
France	43.0	45.7
Germany[2]	19.1	–
Hungary	5.9	28.8
Italy	11.0	16.8
Ireland[1]	25.0	–
Luxembourg	58.0	62.2
The Netherlands	2.4	2.1
Norway	10.2	9.9
Poland	4.5	12.8
Portugal[1]	37.2	–
Spain	24.0	27.0
Sweden	9.0	10.4
Switzerland	8.4	10.5
UK	38.1	40.8
USA	18.9	22.9

2001). Large store developments, mostly by international retailers, have been rapid in Poland and Hungary, although concerns about oversupply and impact are leading to some tightening of planning conditions (Court, 2000).

The impacts of large stores have been extensively studied (e.g. Hallsworth and Worthington, 2000; Morganosky and Cude, 2000) and are considered in more detail in Sec. 7.2. While there is broad consensus as to the nature of these impacts, the timing and nature of restrictions to try to reduce them have varied greatly between countries (Watson, 1996). Although France was the birthplace of hypermarkets, they are now subject to very stringent regulations. These have included a ban on television advertising (Euromonitor, 2000a) and, following the 1996 Raffarin Act, even medium-sized stores required special authorization (Cliquet, 1998). However, governments in France and elsewhere are ambivalent in their attitudes towards large grocery stores:

> *Defend small shopkeepers, by acting against large retailers, or be thankful for large retailers' help in fighting against inflation and developing exportation (Cliquet, 2000b).*

While restrictions have slowed the advance of large store formats in the UK, they certainly have not stopped it. Asda's store development programme in 2001 was its largest ever, featuring store extensions and new hypermarkets under the 'Asda Wal-Mart' banner (Retail Review, 2001d). Tesco has also intensified its moves into wider assortments of non-groceries with its Tesco Extra hypermarket format:

> *Selling everything from cucumbers to hi-fi equipment, Tesco has already put into play 23 of these 60,000 sq.ft.-plus destination-shop hypermarkets, endowing them with a width of assortment that qualifies them as mini-department stores (Retail Review, 2001e).*

The quest for larger formats is by no means exclusive to the grocery multiples. Each of the three main players in the DIY sector, B & Q, Focus and Homebase, is graduating from superstores to 'category-killer' warehouses of hypermarket proportions. IKEA is also moving from large to larger, its new Sheffield store having nearly 300 000 square feet of trading space (Retail Review, 2001f). These 'big-box' formats have developed extensively in Canada and the USA, often grouping together in what have come to be known as 'power centres' (Hahn, 2000; Jones and Doucet, 2000).

Consequently, a combination of competition pressures and superstore saturation have caused retailers to adopt more distinct format strategies, moving away from the 'one size fits all' model of the superstore (European Retail Analyst, 2000). Figure 2.4 illustrates how some retailers have adapted to quite distinctive need segments, which suggest very different solutions. For a major shopping expedition, shoppers expect the widest possible choice and are prepared to travel to find it. As noted earlier, however, large stores are not best equipped to provide instant gratification, top-up needs or minimum hassle. Neither do they invariably seek to provide the lowest possible prices.

2.3.4 Department and Variety Stores

One of the oldest examples of large format retailing is the department store, with over 150 years of history. Claims to be the first department store include Bon Marché, opened in Paris in 1852, and Stewart's 'Marble Dry Good Palace', opened in 1848 in New York (Willans,

Consumer needs	Attributes required	Store format
Major shopping trip with functional and recreational needs	Wide assortment Value for money Interesting environment	Destination store or centre
Immediate gratification with minimal need for planning	Quality, innovation and good service	Boutique Meal solution centre
Lowest possible expenditure	Focused range Keenest prices	Discount store
Less predictable and specialized needs	Convenient location Long hours Understanding of local needs	C-store Specialist local shop
Minimum effort	Remote shopping facility Reliable service	Catalogue shopping E-tailing

Figure 2.4 Needs, attributes and formats

Adapted from: European Retail Analyst (2000).

1997). Some of the trading characteristics of department stores, if not the format itself, were used as far back as 1673 by Japanese retailer Mitsukoshi (Davies and Jones, 1993).

While most people patronize at least one department store (Rousey and Morganosky, 1996), defining them is more problematic. Even the International Association for Department Stores lists seven different definitions on its website. Retail Intelligence (2000) suggest that they are:

> *Stores selling a wide range of goods including significant proportions of clothing and household goods, usually on several floors within one building, with sales area over 2,000m² and at least 25 sales employees.*

Some of the most notable department stores are, of course, far larger than this, both Samaritaine in Paris and Harrods in London being in excess of 50 000 m² (European Retail Digest, 1995). The criterion of 'several floors' cannot be applied to many of the newer department stores in North America, frequently built on just one level or on two.

Defining variety stores presents even greater difficulties, largely because the term (or similar) has been attached to rather different concepts in different countries. In France, department store groups took the leading role in developing variety stores, such as Monoprix (Les Galeries Lafayette). These emulated the American 'Five 'n' Dime' stores, with low fixed price points, a response to the recession and slump in the 1930s (Tordjman, 1993). In Germany and The Netherlands, more than half of variety store sales have traditionally been in foods (European Retail Digest, 1995).

In the UK, Marks & Spencer has epitomized the variety store concept, along with BhS and Littlewoods. Although developing largely on the basis of clothing and other textiles, these stores have diversified into other housewares and food. On the other hand, department stores have become more focused in their ranges, so the distinction between variety and department stores has become blurred. Some sources now classify Marks & Spencer and others as department stores, along with such diversified retailers as Boots, W.H. Smith and Argos (e.g. Business Ratio, 2001).

In spite of some trading difficulties in recent years, Marks & Spencer still holds the largest share of the department/variety store category in the UK. John Lewis and Debenhams are the leaders among the traditional department stores. Table 2.8 illustrated the relative positions of these companies within the clothing sectors. Another area of strength is the housewares sector, within which the department and variety stores hold 22 and 15 per cent respectively (Verdict, 2001).

International comparisons encounter many problems, but Table 2.19 provides an indication of the positions of department and variety stores in several countries. Forecasts for department store shares of non-food sales vary between countries but, overall, the picture is one of a format under some pressure. In the USA, traditional, full-line department stores continue to decline in numbers (Management Horizons, 2000), although the leading

	% share of non-food sales			
	Department stores		**Variety stores**	
	1998	**2003(f)**	**1998**	**2003(f)**
Australia	8.8	7.5	7.5	11.2
Austria	6.9	6.8	3.8	3.3
Canada	16.1	19.2	6.7	7.6
Denmark	6.7	7.0	11.3	12.1
France	2.9	2.7	0.8	—
Germany	5.9	5.1	0.7	0.6
Hungary	5.9	4.6	26.2	23.3
Ireland[1]	13.4	13.4	—	—
Japan	10.8	10.1	—	—
Luxembourg	8.8	7.7	5.9	5.2
The Netherlands	9.7	9.1	3.4	3.6
New Zealand	—	—	16.9	17.1
Norway	—	—	4.4	7.1
Poland	1.3	1.8	4.3	5.6
Russia	36.8	35.4	—	—
Spain	8.0	7.0	—	—
Sweden	2.5	2.7	1.4	1.2
Switzerland	13.8	12.6	—	—
UK	3.6	3.2	18.4	19.8
USA	8.6	8.4	10.2	11.1

Table 2.19 Department and variety stores

Source: derived from Euromonitor (1989; 2000a).

Note: [1] Both categories combined.

edge operators, such as Federated, May & Co. and Dillard's, are making gains through acquisitions and more focused strategies.

Variety stores in France hold a 2 per cent share of food sales, but less than 1 per cent of non-food. Paradoxically, the regulations introduced to limit the power of the hypermarkets have largely obstructed the variety stores from improving their locations (Cliquet, 2000b). In New Zealand, on the other hand, variety stores are the biggest non-food suppliers (Euromonitor, 2000a). In Canada too, the Best Value variety chain, of the Hudson Bay Company, holds a significant share.

The somewhat mixed fortunes of department stores internationally reflect their varying national histories, and their levels of success in coping with competitive pressures. Notable among these difficulties are the following:

1 *Price competition*: almost every part of the department store range has faced waves of price competition from lower cost operators. Superstores now sell many of the more specialized food items; carpet warehouses, electrical superstores and garden/DIY warehouses compete strongly in those areas; and, more recently, clothing discounters such as TK Maxx and Matalan have made their presence felt in the clothing sectors (Retail Review, 2001g).

2 *Assortment competition*: whereas department stores initially offered some of the widest assortments then available under one roof, only the largest can now compete on the depth of assortment of large unit

specialists, where most of their customers also shop (Rousey and Morganosky, 1996).

3 *Fashion competition*: some have found it difficult to compete with the fashionable brand images created by more nimble, specialist competitors. The ageing population is not an answer to this problem, as the 'new old' have fashion expectations shaped by these specialists (Management Horizons, 2000).

4 *Experiential competition*: department stores were early exponents of shopping as a leisure activity (Zola, 1883) but many other stores and centres now offer comparable or better leisure experiences (European Retail Digest, 1995).

5 *Location problems*: while the great department stores of London and Paris retain their appeal to tourists and nationals alike, city centre locations have proved problematic in terms of accessibility, car parking, higher costs of property and maintenance (Willans, 1997).

6 *Management*: some have suffered from a traditional emphasis upon 'form' rather than 'intellectual substance' (Rogers, 1991). Others have had too frequent changes of ownership and direction, to the point of extinction in the case of Galerías Preciados (Gold and Woodliffe, 2000).

Clearly, not all these problems are unique to department stores, neither do they defy solution. Opinions differ as to whether department stores are undergoing a resurgence, or whether they are merely adapting to survive the competitive pressures (e.g. Retail Intelligence, 2000; Verdict, 1999). What is clear is that the most successful players have adopted strategies enabling them to hold or improve upon their market shares.

1 *Consolidation*: the quest for economies of scale has led to many acquisitions and mergers, such as Karstadt and Hertie in Germany (European Retail Digest, 1995), El Corte Inglés and Galerías Preciados in Spain (Campos, 2000) and Federated, Macy's and Bloomingdale's in the USA (Management Horizons, 2000).

2 *Diversification*: these can comprise extensions of the product/service mix, such as in-store restaurants, or more fundamental moves. For example, El Corte Inglés launched the hypermarket chain Hipercor (Gold and Woodliffe, 2000) and a number of department stores moved into mail order or Internet retailing (Verdict, 1999).

3 *New locations*: to counteract the problems of accessibility and parking, many department stores are now the anchor stores of major out-of-town centres. For its first operation outside London, Selfridges became the central anchor of Manchester's Trafford Centre, also benefiting from the experiential appeal of this complex (Retail Review, 1997).

4 *Focus/niches*: rather than presenting a sea of undifferentiated merchandise, Bloomingdale's and others have focused on specific customer segments and tastes (Management Horizons, 2000). Others have played to their particular strengths, for example, Brown Thomas in Dublin opened a designer sportswear store (Wilcox and O'Callaghan, 2001).

5 *Own brands*: while concessions can fill excess space and help fill gaps in the assortment, they do not necessarily help build the retailer's brand (Porter, 1999). Debenham's own-brand/own-bought items yield gross margins of 49 per cent, compared with 20 per cent from concession space (Morgan Stanley Dean Witter, 2001).

6 *Service*: as most price competitors offer lower service levels, department stores can appeal to their slightly older, more affluent clienteles through good service, and a sense of retail theatre (Verdict, 1999).

2.3.5 Discount Stores

As the 'wheel of retailing' theory suggests (Sec. 1.3.1), many companies have started life as discounters, then progressively lost that title. Often they traded up and/or the market became defined at a lower price level. Consequently, the attribution of 'discounter' status is frequently transitory and context dependent.

When Asda first entered southern England it was regarded as a discounter, yet its prices, and those of Morrisons, had come to be the norm within its northern heartlands (McGoldrick, 1988). Likewise, while Wal-Mart and Kmart have redefined price levels around major conurbations, they are described as discounters when entering small-town USA (Brennan and Lundsten, 2000). Customer perceptions, at a given time or place, clearly help to define what is a discounter (Schmidt et al., 1994).

Over the years, discounters have had a profound effect upon retail structure and strategy, in virtually every sector. Discount formats have some characteristics in common (Humphries, 1995):

▸ an emphasis on cost control
▸ low prices
▸ strict range management
▸ a no frills approach to store design and presentation
▸ low levels of customer service.

Drawing together these themes, the IGD (1997) offers the following definition:

> *A retailer that offers a tightly controlled range, at low prices, from premises which are basic by design. The company culture emphasises rigorous cost control and the principal marketing tool is price.*

Limited-line discounting has achieved particular impact in the Danish and German food markets, reflecting the progress of Netto and Aldi, but also restrictions upon larger-scale formats. Table 2.20 estimates penetration into the food markets of seven European countries. Forecasts suggest continued growth in Germany, strong growth in Austria but decline in Hungary, in the face of strong competition from superstores and hypermarkets (Euromonitor, 2000a).

In the UK, food discounters grew at a rate of over 10 per cent annually in the early 1990s, then their progress slowed significantly (Key Note, 2000b; Mintel, 2000c). This reflected a strong response from the existing

Table 2.20 Discounters' share of food markets

Source: derived from Euromonitor (2000a).

Country	% food market	
	1998	**2003(f)**
Austria	6.0	12.3
Denmark	11.3	17.5
Germany	22.8	26.5
Hungary	4.9	3.6
Sweden	8.3	8.0
Switzerland	5.2	7.2
UK	6.0	6.2

multiples, including the (re)introduction of plain-label, grocery generics (Burt and Sparks, 1994), as well as lower-priced petrol (Bidlake, 1995). The superstore operators also became adept in the strategy of multi-segment pricing, which is discussed in Sec. 10.3.3.

Warehouse clubs are another, much larger discount format, typically with in excess of 100 000 square feet, in an out-of-town 'shed' format (Hogarth-Scott and Rice, 1994). They run on a membership basis and stock a wide (but not deep) range of non-foods and foods in bulk packs. They grew rapidly from the early 1980s in the USA, Sam's Club operating 250 out of the total of 590 units by 1992. By the end of the century, however, they were already considered to be in decline (Management Horizons, 2000). In spite of much concern about their entry into the UK, they have made minimal impact. This is due largely to the inconvenient aspects of the format and the strong reactions of the superstore operators to discounters in general.

Discounting has a long history in non-food sectors, representing the early trading format of some variety stores, including Woolworths in the UK and Monoprix in France. In both the UK and the USA, 'extreme value traders' continue to offer a range of merchandise priced at just one pound/dollar. According to Management Horizons (2000):

> *These companies' customers are in the lower income groups in permanent recession and, therefore, are not as affected by economic downturn or upturn as other customers.*

While food discounters attracted most interest in the early-mid 1990s, attention had shifted firmly to the non-food sectors by the new millennium. In 1999 alone, non-food discounters grew by 58 per cent, reflecting particularly the swift growth in the discounting clothing chains (Key Note, 2000a). In fact, the rapid expansion of the Matalan chain was cited by C&A in their decision to exit the UK. From a survey of some of the earlier entrants to the discount clothing market, Robinson and Bailey (1994) found prices at 20–40 per cent below high-street multiple prices:

> *In quality terms, discounters described their clothing as being no higher in quality than good and, in value terms, representing good-to-excellent value for money.*

Although many of the discount clothing chains started or arrived during a period of recession, they have continued their growth during periods of relative prosperity. Table 2.8 showed Matalan's share of the menswear market to have grown rapidly to 2.5 per cent by 2000, slightly ahead of C&A, before its departure. United States discounter TK Maxx had gathered 70 branches since its arrival in the UK in 1994, and Dublin-based Primark had opened 55 (Retail Review, 2001g).

It remains to be seen whether these developments will increase polarization in the clothing market. There can be little doubt that the mid-price clothing market had become a very crowded place (Key Note, 2000c; Verdict, 1998). In the UK, the highest earning 40 per cent of households had an average weekly income of £862; the lowest earning 40 per cent received an average of £153 weekly (Advertising Association, 2001). Although taxation and mortgages reduce the contrasts, there is still a very wide gulf between the discretionary spending powers at each end of the market.

2.3.6 Shopping Centres

In parallel with the development of superstores, hypermarkets and other large store formats, there has also been vigorous development of planning shopping centres over recent decades. The traditional concentrations of shops within town or city centres are referred to by Ghosh and McLafferty (1991) as *shopping districts*. For the International Council for Shopping Centres, these do not fall within their definition of a shopping centre: 'A group of retail and other commercial establishments that is planned, developed, owned and managed as a single property'. A planned shopping centre therefore has far more control over its tenant mix, a crucial determinant of its ultimate success (Kirkup and Rafiq, 1994). Furthermore, it can also be positioned and marketed as a unit (Dawson and Lord, 1985), with the centre management able to control details of design, maintenance, security, etc. Until being largely curtailed by government regulations in the 1990s (see Sec. 7.2), most new shopping centre development in the UK had been out of town, providing easier car accessibility and parking (McGoldrick and Thompson, 1992). Schiller (1987) identified three waves of out-of-town development:

 ▶ *Wave one*: the superstores selling primarily food, with modest non-food ranges.
 ▶ *Wave two*: similarly large stores selling bulky good, such as DIY, carpets, furniture, larger electrical items and garden centres.
 ▶ *Wave three*: clothing and other comparison goods sold in regional shopping centres, a full-scale alternative to traditional town centres.

To an extent, the third wave was reduced in power by a combination of the 1987 stock market crash, the recession that followed, then more stringent planning controls. However, Fernie (1998) identified a fourth wave of decentralization, more fragmented than the first three, including warehouse clubs, factory outlet centres and airport retailing (Freathy and O'Connell, 1999).

The UK has Europe's highest proportion of total retail space within shopping centres, 32 per cent compared with 29 per cent in France and 10 per cent in Germany (Birkett, 2000a). Table 2.21 illustrates again the enormous diversity of retailing within Europe. In France, Denmark and the UK, shopping centre developments were well under way in the 1960s, whereas Italy, Spain, Finland and Sweden started rapid growth in the mid-1980s (Reynolds, 1992). Portugal saw rapid growth in shopping centres in the 1990s, now having considerably more space per capita than many earlier starters. Hungary also experienced a surge in shopping centre activity in the late 1990s (Birkett, 2000a).

These estimates of floor space include a variety of shopping centre types. There are a number of classifications of shopping centre types (e.g. Schiller, 1987) but these are often focused upon one country. Figure 2.5 presents a classification developed by Reynolds (1992), which can be applied on a wider scale. In each case, there are locational and compositional variants, but each category has distinctive characteristics, in terms of size and mix.

Considerable interest has naturally been generated by the regional shopping centres, which come closest to offering the complete alternative to town centre shopping. These are far more common in North America than in Europe, including the 5.0 million square foot Mall of America. The West Edmonton Mall boasts many of the 'world's largest', including a huge indoor wave pool for swimmers, an indoor amusement park with triple-loop roller-coaster, an indoor lake with submarine rides and an NHL-size ice arena. After some decline in visitor numbers in the mid-1990s, West Edmontron resurrected itself by adding gambling and entertainment to its array of available experiences (Wakefield and Baker, 1998).

Table 2.21 Shopping centres in Europe

Sources: derived from Advertising Association (2001); Birkett (2000a); Natwest Markets (1998).

Country	Centres' floor space (million m²)	m² per 1000 population
Austria	1.30	160.6
Belgium	0.68	66.4
Denmark	1.10	206.4
Finland	0.75	145.0
France	12.50	211.9
Germany	4.20	51.2
Greece	0.14	13.3
Hungary	0.40	37.5
Ireland	0.80	213.6
Italy	4.65	80.7
The Netherlands	1.90	120.6
Portugal	1.00	100.0
Spain	5.50	139.5
Switzerland	0.70	97.7
Turkey	0.35	5.4
UK	13.62	228.9

Types		Examples
I: Regional shopping centre (30,000m²+) *(Centres commerciaux régionaux, grandes centros periféricos, regionalen shopping-center)* (Two or more anchors)		
Locational variants	Central area in traditional core Central area adjacent traditional core Non-central suburban growth zone Greenfield site/transport node	Eldon Sqaure, Newcastle, UK La Part-Dieu, Lyon, France Vélizy 2, Versailles, France Curno, Bergamo, Italy
Compositional variants	Hypermarket-dominated Department and variety store-dominated Food, non-food and leisure anchors	A6, Jonkoping, Sweden Lakeside, Thurrock, UK Parquesur, Madrid, Spain
II: Intermediate centres (10,000–20,000m²) *(Centres intercommuneaux, centros intermedios)* (At least one anchor, integrated)		
Locational variants	Non-central suburban community Greenfield site/transport node	Auchan, Torino, Italy Cameron Toll, Edinburgh, UK
Compositional variants	Hypermarket-anchored Speciality non-food anchored	Euromarché BHV, Cergy, France
III: Retail Parks (5,000–20,000m²) *(Centres de magasins d'usine ou parc des entrepôts, parques commerciales, retail warehourse parks)* (Not obviously anchored; not wholly integrated centres)		
Locational variants	Non-central suburban community Greenfield site/transport node	Various, UK Lakeside Retail Park, UK
Compositional variants	Retail warehouse tenant mix Factory outlet tenant mix Hybrid tenant mix	Fairacres Retail Park, Abingdon, UK Direct Usines, Nancy, France Fosse Park, Leicester, UK
IV: Speciality centres (1,000m²) *(Arcades, galeries marchandes, galerias comerciales, Galerien)*		
Locational variants	Central area in traditional core Adjacent to traditional core	Arcades, Lille, France Albert Dock, Liverpool, UK
Compositional variants	Non-food specialist traders Department store conversion	Powerscourt Town House, Dublin, Eire Centre Point, Braunschweig, Germany

Figure 2.5 Shopping centre types

Source: Reynolds (1992).

Notes (1) Floorspace figures are indicative only.
(2) Centres providing for local or neighbourhood needs are excluded.

After earlier, large-scale developments at Brent Cross and Milton Keynes, the MetroCentre on Tyneside became Europe's biggest centre of this type in 1986, with over 2 million square feet of space (McGoldrick and Thompson, 1992). Through the 1990s, more large centres opened, even after the tightening of restrictions on out-of-town developments, usually on the basis of planning permissions initiated at an earlier stage. These include the Trafford Centre, near Manchester, as well as Lakeside in Essex and Bluewater in Kent, these two being just 15 minutes drive time apart (Retail Review, 1999e).

While the right tenant mix remains the primary attraction to major centres, environmental attributes that create excitement are a major influence upon people's desire to stay in centres (Wakefield and Baker, 1998). Although the UK centres are not on the scale of North America's largest, they certainly recognize the importance of experiential marketing (Schmitt, 1999). This is reflected in the excitement of the mix of shops, catering and entertainment facilities, plus the atmospherics of the centres themselves (see Chapter 12). 'Reality engineering' (Solomon et al., 1999) can be experienced at the Rainforest Café and, at times, 'hyperreality' does have is advantages: 'The recreation of Bourbon Street in West Edmonton is a more pleasant environment for many than the decidedly tawdry "original"' (Brown, 1995).

Cinemas have also made a considerable comeback in shopping centres. They were a traditional feature of town centres for much of the last century but had fallen into severe decline, that is, until the 1990s (Jones and Pal, 1998). In Table 2.2 we noted how expenditure at cinemas grew by 157 per cent between 1990 and 2000. In the USA in particular, malls have turned to entertainment to help counteract decreasing mall productivity (LeHew and Fairhurst, 2000). The problems experienced by the malls had several origins:

⦁ Over-saturation of shopping space, with around 35 000 shopping centres in the USA (LeHew and Fairhurst, 2000).
⦁ Too many of the malls look alike, with similar stores and merchandise (Ashley, 1997).
⦁ Time-pressed consumers find the long walks around malls inconvenient (Mundow, 1989).
⦁ As the novel becomes the familiar, fewer consumers report enjoying the mall experience (Wakefield and Baker, 1998).
⦁ Some of the department and variety stores that anchor many malls have declined (Sec. 2.3.4).
⦁ The malls tend to be expensive retailing environments and this is perceived to be reflected in prevailing prices (Solomon, 1993).
⦁ Other formats, such as 'power centres', are offering more focused shopping opportunities (Hahn, 2000).

2.3.7 Variations upon the Mall

The development of power centres in the USA reflected the problems of the malls, plus the fact that only a minority of malls had sufficient experiential appeal to maintain their destination status. Instead of using just a few, large store retailers as anchors, a power centre comprises almost exclusively large stores (Bodkin and Lord, 1997). Many of these are of the 'category killer' variety, offering a powerful proposition of large assortments at low(est) prices. A power centre may therefore include Home Depot, Circuit City, Office Depot, Sport Authority and Toys 'R' Us, as well as Wal-Mart, Kmart and warehouse clubs, such as Price Costco.

These value-oriented retailers operate in large, industrial-style buildings, providing low-cost environments, plus high product choice/size availability. As each is free-standing, customers can park outside the store of choice and shop more quickly: 45 minutes was the average time spent at one power centre, yet 85 per cent of shoppers bought something, compared with 50 per cent of mall shoppers (Solomon, 1993).

Hahn (2000) describes a power centre simply as *an agglomeration of big box retailers*. They usually have the following characteristics:

- more than 250 000 square feet of gross leasable area (GLA), some have more than 1 million square feet
- at least one super-anchor store with at least 100 000 square feet
- at least four smaller anchors of 20 000–25 000 square feet each
- only a few smaller shops of less than 10 000 square feet
- generally an open-air centre
- a total trading area similar to a regional shopping centre
- a unified shopping centre management.

Although the first power centre opened only in 1986, south of San Francisco, there were 713 in the USA by 1998 (Hahn, 2000). While generally operating on a smaller scale, retail parks in the UK have a similar rationale and history. They developed from the early 1980s and, by 2000, there were 539 in operation (Retail Review, 2000i), with an average size of nearly 120 000 square feet.

However, retail parks have evolved during their 20-year history, *from crinkly sheds to fashion parks* (Guy, 2000). Whereas the earliest concentrated upon furniture, carpets, electrical goods and DIY, the 1990s saw the addition of sports goods, clothing, shoes, office supplies and more. Recently, some have added cinemas, bowling alleys, fitness centres, pubs and restaurants (Retail Review, 2000i). They are therefore starting to replicate the mix of covered centres/malls, in lower-cost retailing environments.

Another variation upon this theme is the factory outlet centre/mall, within which clothing tends to be the category most strongly represented. Retail Intelligence (2000) defines them as:

> *A vehicle for suppliers to dispose of merchandise that cannot be sold through conventional retail channels – whether it be surplus stock, last season's ranges, slow-selling products, end-of-line items, returned goods, seconds, discontinued lines, or cancelled orders.*

Which? (2000) found that prices tended to be at least 25 per cent cheaper than on the high street, but products are likely to be last year's stock. Factory shops selling seconds, ends of ranges and old stock have been around for over 100 years (Birkett, 2000b), but the present format of factory outlet centres originated in 1979 (Fernie and Fernie, 1997). There were estimated to be 324 such centres in the USA, accounting for 2.5 per cent of total retail sales (Retail Review, 2000j).

By 2001 there were 34 factory outlet centres in the UK, with a further 18 in the planning/development pipeline (Retail Review, 2001h). Their average size is 130 000 square feet, although the Cheshire Oaks centre is much larger at 300 000 square feet, with around 120 outlets (Natwest Markets, 1998). Some of the outlets in these centres are designer names selling direct to the public, such as Calvin Klein, Ted Baker, Nike and Reebok. However, the high street retail names are also there in force, including Marks & Spencer, Principles, Diesel and Next, as well as the Body Shop's 'Depot' factory outlet stores (Key Note, 2000b).

Clothing was the original focus of factory outlet centres, but the concept has evolved quickly to include a wider range of food/restaurants, jewellery, accessories, mobile phones and housewares. Such centres are not immune to the regulations on out-of-town development (Norris, 1999) but planners take a more favourable attitude to schemes linked to urban regeneration on 'brownfield' locations, such as the Swindon Outlet Centre and Manchester Outlet Mall (Retail Review, 2001h). The latter is adjacent to the Lowry Centre, with its galleries, theatres, exhibition and conference facilities, as well as the War Museum North.

Despite their short history, factory outlet centres are considered to be nearing maturity in the USA and the UK (Birkett, 2000b). Major developers have therefore looked for international expansion (Morgan, 1998), BAA McArthur Glen (BMG) being Europe's leading developer of this format. Table 2.22 estimates factory outlet floor space in 12 countries, including centres not yet built but with definite planning permission. Most of the existing factory outlet centres are in the UK and France but both Germany and Spain have significant schemes 'in the pipeline'. Eastern Europe has also provided opportunities to capture both local and tourist trade, such as RAM Euro Centers' site near Budapest (Fernie and Fernie, 1997). There are also 'virtual' factory outlet malls, such as Haburi.com and BMG Online (Key Note, 2000c).

The cumulative effect of regional shopping centres, retail parks, factory outlet malls and other developments has been to place the future of many town centres in considerable jeopardy. However, many town centres have become involved in town centre management schemes, to become more attractive alternatives to the newer, shopping centre formats. While town centre management can rarely achieve the level of integration of a well-designed and well-managed mall, it can help to overcome many of the competitive disadvantages. Schemes can co-ordinate/provide better security, cleaning, advertising and signage, as well as promoting better car parking and pedestrianization (Medway et al., 1999).

Table 2.22 Factory outlet centres in Europe

Source: based upon Birkett (2000b), estimates of space now open or with planning permission.

Country	000m²	Country	000m²
Australia	23.9	The Netherlands	14.0
Belgium	12.4	Portugal	32.2
France	224.8	Spain	115.7
Germany	91.7	Sweden	23.1
Ireland	14.0	Switzerland	66.9
Italy	18.2	UK	481.0

The stakeholders within town centre management schemes include public sector bodies, such as local authorities and the police, as well as many private sector interests. Some retailers contribute towards the cost of these schemes, usually motivated by enlightened self-interest (Medway et al., 2000). There does appear to be a strong correlation between high standards of town centre management and strong store performance (Birkett, 2000c).

As suburban areas become increasingly besieged by sprawl and traffic, and as the policies of governments shift in favour of public transport (Ibrahim and McGoldrick, 2002), a well-managed town centre can become an increasingly attractive alternative. Indeed, property agent Hillier Parker reported that 90 per cent of floor space in the retail development pipeline was in town centres in 2000, compared with just 45 per cent in 1998 (Retail Review, 2001i).

2.3.8 Home Shopping

In spite of all the innovations within centres and store formats, much attention in recent years has been focused upon home shopping alternatives. Such has been the interest in the prospects and possible consequences of electronic retailing that this is examined in greater detail in Chapter 15. At this stage, it is therefore sufficient to take a brief overview of home shopping in general, notably the catalogue-based formats.

In both the UK and the USA, the history of 'mail order' can be traced back to the nineteenth century. Pioneers in the UK included Kays of Worcester and Fattorini & Sons of Bradford, subsequently trading as Empire Stores (Coopey et al., 1999). By 1900, both had established large networks of local agents, selling through catalogues to 'clubs' of friends, neighbours and fellow workers, as well as collecting their payments. Their customers were primarily urban working class and the major attraction was the credit terms offered.

The origins of mail order shopping in the USA were somewhat different, being focused primarily upon the rural markets, inadequately served by other forms of retailing. The general mail order catalogue of Montgomery Ward dates back to 1872 (Burnett and McCollough, 1994) and its great rival Sears, Roebuck was spending nearly 9 per cent of turnover on advertising by 1902 (Coopey et al., 1999). These companies were proud of their efficient fulfilment centres, as they would now be called: Montgomery Ward's Chicago 'beehive' was featured extensively in company publicity.

By 1970, mail order accounted for 4.2 per cent of total retail trade in the UK, reaching the end of the century at almost the same level (Nielsen, 2001). However, a great deal had changed during that 30-year period, with traditional, 'big book' mail order and the agency networks declining. The entry of Next Directory breathed new life into the sector, appealing directly to a much more up-market clientele (McGoldrick and Greenland, 1991). More recently, other retailer's catalogues, television shopping channels and Internet retailers have brought new impetus to the sector.

Unlike most retail sectors, home shopping is actually becoming less concentrated in the UK, as some of the largest players continue to lose share. As recently as 1990, Great Universal Stores (GUS), which includes Kays and many other catalogue names, held over 30 per cent of the home shopping market: as Table 2.23 shows, this had fallen to under 20 per cent by the end of the decade. Littlewoods also lost share during that period, its second place challenged by OttoVersand of Germany, which acquired both Grattan and Freemans (Retail Review, 1999f).

Next Directory, on the other hand, continues to grow, benefiting from the branding, buying and logistical synergies of this multi-channel retailer. Its achievements inspired Marks & Spencer to expand its home shopping operations, with the benefit of a large existing database of account holders. Corporate Intelligence (1995) identified 27 clothing retailers in the UK with home shopping operations, including Laura Ashley, Benetton and Long Tall Sally.

Great Universal Stores also looked to a multi-channel solution to arrest its decline, through the acquisition of catalogue showroom trader Argos (Retail Review, 2001j). A major advantage of the catalogue showroom format is that goods can be selected at home, then collected (and inspected) at one of the showrooms, without having to wait for home delivery. The combination of GUS and Argos has taken the latter into mainstream home shopping, with the option of home deliveries, an expanded, value-for-money catalogue and a presence on NTL and Telewest digital television (Retail Review, 2000j). The integration of buying, customer service and fulfilment facilities is expected to save the group £80 million over four years.

Home shopping is of varying significance around the world but the prevailing trend is upwards. Table 2.24 is based upon estimates of the non-food shares of home shopping, showing the highest penetrations to be in the USA, Germany, the UK and Austria. In the USA, home shopping is expected to account for 10 per cent of non-food sales in 2003. Canadians have traditionally been less enthusiastic about home

Table 2.23 Home shopping market shares

Source: based upon Nielsen (2001) and Verdict Research.

Company	1995 %	1999 %	Company	1995 %	1999 %
GUS	23.5	19.6	Next Directory	2.3	3.1
Littlewoods	14.3	14.0	Findel	3.1	2.7
Grattan (Otto Versand)	6.7	5.4	Avon	2.5	2.5
Freemans (Otto Versand)	7.7	5.3	QVC	0.6	2.0
Empire (La Redoute)	3.7	4.4	Marks & Spencer	0.4	1.4
N. Brown	3.3	4.0	Others	31.9	35.6
Share of sectors 1999					
Clothing and footwear	13.5%		Furniture and carpets		7.0%
Electrical goods	5.5%		Total retail trade		4.1%

shopping but retailers' catalogues, such as The Bay, and on-line shopping are bringing growth there too. In some markets, including Ireland, the growth of home shopping has been limited by a lower penetration of credit cards (Euromonitor, 2000a).

In theory, home shopping should be highly conducive to international activities, although the varying legislative frameworks and currencies have presented obstacles (Brook and Pioch, 1996). The widespread use of the Euro, and gradual harmonization of regulations, should facilitate cross-border operations in Europe. The merger of Karstadt, Germany's largest department store chain, with mail order group Quelle was motivated largely by Karstadt's ambitions for international expansion (European Retail, 1999b). In the USA, catalogue retailers are also among the leaders in international activity (Samuolis and Morganosky, 1996).

With the diversity of home-shopping opportunities now available, the segments of shoppers using these services have become equally diverse (Freathy and O'Connell, 1998). The risk-aversive may still be less likely to use home shopping systems (Bhuian, 2001) but linkages with well-known stores reduce one major element of risk. Lenient returns policies reduce product-related risk perceptions and do not invariably lead to more returns (Wood, 2001). Risks for home shoppers can also be reduced through good product descriptions and easily understood ordering procedures (Shamdasani and Yeow, 1995).

Motives for using home shopping have also become more diverse, with some providers focusing upon value, others on wide assortments, high service levels, etc. (Eastlick and Feinberg, 1999). The desire for interaction may not be one of the strongest motives for home shopping yet the quality of the call centre service can have a profound effect upon customer satisfaction. Research by Cap Gemini suggested that 26 per cent of customers were irritated after contacting a call centre, 9 per cent were furious (Ody, 1998).

Home shopping may also be seen to lack many of the experiential benefits of store-based retailing, discussed further in Chapter 3. However, Mathwick et al. (2001) found that catalogues do offer a range

Table 2.24 Home shopping: international comparisons

Source: derived from Euromonitor (2000a).

Country	% of non-foods		Country	% of non-foods	
	1998	2003(f)		1993	2003(f)
Australia	1.2	1.6	Japan	2.6	3.1
Austria	6.0	7.5	The Netherlands	3.1	4.6
Canada	1.6	2.8	Norway	2.5	6.3
Denmark	5.3	5.6	Poland	0.5	1.0
France	5.1	5.4	Sweden	4.5	4.2
Germany	7.2	7.0	Switzerland	4.2	4.4
Hungary	0.4	0.9	UK	6.2	7.5
Ireland	0.9	0.8	USA	8.8	10.0
Italy	0.6	0.6			

of experiential value sources, notably entertainment and visual appeal, as well as efficiency and affordability. They conclude:

If retailers hope to design and position their various channel options as an integrated, value-rich package, understanding fundamental differences in the experience delivered by multichannel retail environments is essential.

SUMMARY

The value of consumer expenditure grew by around 28 per cent over the last 10 years but the proportion of that passing through retail outlets continues to fall. With increased spending on housing, health, leisure and financial services, retailers have sought growth outside their traditional product sectors. The demographics of the market are also shifting significantly, with an ageing population profile and more, smaller households. Within households, activities are more fragmented, in terms of leisure and eating patterns, and there is an increased demand for individuality. Shifting consumer values include more concern for the environment but not to the extent of stemming the increase in car ownership. This continues to provide the basis for longer but less frequent shopping trips, although increased suburban and motorway congestion could reverse this trend.

The structure of retailing has also experienced major changes, notably the continued growth of the multiples (corporate chains) in most sectors and most countries. Their growth brings greater buying power and economies of scale, fuelling further growth. This market share has been gained mostly at the expense of independent retailers but smaller multiples and co-operatives have also lost ground. Although significant merging of co-operative societies has occurred, the movement is still far from fully co-ordinated, nationally or internationally. Symbol groups, such as Spar in the grocery sector and Numark in the chemists sector, have offered a lifeline to many independent retailers. Franchising has grown rapidly as a business format, offering a blend of large-scale professionalism and individual enterprise.

Retail formats can be defined in many different ways, based on size, location, product groups, specialization, price levels, store features, etc. The continued fall in shop numbers reflects the concentration of trade into fewer, larger outlets. While small shops are under pressure, their purpose has been refocused in the form of c-stores, including forecourts, neighbourhood stores, city outlets and meal solution centres for busy commuters. At the other end of the scale, superstores and hypermarkets (super centres) continue to claim increasing shares of spending on grocery, DIY, electrical goods and other product sectors. Such large store formats have however become severely restricted, especially in out-of-town locations, by many governments.

With 150 years of history, department stores are one of the oldest large-store formats and they have suffered decline in many countries, in the face to specialist and discounter competition. However, consolidation within the sector and more progressive marketing practices have given some a new lease of life. Variety stores, often established as cheaper alternatives to department stores, have tended to trade up and now face many of the same problems. Discounters continue to influence both retail strategy and structure, although the limited-line grocery discounters made only modest impact in the UK. Discounters, in some shape or form, now exist in virtually all sectors; clothing discounters, such as Matalan and TK Maxx, are expanding rapidly.

Shopping centres are also evolving rapidly, having reached their largest scale in centres such as the West Edmonton Mall in Canada. While offering many experiential benefits for major shopping trips, a combination of saturation (North America), planning restrictions (Europe) and their high operating costs have arrested such developments in many countries. Retail parks, or their larger US equivalent 'power centres', have shown more rapid growth: along with factory/designer outlet centres, these offer lower cost and driver-friendly retail environments for 'big box' retailers. Some traditional town centres are also making a comeback, aided by investments in public transport and more integrative, town centre management schemes.

Home shopping is another retail format with a long history, yet now subject to extensive development through electronic channels. 'Mail order' in the US was originally focused upon rural areas, while in the UK, agents recruited clubs of customers from within their social networks. Catalogue showrooms subsequently offered a hybrid format, with home selection of goods but ordering, payment and collection at showrooms. Now multi-channel solutions proliferate, with many retailers offering remote ordering and/or home delivery options. The development of e-tailing specifically is the focus of the final chapter.

REVIEW QUESTIONS

1 Giving relevant examples, show how forecasts of consumer expenditure are essential to retailers' medium- and long-term planning.

2 Focusing upon one retail company, how should it respond to the long-term changes in the population age structure and in the structure of households?

3 Explain the shift towards fewer, longer journeys when shopping for basic requirements. Will this trend continue?

4 Do you expect that the share of the market held by multiple retailers will continue to grow? Justify your answer.

5 Why have the co-operatives tended to lose market share? Draw up a plan to arrest this trend.

6 What are the main functions of symbol (or voluntary) groups? Explain why these groups hold far more market share in some countries than in others.

7 What are the main advantages of franchising, from the viewpoints of the franchisee and the franchisor? What pitfalls must be avoided to achieve long-term success within franchising arrangements?

8 Suggest some of the dimensions that could be used in the classification of retail formats. Taking any three existing retail formats, show how they are positioned on the dimensions that you have suggested.

9 What are the essential characteristics of the convenience store (c-store) format? Suggest a new application for the c-store concept, in terms of location, product range, services offered, etc.

10 What factors are slowing down the development of superstores and hypermarkets? How much scope do you see for further expansion of these retail formats?

11 Why have department stores been in decline in many countries? What steps should they take if they are to survive and prosper?

12 How would you define a discount store? Which companies stand to lose the most from the proliferation of discount outlets in the clothing sector?

13 Explain why the development of major, out-of-town shopping centres has been virtually halted in many countries.

14 What are the particular benefits and limitations of:

a) Power centres?

b) Retail parks?

c) Factory outlet centres?

15 Taking a traditional town centre that is well known to you, outline a plan of how you, the newly appointed town centre manager, can help that centre to compete more effectively.

16 Outline the main developments in home shopping, before the arrival of the Internet. What lessons can be learned from the successes and failures of the past?

REFERENCES

Aalto-Setälä, V. (2000) 'Economies of scale in grocery retailing in Finland', *Journal of Retailing and Consumer Services*, **7** (4), 207–213.

Advertising Association (2001) *Lifestyle Pocket Book 2001*, NTC Publications, Henley-on-Thames.

Agrawal, D. and R. Lal (1995) 'Contractual arrangements in franchising: an empirical investigation', *Journal of Marketing Research*, **32** (2), 213–221.

Arnold, S.J. (2000) 'Market impacts of large format retailers', *Journal of Retailing and Consumer Services*, **7** (4), iii–v.

Arnold, S.J. and M.N. Luthra (2000) 'Market entry effects of large format retailers: a stakeholder analysis', *International Journal of Retail & Distribution Management*, **28** (4/5), 139–154.

Ashley, B. (1997) 'Are malls in America's future?', *Arthur Anderson Retailing Issues Letter*, **9** (6), Texas A&M University.

Barton, P. and P.J. McGoldrick (2001) 'The provision of total availability. Taking stock of consumer inventory management systems', *7th Retailing and Services Science Conference*, Vancouver.

Bell, D. (1999) 'British food retailing: a comparative analysis', *European Retail Digest*, **21**, 30–35.

Bhat, S. and R. Fox (1996) 'An investigation of jeopardy effects in store choice', *Journal of Retailing and Consumer Services*, **3** (3), 129–133.

Bhuian, S.N. (2001) 'Factors determining consumer interest in catalogs: an examination in an emerging market', *Journal of Marketing Channels*, **8** (3/4), 65–84

Bidlake, S. (1995) 'Stopped in their tracks', *SuperMarketing*, 14 April, 18–20.

Birkett, N. (2000a) 'European property review: shopping centres', *European Retail Digest*, **25** (March), 51–53,

Birkett, N. (2000b) 'European property review: factory outlets', *European Retail Digest*, **26**, 47–49.

Birkett, N. (2000c) 'European property review: town centres', *European Retail Digest*, **27** (September), 44–46.

Bodkin, C.D. and J.D. Lord (1997) 'Attraction of power shopping centres', *International Review of Retail, Distribution and Consumer Research*, **7** (2), 93–108.

Bradach, J.L. (1995) 'Chains within chains: the role of multi-unit franchisees', *Journal of Marketing Channels*, **4** (1/2), 65–81.

Brennan, D.P. and L. Lundsten (2000) 'Impacts of large discount stores on small US towns: reasons for shopping and retailer strategies', *International Journal of Retail & Distribution Mangement*, **28** (4/5), 155–161.

Brook, P. and E. Pioch (1996) 'The strange case of home shopping and the Single European Market', *Journal of Retailing and Consumer Services*, **3** (3), 175–182.

Brown, S. (1986) 'Retail classification: a theoretical note', *Quarterly Review of Marketing*, Winter, 12–16.

Brown, S. (1995) *Postmodern Marketing*, Routledge, London.

Brunso, K. and K.G. Grunert (1998) 'Cross-cultural similarities and differences in shopping for food', *Journal of Business Research*, **42**, 145–150.

Burnett, J.J. and M. McCollough (1994) 'Assessing the characteristics of the non-store shopper', *International Review of Retail, Distribution and Consumer Research*, **4** (4), 433–463.

Burt, S. and M. Gabbott (1995) 'The elderly consumer and non-food purchase behaviour', *European Journal of Marketing*, **29** (2), 43–57.

Burt, S. and L. Sparks (1994) 'Structural change in grocery retailing in Great Britain: a discount reorientation?', *International Review of Retail, Distribution and Consumer Research*, **4** (2), 195–217.

Business Ratio (2001) *Department and Variety Stores*, The Prospect Shop, London.

Campos, E.B. (2000) 'El Corte Inglés: sixty years of business success', *European Retail Digest*, **25** (March), 26–28.

Clarke, I., D. Bennison and C. Guy (1994) 'The dynamics of UK grocery retailing at the local scale' *International Journal of Retail & Distribution Management*, **22** (6), 11–20.

Cliquet, G. (1998) 'Integration and territory coverage of the hypermarket industry in France: a relative entropy measure', *International Review of Retail, Distribution and Consumer Research*, **8** (2), 205–224.

Cliquet, G. (2000a) 'Plural forms in store networks: a model for store network evolution', *International Review of Retail Distribution and Consumer Research*, **10** (4), 369–387.

Cliquet, G. (2000b) 'Large format retailers: a French tradition despite reactions', *Journal of Retailing and Consumer Services*, **7** (4), 183–195.

Competition Commission (2000) *Supermarkets. A Report on the Supply of Groceries from Multiple Stores in the United Kingdom*, The Stationery Office, London.

Coopey, R., S. O'Connell and D. Porter (1999) 'Mail order in the United Kingdom c. 1880–1960: how mail order competed with other forms of retailing', *International Review of Retail Distribution and Consumer Research*, **9** (3), 261–273.

Corporate Intelligence (1995) *High Street Home Shopping*, Corporate Intelligence, London.

Court, Y. (2000) 'Out-of-town retailing in Central Europe', *European Retail Digest*, **26**, 45–46.

Cova, B. (1996) 'The postmodern explained to managers: implications for marketing', *Business Horizons*, **39** (6), 15–23.

Cullen, B. and A. Whelan (1997) 'Concentration of the retail sector and trapped brands', *Long Range Planning*, **30** (6), 906–916.

Dant, R.P., A.K. Paswan and P.J. Kaufman (1996) 'What we know about ownership redirection in franchising: a meta-analysis', *Journal of Retailing*, **72** (4), 429–444.

Davies, G. (2000) 'Co-operation: too late or a new beginning?', *European Retail Digest*, **26** (June), 52–53.

Davies, J.D. and P. Jones (1993) 'International activity of Japanese department stores', *Service Industries Journal*, **13** (1), 126–132.

Dawson, J.A. (1983) 'Independent retailing in Great Britain: dinosaur or chameleon?', *Retail & Distribution Management*, **11** (3), 29–32.

Dawson, J.A. and J.D. Lord (1985) *Shopping Centre Development: Policies and Prospects*, Croom Helm, London.

Eastlick, M.A. and R.A. Feinberg (1999) 'Shopping motives for mail catalog shopping', *Journal of Business Research*, **45**, 281–290.

Ebeltoft Group (1998) *Global Convenience Store Retailing*, Financial Times Publishing, London.

Eliot, S.J. (1994) 'The co-operative difference: asset or handicap?', in *Cases in Retail Management*, P.J. McGoldrick (ed.), Pitman, London, pp. 8–15.

Eliot, S.J. (1996) 'What does the future hold for consumer co-operative societies?', *Journal of Consumer Studies and Home Economics*, **20**, 53–61.

Englis, B.G. and M.R. Solomon (1995) 'To be and not to be: lifestyle imagery, reference groups and the clustering of America', *Journal of Advertising*, **24** (1), 13–28.

Euromonitor (1988) *Voluntary Chains and Buying Groups*, Euromonitor, London.

Euromonitor (1989) *Retail Trade International*, Euromonitor, London.

Euromonitor (2000a) *Retail Trade International*, Euromonitor, London.

Euromonitor (2000b) *Consumer Europe 2000/2001*, Euromonitor, London.

European Retail (1999a) 'ICA angered by PM's comments', *European Retail*, **22** (June), 3–4.

European Retail (1999b) 'Karstadt Quelle to internationalize', *European Retail*, **222** (June), 1–2.

European Retail Analyst (2000) 'The future of the superstore', *European Retail Analyst*, (November), 25.

European Retail Digest (1995) 'Future prospects for department store retailing in Europe', *European Retail Digest*, **5** (Winter), 21–45.

Farhangmehr, M., S. Marques and J. Silva (2001) 'Hypermarkets versus traditional retail stores – consumers' and retailers' perspectives in Braga: a case study', *Journal of Retailing and Consumer Services*, **8** (4), 189–198.

Fernie, J. (1998) 'The breaking of the fourth wave: recent out-of-town retail developments in Britain', *International Review of Retail, Distribution and Consumer Research*, **8** (3), 303–317.

Fernie, J. and S.I. Fernie (1997) 'The development of a US retail format in Europe: the case of factory outlet centres', *International Journal of Retail & Distribution Management*, **25** (11), 342–350.

Foreward, J. and C. Fulop (1996) 'Large established firms' entry into franchising: an exploratory investigation of strategic and operational issues', *International Review of Retail, Distribution and Consumer Research*, **6** (1), 34–52.

Fowler, A., J. Pritchard and A. Gulati (1999) *It Ain't 'Arf Hot, Mum*, Morgan Stanley Dean Witter, London.

Freathy, P. and F. O'Connell (1998) 'In-home shopping methods: experiences from the US', *Research Papers in Retailing*, University of Stirling, Stirling.

Freathy, P. and F. O'Connell (1999) 'A typology of European airport retailing', *Service Industries Journal*, **19** (3), 119–134.

Fulop, C. (1996a) *Overview of the Franchise Marketplace 1990–1995*, City University, London.

Fulop, C. (1996b) *An Investigation of the Needs and Attitudes of the Franchise Marketplace*, City University, London.

Gable, M., M.T. Topol, S. Mathis and M.E. Fisher (1995) 'Entry barriers in retailing', *Journal of Retailing and Consumer Services*, **2** (4), 211–221.

Ghosh, A. and S. McLafferty (1991) 'The shopping center: a restructuring of post-war retailing', *Journal of Retailing*, **67** (3), 253–267.

Gold, P. and L.H. Woodliffe (2000) 'Department stores in Spain: why El Corte Inglés succeeded where Galerías Preciados failed', *International Journal of Retail & Distribution Management*, **28** (8), 333–340.

González-Benito, O. (2001) 'Inter-format spatial competition of Spanish hypermarkets', *International Review of Retail, Distribution and Consumer Research*, **11** (1), 63–81.

Guy, C. (2000) 'From crinkly sheds to fashion parks: the role of financial investment in the transformation of retail parks', *International Review of Retail, Distribution and Consumer Research*, **10** (4), 389–400,

Hahn, B. (2000) 'Power centres: a new retail format in the United States of America', *Journal of Retailing and Consumer Services*, **7** (4), 223–231.

Hallsworth, A.G. and J. McClatchey (1994) 'Interpreting the growth of superstore retailing in Britain', *International Review of Retail, Distribution and Consumer Research*, **4** (3), 315–328.

Hallsworth, A.G. and S. Worthington (2000) 'Local resistance to larger retailers: the example of market towns and the food superstore in the UK', *International Journal of Retail & Distribution Management*, **28** (4/5), 207–216.

Harrison, K. (1994) 'Forget "wrinklies" – life begins at 50', *Supermarketing*, 17 June, 13–16.

Harrison, S. (2000) 'Shouts and whispers: the lobbying campaigns for and against resale price maintenance', *European Journal of Marketing*, **34** (1/2), 207–222.

Hogarth-Scott, S. and S.P. Rice (1994) 'The new food discounters', *International Journal of Retail & Distribution Management*, **22** (1), 20–28.

Humphries, G. (1995) *Prospects for Food Discounters and Warehouse Clubs: Growth or Decline?* Pearson, London.

Ibrahim, M.F. and P.J. McGoldrick (2002) *Shopping Choices with Public Transport Options: An Agenda for the 21st Century*, Ashgate, Aldershot.

IGD (1997) *The European Food Industry*, Institute of Grocery Distribution, Watford.

IGD (1999) *Symbol Groups*, Institute of Grocery Distribution, Watford.

IGD (2000) *Grocery Retailing 2000*, Institute of Grocery Distribution, Watford.

IGD (2001) *Competing in the 21st Century*, Institute of Grocery Distribution, Watford.

Insight Marketing (2001) *The Value Groups*, Insight Marketing, London.

Jones, K. and M. Doucet (2000) 'Big-box retailing and the urban retail structure: the case of the Toronto area', *Journal of Retailing and Consumer Services*, **7** (4), 233–247.

Jones, P. and J. Pal (1998) 'Retail services ride the waves', *International Journal of Retail & Distribution Management*, **26** (9), 374–376.

Key Note (1998) *Franchising*, Key Note, London.

Key Note (2000a) *Franchising*, Key Note, London.

Key Note (2000b) *Discount Retailing*, Key Note, London.

Key Note (2000c) *Clothing Retailing*, Key Note, London.

Key Note (2001a) *Convenience Retailing*, Key Note, London.

Key Note (2001b) *Supermarkets & Superstores*, Key Note, London.

Kirby, D.A. and D.C. Law (1981) 'The birth and death of small retail units in Britain', *Retail & Distribution Management*, **9** (1), 16–19.

Kirkup, M. and M. Rafiq (1994) 'Tenancy development in new shopping centres: implications for developers and retailers', *International Review of Retail, Distribution and Consumer Research*, **4** (3), 345–360.

Knight, A. (2000) 'Greener patios, better neighbours and homes to be proud of: the B&Q approach to responsible retailing', *European Retail Digest*, **27** (September), 6–9.

Le Blanc, G. and N. Nguyen (2001) 'An exploratory study on the cues that signed value to members in retail co-operatives', *International Journal of Retail & Distribution Management*, **29** (1), 49–59.

Leeflang, P.S.H. and W.F. van Raaij (1995) 'The changing consumer in the European Union: a '"meta analysis"', *International Journal of Research in Marketing*, **12**, 373–387.

LeHew, M.L.A. and A.E. Fairhurst (2000) 'US shopping mall attributes: an exploratory investigation of their relationship to retail productivity', *International Journal of Retail & Distribution Management*, **28** (6), 261–279.

Management Horizons (2000) *American Dream: High Performance US Retailing*, Management Horizons Europe, London.

Mathwick, C., N. Malhotra and E. Rigdon (2001) 'Experiential value: conceptualization, measurement and application in the catalog and Internet shopping environment', *Journal of Retailing*, **77** (1), 39–56.

McEvoy, D. and H. Aldrich (1986) 'Survival rates of Asian and white retailers', *International Small Business Journal*, **4** (3), 28–37.

McGoldrick, P.J. (1988) 'Spatial price differentiation by chain store retailers', in *Transnational Retailing*, E. Kaynak (ed.), Walter de Gruyter, Berlin, pp. 167–180.

McGoldrick, P.J. and E. Andre (1997) 'Consumer misbehaviour: promiscuity or loyalty in grocery shopping', *Journal of Retailing and Consumer Services*, **4** (2), 73–81.

McGoldrick, P.J. and S. Greenland (1991) 'From mail order to home shopping: revitalising the mail order channel', *Journal of Marketing Channels*, **1** (1), 59–86.

McGoldrick, P.J. and M.G. Thompson (1992) *Regional Shopping Centres*, Avebury, Aldershot.

Medway, D., A. Alexander, D. Bennison and G. Warnaby (1999) 'Retailers' financial support for town centre management', *International Journal of Retail & Distribution Management*, **27** (6), 246–255.

Medway, D., G. Warnaby, D. Bennison and A. Alexander (2000) 'Reasons for retailers' involvement in town centre management', *International Journal of Retail & Distribution Management*, **28** (8), 368–378.

Mendelsohn, M. (1992) *The Guide to Franchising*, Cassell, London.

Merrilees, B. and D. Miller (1997) 'The superstore format in Australia: opportunities and limitations', *Long Range Planning*, **30** (6), 899–905.

Michael, S.C. (1999) 'Do franchised chains advertise enough?', *Journal of Retailing*, **75** (4), 461–478.

Miller, C.E., J. Reardon and D.E. McCorkle (1999) 'The effects of competition on retail structure: an examination of intratype, intertype and intercategory competition', *Journal of Marketing*, **63** (4), 107–120.

Mintel (1997) *Cooking & Eating Habits*, Mintel, London.

Mintel (2000a) *British Lifestyles*, Mintel, London.

Mintel (2000b) *Retail Review*, Mintel, London.

Mintel (2000c) *Discounting and Loyalty in Retailing*, Mintel, London.

Mintel (2001) *British Lifestyles*, Mintel, London.

Morgan Stanley Dean Witter (1999) *Multiple Compression Factors Evident in the UK*, MSDW, London.

Morgan Stanley Dean Witter (2000) *De-Commissioned by Consolidation off the Agenda*, MSDW, London.

Morgan Stanley Dean Witter (2001) *Debenhams: Room to Grow*, MSDW, London.

Morgan, A. (1998) *Factory Outlet Retailers*, Financial Times Business, London.

Morganosky, M.A. (1997) 'Retail market structure change: implications for retailers and consumers', *International Journal of Retail & Distribution Management*, **25** (8), 269–274.

Morganosky, M.A. and B.J. Cude (2000) 'Large format retailing in the US: a consumer experience perspective', *Journal of Retailing and Consumer Services*, **7** (4), 215–222.

Mueller, R.D. and A.J. Broderick (1995) 'East European retailing: a consumer perspective', *International Journal of Retail & Distribution Management*, **23** (1), 32–40.

Mundow, A. (1989) 'Decline and fall of the mall', *Guardian*, 13 May, 9.

National Statistics (2000a) *1998-Based Population Projections*, The Stationery Office, London.

National Statistics (2000b) *General Household Survey*, The Stationery Office, London.

National Statistics (2001a) *Annual Abstract of Statistics*, The Stationery Office, London.

National Statistics (2001b) *Social Trends, 2001*, The Stationery Office, London.

Natwest Markets (1998) *Store Wars: Sector Update*, NWM, London.

Nielsen (2000) *Retail Pocket Book 2000*, NTC Publications, Henley-on-Thames.

Nielsen (2001) *Retail Pocket Book 2001*, NTC Publications, Henley-on-Thames.

Nooteboom, B., R. Thurik and S. Vollebregt (1986) 'Cases and causes of structural change in retailing', in *Retail Strategies for Profit and Growth*, ESOMAR (ed.), Amsterdam, pp. 177–198.

Norris, S. (1999) 'Factory outlet centres into the new millennium: fact and fiction', *European Retail Digest*, 21, 41–45.

Ody, P. (1998) *Non-Store Retailing*, Financial Times, London.

Oxenfeldt, A.R. and A. O'Kelly (1968) 'Will successful franchise systems ultimately become wholly-owned chains?', *Journal of Retailing*, 44 (Winter), 69–83.

Pilling, B.K., S.W. Henson and B.Yoo (1995) 'Competition among franchises, company-owned units and independent operators: a population ecology application', *Journal of Marketing Channels*, **4** (1/2), 177–195.

Porter, J. (1999) *The Future of Department Store Retailing*, Financial Times Retail & Consumer, London.

Rao, R.C. and S. Srinivasan (2001) 'An analysis of advertising payments in franchise contracts', *Journal of Marketing Channels*, **8** (3/4), 85–118.

Retail Intelligence (2000) *Department Stores in Europe*, Retail Intelligence, London.

Retail Review (1995) 'The voluntary group dimension', *Retail Review*, **211** (April), 8.

Retail Review (1997) 'Department store details', *Retail Review*, **235** (August/September), 27–29.

Retail Review (1999a) 'Population – older and older', *Retail Review*, **253** (June), 1–2.

Retail Review (1999b) 'New technology to spur electricals sales', *Retail Review*, **251** (April), 18–19.

Retail Review (1999c) 'Fifty "Nisa" shops expected by year end', *Retail Review*, **251** (April), 13.

Retail Review (1999d) 'Wal-Mart deal to spark off Euro-merger wave', *Retail Review*, **254** (July), 5–6.

Retail Review (1999e) 'Kent Bluewater hits (out-of-) town', *Retail Review*, **250** (March), 3.

Retail Review (1999f) 'Freeman goes to Versand', *Retail Review*, **251** (April), 20–21.

Retail Review (2000a) 'Boots enlarges on health service functions', *Retail Review*, **266** (October), 15.

Retail Review (2000b) 'Hard slog ahead for grocers, says Verdict', *Retail Review*, **265** (August/September), 7–8.

Retail Review (2000c) 'Furniture retailers – the market shares according to Verdict', *Retail Review*, **265** (August/September), 17.

Retail Review (2000d) 'DIY miscellany', *Retail Review*, **260** (March), 18.

Retail Review (2000e) 'Go-ahead for CWS/CRS merger', *Retail Review*, **260** (March), 8–9.

Retail Review (2000f) 'Acquisitive CWS hungry for more – annual results', *Retail Review*, **262** (May), 10–11.

Retail Review (2000g) 'Spar – an international name', *Retail Review*, **260** (March), 5.

Retail Review (2000h) 'C-store snippets', *Retail Review*, **268** (January/February), 7–8.

Retail Review (2000i) 'The retail park dimension', *Retail Review*, **260** (March), 26.

Retail Review (2000j) 'Argos shines in GUS results as traditional mail order slumps', *Retail Review*, **263** (June), 15–16.

Retail Review (2001a) 'Co-operative Group building on merger platform – annual results', *Retail Review*, **271** (May/June), 8–9.

Retail Review (2001b) 'RPM lifted from OTC medicines', *Retail Review*, **271** (May/June), 11–13.

Retail Review (2001c) 'C-store snippets', *Retail Review*, **268** (January/February), 7–8.

Retail Review (2001d) 'Asda lining up heavy expansion programme', *Retail Review*, **268**, (January/February), 8.

Retail Review (2001e) 'High profile on "Tesco Extra" urban regeneration schemes', *Retail Review*, **271** (May/June), 11.

Retail Review (2001f) 'Ikea lands two more store sites', *Retail Review*, **271** (May/June), 18.

Retail Review (2001g) 'TK Maxx – another discounter in a hurry', *Retail Review*, **270** (April), 16.

Retail Review (2001h) 'Factory outlet malls nearing saturation?', *Retail Review*, **271** (May/June), 2–3.

Retail Review (2001i) 'High Street under pressure – long live the High Street', *Retail Review*, **271** (May/June), 22–23.

Retail Review (2001j) 'Factory outlet centres reviewed', *Retail Review*, **262** (May), 20.

Reynolds, J. (1992) 'Generic models of European shopping centre development', *European Journal of Marketing*, **26** (8/9), 48–60.

Reynolds, J. (1996) 'Changing consumer demands and attitudes', in *The Outlook for West European Retail*, R. Davies (ed.), FT Retail & Consumer Publishing, London, pp. 33–45.

Rinehart, S.M. and D. Zizzo (1995) 'The Canadian and US retailing sectors: important changes over the past 60 years', *Journal of Retailing and Consumer Services*, **2** (1), 33–47.

Robinson, T.M. and J. Bailey (1994) 'Discount clothing retailing in the UK', *International Journal of Retail & Distribution Mangement*, **22** (1), 29–37.

Roddick, A. (1991) *Body and Soul*, Ebury Press, London.

Rogers, D. (1991) 'An overview of American retail trends', *International Journal of Retail & Distribution Mangement*, **19** (6), 3–12.

Rousey, S.P. and M.A. Morganosky (1996) 'Retail format change in US markets', *International Journal of Retail & Distribution Management*, **24** (3), 8–16.

Samuolis, M.E. and M.A. Morganosky (1996) 'International service offerings by catalogue retailers', *International Review of Retail, Distribution and Consumer Research*, **6** (2), 147–160.

Scase, R. (1999) *Britain Towards 2010: The Changing Business Environment*, Department of Trade and Industry, London.

Schiller, R. (1987) 'Out of town exodus', in *The Changing Face of British Retailing*, E. McFadyen (ed.), Newman Books, London, pp. 64–73.

Schmidt, R.A., R. Segal and C. Cartwright (1994) 'Two-stop shopping or polarization', *International Journal of Retail & Distributon Management*, **22** (1), 12–19.

Schmitt (1999) 'Experiential marketing', *Journal of Marketing Management*, **15**, 53–67.

Seiders, K. and D.J. Tigert (2000) 'The impact of supercentres on traditional food retailers in four markets', *International Journal of Retail & Distribution Management*, **28** (4/5), 181–193.

Sen, K.C. (1995) 'Advertising fees in the financial channel', *Journal of Marketing Channels*, **4** (1/2), 83–101.

Sen, K.C. (2001) 'Information asymmetry and the franchise decision', *Journal of Marketing Channels*, **8** (1/2), 91–109.

Shamdasani, P.N. and O.G. Yeow (1995) 'An exploratory study of in-home shoppers in a concentrated retail market', *Journal of Retailing and Consumer Services*, **2** (1), 15–23.

Smails, S. (1996) 'Solos hit the spotlight', *Supermarketing*, **16** February, 18–20.

Smith, A. and L. Sparks (2000) 'The role and function of the independent small shop: the situation in Scotland', *International Review of Retail, Distribution and Consumer Research*, **10** (2), 205–226.

Solomon, B. (1993) 'Power centres: the new fact of retailing', *Management Review*, April, 50–53.

Solomon, M., G. Bamossy and S. Askegaard (1999) *Consumer Behaviour: A European Perspective*, Prentice Hall Europe, London.

Sparks, L. (1994) 'Seven-Eleven Japan Co. Ltd: from licensee to owner in eighteen years', in *Cases in Retail Management*, P.J. McGoldrick (ed.), Pitman, London, pp. 336–351.

Stassen, R.E. and R.A. Mittelstaedt (1995) 'Territory encroachment in maturing franchise systems', *Journal of Marketing Channels*, **4** (1/2), 27–48.

Stern, P. and J. Stanworth (1988) 'The development of franchising in Britain', *The NatWest Bank Review*, May, 38–48.

Stimson, D. (1994) *Use of and Attitudes towards Town Centre and Out-of-Town Shopping*, SRG Information Unit, London.

Strutton, D., L.E. Pelton and J.R. Lumpkin (1995) 'Psychological climate in franchising system channels and franchisor-franchisee solidarity', *Journal of Business Research*, **34** (2), 81–91.

SuperMarketing (1996) 'Win, lose or draw. Co-op: retailing into the future', *SuperMarketing*, **24** May, 22–58.

Swindley, D.G. (1993) 'Central Regional Co-operative Society Ltd: case study', *International Journal of Retail & Distribution Management*, **21** (3), 40–52.

Tordjman, A. (1993) *Evolution of Retailing Formats in the EC*, Group HEC, Jouy-en-Josas.

Treadgold, A. (1996) 'Food retailing in Australia – three retailers, three strategies', *International Journal of Retail and Distribution Management*, **24** (8), 6–16.

Verdict (1998) *Verdict on Clothing Retailers*, Verdict, London.

Verdict (1999) *Verdict on Department Stores*, 1999, Verdict, London.

Verdict (2000) *Verdict on Neighbourhood Stores*, Verdict, London.

Verdict (2001) *Verdict on Housewares Retailers*, 2001, Verdict, London.

Vignali, C., R.A. Schmidt and B.J. Davies (1993) 'The Benetton experience', *International Journal of Retail & Distribution Management*, **21** (3), 53–59.

Wakefield, K.L. and J. Baker (1998) 'Excitement at the mall: determinants and effects on shopping response', *Journal of Retailing*, **74** (4), 515–539.

Ward, R. (1987) 'Small retailers in inner urban areas', in *Business Strategy and Retailing*, G. Johnson (ed.), Wiley, Chichester, pp. 275–287.

Watson, P. (1996) *Hypermarkets and Superstores in Europe: The End of Growth?* Pearson Professional, London.

Which? (2000) 'Bagging a bargain', *Which?* July, 38–41.

Wilcox, M. and E. O'Callaghan (2001) 'The strategic response to Dublin's traditional department stores to intensifying competition', *Journal of Retailing and Consumer Services*, **8** (4), 213–225.

Wileman, A. (1993) 'Destination retailing: high volume, low gross margin, large-scale formats', *International Journal of Retail & Distribution Management*, **21** (1), 3–9.

Willans, J. (1997) 'Department stores: an enduring retail format', *Journal of Fashion Marketing and Management*, **1** (2), 145–149.

Wood, S.L. (2001) 'Remote purchase environment: the influence of return policy leniency on two-stage decision processes', *Journal Marketing Research*, **38** (2), 157–169.

Zanderighi, L. and E. Zaninotto (1994) 'Property rights distribution in European retailing', *International Review of Retail, Distribution and Consumer Research*, **4** (4), 393–409.

Zola, E. (1883) *Au Bonheur des Dames*, translated (1992) *The Ladies' Paradise*, University of California Press, Berkeley, CA.

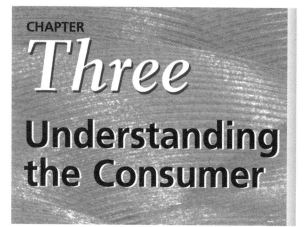

Three

Understanding the Consumer

INTRODUCTION Fundamental to the formulation of retail marketing strategy is a clear understanding of consumer needs, motives and patronage decision processes. It is also easy to forget that every shopper is an individual with a set of needs and motives that differ, at least slightly, from those of other shoppers. In an increasingly competitive trading environment, the best rewards go to retailers who can profitably assemble a product and service mix that is carefully attuned to the requirements of clearly defined consumer segments.

The successful identification of needs does not in itself guarantee a successful marketing strategy, although it is a very logical first step. Without this step, there is a tendency for strategy formulation to dwell upon the range of existing solutions, rather than developing formats to satisfy specific sets of consumer requirements. Insufficient attention to real needs can lead to the copying or continuation of formats that should in fact be evolved or completely superseded. It can also lead to a failure to anticipate or to effectively diagnose declining demand for a particular product/service mix.

Many of the strategic frameworks advanced over recent decades perpetuate the obsession with beating the competition. However, it can be argued that outsmarting the competition is a surer, and probably cheaper, route to success. As Ohmae (1988) observes: 'strategy isn't beating the competition; it's serving customers' real needs'. To further support his argument, he quotes the advice of the great Sun Tzu (500 BC, cited by Ohmae, 1988): 'The smartest strategy in war is one that allows you to achieve your objectives, without having to fight.' The highly visible battles involving prices, promotions, advertising, formats, etc. are in fact only a part of retail strategy. The largest part, often intentionally invisible, is the quest to find ways of satisfying consumer needs, more effectively.

Most retailers would claim to be customer oriented and may also point to the constant interface with shoppers as indicative of an understanding of consumer needs. Although much insight could be gained through the interactions between customers and staff, in reality the full potential is rarely realized. Formal feedback channels between sales staff and senior management may be weak; customer complaints and enquiries are often regarded as something to be dealt with rather than as a valuable information source. In some enlightened companies, however, senior managers do maintain close contact with customers by spending time working on the shop floor or by attending discussion groups of actual/potential customers.

'Internal' channels of communication can provide much insight into consumer needs, but obviously these must be supplemented with 'external' information. The retailer is confronted with an array of secondary sources, presenting research and analysis of various customer, product and store types. The commercial secondary sources tend to be fairly expensive but cost far less than the equivalent primary research. Their main drawbacks, however, are that the information quickly becomes dated, it is available to all competitors, and neither the questions asked nor the samples drawn may be entirely appropriate to a specific retailer's strategic decisions. Most major retailers therefore undertake or commission primary research to try to maintain a competitive edge in monitoring needs, motives and attributes. Many of the research techniques employed will be considered here and in Chapter 5.

This chapter begins by considering shoppers' needs and motives at the most fundamental level, and then some of the specific motives associated with the shopping activity. The criteria employed in selecting between retail outlets are next examined, with some alternative explanations of the consumer's patronage decision process. The penultimate section of the chapter focuses upon the technique of market segmentation; approaches are compared and some typologies of shopping orientations examined. Finally, attention turns to customer retention, the concept of customer loyalty, 'loyalty programmes' and the development of relationship marketing in retailing.

3.1 Motives for Shopping

It is in the interest of the retail strategist to go 'back to basics' in attempting to understand consumer motives; otherwise there is a tendency to confuse needs and solutions. For example, the statement that 'our customers need better service at the checkout' may be perfectly true, but the solution of better checkout service should be carefully appraised in terms of the fundamental needs that it satisfies. The service may satisfy a physical need for greater ease at the checkout, or it may satisfy needs for more human interaction, more security or more prestige. A strategic solution can therefore satisfy several different needs, but it must also be recognized that such needs may be satisfied by several different solutions.

3.1.1 Needs and Motives

One of the most influential theories of human needs has been that of Maslow (1970), which was initially developed in the 1940s. He suggested a hierarchy of needs, from the most basic or primitive through to the most civilized or mature, as Fig. 3.1 illustrates.

Figure 3.1 Maslow's hierarchy of needs

Source: adapted from Maslow (1970).

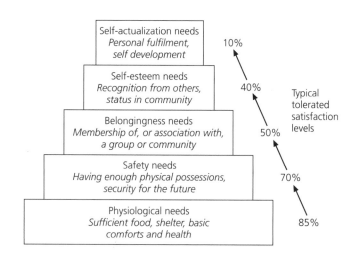

The theory suggests that people seek to progress through this hierarchy and, as needs at one level are satisfied, those at the next level take over. Maslow also estimated 'tolerated satisfaction levels', at which people typically proceed to the next level, even though the lower level needs may not be 100 per cent satisfied.

Inevitable, the theory has been criticized, for the lack of empirical support for the number of categories, the hierarchical order and the satisfaction levels (Betts, 1994). In spite of these criticisms, the theory remains pervasive and accessible (e.g. Maslow and Stephens, 2000). Chenet and Johansen (1999), for example, expand upon the concept of the 'self-actualized consumer':

> *We do not buy products and services anymore—more and more what we buy are concepts and experiences that build up our self-identity and uniqueness (what we eat, drink, wear, drive, where we live, what we do or want to do at work and in our free time, study, believe in, etc.). Concepts and experiences must offer 'unique' requirements.*

Among the other theories of human motivation, McClelland (1967) suggests that needs can be grouped into just three broad categories:

▶ affiliation needs
▶ power needs
▶ achievement needs.

These basic classifications can help to understand the underlying structure of needs that may, potentially, be satisfied by a particular strategic move. For example, in developing its own store card, a retailer may appeal to the need for safety (less cash handling), belongingness ('club' membership), esteem (prestige) and/or power (additional privileges). Similarly, the appeal of a high-status store may be geared to reflect the achievement and self-actualization of customers able to shop there.

The ability of one product, service or store attribute to satisfy a number of different needs is emphasized by Foxall and Goldsmith (1994), who reject the concept of a rigid hierarchy. For example, a struggling artist or writer may seek to achieve self-actualization, while paying scant attention to physiological or safety needs. However, in support of the hierarchy, there is evidence of retrenchment to safety needs, leading to more savings, in times of recession: a form of reverse hierarchy (Betts, 1994).

Foxall and Goldsmith (1994) suggest a 'multidimensional approach' to consumer motivation. Their typology gives more attention to 'higher order' needs, reflecting changes in values and spending power.

1 *Physiological needs*: analogous to Maslow's physiological and safety needs, goods and services that allow consumers to function in day-to-day life.
2 *Social needs*: products or actions that satisfy functional needs may at the same time express membership of a group, or transmit signals about the consumer's social relations.
3 *Symbolic needs*: products or patronage of particular stores may serve as symbols of success, achievement, status or power.
4 *Hedonic needs*: the sensory benefits, such as taste, smell, sound and visual imageries.
5 *Cognitive needs*: the need to know, provoking the use of books, news programmes, store browsing or Internet searching.
6 *Experiential needs*: consumption or patronage because of how it makes consumers feel, producing desired emotions or moods.

Most typologies of needs and motives dwell upon reasons why people do things, rather than reasons for avoiding particular alternatives. The 'dual factor' theory of Herzberg (1966), although developed in relation to job satisfaction/dissatisfaction, has been applied to the understanding of consumer motivations. Herzberg suggested that a distinction should be made between factors causing satisfaction and those causing dissatisfaction. The removal of a 'dissatisfier' would not necessarily produce satisfaction; it would simply overcome one area of dissatisfaction.

For example, a retailer with an awkward returns procedure may not produce a significant attraction by improving this, but may overcome a factor that was inhibiting sales. On the other hand, intensification of 'satisfiers', such as a better selling environment or special offers, would be unlikely to alleviate the blockage to sales caused by the returns procedure. Although essentially a very simple concept, this dual factor theory offers some important insights into the patronage decision process, which is considered in Sec. 3.2.

3.1.2 The Shopping Activity Studies of shoppers' motivations have tended to emphasize the need for the actual products or, alternatively, the reasons for selecting one store/centre as opposed to others. Tauber (1972) made a notable departure from previous patronage research by asking the most basic question, 'Why do people shop?'. He encouraged strategists and researchers to address their attention to the primary motivations that determine the shopping activity, rather than simply to assume that the need to purchase products is the only, or even the main, reason for shopping. Tauber (1972) hypothesized that:

> *People's motives for shopping are a function of many variables, some of which are unrelated to the actual buying of products. It is maintained that an understanding of the shopping motives requires the consideration of satisfactions which shopping activities provide, as well as the utility obtained from the merchandise that may be purchased.*

Based upon in-depth interviews with both male and female shoppers, Tauber suggested several types of personal motive for shopping, classified as follows:

1 *Role-playing*: shopping may be a learned and expected behaviour pattern which, for some, becomes an integral part of their role.
2 *Diversions*: shopping may provide a break from the daily routine, a form of recreation; it can provide a diversionary pastime for individuals or free entertainment for the family.
3 *Self-gratification*: the shopping trip may represent an antidote to loneliness or boredom; the act of purchasing may be an attempt to alleviate depression.
4 *Learning about new trends*: many people enjoy shopping as an opportunity to see new things and get new ideas.
5 *Physical activity*: the exercise provided by shopping is an attraction to some, especially those whose work and travel modes provide little opportunity for exercise.
6 *Sensory stimulation*: the shopping environment can provide many forms of stimulation, through light, colours, sounds, scents and through handling the products.

Tauber's ideas on the shopping activity have proved highly influential and these personal motives have been well substantiated. For example, Piper and Capella (1993) observe that shopping can also be part of the 'modern man' role-play, and Buttle (1992) found various instances of shopping as a diversionary activity. In the area of self-gratification, shopping has been used to cure boredom (Mano, 1999), loneliness (Forman and Sriram, 1991) and for general mood repair (Elliott, 1994). Bloch et al. (1994) report that a quarter of respondents visit malls, in part, for exercise and many go there to learn about new trends. Several studies have addressed the issue of sensory stimulation from the atmospherics of retail stores and centres (e.g. McGoldrick and Pieros, 1998; see also Chapter 12). The term 'experiential retailing' is applied to the creation of retailing experiences that stimulate thought and/or senses (Kim, 2001).

A number of social motives were also hypothesized by Tauber:

1 *Social experiences outside the home*: like the traditional market, the shopping area can provide the opportunity for social interaction, meeting friends or simply 'people-watching'.
2 *Communication with others having a similar interest*: hobby, sports and even DIY shops provide the opportunity for interaction with staff and customers with similar interests.
3 *Peer group attraction*: using a particular store may reflect a desire to be among the group which one chooses or aspires to belong; this may be particularly significant in patronizing a high-status or a 'trend' store.
4 *Status and authority*: in that stores seek to serve the customer, especially when contemplating high-cost, comparison purchases, some shoppers enjoy being 'waited on' while in the store.
5 *Pleasure of bargaining*: some derive satisfaction from the process of haggling or from shopping around to obtain the best bargains.

These social motives have also been extensively corroborated. Bloch et al. (1994) observe how the young and the elderly in particular use shopping areas for social activity. A sense of community is felt when interacting with others of similar interests and values (Oliver, 1999). The aspirational nature of browsing in higher status stores is noted by Buttle (1992). While customers expect respect from staff in all retail settings, the desire for status and authority is most likely to be satisfied where personal service is available (Roy, 1994). Neither is the pleasure of bargaining extinct, whether in the form of negotiations (Lee, 2000) or hunting for bargains at marked-down prices (Betts and McGoldrick, 1996).

Tauber's extended typology of motives underlying the shopping activity represented an important development from the view of shopping as simply a process of economic exchange. Often consumers do not overtly acknowledge these personal and social motives, preferring to justify their shopping behaviour in more 'rational' terms. Many surveys have therefore failed to detect the strength of these factors within the consumer's patronage decision process. However, by using anthropological approaches to the observation of shopping, Underhill (2000) has amassed considerable evidence on the satisfactions derived from the shopping activity.

In its study of the food shopping activity, Mintel (2000) reported that 48 per cent liked to do food shopping as quickly as possible: by no means all consider it as just a burden or a chore. In an earlier study, it was found that younger consumers were the most likely to enjoy shopping (Mintel, 1994). Research by Healey and Baker found the British to be keen shoppers for clothes, if not for food, their enthusiasm being exceeded only by that of the Italians, Belgians and Swedes (Retail Week, 2000).

From an 'enjoyment index' constructed by the Consumers' Association, shopping for new cars or evening wear are considered reasonably enjoyable, much less so when shopping for carpets or basic electrical goods (Childs, 2000). This was not the first attempt to measure the 'fun' element of shopping. Babin et al. (1994) developed measures to indicate levels of hedonic and utilitarian value that consumers derive from shopping.

Table 3.1 indicates differences in levels of enjoyment, according to the type of shop, gender and shopping role. It is interesting to note that, among primary shoppers within households, men are considerably more likely than women to enjoy supermarket shopping. The reverse is true of trips to shopping malls (Dholakia, 1999). While such studies provide useful indications, it is possible to satisfy some motives, such as role playing, without actually enjoying the shopping trip.

Table 3.1 Enjoyment of shopping

Source: derived from Dholakia (1999).

Gender	Male shoppers		Female shoppers	
Shopping role	**Primary %**	**Joint %**	**Primary %**	**Joint %**
Going to supermarket				
Enjoy: A great deal	25.8	16.4	15.3	14.3
Somewhat	65.2	65.6	64.0	69.8
Not at all	9.0	18.0	20.7	15.9
Going to shopping mall				
Enjoy: A great deal	12.5	16.0	23.7	41.2
Somewhat	61.2	64.6	56.5	50.0
Not at all	26.4	19.3	19.8	8.8

3.2 Store Choice

A clear understanding of why consumers patronize one store and not another has long been an objective of retail strategists and researchers. However, as retailers quickly respond to the actions of competitors, there has been convergence of formats in many sectors, so the precise components of the patronage decision are not always obvious. The range of published research data has grown rapidly, but these usually represent broad generalizations across whole sectors, types of store and/or localities. Retailers depending entirely upon standard sources therefore may be led towards standard or follower strategies.

Reasons for selecting a store are normally expressed in terms of the positive attributes which help to fulfil shoppers underlying motives. The connections between these store attributes and consumers' motives are usually left to the imagination or to further investigation, possibly using the technique of means-end chains (e.g. Gengler et al., 1995). Using this technique, researchers probe deeply into the reasons why an attribute is important, establishing the network of linkages between functional attributes and core motives (or values). Figure 3.2 illustrates how a small part of a means-end chain might be configured; the full means-end chain would include far more attributes, consequences, motives and linkages between them. Figure 3.2 does however show how attributes, through a different series of consequences, link to more than one motive, and vice versa (Pieters et al., 1995).

Figure 3.2 Means-end chains

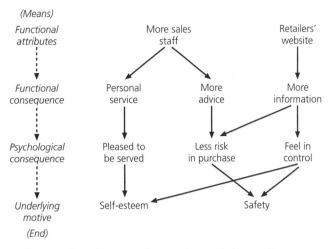

Note: this illustration shows just two attributes and two underlying motives. A full analysis using this technique results in a far more complex means-end chain.

Another complication in researching attributes is that their salience is highly context-specific, varying by shopper type, country, sector, shopping task, etc. There is also a tendency to dwell upon the reasons *for* making a choice, rather than those *against* that choice. Equal attention should therefore be given to all aspects of shopping 'cost', be that money, time, effort, stress or risk.

3.2.1 Store Selection Criteria

Research agencies are broadly in agreement about the attributes which are attractive to consumers when deciding where to shop. Estimates of importance level do, however, vary greatly, in part because of differences in the methods used to measure importance. For example, Table 3.2 lists the most salient attributes identified within two major studies of grocery shoppers' store selection criteria. Both agree on the importance of convenience, price, product assortment and car parking. However, relative importance levels differ somewhat between the studies, and different key attributes emerge from the two studies.

Some of these differences arise because of the methods used to rate importance. Nielsen (2000) ask Homescan panel members to indicate their first and second most important attributes. The Competition Commission (2000), on the other hand, asked which factors were important influences upon the patronage decision, then, which was the main factor. These variations in approach do not alone explain the differences between the most important/main factor percentages.

The ways in which attributes are 'bundled' in a survey can greatly influence ratings of importance. 'Good value for money', for example, is a much wider concept than just prices, potentially including many aspects of product and store quality. Likewise, 'weekly shopping under one roof' is a much broader concept than 'good range of products'. It is not surprising, therefore, that these descriptors received the highest importance ratings in the two studies.

Table 3.2 Reasons for selecting a grocery shop

Source: derived from Competition Commission (2000); Nielsen (2000).

Attributes (Nielsen)	Most important %	Second most important %
Good value for money	18.8	25.3
Convenient location	17.7	11.1
Ease of parking	16.4	8.8
Low prices	14.5	6.4
Good range of products	11.6	18.2
Store is clean and tidy	5.4	4.2
Good quality 'own labels'	4.9	4.1
Good quality fresh produce	3.9	6.7
High quality products	2.7	4.7
Special in-store promotions	2.3	5.7
Helpful staff	1.1	2.7
Attributes (Competition Commission)	**Main factor %**	**An important factor %**
Weekly shopping under one roof	43	69
Prices charged for groceries	18	58
Within easy reach of home	16	55
Large range of groceries	6	45
Sufficient car-parking space	6	38
Products I want always in stock	4	36
Flexible opening hours	4	36
Extra facilities: petrol, coffee shop, etc.	0	12
Shopping experience/style of store	1	6
Proximity to other shops and/or recreational facilities	0	5

The choice of attributes for inclusion within the rating exercise also influences the outcome. For example, 'clean and tidy' is of high importance to nearly 10 per cent in the Nielsen (2000) study, possibly just taken for granted within the other. Conversely, opening hours are of at least some importance to a third of those interviewed for the Competition Commission (2000), yet are not included in the other study. The reason for highlighting these differences is to stress the importance of the methodological context, when interpreting or acting upon survey data.

There is extensive evidence that attribute importance is highly dependent upon shopping/shopper situation. However, only when methods are identical or very closely matched across contexts can these differences be accurately identified.

1 *Place*: Smith (1995) compared store selection factors across five European countries, noting for example that French consumers rate 'wide selection' as relatively unimportant. This again points to the influence of competitive context: many stores in France offer a wide selection, so this becomes less of an issue when choosing between

them. Dunnhumby Associates (2000) likewise observed many points of difference between salience of criteria to shoppers in the UK and the USA. Mintel (1999a) illustrated within-country regional differences, 'attractive prices' being mentioned more frequently in North West England and Scotland.

2 *Period*: Bates and Gabor (1987) found that convenience had increased in rated importance over a 17-year period, whereas cleanliness, good layout, etc. had declined markedly; presumably these are now taken for granted. Mintel (1999a) identified differences over just one year, cash-back facilities having declined in stated importance, probably for the same reason. Betts and McGoldrick (1996) illustrate how attribute importance changes during seasonal 'sale' periods.

3 *People*: it is to be expected that different groups will have different priorities, thus the importance of effective market segmentation. Differences in store selection criteria have been demonstrated between age groups and levels of dependency (Burnett, 1996), life-stages, socio-economic groups (Nielsen, 2000), genders and specific group status (e.g. working women) (Mintel, 1999a).

4 *Purpose*: often store choice is not made in isolation from other purposes that the planned journey must fulfil. For example, the choice of shopping centre, to fulfil these other purposes, may lead to the use of specific stores that do not best match individual selection criteria (Timmermans and Van der Waerden, 1992). The purpose for which a store is visited can also influence criteria salience, as Table 3.3 illustrates. The DIY enthusiast needing large quantities will be most interested in stock availability and prices. Someone looking for ideas will be more concerned with a good choice of the latest products (Van Kenhove et al., 1999).

Table 3.3 Attribute salience varies by task

Source: adapted from Van Kenhove et al. (1999).

DIY store attributes	Rank order of importance by task				
	Urgent purchase	Large quantities	Difficult job	Regular purchase	Get ideas
Store has large enough stock of product I want	1	1	5	4	7
Store is nearby	2	7	6=	5	9
I can get what I want quickly	3	6	6=	7	8
I know for sure that the stores sells those products	4	3	4	1	3
Store carries products of good quality	5	4	2	3	4
Store offers service also after sales	6	5	1	6	5
I can choose between different models of one product	7	8	3	8	1
The store has low prices	8	2	9	2	10
Store carries the latest products	9	9	8	9	2
Store is cozy and elegant	10	10	10	10	6

3.2.2 The Costs of Shopping

So far attention has focused upon the positive attributes of stores, and of the shopping activity, which help to fulfil consumers' motives. It is important, however, to pay attention to the other side of the 'value equation', the elements which potentially detract from the fulfilment of motives. Much attention has been given to the reasons why alternatives are selected, rather less to why they are rejected (Jones and Sasser, 1995).

Economists have traditionally regarded money as primary cost of shopping, prices being traded off against various other non-price attributes. Using spatial interaction models, geographers have typically regarded distance (or time) as the main 'deterence' factor, which is traded off against a number of attraction factors (Sec. 7.1.7) Bell et al. (1998) include both price and travel costs within their model of total shopping costs. However, a more complete view of the costs of shopping demands the recognition of other non-monetary costs, including time, effort and stress (Cassill et al., 1997). Figure 3.3 adds risk to the negative side of the value equation, this being another factor that consumers normally seek to minimize in choosing a store, centre, product or brand (Mitchell and McGoldrick, 1996).

Figure 3.3 The value equation

Source: adapted from Chain Store Age Executive (1994).

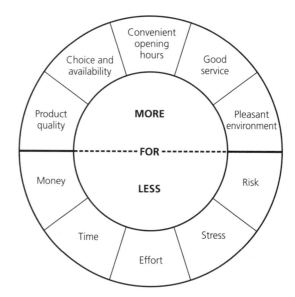

Of course, not all shoppers seek to minimize money, time, effort, stress and risk. Those involved in conspicuous consumption may see merit in spending more, while others see the filling of time as an objective (McGoldrick and Andre, 1997). As noted earlier, some regard high-effort shopping as a form of exercise or role fulfilment (Tauber, 1972). Under certain circumstances, stress and risk can also have positive connotations, thus the liking for white-knuckle rides or visits to Las Vegas. Just as store selection criteria are person and context dependent, so too is the extent to which 'costs' may sometimes become benefits.

It may also be argued that money, time, effort, stress and risk are simply consequences of various fundamental attributes. Thus, they could occupy intermediary roles within a means-end chain (e.g. Fig. 3.2), helping to understand how negative attributes can contribute to a lack of gaol fulfilment. For example:

higher prices or car park charges	= more money
distant location or long queues	= more time
difficult access or self service	= more effort
layout changes or information overload	= more stress
unknown brands or unsafe parking	= more risk

Although these factors do reflect (usually) adverse consequences of various attributes, there is merit of giving them explicit attention. It helps to counter the research bias towards the positive factors which attract shoppers. It is also consistent with the increased attention now being given to customer retention (Sec. 3.4).

The monetary costs of a 'basket' of goods has been given extensive attention within the context of retail pricing (Chapter 10). However, this is not the full extent of the financial cost of shopping, as many shopping journeys also incur fuel/motoring costs, car-parking charges or public transport fares (Bell et al., 1998). These become all the more relevant as governments increasing tax and discourage the use of car-borne transportation. Additionally, a shopper may incur other monetary costs by making a particular shopping choice, for example, the need to buy a snack, a meal or peace offerings for children, having travelled some distance.

Expressions such as 'saving time', 'investing time' and 'time is money' emphasize that time, like money, is a scarce resource (Betts et al., 1998). As Leclerc et al. (1995) point out: 'Even the wealthy are limited to 24 hours per day. For many, time is not just a scarce resource, it is *the* scarce resource.' However, they also note the major differences between time and money. Time cannot be stored and it is also less transferable than money. Consequently, consumers may be more willing to risk the possible loss of money than time, as the latter is less easily recouped, if lost.

Like money, clock time is divided into discrete, immutable units which are external to the individual. Davies (1994) observes that the emphasis upon clock time is a particular characteristic of industrialized and urbanized societies. However, psychological time, or the subjective perception of a time period, may be of equal or greater importance in understanding consumers' time costs.

If people are active and stimulated during a given time period, it will seem to pass more quickly than time spent bored. In retrospect, there is the opposite tendency to overestimate the duration of the active time, while empty time is underestimated (Davies and Omer, 1996). Consequently, 'time flies' when an hour is spent in a stimulating and attractive store or centre: conversely, 'time drags' if the hour is spent in a dismal environment with long checkout queues. However, even waiting time can seem to pass more quickly if ways are found to make this more pleasant (Pruyn and Smidts, 1998).

Time is frequently used as an indication of the effort required to get to a shop, and to complete the shopping. It is, however, an inadequate measure of effort, as many aspects of accessibility can influence the physical effort required to get to a store. Stairs, steep slopes, crowds, exposure to weather and large car parks all increase effort. Once in the store, awkward trolleys, bad layouts and long aisles increase the work of shopping. While ergonomists have researched extensively the work of store staff (e.g. Slappendel, 1992), the overall effort of shopping has received less attention. The effort required to make value comparisons in-store was considered by Betts et al. (1998): other specific elements of the shopping task, such as trolley design, have also been the subject of proprietary studies.

Slightly more attention has been given to stress and shopping (e.g. Aylott and Mitchell, 1998). As noted earlier, stress can be either positive (eustress) or negative (distress). Some people actively seek the input of pressure to their lives to combat understimulation (McGoldrick and Andre, 1997). However, reports of 'trolley rage' and other manifestations of negative stress have drawn attention to some of its causes in the retail environment (Moody, 1996).

According to IGD (2001) research, changes to a store's layout are guaranteed to wind up shoppers, as they interrupt shopping patterns and are usually considered to be manipulative. Lewis (2000) reports on the major stresses to afflict 'old' and 'new' consumers, summarized in Table 3.4. His new consumers, who may be of any age category, are characterized by individualism, independence and greater product knowledge. They are very likely to be stressed by queues, blocked aisles, unhelpful staff and other time-wasting attributes. More traditional shoppers, on the other hand, are most likely to be stressed by factors which disrupt or complicate their shopping routine. In practice, however, virtually any aspect of store performance that fails to meet expectations can induce some stress, especially if a shopper is already stressed from work and/or home.

Table 3.4 Sources of shopping stress

Note: for the purpose of this study, 'new' consumers transcend all ages, ethnic and even social groups. They are as likely to be affluent over 50s as ambitious under 30s.

Source: adapted from Lewis (2000).

'Old' consumers	'New' consumers
Favourite brand out of stock	Narrow / congested / blocked aisles
Product relocation / layout changes	Checkout queues
Too much choice	Loud music / many tannoy announcements
Poor signage / labelling	Insufficient / unhelpful / ignorant staff
Information overload	Lack of time
Being watched by security cameras	Trolley manoeuvrability

Perceived risk is also a concept that pervades many aspects of the store and product selection process. An extensive body of evidence on the role of perceived risk within consumers' choice processes has accumulated (see Mitchell, 1999). Most of this has focused upon product choice, although product risks can clearly influence store choice, for example, retailers' stances on genetically modified (GM) foods (Pearce and Hansson, 2000). The concept of risk has been increasingly deployed within the study of store choice (Mitchell and Kiral, 1999), the influence of store effects upon choice (Sweeney et al., 1999) and in the choice between home or store-based shopping (Van den Poel and Leunis, 1996).

A risk perception comprises an evaluation of the probability of an unwelcome outcome, combined with the likely consequences of that outcome. Thus, it may be highly probable that a store will be crowded on Saturday, but the consequences are modest, unless the consumer is extremely time-pressured or claustrophobic. On the other hand, the probability of the car being stolen from the store or centre's car park is low, but the consequences very troublesome. The extent to which an option is avoided therefore depends upon the consumer's assessment of risk probability and likely consequences.

Table 3.5 lists five different forms of perceived risk, illustrating that each can apply to store (or centre) choice and to product (or brand) choice. Consumers develop a repertoire of risk reduction strategies to help minimize the probability and/or consequences of risks that they perceive. This framework can also help retailers to identify the many ways in which they too can minimize consumers' perceptions of risk. Herzberg's (1966) 'dual factor' theory points to the importance of removing potential 'dissatisfiers' (Sec. 3.1.1). This may suggest more effective strategy options than simply continuing to raise levels of other 'satisfiers' in the retail mix.

Table 3.5 Examples of perceived risks in store patronage

Source: based upon Mitchell and McGoldrick (1996).

Type of perceived risk	Example of risks perceived	Possible risk reduction strategies	
		By retailer	**By consumer**
Physical risks	Concern for personal safety	High-profile security	Shop in safe areas / times
	Concern for health ranges	Information and special	Check fat / salt / calorie levels
Financial risks	Spend too much in superstore	Self-scanning technology	Buy generics / cheaper brands
	Item beyond current means	Offer credit terms	Shop during 'sale' times
Performance risks	Store may not stock all needs	Well-targeted assortment	Stay with a familiar store
	Product may not satisfy	Easy returns arrangements	Buy expensive or familiar brand
Psychosocial risks	Unknown store environment	Display layout diagrams	Visit store with a friend
	Embarrassed by store brand	Develop image of store brand	Buy different brands to offer friends
Time risks	Congestion/queues may be bad	Checkout service guarantees	Shop at off-peak times
	Self-assembly may take ages	Good instructions / video guides	Buy furniture fully assembled

3.3 The Patronage Decision Process

The study of the consumer's patronage decision process and the development of store choice models holds out the prospect of being able to influence this process more precisely, rapidly and / or economically. In the general field of consumer behaviour, significant advances have been made in the construction and refinement of comprehensive models, notably those of Sheth (1974) and Engel et al. (1986). These offer helpful insights into the patronage decision process, especially in relation to single-item, major purchases. There are however important differences between the processes of selecting a store and selecting a product.

It is argued that the two processes and their determinants are significantly different and therefore cannot be combined into a single conceptual framework with a common set of constructs (Sheth, 1983).

Attempts to depict, explain or predict retail patronage have deployed a considerable diversity of perspectives and approaches. At one extreme, arising from the interface between marketing and urban geography, there has been the development of models emphasizing the location factor, generally depicting patronage behaviour at the most aggregate level. These spatial models are considered in Chapter 7 in relation to store location decisions. In contrast, behavioural models have been developed which focus upon the decision process of individual shoppers. Some are essentially descriptive, while others are of a stochastic nature, with detailed formulations attempting to predict probably behavioural outcomes. A few models attempt to provide an overall view, while the majority focus upon a particular element of the decision process. Some relate primarily to the choice of a centre, others to the choice of a specific retailer.

It would be beyond the scope and purpose of this section to provide a full review of these various modelling approaches or of the extensive body of work on retail patronage behaviour. To explore these areas in greater depth, readers may wish to consult the comprehensive review by Laaksonen (1993) as an excellent starting point. Here it is sufficient to draw from the different approaches some of the specific insights they provide into how consumers process and evaluate marketing cues in order to arrive at a patronage decision.

3.3.1 Multi-Attribute Models

An element of the patronage decision that has received considerable attention is the process by which attitude towards the store is formed, given a range of perceptions relating to individual attributes. The approach of Fishbein (1967) has been widely applied to the modelling and measurement of overall attitude; this holds that 'an individual's attitude towards any object is a function of his [sic] beliefs about the object and the evaluative aspects of those beliefs'. The overall attitudes towards the object (store) could therefore be expressed as a uni-dimensional construct, representing a function of the individual evaluations (A-scales) weighted according to their salience (B-scales). The Fishbein model was adapted slightly by Bass and Talarzyk (1972) to relate more specifically to attitudes towards stores. Termed a 'multi-attribute attitude model', this involved the summation of attribute ratings, each weighted according to its importance as rated by consumers. Expressed more formally:

$$A_{jk} = \sum_{i=1}^{n} W_{ik} \, B_{ijk}$$

A_{jk} = consumer k's attitude score for j

W_{ik} = importance weight assigned by consumer k to attribute i

B_{ijk} = consumer k's belief as to the amount of attribute i offered by store j

n = number of important attributes in the selection of given type of store

Fishbein claimed that about twelve attributes were capable of being effectively researched in this way. Given the problem of handling multi-attribute judgements with a large number of attributes, Louviere and Gaeth (1987) suggested the solution of 'hierarchical information integration'. Using this approach, individual attributes (e.g. parking, travel time, width of aisles) are combined to form higher-order constructs (e.g. convenience). The authors claim that the procedure could offer an explanation of how consumers may simplify their complex decision tasks; they warn against such simplification procedures simply to produce tractable research designs or to satisfy the preconceived notions of management or researchers.

A major drawback of the multi-attribute model is the unrealistic implication that consumers make an almost simultaneous evaluation of the many attributes in arriving at their store choice. Such decisions are more likely to involve a hierarchical evaluation of alternatives. If stores are eliminated progressively from the active choice set, then the importance or weighting of attributes used to distinguish between the remaining stores will change at each stage in the decision. As Meyer and Eagle (1982) observed:

> *There is evidence that consumers are not likely to make choices by noting how good various alternatives are with respect to a multi-attribute utility function. Rather, choices often appear to be made hierarchically; that is, the attributes used to discriminate among alternatives (the parameters and elements of the utility function) change as various candidates are eliminated from consideration.*

From the viewpoint of the model builder, this presents serious problems in estimating the large numbers of parameters involved. Meyer and Eagle (1982) addressed the 'context effect', whereby the salience of attributes varies according to the amount of variability across the remaining alternative choices on that attribute. They proposed a 'bilinear differences model', which takes into account the shifting importance weights and also assumes that choices are made on a 'paired' basis, even when several alternative stores are available:

> *The model implies a choices process whereby an individual's 'focus of attention' may shift to minor attributes (such as subtle aspects of appearance) as alternatives become increasingly similar on major attributes (such as price).*

Figure 3.4 provides a simple illustration of these concepts, helping to explain why attribute importance ratings can differ greatly from study to study (see Table 3.2). When superstores first appear in an area, their particular points of difference, such as good prices and choice, may become particularly salient within consumers' choices. As more open in the area, and some existing competitors respond, these attributes may become minimum expected requirements for a store to enter the 'choice set'. Other attributes, such as hours, service and ambience may then define the two (or few) within the final choice. By that stage, the two remaining stores may be finely balanced on all these attributes. The final choice may therefore be made on the basis of attributes which, at the first stage, would have been rated as less important.

Figure 3.4 Competitive context and attribute salience

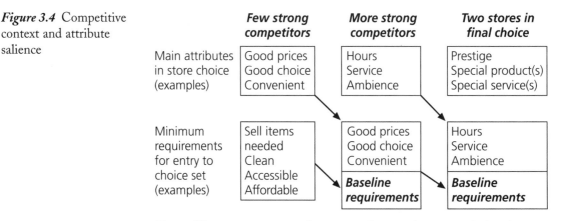

Note: different consumer preferences and competitor strengths/weaknesses will produce different groupings of attributes at each level.

An unrealistic within the conventional multi-attribute model is that consumer attitude responses to attribute differences are linear or consistent across the whole range. It may be reasonably assumed that consumers have certain 'thresholds' of acceptable prices, location, range, services, etc. Within these thresholds, there are likely to be 'zones of indifference' in relation to specific attributes. Some evidence of response thresholds was provided by Malhotra (1983) in relation to the patronage of record shops by students. The stores' images for variety, service, price, location and facilities were found to be salient but a threshold, rather than a linear, function was indicated. Murphy and Suntook (1998) refer to the 'danger zone', where attributes fail to meet threshold levels, resulting in a sharp decline in customer acceptance.

If one adopts the assumption of threshold of acceptability within the patronage decision process, then the task of modelling can be reduced to the subset of stores that comprise the actual choice set. This concept has been applied in relation to spatial models, where distance or lack of information may limit the consumer's choice set (e.g. Black, 1984). The concept may be extended further to exclude stores that are not within the choice set of a particular consumer or segment for reasons other than distance; for example, some stores may be regarded as too small, too dirty, too difficult for parking, etc. Malhotra (1986) suggested that store choice models should be based upon 'censored preference data', excluding stores that are declared unacceptable by consumers. Not only does this procedure slightly simplify the modelling process, it also reduces errors introduced by including stores that are irrelevant to the consumers' patronage decision.

3.3.2 Models of Store Choice

Flowcharts can help to depict and to understand the probable sequence of, and elements within, the store choice process. Two notable examples are those of Monroe and Guiltinan (1975), based upon time-path analysis, and Laaksonen (1993). No single model fully incorporates the vast diversity of factors and processes that can, potentially, influence store choice. However, while necessarily a simplification of complex realities, a model can assist in drawing together some of the empirically and/or theoretically derived generalizations regarding store choice.

Figure 3.5 is based primarily upon these two models but is extended to incorporate additional influences. It sets out to provide a framework to integrate many of the concepts discussed within this and subsequent chapters. Some of the particular characteristics of this model are explained below.

1 *Habitual behaviour*: a great deal of regularity has been observed in consumers' patterns of store patronage (e.g. Uncles et al., 1995). Sheth and Raju (1973) conclude that consumers often make a binary choice between their usual alternative and any other choice. The shopper may have a belief structure relating to the habitual store but it is not consciously or actively taken into account within the actual choice (Woodside and Trappey, 1996). Consequently, if the experience of the store is reasonably within expectations, a greatly simplified choice sequence is likely to ensue: the customer remains 'loyal'.

2 *Expectations and experiences*: the role of expectations is crucial in determining whether the experience of a store, and its products, will lead to repeat patronage. Swinyard and Whitlark (1994) draw upon prospect theory to illustrate that a failure to meet expectations can have a much stronger (negative) effect upon return intentions that the (positive) effect of equivalently exceeding expectations. Expectations are fundamental to the 'gaps model', developed primarily for the

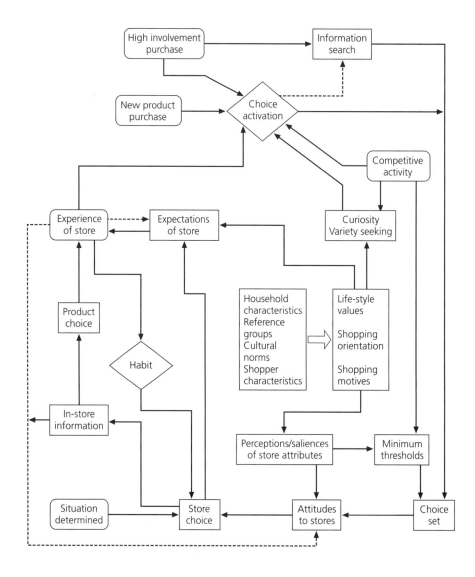

Figure 3.5 Patronage decision processes

Sources: developed from Laaksonen (1993); Monroe and Guiltinan (1975); and various sources.

measurement of service quality (Parasuraman et al., 1991), but applicable to all forms of experience-expectation gap. These models are considered further in Chapter 13.

3 ***Choice activation***: a failure to meet expectations is just one type of occurrence that can activate a more elaborate and conscious choice process. Products purchased for the first time, or other high involvement purchases, are likely to trigger fuller evaluations of alternatives (Walker and Knox, 1997). Likewise, competitors' moves may activate choice, possibly by stimulating curiosity or variety seeking behaviour (McGoldrick and Andre, 1997). This may or may not involve the consumer in a phase of increased information search using print media, the Web and/or store visits.

4 ***Attribute saliences***: attitudes to stores are not depicted in terms of a rigid relationship between perceptions and importance of attributes.

As discussed in the previous section, it is accepted that an attribute of critical importance at one time (or in one place) can cease to be as salient in another context (Meyer and Eagle, 1982). A certain level of performance on that attribute may become a minimum threshold for entry to the consumer's choice set (Malhotra, 1983).

5 *Situation determined*: store choice may be determined neither by habit nor by the selection from the preferred choice set. It may be the result of a planned journey, the store used becoming a subsidiary consideration, for example, in a work-related or recreational trip. Alternatively, the choice of shopping centre may take priority over the choice of store (Timmermans, 1996).

6 *Store-product choice*: Monroe and Guiltinan (1975) emphasize within their model the different processes involved in the selection of stores and the choice of products / brands within those stores. In-store decision making is given detailed attention in Chapter 12. As Sheth (1983) observes, the determinants of store and product choice processes are quite different, yet they are interlinked. Stores may be selected on the basis of their product choice, quality or exclusivity: these attributes also contribute to loyalty or 'defection' from the store. Neither can it invariably be assumed that the store choice is primary, product choice secondary. Sometimes a shop is sought to supply the particular product, which is already chosen (Kahn and Lehmann, 1991).

7 *Segmentation variables*: in common with most of the descriptive models of consumer behaviour (e.g. Engel et al., 1986; Laaksonen, 1993), the characteristics of the household, reference groups, cultured norms and the individual shopper are central. They influence the lifestyle, values, motives and shopping orientation, which in turn help to determine expectations, attribute salience and propensities towards variety seeking. The many ways of segmenting retail markets will now be considered.

3.4 Segmenting Retail Markets

The previous sections have illustrated the wide range of needs and wants that can motivate product purchases and the shopping activity. Every customer has a different set of needs, wants and motives, but in few consumer goods markets it is feasible fully to tailor the retailing mix to the level of the individual customer. Hence the need to identify reasonably homogeneous groupings, or segments, of shoppers to be the target(s) of retail marketing efforts. There are many different ways in which a retailer can define market segments, based upon consumer characteristics and/or their shopping orientations; examples of each are considered in this section.

The need for more systematic forms of market segmentation has increased with the intensification of retail competition and with the growth of the multiple chains. Meeting the competition 'head on' in a very broadly defined market, such as electrical goods, is usually a viable strategy only for the retailer(s) that enjoy the greatest economies of scale and cost advantages; even for them, it may well not be the most profitable strategy. Ironically, as the multiples grew rapidly, there was an intensive phase of standardization, both in product ranges and in outlet formats. However, the likelihood of the same mix being appropriate in all areas is remote, a realization that has brought a phase of greater adaptation, either within an overall format or by developing various clearly differentiated formats designed to appeal to different market needs.

3.4.1 Approaches to Market Segmentation

There are numerous possible bases for market segmentation, including demographics, geographical location, lifestyles and psychographics. The most important characteristics of the segmentation variables are that they should be indicative, directly or indirectly, of relevant need, preference, consumption or behaviour patterns. The segments must also be:

1 *Measurable*: for this reason, variables that can easily be identified and measured, such as age or residential areas, may be preferred to variable or attributes requiring more elaborate measurement techniques (González-Benito et al., 2000).
2 *Economically viable*: the segment must be capable of producing the profit contribution to justify the effort and cost of target marketing and possible repositioning.
3 *Accessible*: even a segment that is clearly identified and obviously viable may not be accessible, either geographically or in terms of cost/effective media communications.
4 *Actionable*: the degree to which, given limited time and resources, a firm can formulate effective programmes to attract and serve the segments (Segal and Giacobbe, 1994).

Table 3.6 provides a summary of some frequently used segmentation bases and variables. Some of these are relatively simple variables, while others represent more complex clusters of attributes. Some categories are entirely discrete, whereas others, such as ownership categories or lifestyle orientations, can overlap: Thus, a person can be time poor, individualistic, health conscious *and* environmentally concerned.

There are numerous other techniques available to identify segments of consumers with relatively homogeneous requirements from retailers (Steenkamp and Wedel, 1991). From a study of 37 characteristics that may correlate with store selection, Bellenger et al. (1976) concluded that the relatively simple variables, such as age and income, provided the most useful and manageable bases for segmentation. González-Benito et al. (2000) have also confirmed the importance of easily measurable demographic and socio-economic variables as indicators of shopping behaviour.

Retailers have often been criticized for their fixation upon younger adults and ignoring the opportunities within older groups (Burt and Gabbott, 1995). Used sensibly, however, age can be a valuable segmentation variable, and interest is extending both to younger and to older groups (e.g. Hare et al., 2001). The 14–18 year-old market is the

Bases/variables	Typical categories/scales
Demographic	
Age	Under 3, 3–4, 5–8, 9–11, 12–15, 16–18, 19–23, 24–29, 30–39, 40–49, 50–59, 60–69, 70+
Sex	Male, female
Education	Minimum GCSEs, A levels, degree or equivalent, postgraduate
Occupation	AB, C1, C2, DE
Family	1, 2, 3–4, 5+
Lifestyle	Pre-family, new family, maturing family, established family, post family, older couples, older singles
Income	Under £5K, £5K–£9K, £10K–£14K, £15K–£19K, £20K–£29K, £30K–£39K, £40K–£49K, £50K–£74K, £75K–£99K, over £100K
Durables owned	Home PC, digital television, CD player, video/DVD, telephone/fax, washing machine, dishwasher, microwave, car(s)
House	Fully owned, mortgaged, renting
Geographic	
Area type	Metropolitan area, small city, town, village
Area density	Urban, suburban, rural
Neighbourhood types	ACORN (Table 3.8), MOSAIC (Table 7.5)
House type	Detached, semi-detached, terrace, flat
Regions	Scotland, North East, Yorkshire, North West, Midlands, Wales, South West, South East, Anglia, London
Behavioural	
User/spending status	Non-user, under £50 per year, £50–£199, £200–£499, £500–£999, £1000–£1999, £2000–£3000, over £3000
Frequency	Most days, 2–3 times weekly, weekly, fortnightly, monthly, 5–10 times yearly, 2–4 times yearly, yearly, non-user
Loyalty	None, under 10%, 10%–29%, 30%–49%, 50%–69%, 70%–90%, over 90%
Psychographic	
Lifestyles	Instant gratification, time poor, health conscious, individualistic, hedonistic, experiential, environmental concerns
Fashion orientation	Leader, follower, independent, neutral, uninvolved, negative, rejecter
Benefits sought	Convenience, lowest price, value for money, highest quality, style and design, choice, enjoyment
Values	'VALS' value lifestyle groups; 'RVS' Rokeach's value survey; 'LOV' list of values

Table 3.6 Examples of segmentation bases

target of some fashion retailers (e.g. Thomas et al., 2000) and the influence of much younger children within the purchase decision is increasingly recognized (Darian, 1998):

> *Families are big business—they're high spenders, regular shoppers, and they come with their own brand-loving, TV watching mini-consumers. Parents and their children are a retailer's dream (Drummond, 1996a).*

Given the importance of families as initiators and influences of patronage decisions, life-stage segmentation provides a focus upon family characteristics. Table 3.7 illustrates the life-stage profiles of five retail companies. If new families are seen as an investment in the future, both Tesco and Asda are clearly attracting this segment, while J. Sainsbury performs well with the pre- and post-family groups. The later life-stage bias within the clienteles of both Marks & Spencer and the Co-op are also illustrated.

Life-stage	Tesco	Sainsbury	Asda	Co-op	Marks & Spencer
Pre-family	120	151	95	45	92
New family	142	62	132	23	66
Maturing family	106	74	132	46	66
Established family	84	98	130	118	78
Post-family	104	114	83	100	107
Older couples	100	99	88	119	133
Older singles	63	100	69	201	121

Table 3.7 Life-stage comparisons

Note: a value of 100 indicates average participation by that life-stage category.

Source: Nielsen (2000) based on AC Nielsen Homescan.

Within new families, females still tend to take the major role in food shopping (Marshall and Anderson, 2000) but shopping has increased in importance for males (Evans et al., 1996; Torres et al., 2001). Underhill (2000) identified various opportunities to retail more successfully to the male shopper. The growing number of single-person and single-sex households has contributed to a blurring gender roles in shopping (Davies and Bell, 1991). This has led some retailers to identify opportunities to target the 'opposite sex' as customers, for example, women in automotive supply stores and men in gourmet food shops (Stern et al., 1993).

Although most of the demographic variables score highly on the criteria of being easily identified and measured, it has long been asserted that psychographic segmentation can improve our ability to predict and understand consumer behaviour. Yankelovich (1964) had already noted the need for segmentation bases that relate more to attitudes and opinions than to demographic characteristics:

> We should discard the old, unquestioned assumption that demography is always the best way of looking at markets.

> Markets should be scrutinised for important differences in buyer attitudes, motivations, values, usage patterns, aesthetic preferences or degree of susceptibility.

It is becoming increasingly difficult to predict behaviour patterns on the basis of demographic alone. As Huie (1985) pointed out:

> There is a blurring of the behavioural patterns into which we used to neatly pigeon-hole people. Rich-poor, old-young, boy-girl — they are not the predictable labelling they used to be.

Some of the lifestyle trends (see Chapter 2) cut across traditional classifications. For example, the health-conscious or the environmentally concerned consumer may be 21 or 60 years of age, may earn £8000 a year or £50 000. Although the age and income level will inevitably influence the level and type of consumption, it may be the lifestyle characteristic that forms the most suitable focus for the retailer (see Sec. 4.4.1).

Much interest has been shown in the use of values for segmentation purposes, resulting in the development of various classifications and scales. As Kamakura and Novak (1992) observe:

> *A value refers to a single belief that transcends any particular object, in contrast to an attitude, which refers to beliefs regarding a specific object or situation.*

One of the most commonly used instruments for the measurement of values is the Rokeach (1973) value survey (RVS). However, this is somewhat complex and wide-ranging set of measures. It has been suggested the abbreviated LOV (list of values) instrument is more appropriate for consumer behaviour research (Beatty et al., 1985). This comprises the following items, representing the major motivational domains (Kamakura and Novak, 1992).

Motivational domain	*LOV item*
Self-direction	Self-respect; self-fulfilment
Achievement	Accomplishment; well respected
Enjoyment	Fun and enjoyment; excitement; warm relationships
Maturity	Belonging; warm relationships
Security	Security

Drawing upon measures of both values and lifestyles, the 'VALS' (value lifestyle) groups were classified by Mitchell (1983). The VALS categories are: survivors; sustainers; belongers; emulators; achievers; I-am-me; experentials; societally conscious; intergrateds.

Geodemographic segmentation systems, such as ACORN (A Classification of Residential Neighbourhoods) incorporate various demographic, geographic and lifestyle characteristics. A major strength of these systems is their ability to link together different data sets, provided that they have been geocoded (Mitchell and McGoldrick, 1994). Table 3.8 shows the six ACORN categories and 17 ACORN groups: a further level of disaggregation goes down to 54 ACORN types, some depicting as few as 0.4 per cent of the population.

Clearly, some of the neighbourhood types are more homogeneous than others, therefore better predictors of purchasing and shopping behaviours. The segments are however extremely measurable and accessible. With geocoding, lists of addresses within specified groups can be produced for promotional or research purposes. Applications of geodemographic data for retail location and localization decisions are discussed in Chapter 7.

ACORN category	ACORN group	% of population
A—Thriving	1. Wealthy achievers, suburban areas	15.2
	2. Affluent greys, rural communities	2.3
	3. Prosperous pensioners, retirement areas	2.4
B —Expanding	4. Affluent executives, family areas	3.8
	5. Well-off workers, family areas	7.8
C—Rising	6. Affluent urbanites, town and city	2.3
	7. Prosperous professionals, metropolitan	2.2
	8. Better-off executives, inner city	3.5
D—Settling	9. Comfortable middle-agers, mature home-owning areas	13.5
	10. Skilled workers, home-owning areas	10.6
E—Aspiring	11. New homeowners, mature communities	9.7
	12. White-collar workers, better-off multi-ethnic areas	4.0
F—Striving	13. Older people, less prosperous areas	3.6
	14. Council estate, better-off	11.5
	15. Council estate, high unemployment	2.7
	16. Council estate, greatest hardship	2.7
	17. Multi-ethnic, low-income areas	2.2

Table 3.8 A classification of residential neighbourhoods

Source: adapted from Nielsen (2001), based upon information supplied by CACI Information Solutions.

3.4.2 Segmentation by Shopping Orientation

Having looked at segmentation approaches using variables only indirectly connected with the shopping activity, attention now turns to typologies based upon shopping orientations. At one time, this approach to segmentation may have been criticized on the grounds of being difficult to measure and to access. With the proliferation of 'loyalty' and other store cards, however, some retailers now find shopping pattern variables more measurable and accessible than household-level demographic data (Kim et al., 1999).

In spite of earlier operational difficulties, segmentation by shopping orientation has a long history, reflecting its direct relationship with patronage behaviour and motives. Considerable attention has been given to four orientation segments in particular, which were defined by Stephenson and Willett (1969):

1 The convenience shopper.
2 The recreational shopper.
3 The price-bargain shopper.
4 The store-loyal shopper.

Given the interest in loyalty and loyalty schemes over recent years, category four is considered in more detail in the section that follows. Among the other categories, convenience shoppers are not necessarily apathetic about shopping activity: they may be demonstrating more positive acceptance of the price-convenience trade-off (Williams et al., 1978). Berry (1979) refers to the 'time-buying consumer', reflecting growing time scarcity and the pressure both for convenience products and convenient shopping. A number of typologies have focused upon time orientations (e.g. McDonald, 1994) and upon income and time pressures (e.g. Van Kenhove and De Wulf, 2000).

While some people suffer from time scarcity, others have too much discretionary time. For the recreational shopper, the activity may offer a way of filling time, both in the number of trips undertaken and the way these are conducted: more browsing and pre-search activity is likely to be undertaken (Holman and Wilson, 1982). Search behaviour has also been suggested as segmentation basis. Putrevu and Lord (2001) identified three search segments:

1 High-search (42 per cent).
2 Selective-search (47 per cent).
3 Low-search (11 per cent).

It should not be assumed that those seeking recreational shopping are invariably the time rich. Boedeker (1997) found recreational shoppers to have higher exploratory tendencies and high preferred arousal levels. Such shopper could use high-stimulus retail environments as an escape from work or other pressures.

The price bargain segment has also been extensively studied, being a fairly large proportion of shoppers. Mintel (2000) claims that 41 per cent of shoppers look out for bargains when shopping for non-foods. Rinne and Swinyard (1995) identified segments among discount store shoppers, the largest (43 per cent) being the 'difficult discount core'. This category demands much from their stores, in terms of prices, product quality/choice and service, often choosing to shop at Wal-Mart. In the context of durable goods, Swait and Sweeney (2000) proposed value, rather than simply price, oriented segments:

1 Price conscious (28.5 per cent): those who seek the lowest price, quality is less important
2 Value conscious (26.4 per cent): those who seek the best value for money, based on price and quality, when considering a durable good.
3 Quality conscious (45.1 per cent): those who seek the best quality price is less important.

In the purchasing of women's clothes, the proportions prepared to pay for the best are much smaller, reflecting the high costs involved. Table 3.9 shows four categories of fashion orientation, illustrating how the 'top' 20 per cent of consumers can represent 58 per cent of expenditures. This typology underlines the very different product and pricing strategies required for these different orientation segments.

Numerous other typologies of shopping orientations have been published: the reader may wish to consult reviews by Lesser and Hughes

Table 3.9 Fashion orientations: women's apparel market

Source: based on study conducted for Glamour Magazine, reported in Ghosh (1994, p. 153).

(1986) and Jarratt (1996). Increasingly, retailers are now able to draw upon their own databases to produce 'customized' shopper typologies, providing for targeted retail strategies and marketing communications. However, Buttle (1992) warns against the assumption that a person or household has one, fixed shopping orientation. Shopping motives and orientations have been shown to vary according to product class, location, which member of the family is doing the shopping and whether he or she is accompanied.

Segment	Percentage of consumers	Shopping behaviour
Fashion enthusiasts	8% of consumers. Along with style seekers, account for 58% of expenditures on clothing.	Confident. Highly motivated by style, social status and high-quality clothing.
Style seekers	12% of consumers	Keep close eye on latest styles. More oriented towards quantity than quality.
Classics	20% of consumers 20% of expenditures	Look for traditional, good quality styles that have stood the test of time.
Timids and uninvolved	60% of consumers 22% of expenditures	Little or no interest in fashion. Shop only when they have to. Spend as little as possible.

3.5 Customer Retention

So far, more attention has been given to the factors which attract shoppers to a given company or store. It is now a major preoccupation of retailers to maintain the loyalty of those shoppers, once attracted. The cost of recruiting a customer is usually considerably higher than the cost of retention, even in the supermarket context (Sirohi et al., 1998). Loyal shoppers are far more likely to 'forgive' occasional service failures (Bolton, 1998), and the inertia factor within loyalty makes them less likely to switch stores (Rust and Zohorik, 1993). Customers with strong commitment to a store are also more resilient to the counter persuasion of others, and less likely to extend their search to other stores (Dick and Basu, 1994).

Since store loyalty was suggested as a valuable basis for market segmentation (Enis and Paul, 1970), there have been numerous different definitions and measures. Although a surprisingly elusive concept, loyalty has been the focus of extensive retail marketing effort. At their most basic level, loyalty programmes are little more than sales promotions. More sophisticated programmes however can greatly enhance the retailer's understanding of its customers. They also open up the possibility of relationship marketing driven largely by systems, rather than depending entirely upon person–person interactions.

3.5.1 Loyalty Concepts and Measures

Used loosely, as it often is, the term 'loyalty' conjures up various notions of affection, fidelity or commitment. Even so, in their attempts to measure this illusive commodity, researchers often resort to behavioural measures of loyalty. For example, the Enis-Paul Index (Burford et al., 1971; Enis and Paul, 1970) uses three behavioural components to construct a measure of loyalty, namely:

1 The percentage of budget allocation to the store (budget ratio).
2 The amount of switching (switching ratio).
3 The number of alternatives explored (patronage ratio).

This index has been used in a number of subsequent studies (e.g. Denison and Knox, 1993; Knox and Denison, 2000; McGoldrick and Andre, 1997). While such indices provide convenient, single measures of behavioural loyalty, it can be beneficial to examine measures individually. For example, Table 3.10 shows three measures of behavioural loyalty, illustrating that different occupation and age groups use an Aldi store in rather different ways. The more affluent consumers visit less frequently and undertake a lower proportion of their shopping at Aldi. There is, however, no significant difference between the average weekly spending at Aldi of the various groups. In other words, although the lower income groups appear more loyal to Aldi on two measures, visit frequency and percentage of budget, each group is of equal value in terms of turnover.

Table 3.10 Alternative measures of loyalty

Source: adapted from McGoldrick and Andre (1997).

	Visits per week	£ per week at Aldi	% grocery shopping
Occupation			
AB	0.77	29.28	64.2
C1	0.89	29.73	67.5
C2	1.21	31.43	68.8
DE	1.52	31.11	79.4
(significance)	(yes)	(no)	(yes)
Age			
Under 35	0.93	30.93	71.4
35–54	1.13	31.00	70.1
55 or above	1.57	27.25	61.2
(significance)	(yes)	(no)	(no)

East (1999) has argued strongly in favour of behaviour-based measures of loyalty, noting that profits are made from behaviour, not sentiment or thought. This is consistent with Enis and Paul's (1970) definition of store loyalty: 'Consumer inclination to patronise a given store during a specified time period'. Others, however, support the concept of hybrid measures that include both behavioural and attitudinal measures (e.g. Bloemer and Ruyter, 1998; Dick and Basu, 1994;). Something of a gap therefore exists between the different connotations of 'loyalty', in that it comprises both behavioural and affective (or commitment) components. The concept of commitment has been defined as 'an emotional or psychological attachment to a brand' (Beatty et al., 1988). In a similar vein, Chenet and Johansen (1999) describe *real* loyalty as: 'A state of mind, an intellectual and emotional link between the customer and the firm'.

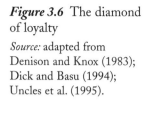

Figure 3.6 The diamond of loyalty

Source: adapted from Denison and Knox (1983); Dick and Basu (1994); Uncles et al. (1995).

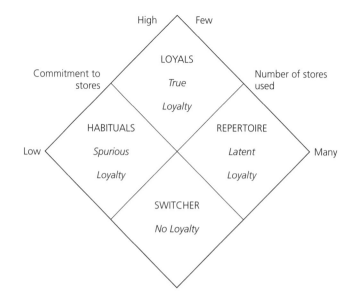

Figure 3.6 illustrates the 'diamond of loyalty', variations of which have been proposed by Denison and Knox (1993) and by Dick and Basu (1994). It draws attention to the major differences between the 'loyals', with high commitment, and 'habituals', with low commitment. Most measurement systems would place these two types within the same category, with obvious dangers for strategy formulation. The habituals are clearly more likely to be poached by a new rival entering, or diversifying, into the area (Bendapudi and Berry, 1997). On the other side of the diamond, the 'promiscuous' shoppers can be similarly divided, with very different strategies being appropriate in each case.

Aspects of geography can easily lead to shopping behaviour that includes two or more stores. The practice of patronizing 'repertoires' of stores is by no means uncommon (Uncles et al., 1995). A customer, therefore, may be strongly committed to a store but, as time and distance are key shapers of behaviour, this commitment may not result in high visit frequency. The need to obtain perishable goods, for example, may necessitate visits to other, closer stores (Krider and Weinberg, 2000). Paradoxically, many loyalty programmes penalize, perhaps also alienate, customers in this category.

Table 3.11 provides an indication of the behavioural loyalty of UK grocery shoppers. Around a third are usually loyal, unless their routines are disrupted by different travel patterns, out-of-stock 'emergencies', etc. The largest proportion, 43 per cent, shops mainly in one store but 'admit' to occasional disloyalty. Some 25 per cent are not loyal at all. Given the intensive use of loyalty programmes through the duration of this analysis, it is interesting to note that behavioural loyalty actually declined slightly

Although behavioural loyalty measures the outcome, it says very little about the causes of loyalty. An understanding of these is clearly critical to the task of building 'sustainable loyalty', more resilient to competitors' moves. A number of researchers have investigated the root causes of

Category	1994 %	1999 %
Loyals (usually do all grocery shopping in one shop)	34	33
Occasional disloyals (most in one shop but sometimes elsewhere)	43	43
Often disloyals (often go elsewhere but most in one store)	17	20
Variable source (do not shop regularly in any one store)	5	5

Table 3.11 Loyalty behaviour

Source: derived from Mintel (1999b).

loyalty (e.g. East et al., 1995; Flavian et al., 2001; McGoldrick and Andre, 1997; Reynolds, 1995):

▪ *Laziness*: the 'loyal' shopper cannot be bothered to visit more than one store: money saving is not the main preoccupation.
▪ *Habit*: he or she is used to visiting the same store each week and does not feel like changing this habit.
▪ *Time saving*: he or she is too busy with other aspects of life to visit more stores than is necessary.
▪ *Switching costs*: visiting other stores requires travel and time to familiarize with products, layout, deals, systems, etc.
▪ *Risk avoidance*: using less familiar stores may expose shopper to greater performance (product) risk and economic (price) risk.
▪ *Convenience*: the store is the nearest or open long hours.
▪ *Full satisfaction*: the overall value offered is better than that of rivals.
▪ *No real choice*: in a remote geographical area or the only store specializing in a particular category.

A number of reasons have also been advanced for shoppers being 'promiscuous' in their patronage behaviour:

▪ *Money saving*: shopping around for some is the way to find the best prices and bargain offers.
▪ *Cleverness*: he or she feels like a smart shopper by tracking down better prices, or better quality for the same price.
▪ *Dedication*: he or she considers it to be normal behaviour to cross-shop, his or her duty when shopping.
▪ *Variety shopping*: he or she finds it enjoyable to visit more than one format and have more shopping experiences.
▪ *Curiosity*: he or she likes to acquire knowledge about different products, brands, fashions and store formats.
▪ *Time availability*: having got plenty of time, it is a pity not to take advantage of different stores.
▪ *Time killing*: using several stores is a way of filling surplus time.
▪ *Distance*: the preferred store is too far away to visit for urgent or top-up shopping needs.

Table 3.12 provides some indication of how time, distance and other factors create a difference between the actual main store used and the preferred main store. This example is based upon housewares purchasing and suggests that some stores, with extensive branch networks, enjoy more behavioural loyalty than commitment. IKEA, on the other hand, is a store that many more people would use, if they had reasonable access to a store. In fact, if all the shoppers were equally aware of all these companies, the gaps may have been larger.

Table 3.12 Current and potential shares

Source: derived from Verdict (1999).

Note (1): would prefer to use if convenient.

Store supplying housewares	Main use current %	Share potential [1] %	Potential change %
Argos	13.1	11.8	–9.7
Asda	3.5	3.1	–8.8
Debenhams	3.5	3.2	–8.6
Marks & Spencer	3.8	3.5	–8.1
Woolworths	5.6	5.2	–6.5
John Lewis	6.8	7.0	+1.8
The Co-op	3.0	3.1	+2.0
Homebase	3.0	3.1	+4.0
IKEA	4.8	6.5	+35.4

Whether people who visit a store adopt it as their main source is another indicator of its ability to satisfy their needs within a category. Table 3.13 shows the 'conversion' rates of various food and grocery stores, that is, the percentage of visitors who are main users. Each of the top three grocery retailers have conversion rates of just over 50 per cent, considerably higher than their two main rivals. The low conversion rate of Waitrose is attributed to a high visiting rate, relative to the size of its branch network, suggesting that people make special trips from time to time. In the case of the 'hard discounters', low conversion rates suggest two-stop or repertoire shopping, as many people use them to get low prices on their basic grocery needs (Schmidt et al., 1994).

Table 3.13 Conversions to main users

Source: adapted from Verdict (2000).

Grocery store	Store users %	Main users %	Conversion rates %
Tesco	42.8	22.4	52.2
Asda	27.1	13.8	51.0
J. Sainsbury	34.5	17.6	51.0
Somerfield	14.5	6.1	42.3
Safeway	20.6	8.5	41.5
Kwik Save	20.6	8.4	41.0
The Co-op	17.3	5.8	33.4
Netto	4.3	1.1	26.0
Waitrose	5.9	1.4	24.0
Aldi	9.3	2.1	22.2
Lidl	4.4	0.9	20.9

3.5.2 Loyalty Programmes

In theory, and in practice in a number of cases, loyalty programmes offer an important step towards one-to-one marketing, or at least, far more closely defined and observed segments. A definition of loyalty programmes / schemes from the Coca-Cola Retail Research Group is quoted by Reynolds (1995):

> *An initiative where a specific mechanism is used to incentivise the customer to give a higher share of his/her grocery spend to a retailer— over and above that warranted by the attractiveness of the retailers' core offering of location, product, service, price, etc.*

Interestingly, this definition emphasizes the promotional aspect of loyalty programmes, ignoring their information value in providing detailed knowledge of customers' purchase patterns.

The main avalanche of loyalty schemes occurred around the mid-1990s but they continued to proliferate. This was inspite of some high-profile withdrawals, such as Safeway's ABC card (Retail Review, 2000). The originality of the loyalty programme concept is frequently overestimated, bearing in mind that the co-operatives distributed dividends to customers, proportionate to their purchases, over 150 years ago (McGoldrick and Andre, 1997). A major difference now is in the technology available to collect, store and 'mine' the purchase data.

While technology facilitated the process, other factors precipitated the spread of these schemes. Retailers were searching for new ways to differentiate themselves, although much of that benefit was neutralized by competitors launching their own schemes (Drummond, 1996b). It was also well known, especially in business-to-business contexts, that it is much cheaper to retain an existing customer than to recruit a new one (Sopanen, 1996). Customer expectations also played their part, as air miles and petrol promotions had already created familiarity and acceptance of the loyalty scheme concept (Reynolds, 1995).

Frequent-flyer programmes and the loyalty schemes of Tesco and J. Sainsbury have come to characterize loyalty programmes for many people. However, there are many variations upon the theme, as Fig. 3.7 summarizes. Some schemes operate in just a local area (Worthington and Hallsworth, 1999), others are national or international in scope. Local schemes often use simple, cardboard cards, contrasting with the high-tech smart cards used by such retailers as Boots the Chemist (Baxter, 1998). Some are used as short-term, tactical devices, while others are long-term elements of retail marketing strategy.

Baxter (1998) depicts a continuum of levels at which loyalty programmes can operate, from the most tactical to the most strategic:

1 Profit uplift from increased sales.
2 Targeted promotion tool.
3 Strategic decision support from better understanding of customer behaviour.

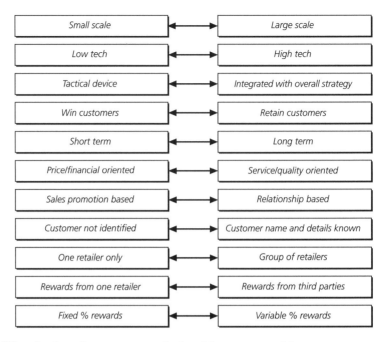

Figure 3.7
Characteristics of loyalty
schemes

Source: adapted from Mintel
(1999b); Reynolds (1995).

Small scale	↔	Large scale
Low tech	↔	High tech
Tactical device	↔	Integrated with overall strategy
Win customers	↔	Retain customers
Short term	↔	Long term
Price/financial oriented	↔	Service/quality oriented
Sales promotion based	↔	Relationship based
Customer not identified	↔	Customer name and details known
One retailer only	↔	Group of retailers
Rewards from one retailer	↔	Rewards from third parties
Fixed % rewards	↔	Variable % rewards

4 The basis of customer relationships, competitive strategy, store
format / location decisions and company culture.

Clearly, a scheme that achieves the highest level of strategic objectives
can also enjoy the other, more tactical advantages.

Not all schemes depend upon giving money away. For example, the
Marks & Spencer store card produces a valuable database but does not, in
itself, convey a discount. However, cardholders do receive mail-outs and
invitations to special events. Far from being free, the Johnsons 'Priority
Club' actually costs money to join, although members do then receive a
discount, vouchers and faster service at their dry cleaning branches.

If customer details are collected when a card is issued, then there
clearly is scope for data-mining and relationship-building. However, given
the vast scale of the data that can accumulate, not all retailers can harness
its full power. Most larger schemes do include the collection of customer
details, although too intrusive an application form can deter joining. At one
leading supplier of car tyres, their form actually asked for the name of next
of kin! Simply knowing a customer's address and postcode can provide a
link into other geodemographic databases, as well as providing invaluable
data on location, travel patterns and shopping frequencies.

Some schemes involve more than one company (Cuthbertson, 1998),
for example Tesco points can be earned on spending with electricity
suppliers and Co-op Travel Care. More common is the ability to use
points for goods or services provided by third parties. The consumer
gains by being offered more choice of redemption modes: a trip to Rome
or Paris will have stronger aspirational value than a series of small
discounts at the checkout (O'Brien and Jones, 1995). The retailer also
gains, as the third party is likely to pick up some or all of the cost of the

incentive. Table 3.14 shows J. Sainsbury's third party arrangements: the discounts are generally at a higher rate than the voucher would earn if exchanged at Sainsbury's own stores.

Third party	The offer
Arcadia (incl. Burton, Dorothy Perkins, Principles, Top Shop, Top Man)	Exchange £2.50 reward voucher for £5.00 discount on every £25.00 spent
Burger King	Voucher is full payment for Whopper Meal or Big King Meal
British Gas (Electricity only)	Voucher qualifies for £5.00 off quarterly bill
Blockbuster, Xtra Vision	Voucher rents one movie
Harry Ramsden's	Voucher buys meal of Haddock & Chips or Cod & Chips
Whitbread (Brewers Fayre, TGI Fridays, Beefeater)	Voucher gets £5.00 off adult main course meal at designated outlets
BT Talktime	Voucher buys 250 BT Talktime minutes at BT local weekend rate
NSPCC, The Blue Cross	Donation to charities at voucher face value (£2.50)

Table 3.14
J. Sainsbury's third party arrangements

Source: Retail Review (1999).

Where a discount is given to loyalty cardholders, the rates vary considerably. If points are simply used to obtain a discount on subsequent purchases, they are worth 1 per cent at Tesco, J. Sainsbury and Argos (Mintel, 1999b). There are typically many incentives to save points to acquire rewards of higher value. However, Parker and Wothington (2000) found that the 'points junkies', who saved diligently within the former Safetway ABC scheme, were not always equitably rewarded. The discount from WhS Clubcard points is 2 per cent, Boots Advantage card 4 per cent. The Bhs Choice card used a sliding scale of discounts, zero on the first £100 spent in a given year, climbing to 12.7 per cent by the time £2500 had been spent.

The decision to implement a loyalty programme is by no means straightforward, given their many advantages and disadvantages. Figure 3.8 summarizes a number of these, both from the retailer and the consumer perspective. Among the less obvious benefits is the fact that the retailer's brand name establishes a presence in the consumer's wallet or purse, which may facilitate retailers' moves into banking and financial services (Cuthbertson, 1998). It has also been shown that loyalty programme members are more likely to 'forgive' the occasional lapse in the service provided by the retailer (Bolton et al., 2000).

On the negative side, cost is undoubtedly a major issue for retailers with loyalty programmes. Some of the discount costs can be mitigated through the use of third parties (Table 3.14). Tesco have also generated a revenue stream in the sale of non-personal loyalty card data to manufacturers and others, following the partial acquisition of data consultancy Dunnhumby (Kleinman, 2001). These measures go some way towards alleviating the major costs of start-up, investment in IT, mailing costs, administration, call centres, etc. 'We're talking about a cost

Retailer Perspective	
FOR	**AGAINST**
Reinforces loyalty and / or heavy spending	Cost of financial and other incentives
Achieves competitive advantage or parity	Cost of IT systems and cards
Customers more likely to forgive errors or service lapses	Launch costs: media, staff training, etc.
Third parties finance some of offers and costs	Cost of administration and enquiry handling
Points promotions as alternative to price promotions	Cost of mail-outs and coupons
May reduce number of mark-downs	Most schemes easy to copy
May save on media advertising	Many customers also join competitors' scheme
Customers carry brand name in wallets / purses	Withdrawal of a scheme may lose goodwill
More precise segmentation and targeting	Most discounts given to all, not just loyal card holders
Opportunities for mail-outs and relationship building	May convey an association with higher prices
Facilitates cross-selling	Rivals without schemes will exploit this
Detailed knowledge of purchase patterns	Not a key patronage determinant for most shoppers
More extensive knowledge of customer's personal details	May distract from more crucial aspects of strategy
Customer Perspective	
FOR	**AGAINST**
Extra discounts	Discounts usually small
'Something for nothing'	Points take a long time to accumulate
Personalized offers	Too much plastic to carry
Other services, invitations to events, etc.	Inconvenient redemption systems
Membership of a 'club'	Hassle of filling out form
Choice of redemption options	More junk mail received
Satisfaction of saving points	Invasion of privacy

Figure 3.8 Pros and cons of loyalty schemes

Source: based upon Baxter, 1998; Bolton et al., 2000; Davies, 1998; McGoldrick and Andre, 1997; Mintel, 1996; O'Brien and Jones, 1995; Uncles, 1994; Wright and Sparks, 1999.

of millions of pounds to give 1 per cent of your hard-earned profits away —it's big bucks' (Drummond, 1996b). Detailed costings are elusive but Deloitte & Touche (1999) found that loyalty programmes were consuming around half of the marketing expenditures of major food retailers. Retail Review (1995) pointed to evidence of increased inflation, and a reduction in retailer sponsored promotions, after the launch of the major programmes. There is also a risk, as retailers polarize between enthusiasts and rejecters of loyalty schemes, that the schemes may convey an image of higher prices.

Indeed, when Safeway abandoned its well-established ABC loyalty card, it vigorously sought to minimize the public relations damage by emphasizing its new-found ability to offer more price cuts. The strategy appeared to work initially for Safeway, with volume increases and more people attracted into the stores (Retail Review, 2000). Critics would argue that these include many promotional 'cherry-pickers', although loyalty cards in themselves do not guarantee loyalty either: 'I have accumulated nine "loyalty" cards from various stores and supermarkets, does that make me more loyal or less?' (The Times, 1998).

By 1999, 75 per cent of shoppers were participating in at least one store card or loyalty scheme (Mintel, 1999b). Thirty-seven per cent held a Tesco card, 30 per cent a Sainsbury card. The incidence of cross-shopping is clear, however, with over half of Sainsbury card holders also having a Tesco card.

Evidence from A.C. Nielsen suggested that loyalty cards can actually damage loyalty, unless part of an effective customer relationship programme (Davies, 1998). A survey by Wright and Sparks (1999) pointed to 'loyalty saturation', some people refusing to join schemes because they had too many cards already. Mintel's (1996) research also found card fatigue, as well as frustration with the small rewards, and the time taken to accumulate them. Some, however, enjoyed saving up for a special gift or reward, possibly a short holiday. According to O'Brien and Jones (1995), five elements are critical determinants of a programme's value to consumers:

> *Cash value, choice of redemption options, aspirational value, relevance and convenience. Few programmes offer all five, but companies that want to play the rewards game should be sure their value measures up to customers' alternatives.*

3.5.3 Relationship Marketing

A growing recognition of the value of relationships has led many to question the traditional, transaction-oriented view of marketing. Reflecting this shift of emphasis, Grönroos (1994) offers a revised definition of marketing, which seeks to incorporate both its transactional and relationship qualities:

> *Marketing is to establish, maintain and enhance relationships with customers, and other partners, at a profit, so that the objectives of the parties involved are met.*

There has been a proliferation of terms to describe the 'new' emphasis upon relationships, including:

▶ relationship marketing
▶ one-to-one marketing
▶ database marketing
▶ loyalty marketing
▶ wrap-around marketing
▶ customer partnering
▶ symbiotic marketing
▶ interactive marketing
▶ lifetime-value marketing
▶ customer relationship management (CRM)

(Buttle, 1996; Davids, 1999).

While some writers ascribe more specific meanings to these terms, collectively they represent the continued progression from mass-marketing to micromarketing, theoretically down to segments of one. However, the 'newness' of the relationship concept has been challenged: as Gilmore and Pine (1997) point out:

> *As the concept of a mass market gained currency ... all too many managers lost sight of the simple fact known for ages by every butcher, cobbler and corner grocer: every customer is unique.*

As Healy et al. (2001) observe, relationship marketing may be a new term but it describes an old phenomenon. Indeed, the relationships between some customers and their local stores are still of a far closer and more personal nature than their computer-mediated relationships with major multiples. That said, many of these same customers still patronize primarily the multiples, raising questions about the importance to customers of such relationships, compared with value, choice, etc. (O'Malley and Tynan, 2000).

The origins of relationship marketing can be traced to four main sources:

- business to business marketing
- marketing channel relationships
- database / direct marketing
- services marketing (Buttle, 1996; Möller and Halinen, 2000).

In each of these contexts, the importance of the relationship is apparent and one-to-one marketing is often feasible. Within marketing channels and other business-to-business contexts, key account staff have given priority to maintaining effective relationships with clients. Now category management has widened the relationship interface between many retailers and their suppliers (see Chapter 8). Banks and other financial service providers have tried to emulate the key account principle by allocating specific members of staff as 'personal bankers' to highly valued clients. Staff within more exclusive fashion stores can also maintain a personal and effective relationship with key customers, given their higher staff-customer ratios (Beatty et al., 1996; Reynolds and Beatty, 1999).

Relationships of this type are more problematic for large-scale retailers of groceries and other fast-moving consumer goods (fmcg). Stores are usually large and open for long hours, employing numerous staff, many part time and/or short term. These staff will be important elements in the performance element of the retailer–customer relationship but information systems must, in these circumstances, also play a major part.

Figure 3.9 depicts some of the main components of retailer–customer relationships. The relationship may be seen to be favourable if it leads to the customer both liking and trusting the retailer (Chenet and Johansen, 1999), hopefully leading to loyalty. Hoekstra et al. (1999) discuss the

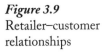

Figure 3.9
Retailer–customer
relationships

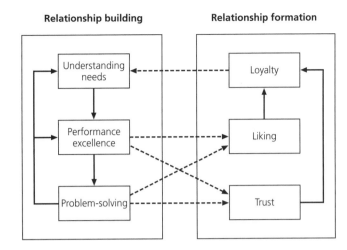

numerous individual facets involved in the development of customer relationships. These can be summarized as understanding the customer's needs, performance excellence and effective problem-solving.

In the more personal relationship contexts, such as business-to-business marketing, much of the understanding and problem-solving is achieved by the staff who know the customer well. In fmcg retailing, understanding can be enhanced through loyalty card data and other ways of researching customer behaviour. However, these often leave gaps in knowledge about needs that are not being met (Hoekstra et al., 1999) and about customers' behaviour outside the store (Davies, 1998). These information deficiencies can make excellent performance, as required and perceived by the customer, more difficult to achieve.

Problem-solving is also an area in which less personal forms of relationship marketing can be slow or ineffective. According to Chenet and Johansen (1999), 96 per cent of dissatisfied customers never complain, but 90 per cent never come back either. Clearly, this proportion varies according to the number of real choices available to the customers. Queues at 'customer service' desks, and the ponderous procedures in getting through to some call centres, do not encourage dialogue or effective problem-solving.

When a customer encounters a problem or has a suggestion, this should not become just another statistic about customer (dis)satisfaction. It is an opportunity to develop the relationship and continuously to review the effectiveness of current strategy. In Ireland, the Superquinn chain places great emphasis upon dialogue between customers and store managers, whose desks are positioned at the customer service points. They refer to the 'boomerang effect', doing everything possible to get the customer back (Chenet and Johansen, 1999).

While customer retention remains a key objective of relationship marketing, retailers must focus their strongest efforts upon their best customers. One retailer, for example, found that its top 30 per cent of customers accounted for 75 per cent of sales. At the other end of the scale, the bottom 20 per cent of customers produced only 3 per cent of sales (Sopanen, 1996). Similar ratios are quoted by Seiders and Tigert (1997), with a retailer reportedly losing money on its bottom 30 per cent of customers. Where top customers account for most of the business, relationship marketing tends to be most cost-efficient (Peppers et al., 1999). These costs clearly depend upon the balance between personal relationship-building and system-driven approaches.

Sheth and Sisodia (1999) observe that AT&T lost money on 35 per cent of its residential customers: 'outsourcing' these customers to other telephone companies may therefore increase profits. However, a retailer should be wary of underinformed strategies of customer outsourcing. These (currently) low-value customers may, in fact, include a rival's most valuable customers, suggesting an altogether more positive approach towards their 'conversion'. Mintel (1999b) quotes a number of loyalty scheme managers from the grocery sector who admit to a degree of information overload:

> *There is more information than we can cope with. It is impossible to look directly at an individual, but clusters and segments can be constructed on the basis of common behaviour and that helps us to pitch our marketing effort.*

Whether or not it would be impossible is questionable, but it would certainly involve a huge investment of managerial time. The compromise is to use the database to tailor offers and communications to much smaller, more closely defined segments. For example, Tesco now mails 100 000 variations of its quarterly statement, each offering a different mix of incentives (Marsh, 2001).

It is also likely that customers would become more sensitive to privacy issues, if it became clear that someone was watching their purchase patterns (O'Malley and Tynan, 2000). Boots the Chemist deliberately avoids individual analysis, as its health-related products can include highly personal items (Retail Intelligence, 1999). It does however use its data to undertake various segmentation exercises, for example, in relation to its promotional offers:

- *deal seekers*, only ever buying promotional lines
- *stockpilers*, who buy in bulk when on offer, then do not visit the store for weeks.
- *loyalists*, who buy more of an item when on offer but soon revert to their usual brand or buying patterns.
- *new market*, customers who start buying when on promotion, then continue to buy the same product when it reverts to normal price.

These forms of segmentation, difficult to achieve without loyalty/store card data, have the advantage of reflecting actual behaviour, rather than characteristics considered typical of age or lifestyle groups. As Bolton et al. (2000) point out:

Figure 3.10 The relationship marketing ladder

Source: Christopher et al. (1991).

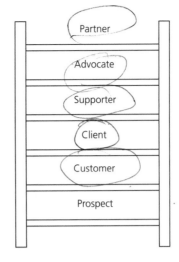

It is theoretically more profitable to segment and target customers on the basis of their (changing) purchase behaviour and service experiences, rather than on the basis of their (stable) demographics or other classification variables.

Forms of segmentation have also been suggested which reflect the state of the relationship, as well as customer behaviour. Christopher et al. (1991) suggest the idea of a relationship marketing ladder, illustrated in Fig. 3.10. The potential customer starts as a prospect, then progresses up several 'rungs' of the ladder, becoming a customer, client, supporter, advocate and, at best, a partner. The task of relationship marketing is clearly to develop many advocates and partners. Not only are these typically very loyal purchasers, they also influence others through positive, word-of-mouth recommendation.

The concept of relationship quality segmentation was developed further by Heskett et al. (1994). Figure 3.11 shows how six categories may be identified, based on a combination of relationship strength, and the product / service benefits to the customer. Thus, if the retail offer is highly beneficial to the customer, yet the relationship is poor, the result may be ambivalence. More positive combination of benefits and relationship can result in supporters or ambassadors, equivalent to the upper part of the ladder in Fig. 3.10.

The matrix in Fig. 3.11, however, differs from the ladder in another important respect: it does not assume that customers progress towards more positive dispositions towards the company. If the benefits are low or the relationship is poor, they may well become 'opponents', dispersing negative word-of-mouth. Low benefits and poor relationships combined may produce 'terrorists', people who are so disappointed that they seek revenge. In one study, terrorists comprised of 15 per cent of users, opponents 17 per cent; so, nearly a third of users were likely to express strong negative opinions about this firm (Chenet and Johansen, 1999).

Figure 3.11
Relationship quality
segmentation

Adapted from: Heskett et al.
(1994); Chenet and
Johansen (1999).

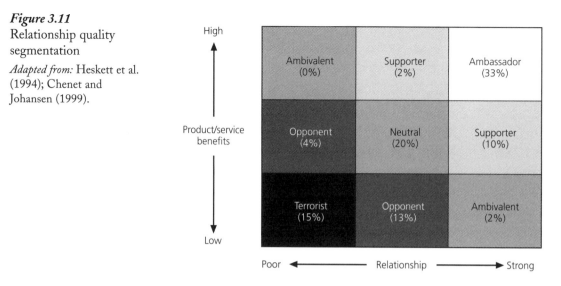

Note: percentages relate to one case study company, they are not generalized proportions.

While relationship marketing for many retailers may stop short of genuine, one-to-one marketing, it can still be of considerable value for segmentation, closer targeting and diagnostics. Indeed, if not done well, one-to-one marketing can do more harm than good. For example, Colgate and Danaher (2000) report how poorly performing 'personal bankers' led to lower levels of customer satisfaction than if no personal banker had been available. Exponents of relationship marketing often fail to address the issues of cost and economies of scale in staff/management time, when the concept is applied to lower-value, high-frequency products or services (Peppers and Rogers, 1993).

It is also questionable whether customers actually want relationships with all the companies with which they deal (Egan, 2000). Buttle (1996) suggested the possibility of segmentation by 'relationship proneness', bearing in mind the motivation of relationship-seeking among some shoppers (Buttle, 1992; Tauber, 1972). Other shoppers however are becoming alarmed about the amount and depth of information being collected about them, fuelling concerns of a possible privacy backlash (Hagel and Rayport, 1997). In common with all customer-focused activities, relationship marketers must consider the value added for the customer. As Davids (1999) points out:

> *Viewing CRM as a sales or customer service solution is the shortest trip to failure ... no customer wants to bother with a program that is really designed only to help the retailer.*

SUMMARY

An understanding of consumers' needs and motives is an essential prerequisite of successful retail marketing strategy. The identification and satisfaction of consumer needs is one of the most fundamental principles of retail marketing; without this focus, strategic planning can easily become dominated by the actions of competitors or internal influences. The most successful examples of innovation and evolution in retail formats represent accurate and profitable responses to previously unsatisfied needs. The constant interface with customers does not necessarily lead to a clear understanding of their needs, or of those of potential target groups. Effective research procedures and information systems, both internal and external, are required.

A common flaw in strategic planning is failing to distinguish between solutions and needs. Sometimes overlooked is the fact that most strategic solutions satisfy more than one underlying need, which in turn may be satisfied by alternative or better solutions. Some of the basic classifications of human needs could provide frameworks for understanding why shoppers act and react in certain ways. The shopping activity itself, for example, may satisfy many personal and social motives, some not related to the buying of products. These may include the need for diversion, physical activity, sensory stimulation or social experiences. While some regard shopping as mainly a chore, many see it as satisfying other more diverse needs.

There have been numerous studies of consumers' store criteria, as retailers and researchers seek to identify the store attributes that are most instrumental in store choice decisions. Means-end chains can be a useful analytical device in helping to understand linkages between attributes, consequences and underlying motives. There is some evidence of shifting priorities over time, shifts that have been both reflected in and influenced by changes in retailers' strategic emphasis. It is also dangerous to generalize from the findings of studies based upon a diversity of samples, methodologies, locations and sectors. The choice of a store is in part a function of the choice of a shopping centre, and of the needs that precipitated the shopping trip.

Decisions between stores and centres also involve evaluation of the relative shopping 'costs'. Monetary costs include not only the money paid for goods but also the travel and incidental expenses. Time is often equated with money, but that is an oversimplification of its 'cost', as time used shopping may in part be considered beneficial and enjoyable. Shopping can also involve physical effort, which can be reduced through provision of bag-packing/carrying and other personal services. Stress is another shopping cost that retailers should generally seek to minimize. In evaluating retail options, consumers also typically perceive risks, representing the probability and consequences of various undesirable outcomes.

An understanding of the process by which attitudes are formed and patronage decisions are made is an important but elusive goal of retail strategists and researchers. It is clear that attitudes are influenced not only by shopping experiences and retailer strategies but also by the economic, demographic, psychographic and lifestyle characteristics of the shopper. Various simple formulations, such as multi-attribute attitude model, have been suggested as ways in which individual attribute evaluations may be combined. There is evidence, however, that consumers have certain thresholds of acceptability and zones of indifference in evaluating store attributes. The salience of particular attributes may also be highly specific to a competitive situation, depending upon the elements of differentiation between the stores within the consumers' active choice set.

In most retail sectors it is appropriate to target marketing efforts at groupings, or segments, of shoppers who are likely to share some common characteristics, in terms of their needs, motives and patronage criteria. There are many different possible bases for market segmentation; in practice, the defined segments must be measurable, economically viable, accessible and actionable. A great deal of segmentation uses relatively simple demographic variables, such as age or income, and geographical variables, such as region or area type. Increased use is now being made of psychographic segmentation bases, such as values, attitudes or lifestyle orientations. With the rapid development of geographical information systems in recent years, detailed classifications and databases of residential neighbourhoods have also become available for segmentation purposes.

Another approach is to use typologies of shopping orientations, for example convenience, recreational, price-bargain and store-loyal shoppers. There are now many available typologies based on shopping orientations, and retailers can also develop their own, using customer loyalty databases. However, care should be taken not to 'pigeon-hole' shoppers or households, as orientations can vary according to the context of the shopping trip.

The achievement of store loyalty among their customers is a goal to which most retailers aspire. The concept of loyalty, however, has been defined and measured in many different ways. For some, behavioural loyalty is the key factor, although there are several measures of loyal behaviour. For others, commitment to a store, involving an emotional or psychological attachment, is at least as important. While the majority of shoppers have one main source of supply, most use other stores at least occasionally.

Loyalty programmes offer retailers the opportunity to learn a great deal more about their customers, as well as providing an incentive for them to visit more frequently, spend more and/or be more loyal. Knowing customers' addresses and some other basic details is in itself a powerful segmentation tool: when coupled with long-term transaction data, the power of this information is further enhanced. As well as informing location, format, product selection and many other decisions, these data can also be used for product-awareness promotions and cross-selling activities.

It makes sense to develop good relationships with top customers especially, through understanding their needs, performing excellently in their eyes, and by solving problems quickly and effectively. By developing their loyalty, liking and trust, these customers can be developed into supporters, even ambassadors of the company. Relationship marketing can however be expensive and counter-productive, if not done well. Neither do all customers seek or value the types of relationships that companies seek: some are also becoming concerned about the intrusiveness of the information being given to retailers.

REVIEW QUESTIONS

1 Discuss, with examples, the major pitfalls in developing retail strategy without an adequate understanding of consumer needs.

2 What are the principal research approaches and information systems that could be utilized by a large retail organization to maintain contact with consumer needs?

3 Identify the underlying needs that may be satisfied by offering a counter service delicatessen in a supermarket. Suggest some of the possible alternative solutions to these same needs.

4 How can the shopping activity itself satisfy personal and social motives that are not necessarily related to the actual buying of products?

5 Why is it dangerous to assume that store selection criteria identified in previous studies can be applied to similar store choice situations?

6 Give examples of different types of risk that consumers may perceive when selecting a shopping option. What steps could the retailer take to reduce each of these perceived risks?

7 Outline the basic principles of the multi-attribute attitude model. What are the main limitations of this concept as a model of the consumer's patronage decision?

8 Taking an actual store choice situation within your recent experience, try to depict the major influences and the sequences of effects in your patronage decision.

9 What factors should be considered in selecting possible bases for retail market segmentation?

10 Explain what is meant by psychographic segmentation. Give examples of psychographic segments that would be relevant to a clothing sector.

11 Evaluate the advantages and problems of segmenting retail markets on the basis of consumers' shopping orientations.

12 What can retailers gain from measuring not just behavioural loyalty but also customers' commitment to their stores? Why does high commitment not always lead to high behavioural loyalty, or low commitment to disloyalty?

13 You have been employed as a consultant by a major grocery retailer to advise on whether or not to continue with its loyalty card programme. Some competitors have withdrawn their programmes and there is some evidence of 'loyalty card fatigue' among consumers. Against this background, would you advise your client to continue or to abandon its loyalty card? Present a case for and against each option and justify your recommendation.

14 Outline they ways in which the relationship marketing concept may be put into practice by:

a) an exclusive ladies' fashion store

b) a chain of chemists' shops.

Highlight the particular pitfalls to be avoided in each of the two cases.

REFERENCES

Aylott, R. and V.-W. Mitchell (1998) 'An exploratory study of grocery shopping stressors', *International Journal of Retail & Distribution Management*, **26** (9), 362–373.

Babin, B.J., W.R. Darden and M. Griffin (1994) 'Work and/or fun: measuring hedonic and utilitarian shopping value', *Journal of Consumer Research*, **20**, 644–656.

Bass, F.M. and W.W. Talarzyk (1972) 'An attitude model for the study of brand preference', *Journal of Marketing Research*, **9** (1), 93–96.

Bates, J.M. and A. Gabor (1987) 'Changes in subjective welfare and purchasing behaviour: report on an enquiry', *Journal of the Market Research Society*, **29** (2), 183–207.

Baxter, A. (1998) 'Retailer case study: Boots the Chemists—Advantage Card Scheme', *European Retail Digest*, **10**, 14–17.

Beatty, S.E., L.R. Kahle and P. Homer (1988) 'The involvement-commitment model: theory and implications', *Journal of Business Research*, **16** (2), 149–167.

Beatty, S.E., L.R. Kahle, P. Homer and S. Misra (1985) 'Alternative measurement approaches to consumer values: the List of Values and Rokeach Value Survey', *Psychology and Marketing*, **2** (3), 181–200.

Beatty, S.E., M. Mayer, J.E. Coleman, K.E. Reynolds and J. Lee (1996) 'Customer-sales associate retail relationships', *Journal of Retailing*, **72** (3), 223–247.

Bell, D.R., T.-H. Ho and C.S. Tang (1998) 'Determining where to shop: fixed and variable costs of shopping', *Journal of Marketing Research*, **35** (3), 352–369.

Bellenger, D.N., D.H. Robertson and E.C. Hirschmann (1976) 'Age and education as key correlates of store selection for female shoppers', *Journal of Retailing*, **52** (4), 71–78.

Bendapudi, N. and L.L. Berry (1997) 'Customers' motivations for maintaining relationships with service providers', *Journal of Retailing*, **73** (1), 15–37.

Berry, L.L. (1979) 'The time-buying consumer', *Journal of Retailing*, **55** (4), 58–69.

Betts, E. (1994) 'Understanding the financial consumer', in *Retailing of Financial Services*, P.J. McGoldrick and S.J. Greenland (eds), McGraw-Hill, Maidenhead, pp. 41–84.

Betts, E. and P.J. McGoldrick (1996) 'Consumer behaviour and the retail "sales" modelling the development of an attitude problem', *European Journal of Marketing*, **30** (8), 40–58.

Betts, E., P.J. McGoldrick, V.-W. Mitchell and D. Lennard (1998) *Investigating the Temporal Cost of Packaging Information Comparisons for Optimum Buys*, DTI, London.

Black, W.C. (1984) 'Choice-set definition in patronage modelling', *Journal of Retailing*, **60** (2), 63–85.

Bloch, P.H., N.M. Ridgway and S.A. Dawson (1994) 'The shopping mall as consumer habit', *Journal of Retailing*, **70** (1), 23–42.

Bloemer, J. and de Ruyter, K. (1998) 'On the relationship between store image, store satisfaction and store loyalty', *European Journal of Marketing*, **32** (5/6), 499–513.

Boedeker, M. (1997) *Recreational Shopping: The Role of the Basic Emotional Dimension of Personality*, Turku School of Economics, Finland.

Bolton, R.N. (1998) 'A dynamic model of the duration of the customer's relationship with a continuous service provider: the role of satisfaction', *Marketing Science*, **17** (1), 45–65.

Bolton, R.N., P.K. Kannan and M.D. Bramlett (2000) 'Implications of loyalty program membership and service experiences for customer retention and value', *Journal of the Academy of Marketing Science*, **28** (1), 95–108.

Burford, R.L., B.M. Enis and G.W. Paul (1971) 'An index for the measurement of consumer loyalty', *Decision Sciences*, **2** (2), 17–24.

Burnett, J. (1996) 'Comparing the patronage selection criteria of the elderly: chronological age versus dependency', *International Review of Retail, Distribution and Consumer Research*, **6** (3), 243–257.

Burt, S. and M. Gabbott (1995) 'The elderly consumer and non-food purchase behaviour', *European Journal of Marketing*, **29** (2), 43–57.

Buttle, F. (1996) *Relationship Marketing: Theory and Practice*, Paul Chapman, London.

Buttle, F.A. (1992) 'Shopping motives: a constructionist perspective', *Services Industries Journal*, **12** (3), 349–367.

Cassill, N.L., J.B. Thomas and E.M. Bailey (1997) 'Consumers' definitions of apparel value: an investigation of department store shoppers', *Journal of Fashion Marketing and Management*, **1** (4), 308–321.

Chain Store Age Executive (1994) 'Retailing in the 21st century', *Chain Store Age Executive*, **69** (12), special issue.

Chenet, P. and J.I. Johansen (1999) *Beyond Loyalty: the Next Generation of Strategic Customer Relationship Marketing*, Oak Tree Press, Dublin.

Childs, M. (2000) 'Personal perspective on 2010', in *Retail and Consumer Services Panel: Personal Perspectives*, DTI (ed.), DTI, London, pp. 8–12.

Christopher, M., A. Payne and D. Ballantyne (1991) *Relationship Marketing: Bringing Quality, Customer Service and Marketing Together*, Butterworth-Heinemann, Oxford.

Colgate, M.R. and P.J. Danaher (2000) 'Implementing a customer relationship strategy: the asymmetric impact of poor versus excellent execution', *Journal of the Academy of Marketing Science*, **28** (3), 375–387.

Competition Commission (2000) *Supermarkets*, The Stationery Office, London.

Cuthbertson, R. (1998) 'Loyalty card schemes in retailing across Europe', *European Retail Digest*, **20**, 5–7.

Darian, J.C. (1998) 'Parent-child decision making in children's clothing stores', *International Journal of Retail & Distribution Management*, **26** (11), 421–428.

Davids, M. (1999) 'How to avoid the 10 biggest mistakes in CRM', *Journal of Business Strategy*, **20** (6), 22–26.

Davies, G. (1994) 'What should time be?', *European Journal of Marketing*, **28** (8/9), 100–113.

Davies, G. (1998) 'Loyalty cards can erode loyalty. Only customer relationship programmes can build it', *European Retail Digest*, **20**, 8–13.

Davies, G. and J. Bell (1991) 'The grocery shopper—is he different?', *International Journal of Retail & Distribution Management*, **19** (1), 25–28.

Davies, G. and O. Omer (1994) 'Time allocation and marketing', *Time and Society*, **5** (2), 253–268.

Deloitte & Touche (1999) *Retail Benchmarking Study*, Deloitte & Touche, London.

Denison, T. and S. Knox (1993) 'Cashing in on loyal customers: The divi and the indemnity for retailers', in *ESRC Seminar: Strategy Issues in Retailing*, P.J. McGoldrick and G. Davies (eds), ICRS, Manchester, pp. 225–252.

Dholakia, R.R. (1999) 'Going shopping: key determinants of shopping behaviours and motivations', *International Journal of Retail & Distribution Management*, 27 (4), 154–165.

Dick, A.S and K. Basu (1994) 'Customer loyalty: toward an integrated conceptual framework', *Journal of the Academy of Marketing Science*, 22 (2), 99–113.

Drummond, G. (1996a) 'Happy families', *SuperMarketing*, 29 November, 20–22.

Drummond, G. (1996b) 'Is anyone 100% loyal', *SuperMarketing*, 2 February, 22–24.

Dunnhumby Associates (2000) *The Millennium Shopper*, Dunnhumby Associates, London.

East, R. (1999) 'Fact, fiction and fallacy in retention marketing', *Working Paper*, Kingston Business School, Kingston.

East, R., P. Harris, G. Willson and W. Lomax (1995) 'Loyalty to supermarkets', *International Review of Retail, Distribution and Consumer Research*, 5 (1), 99–109.

Egan, J. (2000) 'Drivers to relational strategies in retailing', *International Journal of Retail & Distribution Management*, 28 (8), 379–386.

Elliott, R. (1994) 'Addictive consumption: function and fragmentation in postmodernity', *Journal of Consumer Policy*, 17, 159–179.

Engel, J.F., R.D. Blackwell and P.W. Miniard (1986) *Consumer Behaviour*, Holt, Rinehart & Winston, New York.

Enis, B.M. and G.W. Paul (1970) '"Store loyalty" as a basis for market segmentation', *Journal of Retailing*, 46 (3), 42–56.

Evans, K.R., T. Christiansen and J.D. Gill (1996) 'The impact of social influence and role expectations on shopping center patronage intentions', *Journal of the Academy of Marketing Science*, 24 (3), 208–218.

Fishbein, M. (1967) *Attitude Theory and Measurement*, Wiley, New York.

Flavian, C., E. Martinez and Y. Polo (2001) 'Loyalty to grocery stores in the Spanish market of the 1990s', *Journal of Retailing and Consumer Services*, 8, 85–93.

Foreman, A.M. and V. Spiram (1991) 'The depersonalization of retailing: its impact on the "lonely" consumer', *Journal of Retailing*, 67 (2), 226–243.

Foxall, G. and R. Goldsmith (1994) *Consumer Psychology for Marketing*, Routledge, London.

Gengler, C.E., D.B. Klenosky and M.S. Mulvey (1995) 'Improving the graphic representation of means-end results', *International Journal of Research in Marketing*, 12 (3), 245–256.

Ghosh, A. (1994) *Retail Management*, Dryden Press, Fort Worth, TX.

Gilmore, J.H. and B.J. Pine (1997) 'The four faces of mass customization', *Harvard Business Review*, 75 (1), 91–101.

González-Benito, O., M. Greatorex and P.A. Munoz-Gallego (2000) 'Assessment of potential segmentation variables. An approach based on a subjective MCI resource allocation model', *Journal of Retailing and Consumer Services*, 7 (3), 171–179.

Grönroos, C. (1994) 'From marketing mix to relationship marketing: towards a paradigm shift in marketing', *Management Decision*, 32 (2), 4–20.

Hagel, J. and J.F. Rayport (1997) 'The coming battle for customer information', *Harvard Business Review*, 75 (1), 53–65.

Hare, C., D. Kirk and T. Lang (2001) 'The food shopping experience of older consumers in Scotland: critical incidents', *International Journal of Retail & Distribution Management*, 29 (1), 25–40.

Healy, M., K. Hastings, L. Brown and M. Gardiner (2001) 'The old, the new and the complicated: a trilogy of marketing relationships', *European Journal of Marketing*, 35 (1/2), 182–193.

Herzberg, F. (1966) *Work and the Nature of Man*, Staples Press, London.

Heskett, J.L., T.O. Jones, G.W. Loveman and W.E. Sasser (1994) 'Putting the service-profit chain to work', *Harvard Business Review*, 72 (2), 164–174.

Hoekstra, J.C., P.S.H. Leeflang and D.R. Wittink (1999) 'The customer concept: the basis for a new marketing paradigm', *Journal of Market Focused Management*, 4, 43–76.

Holman, R.H. and R.D. Wilson (1982) 'Temporal equilibrium as a basis for retail shopping behavior', *Journal of Retailing*, 58 (1), 58–81.

Huie, J. (1985) 'Understanding the new breed of consumer' in *Insights in Strategic Retail Management*, J. Gattorna (ed.), MCB, Bradford, pp. 45–48.

IGD (2001) *Consumer Watch*, 4th edn, IGD, Watford.

Jarratt, D. (1996) 'A shopper taxonomy for retail strategy development', *International Review of Retail, Distribution and Consumer Research*, 6 (2), 196–215.

Jones, T.O. and W.E. Sasser (1995) 'Why satisfied customers defect', *Harvard Business Review*, 73 (6), 88–99.

Kahn, B.E. and D.R. Lehmann (1991) 'Modelling choice among assortments', *Journal of Retailing*, 67 (3), 274–299.

Kamakura, W.A. and T.P. Novak (1992) 'Value-system segmentation: exploring the meaning of LOV', *Journal of Consumer Research*, 19 (June), 119–132.

Kim, B.-D., K. Srinivasan and R.T. Wilcox (1999) 'Identifying price sensitive consumers: the relative merits of demographic vs. purchase pattern information', *Journal of Retailing*, 75 (2), 173–193.

Kim, Y.-K. (2001) 'Experiential retailing: an interdisciplinary approach to success in domestic and international retailing', *Journal of Retailing and Consumer Services*, 8, 287–289.

Kleinman, M. (2001) 'Tesco to offer profiles of Clubcard customers', *Marketing*, 8 February, 1.

Knox, S.D. and T.J. Denison (2000) 'Store loyalty: its impact on retail revenue', *Journal of Retailing and Consumer Services*, 7 (1), 33–45.

Krider, R.E. and C.B. Weinberg (2000) 'Product perishability and multistore grocery shopping', *Journal of Retailing and Consumer Services*, 7 (1), 1–18.

Laaksonen, M. (1993) 'Retail patronage dynamics: learning about daily shopping behavior in contexts of changing retail structures', *Journal of Business Research*, 28 (1/2), 3–174.

Leclerc, F., B.H. Schmitt and L. Dube (1995) 'Waiting time and decision making: is time like money?', *Journal of Consumer Research*, 22 (June), 110–119.

Lee, D.Y. (2000) 'Retail bargaining behaviour of American and Chinese customers', *European Journal of Marketing*, 34 (1/2), 190–206.

Lesser, J.A. and M.A. Hughes (1986) 'Towards a typology of shoppers', *Business Horizons*, 29 (6), 56–62.

Lewis, D. (2000) 'That sales pressure', *The Grocer*, 11 March, 42–43.

Louviere, J.J. and G.J. Gaeth (1987) 'Decomposing the determinants of retail facility choice using the method of hierarchical information integration: a supermarket illustration', *Journal of Retailing*, **63** (1), 25–48.

Malhotra, N.K. (1983) 'A threshold model of store choice', *Journal of Retailing*, **59** (2), 3–21.

Malhotra, N.K. (1986) 'Modelling store choice based on censored preference data', *Journal of Retailing*, **62** (2), 128–144.

Mano, H. (1999) 'The influence of pre-existing negative affect on store purchase intentions', *Journal of Retailing*, **75** (2), 149–172.

Marsh, H. (2001) 'Dig deeper into the database goldmine, *Marketing*, 11 January, 29–30.

Marshall, D.W. and A.S. Anderson (2000) 'Who's responsible for the food shopping? A study of young Scottish couples in their "honeymoon" period", *International Review of Retail, Distribution and Consumer Research*, **10** (1), 59–72.

Maslow, A.H. (1970) *Motivation and Personality*, Harper & Row, New York.

Maslow, A.H. and D.C. Stephens (2000) *The Maslow Business Reader*, Wiley, Chichester.

McClelland, D.C. (1967) *The Achieving Society*, Free Press, New York.

McDonald, W.J. (1994) 'Time use in shopping: the role of personal characteristics', *Journal of Retailing*, **70** (4), 345–365.

McGoldrick, P.J. and E. Andre (1997) 'Consumer misbehaviour: promiscuity or loyalty in grocery shopping', *Journal of Retail & Consumer Services*, **4** (2), 73–81.

McGoldrick, P.J. and C.P. Pieros (1998) 'Atmospherics, pleasure and arousal: the influence of response moderators', *Journal of Marketing Management*, **14**, 173–197.

Meyer, R.J. and T.C. Eagle (1982) 'Context-induced parameter instability in a disaggregate-stochastic model of store choice', *Journal of Marketing Research*, **19** (1), 62–71.

Mintel (1994) 'Shopping—who enjoys it?', *Retail Intelligence*, **3**, 72.

Mintel (1996) *Customer Loyalty in Retailing*, Mintel, London.

Mintel (1999a) 'Consumer shopping', *Retail Intelligence*, June, 32–42.

Mintel (1999b) *Customer Loyalty in Retailing*, Mintel, London.

Mintel (2000) *Retail Review*, Mintel, London.

Mitchell, A. (1983) *The Nine American Life Styles*, Warner, New York.

Mitchell, V.-W. (1999) 'Consumer perceived risk: conceptualisations and models', *European Journal of Marketing*, 33 (1/2), 163–195.

Mitchell, V.-W. and H.R. Kiral (1999) 'Risk positioning of UK grocery multiple retailers', *International Review of Retail, Distribution and Consumer Research*, **9** (1), 17–39.

Mitchell, V.-W. and P.J. McGoldrick (1994) 'The role of geodemographics in segmenting and targeting consumer markets: a Delphi study', *European Journal of Marketing*, **28** (5), 54–72.

Mitchell, V.-W. and P.J. McGoldrick (1996) 'Consumers' risk reduction strategies: a review and synthesis', *International Review of Retail, Distribution and Consumer Research*, **6** (1), 1–33.

Möller, K. and A. Halinen (2000) 'Relationship marketing theory: its roots and direction'. *Journal of Marketing Management*, **16**, 29–54.

Monroe, K.B. and J.P. Guiltinan (1975) 'A path-analytic exploration of retail patronage influences', *Journal of Consumer Research*, **2**, 19–28.

Moody, A. (1996) 'Shock horror!', *SuperMarketing*, 25 October, 18–20.

Murphy, J. and F. Suntook (1998) 'Keeping the satisfied customer', *Mastering Management Review*, **11** (April), 32–35.

Nielsen (2000) *Retail Pocket Book*, NTC, Henley-on-Thames.

Nielsen (2001) *Retail Pocket Book*, NTC, Henley-on-Thames.

O'Brien, L. and C. Jones (1995) 'Do rewards really create loyalty?', *Harvard Business Review*, 73 (3), 75–82.

O'Malley, L. and C. Tynan (2000) 'Relationship marketing in consumer markets: rhetoric or reality?', *European Journal of Marketing*, **34** (7), 797–815.

Ohmae, K. (1988) 'Getting back to strategy', *Harvard Business Review*, **66** (6), 149–156.

Oliver, R.L. (1999) 'Whence consumer loyalty?', *Journal of Marketing*, **63** (4), 33–44.

Parasuraman, A., L.L. Berry and V.A. Zeithaml (1991) 'Understanding customer expectations of service', *Sloan Management Review*, **32** (3), 39–48.

Parker, C. and S. Worthington (2000) 'When lemonade is better than whisky: investigating the equitableness of a supermarket's reward scheme', *International Journal of Retail & Distribution Management*, **28** (11), 490–497.

Pearce, R. and M. Hansson (2000) 'Retailing and risk society: genetically modified food', *International Journal of Retail & Distribution Management*, **28** (11), 450–458.

Peppers, D. and M. Rogers (1993) *The One to One Future: Building Relationship One Customer at a Time*, Currency Doubleday, New York.

Peppers, D., M. Rogers and B. Dorf (1999) 'Is your company ready for one-to-one marketing?', *Harvard Business Review*, **77** (1), 151–160.

Pieters, R., H. Baumgartner and D. Allen (1995) 'A means-end chain approach to consumer goal structures', *International Journal of Research in Marketing*, **12** (3), 227–244.

Piper, W.S. and L.M. Capella (1993) 'Male grocery shoppers' attitudes and demographics', *International Journal of Retail & Distribution Management*, **21** (5), 22–29.

Pruyn, A. and A. Smidts (1998) 'Effects of waiting on the satisfaction with the service: beyond objective time measures', *International Journal of Research in Marketing*, **15**, 321–334.

Putrevu, S. and K. R. Lord (2001) 'Search dimensions, patterns and segment profiles of grocery shoppers', *Journal of Retailing and Consumer Services*, **8**, 127–137.

Retail Intelligence (1999) 'Boots gains insights', *UK Retail Report*, **103**, 92–93.

Retail Review (1995) 'Loyalty cards catching on?', *Retail Review*, **207** (July), 4.

Retail Review (1999) 'Sainsbury reward card extended to more third party retailers', *Retail Review*, **248** (January), 12–13.

Retail Review (2000) 'Safeway culture change: so far, so good', *Retail Review*, **265** (August), 14–14.

Retail Week (2000) 'British shoppers prefer shopping for new outfits to buying groceries', *Retail Week*, **24** March, 4.

Reynolds, J. (1995) 'Database marketing and customer loyalty: examining the evidence', *European Retail Digest*, **7** (Summer), 31–38.

Reynolds, K.E. and S.E. Beatty (1999) 'A relationship customer typology', *Journal of Retailing*, **75** (4), 509–523.

Rinne, H. and W.R. Swinyard (1995) 'Segmenting the discount store market: the domination of the "difficult discounter core"', *Review of Retail, Distribution and Consumer Research*, **5** (2), 123–146.

Rokeach, M. (1973) *The Nature of Human Values*, Free Press, New York.

Roy, A. (1994) 'Correlates of mall visit frequency', *Journal of Retailing*, **70** (2), 139–161.

Rust, R.T. and A.J. Zohorik (1993) 'Customer satisfaction, customer retention and marketing share', *Journal of Retailing*, **69** (2), 193–215.

Schmidt, R.A., R. Segal and C. Cartwright (1994) 'Two-stop shopping or polarization: whither UK grocery shopping?', *International Journal of Retail & Distribution Management*, **22** (1), 12–19.

Segal, M.N. and R.W. Giacobbe (1994) 'Market segmentation and competitive analysis for supermarket retailing', *International Journal of Retail & Distribution Management*, **22** (1), 38–48.

Seiders, K. and D.J. Tigert (1997) 'Impact of market entry and competitive structure on store switching/store loyalty', *International Review of Retail, Distribution and Consumer Research*, **7** (3), 227–245.

Sheth, J. (1974) *Models of Buyer Behaviour*, Harper & Row, New York.

Sheth, J. (1983) 'An integrative theory of patronage preference and behaviour', in *Patronage Behavior and Retail Management*, W. Darden and R. Lusch (eds), Elsevier-North Holland, New York, pp. 9–28.

Sheth, J.N. and P.S. Raju (1973) 'Sequential and cyclical nature of information processing models in repetitive choice behavior', *Advances in Consumer Research*, **1**, 348–358.

Sheth, J.N. and R.S. Sisodia (1999) 'Revisiting marketing's lawlike generalizations', *Journal of the Academy of Marketing Science*, **27** (1), 71–87.

Sirohi, N., E.W. McLaughlin and D.R. Wittink (1998) 'A model of consumer perceptions and store loyalty intentions for a supermarket retailer', *Journal of Retailing*, **74** (2), 223–245.

Slappendel, C. (1992) 'An ergonomic evaluation of scanner checkouts in supermarkets', *Journal of Occupational Health and Safety*, **8**, 331–334.

Smith, J. (1995) *Category Killers in Europe*, FT/Pearson, London.

Sopanen, S. (1996) 'Customer loyalty schemes: the bottom line', *European Retail Digest*, **11** (Summer), 12–19.

Steenkamp, J.E.M. and M. Wedel (1991) 'Segmenting retail markets on store image using a consumer-based methodology', *Journal of Retailing*, **67** (3), 300–320.

Stephenson, D. and R.P. Willett (1969) 'Analysis of consumers' retail patronage strategies', in *Marketing Involvement in Society and Economy*, P.R. MacDonald (ed.), AMA, Chicago, pp. 316–322.

Stern, B.B., S.J. Gould and S. Tewari (1993) 'Sex-typed service images: an empirical investigation of self-service variables', *Service Industries Journal*, **13** (3), 74–96.

Swait, J. and J.C. Sweeney (2000) 'Perceived value and its impact on choice behavior in a retail setting', *Journal of Retailing and Consumer Services*, **7** (2), 77–88.

Sweeney, J.C., G.N. Soutar and L.W. Johnson (1999) 'The role of perceived risk in the quality-value relationship: a study in a retail environment', *Journal of Retailing*, **75** (1), 66–105.

Swinyard, W.R. and D.B. Whitlark (1994) 'The effect of customer dissatisfaction on store repurchase intentions: a little goes a long way', *International Review of Retail, Distribution and Grocery Research*, **4** (3), 329–344.

Tauber, E.M. (1972) 'Why do people shop?', *Journal of Marketing*, **36** (4), 46–49.

The Times (1998) 'Plastic padding', *The Times*, 9 January, 21.

Thomas, J.B., G.A. Woodward and D. Herr (2000) ' An investigation of the effect of jean purchase criteria and store selection on US teenagers' purchasing behaviours', *Journal of Fashion Marketing and Management*, **4** (3), 253–262.

Timmermans, H. (1996) 'A stated choice model of sequential mode and destination choice behaviour for shopping trips', *Environment and Planning A*, **28**, 173–184.

Timmermans, H. and P. Van der Waerden (1992) 'Modelling sequential choice processes: the case of two-stop trip chaining', *Environment and Planning A*, **24**, 1483–1490.

Torres, I.M., T.A. Summers and B.D. Belleau (2001) 'Men's shopping satisfaction and store preferences', *Journal of Retailing and Consumer Services*, **8**, 205–212.

Uncles, M. (1994) 'The seven perils of loyalty programmes', *Marketing Society Review*, Autumn, 18–20.

Uncles, M., A. Ehrenberg and K. Hammond (1995) 'Patterns of buyer behaviour: regularities, models and extensions', *Marketing Science*, **14** (3:2), G71–G78.

Underhill, P. (2000) *Why We Buy: The Science of Shopping*, Touchstone, New York.

Van den Poel, D. and J. Leunis (1996) 'Perceived risk and risk reduction strategies in mail-order versus retail store buying', *International Review of Retail, Distribution and Consumer Research*, **6** (4), 351–371.

Van Kenhove, P. and K. De Wulf (2000) 'Income and time pressure: a person-situation grocery retailing typology', *International Review of Retail, Distribution and Consumer Research*, **10** (2), 149–166.

Van Kenhove, P., K. De Wulf and W. Van Waterschoot (1999) 'The impact of task definition on store-attribute saliences and store choice', *Journal of Retailing*, **75** (1), 125–137.

Verdict (1999) *How Britain Shops Housewares*, Verdict, London.

Verdict (2000) *How Britain Shops 2000*, Verdict, London.

Walker, D. and S. Knox (1997) 'Understanding consumer decision making in grocery markets: does attitude-behaviour consistency vary with involvement?', *Journal of Marketing Communications*, **3**, 33–49.

Williams, R.H., J.J. Painter and H.R. Nicholas (1978) 'A policy-oriented typology of grocery shoppers', *Journal of Retailing*, **54** (1), 27–42.

Woodside, A.G. and R.J. Trappey (1996) 'Customer portfolio analysis among competing retail stores' *Journal of Business Research*, **35**, 189–200.

Worthington, S. and A. Hallsworth (1999) 'Cards in context—the comparative development of local loyalty schemes', *International Journal of Retail & Distribution Management*, **27** (10), 420–428.

Wright, C. and L. Sparks (1999) 'Loyalty saturation in retailing: exploring the end of retail loyalty cards?', *International Review of Retail & Distribution Management*, **27** (10), 429–439.

Yankelovich, D. (1964) 'New criteria for market segmentation', *Harvard Business Review*, **42** (2), 83–90.

Retail Strategy and Planning

INTRODUCTION
Formal structures and processes for strategic planning do not have a long history in most retail companies. The widespread recognition of the need for marketing orientation was not initially coupled with a propensity for long-term strategic planning:

> *[retailing executives] are used to reacting quickly and decisively to meet the problems of operating their business in a rapidly changing and highly competitive market. They like to see themselves as 'quick on their feet' and take pride in being so. Strategic planning however requires a longer term and a more sober posture if it is to be done properly (Rosenbloom, 1980).*

The prolific use of the word 'strategy' over the last 20 years, both by academic and industry writers, could suggest that short-termism and reactive management are now things of the past. Alas, an overview of the same two decades sees abundant evidence of both these traits, as the industry became collectively fixated upon price-cutting, then advertising, then store redesigns, then customer service, then loyalty schemes, then e-tailing. Reviewing the recent history of competitive advantage in retailing, Harris and Ogbonna (2001) identify 'competitive eras'. McGoldrick and Andre (1997) observed that most retail strategies were, in fact, formed in someone else's head office. Having reflected upon the difficulties of major retailers that had lost their leadership positions, Walters and Hanrahan (2000) concluded that: 'perhaps a well thought through strategy would help?'

In fairness to some of the best managed retail companies, considerable strides have been made in the development of strategic planning. Some have specialist strategic planners, largely free of 'line' responsibilities, working close to the chief executive. Others have created 'incubator units' to help hatch innovative strategic plans and solutions. It is noticeable that some companies adapt to competitive pressures, without abandoning their core strategy. Others seem to adopt a new 'strategy' at very regular intervals, often associated with rapid turnover among senior executives.

A problem for many, in developing an effective strategic planning function, is a lack of clarity as to its role. Even the word 'strategy' has been subject to diverse interpretations of its meaning and scope (e.g. Johnson and Scholes, 1999; Mintzberg, 1994; Whittington, 1993). The contrasting perspectives upon strategy were illustrated by use of '5 Ps' (Mintzberg, 1994):

1 Strategy is a *plan*, a direction, a guide or course of action for the future.
2 Strategy is a *pattern* of behaviour over time, such as innovating or following.
3 Strategy is a *position* in the market, such as up-market.
4 Strategy is *perspective*, a way of doing things, a business concept.
5 Strategy is a *ploy*, a specific manoeuvre to outwit a competitor.

Contrasting views are also expressed by various leading industrialists, as the following selection from the *Journal of Business Strategy* (1996) demonstrates:

> *Strategy is knowing your customers and their needs and helping them espouse those needs.*

> *Strategy is part of the overall planning process. It is the part that gets you from where you are to where you want to be.*

> *Strategy is the blueprint to achieve the identified goals of an organisation. It goes beyond just being a document to follow, but extends into the thought process and, ultimately, the culture of an organisation.*

These definitions give some impression of the scope of strategy, from establishing a customer-driven direction, through the process of planning, to the organizational process required for effective implementation. So, what should be the scope of strategic planning in retail organizations? Using the example of IKEA, Johnson and Scholes (1999) suggest four main characteristics of strategy:

1 **Long-term direction**: in its early days, IKEA was defined as a Scandinavian furniture retailer; now it has shifted to a global scale.
2 **Achieving some advantage**: IKEA was successful because it offered different benefits, compared with other retailers.
3 **Scope of an organization's activities**: the boundaries of the business, in terms of products, mode of service, design functions, etc.
4 **Search for strategic fit**: matching the activities of an organization to the environment in which it operates.

Having established a focus on consumer needs in the previous chapter, this chapter now examines some of the logical steps in formulating retail strategy. Various strategic frameworks and approaches have been applied to retailing, including strategic audits, mission statements, differentiation strategies, value chain analysis and the balanced scorecard. The chapter then moves on to look at ways of achieving growth, either through internal growth or through acquisitions and alliances. Finally, the chapter turns to the closely linked processes of targeting and positioning. Having established the segment(s) in which to compete, alternative approaches to positioning strategy are considered.

4.1 Strategic Analysis

A number of frameworks have emerged to assist in the early stages of the strategic planning process: these are now utilized within many retail companies (e.g. Johnson, 1987; Walters and Hanrahan, 2000). A strategic audit is a logical starting point, in helping to identify salient elements of the external and internal environments. This section looks at three well-established approaches, used to audit the macroenvironment, competitive forces and an overall business situation analysis. Although these approaches do not in themselves produce a strategy, they provide valuable insights into the company's current position, and the constraints that need to be overcome.

4.1.1 PEST Analysis

Successful retail companies often seem to be moving ahead with far less effort than their struggling competitors. Like an experienced driver, compared with a learner, the company is probably very aware of what is going on around it, and also what lies ahead. Given the complexity of the environments within which retailers now operate, however, few individuals have the experience, time or information to be constantly aware of all salient factors. A systematic audit can therefore help to review the elements that may help to shape, constrain or even derail a retail strategy. The old adage that 'retail is detail' is true also of strategic analysis, and checklists can help to cope with that necessary detail.

PEST analysis focuses upon the political sociocultural, economic and technological forces at work in the macroenvironment. Figure 4.1 illustrates some of the factors that may be considered within such analysis. For example, food retailers studied in great detail the findings of the Competition Commission (2000), as these could influence the political/legal environment within which they may operate in the future. Others have identified sociocultural factors such as environmental concerns, as potential sources of competitive advantage (e.g. Beharrell, 1991; Simms, 1992). Most retailers pay great attention to budget speeches and announcements on interest rates, which can cause immediate changes in the economic environment. Changes in the technological environment affect all retailers through new channels, cost saving technologies and, for some, potential obsolescence of products sold.

PEST analysis can be a valuable 'brainstorming' exercise, encouraging busy executives to think outside the immediate realms of their organizations and marketplaces. Figure 4.1 suggests a few of the headings that may be relevant, but a planning group should ask:

1 What environmental factors are currently affecting the company?
2 Which are the most important?
3 What new factors may be relevant in the future?

Figure 4.1 Example of retailer's PEST analysis

Political/Legal	Economic
• Change of government • Tax policies • Employment law • Minimum wage • Trading hours restrictions • Planning guidelines • Monopoly legislation • Terms of trade codes/laws • Bargain offer regulations • Environmental laws	• GNP trends • Regional economies • Disposable incomes • Savings ratio • Interest rates • Exchange rates • Fuel costs • Employment levels • National competition • International competition
Sociocultural	**Technological**
• Environmental concerns • Consumerism • Changing work patterns • Income distribution • Holiday/leisure time • Exercise/sport participation • Food concerns • Levels of education • Ageing population • Delays in starting family	• High-tech products • Food processing/presentation • Internet/interactive television • Electronic funds transfer • Electronic data interchange • Warehouse technology • Greener vehicles • Satellite tracking • International teleconferencing • Security technologies

Particular types of retail company will need to drill down far deeper than some of the general headings suggested here. For example, a sportswear retailer needs to be alert to trends in wearing trainers, tracksuits, etc. for general leisure wear, and the social/age groups most likely to do this. All retailers will require more in-depth analysis of its competitive environments, possibly employing a variation upon Porter's (1980) 'Five forces' model.

4.1.2 Analysis of Competitive Forces

Porter argued that intense competition is entirely natural, and that the level and form of that competition is defined by the interplay of five basic forces, namely:

▶ competitive rivalry
▶ buying power
▶ power of suppliers
▶ threat of substitutes
▶ threat of entrants.

While the idea of increasing turbulence in retailing is well supported (e.g. Dawson, 1995; Morgan Stanley Dean Witter, 1999a), the five forces concept has its critics (e.g. McDonald, 1992; O'Shaughnessy, 1988; Warnaby and Woodruffe, 1995). Criticisms include the choice of the five forces and their extreme variability in particular industry situations. Kay (1993) also points to evidence that a company's

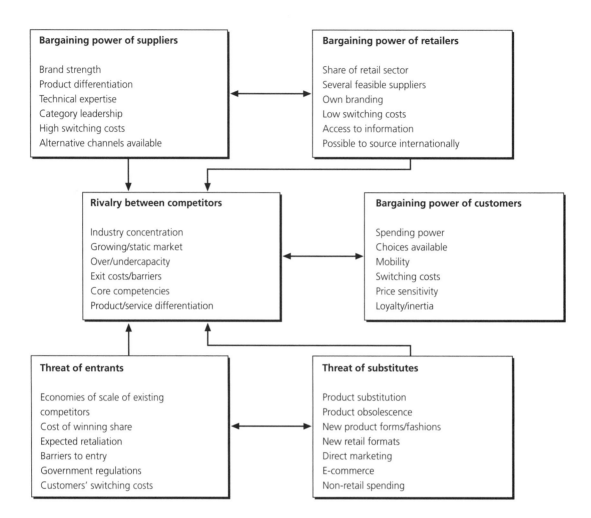

Bargaining power of suppliers

Brand strength
Product differentiation
Technical expertise
Category leadership
High switching costs
Alternative channels available

Bargaining power of retailers

Share of retail sector
Several feasible suppliers
Own branding
Low switching costs
Access to information
Possible to source internationally

Rivalry between competitors

Industry concentration
Growing/static market
Over/undercapacity
Exit costs/barriers
Core competencies
Product/service differentiation

Bargaining power of customers

Spending power
Choices available
Mobility
Switching costs
Price sensitivity
Loyalty/inertia

Threat of entrants

Economies of scale of existing
competitors
Cost of winning share
Expected retaliation
Barriers to entry
Government regulations
Customers' switching costs

Threat of substitutes

Product substitution
Product obsolescence
New product forms/fashions
New retail formats
Direct marketing
E-commerce
Non-retail spending

Figure 4.2 Forces
influencing competition
in the retail sector

performance within an industry is far more influential upon profit levels than the conditions within and around that industry.

However, if used as a diagnostic/predictive checklist, rather than as an analytical model, the 'forces' concept has value as an audit tool. When applied to retailing, ambiguity tends to arise as to whether 'buying power' relates to that of consumers, or that of the retail buyers. Figure 4.2 therefore distinguishes between these two elements of competitive pressure: both are critical issues but quite different in their sources and effects.

It is important for a retailer to maintain vigilance in all areas of potential turbulence and competitive activity. At any point in time, retail attention can easily become focused primarily upon just one of these areas. For example, the grocery industry tended to focus upon rivalry between current competitors, until a new threat looms. When warehouse clubs were thought to be a major threat, competitors quickly teamed up to mount a legal and PR counter-attack. Likewise, many retailers around the world have, at various times, focused upon the 'Wal-Mart threat'. In terms of threats from substitutes, most retailers are conscious of the risk of 'disintermediation', being cut out of the channel by e-commerce.

Forces on the supply side, and the relative bargaining power of retailers and their suppliers, are given detailed treatment in Chapter 8. Clearly, factors that increase the retailer's bargaining power tend to have the inverse efforts upon that of suppliers. Sheth and Sisodia (1999) and Hughes (1996) have challenged this element of the five forces model, in failing to accommodate increased co-operation between companies and their suppliers. Indeed, co-operation can also be extended to new entrants and substitute channels, as in the development of 'clicks and mortar' retailing. However, forces which change relative bargaining power can easily destabilize or change the nature of such collaborative arrangements.

4.1.3 SWOT Analysis

Potentially a most comprehensive form of business situation analysis, SWOT involves producing a systematic evaluation of the company's strengths and weaknesses, plus the opportunities and threats within the competitive environment. It therefore brings together the findings of PEST and competitive forces analysis, and relates these to the strategic capabilities of the retail organization. McDonald and Tideman (1993) observe how such audits are sometimes used only in last-ditch attempts to define a marketing problem, or entrusted to consultants to administer from time to time. They recommend that the process should be concluded internally, if possible, and repeated annually, at the start of the planning cycle.

Table 4.1 illustrates some of the items that should be appraised, although the list is designed to be illustrative, not exhaustive.

In fact, the number of areas that may potentially be considered is enormous, but the analysis normally focuses upon the issues of particular relevance to strategic planning and implementation. Many of the external issues, generally representing the opportunities and threats, have already been discussed. The internal aspects of the company, upon which the evaluations of the strengths and weaknesses are mainly based, are considered in the chapters that follow.

Although in essence a very simple concept, SWOT analysis can be developed to a high degree of sophistication, involving an extensive network of internal and external information systems. While some attributes can be quantified with a reasonable degree of precision, others require qualitative judgements. Another problem in appraising strengths and weaknesses is to maintain the necessary objectivity in evaluating the company's capabilities, aspects that are sometimes ignored in the pursuit of opportunistic ventures (Markides, 1997; Mintzberg and Waters, 1982). For example, not all of the attempts by UK grocery retailers to diversify into wider ranges of non-foods have been successful, largely because of a lack of buying and marketing capability in those areas (e.g. Retail Review, 1996a).

As a step from business situation analysis towards strategy formulation, Johnson and Scholes (1999) illustrate how a SWOT analysis can be charted as a matrix, issues in the environment on one axis, internal strengths/weaknesses on the other. This enables the analyst

Components	Examples of issues
STRENGTHS/WEAKNESSES (internal)	
Stores	Size profile, locations, design characteristics, development potential
Buying	Buying power, product category experience, breadth of buying expertise, outside agents or networks
Product range	Width and depth of assortment, distinctive/innovatory products, own-brand penetration
Management	Skills and expertise, leadership and vision, organization structure, cohesiveness of organization
Marketing	Advertising effectiveness, pricing policies, merchandising skills, customer service levels, marketing research
Personnel	Numbers and age structure, flexibility, skill levels, training resources
Systems	Order/payment systems, PoS information, reporting/communications, returns/complaints procedures, financial accounting
Distribution	Warehouse location/capacity/type, transportation systems, out-of-stock levels, order lead times
Finance	Cost structures, gross/net margins, return on investment, working capital, total assets
OPPORTUNITIES/THREATS (external)	
Economic changes	Unemployment levels, distribution of wealth, interest rates, disposable incomes
Social changes	Ageing population, more smaller households, two-career families, changing lifestyles
Consumer changes	Different needs and wants, beliefs and attitudes, perceptions (images) of company, loyalty and patronage patterns
Suppliers	Bargaining power, production capacity, flexibility, reliability, R & D capacity
Market structure	Relative market shares, leader/follower roles, oligopoly/monopolistic competition, mergers and acquisitions
Competitors	Existing/new competition, direct/indirect competition, SWOT of competitors, competitor strategies, likely competitor reactions
Legislation	Competition policy, codes/laws on terms of trade, planning policy guidelines, bargain offer regulations, advertising restriction

Table 4.1 Typical components of a SWOT analysis

to score how well/badly the company can respond to specific opportunities or threats, given its particular strengths and weaknesses. Clearly, this form of analysis requires the selection of subsets of key issues, otherwise the matrix would become unwieldy. The SWOT framework can also be usefully extended to the assessment of competitors' capabilities (Porter, 1980).

4.2 Strategic Direction

Having taken stock of its situation, with regard to its macroenvironment, marketplace(s) and capabilities, a retailer needs then to define the direction in which it should progress. A mission or vision statement can help to crystallize and to communicate the retailer's strategic objectives. Various approaches to gaining competitive advantage may be considered, including cost leadership, differentiation and focus strategies. The concept of the value chain can assist in identifying the means to achieve competitive advantage. When formalizing its plans, the application of the balanced scorecard can help to ensure that progress towards one set of objectives is not achieved to the neglect of other objectives.

4.2.1 Defining a Strategic Mission

Before a company can move to the stage of defining its strategic objectives in detail, it is essential to define the overall vision or mission of the organization.

> *A vision is the antecedent to a strategy. A strategy is dependent on a vision in order to give it form and direction. A vision is a description of a place, or a state where you wish to be. It's what you want to be (Journal of Business Strategy, 1996).*

Johnson and Scholes (1999) suggest a distinction between a mission statement and a statement of strategic intent. The former is regarded as a generalized statement of the overriding purpose of the organization, whereas strategic intent is the desired future state or aspiration of the organization. In practice, many mission statements are quite specific about the retailer's aspirations, for example:

> *Iceland's aim is to provide profitable growth and long term customer satisfaction by selling the widest possible range of frozen foods, all offering honest value in a clean environment with friendly efficient service.*

While mission statements have tended to be concerned mostly with economic aspects, increasing numbers of companies are including social or moral elements, in terms of service to the customers and/or the wider community. Many have backed up this type of commitment with a range of community projects and sponsorships (Chapter 11). Four 'constituencies' may therefore be referred to in the mission statement, namely, customers, employees, shareholders and communities. To retain brevity in the mission statement, two further 'constituencies', suppliers (Burt and Davis, 1999) and the environment (Bansal and Kilbourne, 2001; Bartlett and Barrett, 1992; McKinnon and Woodburn, 1994), are often the subjects of separate statements.

For some retailers, corporate socially responsible (CSR) activities occupy a key role within the company's proclaimed mission (Arnold et al., 1996; Piacentini et al., 2000). These may include 'green' issues, ethical supply policies and charitable links. Being positioned as a socially responsible company, as in the case of the Body Shop, engenders liking and trust, but can also open up the company to a range of criticisms, as Benetton discovered.

The definition of corporate mission requires finding answers to some very basic but none the less difficult questions, such as:

▶ Where are we?
▶ How did we get here?
▶ Where should we be?
▶ How would we get there?

The strategic audits, already discussed, should help the retailer to answer the earlier questions. However, even the first of the questions requires a careful definition of the business within which the company operates: this may be less obvious than it first appears. For example, Piercy (1983) suggested a progression of possible business definitions for a retailer operating garden centres:

1 Horticulture—selling plants and related products.
2 Providing a comprehensive gardening service.
3 Making gardening easier.
4 Filling people's disposable time.
5 Entertainment/leisure.
6 Fulfiling people's dreams.

Each of these possible business definitions says something different about the consumer needs that may be satisfied by the garden centre. More importantly, they help to avoid the classic pitfalls of 'marketing myopia' (Levitt 1960) and to provide alternative insights into where the company could be. In his analysis of strategies in American retailing, Savitt (1987) referred to an emerging 'production orientation', whereby retailers produce a far more complete and integrated product/service offering, to become in effect a part of their customers' consumption system. Thus, a supplier of hardware products offering some advice could progress to become an integral part of the consumer's home maintenance operation. This could include not only the supplying of the required product but also a full range of gardening and household repair/maintenance services. This involves moving away from a perception of being a store supplying merchandise, with a few additional services, to being a complete system for satisfying the particular set of customer needs.

A mission statement is usually agreed by senior management, although its final form may well be crafted by the PR department or an outside agency. Somewhat unusually, Superdrug involved all its 12 000 employees in a competition to produce a mission statement, based upon a set of mission characteristics provided by the executive team (Gatley and Clutterbuck, 1998). Around 1300 entries were received and, in the end, the mission statement was based upon three of these: 'Our mission is to be customer's favourite, up-to-the-minute health and beauty shop, loved for its value, choice, friendliness and fun.'

This approach was not indicative of any lack of leadership, rather a recognition of the need to get all employees to 'buy into' the strategic vision. Indeed, the importance of leadership in retailing has frequently been acknowledged (e.g. Thomas, 1991; Collins, 1992). Without strong leadership, strategic planning and implementation can be greatly hampered by interfunctional rivalries, vested interests and lack of vision (Green, 1987). However, that leadership does not have to be the source of all strategic vision. Gush (1999) reflects upon the changing leadership styles at the Burton Group, from the 'inspired despot' Ralph Halpern in the 1980s, to John Hoerner, 'a lateral thinker who retains an exasperating eye for detail'. Whittington (1993) refers to the notion of 'middle-up-down' management, recognizing the role of middle management in the creation of strategy. Heifetz and Laurie (1997) go further, emphasizing the value of the protection, rather than suppression, of the voices of leadership from lower down in the organization.

4.2.2 Routes to Competitive Advantage

Porter (1985) observed that 'sustainable competitive advantage' is the key to long-term, above average performance. Although a company may have numerous specific strengths and weaknesses compared with its competitors, Porter maintained that there are in essence two basic types of competitive advantage: low cost and differentiation. Either through effective differentiation or through a low cost proposition, a company can pursue a broad target or focus upon a narrow segment or need. On the basis of this, Porter suggested three 'generic strategies':

1 Overall cost leadership.
2 Differentiation.
3 Focus.

Although presented initially in relation to manufacturing industries, these have been adapted and applied to the retailing industry. The overall cost leadership position is typically associated with sustained investment and access to capital, intense supervision of labour, low-cost distribution and tight control systems. In the case of retailing, the required attributes would also be likely to include strong buying, merchandising expertise and highly efficient store management systems. This 'productivity-led' form of competitive advantage may be translated into strict range control and a price leadership position. Competitive advantage through differentiation is likely to be associated with strong marketing abilities, creative flair and a good reputation for quality and/or innovation. In retailing, this may translate into particular advantages in terms of product range, locations, store design/ambience, services and/or promotion. A focus strategy is likely to involve some of the cost leadership of differentiation attributes, but directed at a particular target market segment. Approaches to target marketing are considered in Sec. 4.4.1.

Each of these 'generic strategies' has its risks, as Table 4.2 summarizes. While manufacturers can protect some of their innovations through patents, rarely can the differentiation methods that are more readily accessible to retailers be legally protected. If they work, then they are likely to be copied. Cost leadership is also a problematic concept in retailing, as retailers have less variability in cost structures than industrial businesses (Helms et al., 1992).

Table 4.2 Generic strategies and risks

Source: derived from Porter (1980, 1985).

Overall cost leadership, e.g. Comet

- May be lost if inflation, competitors' innovations or technological change reduce cost advantage
- Cost emphasis may make company less sensitive to required changes in assortment or marketing mix
- Price leadership is a game that has to be won: being second cheapest does not attract the price shopper

Differentiation, e.g. Harrods

- The need for the differentiating factor(s) may diminish
- The price differential vis-à-vis low-cost competitors may become too great to retain customer loyalty
- Imitation, real or superficial, tends to reduce perceptions of differentials over time

Focus, e.g. Tie Rack

- Requirements of the strategic target and of the market as a whole may converge
- Competitors may invade particular lucrative sub-markets within the strategic target, i.e., outfocus the focuser,
- The chosen focus may restrict scope for growth, therefore restrict economies of scale and increase relative costs.

The main cost for most retail businesses is the cost of goods sold, so size and buying power may be the key to cost leadership. Consequently, although Kwik Save may have low operating costs, it does not have the buying power of either Tesco or J. Sainsbury (Kay, 1993). Like differentiation strategies, focus strategies may also be copied, or assimilated into mainstream retailing, if the segment is attractive (Collins, 1992). Consequently, the pursuit of one generic strategy may not in fact provide 'sustainable competitive advantage', defined by Hoffman (2000) as:

> *The prolonged benefit of implementing some unique value-creating strategy not simultaneously being implemented by any current or potential competitors, along with the inability to duplicate the benefits of that strategy.*

Porter maintained that a company must usually decide between the alternative generic strategies: otherwise it is likely to become 'stuck in the middle'. This proposition has been challenged in contexts other than retailing. Miller (1992), for example, refers to a 'virtuous circle' in strategy, whereby the search for low cost provides surpluses, which are reinvested in differentiation. The generic strategies have also been criticized as reflecting aggregate market behaviours, failing to reflect the shift towards more intricate and close targeted price/value propositions (Sheth and Sidosia, 1999).

While the generic strategies may represent different zones on a 'strategy positioning map', there is considerable evidence that retailers can successfully deploy elements of more than one of them. Rosenbloom and Dupuis (1994) traced the belief in the incompatibility of low cost/price and differentiation back to the 'wheel of retailing' concept, which holds that retailers tend to enter the market at the low-price/low-service position, then trade up from there (Hollander, 1960). However, they demonstrate a number of challenges to this conventional wisdom, examples of retailers combing low prices with value adding services. For example, Wal-Mart offers a large assortment, high product quality standards and efficient checkout services, while also offering highly competitive prices.

Such 'combination strategies' do not invariably feature low prices. Cappel et al (1994) observe that Dillard's Department Stores achieve lower than average cost through improvements in staffing and inventory control. At the same time, they maintain an image of exclusivity, based on good service and high quality merchandise, enabling them to charge a premium price. Warnaby and Woodruffe (1995) propose the combination strategy of 'cost effective differentiation'; building upon the audit of competitive forces (Sec. 4.1.2). They maintain that, through the most appropriate response to other 'actors' within their trading environments, retailers can achieve a form of competitive advantage that is as sustainable as possible. Figure 4.3 illustrates this concept. While

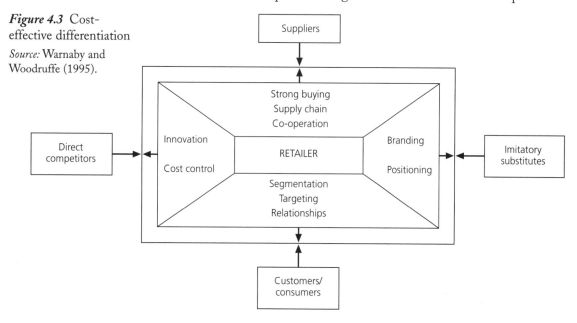

Figure 4.3 Cost-effective differentiation

Source: Warnaby and Woodruffe (1995).

specific activities are most closely associated with particular 'forces', Warnaby and Woodruffe emphasize the need to achieve co-ordination between the activities.

A shift in attention from strategic positioning to operational effectiveness has been noted by Porter (1996):

> *Under pressure to improve productivity, quality and speed, managers have embraced tools such as TQM [total quality management], benchmarking, and re-engineering. Dramatic operational improvements have resulted, but rarely have these gains translated into sustainable profitability. Gradually, the tools have taken the place of strategy.*

Porter (1996) suggests that the 'productivity frontier', the sum of all existing best practices at any given time, is constantly shifting outwards. This recognizes that management has the facility to improve on multiple dimensions of performance at the same time. However, there is little point in moving this frontier outwards in an indiscriminate way (Walters and Hanrahan, 2000). Rather, the company should seek to stretch the frontier in a planned response to a market–defined opportunity.

Figure 4.4. illustrates this concept, and the ways in which a recently established productivity frontier has been stretched by various food retailers. However, different levels of success and sustainability have been enjoyed by retailers at the different positions. For example, Kwik Save has shown symptoms of being 'stuck in the middle', not between Harrods and Aldi, but between Asda/Wal-Mart and Aldi. Marks & Spencer foods, on the other hand, enjoyed a highly profitable middle ground between the superstores and the exclusive, department store food halls. This advantage however was eroded, as the superstores upgraded their convenience food offerings.

It is appropriate therefore to conclude that a retailer needs both strategic and operational effectiveness. In essence, strategic effectiveness is doing the right things; operational effectiveness is doing the right things right (Walters and Hanrahan, 2000).

Figure 4.4 Stretching the productivity frontier

Source: adapted from Porter (1996); Walters and Hanrahan (2000).

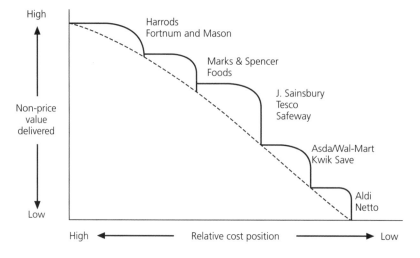

This is compatible with what Markides (1999) describes as 'breakthrough strategies', which involve both playing the game better, while also playing the game differently. To achieve the latter, a company needs to search for:

▶ new or unexploited customer segments to focus on (a new *who*)
▶ new customer needs that no competitor is currently satisfying (a new *what*)
▶ new ways of delivering the service (a new *how*).

Porter (1996) emphasizes that trade-offs are an essential feature of strategy: they create the need for choice and purposefully limit what a company offers. Companies, particularly retailing companies, cannot be 'all things to all people', a point made over 40 years ago by Martineau (1958). However, much has been learnt within that time about how to create customer value within a cost-effective retail strategy.

4.2.3 Creating Customer Value

The concept of the 'value chain' is helpful in assessing potential sources of competive advantage. Porter (1985) held that:

every firm is a collection of activities that are performed to design, produce, market, deliver and support its product (or service).

An analysis of the value chain, rather than value added, is the appropriate way to examine competitive advantage.

There have been a number of applications of the value chain concept to the retailing context. Figure 4.5 presents a matrix comprising operational elements and the major corporate functions. Each of many elements can serve to increase value, real or perceived, and therefore contribute to competive advantage. A particular merit of the value chain concept is in helping to highlight the specific components, their relative contributions to the value creation process, and their relative costs.

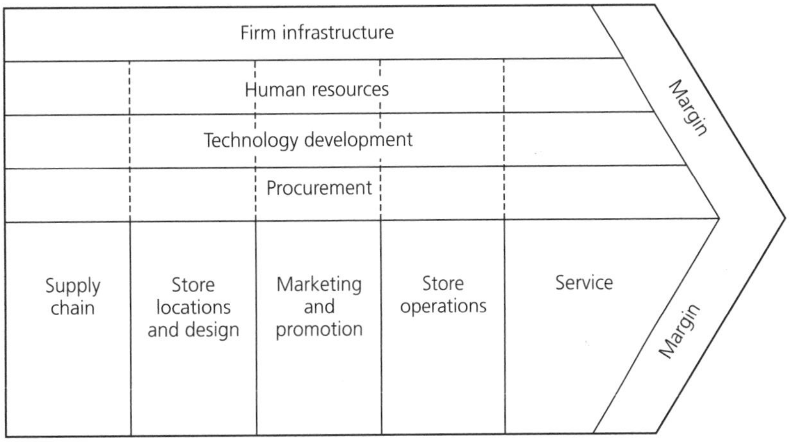

Figure 4.5 Retail value chain

Source: adapted from McGee (1987); Porter (1985).

It also emphasizes that retailers are not just random collections of stores, departments, people, products and money. These resources are of little value, unless deployed into activities which ensure that products and services valued by the final consumer are available. It is these competencies to perform particular activities, and the ability to manage linkages between activities, which are the sources of competitive advantage (Johnson and Scholes, 1999). Few of these competencies are likely to be unique on their own. It is the combination of resources, leveraged to appropriate effect, than can be unique (Prahalahad and Hamel, 1990).

At first inspection, the link between value creation and business success may appear obvious. However, even the term 'value' has proved difficult to define, and extremely variable in its properties. De Chenatony et al. (2000) point to evidence of variability between customers, between cultures, in different situations, before and after patronage, and between tangible and intangible offerings. An attempt by Woodruff (1997) to consolodate various definitions is adjusted, for the retail context, below:

> *Customer value is a customer's perceived preference for, and evaluation of, those attributes, attribute experiences and consequences that facilitate or block the achievement of the customer's goals and purposes.*

This points to a need to refocus the traditional value chain, which has emphasized the functions and competencies with organizations, leaving the customer as the recipient of the value generated. To be consistent with the marketing concept, the value chain should start with analysis of the target customers and their particular needs. Chan Kim and Mauborgne (1997) give examples of how various organizations have achieved success, by focusing upon what customers need most, rather than less salient attributes.

This does not diminish the importance of organizational competencies. Indeed, their analysis may show the company unable to respond to a particular needs profile. In some cases, this may be overcome by organizational changes, through alliances or by outsourcing some activities. In Chapter 8, the outsourcing of some category management and logistical functions is discussed. In other cases, however, the company may be better employed searching for a different needs profile, that it is equipped to satisfy better than the competition.

Figure 4.6 illustrates the idea of a value chain which starts with the target consumer, then identifies which of their many diverse needs comprise the opportunity. The activities of the organisation are then co-ordinated and focused around the provision of attributes, at appropriate levels, to meet these needs. Having provided the required value, this is then communicated by customer satisfaction, through to the wider consumer market and also to the financial markets.

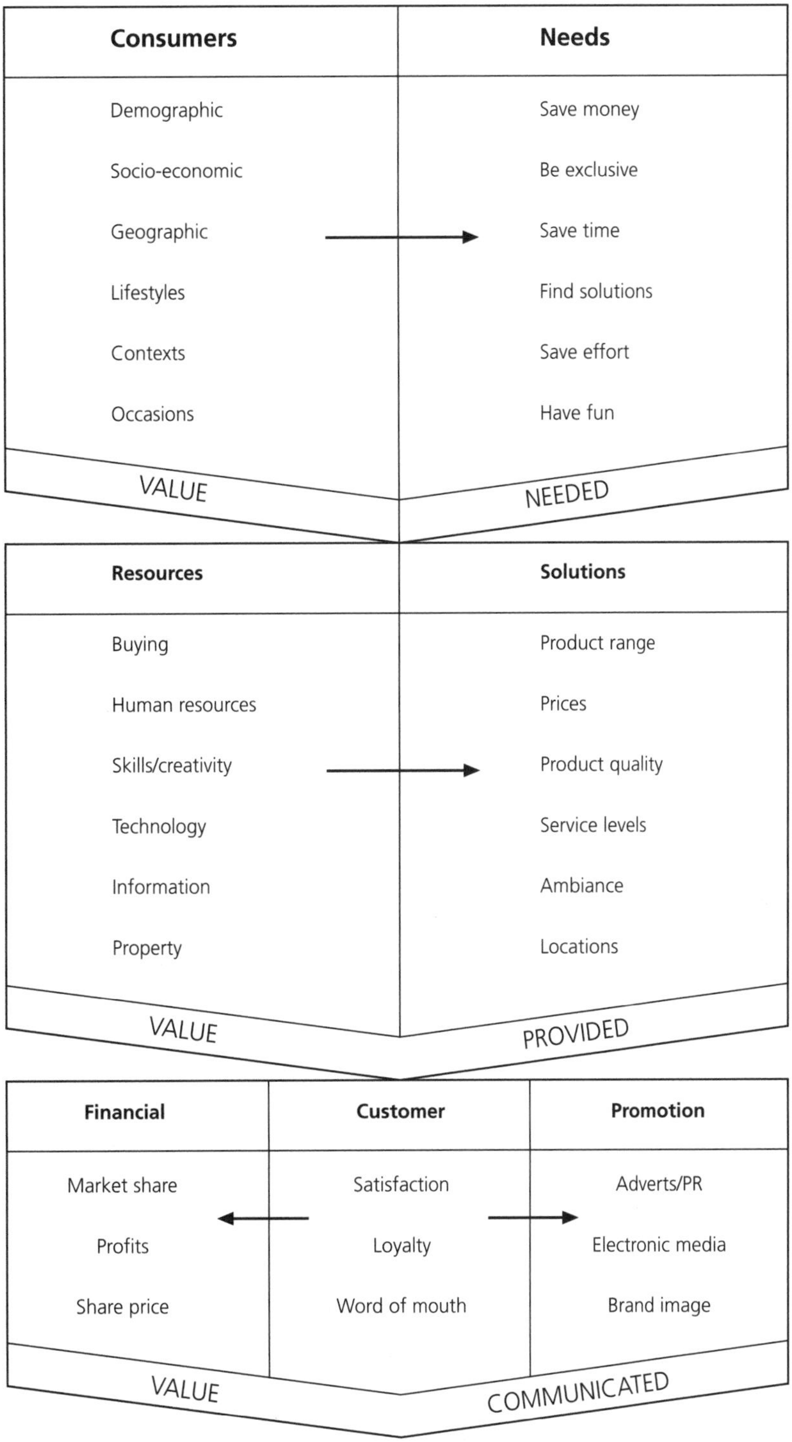

Figure 4.6 Customer-driven value system

Consumers	Needs
Demographic	Save money
Socio-economic	Be exclusive
Geographic	Save time
Lifestyles	Find solutions
Contexts	Save effort
Occasions	Have fun

VALUE NEEDED

Resources	Solutions
Buying	Product range
Human resources	Prices
Skills/creativity	Product quality
Technology	Service levels
Information	Ambiance
Property	Locations

VALUE PROVIDED

Financial	Customer	Promotion
Market share	Satisfaction	Adverts/PR
Profits	Loyalty	Electronic media
Share price	Word of mouth	Brand image

VALUE COMMUNICATED

There are many examples of companies that have accepted trade-offs between attributes, to satisfy a different needs profile. Although IKEA, with its self-assembly furniture, is sometimes portrayed as a low-service retailer, it does provide various forms of need-satisfying services (Rosenbloom and Dupuis, 1994):

▶ complexity saving—catalogues, product information, easy to find merchandise
▶ time saving—many items available from stock, one-stop shopping for furniture and accessories
▶ uncertainty saving—product guarantees
▶ recreation—shop and have lunch in the Scandinavian restaurant.

In developing the concept of activity system maps, Porter (1996) illustrates how numerous activies at IKEA interlock to create key attributes. For example, self-selection by customers permits less sales staffing but requires ample stock on site and suburban locations with large car parks, as customers mostly provide their own transport.

The value that Wal-Mart has set out to create is simple to define but hard to execute. It involves providing customers access to quality goods, to make these goods readily available and to develop cost structures that enable competitive pricing (Stalk et al., 1992). This has been achieved through a 'productivity loop' of continuous growth in both volume and productivity (Maximov and Gottschlich, 1993). Thus, while competitors know about Wal-Mart's superior logistics strategy, they cannot easily imitate it because it is embedded in a complex management process.

The more complex the process underlying superior value creation, and the wider it cuts across functional groups, the more difficult it is to imitate (Shoham and Fiegenbaum, 1999). To deliver the lowest prices, Wal-Mart invested in cross-docking distribution, plus the network of interorganizational relationships to make it work. The Limited invested in speed sourcing (Pollack, 1994). Dillard's invested in technology to become the low-cost department store. To ensure customer loyalty, Nordstom attracts and empowers superior-quality employees.

These investments in value-delivery competences have created a more sustainable competitive advantage for the leaders. They can be replicated by others, but only at high cost and over long periods of time.

4.2.4 The Balanced Scorecard

In attempting to implement its strategic vision, it is clear that a company can easily focus upon one 'constituency' of its mission statement, to the neglect of others. The need to balance financial and marketing outcomes has been recognized for some time (e.g. Cronin and Skinner, 1984; Goodman, 1985), but this concept was extended further by Kaplan and Norton (1992) with their 'balanced scorecard'. This urged organizations to translate their strategic visions into specific, measureable goals, from four perspectives:

1 Financial stakeholders
2 Customers
3 Internal business processes
4 Innovation, learning and growth.

The balanced scorecard acknowledges the importance of internal business processes in the creation of value; it recognizes too the importance of innovation, learning and growth to the sustainability of the strategy and the company. It also tackles the problem that mission statements are often poorly communicated, understood and/or accepted within organizations. Even if none of the above is a problem, managers and staff at lower levels may find it difficult to relate to lofty statements of strategic aims in their day-to-day activities. Kaplan and Norton (1993) therefore suggest that success factors, critical to the achievement of the vision, should be identified within each perspective. From these, goals, measurements and targets can be established, which can include all areas and levels within the organization.

Figure 4.7 outlines the balanced scorecard that a retailer might use, illustrating the necessary integration between the four perspectives, and the pivotal role of the strategic vision. The customer perspective is the subject of Chapter 5, the financial perspective Chapter 6. These will demonstrate the numerous goals and measures that could be used in these sectors of the scorecard. Norton and Kaplan's *internal* business processes are considered too restrictive for the retail context, as this would seem to exclude important interorganizational processes, such as category management and efficient customer response (Chapter 8). It could also be argued that retailers may wish to set goals with regard to the environment and/or their community involvement (e.g. Mitchell, 1992).

Although the number of goals and measures is potentially vast, it is suggested that the scorecard should be limited to 15 to 20 measures. This ensures transparency: an observer should be able to understand the company's strategy from the scorecard (Kaplan and Norton, 1993). While targets and measurements are important elements of the scorecard, important goals that are more difficult to quantify should not be excluded. For example, evaluations of creativity and design may have to depend upon management estimates. Drawing upon an earlier study of retail store efficency, Thomas et al. (1999) suggest a number of possible measures for a retailer's scorecard. They point out that, while multiple measures can be confusing for some, advances in technology and software make it more feasible to utilize integrated decision frameworks.

Early experiences with the scorecard helped to evolve a series of planning stages for its development and implemenation. Kaplan and Norton (1996) suggest four main processes, which form a continuous feedback loop.

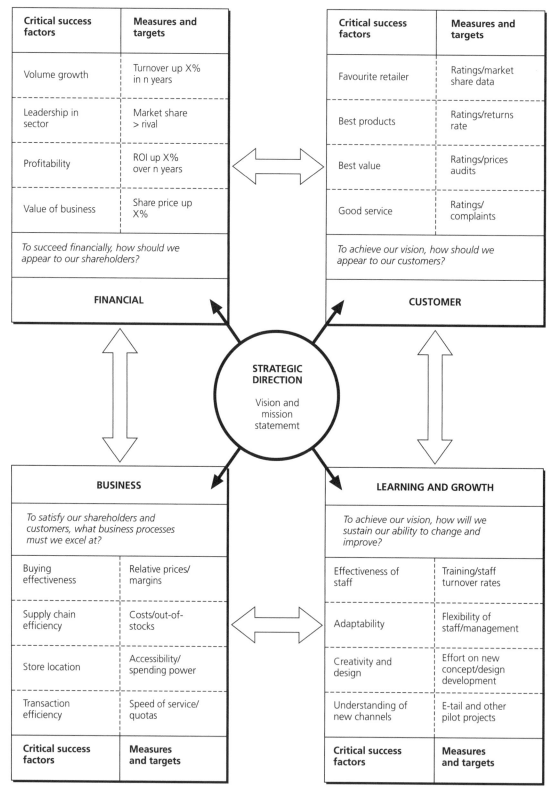

Critical success factors	Measures and targets
Volume growth	Turnover up X% in n years
Leadership in sector	Market share > rival
Profitability	ROI up X% over n years
Value of business	Share price up X%
To succeed financially, how should we appear to our shareholders?	

FINANCIAL

Critical success factors	Measures and targets
Favourite retailer	Ratings/market share data
Best products	Ratings/returns rate
Best value	Ratings/prices audits
Good service	Ratings/ complaints
To achieve our vision, how should we appear to our customers?	

CUSTOMER

STRATEGIC DIRECTION

Vision and mission statememt

BUSINESS

To satisfy our shareholders and customers, what business processes must we excel at?	
Buying effectiveness	Relative prices/ margins
Supply chain efficiency	Costs/out-of-stocks
Store location	Accessibility/ spending power
Transaction efficiency	Speed of service/ quotas
Critical success factors	**Measures and targets**

LEARNING AND GROWTH

To achieve our vision, how will we sustain our ability to change and improve?	
Effectiveness of staff	Training/staff turnover rates
Adaptability	Flexibility of staff/management
Creativity and design	Effort on new concept/design development
Understanding of new channels	E-tail and other pilot projects
Critical success factors	**Measures and targets**

Figure 4.7 A retailer's balanced scorecard

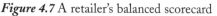

Source: adapted from Kaplan and Norton (1992; 1993; 1996).

1 *Translating the vision*: clarifying the vision and gaining consensus within the organization. Strategy statements expressed and agreed as an intergrated set of objectives and measures, describing the long-term drivers of success.

2 *Communicating and linking*: communicating the strategy up and down the organization. Setting goals and linking rewards to performance.

3 *Business planning*: setting targets, aligning strategic objectives, allocating resources and establishing milestones.

4 *Feedback and learning*: widens the focus from financial targets to broader perspectives. Facilitates strategy review and learning: strategies can be modified to reflect real-time learning.

Financial results can be a slow indicator of a company's overall performance. The diagnostic properites of the balanced scorecard could therefore give earlier warning of problems in the process required to create customer value, or in customer perceptions of the value. However, some would argue that far more detailed and rigorous analyses of customer perceptions (images) are required. Furthermore, there is a danger that the scorecard, like other management tools, could take the place of effective strategy (Porter, 1996). It may also be deployed by managers simply wishing to demonstrate their command of contemporary techniques (Whittington, 1993). If used with a weak strategy, or merely symbolically, the scorecard could impose an additional burden of time and cost upon the organization.

As a contribution to 'joined-up thinking' within organizations, the balanced scorecard does hold great promise. Its greatest benefit is the potential to integrate better the activities of each part of the organization, or business unit, towards a common set of goals. It also helps employees, at all levels, to see more clearly how their efforts contribute to the survival or prosperity of the organization. Some retailers regularly update a large scorecard diagram, displayed in a prominent position passed by all staff as they enter the sales floor.

4.3 Strategies for Growth

In retailing, as in most other areas of business, the option of standing still is not really available. As the earlier analysis of competive forces illustrated, existing and new competition is constantly seeking to acquire market share, tending also to erode margins. Even if existing share can be defended, the growth of other competitors may give them formidable economies of scale, making future defence of share all the more difficult (Morgan Stanley Dean Witter, 1999a).

Retailers are therefore constantly seeking profitable ways to grow their businesses, whether through internal expansion or through acquisitions. This section looks first at some of the growth vectors available to retailers, extending the concept of product-market strategy. The alternatives of specialization and diversification are then considered, as many of the growth vectors involve some form of diversification.

Acquisitions and mergers have helped many companies to achieve growth; scale may also be achieved through alliances and various collaborative arrangements.

4.3.1 Retail Growth Vectors

Ansoff (1988) referred to the 'sales gap' (or 'planning gap'), which represents the increasing difference between what is likely to be achieved without strategic change, and what could be achieved through expansion and/or diversification. Strategic change was defined as a realignment of the firm's product-market environment: Ansoff's 'product-mission matrix' suggested four, generalized growth options:

1 Market penetration (present product/present mission)
2 Market development (present product/new mission)
3 Product development (new product/present mission)
4 Diversification (new product/new mission).

Figure 4.8 Product-market matrix

Source: adapted from Ansoff (1988); Knee and Walters (1985); McDowell Mudambi (1994).

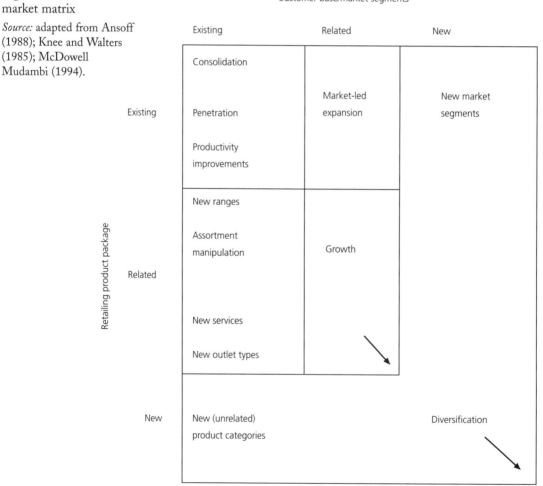

This matrix, originally published in 1965, has played an influential role but requires adaption for the retail context. Kristenson (1983) replaces the 'product' dimension with 'assortment', given that most retailers are concerned with very large number of product assortment decisions. Likewise, the mission (or market) dimension may be better described in terms of existing or new market segments. This draws attention to the fact that market expansion opportunities for a retailer may well exist within the existing geographical markets.

Knee and Walters (1985) suggested a distinction between related and new products/markets, as movement into related fields typically involves less risks. The firm is more likely to be able to benefit from its existing scale and competencies, and its image is more likely to be conguent with the related development. Figure 4.8 incorporates some of these elaborations upon Ansoff's matrix. It does however retain an essential feature of the original: as you move from the upper left corner, the alternatives involve increasing risk.

The strategic options for growth are, in fact, numerous, well exceeding the capacity of any two dimensional matrix. For example, Omura (1986) identified 20 growth options, having taken into account possibilities for assortment manipulation, change in delivery and different service requirements. Howe (1990) also refers to 'vertical' strategies, involving taking over or controlling aspects of distribution and/or production. As the dimensions proliferate, the distinctions between strategic options, marketing options and operational efficiencies tend to become blurred.

Figure 4.9 summarizes the principle growth vectors that retailers are likely to consider when examining their strategic options (e.g. Quarmby, 1995). There are clearly many interrelationships between these. For example, internationalization may require modifications to format and some alterations to the product/services mix. There are also many optional points along each vector, not just the three (existing/related/new) choices, as depicted. However, even in its simplified form, the 'strategic space vehicle' in Fig. 4.9 implies over 700 combinations of growth strategy!

Growth within the existing proposition may appear the least adventurous option, but it does have great benefits, if it can be achieved. It tends to involve the lowest risks, as it utilizes to the full the organization's existing knowledge and experience. The Strategic Planning Institute, through its PIMS (Profit Impact of Market Strategy) database, has demonstrated the association between relative market share and return on investment (Buzzell and Gale, 1987). Tesco in the UK and Wal-Mart in the USA are both clear beneficiaries of their high market shares. Ironically, Tesco is working to expand its national scale into global scale, while its rival Asda seeks to leverage its global scale (via Wal-Mart) to achieve greater national scale (Retail Review, 2000a).

There are, however, limits to the market share growth route, defined largely by the size of the market, and the concerns of competition authorities about local or national monopolies/oligopolies (e.g. Competition Commission, 2000). In practice, therefore, retailers who are intent upon growing are likely also to move along some or all of the other vectors. Tesco has achieved some of its growth by widening the appeal of its store to attract adjacent segments, in terms of their characteristics and preferences. In the DIY sector, some superstores chose to widen their appeal to other domestic market segments; B & Q Warehouses go further by adding essentially different segments, that is, builders and other small businesses.

Figure 4.9 Retail growth vectors

Expansion through new or modified formats was identified as an important growth vector by Duke (1991). McDowell Mudambi (1994)

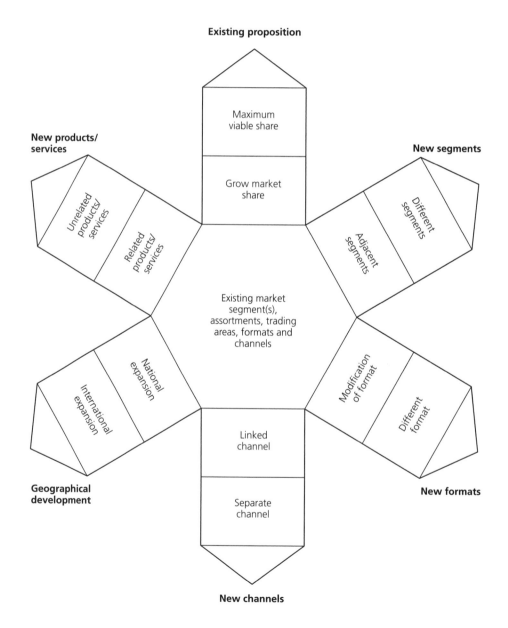

refers to 'migrational strategies', which can include stores of radically different size or type. The format may involve compression of the standard format, such as Sainsbury's 'community supermarkets', at around 10 000 square feet (compared with superstores of 25 000 square feet or more). Alternatively, it may involve a fundamentally different format, such as Wal-Mart's 'Sam's' warehouse club stores (Retail Review, 2000a).

New channels have represented a popular growth vector in recent years (e.g. DTI, 2000; Morgan Stanley Dean Witter, 2000). The addition of home delivery and telephone ordering services represented a logical progression for catalogue retailer Argos. Full-scale e-tailing has required considerable development of new skills in electronic interfaces and home delivery logistics for many retailers (see Chapter 15). Equally topical is the internationalization option, regarded as a primary growth vector for retailers (e.g. *Robinson and Clarke-Hill, 1990*; *Pellegrini, 1995*), especially those that have already entered the most viable geographical areas at home. The movement from national to international expansion does, however, involve significant risk, as many retailers have found to their cost (see Chapter 14).

The product/services vector comprises numerous opportunities for diversification. This can be at the modest level of product innovations, or diversification into new categories of products/services. Over the years, J. Sainsbury has added CDs, videos, photo processing, dry cleaning, pharmacies, post offices and petrol stations to their stores. The 'common thread' (Ansoff, 1988) between these is that they form part of most people's weekly shopping needs (Quarmby, 1995). Its move into personal banking, although requiring a different set of competencies, is still consistent with that 'common thread'.

4.3.2 Diversification or Specialization

The 'retail accordion theory' suggests that the pattern of retail evolution has tended to alternate between domination by wide-assortment retailers and domination by narrow-line, specialized retailers (Hollander 1966). Most support has been given to this theory by the pattern of evolution of retailing in the USA. In early settlements, the general store stocked a very diverse range, but as settlements grew and developed, so did more specialized stores. Department stores subsequently emerged, offering wide assortments, but these then lost ground to more specialized chains. From the 1950s, many of the specialists started to proliferate their product ranges, notably the supermarkets and drug stores. The term 'scrambled merchandising' described the practice of selling product lines not traditional in the type of outlet. This form of merchandising sought to satisfy the demand for one-stop shopping. However, as consumers became more demanding of choice, some of the more specialist stores proved best able to meet the demand for choice in depth.

The retail accordion certainly should not be viewed as a predictive tool or a precise explanatory model. It does, however, draw attention to this curious facet of retail evolution, and also serves to emphasize that both diversification and specialization strategies have succeeded under certain sets of circumstances.

The wide-narrow-wide pattern of the accordion is still observed at the level of corporate strategy: 'Diversification as a corporate strategy goes in and out of vogue on a regular basis' (Markides, 1997). A number of different strategies have been described as specialization (Poyner, 1886):

1 Broad category range – narrow target market, for example, Harvey Nichols
2 Narrow category range – specific target market, for example, Tie Rack
3 Narrow category range – deep choice within categories, for example, Toys 'R' Us.

The 'category–killer' approach made a considerable impact in the 1990s, with stores such as IKEA, B & Q Warehouse and Toys 'R' Us achieving success in their areas of specialization. 'Category killers' been defined in various ways (Smith, 1995) but share certain characteristics:

1 Specialized product range, featuring depth, rather than breadth, of selection
2 Mainly branded goods that are hard for other retailers to differentiate
3 Large stores, typically in suburban 'power shopping centres' (retail parks in UK terminology)
4 Appeal to car-borne shoppers with more concern for selection and price than nearby location
5 Through the 'virtuous circle' productivity loop, attempt to offer lower prices than smaller, or more generalist, competitors (Rogers, 1996).

In other words, category killers are 'top-of-mind' destination stores that attempt, through the combined appeal of deep selections and low prices, to dominate a fairly narrowly defined market of infrequently purchased goods. Most commentators regard 'category killers' and 'power retailer' as virtually synonymous. However, Wal-Mart and Nordstrom have also been described as 'power retailers'; the term is also being used loosely to describe any retailer enjoying significant consumer success and market power, based on buying, technology and/or merchandising skills (Rogers, 1996). Although food superstores have achieved considerable category dominance, they are rarely described as category killers. This is due to the competition between them, and the continued survival of many convenience food stores (Smith, 1995).

Among the many benefits of deep assortment specialization is the ability to offer expert advice, more characteristic of smaller, specialist outlets. Golfing section salesmen at a sports category killer were required to play off a handicap of around ten or better, besides possessing the appropriate retail skills (Retail Review, 1996b). B & Q Warehouses employ experienced electricians, plumbers, builders, etc. to give customers the most practical advice. The category killer strategy is considered most suitable where there is low diversity within each purchase, combined with low purchase frequency. Office supplies, housewares, furniture and consumer electricals are other categories considered to be highly suitable (Smith, 1995).

The strategy is not without its risks. Too much choice can cause overload and confusion, causing some customers to retreat and not make a purchase at all (Huffman and Kahn, 1998; Kahn, 1998). The need to stock slow-moving items, as well as the fast movers, can also lead to high levels of stockholding, although it may be possible to 'share' this problem with suppliers. A problem for Toys 'R' Us has also been the 'cherry-picking' of more profitable, fast-moving product sales by wider range competitors, such as Carrefour and Wal-Mart. For example, Wal-Mart retains its presence in toy selling with around 1500 SKUs (stock-keeping units) through the year, but increases this to 3500 SKUs in the Christmas season (Tordjman, 1996).

There are several reasons that can trigger a move towards greater diversification (Johnson and Scholes, 1999):

- escape from present sector, if it is in decline or under attack
- spreading risk: avoiding placing all 'eggs in one basket'
- even out cyclical effects, for example, in the toy or garden care sectors
- opportunity to utilize excess cash in a short-term tax loss situation
- exploiting underutilized resources and competencies
- enjoy synergies from activities in different sectors, for example, customer databases.

The major grocery retailers have been able to expand into takeaway foods and restaurants, including a 'drive-thru' at Asda, Canterbury (Webb, 1999), but the limitations of overall food market have encouraged diversification. Tesco has used its larger stores, notably its 'Extra' hypermarkets, to develop distinct in-store entities for some of its non-food sectors. These include Electricals (kettles to computers). Cookshop, Health and Beauty, Baby and Children's world, Music and Leisure, Sportsworld and Print and Paper (Retail Review, 1999b). Its diversifications also include eyetests and spectacles, building upon the theme of its well established pharmacies. Tesco also won awards for its credit card, insurance and other financial services (Retail Review, 2000b).

Asda was the first grocery chain to contribute its sales figures to the BBC's weekly top 40 CD listings, a move, according to Asda, to make it *a serious place to buy music, unique among supermarkets*. Evidence suggested that the company achieved considerable growth in the music and video, home and leisure and clothing categories (Webb, 1999). Prior to leaving Asda in 2000, George Davies had built their clothing operation to around 2 per cent of the clothing market (Retail Review 2000c).

Some of the other grocers have demonstrated ambivalence regarding clothes, with accordion-like expansions and withdrawals from the sector. As Table 4.3 illustrates, Hart and Davies (1996) discovered similar

Category Perception	Household Goods %	Health & Beauty %	Stationery %	Entertainment %	Clothing %
Inappropriate	1.0	2.6	8.7	24.0	25.0
Neutral	6.7	10.3	15.2	14.7	15.0
Appropriate	92.3	87.1	76.1	61.3	60.1

Table 4.3
Appropriateness of
supermarket non-foods
Adapted from: Hart and
Davies (1996).

ambivalence among consumers, as to whether or not clothing was appropriate supermarket merchandise.

However, for a superstore to become a 'serious place to buy clothes', it needs more than a few racks of miscellaneous garments, placed in a quiet corner of the store. It requires commitment of buying/design expertise, a viable floor-space allocation and considerable initial promotional support.

As the grocers have moved in on the pharmarcy and health and beauty categories, Boots has sought more diverse ways to pursue its mission of helping customers to look and feel better. From its well-established optician service, it has entered dentistry, chiropody, physiotherapy and a range of 'alternative' treatments. Its in-store health services also include advice on weight, smoking, sleep patterns and stress. Expansions beyond the store now include fitness clubs, complete with swimming pools and the usual facilities.

While requiring different retail/service expertise, these diversifications are strongly linked by the 'common thread' of health and personal well-being (Retail Review, 2000d). Given the consistency of positioning, most qualify as the type of brand extensions that can 'safely' carry the Boots name (Doyle, 1989). For the fitness club initiatives, the company has chosen to use the 'Body 360' name. Many retailers' 'brand extensions' are far less congruent with the core image of the company, running the risk of diluting beliefs associated with the brand name (Roedder et al., 1998).

Prior to diversifying from their core areas, retailers should answer a number of critical questions (Collins, 1992; Omura, 1986):

1 Have we really exhausted opportunities to increase profits in our existing sectors?
2 If not, would this not be a lower risk and quicker source of growth?
3 Are we going to be distracted from the core business that is going to fund our new venture?
4 What skills do we have that are genuinely transferable?
5 Is our image compatible with the new products/services, in terms of status or reduction of consumers' perceived risk?
6 Will economies of scale in marketing, buying and distribution carry over into the new ranges?
7 Can we compete with existing specialists if our diversified assortments offer little depth of choice?

4.3.3 Acquisitions and Mergers

Probably the most rapid route towards diversification at the corporate level is that of acquisition or merger. The retailing sector has experienced a great deal of acquisition activity, in the pursuit of both national and international growth (Hubbard and Kelly, 1999; Keep et al., 1996). Table 4.4 shows some examples of UK groups and their main trading names, many of which are the result of earlier acquisitions. However, the mosaic is constantly changing, for example, with the decision to divide the Kingfisher interests into specialists (B & Q, Comet, etc.) and more general merchandise stores (Woolworths, Superdrug) (Retail Review, 2000e).

Table 4.4 Who owns whom?

Note: (¹) Arcadia subsequently disposed of the formats italicized.

Derived from: Nielsen (2000).

There are many other examples of de-merger activity, such as the division of Debenhams from the rest of the (former) Burton Group, now Arcadia (Gush, 1999).

As a means to diversify, acquision has considerable risks. Having studied the acquisitions of 33 prestigious companies in the USA,

Group	Activity	Outlets
Arcadia¹	Men's clothing	Burton, Top Man, *Principles for Men, SU24*
	Women's clothing	Dorothy Perkins, Evans, Top Shop, Wallis, *Principles, Richards,* Miss Selfridge, *Warehouse, Outfit*
	Camping, leisurewear	*Racing Green, Hawkshead*
Kingfisher	Variety stores	Woolworths, Big W
	Drugstores	Superdrug
	DIY	B & Q
	Electrical	Comet
	Music, entertainment	MVC
Alexon	Women's clothing	Eastex, Envy, Alexon, Dash, Kaliko, Ann Harvey, Minuet
	Footwear	Dolcis
Dixons	Electrical/photographic	Dixons, Currys
	Computers	PC World, @ Jakarta
	Telephones etc	The Link
Tulchan	Hosiery	Sock Shop
	Knitware	Jumper
Storehouse	Children's clothing	Mothercare
	Variety stores	BhS
John Lewis Partnership	Supermarkets	Waitrose
	Department stores	John Lewis, Peter Jones, Bainbridge, Jessops, George Henry Lee, Tyrell & Green, Cole Bros.

Porter (1987) found that most had divested themselves of many more acquisitions than they had retained. He offered some explanations:

1 It is the individual business units that compete, not the diversified company. The strategy therefore fails unless each business unit is carefully nurtured.
2 Corporate diversification adds costs and constraints to the business units, such as the need to comply with corporate planning, control or personnel systems/policies.
3 Shareholders themselves can often diversify more cheaply, to their own preferences. A company typically incurs a sizeable acquisition premium.

Given the chequered history of corporate diversification, companies are urged to ask themselves a number of searching questions, prior to diversifying by acquisition. Unfortunately, companies often make such decisions in an atmosphere not conducive to thoughtful deliberation. With the competitive/opportunistic nature of many acquisitions, senior mangers are often required to digest mountains of data, under intensive time presssure (Markides, 1997). Table 4.5 suggests some of the questions that should be answered, before using the acquisition approach to diversification.

Table 4.5 Questions before diversifying through acquisition

Source: derived from Collins (1992); Whittington (1993); Markides (1997).

One of the few systematic studies of post-acquisition performance among retailers produced mixed results (Keep et al., 1996). Some retailers improved their performance as they reduced their diversification, while others that remained consistently diversified outperformed industry averages.

1. What are our sources of competitive advantage in our existing market?

2. Can we compete effectively with the new competitors at their own game?

3. What strategic assets do we need in order to succeed in the new market?

4. Will our strategic assets be as effective, when used in different ways and combinations?

5. Will we be simply a player or emerge as a winner in the new market?

6. What can we learn from the acquired business and are we sufficiently organized to learn it?

7. If we buy the company, are we really going to retain the people whose skills we lack?

8. Are personal motives, such as power, prestige, more overseas trips, etc., playing too large a part in our decision?

This appears to confirm the view that acquisition to diversify can be successful, if well conceived and managed, but frequently it is not. Focusing upon acquisitions for the purpose of growth, Cushman and Dyer (1997) found that post-acquisition retailers, in relative terms, fared better than acquiring companies in other industries. However, two-thirds experienced some loss in return on equity (ROE) performance: 'The lack of significant gains overall could lead one to believe that acquisition may not be the prosperous vehicle for growth that many had hoped for.'

Acquisitions must be evaluated in terms of the strategic objective(s) being pursued, which may be more concerned with long term survival/prosperity than immediate profit gains:

1 *Diversification*: the Kingfisher group has become highly diversified from its original Woolworths base. This provided protection from decline in the core market, and the cyclical nature of some of the new markets.

2 *Defensive*: the agreed merger between Carrefour and Promodes came within three months of Wal-Mart taking over Asda in the UK (Vaughan, 1999). Kumar et al. (1991) identified some of the characteristics of retailers most vulnerable to acquisition.

3 *Market share/economies of scale*: the Wm Low chain was an expensive acquisition for Tesco but it expanded their scale and share, especially in Scotland (Drummond, 1995). The Somerfield acquisition of Kwik Save was also motivated by scale and geographical coverage (Smith, 1998), but the attempted integration of the chains hit major problems of local repositioning. (Retail Review, 1999).

4 *Synergy/skills transfer*: in theory, most acquisitions/mergers are supposed to create synergy, that is, produce benefits over and above those that could have been produced by the business units operating independently. These synergies may include combined buying power/expertise, reduced logistical and head office overheads, and the savings/benefits of combined IT systems (Morgan Stanley Dean Witter, 1999b).

5 *Alternative channel development*: the acquisition of the Grattan mail order business by Next preceded the launch of the 'Next Directory' catalogue. Alliances can also play a part in channel development, such as Tesco's entry to mortgages on line, through tie-ups with CGU and John Charcoal (Retail Review, 2000b).

6 *Internationalization*: acquisition has been a major vehicle for international growth, such as Wal-Mart's acquisitions in the UK and Germany. These are considered further in Chapter 14.

Whether retailers diversify through acquisition or through internal growth, they are advised to re-evaluate their portfolio on a regular basis (Ghosh, 1994). Portfolio planning models have been in use for many years (e.g. Day, 1977), and have been criticized as being time/data-demanding, as well as oversimplified in their recommendations.

Figure 4.10 illustrates how portfolio planning may be applied by a diversified retailer. Activities can be positioned on the matrix in terms of the retailer's competitive advantage in the sector, and the attractiveness of the product/service sector. Attractiveness may be measured by expected growth rates, overall size, competition, bargaining position vis-à-vis suppliers, and profit margins. Evaluating sectors for superstore diversification, Moore (1996) classifies personal care, pharmacy, music

Figure 4.10

Portfolio planning

Source: adapted from Ghosh (1994).

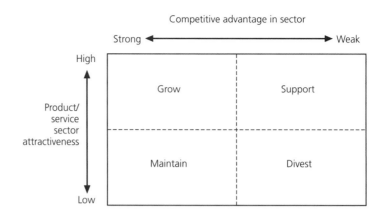

and entertainment as growth areas, whereas petrol, cards and household goods are mature sectors.

Portfolio analysis can be used at various different levels of analysis, depending upon how the retailer defines its strategic business units (SBUs):

▶ *Store brand names*: the different named outlets within the Arcadia or Dixons groups (Table 4.4) may be treated as SBUs.
▶ *Store formats*: for example, the superstores, compacts, city centre outlets and forecourt convenience stores run by the major grocery retailers.
▶ *Product/service categories*: department stores or superstores may look upon financial services, health and beauty, household goods, food, etc. as SBUs.
▶ *Geographical location*: international operations are usually regarded as separate business units, as market and competitive conditions differ.

A retailer can employ portfolio analysis to assist in prioritization and allocation of financial and managerial resources. If the sector is not attractive, and the retailer's position weak, to divest may be the obvious solution. That is, of course, unless the activity forms a crucial link to future planned activities, or if it is better to invest some resources to secure a better disposal price in the future. Even where property is leased, disposal may be difficult and expensive due to lease terms, as the British Shoe Corporation found to its cost (Guy, 1999).

Likewise, the decision to support, grow or maintain inputs to an activity must always be taken with regard to competitor activity and the retailer's longer-term plans. In common with most strategic planning models, portfolio analysis is of value in raising questions, potentially dangerous if relied upon to provide all the answers.

4.3.4 Alliances and Concessions

Diversification through acquisition can bring problems and risks, especially when used to enter entirely new product-markets. However, many retailers are facing a growing consumer demand for choice in depth, requiring specialist assortments, while at the same time wishing to diversify and escape the constraints of their current markets. Possible solutions to this dilemma include various forms of alliances, which range from loose, opportunistic alliances through to formalized joint ventures (Johnson and Scholes, 1999).

The Homebase chain found its origins in a joint venture between J. Sainsbury and the Belgian retailer GB-Inno-BM. This brought in extensive experience in the buying and merchandising of home improvement and garden products, skills that J. Sainsbury would have had to develop from scratch. J. Sainsbury, for its part, contributed its expertise in the UK market and in site acquisition. The development of the chain was further boosted in 1995 by the takeover of Texas Homecare. Inspite of achieving the number two position, behind B & Q, the decision was made in 2000 to dispose of the chain (Morgan Stanley Dean Witter, 2001). This reflected the strong position of market leader B & Q, the possiblility of further competition in the sector, and the need to invest to recover lost ground in J. Sainsbury's core grocery business.

Several strategic partnerships have been developed between grocery retailers and oil companies to develop forecourt convenience stores. Webb (1999) recorded the following agreements:

- Tesco with Esso
- Safeway with BP
- Somerfield with Elf
- Alldays with Total
- Budgens with Q8.

Prior to its partnership with Esso, Tesco has been developing independently its 'Tesco Express' format. However, the link-up with Esso increased the pace of this development, giving access to a wider choice of larger, high-volume forecourts. The activity also has a logical link with Tesco's diversification into car insurance (Retail Review, 2000f). Prior to these developments, the major oil companies had lost a great deal of their petrol market share to the superstore filling stations. Their motivation to enter agreements was therefore largely defensive. As one industry commentator remarked: 'It is easier for the supermarket chains to sell petrol than it is for the oil companies to sell food' (Arnold, 1996).

Joint developments do not necessarily involve the development of a joint operation. Marks & Spencer and Tesco have developed side by side in a number of edge/out-of-town centres. The first of these, the Brookfield Centre in Hertfordshire, was essentially opportunistic. As it was deemed to be a success, others followed. Marks & Spencer also collaborated with Asda and with J. Sainsbury in developing specific sites (Davies, 1993). The incentives for the grocery retailers were:

- to increase the catchment area, by much as 50 per cent, compared with a stand-alone superstore
- to improve chances of getting planning permission.

On these joint sites, the partners compete, particularly in the areas of convenience foods, wines, toiletries, cosmetics and baby-care items. Far from being a deficit, these areas of competition can contibute to the cumulative attraction of the joint development.

Another solution to the problems of offering specialization within diversity is to utilize concessionaires, often referred to as 'shops within shops'. The term 'leased departments' tends to be used for similar arrangements in the USA (e.g. Berman and Evans, 1998). While the terms are largely interchangeable, 'shop within shop' is often used to refer to a unit run by another, established retailer. 'Concession', on the other hand, more often describes a unit run by a company regarded primarily as a manufacturer.

A wide variety of agreements exist between concessions and host retailers, and payments for space usually take the form of:

1 A percentage of the concession's sales.
2 As above, but with a minimum payment.
3 A fixed rental for the space occupied.
4 A fixed rental plus a percentage of sales.
5 A rental proportional to the host retailer's sales.

The first concession in the UK was probably a Jaeger ladies fashion concession, opened in Selfridges in 1935. Jaeger continued to use concessions, as well as running their own, usually larger outlets (Buttle, 1994). In common with other concessionaires, they enjoy the benefits of the traffic flow generated by the host retailer, while also contributing to the overall attraction of the store. However, they also suffer restrictions in some stores, for example, in the use of music or providing customers with cups of coffee.

Table 4.6 Pros and cons of using concessions

Source: adapted from McGoldrick (1989).

Table 4.6 summarizes the potential advantages and disadvantages of using concessions, from the viewpoint of the host retailer. Sometimes a genuine win–win situation can be achieved, with the concession contributing more profit per unit of space than the host retailer could

Possible advantages	Possible problems
Flexibility of short-term contracts	Diversity of design formats instore
Gain specialist expertise	Less coherent image for store
Learning from concessions	Concession can damage reputation
Offer specialization within diversity	Merchandise positioning mismatch
Provide attraction to the store	Confusion in store layout
Superior supply terms	A substitute for real innovation
Pressure upon concession to perform	Diversion of sales to concession
Reduction in staff and other costs	Less control over prices, stock, etc.
Reduced risk of unsold stock	Staff less/not loyal to store
Guaranteed income to store	Concession–store staff conflicts
Productive use of excess space	More admin for store manager
Higher profit per square metre than own department	Lower realized gross margins leading to less net profit

generate itself. However, there are dangers, especially if the strategy is overused. In its hostile bid for Debenhams, the Burton Group was highly critical of the excessive use previously made of concessions; referring to a hotch-potch of shops-in-shops, with conflicting marketing images, and confused merchandising and floor layouts (McGoldrick, 1989).

4.4 Customer Targeting

In the previous chapter, many different approaches to segmenting retail markets were discussed. Market segmentation assists in the understanding and satisfaction of consumer needs; it can also be a first step towards deciding upon the areas of the market in which to compete. It has long been recognized that very few retailers can, in reality, regard the whole market as 'their oyster'. Quoting from one retailer almost 50 years ago, Martineau (1958) stressed this aspect of retail marketing:

> *It is high time we retailers realised that we cannot be all things to all people. When we try to do that, we end up with no particular appeal for anybody.*

> *It is up to us to decide where we fit, who comprises our customer body, and then to fulfill, as completely and satisfactorily as possible, the expectations of our particular group and our logical market.*

Sound advice indeed, but advice which has been frequently ignored, misunderstood or applied in simplistic manner. This section starts by looking at trends in target marketing, including the emergence of the lifestyle retailer. Positioning strategies are then considered, as retailers seek to achieve effective differentation from competition.

4.4.1 Target Marketing

A prerequisite for effective targeting is an understanding of the needs of viable market segments. Figure 4.11 summarizes the logical sequence of

Figure 4.11 From segmentation to positioning

Source: adapted from Dibb and Simkin (1991).

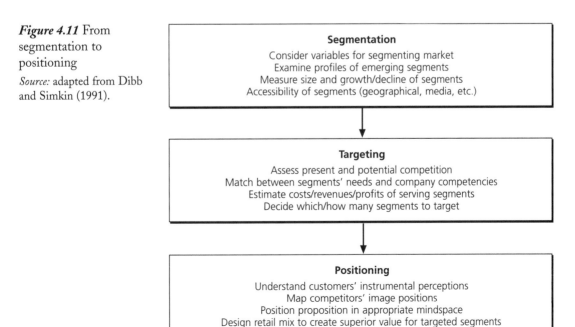

Segmentation
Consider variables for segmenting market
Examine profiles of emerging segments
Measure size and growth/decline of segments
Accessibility of segments (geographical, media, etc.)

Targeting
Assess present and potential competition
Match between segments' needs and company competencies
Estimate costs/revenues/profits of serving segments
Decide which/how many segments to target

Positioning
Understand customers' instrumental perceptions
Map competitors' image positions
Position proposition in appropriate mindspace
Design retail mix to create superior value for targeted segments

events from segmenting the market, through to positioning the retail proposition for maximum appeal and value to the target market(s). These stages could be succinctly expressed as *define*, *decide*, *design* and *deliver*.

Some clothing retailers in particular have focused upon relatively narrow target markets in their quest for competive advantage. This is in contrast with the broad appeal which, for example, Marks & Spencer has tried to maintain. In their attempts to combat more targeted competition, groups such as Sears and British Shoe Corporation used their multiplicity of outlets and trading names to target different segments. Their efforts however were not successful, in part because they were based on rather simplistic notions of segmentation (Collins, 1992). These problems led to numerous store closures and acute difficulties for Sears in the disposal of property freeholds and leaseholds (Guy, 1999).

Arcardia also deployed its various trading names to target different segments and needs, as Table 4.7 illustrates. In addition to usual gender/age/income-based targeting, this also differentiated on the basis of fashion orientation. Hawkshead served a broad range of customer types but with a specific target need: outdoor clothing. Evans is well established as the shop catering for size 16s and above. Each of these 'brands' could be regarded as SBUs within Arcadia's portfolio. In 2001,

Store fascia	Target consumers	Assortment characteristics
Burton Menswear	Men	Mainstream/value clothing
Dorothy Perkins	Women	Mainstream/value clothing
Evans	Women	Size 16 and above
Hawkshead	Women, men and children	Outdoor clothing
Miss Selfridges	Young women	Clubwear, accessories and cosmetics
Outfit	Women, men and children	Out-of-town retailer of Arcadia brands
Principles for Men	Men	Formal/casual clothing
Principles for Women	Women	Formal/casual clothing and accessories
Racing Green	Women and men	Clothing and homeware
SU214	Women and men	Branded designer fashion
Topman	Young men	Fun, fast-moving fashion
Topshop	Young women	Fun, fast-moving fashion
Wade Smith	Women, men and children	Branded designer clothing
Wallis	Women	Higher-quality clothing
Warehouse	Women 20–30	Accessibly priced fashion

Table 4.7 Arcadia targets and characteristics

Note: Fascias in italics identified for closure in 2001.

Sources: IGD (2000b); Retail Review (2001).

the company decided to reduce the number of separate entities within this portfolio, from fifteen to just the six most successful trading formats (Retail Review, 2001).

A major problem in the implementation of target marketing has been the tendency of many retailers to pursue the same targets. Clearly, the whole point of target marketing is lost if everyone shoots at the same target. There has been an infatuation with the 25–44-year-old market, in spite of the fact that over half of shoppers (over 15 years old) are now 45 or older (Nielsen, 2000). Those in the 45-60 age band often have higher disposable incomes, especially where children have ceased to be a financial burden, the mortgage is paid off and, in many cases, both partners are working again. The retired are also becoming a more numerous and increasingly attractive market, as institutional and/or index-linked pensions progressively supplement or replace meagre state pensions. However, it would be equally misguided to regard the 'grey market' as one segment: it incorporates a great diversity of needs, preferences and lifestyles (Tantiwong and Wilton, 1985).

Part of the preoccupation with age in targeting can be put down to the strong links between age, life stage and disposable income. It is not however a good predictor of lifestyles, which have been the key targeting variables of a number of retailers.

> *A lifestyle retail organization is one that bases its strategy and operations on unique living patterns of its target customer, rather than on demographics or merchandise strength (Blackwell and Talarzyk, 1983).*

The Body Shop targets consumers who are socially aware, caring and concerned about the environment. Another successful lifestyle retailer, the Limited, describes its target as educated, affluent, gregarius, fashion-oriented and, more often than not, a working woman who lives in or near a major metropolitan area. Both retailers initially saw their targets as younger shoppers but these lifestyles are now applicable to a wider age range. Part of the early success of Next was attributed to the fact that it missed its target:

> *The genius of Next is that it missed its target market. No criticism here of its cohesive lifestyle product policy but a reference to the fact that Next reaches a far wider age range than was originally planned (Poynor, 1986).*

Lifestyle retailing is an intuitively appealing, sometimes highly successful concept. Its success derives in part from the fact that lifestyles can be defined in so many different ways. This in itself make effective differentation more likely than when using just age and/or income for targeting. Just as store images can vary on numerous different attributes, so too can shoppers' images and self-images (see Chapter 5). Among the many attributes used to define lifestyles are the following:

- cultural or subcultural values, norms and customs
- reference groups—people who influence patronage and buying decisions
- family life cycle—children's clothes/toys, school wear, students, empty nesters
- career orientation—success, mobility, ambition.
- time utilization—need to minimize purchase time, or maximize in-store experience
- personality—gregarious, conscientius, self-confident, risk aversive

- status consciousness—'snob' or bargain appeal, symbolic patronage/consumption
- ethical and environmental concerns, organic foods, cruelty-free furs/cosmetics
- environmental dispositions—preferences for crowds/space, urban/rural
- fashion orientation—trendy, sophisticated, conservative
- sports, hobbies and recreational activities

4.4.2 Positioning Strategies

Having evaluated and selected the most appropriate target market(s), the retailer is faced with the task of positioning the retail mix to serve the target customers most effectively and profitability. The concept of positioning found its origins in product marketing but its scope of application soon grew far wider:

> *Positioning starts with a product, a piece of merchandise, a service, an instituion or even a person.*
>
> *But positioning is not what you do a product. Positioning is what you do to the mind of the prospect. That is, you position the product in the mind of the prospect (Ries and Trout, 1982).*

This definitions correctly emphasizes the issue of perception in relation to positioning: no amount of manipulation of the retail mix will add up to effective positioning, unless it produces a coherent and favourable image within the minds of target customers. It must be noted, however, that Ries and Trout were writing from the advertiser's perspective, and so were primarily concerned with communication strategies. Effective positioning must embrace the total retail marketing effort, if the results are to be credible and sustainable.

There have been many cases of retailers attempting to reposition simply by switching advertising messages; unless these are reinforced by customers' experiences in the store, the chances are that the retailer has just wasted a great deal of advertising expenditure. At the other extreme, repositioning may amount to rebranding, as in the case of River Island. As Britain recovered from post-war gloom, the Lewis separates chain was repositioned as Chelsea Girl, capturing the spirit of the 'swinging 60s':

> *its image was of loud music, affordable up-to-date merchandise 'served' by gum-chewing assistants; then, during the 1970s and 1980s, it fine-tuned its offering to accommodate shifting tastes of more discerning consumers (Lea-Greenwood, 1993).*

By the late 1980s, the Chelsea girl image was looking dated and was not fully integrated with its partner chain, Concept Man. The repositioning under the River Island brand overcame both these problems, as well as broadening the appeal of the stores. Table 4.8 illustrates that River Island is perceived as a significant competitor, both by Next for Men and Burton Menswear. Interestingly, the management at Next do not perceive Burton Menswear as occupying the same market segment. In contrast,

Competitors	Next for Men	Burton Menswear
Marks & Spencer	Main competitor, used for benchmarking on prices and quality	Higher priced main competitor
River Island	Fashion led; used by younger customers	Higher priced and fashion led
Principles for Men	Competitior on quality and style	Fashion led for middle age group
Top Man	Competitor at lower-end price ranges; used by younger customers	Fashion-led competitor for the younger age groups
Next for Men	n/a	Second main competitor
Burton Menswear	Not perceived as a competitor by management at Next	n/a
French Connection, Reiss, Jigsaw	Strong competition in fashion forward ranges	n/a
Cruise and upmarket independents	Local competition on designer fashion	n/a
Sportswear retailers	Some basic competition at the lower end	Strong local competition
Discount fashion retailers	n/a	Strong local competition in casual and formal wear

Table 4.8 Competitive positioning: Next and Burton

Note: based upon management perceptions of competitors.

Source: Birtwistle and Freathy (1998).

Burton Menswear considers Next to be one of their main competitors (Birtwistle and Freathy, 1998).

The need for strategic positioning is very obvious in the case of fashion stores but grocery chains are by no means oblivious to the concept. Their appeal however tends to be wider, as a major grocery store will seek to attract at least a quarter of food business from within its catchment area (Competition Commission, 2000). This makes it difficult for superstores to target too tightly, for example, providing carpets for some shoppers, floor tiles for others (Corstjens and Corstjens, 1995). Grocery chains do, however, adjust the positioning of their stores between localities, varying prices, promotions, assortments, service(s) and some aspects of ambience: within a superstore, different zones and categories also target different shoppers.

Even ignoring such local differences, there are still significant positioning differences between the major grocery chains. Figure 4.12 maps positions on just two dimensions, age and socioeconomic group. This illustates the favourable positioning of Tesco, with mass-market appeal but a bias towards younger, more affluent shoppers. It also helps to explain the problems that Somerfield encountered when they tried to reposition Kwik Save stores under the Somerfield banner (Retail Review, 1999). Positioning maps can also help to understand the dynamics of

Figure 4.12 Positioning by age and socioeconomic group

Source: derived from Nielson (2000).

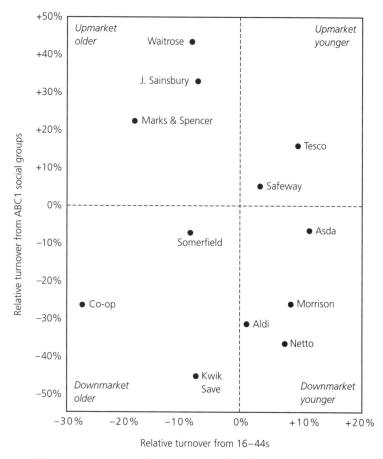

Note: zero per cent on each scale represents the national average penetration in those age/social bands.

competition within a market (Ghosh, 1994). A Netto store is likely to suffer more from the arrival of a new Aldi, which occupies a similar position, than from the opening of a Marks & Sainsbury store.

Instances of grocery retailers operating under completely different store names have generally been short-lived, often being the legacy of merging two or more dissimilar chains. There have been many instances of multi-positioning in the fashion sectors, the various names of the Arcadia group being just one such case (Table 4.7). Multi-positioning does not invariably involve the use of different names: Boots, for example, have eight different stores types in their portfolio, all operating under the Boots banner (IGD, 2000a). Tesco, Tesco Extra, Tesco Metro and Tesco Express illustrate another approach, each format drawing upon and reinforcing the power of the main brand, while signalling different positions and purposes.

In their seach for new and profitable market positions, retailers should not be constrained by the convention of the two dimensional matrix. The majority of positioning diagrams, such as Fig. 4.12, are still based upon two axes, which can obscure opportunities to position on numerous other dimensions. For example, a matrix based upon price and service would produce just four quadrants (e.g. Lucas and Gresham, 1988):

1 Low price–high service (low profit).
2 High price–high service (service oriented).
3 Low price–low service (price oriented).
4 High price–low service (poor value).

Conventional wisdom would suggest that only quadrants 2 and 3 offer viable strategies. However, Wal-Mart and others have 'broken the rules' by looking far more carefully at what aspects of service people actually value most. Coupled with many cost-saving measures, this has enabled them to position as low price–high (required) service retailers, and still trade profitablity in most cases.

Simplistic concepts of positioning are just one reason for the lack of effective differentation by many retailers. Kim and Mauborgne (1999) also point to a reinforcing cycle, whereby companies' behaviour affects customers' expectations. They have trained shoppers in what to expect, making it less likely that basic market research will yield new insights. When surveyed, customers tend to echo back: more of the same for less money.

The 'creation of new market space' requires that companies probe deeper in terms of profiling cutomers needs and how well these are satisfied by existing competitors. Table 4.9 shows how Barnes & Noble positioned themselves on multiple dimensions, vis-à-vis other book retailers in the USA. As well as offering better prices, the company employs staff, often with degrees, with extensive knowledge of books. The book superstores stock over 150 000 titles, compared with 20 000 in the average bookstore. They stay open until 11.00 p.m., and their coffee bars, armchairs, classical music and wide aisles invite people to linger comfortably. While being hailed as 'value innovations', such success stories are really the application of a simple, if elusive, principle:

> *strategic positioning involves providing unique value. The retailer must first identify a specific consumer segment, then gain a thorough understanding of it—including what kind of goods these people want to buy, how they want to shop for them, and what auguented benefits and services they expect (Wortzel, 1987).*

Table 4.9 Value innovation in US book retailing

Note: based on a scale from 0 (low) to 10 (high).

Source: adapted from Kim and Mauborgne (1999).

Dimension	Barnes & Noble	Independent bookstores	Mall bookstores
Price	1.0	3.0	2.0
Knowledgeable staff	6.2	5.1	1.8
Selection of books	8.0	2.1	0.9
Store ambience	8.5	2.9	1.2
Store hours	7.2	1.7	2.8
Café and lounge area	8.1	n/a	n/a

Letting customer needs determine the dimensions of positioning opens up far more opportunities than are implied by conventional positioning matrices. In Chapter 3, numerous diverse needs were identified, associated with the shopping experience as well as the prices, products, etc. Many of these needs are far from satisfied. The use of 'catch-all' terms, such as service and convenience, can also mask positioning opportunities. In the following chapter, techniques for disaggregating such terms are discussed, often revealing a rich diversity of more specific attributes. The right combination and level of these attributes offers the formula for the next 'value innovation'.

SUMMARY

The retail industry has a tradition of fast and reactive decision-making, which was slow to give way to more formal strategic planning. We still see 'lemming-like' behaviour, with many retailers pursuing the same markets, with similar assortments, using the same promotional tools. It has become apparent that expenditures on price cuts, advertising, design refits, loyalty programmes, etc. are often wasted, unless they form part of a coherent, overall strategy. There has certainly been no shortage of 'strategic prescriptions' in recent decades, formulated by strategy 'gurus' and dispensed vigorously by management consultants. However, ambiguity remains, even as to the meaning of the term 'strategy', with varying interpretations and perspectives.

A logical first step in strategic planning is to conduct a strategic audit of the company's environment, competitive situation and internal capabilities. A PEST analysis focuses upon political/legal, economic, social and technological issues in the macroenvironment, which are potentially relevant to the future plans and progress of the company. Analysis of the competitive forces surrounding the organization draws attention to possible changes in bargaining power on both supply and demand sides, as well as the threats of substitute products/channels and possible new entrants to the market. SWOT analysis helps to draw these strands together, by assessing these opportunities and threats in conjunction with the company's own strengths and weaknesses.

At the core of a strategic plan should be a clear statement of the company's overall direction and what it plans to accomplish. This can be defined and communicated in the form of a misson or vision statement. This may refer to various 'consituencies' with which the retailer is concerned, including customers, employees, shareholders, communities, suppliers and the environment. While mission statements are the responsiblility of senior management, organizations are increasingly involving other levels in the creation of a strategic vision.

For many years, retailers have been urged to select between the available 'generic strategies', in order to achieve sustainable competitive advantage. However, differentiation, cost leadership and focus strategies each have their risks. Furthermore, some retailers have achieved great success through combination strategies, using elements of each of these stategies. It is clear that strategic effectiveness needs to be combined with operational effectiveness; as the 'productivity frontier' in retailing continues to be pushed forwards, efficiency and appropriate strategic positioning are both prerequisites.

The concept of the value chain is useful in identifying the components within organizations, their contributions to the creation of value, their necessary harmonization and their costs. Often the customer is depicted as the recipient of the value generated, however, the target customers' specific needs should be the focus of the value chain's construction. Companies that have developed well–focused, complex technical/human systems, effective cross–functional working and strong inter-organizational relationships tend to find that their value propositions are harder to imitate.

The communiation and implementation of a defined strategy can be facilitated through the use of the 'balanced scorecard'. This takes four perspectives: those of financial stakeholders, customers, business processes and the organization's learning and growth. By identifying critical success factors from each of these perspectives, goals can be set, along with appropriate measures and targets. This helps to co–ordinate the efforts of all parts of the organization, as well as providing early feedback that specific goals, or strategies, may require modification.

Given turbulence in markets and competitive conditions, retailers must constantly examine growth opportunities, if only to avert decline. Strategies include consolidation within the existing product-market position, building share and enjoying greater economies of scale. Most retailers must also explore other 'growth vectors' into related or new areas. These can include related/new market segments, retail formats, delivery channels, geographical regions/countries and different product/service propositions.

While some retailers seek growth through product/service diversification, others prosper through specialization upon a particular category or target market. Category killers, such as IKEA, B & Q Warehouses and Toys 'R' Us, have emerged as a powerful force, but the strategy does have risks, notably 'cherry-picking' by competitors. Many retailers have been persuaded to diversify because of static, declining or overcrowded product/service sectors. These moves are most likely to be successful when they have a coherent link with the retailer's core proposition and/or fulfil different needs of the same/similar customers.

Retailers may also utilize the options of acquisition or merger to pursue their strategic goals at the corporate level. This approach may be used to diversify out of saturated, static or declining markets, to buy market share and increase economies of scale, to share/transfer skills or strengths to create synergistic benefits, or to develop alternative channels of distribution. Many acquisitions have not achieved the intended results, usually because insufficient synergy is achieved to outweigh the additional costs and constraints upon the individual business units. Portfolio analysis may be applied to help identify which business units to develop, maintain or phase out. Alternatives to acquisition include two or more separate companies collaborating in jointly owned companies or joint development programmes. Another approach is to utilize concessionaire agreements, whereby space within stores is allocated to other retailers or manufacturers to operate as shops within shops.

A key element of retailing strategy is the decision upon the market segment(s) within which to compete. These may be selected on the basis of segment size, growth potential, competition, company capabilities, required investment and/or profit potential. Many companies express their target markets in terms of age or class characteristics, but this has led to many pursuing the same targets, often ignoring strong potential in other segments. There are many opportunities to target on the basis of lifestyles, which are more diverse, offering more scope for effective differentiation.

Positioning requires a clear understanding of the needs and motives of the target segments. Some retailers, notably in the fashion sector, use different stores names to achieve multiple positioning objectives. However, mob positioning still prevails, as many retailers deploy the same positioning dimensions. Value innovations tend to occur when retailers identify sets of needs that are not currently well served, and position accordingly.

REVIEW QUESTIONS

1 What is strategy? Relate your answer to the activities of a particular retailer.

2 Taking a retail sector and country of your choice, what are the major issues that would emerge from a PEST analysis of the macroenvironment?

3 Focusing upon one retailer with which you are familiar, conduct a SWOT analysis for that company. Discuss how its strengths and weaknesses will affect its ability to respond to specific opportunities and threats that you identified.

4 Select a retail company within the fashion sector or the home furnishing sector. How would you define the corporate mission for that company? By visiting its website, or other sources, critically compare your version of its mission statement with that published by the company.

5 Give examples of retailers pursuing each of Porter's three 'generic strategies'. What are the risks associated with each of these strategies?

6 When pursuing 'combination strategies', some retailers appear to be 'stuck in the middle'; for others, combination strategies work very well. Why?

7 Taking a retailer that is clearly successful within its sector, how would you chart the value chain for that company. Illustrate how that value chain delivers benefits that are valued by the customers.

8 Starting with a retailer's mission statement (e.g. from question 4), construct a balanced scorecard, showing the success factors critical to achieving success in that mission. What measurements are most suitable to evaluate progress towards each of the defined goals?

9 How would you adapt the product-market strategy concept to help a retailer to identify alternative growth vectors?

10 Why have 'category killers' achieved success in some sectors but not in others? What are the risks associated with the 'category killer' strategy?

11 Give an example of (a) successful and (b) unsuccessful diversification by retail companies. Why did one fail and the other succeed?

12 What factors have motivated acquisitions and mergers by retail companies? What are the major drawbacks of this strategic approach?

13 What methods could a retailer use in applying portfolio analysis to its strategic business units?

14 Outline the different types of strategic alliance that have been used by retailers. What advantages do such alliances offer, compared with acquisition or merger?

15 You have been commissioned to advise a chain of small to medium-sized menswear shops. How should they define and decide upon the target markets in which to compete?

16 Why have so many attempts at positioning failed to produce effective differentiation? Taking a sector of your choice, suggest how a retailer could approach the task of finding new market space.

REFERENCES

Ansoff, H.I. (1988) *New Corporate Strategy: An Analytical Approach to Business Policy for Growth and Expansion*, Wiley, New York.

Arnold, H. (1996) 'Pump up the volume', *SuperMarketing*, **9** February, 18–20.

Arnold, S.J., J. Handelman and D.J. Tigert (1996) 'Organizational legitimacy and retail store patronage', *Journal of Business Research*, **35** (3), 229–239.

Bansal, P. and W.E. Kilbourne (2001) 'The ecologically sustainable retailer', *Journal of Retailing and Consumer Services*, **8**, 139–146.

Bartlett, R.C. and L. Barrett (1992) 'A retailer's perspective on the environmental challenge', *Retailing Issues Letters*, **4** (3), 1–4.

Beharrell, B. (1991) 'Introduction: an environmentally friendly policy for retailing', *British Food Journal*, **93** (3), 3–7.

Berman, B. and J.R. Evans (1998) *Retail Management: A Strategic Approach*, Prentice-Hall, Englewood Cliffs, NJ.

Birtwistle, G. and P. Freathy (1998) 'More than just a name above the shop: a comparison of the branding strategies of two UK fashion retailers', *International Journal of Retail & Distribution Management*, **26** (8), 318–323.

Blackwell, R.D. and W.W. Talarzyk (1983) 'Lifestyle retailing: competitive strategies for the 1980s', *Journal of Retailing*, **59** (4), 7–27.

Burt, S. and S. Davis (1999) 'Follow my leader? Lookalike retailer brands in non-manufacturer-dominated markets in the UK', *International Review of Retail, Distribution and Consumer Research*, **9** (2), 163–185.

Buttle, F. (1994) 'Jaeger Ladies', in *Cases in Retail Management*, P.J. McGoldrick (ed.), Pitman, London, pp. 259–277.

Buzzell, R.D. and B.T. Gale (1987) *The PIMS Principles*, Free Press, New York.

Cappel, S.D., P. Wright, D.C. Wyld and J.H. Miller (1994) 'Evaluating strategic effectiveness in the retail sector: a conceptual approach', *Journal of Business Research*, **31** (November), 209–212.

Chan Kim, W. and R. Mauborgne (1997) 'Value innovation: the strategic logic of high growth', *Harvard Business Review*, **75** (1), 103–112.

Collins, A. (1992) *Competitive Retail Marketing*, McGraw-Hill, Maidenhead.

Competition Commission (2000) *Supermarkets*, HMSO, London.

Corstjens, J. and M. Corstjens (1995) *Store Wars: The Battle for Mindspace and Shelfspace*, Wiley, Chichester.

Cronin, J.J. and S.J. Skinner (1984) 'Marketing outcomes, financial conditions and retail profit performance', *Journal of Retailing*, **60** (4), 9–22.

Cushman, L.M. and C.L. Dyer (1997) 'Post-acquisition performance of apparel retailers: is bigger necessarily better?', *Journal of Fashion Marketing and Management*, **2** (1), 34–40.

Davies, G. (1993) 'Patterns in cross shopping for groceries and their implications for co-operation in retail location', *British Journal of Management*, **4**, 91–101.

Dawson, J. (1995) 'Strategies of retailers in the European societies of the late 1990s', *University of Edinburgh Working Paper Series*, 95/18.

Day, G.S. (1977) 'Diagnosing the product portfolio', *Journal of Marketing*, **41** (2), 29–38.

De Chernatony, L., F. Harris and F. Dall'Olmo Riley (2000) 'Adding value: its nature, roles and sustainability', *European Journal of Marketing*, **34** (1/2), 39–56.

Dibb, S. and L. Simkin (1991) 'Targeting, segments and positioning', *International Journal of Retail & Distribution Management*, **19** (3), 4–10.

Doyle, P. (1989) 'Building successful brands: the strategic options', *Journal of Marketing Management*, **5** (1), 77–95.

Drummond, G. (1995) 'Tesco's takeover of Wm Low', *SuperMarketing*, 17 February, 14–16.

DTI (2000) *Clicks and Mortar: The New Store Fronts*, Department of Trade and Industry, London.

Duke, R. (1991) 'Post-saturation competition in UK grocery retailing', *Journal of Marketing Management*, **7** (1), 63–75.

Gatley, L. and D. Clutterbuck (1998) 'Superdrug crafts a mission statement—with the help of 12 000 employees', *International Journal of Retail & Distribution Management*, **26** (10), 394–395.

Ghosh, A. (1994) *Retail Management*, Dryden Press, Fort Worth, TX.

Goodman, C.S. (1985) 'On output measures of retail performance', *Journal of Retailing*, **61** (3), 77–82.

Green, S. (1987) 'From riches to rags: the John Collier story: an interpretative study of strategic change', in *Business Strategy and Retailing*, G. Johnson (ed.), Wiley, Chichester, pp. 215–233.

Gush, J. (1999) 'Burton Group (C): John Hoerner 1991–7', in *Exploring Corporate Strategy*, by G. Johnson and K. Scholes, Prentice-Hall, Harlow, pp. 882–890.

Guy, C. (1999) 'Exit strategies and sunk costs: the implications for multiple retailers', *International Journal of Retail & Distribution Management*, **27** (6), 237–245.

Harris, L.C. and E. Ogbonna (2001) 'Competitive advantage in the UK food retailing sector: past, present and future', *Journal of Retailing and Consumer Services*, **8**, 157–173.

Hart, C.A. and M.A.P. Davies (1996) 'Consumer perceptions of non-food assortments: an empirical study', *Journal of Marketing Management*, **12**, 297–312.

Heifetz, R.A. and D.L. Laurie (1997) 'The work of leadership', *Harvard Business Review*, **75** (1), 124–134.

Helms, M.M., P.J. Haynes and S.D. Cappel (1992) 'Competitive strategies and business performance within the retailing industry', *International Journal of Retail & Distribution Management*, **20** (5), 3–14.

Hoffman, N.P. (2000) 'An examination of the 'sustainable competitive advantage' concept: past, present and future', *Academy of Marketing Science Review* (on line) http://www.amsreview.org/amsrev/theory/hoffman00-04.html.

Hollander, S.C. (1960) 'The wheel of retailing', *Journal of Marketing*, **24** (3), 37–42.

Hollander, S.C. (1966) 'Notes on the retail accordion', *Journal of Retailing*, **42** (2), 24–40.

Howe, W.S. (1990) 'UK retailer vertical power, market competition and consumer welfare', *International Journal of Retail & Distribution Management*, **18** (2) 16–25.

Hubbard, N. and J. Kelly (1999) 'Mergers changing the face of retailing', *European Retail Digest*, **24**, 5–6.

Huffman, C. and B.E. Khan (1998) 'Variety for sale: mass customization or mass confusion', *Journal of Retailing*, **74** (4), 491–513.

Hughes, A. (1996) 'Forging new cultures of food retailer–manufacturer relations?', in *Retailing, Consumption and Capital: Toward the New Retail Geography*, N. Wrigley and M. Lowe (eds), Longman, Harlow, pp. 90–115.

IGD (2000a) *Grocery Retailing 2000*, Institute of Grocery Distribution, Watford.

IGD (2000b) *Non-Food Retailing 2000*, Institute of Grocery Distribution, Watford.

Johnson, G. (1987) *Business Strategy and Retailing*, Wiley, Chichester.

Johnson, G. and K. Scholes (1999) *Exploring Corporate Strategy*, Prentice-Hall, Harlow.

Journal of Business Strategy (1996) 'Strategy: what the heck is it?', *Journal of Business Strategy*, **16** (3), 64.

Kahn, B.E. (1998) 'Dynamic relationships with customers: high-variety strategies', *Journal of the Academy of Marketing Science*, **26** (1), 45–53.

Kaplan, R.S. and D.P. Norton (1992) 'The balance scorecard— measures that drive performance', *Harvard Business Review*, **70** (1), 71–79.

Kaplan, R.S. and D.P. Norton (1993) 'Putting the balanced scorecard to work', *Harvard Business Review*, **71** (5), 134–147.

Kaplan, R.S. and D.P. Norton (1996) 'Using the balanced scorecard as a strategic management system', *Harvard Business Review*, **74** (1), 75–85.

Kay, J. (1993) 'Economics in business', *Economics and Business Education*, **1** (1), 74–78.

Keep, W.W., S.C. Hollander and R.J. Calantone (1996) 'Retail diversification in the USA', *Journal of Retailing and Consumer Services*, **3** (1), 1–9.

Kim, W.C. and R. Mauborgne (1999) 'Creating new market space', *Harvard Business Review*, **77** (1), 83–93.

Knee, D. and D. Walters (1985) *Strategy in Retailing: Theory and Application*, Philip Allan, Oxford.

Kristenson, L. (1983) 'Strategic planning in retailing', *European Journal of Marketing*, **17** (2), 43–59.

Kumar, V., R.A. Kerin and A. Pereira (1991) 'An empirical assessment of merger and acquisition activity in retailing', *Journal of Retailing*, **67** (3), 321–338.

Lea-Greenwood, G. (1993) 'River Island Clothing Co.: a case study on changing an image', *International Journal of Retail & Distribution Management*, **21** (3), 60–64.

Levitt, T. (1960) 'Marketing myopia', *Harvard Business Review*, **38** (4), 45–56.

Lucas, G.H. and L.G. Gresham (1988) 'How to position for retail success', *Business*, **38** (2), 3–13.

Markides, C. (1999) 'Six principles of breakthrough strategy', *Business Strategy Review*, **10** (2), 11–18.

Markides, C.C. (1997) 'To diversify or not to diversify', *Harvard Business Review*, **75** (6), 93–99.

Martineau, P. (1958) 'The personality of the retail store', *Harvard Business Review*, **36** (1), 47–55.

Maximov, J. and H. Gottschlich (1993) 'Time-cost-quality leadership', *International Journal of Retail & Distribution Management*, **21** (4), 3–13.

McDonald, M.H.B. (1992) 'Strategic marketing planning: a state of the art review', *Marketing Intelligence and Planning*, **10** (4), 4–22.

McDonald, M.H.B. and C.C.S. Tideman (1993) *Retail Marketing Plans*, Butterworth-Heinemann, Oxford.

McDowell Mudambi, S. (1994) 'A topology of strategic choice in retailing', *International Journal of Retail & Distribution Management*, **22** (4), 32–40.

McGee, J. (1987) 'Retailer strategies in the UK', in *Business Strategy and Retailing*, G. Johnson (ed.), Wiley, Chichester, pp. 89–106.

McGoldrick, P.J. (1989) 'Department store concessions: strategic decisions and consumer reactions', in *Retail and Marketing Channels*, L. Pellegrini and S.K. Reddy (eds), Routledge, London, pp. 287–310.

McGoldrick, P.J. and E. Andre (1997) 'Consumer misbehaviour: promiscuity or loyalty in grocery shopping', *Journal of Retailing and Consumer Services*, **4** (2), 73–81.

McKinnon, A.C. and A. Woodburn (1994) 'A consolidation of retail deliveries: its effects on CO_2 emissions', *Transport Policy*, **1** (2), 125–136.

Miller, D. (1992) 'The generic strategy trap', *Journal of Business Strategy*, **13** (1), 37–42.

Mintzberg, H. (1994) *The Rise and Fall of Strategic Planning*, Prentice-Hall, Hemel Hempstead.

Mintzberg, H. and J.A. Waters (1982) 'Tracing strategy in an entrepreneurial firm', *Academy of Management Journal*, **25** (3), 465–499.

Mitchell, R. (1992) 'How The Gap's ads got so-o-o cool', *Business Week*, 9 March, 64.

Moore, L. (1996) 'On the catwalk', *SuperMarketing*, 16 February, 14–16.

Morgan Stanley Dean Witter (1999a) *Four Prerequisites of Success*, MSDW, London.

Morgan Stanley Dean Witter (1999b) *Laurus: Spice or Splice?* MSDW, London.

Morgan Stanley Dean Witter (2000) *Clothing on the Internet: Retail is Detail + E-tail*, MSDW, London.

Morgan Stanley Dean Witter (2001) *J. Sainsbury: Still Everything to Prove*, MSDW, London.

Nielsen (2000) *Retail Pocket Book*, NTC, Henley-on-Thames.

O'Shaughnessy, J. (1988) *Competitive Marketing: A Strategic Approach*, Unwin Hyman, Boston, MA.

Omura, G.S. (1986) 'Developing retail strategy', *International Journal of Retailing*, **1** (3), 17–32.

Pellegrini, L. (1995) 'Alternative growth strategies: the options for the future', *European Retail Digest*, **8** (Autumn), 15–21.

Piacentini, M., L. MacFadyen and E. Eadie (2000) 'Corporate social responsibility in food retailing', *International Journal of Retail & Distribution Management*, **28** (11), 459–469.

Piercy, N. (1983) 'Analysing corporate mission: improving retail strategy', *Retail & Distribution Management*, **11** (2), 31–35.

Pollack, E. (1994) 'Raising the bar: keys to high-performance retailing', *Chain Store Age Executive*, **70** (1), 2MH–5MH.

Porter, M. (1996) 'What is strategy?', *Harvard Business Review*, **74** (6), 61–78.

Porter, M.E. (1980) *Competitive Strategy: Techniques for Analysing Industries and Competitors*, Free Press, New York.

Porter, M.E. (1985) *Competitive Advantage: Creating and Sustaining Superior Performance*, Free Press, New York.

Porter, M.E. (1987) 'From competitive advantage to corporate strategy', *Harvard Business Review*, **87** (3), 43–59.

Poynor, M. (1986) 'There's no business like shop business', *Retail & Distribution Management*, **14** (4) 6–9.

Prahalahad, C.K. and G. Hamel (1990) 'The core competence of the corporation', *Harvard Business Review*, **68** (3), 79–91.

Quarmby, D. (1995) 'Growth strategies—a personal view', *European Retail Digest*, **8** (Autumn), 33–38.

Retail Review (1996a) 'Sainsbury drops clothing as Asda plays up childrenswear', *Retail Review*, **222** (May), 6.

Retail Review (1996b) 'What is a "category killer"?', *Retail Review*, **222** (May), 18–19.

Retail Review (1999) 'Somerfield snags on Kwik Save conversations', *Retail Review*, **254** (July), 6–8.

Retail Review (2000a) 'Wal-Mart's global push', *Retail Review*, **266** (October), 5–6.

Retail Review (2000b) 'Tesco goes into mortgage advice via Internet tie-up', *Retail Review*, **262** (May), 14.

Retail Review (2000c) 'George designer leaves all-action Asda', *Retail Review*, **267** (December), 11.

Retail Review (2000d) 'Boots enlarges on health services function', *Retail Review*, **266** (October), 15.

Retail Review (2000e) 'Kingfisher drops demerger bombshell', *Retail Review*, **265** (September), 1–3.

Retail Review (2000f) 'Tesco/Esso forecourt alliance near to contractual commitment', *Retail Review*, **259** (February), 12.

Retail Review (2001) 'Arcadia on the up', *Retail Review*, **270** (April), 13.

Ries, A. and J. Trout (1982) *The Battle for your Mind*, Warner Books, New York.

Robinson, T.M. and C.M. Clarke-Hill (1990) 'Directional growth by European retailers', *International Journal of Retail & Distribution Management*, **18** (5), 3–14.

Roedder J. D., B. Loken and C. Joiner (1998) 'The negative impact of extensions: can flagship products be diluted?', *Journal of Marketing*, **62** (January), 19–32.

Rogers, D. (1996) 'American power retailing: what is it?', *European Retail Digest*, **10** (Spring), 13–16.

Rosenbloom, B. (1980) 'Strategic planning in retailing: prospects and problems', *Journal of Retailing*, **56** (1), 107–118.

Rosenbloom, B. and M. Dupuis (1994) 'Low price, low cost, high service: a new paradigm for global retailing?', *International Review of Retail*, Distribution and Consumer Research, **4** (2), 149–158.

Savitt, R. (1987) 'American retailing strategies and the changing competitive environment', in *Business Strategy and Retailing*, G. Johnson (ed.), Wiley, Chichester, pp. 117–132.

Sheth, J.N. and R.S. Sisodia (1999) 'Revisiting marketing's lawlike generalizations', *Journal of the Academy of Marketing Science*, **27** (1), 71–87.

Shoham, A. and A. Fiegenbaum (1999) 'Extending the competitive marketing strategy paradigm: the role of strategic reference points theory', *Journal of the Academy of Marketing Science*, **27** (4), 442–454.

Simms, C. (1992) 'Green issues and strategic management in the grocery retail sector', *International Journal of Retail and Distribution Management*, **20** (1), 32–42.

Smith, J. (1995) *Category Killers in Europe*, FT/Pearson, London.

Smith, P. (1998) 'Somerfield and Kwik Save: the inside story', *European Retail Digest*, **20**, 46–49.

Stalk, G., P. Evans and L.E. Shulman (1992) 'Competing on capabilities: the new rules of corporate strategy', *Harvard Business Review*, **70** (2), 57–69.

Tantiwong, D. and P.C. Wilton (1985) 'Understanding foodstore preferences among the elderly using hybrid conjoint measurement models', *Journal of Retailing*, **61** (4), 35–64.

Thomas, A.B. (1991) 'Leadership and change in British retailing 1955–84', *Service Industries Journal*, **11** (3), 381–392.

Thomas, R., M. Gable and R. Dickinson (1999) 'An application of the balanced scorecard in retailing', *International Review of Retail, Distribution and Consumer Research*, **9** (1), 41–67.

Tordjman, A. (1996) 'Toys "R" Us', *European Retail Digest*, **10** (Spring), 17–23.

Vaughn, C. (1999) 'Retail consolidation in European food retailing', *European Retail Digest*, **24**, 11–13.

Walters, D. and J. Hanrahan (2000) *Retail Strategy: Planning and Control*, Macmillan, Basingstoke.

Warnaby, G. and H. Woodruffe (1995) 'Cost effective differentiation: an application of strategic concepts to retailing', *International Review of Retail, Distribution and Consumer Research*, **5** (3), 253–269.

Webb, S. (1999) 'Grocery retailing in the UK', *European Retail Digest*, **21**, 36–38.

Whittington, R. (1993) *What is Strategy—and Does it Matter?*, Routledge, London.

Woodruff, R.B. (1997) 'Customer value: the next source for competitive advantage', *Journal of the Academy of Marketing Science*, **25** (2), 139–153.

Wortzel, L.H. (1987) 'Retailing strategies for today's mature marketplace', *Journal of Business Strategy*, **7** (4), 45–56.

CHAPTER

Five

Monitoring
Marketing
Performance

INTRODUCTION   In Part One, so far, we have looked at ways of assessing the marketing environment, identifying consumers' needs and formulating retail strategy. Attention now focuses on ways of evaluating the performance of the company, either in its entirety or in terms of its individual elements. This chapter looks at retail performance from the first of two crucial perspectives. Here, the assessment of image is examined as a means of evaluating the marketing performance from an all-important perspective, that of actual and potential customers. In the next chapter, means of analysing the financial performance of the company are considered, using more traditional tools of cost and profit analysis.

This combination of performance indicators reflects the increased recognition of linkages between marketing and financial outcomes (e.g. Cronin and Skinner, 1984; Egan and Guilding, 1994).

> *Target market satisfaction is, after all, the measure of the output of a service industry. Value added, in its conventional sense of sales price less costs of inputs acquired from outsiders, may be a flawed proxy for consumer satisfaction, to the extent that sales are (in part) caused by exogenous factors (Goodman, 1985).*

The image accumulated is therefore a major component of a retailer's 'brand equity' (Aaker, 1991; 1994). This is a more sophisticated development upon the accounting practice of allocating a value for 'goodwill' when a shop is sold. From 1998, The Accounting Standard Board's directive, Financial Standard 10 (FRSO 10), required UK companies to capitalize newly acquired goodwill and intangibles (Brand Finance, 1999). The treatments of existing brand values are extremely varied and methodologies for quantifying those values are still evolving (Kerin and Sethuraman, 1998; Wood, 1995). However, the financial importance of images and brands is now widely accepted: 'The assets that really count are the ones accountants can't count' (Stewart, 1995). It is important to appreciate that some of the traditional financial criteria provide only a short-term perspective: they also do little to disaggregate or diagnose elements of marketing performance.

The first section addresses the importance of image monitoring to the evaluation and formation of retail marketing strategies. Concepts of image and brand equity are discussed, then a summary is provided of the many components identified within studies of image. Alternative approaches to image analysis are evaluated, recognizing the value of the many qualitative and quantitative techniques that can now be applied to the task. The final section recognizes that performance evaluation usually involves comparisons: examples are given of image comparisons between companies, stores, customers, product groups and shopping centres.

5.1 Store Image and Brand Equity

The importance to retailers of effectively monitoring their images has been firmly established and documented over the last five decades. In one of the earliest and most inspirational of the many papers on retail images, Martineau (1958) quoted several case studies, illustrating how the success or failure of stores could often be attributed to undertested or underemphasized elements of their image. While image monitoring has been assimilated into mainstream, practical retail marketing, researchers recently have given much attention to the concepts of branding and brand equity. With the exception of retailers' own-brand products, the subject of Chapter 9, most of this work has been focused upon manufacturer branding. However, the emerging concepts can further contribute to our understanding of the nature and strategic importance of image.

5.1.1 Importance of Image Evaluation

Among Martineau's classic case studies were two grocery chains, with similar prices, services and product choice, yet one was significantly outperforming its rival. Image research revealed that management of the struggling chain had not identified the key areas of differentiation. The successful chain was distinctive in being perceived as 'clean and white', 'the store where you can see your friends' and 'the store with helpful personnel'.

Links between retail patronage and image attributes have been confirmed by many researchers subsequently (e.g. Baker et al., 1994; Darden and Babin, 1994). Further evidence has also emerged that store image is positively related to store loyalty (e.g. Mazursky and Jacoby, 1986; Osman, 1993). However, it is likely that store satisfaction strengthens the causal linkage between image and store loyalty (Bloemer and de Ruyter, 1998). The fundamental importance of image is, however, widely accepted: 'retail management is, explicitly or implicitly, related to image management' (Samli et al., 1998).

Oxenfeldt (1974) pointed to the problems and importance of image monitoring, in terms of the strong possibility that a store might have an image other than that which it 'deserves', in terms of relatively objective measures. In particular, he identified five conditions under which images may be better or worse than they deserve:

1 Past circumstances which still exert strong effect on present images; there seems to be a very long lag of impressions behind store realities.
2 Effects of premeditated image-building by rivals, i.e. their failures will help, their successes will hurt.
3 Errors or accidents by the retailer itself or by rivals.
4 The role of certain influential persons who praise or attack the store.
5 Present benefits that are not seen or recognized by potential customers.

It may be expected that image monitoring is more important to manufacturers than to retailers, as retailers are in constant daily contact with their customers. Given, however, that some senior retail decision-makers do not have a great deal of direct contact with consumers, this is not always the case. From a comparative study to retailers' and customers' perceptions of the most important criteria in purchasing electrical appliances, McClure and Ryans (1968) concluded that:

> *Their familiarity and frequency of contact with customers make them the envy of many manufacturers operating from remote corporate offices. Yet this familiarity and frequency of contact do not seem to give retailers a highly accurate understanding of consumers.*

From her wide range of retail image studies, May (1974) confirmed that the way in which stores are perceived by managers is often in sharp disagreement with the perceptions of customers. She also noted that there were substantial dissimilarities between the images held by different members of management. A systematic comparison of management and customer images was undertaken by Pathak et al. (1974), who concluded that store managers tend to overate their stores, compared with customers' ratings, especially in the cases of low-status stores.

More recent evidence shows that retailers' perceptions can also be lower than those of customers, on some attributes. In one store, studied by Birtwistle et al. (1999), the staff's evaluation of merchandise fashion and style was far lower than that of customers. Samli et al. (1998) also found several instances of customer perceptions that were better than management perceptions, reflecting their greater knowledge of what could be achieved, especially in terms of service and product choice. Even this type of incongruity can be problematic, especially if the staff's lower opinions are communicated to customers. Both studies also revealed a number of areas in which staff/management overrated elements of image.

In spite of the plethora of in-house or agency research available to retailers, evidence continues to emerge of major gaps between retailer and customer perceptions. Osman (1993) suggested that retailers should measure congruity between their perceptions and those of customers, to provide rapid feedback on trading strategy. Samli et al. (1998) proposed a diagnostic tool, based both upon the levels of image ratings, and upon the congruity between retailer–customer ratings. Figure 5.1 summarizes

Example attributes	Below average ratings	Above average ratings
Suggested actions		
Customers' images better	**In-stock position** **Layout** **Checkout speed** *Vulnerable to competition* *Act quickly*	**Range of goods** **Car parking** *Use of attributes to promote store*
No significant difference	**Helpful, friendly, knowledgeable staff** **Displays** **Décor** *Problem areas* *Correct deficits*	**Clean** **Comfortable** **Good prices** **Convenient location** **Quality of goods** *Maintain position* *Opportunities to promote*
Management images better	**Community involvement** *Check relevance of causes* *supported for target customers* *Communicate what is being done*	**No-hassle returns** **Warranties** *Investigate with field research* *Mystery shoppers*

Figure 5.1 Management–customer image congruence
Source: derived from Samli et al. (1998).

some of the areas in which congruence or incongruity were identified, and the recommended managerial actions.

5.1.2 Concepts of Image and Brand Equity

Definitions of store image have proliferated as the study of the subject has advanced. One of the earliest definitions of image, specifically in relation to retail stores, was that of Martineau (1958): 'The way in which the store is defined in the shopper's mind, partly by its functional qualities and partly by an aura of psychological attributes.' This definition emphasizes the need to consider not only the more visible or measurable factors but also the less tangible factors, such as the 'personality' of the store. Martineau continued to explain how architecture, displays, symbols, colours and staff attitudes are all 'key personality variables'. This definition can however be criticized for tending to ascribe a 'mystique' to the concept that is not entirely warranted. As Doyle and Fenwick (1974) pointed out:

> *Many of the examples of successful image creation cited by Martineau and other studies depend upon physical, but non-price aspects of the store. Thus, rather than classifying image as part of the 'non-logical basis of shopping behaviour,' as Martineau suggests, it is reasonable to view the customer as rationally evaluating the store on a multi-attribute utility function.*

Many of the definitions that have emerged could be criticized for implying a stability in store image that is not likely to exist. Images can be changed as a result of relatively minor observations or occurrences, which happen to be noticeable and salient to particular shoppers. This limitation was largely overcome by Berry (1969) who, following an in-depth study of department store image, defined image in behavioural terms:

An image is the result of differential reinforcement in the context of a given stimulus or set of stimuli. Specifically, department store image is the result at any one point in time of differential reinforcement, in the context of a department store, previous to that time. Stated differently, department store image is the total conceptualised or expected reinforcement an individual associates with a particular store.

Berry further explained that the effect of any specific stimulus was largely determined by a number of individual 'state variables' or conditions of deprivation/satiation, and 'societal and sub-cultural norms'. In other words, many personal characteristics and expectations of the society within which the individual lives influence perceptions, reactions and, therefore, the nature of the images formed.

The limited amount of information upon which images can be formed has been observed by other researchers. Lindquist (1974) found that this characteristic of image has been recognized in other contexts for many years. Drawing upon the early work of Boulding (1956), Lindquist noted that:

The behaviour of a human is not directed by mere knowledge and information but is a product of the images that a man perceives. [Boulding] argues that we function or react not in response to what is true but to what we believe to be true. He asserts further that we use subjective values and knowledge to mediate between ourselves and the world around us.

The human mind can handle only a certain number of complex situations and stimuli; therefore, it attempts to oversimplify circumstances and thus abstracts only a few meanings that appear salient.

This aspect of image is clearly of fundamental significance in retail marketing and will be given further consideration in future chapters, notably in relation to price images in Chapter 10. It has also been noted that, while images are usually formed on the basis of limited information, they none the less assume a greater proportion and significance than the individual contributory components. This characteristic, and the subjective nature of image, was stressed by Oxenfeldt (1974):

What exactly do we mean by the image of a store? I submit that it is more than a factual description of its many characteristics. In many cases, it is less like a photograph than a highly interpretative portrait. In other words, an image is more than a sum of its parts.

The images held by consumers are thus formed, somewhat selectively, from a combination of factual and emotional material. Sometimes the term 'image' is used in a very limited sense to denote just the less tangible aspects of a store. This does however imply an artificial distinction between the tangible and the intangible components of image which is potentially dangerous for two main reasons:

1 Although consumers could, in theory, obtain precise and objective measures of such tangible attributes as prices and location, in reality their images are likely to be formed from more subjective impressions based upon various cues (Mazursky and Jacoby, 1986), which signal something about the level of prices or the convenience of the location.
2 Some elements previously regarded as intangible, such as store atmosphere, are increasingly being disaggregated and studied as a collection of fairly tangible attributes, such as music, lighting, space, colours and aromas, etc. (see Chapter 12).

The convergence between concepts of image and concepts of branding has become more apparent as brands cease to be regarded primarily as inputs by marketers. Indeed, it is more constructive to regard them as outputs, in terms of the images consumers' hold of the product or company (de Chernatony, 1993).

> *Brands are complex entities that are conceived in planning documents but ultimately they reside in consumers' minds.*

> *But, because of the perceptual process, consumers' interpretations of brands may differ from that intended by marketers.*

Part of the reluctance to refer to retailers' brand images stems from the ambiguity of terminologies. Retailer brands are usually regarded as the 'own brand' products stocked by many retailers (see Chapter 9).

However, names such as Tesco, Wal-Mart and Harrods may equally be regarded as brands in themselves, just as McDonald's and Hertz are powerful brands in their sectors (Davies, 1992). The developing concepts of brand equity can therefore help to move forward our understanding of the instrumental role of images for retailers.

In common with the development of the image concept, various definitions have added different shades of meaning to the brand equity concept.

> *Brand equity is a set of brand assets and liabilities linked to a brand, its name and symbol, that add to or subtract from the value provided by a product or service to a firm and/or to that firm's customers (Aaker, 1991).*

> *Brand equity represents the value (to a consumer) of a product, above that which would result for an otherwise identical product without the brand's name (Leuthesser et al., 1995).*

Feldwick (1996) identified three, relatively distinct uses of the expression 'brand equity':

1 *Brand value*: the total value of a brand as a separable asset.
2 *Brand strength*: a measure of the strength of consumer's attachment to a brand.
3 *Brand description*: the associations and beliefs the consumer has about the brand.

Figure 5.2 The value of a retailer's brand

Source: adapted from Aaker (1991; 1994).

Various attempts have been made to quantify brand value, including Young and Rubican's Brand Asset Valuator project (Agres and Dubitsky, 1996). This is based around four main pillars of brand strength, namely:

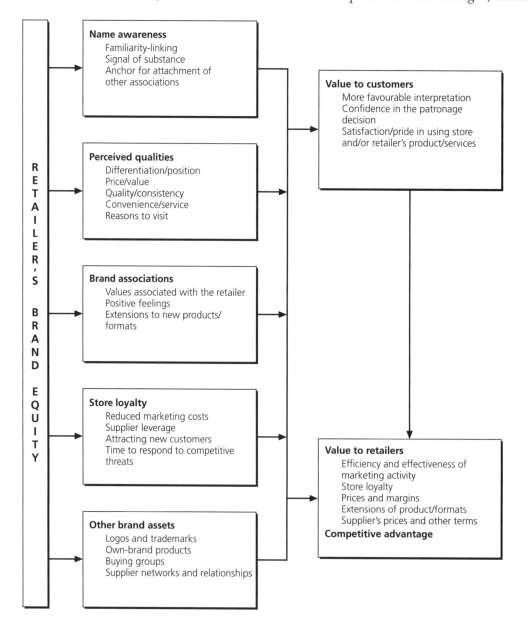

1 *Differentiation*, what distinguishes the brand from others?
2 *Relevance*, is the brand appropriate to target consumers?
3 *Esteem*, how highly is the brand regarded by consumers?
4 *Knowledge*, awareness, not only of the brand, but what it stands for.

Although applied primarily to branded products, these concepts are equally applicable to the evaluation of a retailer's brand (image) value. Not all writers are entirely convinced of the power of brand equity. From a study across five product categories, Bello and Holbrook (1995) found only one in which brand equity appeared to result in price premiums. However, this study addressed only one of the potential benefits or outcomes of brand equity.

The most substantial accounts of these benefits were presented by Aaker (1991; 1994). Figure 5.2 is adapted from these sources to emphasize further the relevance to retail image evaluation. It illustrates how the brand equity accumulated by retailers can generate value in a number of ways, through improved loyalty, awareness, image, associations and other brand assets. Collectively, these benefits add value, both for the customer and for the retailer.

A store with strong brand equity conveys clear values to customers, which may relate to prices, quality, convenience, ethical stance, etc. Confidence in the patronage decision is increased, both at store and product level, and the experience may also be enhanced. The retailer, for its part, is likely to enjoy greater loyalty, marketing programmes will be more effective and margins may also be better. It could also enjoy more bargaining power with suppliers, and find it easier to extend into new formats or product categories. Overall, strong brand equity can contribute towards the key components in achieving competitive advantage in retailing.

5.2 Image Elements and Measurement

Having established the importance of image in the monitoring of marketing performance, it is necessary now to operationalize the relevant concepts. The logical next step is to try to identify the component parts of images, accepting that these are not confined to evaluations of tangible attributes. Images also comprise feelings, pictures and associations. This must also be recognized in the choice of methods used to measure images, ranging from highly structured scales to in-depth elicitation techniques.

5.2.1 Components of Store Image

Many academic researchers and consultants have attempted to identify and classify the components of store image. Some writers have ascribed more specific meanings to the terms 'attribute', 'components' and 'dimension'. For example, 'attributes (the narrowest, most specific constructs), components (aggregation of similar attributes), and dimensions (the most general constructs)' (Hansen and Deutscher 1977). Unfortunately, these definitions are neither precise nor consistently utilized across the various image studies.

Table 5.1 Elements of store image

Sources: derived from many sources, including Aaker (1997); Darden and Babin (1994); de Chernatony and Dall'Olmo Riley (1998); Keaveney and Hunt (1992); Kim (2000); Kunkel and Berry (1968); Lindquist (1974).

Price of merchandise	Services provided
Low prices	Choice of payment methods
Discounts and bargains	Extended credit
Good value prices	Restaurant/café
Fair or competitive prices	Toilets
High or prestige prices	Other services
Quality of merchandise	**Home services**
Good/poor quality products	Catalogue available
Good/poor departments/categories	Telephone orders
Branded/designer goods	Internet orders
Well designed products	Home deliveries
Fashionable products	Delivery reliability
Range of merchandise	**Promotions**
Breadth of choice	Seasonal sales
Depth of choice	Competitions
Carries items I like	Loyalty programme
Choice of brands	Special events
Good for gifts	Fashion shows
Sales personnel	**Advertising**
People who care	Impact of advertising
Number/availability of staff	Style and quality
Knowledgeability of staff	Media vehicles used
Polite and courteous	Personalities involved
Efficient (checkout) service	Truth of advertising
Locational convenience	**Store atmosphere**
Location from home	Interior/exterior decor
Location from work	Symbols and colours
Accessibility	Active/sleepy
Public transport options	Pleasant/unpleasant
Desirable locations	Basic/stylish
Other convenience factors	**Store layout**
Availability of parking	Ease of circulation
Safety of area	Level of congestion
Hours of opening	Lifts and escalators
Proximity of other stores	Ease of finding goods
General ease of use	Quality of displays
Clientele	**Reputation on adjustments**
Mostly older/younger	Warranties/guarantees
Trend setters/followers	Returns policies
Higher/lower incomes	Ease of returns
More/less intelligent	Exchange policies
Mostly singles/couples/families	Reputation for fairness
Personality of store	**Institutional image**
Sincere	Conservative/modern
Exciting	Trustworthy
Competent	Reliable
Sophisticated	Ethical
Rugged	Campaigning
Associations	**Visual imagery**
People	Pictures
Animals	Icons
Political parties	Scenes
Countries	Episodes
Cultures	Fantasies

Where image analysis is conducted for diagnostic purposes, it is important to drill down from the level of generalized components. So often, the 'devil is in the detail', and this detail may easily remain undetected, if comparisons are based upon broad, descriptive terms. Table 5.1 lists 18 general areas and 90 more specific elements that have been identified in previous studies of image and brand identity.

This is by no means an exhaustive list but it is sufficient to illustrate that a measure of 'convenience', for example, could relate to at least ten different, more specific attributes. Likewise, the expression 'good service' can have numerous specific interpretations, an issue that is further explored in Chapter 13, in connection with the SERVQUAL model (Parasuraman et al., 1988; 1991)

The relative importance of the various image components can be partially derived from the studies of patronage motives, discussed in Chapter 3. It should be re-emphasized, however, that the importance of components varies considerably between markets, sectors, competitive situations and customer segments. Hirschman et al. (1978) asked respondents in seven locations to rate the importance of 10 store image dimensions. Although there was some stability in the rank orders of importance, there were significant differences:

> *The belief that the major dimensions composing these images are consistent from one market to another is not supported by this research. Thus, to assure himself that he is positioning a store on relevant dimensions, a retailer should determine what are the major dimensions within each market the store is operating.*

This finding is completely in accord with those of Arnold et al. (1983) who noted very considerable differences between geographically separated markets. There are sound reasons why the relative importance of attributes should vary between markets, whether the comparison is on an international, regional or even at the locality scale. First, in so far as different localities are likely to be dominated by different shopper segments, however these be defined, they will inevitably have some different attitudes, needs and priorities. Second, competition varies within each market. Even if consumers perceived few differences between the stores on the attributes that are usually the most salient, they would probably discriminate between the stores on attributes that would usually be given only low rankings.

Early researchers of store image (e.g. Kunkel and Berry 1968; Lindquist, 1974; May 1971) tended to classify image attributes in a way that relates to elements of the retail marketing mix. This provided a valuable elaboration upon such broad expressions as 'prices' or 'quality', but it tended to overlook some of the more emotional components of a store's identity. Further insights can be drawn from studies of branding, which have tended to give more attention to these elements. Urde (1999) expresses a strong view on this issue:

Intellectually explaining and emotionally communicating are in principle two ways of communicating a message. When we interpret a brand, we use both our 'brain' (i.e., reference function) and our 'heart' (i.e., emotional function). A brand is experienced in its entirety. Intellectually explaining a brand thus becomes just as fruitless as attempting to explain a work of art.

In the retail context, Keaveney and Hunt (1992) observe an inconsistency between the concepts of store image, which tend to stress the gestalt view, and image measures, which tend to adopt the piecemeal approach:

Attribute-based measurement cannot account for the symbolic nature of images or the tendency for individuals to assign human-like personalities to inanimate objects, like stores.

No doubt it was time to challenge the implicit view that consumers classify stores according to attributes of marketing strategy. Clearly, feelings, emotions, and values which consumers associate with stores are as much a part of store imagery. However, in a world which can digitize even the most complex pictures and images, researchers and practitioners should not abandon their tools of image research; they may, however, require considerable elaboration and sharpening!

Various attempts have been made to expand upon measures of store personality (e.g. Darden and Babin, 1994) and brand personality (e.g. Aaker, 1997). Kim (2000) adopted Aaker's (1997) measures to compare brand (and store) personalities, including The Limited and Victoria's Secret. The measures used could be equally applicable to human personality traits:

- *Sincerity*: down-to-earth, honest, wholesome, cheerful.
- *Excitement*: daring, spirited, imaginative, up to date.
- *Competence*: reliable, intelligent, successful.
- *Sophistication*: upper class, charming.
- *Ruggedness*: outdoorsy, tough.

It is widely accepted that the purchasing of some products or brands involves elements of self-expression and identification. Furthermore, consumers tend to prefer brands that are congruent with their self-concept or ideal self (Malhotra, 1988; Sirgy, 1982). The relevance of self-image/store-image congruence has not been ignored in the context of store choice (e.g. Bellenger et al., 1976; Manrai and Manrai, 1995). However, there is still a tendency for the self-image measures to mirror store attributes rather than people attributes.

Turning again to the research on branding, Fig. 5.3 illustrates characteristics of the Volvo brand proposition. Various tangible attributes can be seen to support the car's core proposition of being a safe, reliable family car. However, it is also important to recognize the inner directed values associated with the brand, such as feelings of being

Figure 5.3 A brand proposition

Source: Sherrington (1995, p. 514).

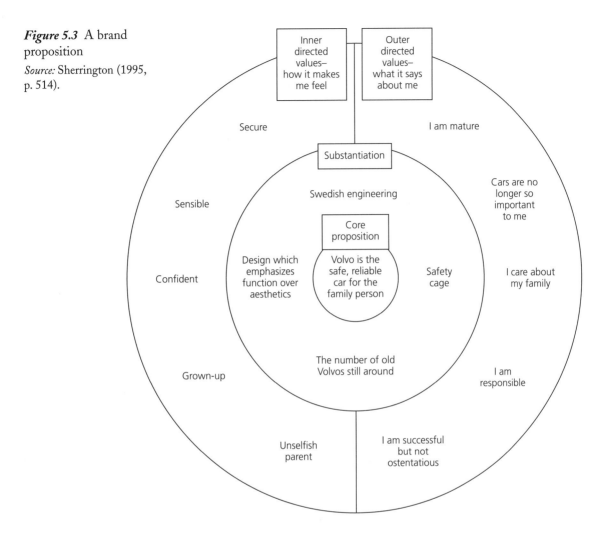

sensible, grown-up and an unselfish parent. The brand also says various things about the owner, i.e., the outer directed values, just as patronizing a particular store can be a form of expression to others. Although it was tempting to adapt Fig. 5.3 to a named retailer, that challenge forms one of the review questions at the end of this chapter.

5.2.2 Measurement of Images

Given that image research is concerned with the measurement of attitudes and opinions, rather than more easily quantifiable factors, it is appropriate to summarize the principal measurement techniques and some of the issues that have arisen. Even the most statistically significant set of results cannot be more reliable or valid than the initial measurement system.

The choice of measurement technique, sample design and study focus must attempt to minimize the factors that can confound and distort image measures. Peterson and Kerin (1983) represented these potentially confounding influences in the form of an equation:

$$R = f(SO, SC, MI, M, EN, E)$$

Where:

R   =   image response
SO   =   stimulus object (retail store) characteristics
SC   =   subject (consumer) characteristics
MI   =   measurement instrument characteristics
M   =   mode of data collection
EN   =   data collection environment
E   =   extraneous or error (i.e., all other) factors.

Scaling Techniques

The semantic differential is probably still the most widely used scaling system in retail image research. The device was evolved by Osgood et al. (1957) and generally consists of a number of seven- or five-point scales that are bipolar, i.e., with the extremes defined by contrasting adjectives, such as 'clean-dirty'. Figure 5.4 shows some of the scale formats that may be applied in store image research. Using the traditional semantic differential, each retailer (or store or department) in turn would be rated on all attributes.

A modification of this approach is to rate each retailer in turn on a single attribute, and then go on to rate each one on the next attribute. The graphic positioning scale uses a slightly different format; respondents place a symbol, typically a letter, to represent their perceptions of each retailer's position in a scale between bipolar adjectives. Compared with traditional scales, this has the particular advantage of saving space on the questionnaire. The main drawbacks, however, are the difficulties of coding the data for computer analysis and the more complex instructions for respondents.

A modified technique to overcome these drawbacks is the numerical comparative scale, also illustrated in Fig. 5.4. This is very economical on questionnaire space as the scale does not have to be repeated for each store. Rating on an attribute-by-attribute basis can also lead to better discrimination between the stores (Teas, 1994). The ratings given to any one store are however likely to be influenced by the choice of other stores within the comparison. Wong and Teas (2001) present extensive evidence on the effects of using different scaling formats. Clearly, evidence derived by using different image scale formats cannot readily be compared.

Other approaches include unipolar attitude scales, such as used by James et al. (1976), wherein single attributes are rated on a scale, such as 'very good-very bad'. An alternative form of unipolar scale is the 'staple scale', wherein a single adjective is rated on a non-verbal scale, which may run from +5 to −5. This approach was tested by Hawkins et al. (1976) in the measurement of store images and was found to have high levels of test-retest reliability. It also overcomes the problem that items such as 'high-priced' and 'low-priced', while seemingly direct opposites, may in fact reflect different concepts in consumers' minds.

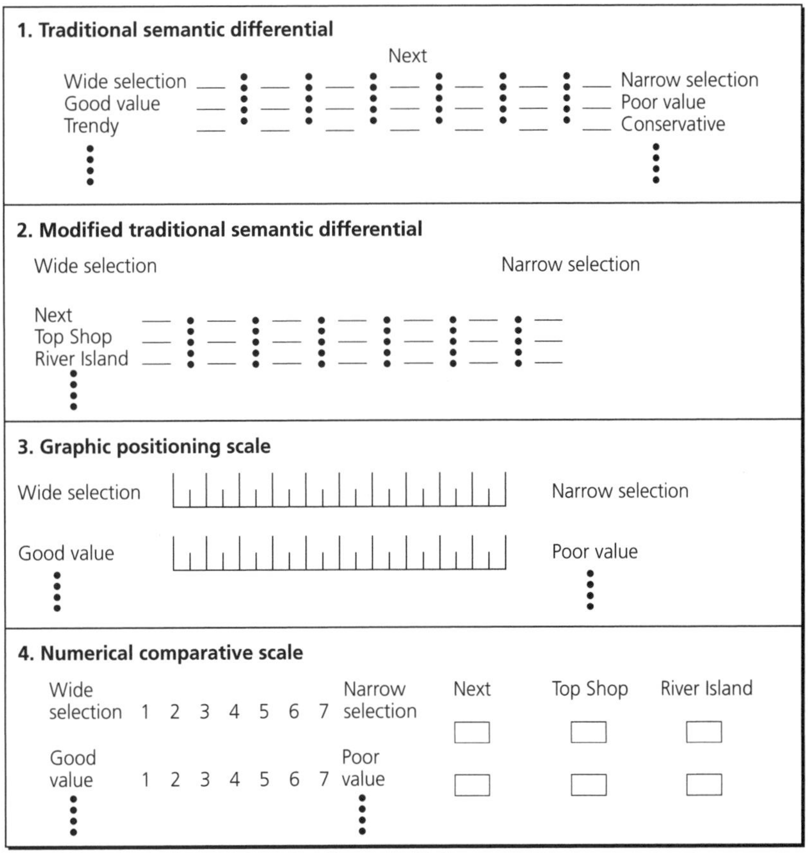

Figure 5.4 Examples of scale formats in image research

Source: adapted from Golden, Albaum and Zimmer (1987).

1. Traditional semantic differential

Next

Wide selection — Narrow selection
Good value — Poor value
Trendy — Conservative

2. Modified traditional semantic differential

Wide selection   Narrow selection

Next
Top Shop
River Island

3. Graphic positioning scale

Wide selection   Narrow selection

Good value   Poor value

4. Numerical comparative scale

| Wide selection | 1 2 3 4 5 6 7 | Narrow selection | Next | Top Shop | River Island |
| Good value | 1 2 3 4 5 6 7 | Poor value | | | |

Another structured and, essentially, unipolar technique is the 'agree-disagree' scale, originally evolved by Likert (1932). This is usually administered as a single, five- or seven-point scale, measuring responses from strongly disagree to strongly agree. Alternatively, it can be split into two scales, one to measure direction, the next to measure the strength of disagreement/agreement (Albaum, 1997). Likert-type scales measure levels of agreement with a given set of sentences, especially useful when the attitude or belief cannot be reduced to one or two adjectives.

Semantic differentials and other rating scales have considerable advantages in allowing comparisons between different groups of respondents in relation to common and defined attributes. Osgood et al. (1957) presented extensive evidence as to the validity, reliability and sensitivity of semantic differentials. They do, however, have certain conceptual and analytical problems. For example, Oppenheim (1976) questioned: 'are we justified in basing our calculations on the assumption of equality of intervals, both within each scale and between different scales?' The problem of this linear assumption, which is implicit within most rating scales, was discussed further in Chapter 3. This particular problem has been ignored by many researchers or, at least, the linear form has been accepted as a reasonable approximation.

Open-Ended Techniques

A fundamental problem of attitude scales is that they involve forced-choice measures that may not isolate critical image components (e.g. Blawatt, 1995; Keaveney and Hunt, 1992; Kunkel and Berry, 1968; McDougall and Fry, 1974). Criticizing the use of rigid scales, Kunkel and Berry (1968) observed that: 'people are encouraged to respond to characteristics that do not necessarily comprise the image they have of the store being studied'.

Cardozo (1974) also noted the problem that factors relevant in the purchase of one type of product may be largely irrelevant to another: 'dimensions may not by any means be the same as those which the consumer considers meaningful in the purchase of a particular product'. In order to overcome some of these problems, he adopted a psycho-linguistic approach. This was essentially open-ended but encouraged respondents to build their own image structures by noting the stores mentioned and the adjectives (dimensions) used to describe them. Using name-tags and a peg-board, respondents were then asked to position the stores on the board according to their level of similarity or difference. This procedure evoked further discussion of why the stores were thus placed. The technique therefore developed some structure and allowed limited quantification of 'mentions', without imposing a structure upon the respondents.

Among the problems in classifying open-ended responses to an image survey are the possible subjectivity of the analyst and the possible inconsistencies in the approaches used when more than one analyst is involved. Having obtained open-ended image responses from a sample of nearly 900 mail panel members, Zimmer and Golden (1988) used content analysis largely to overcome these problems. Content analysis is a research technique for the objective, systematic and quantitative description of the manifest content of communication. It has been used in a number of contexts, including an intriguing analysis of shopping and brand name references in popular works of fiction (Brown, 1995).

Using a clearly formulated set of rules and procedures, Zimmer and Golden (1988) found a reasonable level of consistency between the categories formed by three different analysts. It is noticeable from this study that many of the responses related to overall, global impressions of stores, although such impressions may well be rooted in perceptions of specific attributes. It led the researchers to conclude:

> *when the researcher elicits store image in terms of specific attributes, some of the richness of the consumer's own imagery is lost, as consumers do not limit thinking to specific store attributes, nor do they necessarily think of store attributes at all.*

Keaveny and Hunt (1992) also reflect on the divergence between the conceptualisation and the measurement of store images. Whereas the definitions and conceptualizations tend to emphasize the holistic nature of image, measures usually adopt the 'piecemeal', attribute-by-attribute approach: 'in short, an image was believed to be a picture, but was measured with a list'.

The pictorial aspects of images may not lend themselves easily to measurement by verbal scales. These aspects are not required to obey the laws of logic, such as the rule of non-contradiction, and they may not accord with reality (Elliott, 1994). Blawatt (1995) highlights the importance of theories of 'dual coding' in information processing, whereby both verbal and non-verbal images are consigned to, and retrieved from, memory. The dual-coding theory appears to have some association with hemispheric functions, whereby left-brain processing is presumed literal, while right-brain functions include emotion and visual imagery.

Researchers in the related field of brand equity have offered some practical suggestions on how to elicit the elements of image that may be more difficult to verbalize. Aaker (1991) suggest nine approaches to the elicitation of brand associations that consumers may be unwilling, or unable, to verbalize, without the help of in-depth techniques.

1 *Free association techniques*: measures to bypass the inhibiting thinking process of the respondent, including word association or sentence completion.
2 *Picture interpretation*: the picture has the power to elicit feelings associated with the store. The consumer may be given a scene and asked to project him or herself into the scene. Projective techniques may also be used to attribute feelings or impressions to others, to avoid embarrassment or guilt.
3 *Store/brand as a person*: valuable to elicit personality issues, such as lively or dull. A respondent may be asked to act out being a store, then describe how old/young they are, whether masculine or feminine, what sort of personality they have, etc.
4 *Places, animals, activities and magazines*: this helps people to go beyond obvious, mundane description. From lists of possibilities, respondents associated Kentucky Fried Chicken with Puerto Rico, a zebra (stripes on the chicken bucket), a housewife dressed in denim, camping and reading *TV Guide* (Plummer, 1984/85).
5 *Use experience*: brings out associations, feelings and contexts that were part of the experience, such as realistic elements of shopping in seasonal sales.
6 *Decision process*: can tease out associations not part of a person's stated image of a store, such as people who recommend it, or the experience of other people.
7 *What the user is like*: how does the user of one brand/store differ from the user of another? This can elicit responses that go beyond a 'logical' rationale for their choices.

8 *What distinguishes brands/stores from each other*: this can evoke a customer-driven vocabulary to describe points of difference, that would not necessarily have been identified as important, using standard scales.

9 *Means-end analysis*: pushing respondents beyond attributes towards consumer benefits and personal values (Reynolds and Gutman, 1984). Well trained/motivated staff, for example, may provide good service, making customers feel important and contributing to their self-esteem. Typically, a researcher must repeatedly ask why, sometimes known as the 'five whys', to encourage respondents to reveal the benefits and values behind the stated attributes.

A large proportion of imagery is acquired under low involvement conditions, therefore is not subjected to conscious processing by the brain. Consequently, many associations are unconsciously stored in a non-verbal mode (Zaltman, 1997). Around two-thirds of all stimuli that reach the brain are visual (Kosslyn et al., 1990). Only a small minority,

Table 5.2 In-depth elicitation of associations

Source: adapted from Supphellen (2000).

Purpose	Suggested techniques
ACCESS: *a major challenge is to obtain access to less conscious associations*	▸ Include one or more visual technique ▸ Probe for secondary associations ▸ Probe for relevant situations ▸ Address sensory associations directly ▸ Use real stimuli when practicable ▸ Use more than one sample
↓	↓
VERBALIZATION: *unconscious associations are mainly non-verbal, existing in visual, sensory or emotional modes*	▸ Use established scales to elicit emotional and personality associations ▸ Take your time and create acceptance of pauses: verbalization may not be easy ▸ Adapt to individual differences in response styles
↓	↓
CENSORING: *impression management and self-deception can lead to the holding back of associations*	▸ Assure confidential treatment of responses ▸ Use person-projective techniques, such that the elicited association can be ascribed to other people
↓	↓
VALIDATION: *associations can be elicited that are spurious or irrelevant, a major criticism of in-depth interviews*	▸ Validate minority associations on a subsample of the majority, to confirm relevance to others ▸ Simplistic measures of salience, such as frequency or order of mention, should not be the only test used ▸ Follow-up surveys may be appropriate to assess importance, uniqueness and relationships between associations

those subjected to cognitive elaboration, will have a verbal description attached to them when entering memory. Supphellan (2000) draws upon a wide range of in-depth techniques to construct a combination methodology for the elicitation of brand associations: this is summarized in Table 5.2. It addresses first the issue of gaining access to less conscious associations, then the task of verbalizing, when many are not stored in verbal form. The researcher then faces the problems of censoring, resulting from impression management or a tendency towards socially desirable responding (SDR) (Mick, 1996). As a final stage, the findings should be validated across subsamples, using larger surveys or involving managers most closely involved.

Multidimensional Scaling and Conjoint Analysis

An approach which permits some structuring and quantification of images, while avoiding the rigidity of fixed scales, is multidimensional scaling (MDS). This has been used in various forms by, for example, Doyle and Fenwick (1974), Singson (1975), Jain and Etgar (1976), Davies (1987), Green et al. and Hodgkinson et al. (1991). The benefits of this approach were described by Singson (1975):

> *MDS starts with only one piece of information, namely, judgement of similarities between all pairs of stimuli within the stimulus set under study. From this set of similarities judgements, the researcher attempts to infer the basic attribute(s) that underlie people's perceptions about the set of objects or stimuli. Since the researcher does not start with preselected attributes, he [sic] avoids the possibility of superimposing his own perception about the set of stimuli under study upon the respondents. Thus, MDS represents an unobtrusive way of getting at people's perceptions.*

By this approach, a multidimensional map can be evolved, indicating the perceived similarities between stores and the most salient dimensions by which these are assessed. The technique has the potential of exposing judgement criteria of which the respondents are not consciously aware or that they are less willing to discuss. Based upon a study of the images of five stores in Manchester city centre, Davies (1987) used MDS to produce two- and three-dimensional maps, an example of which is shown in Fig. 5.5. Maps of this type show the relative positions of the five stores in a form of 'image space' (Doyle, 1975).

Ways of collecting the data have varied between the studies that used MDS. Doyle and Fenwick (1974) and Singson (1975) asked respondents to rate the similarities of all possible pairs of stores, then used relatively conventional scaling techniques to help them to identify and label the dimensions upon which store similarities were being evaluated. In common with some other multivariate techniques, such as factor analysis, this final stage requires considerable judgement on the part of the researchers and represents a significant limitation. There are also problems in assessing the statistical significance of the results (Amirani and Gates, 1993).

Figure 5.5
Multidimensional
scaling map

Source: 'Monitoring
retailing strategy by
measuring customer
perception' by G. Davies in
G. Johnson (ed.), *Business
Strategy and Retailing*,
Copyright © 1987 John
Wiley & Sons Ltd.
Reprinted by permission of
John Wiley & Sons Ltd.

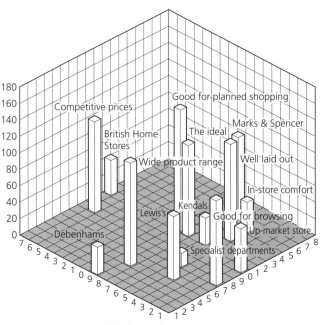

Manchester department stores

One approach to overcoming these limitations is to combine the use of MDS with other analytical techniques. Green et al. (1987) noted the display power of MDS but also the difficulty of interpreting axes. They therefore utilized a combination of MDS, conjoint analysis and cluster analysis to achieve greater analytical and predicative capabilities. Within conjoint analysis studies, respondents are presented with a number of hypothetical store profiles, based upon previously established attributes. These are then sorted according to their perceived similarity to the stores upon which the study is focused (Amirani and Gates, 1993). Finally, the respondent rates preferences for each of the actual stores.

These similarity judgements, combined with preference ratings, enable the analyst to estimate the salience of each attribute, and the desirability of each attribute combination. A variation upon this 'attribute-anchored' conjoint approach is the 'brand-anchored' conjoint approach. Within this, the hypothetical store profiles are anchored to characteristics of existing, known shares, for example:

▶ value for money like Sears.
▶ location convenience like Bloomingdale's.
▶ service like Wal-Mart.

Louviere and Johnson (1990) claim that this approach helps to analyse positioning strategies associated with changing images attributes, over a domain spanned by sets of existing retail concepts. An essential prerequisite, however, is the effective elicitation of the salient attributes to be included within the conjoint analysis.

5.3 The Comparison of Images

However sophisticated or basic the measurement technique, realizing the full value of image monitoring often requires simultaneous comparison and, if possible, comparisons over time. The advantages of also tracking images over a period of time is that a 'moving picture' of the store's positioning is created (Pessemier 1980). This can assist in monitoring the effects of strategic moves, marketing activities, competitors' actions and, especially in new markets, the evolution of the image (McGoldrick, 1998).

So far the impression may have been gained that store image is concerned exclusively with comparing one retailer with its rivals. While this is true in many cases, there are other important contrasts that can be drawn, notably the images of individual branches, their customers, individual departments, shopping centres and stores in different countries. Examples will be given of each of these types of image comparison.

5.3.1 Retailers and their Clients

Retailer comparisons are the most usual application of image research, of which many case studies may be found within the literature (e.g. Davies, 1987; Doyle and Fenwick 1974; KPMG, 2000). Figure 5.5 illustrates this type of comparison, based upon the technique of multidimensional scaling. Where more basic rating scales are used, the comparisons are usually expressed in terms of the average (mean) values of ratings given to each store on each dimension. Alternatively, the percentages agreeing with a particular statement may be reported.

Table 5.3 Organizations trusted to be honest and fair

Source: derived from KPMG (2000), based upon Henley Centre data.

Your GP	85%	Your bank	72%
Kellogg's	84%	Tesco	71%
Boots	83%	Asda	67%
Marks & Spencer	83%	Coca-cola	65%
Cadbury	83%	Your church	64%
Heinz	81%	Safeway	64%
Nescafé	77%	The police	62%
Sainsbury	74%	Your MP	29%
Rowntree	74%		

Table 5.3 shows the numbers of respondents who considered various organizations to be honest and fair. This provides a comparative measure of trust, a key component within a retailer's brand equity. In this study, the retailers are also compared with the levels of trust enjoyed by selected manufacturers and institutions. Long established retailers, such as Boots and Marks & Spencer, rank alongside Kellogg's, Cadbury and doctors on this trust scale. Likewise, the leading grocery chains enjoy similar trust levels to customers' own banks (KPMG, 2000).

A different approach to the comparison of images is to focus upon the image of the clientele of various stores, rather than upon the images held by them. It is clear from many studies that particular types of shoppers patronize particular stores, reflecting the association between store and self-image. This association can be put to effective use by retail management: 'projecting a store image which is consistent with the target markets' self-image will increase loyalty among those shoppers' (Bellenger et al., 1976). This aspect of image has been curiously neglected by researchers, in spite of the strong influence of other customers on store choice, and upon the service experience when among other customers (Grove and Fisk, 1997).

One of the most direct comparisons of clientele images was that of Burstiner (1974). He developed a 15-scale semantic differential to compare perceptions of the social class, personality and lifestyles of shoppers patronizing three New York department stores. Table 5.4 shows the average (mean) rating for each of the three stores on each of 15 semantic differential scales. The ratings were on a scale of 1 to 7; the lower the mean ratings, the closer the ratings were to the word on the left, and vice versa. Thus, for example, shoppers at store B were perceived as being more sophisticated, extravagant and intelligent, especially when contrasted with the shoppers at store C.

Table 5.4 Images of store clientele

Source: adapted from Burstiner (1974, p. 30).

Comparative mean ratings				
Scale (1–7)		**A**	**B**	**C**
Modern	Old-fashioned	3.50	2.55	3.36
Unfriendly	Neighbourly	4.20	4.12	4.28
Rugged	Delicate	3.93	4.87	3.29
Quality-seekers	Bargain-hunters	3.76	2.31	5.85
Serious	Humorous	3.36	3.07	3.93
Plain	Sophisticated	3.79	5.48	2.68
High-income	Low income	3.78	2.46	5.20
Apartment dwellers	Homeowners	3.63	3.64	3.25
Economical	Extravagant	3.33	5.13	2.13
Mostly married	Mostly single	2.93	3.77	3.01
Leaders	Followers	4.39	3.18	5.00
Middle class	Lower class	2.85	2.05	4.51
Dull people	Intelligent people	4.33	5.09	3.74
Executives	Workers	4.80	2.89	5.70
Mostly young	Mostly older	4.54	3.69	3.63

A subsequent study of shoppers at the Cheshire Oaks factory outlet centre, using variations upon Burstiner's scales, showed them to be predominantly fashionable and style conscious, yet economical and down to earth (Vazquez et al., 1999).

Alternative approaches to comparing clients, especially in relation to their perceived social class, were demonstrated by Marcus (1972). In one stage of the study, respondents were shown a picture depicting a high-, middle- or low-class shopper; they were asked to indicate the store to which that shopper was going. In another stage, respondents were asked which store six 'types of people' were most likely to use; the 'types of people'

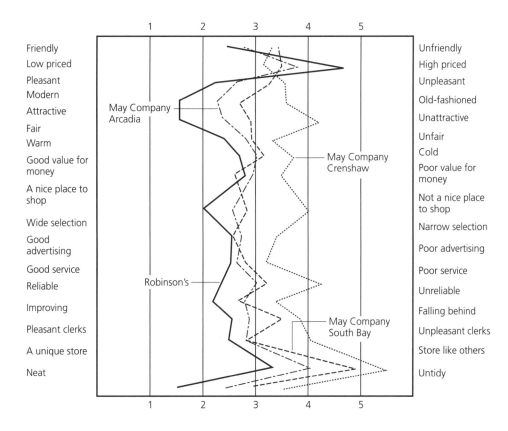

Figure 5.6 Inter-store
image comparisons

Source: Marcus (1972, p. 39).

5.3.2 Inter-Branch Image Comparisons

were chosen to reflect different social levels. These projective techniques were used to minimize problems of self-image by making the image evaluations more detached from the respondents' own patronage decisions.

Many comparisons of specific retailer's images have left the impression that the findings can be generalized, to a greater or lesser extent, across all stores within the chain. Marcus (1972) effectively challenged this assumption by showing that image ratings given to three branches of the May Company in various districts of Los Angeles differed significantly. Figure 5.6 shows the positions of the mean ratings of the three stores compared with those of the fairly upmarket Robinson's store. The 17 scales were selected to reflect some of the tangible and less tangible image components.

Figure 5.6 shows that the May stores in general received less favourable ratings than the Robinson's store. The most notable exception was in respect of price, although a higher price rating is obviously consistent with the higher-status image of Robinson's. The most important outcome of this comparison, however, is the difference between the individual May stores. For example, the image of May's Arcadia branch was closer to that of Robinson's than it was to that of May's Crenshaw branch, which was the least well perceived store.

There are three main reasons why images can differ considerably between branches:

1 In spite of the standardized formats of many chains, every store differs at least slightly in terms of size, location, layout and/or staff.
2 No two localities are exactly alike in terms of competition mix and strength; shoppers therefore have different expectations and bases for comparison.
3 While most retailers seek out locations with specific customer characteristics in mind, there are always some local differences that are likely to influence patronage motives and customer reactions.

It is important, therefore, to be sensitive to local differences, rather than simply to assume that national marketing leads to a national image. Local image monitoring can also be helpful in suggesting modifications to the assortment, prices, service levels or communications mix. The opportunities for 'localization', provided by geographical information systems (GIS), are discussed in Chapter 7 (e.g. O'Malley et al., 1997). The importance of local pricing is highlighted in Chapter 10.

Surprisingly little research attention has been given to the images of retail outlets of the same chain in different countries. In Chapter 14, differences are demonstrated in the images of Marks & Spencer stores in the UK, France and Hong Kong (McGoldrick, 1998; McGoldrick and Ho, 1992). In part, these differences could be ascribed to positioning strategies vis-à-vis pricing, services or assortments. To a large extent, however, they relate to the different competitive contexts and consumer expectations.

International image monitoring, while presenting additional research challenges, offers more than just an evaluation of international positioning outcomes. If conducted on a time-series basis, it offers the opportunity to track the growth of an image within a 'new' market. Both the quantity (awareness) and qualities of the image are important as the company develops within markets where it was relatively unknown. With sufficient advertising and promotion, some elements of brand equity can be developed fairly rapidly. Others, such as trust and reliability, take much longer to develop.

5.3.3 Images of Departments or Categories

As many stores become increasingly diversified, there are sound reasons for believing that both the importance and the ratings of image components will differ by department within a store. This proposition was explored by Cardozo (1974), who investigated the images of stores in relation to the health and beauty aids and the housewares product groups. For both product groups, price was the most frequently mentioned factor (using the psycho-linguistic approach), but there were major differences between both the implied importance and the evaluations of image dimensions in respect of the two groups.

McGoldrick (1979) compared consumers' ratings of major image dimensions relating to 11 product groups/departments within one

	Price ratings (%)				Quality ratings (%)			
	Lower than ave.	About ave.	Higher than ave.	Don't know	Below ave.	About ave.	Above ave.	Don't know
Ladies' and men's knitwear	9	63	24	4	1	16	80	3
Ladies' nightwear and underwear	12	56	26	6	1	20	74	5
Men's nightwear and underwear	9	50	15	26	1	25	50	24
Other ladies' clothes	9	55	28	8	3	27	62	8
Other men's clothes	8	48	19	25	3	25	49	23
Footwear	13	45	14	28	11	32	33	25
Children's clothes	8	36	27	29	1	18	55	26
Food and drinks	5	33	58	4	1	15	80	4
Household goods	3	43	28	26	2	28	48	22
Cosmetics	4	39	17	40	5	25	31	39
Plants	7	41	17	35	2	24	41	33

Table 5.5 Departmental price and quality ratings
Source: McGoldrick (1979, p. 22).

Marks & Spencer store. Table 5.5 summarizes the price and quality ratings given to the various 'departments' of the store. Most of the departmental ratings were broadly consistent with the store's overall image for good quality and good value. There were exceptions, however, notably footwear and cosmetics, which were sufficient to warrant action in these areas.

A subsequent study by Stewart and Hood (1983) extended the study of product category images to include also those of Littlewoods and BhS; again, some differences in the images and competitive positions of individual departments were revealed. Clearly, such intra-store image differences may not necessarily work to the detriment of the retailer. For example, the relatively high-price image of Marks & Spencer's food (Table 5.5) did not prevent them from being successful in that area; indeed, it may have actually contributed by positioning the company distinctively on the price-quality dimensions. Subsequently, many supermarket chains have followed their lead into high value-added convenience foods.

Hart and Davies (1996) note that supermarkets have not been the focus of department-level image analysis, in spite of their diversifications into various non-food areas. Adverse image differences can be most detrimental to a store's overall image; at least occasionally, retailers should disaggregate their image monitoring by product class, especially if they are selling a diverse product assortment. There is also clearly a series of linkages between store images and the brands sold; the positive or negative effects of selling strongly branded manufacturer's products should also be considered (Jacoby and Mazursky, 1984).

5.3.4 Shopping Centre Images

The relative positioning of shopping centres can also be evaluated through image measurement techniques. One of earlier studies that has focused upon shopping centre images was that of Nevin and Houston

Table 5.6 Images of two centres

Note: 27 attributes and 'overall image' were compared in this study.

Source: McGoldrick and Thompson (1992).

(1980), who utilized factor analysis to extract three major dimensions from 16 image rating scales. More recently, shopping centre images have attracted the interest of researchers in several countries (e.g. Bell, 1999; Blawatt, 1995; Hackett and Foxall, 1994; Ruiz, 1999). Finn and Louviere (1996) demonstrated some of the characteristics that contribute to a centre's image, notably the anchor stores. 'Image transference', between anchor stores and lesser known stores within shopping centres, has also been illustrated (Burns, 1992).

	MetroCentre		Eldon Square	
	1987	**1990**	**1987**	**1990**
Quality of stores	80	83	81	80
Spaciousness	95	94	58	68
'In-place' to go	79	81	65	67
For eating or drinking	74	76	64	67
Friendliness of atmosphere	77	77	65	70
Parking facilities	88	93	43	40
Product selection in stores	78	80	82	80
General layout	88	87	67	72
Place to take children	85	89	53	57
Level of crowds	49	68	81	71
General price level	60	62	52	58
Undesirable characters	14	40	59	51

The images of Eldon Square, in Newcastle, and the nearby MetroCentre were compared by McGoldrick and Thompson (1992). The study was initially conducted one year after the MetroCentre opened, then was replicated three years later. The centres were compared on a total of 28 scales, 12 of which are shown in Table 5.6. The centres were fairly evenly matched on perceptions of store quality and product selection but the newer MetroCentre scored well on amenities and as a place to visit. Over the three-year period, refurbishments at Eldon Square seemed to contribute to a perception of increased prices. Ironically, as MetroCentre became more accessible by public transport and increased its leisure facilities, its image for 'undesirable characters' became less favourable.

Although the image of a centre may be somewhat beyond the control of the individual retailer, such an evaluation can assist in location decisions, helping to identify the centres that are compatible with the retailer's image. The choice of a centre usually precedes the choice of a store (Bell, 1999), although there are circumstances where store choice, or even brand choice, may determine which centre is visited. Knowledge of a centre's image can also help in evaluating or predicting the performance of a store within that centre.

SUMMARY

It is of vital importance for retailers to evaluate and frequently re-evaluate the performance of their retailing strategy. A number of accounting measures are applied to assess the financial health of the company but such measures should be supplemented with a detailed evaluation of retail marketing performance, from the viewpoint of the target customers. Such evaluations can provide early warnings of problems which, if not corrected, would exert a negative impact upon the balance sheet.

The linkages between store image, patronage and loyalty are well established. However, a serious gulf can exist between retailers' evaluations of their own stores and the images held by consumers. Most senior retail managers have little direct contact with existing or potential customers. Even at store level, managers tend to be optimistic in their estimates of their own store image. The importance of systematic image monitoring is therefore paramount, to assess the strength of the organization's brand equity.

An appropriate first stage is to identify the detailed set of potentially salient attributes. Some studies have identified around 50 such attributes, often with further subcategories. It is dangerous to overgeneralize these, or to assume that images are composed of just broad, functional dimensions, such as price, range or location. It is important also to elicit the emotions, feelings, values and associations within customers' images of the retailer.

Semantic differential scales have been widely used for image measurement, along with more compact variants, such as the numerical comparative scale. Open-ended techniques are a necessary prerequisite to the use of scales, as well as providing insights into non-verbal imagery. A number of techniques from branding and advertising research can be deployed in this context. Multivariate techniques have also played their part in image research, including conjoint analysis, factor analysis and multidimensional scaling.

Many image studies have compared two or more retailers; management also need to track these comparisons over time. Image analysis can be employed to evaluate a retailer's stores in different areas, or even in different countries. Within the individual store, it is also possible that different departments or merchandise groupings may be achieving very different images. Shopping areas and centres also have distinctive images, reflecting their attractiveness to retail tenants and to customers.

REVIEW QUESTIONS

1 Illustrate how the use of financial analysis alone can fail to detect problems in retail marketing strategy.

2 Why do retailers' images of their own stores often differ from those held by customers? Show how the identification of such differences can assist the retailer in formulating and refining retail strategy.

3 'Store image is less like a photograph than a highly interpretative portrait.' Discuss.

4 In Fig.5.3, the brand proposition model is applied to Volvo cars. Apply this model to a retailer of your choice. Determine the core proposition of that retailer and identify how it is substantiated at the functional level. Then add what you perceive to be the inner and outer directed values associated with being a customer of that retailer.

5 Compare the advantages and problems of using the following types of scales in the evaluation of store images:

a) semantic differential scales

b) graphic positioning scales

c) numerical comparative scales

d) Likert scales.

6 Outline the general principle of multi-dimensional scaling (MDS) in the evaluation of store images. What complementary techniques can be deployed to assist in the interpretation of MDS results?

7 An in-depth understanding of image requires access to associations that consumers may be unable, or unwilling, to verbalize. Outline some of the techniques that can be deployed to elicit less conscious associations.

8 Why is it important to know how customers perceive clients of various stores? What marketing actions may be guided by comparisons of clientele images?

9 Studies have shown there to be major differences between the images of different stores of the same chain. Explain why this might be the case, and discuss the implications for the localization strategies of chainstore retailers.

10 Just as manufacturers have engaged in brand extensions, retailers too have diversified into many new categories. The choice of these may be more driven by margins than by image considerations. From your own experience, compare two examples of range extension, one of which fits well with the retailer's image, while the other one does not.

11 Taking two shopping centres with which you are familiar, list the elements of their images upon which they differ, in your view. Identify the clothing retailers that are best matched to the images of these two centres.

REFERENCES

Aaker, D.A. (1991) *Managing Brand Equity: Capitalising on the Value of a Brand Name*, Free Press, New York.

Aaker, D.A. (1994) 'The value of brand equity', *Journal of Business Strategy*, **13** (4), 27–32.

Aaker, J.L. (1997) 'Dimensions of brand personality', *Journal of Marketing Research*, **34** (3), 347–356.

Agres, S.J. and T.M. Dubitsky (1996) 'Changing needs for brands', *Journal of Advertising Research*, **36** (1), 21–30.

Albaum, G. (1997) 'The Likert scale revisited: and alternate version', *Journal of the Market Research Society*, **39** (2), 331–348.

Amirani, S. and R. Gates (1993) 'An attribute-anchored conjoint approach to measuring store image', *International Journal of Retail & Distribution Management*, **21** (5), 30–39.

Arnold, S.J., T.H. Oum and D.J. Tigert (1983) 'Determinant attributes in retail patronage: seasonal temporal, regional and international comparisons', *Journal of Marketing Research*, **20** (2), 149–157.

Baker, J., D. Grewal and A. Parasuraman (1994) The influence of store environment on quality inferences and store image', *Journal of the Academy of Marketing Science*, **22** (Fall), 328–339.

Bell, S.J. (1999) 'Image and consumer attraction to intraurban retail areas: an environmental psychology approach', *Journal of Retailing and Consumer Services*, **6**, 67–78.

Bellenger, D.N., W.W. Stanton and E. Steinberg (1976) 'The congruence of store image and self image as it relates to store loyalty', *Journal of Retailing*, **52** (1), 17–32.

Bello, D.C. and M.B. Holbrook (1995) 'Does an absence of brand equity generalize across product classes?', *Journal of Business Research*, **34** (2), 125–131.

Berry, L.L. (1969) 'The components of department store image: a theoretical and empirical analysis', *Journal of Retailing*, **45** (1), 3–20.

Birtwistle, G., I. Clarke and P. Freathy (1999) 'Store image in the U.K. fashion sector: consumer versus retailer perceptions', *International Review of Retail Distribution and Consumer Research*, **9** (1), 1–16.

Blawatt, K. (1995) 'Imagery: an alternative approach to the attribute-image paradigm for shopping centres', *Journal of Retailing and Consumer Services*, **2** (2), 83–96.

Bloemar, J. and K. de Ruyter (1998) 'On the relationship between store image, store satisfaction and store loyalty', *European Journal of Marketing*, **32**, 5/6, 499–513.

Boulding, K.E. (1956) *The Image*, University of Michigan Press, Ann Arbor, MI.

Brand Finance (1999) *The Brand Finance Report*, Brand Finance, London.

Brown, S. (1995) 'Sex 'n' shopping: a "novel" approach to consumer research', *Journal of Marketing Management*, **11**, 769–783.

Burns, D.J. (1992) 'Image transference and retail site selection', *International Journal of Retail & Distribution Management*, **20** (5), 38–43.

Burstiner, I. (1974) 'A three-way mirror: comparative images of the clienteles of Macy's, Bloomingdale's, Korvettes', *Journal of Retailing*, **50** (1), 24–36, 90.

Cardozo, R.N. (1974) 'How images vary by product class', *Journal of Retailing*, **50** (4), 85–98.

Cronin, J.J. and S.J. Skinner (1984) 'Marketing outcomes, financial conditions and retail profit performance', *Journal of Retailing*, **60** (4), 9–22.

Darden, W.R. and B.J. Babin (1994) 'Exploring the concept of affective quality: expanding the concept of retail personality', *Journal of Business Research*, **22** (February), 101–109.

Davies, G. (1987) 'Monitoring retailing strategy by measuring customer perception', in *Business Strategy and Retailing*, G. Johnson (ed.), Wiley, Chichester, pp. 133–152.

Davies, G. (1992) 'The two ways in which retailers can be brands', *International Journal of Retail & Distribution Management*, **20** (20), 24–34.

De Chernatony, L. (1993) 'Categorizing brands: evolutionary processes underpinned by two key dimensions', *Journal of Marketing Management*, **9**, 173–188.

De Chernatony, L. and F. Dall'Olmo Riley (1998) 'Modelling the components of the brand', *European Journal of Marketing*, **32** (11/12), 1074–1090.

Doyle, P. (1975) 'Measuring store image', *Admap*, **11** (11), 391–393.

Doyle, P. and I. Fenwick (1974) 'How store image affects shopping habits in grocery chains', *Journal of Retailing*, **50** (4), 39–52.

Egan, C. and C. Guilding (1994) 'Dimensions of brand performance: challenges for marketing management and managerial accountancy', *Journal of Marketing Management*, **10**, 449–472.

Elliott, R. (1994) 'Exploring the symbolic meaning of brands', *British Journal of Management*, **5** (June), 513–519.

Feldwick, P. (1996) 'What is brand equity anyway, and how do you measure it?', *Journal of the Market Research Society*, **38** (2), 85–104.

Finn, A. and J.J. Louviere (1996) 'Shopping centre image, consideration and choice: anchor store contribution', *Journal of Business Research*, **35**, 241–251.

Golden, L.L., G. Albaum and M. Zimmer (1987) 'The numerical comparative scale: an economical format for retail image measurement', *Journal of Retailing*, **63** (4), 393–410.

Goodman, C.S. (1985) 'On output measures of retail performance', *Journal of Retailing*, **61** (3), 77–82

Green, P.E., A.M. Krieger and J.D. Carroll (1987)' Conjoint analysis and multidimensional scaling a complementary approach', *Journal of Advertising Research*, **27** (5), 21–27.

Grove, S.J. and R.P. Fisk (1997) 'The impact of other customers on service experiences: a critical incident examination of "getting along"', *Journal of Retailing*, **73** (1), 63–85.

Hackett, P.M.W. and G.R. Foxall (1994) 'A factor analytic study of consumers' location specific values: a traditional high street and a modern shopping mall', *Journal of Marketing Management*, **10**, 163–178.

Hansen, R. and T. Deutscher (1977) 'An empirical investigation of attribute importance in retail store selection', *Journal of Retailing*, **53** (4), 59–73.

Hart, C.A. and M.A.P. Davies (1996) 'Consumer perceptions of non–food assortments: an empirical study', *Journal of Marketing Management*, **12**, 297–312.

Hawkins, D.I., R. Best and G. Albaum (1976) 'Reliability of retail store images as measured by the stapel scale', Journal of Retailing, **52** (4), 31–38, 92.

Hirschman, E.C., B. Greenberg and D.H. Robertson (1978) 'The intermarket reliability of retail image research: an empirical examination', *Journal of Retailing*, **54** (1), 3–12.

Hodgkinson, G.P., J. Padmore and A.E. Tomes (1991) 'Mapping consumers' cognitive structure: a comparison of similarity trees with multidimensional scaling and cluster analysis', *European Journal of Marketing*, **27** (7), 41–60.

Jacoby, J. and D. Mazursky (1984) 'Linking brand and retailer images—do the potential risks outweigh the potential benefits?', *Journal of Retailing*, **60** (2), 105–122.

Jain, A.K. and M. Etgar (1976) 'Measuring store image through multidimensional scaling of free response data', *Journal of Retailing*, **52** (4), 61–70, 95.

James, D.L., R.M. Durand and R.A. Dreves (1976) 'The use of a multi-attribute attitude model in a store image study', *Journal of Retailing*, **52** (2), 23–32.

Keaveney, S.M. and K.A. Hunt (1992) 'Conceptualisation and operationalization of retail store image: a case of rival middle-level theories', *Journal of the Academy of Marketing Science*, **20** (2), 165–175.

Kerin, R.A and R. Sethuraman (1998) 'Exploring the brand value-shareholder value nexus for consumer goods companies', *Journal of the Academy of Marketing Science*, **26** (4), 260–273.

Kim, H.–S. (2000) 'Examination of brand personality and brand attitude within the apparel product category', *Journal of Fashion Marketing and Management*, **4** (3), 243–252.

Kosslyn, S., M.C. Segar, J. Pani and L.A. Hillger (1990) 'When is imagery used?', *Journal of Mental Imagery*, **14**, 131–152.

KPMG (2000) *Customer Loyalty and Private Label Products*, KPMG, London.

Kunkel, J.H. and L.L. Berry (1968) 'A behavioural concept of retail images', *Journal of Marketing*, **32** (4), 21–27.

Leuthesser, L., C.S. Kohli and K.R. Harich (1995) 'Brand equity: the halo effect measure', *European Journal of Marketing*, **29** (4), 57–66.

Likert, R. (1932) 'A technique for the measurement of attitudes', *Archives of Psychology*, **140**, 44–53.

Lindquist, J.D. (1974) 'Meaning of image: a survey of empirical and hypothetical evidence', *Journal of Retailing*, **50** (4), 29–38, 116.

Louviere, J.J. and R.D. Johnson (1990) 'Reliability and validity of the brand-anchored conjoint approach to measuring retailer images', *Journal of Retailing*, **66** (4), 359–382.

Malhotra, N.K. (1988) 'Self-concept and product choice: an integrated perspective', *Journal of Economic Psychology*, **9** (1), 1–28.

Manrai, A.K. and L.A. Manrai (1995) 'A comparative analysis of two models of store preference incorporating the notion of self-image and store image: some empirical results', *Journal of Marketing Channels*, **4** (3), 33–51.

Marcus, B.H. (1972) 'Image variation and the multi-unit retail establishment', *Journal of Retailing*, **48** (2), 29–43.

Martineau, P. (1958) 'The personality of the retail store', *Harvard Business Review*, **36** (1), 47–55.

May, E.G. (1971) *Selection and Clustering of Image Dimensions*, Working Paper 71–137, Marketing Science Institute, Cambridge, MA.

May, E.G. (1974) 'Practical applications of recent store image research', *Journal of Retailing*, **50** (4), 15–20, 116.

Mazursky, D. and J. Jacoby (1986) 'Exploring the development of store images', *Journal of Retailing*, **62** (2), 145–165.

McClure, P.J. and J.K. Ryans (1968) 'Differences between retailers', *Journal of Marketing Research*, **5** (1), 35–40.

McDougall, G.H.G. and J.N. Fry (1974) 'Combining two methods of image measurement', *Journal of Retailing*, **50** (4), 53–61.

McGoldrick, P.J. (1979) 'Store image: how departmental images differ in a variety chain', *Retail & Distribution Management*, **7** (5), 21–24.

McGoldrick, P.J. (1998) Spatial and temporal shifts in the development of international retail images', *Journal of Business Research*, **42** (2), 189–196.

McGoldrick, P.J. and S. Ho (1992) 'International positioning: Japanese department stores in Hong Kong', *European Journal of Marketing*, **26** (8/9), 63–76.

McGoldrick, P.J. and M.G. Thompson (1992) 'The role of image in the attraction of the out-of-town centre', *International Review of Retail, Distribution and Consumer Research*, **2** (1), 81–98.

Mick, D.G. (1996) 'Are studies of dark side variables confounded by socially desirable responding? The case of materialism', *Journal of Consumer Research*, **23** (3), 106–119.

Nevin, J.R. and M.J. Houston (1980) 'Image as a component of attraction to intraurban shopping areas', *Journal of Retailing*, **56** (1), 77–93.

O'Malley, L., M. Patterson and M. Evans (1997) 'Retailer use of geodemographic and other data sources: and empirical investigation', *International Journal of Retail & Distribution Management*, **25** (6), 188–196.

Oppenheim, A.M. (1976) *Questionnaire Design and Attitude Measurement*, Heinemann, London.

Osgood, C.E., G.J. Suci and P.H. Tannenbaum (1957) *The Measurement of Meaning*, University of Illinois Press, Urbana, IL.

Osman, M.Z. (1993); 'A conceptual model of retail image influences on loyalty patronage behaviour', *The International Review of Retail, Distribution and Consumer Research*, **3** (2), 133–148.

Oxenfeldt, A. (1974) 'Developing a favourable price-quality image', *Journal of Retailing*, **50** (4), 8, 8–14, 115.

Parasuraman, A., L.L. Berry and V.A Zeithaml (1991) 'Refinement and reassessment of the SERVQUAL scale', *Journal of Retailing*, **67** (4), 420–450.

Parasuraman, A., V.A. Zeithaml and L.L. Berry (1988) 'SERVQUAL: a multiple-item scale for measuring consumer perceptions of service quality', *Journal of Retailing*, **64** (1), 12–40.

Pathak, D.S., W.J. Crissy and R.W. Sweitzer (1974) 'Customer image versus the retailer's anticipated image', *Journal of Retailing*, **50** (4), 21–28, 116.

Pessemier, E.A. (1980) 'Store image and positioning', *Journal of Retailing*, **56** (1), 94–106.

Peterson, R.A. and R.A. Kerin (1983) 'Store image measurement in patronage research: fact and artifact', in *Patronage Behaviour and Retail Management*, W.R. Darden and R.F. Lusch (eds), Elsevier North-Holland, New York, pp. 293–306.

Plummer, J.T. (1984/85) 'How personality makes a difference', *Journal of Advertising Research*, **24** (December/January), 27–31.

Reynolds, T. J. and J. Gutman (1984) 'Advertising is image management', *Journal of Advertising Research*, **25** (February/March), 29–37.

Ruiz, F.J.M. (1999) 'Image of suburban shopping malls and two-stage versus uni-equational modelling of the retail trade attraction', *European Journal of Marketing*, **33** (5/6), 512–530.

Samli, A.C., J.P. Kelly and H.K. Hunt (1998) 'Improving the retail performance by contrasting management—and customer-perceived store images: a diagnostic tool for corrective action', *Journal of Business Research*, **43**, 27–38.

Sherrington, M. (1995) 'Branding and brand management', in *Companion Encyclopedia of Marketing*, M.J. Baker (ed.), Routledge, London, pp. 509–527.

Singson, R.E. (1975) 'Multidimensional scaling analysis of store image and shopping behaviour', *Journal of Retailing*, **51** (2), 38–52, 93.

Sirgy, J. (1982) 'Self-concept in consumer behaviour: a critical review', *Journal of Consumer Research*, **9** (4), 287–300.

Stewart, D and N. Hood (1983) 'An empirical examination of customer store image components in three U.K. retail groups', *European Journal of Marketing*, **17** (4), 50–62.

Stewart, T.A. (1995) 'Trying to grasp the intangible', *Fortune*, **132** (7), 157–158.

Supphellan, M. (2000) 'Understanding core brand equity: guidelines for in-depth elicitation of brand associations', *International Journal of Market Research*, **42** (3), 319–338.

Teas, R.K. (1994) 'Retail services image measurement: an examination of the stability of a numerical comparative scale', *International Review of Retail, Distribution and Consumer Research*, **4** (4), 427–442.

Urde, M. (1999) 'Brand orientation: a mindset for building brands into strategic resources', *Journal of Marketing Management*, **15**, 117–133.

Vazquez, D., H. Dirania and P.J. McGoldrick (1999) 'Consumer images, beliefs, motives and satisfaction with a factory outlet centre: the case of Cheshire Oaks', *Proceedings of the 10th International Conference on the Distributive Trades*, Stirling, pp. 212–221.

Wong, J.K. and Teas, R.K. (2001) 'A test of the stability of retail store image mapping based on multi-entity scaling data', *Journal of Retailing and Consumer Services*, **8**, 61–70.

Wood, L.M. (1995) 'Brands: the asset test', *Journal of Marketing Management*, **11**, 547–570.

Zaltman, G. (1997) 'Rethinking market research: putting people back in', *Journal of Marketing Research*, **34** (4), 424–437.

Zimmer, M.R. and L. L. Golden (1988) 'Impressions of retail stores: a content analysis of consumer images', *Journal of Retailing*, **64** (3), 265–293.

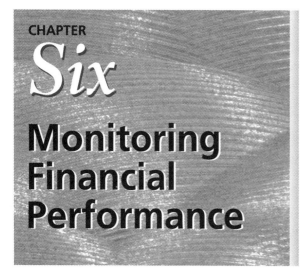

CHAPTER

Six

Monitoring Financial Performance

INTRODUCTION

The concept of the balanced scorecard, discussed in Chapter 4, emphasized the importance of taking an holistic view, both in the planning and the evaluation of business activities (Kaplan and Norton, 1996; Thomas et al., 1999). The linkages between marketing and financial performance have become increasingly recognized (e.g. Cronin and Skinner, 1984; Egan and Guilding, 1994). This is not to imply that measures of financial performance are of diminished significance. With national and international predators always alert to bargains, a retailer ignores its balance sheet at its peril!

To help establish the bridge between concepts of marketing and financial performance, this chapter first examines measures and concepts of productivity in retailing. While providing valuable benchmarking and diagnostic tools, productivity measures based upon financial criteria alone do not provide a full picture of retail effectiveness. Attention must also be given to the 'output' or overall service that a retailer provides.

To assess elements of overall financial performance, a very wide range of ratios is available: some of the key ratios are explained and illustrated. Processes for auditing the financial structure of a retail company are then examined, including internal and external benchmarking. Major costs for retailers are identified, including the cost of goods sold, labour, land, premises, transport and energy. Finally, profitability of the item level is considered, notably direct product profitability, a form of activity-based costing.

6.1 Productivity and Profitability

In view of the scale of the retail industry, surprisingly little research attention has been devoted to retail financial management in general (Cowton and Pilz, 1995; McCaffery et al., 1997). Retail productivity, on the other hand, has been extensively studied. With the interest generated by the concept of the balanced scorecard, however, it is likely that researchers and retailers will strive increasingly to integrate financial and marketing performance measures (Thomas et al., 1998; 1999).

6.1.1 Productivity and Effectiveness

Many different measures have evolved to assess aspects of retail productivity and profitability, most of which provide useful indicators of retail performance. The study of productivity in retailing has a long history (e.g. Bucklin, 1981; Cox, 1948; Hall et al., 1961) but has attracted renewed interest over the last 20 years. It is not the purpose of this section to provide a full appraisal of all these theoretical and empirical developments. An excellent collection of papers addressed this topic in the Fall 1984 issue of the *Journal of Retailing* (e.g. Achabal et al., 1984; Good, 1984): more recent contributions appeared in issues of the *International Journal of Research in Marketing* (e.g. Bultez and Parsons, 1998; Thomas et al., 1998) and the *International Review of Retail, Distribution and Consumer Research* (e.g. Keh, 1997; Kuwahara, 1997).

The meanings of the terms 'productivity', 'efficiency' and 'effectiveness' have frequently been blurred in discussions of retail performance. More distinct definitions were developed by Achabal et al. (1984) and were subsequently summarized by Goodman (1985):

1 *Productivity* relates a single input factor to an output measure, other inputs assumed constant.
2 *Efficiency* measures the effects of all inputs in combination and thus recognises that all inputs and the proportions in which they are employed may vary.
3 *Effectiveness* takes into account goal achievement as well.

These concepts are therefore quite distinct in their scope, but a hierarchical relationship may be seen to exist between them:

> *High productivity is a necessary but not sufficient condition for high efficiency, as individual productive factors may not be combined in an optimal manner. Similarly, high efficiency is a necessary but not sufficient condition for high effectiveness, as the efficient combination may be directed to less that optimal goals (Goodman, 1985).*

Various different ratios can be calculated to measure aspects of retail productivity. Two of the most commonly quoted are sales per square metre (or foot) of selling space, and sales per employee (full-time equivalent). Examples of these two ratios are given in Table 6.1. These illustrate considerable differences, both within and between sectors. However, a lower value on these measures does not necessarily mean lower effectiveness. A relatively high number and/or quality of staff *may* be a natural outcome of higher service positioning. Likewise, more space per unit of sales *could* reflect a more comfortable selling environment. Goldman (1992), for example, demonstrated that Japanese retailing seemed to show low productivity of labour, yet achieve high levels of effectiveness, in terms of good service and accessibility to all shoppers. Similarly, Gadrey and Jany-Catrice (2000) observe that the retail labour force per inhabitant is 68 per cent higher in the USA than in France; this difference however was explained by the more extensive services provided in the USA. These ratios do, however, provide benchmarks, so that retail managers can identify and explore instances of lower 'productivity'.

Company	Sales £ per sq. metre	Company	Sales £000 per FTE employee
Tesco	92	Tesco	146
Sainsbury	98	Sainsbury	139
Asda	81	Asda	163
Safeway	69	Safeway	138
Woolworth	28	Woolworth	116
W.H. Smith	33	W.H. Smith	112
Superdrug	37	Superdrug	122
Marks & Spencer	51	Marks & Spencer	160
Storehouse	17	Storehouse	123
Debenhams	19	Boots	98
Arcadia	29		

Table 6.1 Productivity measures

Source: derived from IGD (2000).

When applied at the individual store level, productivity measures can help to evaluate store management performance (Thomas et al., 1998). They can also identify critical success factors (CSFs), in order that best practices can be identified, described and used as benchmarks for other stores in the chain. When applied at store level, account must be taken of the particular advantages and disadvantages of specific stores, notably location, competitive intensity and varying levels of 'customer efficiency' in the use of the store's services (Kamakura et al., 1996). Other factors may also be beyond the control of store managers, for example wage rates if set by head office.

There has been a tendency to 'borrow' concepts and measure of productivity from the manufacturing industry, although these may be less than appropriate as measures of retail performance. As Nooteboom (1986) observed:

> *[Manufacturing] industry provides a utility of form, while retailing provides a utility of time and place. In view of those differences, one should not too readily and uncritically employ concepts and tools from studies of productivity in industry.*

The 'output' function in retailing is therefore especially difficult. Good (1984) pointed out that a retailer's output is essentially a set of tangible services that make the goods sold more useful to consumers. It is because of these services that a margin can be earned between buying and selling prices. Indeed, further convergence is likely to occur between measures of productivity and effectiveness. Reardon and Vida (1998), for example, refer to a 'productivity measurement crisis', and the growing appreciation that output measures should also include factors such as customer satisfaction and loyalty. As discussed in Chapter 5, brand equity is a major output of retail activity but not one that is traditionally included in productivity measures.

6.1.2 Profitability Measures

In appraising the financial performance of retail companies, the wide range of financial ratios, applicable to most types of business, are commonly used. The retail industry does, however, have some particular accounting conventions, sometimes used to mask underlying performance (Cotter and Hutchinson, 1999; Treadgold, 1991). A full treatment of retail accounting would be beyond the scope of this text but discussion of the major financial ratios, applied to retailing, were provided by Zimmerman et al. (1990) and Business Ratio Plus (1998).

A summary of the more frequently used ratios is provided in Table 6.2, where these ratios are subdivided into profitability, liquidity, leverage and activity ratios. The first of the profitability ratios, gross margin, indicates the total margin available to cover operating expenses and interest, then yield a profit. It is a ratio that is used at the company, category or individual item level, although some of its limitations are discussed in the next section. Most of the gross margin data were excluded from the report of the Competition Commission (2000), although gross margins of five major grocery companies were compared with those of selected retailers elsewhere:

- five grocers (GB) 25.1 per cent
- Wal-Mart (US) 21.0 per cent
- Ahold (NL) 23.4 per cent
- Delhaize (B) 24.3 per cent
- Carrefour (F) 21.1 per cent
- Metro (D) 22.2 per cent

Table 6.3 provides a more comprehensive comparison across countries and sectors, albeit based upon older data. Although there have been some minor adjustments in relative margin levels, it is still clear that percentage gross margins are much higher in clothing, footwear and jewellery, compared with food, liquor and tobacco. Within all the countries there are specific exceptions to these generalizations, for example, high-margin food operations and relatively low-margin footwear stores.

Operating profit margins indicate retailers' profitability from current operations, before taking into account the interest charges accruing from the capital structure. Net profit margins express profitability after all costs have been deducted. However, conventions differ as to whether this is reported before or after taxes. Table 6.4 compares the pre-tax net margins of 10 UK retailers in various sectors. Pariente (1994) compared the net margins of several UK and French retailers, noting that the UK net margins were mostly considerably higher. This was attributed primarily to lower labour costs, better logistic know-how and a higher penetration of retailer-branded products in the UK.

Table 6.2 Summary of key financial ratios

Sources: derived from Business Ratio Plus (1998); Thompson and Strickland (1987), Zimmerman et al. (1990).

Ratio	Method of calculation
Profitability ratios	
Gross profit margin	$\dfrac{\text{Sales} - \text{cost of goods sold}}{\text{Sales}}$
Operating profit margin	$\dfrac{\text{Profit before taxes and interest}}{\text{Sales}}$
Net profit margin (or return on sales)	$\dfrac{\text{Profit after interest}}{\text{Sales}}$
Return on total assets	$\dfrac{\text{Net profit}}{\text{Total assets}}$
Return on equity (or return on net worth)	$\dfrac{\text{Net profit}}{\text{Total shareholders' equity}}$
Return on capital employed	$\dfrac{\text{Net profit}}{\text{Total capital employed}}$
Earnings per share	$\dfrac{\text{Profits after taxes} - \text{Performance dividends}}{\text{Number of ordinary shares}}$
Price earnings ratio (or PE multiple)	$\dfrac{\text{Average price of a company share}}{\text{Earnings per share (most recent)}}$
Liquidity ratios	
Current ratio	$\dfrac{\text{Current assets}}{\text{Current liabilities}}$
Quick ratio (or acid test)	$\dfrac{\text{Cash and accounts receivable}}{\text{Current liabilities}}$
Leverage ratios	
Debt to assets ratio	$\dfrac{\text{Total debt}}{\text{Total assets}}$
Debt to equity ratio	$\dfrac{\text{Total debt}}{\text{Total shareholders' equity}}$
Times – interest – earned (or coverage ratio)	$\dfrac{\text{Profits before taxes and interest}}{\text{Total interest charge}}$
Activity ratios	
Inventory turnover	$\dfrac{\text{Sales}}{\text{Inventory}}$
Asset turnover (asset utilization)	$\dfrac{\text{Sales}}{\text{Total assets}}$
Accounts receivable turnover	$\dfrac{\text{Annual credit sales}}{\text{Accounts receivable}}$
Average collection period	$\dfrac{\text{Accounts receivable}}{\text{Average daily sales}}$

Table 6.4 also shows returns on total assets (ROTA) of the ten companies. The assets include fixed assets, such as land and property, and current assets, including stock, debtors and cash, with a deduction for current liabilities, notably creditors. *The Times* (1999) compared the land and property assets of UK retailers with their market capitalization,

Table 6.3 Percentage gross margins: international and sector comparisons

Notes: [1] Based upon West German data.
[2] Confectionery, newsagents and tobacco.

Source: derived from O'Riordan (1993).

Sector	GB	F	D[1]	NL	DK	IRL	USA
Food	22.8	20.1	26.4	21.9	19.4	17.1	25.6
Liquor	17.0	38.8	26.6	16.4	14.9	17.0	16.3
CTN[2]	18.5	20.4	14.6	14.5	16.8	18.7	–
Household	35.9	36.9	35.2	36.6	35.1	26.4	44.0
Electrical	31.9	29.5	26.4	27.4	40.6	26.9	34.9
Stationery, books	38.6	35.1	33.5	31.1	32.2	28.5	–
Jewellery	43.2	46.7	43.6	45.4	48.8	40.5	–
Department stores	30.6	33.0	–	–	38.6	33.2	32.9
Clothing	43.7	39.2	38.0	38.4	36.8	27.3	42.9
Footwear	43.0	37.0	37.5	37.2	39.5	33.1	46.7

showing several to be vulnerable to takeover for asset-stripping purposes. It was questionable, however, whether many of the book values of these assets could actually be realized in the property market. The Competition Commission (2000) observed that UK grocery multiples tended to depreciate their property assets over 40 years, compared with 18–20 years for continental European and US retailers.

Table 6.4 Profit measures: selected retailers

Source: derived from Business Ratio Plus (1998).

Company	Return on capital employed %	Return on total assets %	Net margin before tax %
Boots	57.0	22.2	9.4
Next	77.4	30.1	11.7
River Island	78.5	28.8	13.2
Allied Carpets	39.2	16.5	6.5
IKEA	24.7	16.2	8.9
Woolworth	34.9	14.9	5.2
John Lewis	11.0	7.5	4.8
Tesco	16.6	11.3	5.4
Sainsbury	13.6	8.4	4.3
Asda	17.7	11.2	3.9

Return on equity (ROE), often termed return on net worth (RONW), measures the rate of return on shareholders' investment in the company. Return on capital employed (ROCE) is often taken as the primary measure of performance, indicating the profit a business yields relative to all the money invested in it (Business Ratios Plus, 1998). Definitions vary, but the Competition Commission (2000) took capital employed to be shareholders' equity plus long-term debt. On many non-UK company balance sheets, capital employed also includes 'intangibles', such as goodwill.

Another widely used ratio to assess the profitability of a company is earnings per share (EPS). This expresses the earnings available to ordinary shareholders. The price earnings ratio (PER) relates EPS to the average price of a company share over the relevant accounting period, or the price at a given point in time. It measures the price that investors are willing to pay for each unit of earnings. The PER includes a measure of the returns on existing operations and, crucially, a measure of expected future performance (Cotter and Hutchinson, 1999).

Liquidity ratios indicate the ability of the company to convert assets to cash. The current ratio indicates the extent to which the claims of creditors are covered by assets that are convertible on an appropriate timescale. A current ratio in excess of two is normally the sign of a strong business (Zimmerman et al., 1990). The quick ratio, or acid test, measures ability to meet liabilities without selling inventories. Creditors are especially interested in this ratio, being indicative of a company's ability to meet current obligations. Cash flow problems have been a major precursor of business failures in retailing (McGurr and DeVaney, 1998).

Leverage or gearing ratios provide an indication of the degree of risk that the company represents for lenders. The debt-to-assets ratio indicates the extent to which the firm's operations have been financed by borrowed funds. The debt-to-equity ratio relates funds provided by creditors to funds provided by shareholders. Pariente (1994) observed that British retailers generally rely less on borrowed funds than their French counterparts, although some UK retailers do make extensive use of long-term debt as a funding source (Business Ratios Plus, 1998).

In the USA, a phase of leveraged buyouts (LBOs), financed by loans from banks and others, created a legacy at some major retail firms coping with very high levels of interest payments (Weinstein, 1993). There can be a positive incentive towards debt, where interest costs are tax deductible. However, as interest costs may remain the same in times of difficult trading, the risk of financial distress and bankruptcy is increased (Hutchinson and Hunter, 1995). The survival of department store E1 Corte Inglés in Spain, while its major rival failed, was attributed in part to its modest range of borrowings (Gold and Woodliffe, 2000). Times-interest-earned, or the coverage ratio, shows how far earnings can decline before the company would become unable to meet its interest commitments.

Among the activity ratios, inventory turnover is a key measure of how quickly the goods purchased are resold. Stockturn tends to vary greatly between sectors and between individual product lines, a factor that is further discussed in the final section. Fixed/total assets turnover indicates whether a sufficient volume of business is being generated, relative to the scale of the company's assets. The measures of credit repayment periods are of increasing significance, especially of retailers financing their own credit schemes or store cards (see Chapter 13).

This brief overview of financial ratios will have illustrated that no single measure of performance fully reflects the financial well-being of a company. Accord to Stern et al. (1996), the financial performance of retailers is multidimensional, requiring the examination of profitability, liquidity, leverage and growth patterns/potentials, both of sales and of profits. Bates (1990) urges retailers to look beyond price and think more directly about gross margin planning. However, operating costs and the effective use of assets are also critical components of overall profitability.

6.2 Elements of Cost and Profitability

It is very easy to spend money in the pursuit of increased market share or in the implementation of a new market strategy. As will be demonstrated in the following chapters, few of the tools of retail marketing can be utilized without the adjustment of cost structures. The most successful and profitable retail companies are those that have developed a coherent position in the market, while maintaining constant vigilance in all areas of productivity and cost control.

6.2.1 Auditing Financial Structure

Financial control is not synonymous with lowest costs, except for the most price-driven of discount operations. The greatest financial achievement of successful retailers has been to challenge the 'rules' about relationships between costs, quality and service levels. Companies such as Next and Tesco have established strong positions in their respective markets, while yielding healthy profits in recent years. This has been achieved through maximizing efficiencies across the system as a whole, including purchasing, distribution, store operations and marketing.

To an extent, retailers have deployed the concept of business process re-engineering to their organizations, in order to identify and possibly eliminate parts of their processes that were not vital in the delivery of value to customers. Hammer and Champy (1993) defined business process re-engineering as:

> *the fundamental rethinking and radical redesign of business processes to achieve dramatic improvements in critical contemporary measures of performance, such as cost, quality, service and speed.*

Like many 'new' concepts, it was deployed badly within some organizations, severely damaging staff morale or losing sight of future market needs (Hamel and Prahalad, 1994). It has however achieved some good results within the logistics function, where the focus upon speed and service is naturally congruent with customer expectations from that function (Micklethwait and Woolridge, 1996). As the concept starts to mature, the abiding importance of customer perceptions has become more explicit:

> *organisations have restructured around business processes rather than functions. Someone needs to be accountable to the customer for the entire process and measured on their perceptions of performance (Knox and Maklan, 1998).*

Doyle and Cook (1985) suggested a systematic framework for auditing the financial structure of a retail company. This has been updated in Fig. 6.1. It takes the form of 31 questions, to which retailers may add to reflect their own circumstances. In the nature of any audit, this should be administered periodically to maintain pressure on costs, and to avoid

---

A SALES VOLUME

1) Can the market be expanded through innovation or modified strategy?
2) What opportunities exist for extending product, service or delivery options?
3) Can market share be won from competitors?
4) How can the marketing strategy and store image be improved?
5) Does a clear, long-term marketing plan exist, and is it appropriate for current/predicted trading conditions?

B MARGINS

1) Can prices on certain lines be increased without eroding competitive position?
2) Does an effective system exist for planning target mark-ups?
3) Is the balance of manufacturer and own-brands appropriate?
4) Can the present level of markdowns be reduced?
5) If the breath or depth of assortment is modified, could more space be given to high margin lines?

C COST OF GOODS SOLD

1) Can buying discounts be improved?
2) Are all feasible allowances and overriders being negotiated?
3) Should purchasing be focused around fewer buyers or category managers?
4) Should more use be made of buying alliances or direct international sourcing?
5) Are buying decisions effectively centralised?

D OPERATING EXPENSES

1) Does a sound information and accounting system exist for monitoring expense centres and selling units?
2) Is there an effective budgetary control system for planning expenses and relating them to financial goals?
3) Can business process re-engineering reduce costs while maintaining or enhancing the required outputs?
4) Is technology able to reduce costs in the supply chain or store processes?
5) What steps can be taken to reduce the costs of crime?
6) Are advertising and promotional budgets cost-effective and clearly related to store strategy?

E ASSET TURNOVER

1) What are the costs and benefits of de-listing marginal brands?
2) Should stores, warehouses and other fixed assets be leased, not owned?
3) Do display techniques make maximum use of store facilities?
4) Would a reduction in slow-moving sizes or brands cut costs sufficiently to offset any volume loss?
5) Can efficient customer response (ECR) and just-in-time (JIT) delivery further reduce inventory and improve stock turnover?
6) Are accounts receivable being systematically monitored?

F LEVERAGE RATIO

1) What is the appropriate current ratio and debt-enquiry ratio for this type of retailing?
2) Does the times-interest-earned ratio indicate a problem if trading slowed down significantly in a recession?
3) Can supplier finance be used more effectively?
4) Should future expansion be financed by debt or equity?

Figure 6.1 Auditing financial structure

Sources: these include Doyle and Cook (1985); Walters and Laffy (1996).

slippage towards higher costs that do not result in higher performance. Larger organizations keep many of these questions under constant review, through advanced management information systems.

Since much of the attention within this book is upon the maximization of sales and margins, it is appropriate now to focus upon major costs and other issues that impact upon overall profitability. Most major retailers utilize benchmarking to compare their costs and productivity ratios with industry norms. Deloitte and Touche (1999) undertook a survey of retailers, large and small, to establish some valuable benchmark cost data. It is also common to apply internal benchmarking between stores or divisions: Asda consider this to be more important than external benchmarking (Competition Commission, 2000). The next section therefore addresses the main areas of cost that represent the difference between gross and net margins.

6.2.2 Components of Retail Cost

The cost of goods sold (COGS) represents the major cost for the vast majority of retailers. If we refer back to Table 6.3, showing gross margins, these indicate the significance of COGS as a percentage of sales. For example, gross margins of 22.8 per cent among UK food retailers indicate that, on average, COGS comprise 77.2 per cent of the selling price, compared with 56.3 per cent in the clothing sector.

This illustrates the critical importance to cost control of professional and powerful retail buying units. The largest multiples do not invariably enjoy the best terms on each individual item. Table 6.5 is based only upon the top five lines of 26 leading suppliers. However, it provides powerful evidence of the effects of buying power upon the cost of goods sold. Sainsbury was paying 1.6 per cent more than Tesco for these lines, Booth's around 9 per cent more. Table 6.5 also illustrates the competitive disadvantage of warehouse clubs and many wholesalers, in terms of buying power. The buying function and terms of trade are considered further in Chapter 8.

Table 6.5 Relative cost of goods

Notes: [1] Average of prices paid by 24 multiples (including 10 large co-operative societies) for the top five lines of 26 large suppliers.
[2] Comparisons in the lower section of the table should be regarded as indicative only.

Source: Competition Commission (2000).

Organization	Lines	% of average[1]	% of lines bought for less than average
Tesco	126	96.2	80
Sainsbury	125	97.7	74
Asda	127	97.8	66
Somerfield	130	98.4	65
Safeway	123	98.8	65
Morrison	122	99.8	46
Iceland	66	101.0	38
Budgens	85	103.6	24
Netto	24	104.2	21
Waitrose	103	104.4	23
Booths	74	104.7	26
Co-ops[2]	n/a	100.5	n/a
Voluntary chains	114	105.4	n/a
Warehouse clubs and wholesalers	114	108.7	n/a

Operating costs arise in every stage of the retailing and distribution process. For the leading grocery chains, these costs could be broken down into:

- store costs (75 per cent)
- distribution costs (13 per cent)
- overheads (12 per cent).

The largest single element of operating cost is staff cost, for the majority of retail companies. In the Deloitte and Touche (1999) benchmarking study, only the household goods stores placed rent ahead of staff, in the ranking of costs. Table 6.6 illustrates the great diversity of staff costs among retailers. At Body Shop, staff costs comprise around 20 per cent of sales, compared with less than 5 per cent at discount chain Netto.

International comparisons conducted by the European Retail Digest (1996) and Burt and Sparks (1997) revealed a similar spread of staff costs. These costs, more than most, focus retail minds upon the possible trade-offs between competitive pricing, margin enhancement and the provision of good service.

Table 6.6 Employee cost as percentage of sales

Source: derived from Business Ratio Plus (1998).

Company	Pay/sales %	Company	Pay/sales %
Boots	11.5	Marks & Spencer	8.8
Next	12.6	House of Fraser	12.9
River Island	15.2	Harrods	14.9
Etam	18.6	Dixons	9.7
Body Shop	20.6	Comet	11.5
DFS Furniture	7.0	Netto	4.4
IKEA	7.3	Asda	7.5
Argos	8.5	Tesco	8.8
B & Q	11.8	Sainsbury	9.6
Allied Carpets	13.0	Oddbins	9.7

Retailers are frequently urged to consider technological solutions to increasing labour productivity (e.g. Reardon et al., 1996). As discussed in connection with the 'wheel of retailing' theory, retailers have sometimes been induced to adopt technology that added, rather than subtracted, from costs. However, the widespread adoption of EPoS is an example of technology that has, in the long term, both reduced costs and enhanced service. Likewise, technologies that track customer flows and help in predicting demand for checkout staff also provide cost-effective, enhanced service (see Chapter 12).

It may be expected that larger stores would enjoy greater labour productivity, but such economies of scale have not proved easy to measure (e.g. Dawson and Kirby, 1977; Tucker, 1975). Part of the problem is that larger stores may offer better services, which mask underlying efficiencies in management and staff costs. Notwithstanding this, Shaw et al. (1989) did find evidence of slight economies of scale. The Competition Commission (2000) concluded that, for larger stores in excess of 3000 sq. metres, the economies of scale are modest and, for some companies, seem to disappear completely. Inevitably, the optimum store size varies according to the product lines sold (Santos-Requejo, 2001).

Marketing costs are generally within the range of between 1 and 2.5 per cent of sales for large-scale retailers, although some spend more than this (Deloitte and Touche, 1999). Expenditure on advertising has traditionally been the largest area of marketing costs, which is analysed further in Chapter 11. However, loyalty programmes accounted for around 40 per cent of marketing spending by the large food multiples included within the Deloitte and Touche (1999) benchmarking study. In no other sector did loyalty programmes account for more than 10 per cent, on average, of marketing spending.

Among the other areas of cost, much attention has been given to crime, which has cost UK retailers £1500 million in one year alone (Bamfield, 1996). In the same year, a further £525 million was spent by retailers on security. Customer thefts comprised 45 per cent of the crime losses, followed by staff thefts (30 per cent) and other forms of criminal activity. These costs represent over 1 per cent of overall turnover, or £90 per household per annum (Retail Review, 1996). In addition to surveillance systems, effort has therefore been expended on understanding the psyche of the shoplifter (e.g. Cox et al., 1993; Strutton et al., 1994) and on examining the retailer's legal remedies (e.g. Bamfield, 1996; Leaver, 1993). Observing that US retailers lose between 0.5 and 2 per cent of revenues to employee, customer, vendor and other forms of fraud, Caruana et al. (2001) suggest ways to avoid recruiting staff who are more likely to condone fraud.

Energy costs represent over 1.0 per cent of turnover for retailers in general (Moir, 1987): paradoxically, the percentages are generally higher for clothing retailers than for supermarkets. Although the latter incur the costs of frozen/chill storage, these costs tend to be spread over more turnover per square metre of space. Many innovations have been introduced to minimize energy costs, most of which are deployed at Sainsbury's experimental 'green' store at Greenwich. Among its many features, this store includes:

- one-third of a mile of north-facing windows to provide light, without excess heat
- wind turbines and solar panels
- gas-fired power station providing both heat, when needed, and power
- banks of earth surrounding the store for insulation against cold or heat
- recharging points for electric vehicles.

While most of these features increased building costs, the savings on energy and the PR benefits to the company's image made the Greenwich store a worthwhile venture. Bansal and Kilbourne (2001) point to a lack of attention to the natural environment within the retailing literature, depicting a model for the 'ecologically sustainable retailer' of the future.

As well as energy costs, maintenance costs also vary greatly by store type, lifts and escalators being particularly expensive in this respect. For Selfridges, maintenance costs are around 1.8 per cent of turnover, compared with 0.65 per cent at Next (Morgan Stanley Dean Witter, 1999). Superstores with parking above or below the store are considerably more expensive to construct and maintain, although this may sometimes be justified if land is scarce and expensive.

Land costs are considered to be high in the UK, at around $3000 to create each square metre of selling space. This compares with $1200 in France and $500 in the USA (Competition Commission, 2000). In general, it requires 8 square metres of land to produce 1 square metre of superstore selling space, the rest being needed for car parks, access roads and non-selling areas within the store. Guy (1995) estimated that Tesco could afford to pay over £20 million for a site, given its sales per square foot ratio and its ability to 'squeeze' more selling space out of a given size of building. However, he questioned whether these land costs were sustainable, as price competition increases and as retailers are obliged to consider more marginal sites.

Given the high costs of space, UK retailers in particular have a strong motivation to achieve rapid turnover of stock. Table 6.7 shows the average days of stock held by selected retailers, varying from 70.4 days at Comet to just 12.4 days at Netto. In a comparison of food retailers in the UK and France, Burt and Sparks (1997) found the averages to be 20.3 and 35.4 days stock, respectively. The *European Retail Digest* (1996) identified retailers in continental Europe which held over 100 days of stock. Companies that have been successful in reducing inventories have usually invested heavily in point-of-scale and supply chain technologies (Switzer, 1994).

Table 6.7 Days stock: selected retailers

Source: adapted from Business Ratio Plus (1998).

Company	Days stock	Company	Days stock
Boots	26.3	Comet	70.4
Etam	35.8	Netto	12.4
Next	48.9	Tesco	14.6
IKEA	19.7	Asda	15.3
B & Q	61.3	Sainsbury	19.0
Marks & Spencer	20.8	W.H. Smith	40.1
John Lewis	30.7	Toys 'R' Us	69.0

Faster stockturn improves space productivity, as well as reducing the risk of obsolescence or product deterioration. It also increases the probability that the stock will be sold before payment is required by the supplier, with obvious cash flow benefits for the retailer. The major UK grocery retailers take around 28 days to pay their suppliers (Competition Commission, 2000). This is broadly in line with German retailers but considerably faster than is the norm in many other European countries (Libre Service Actualités, 1991).

6.3 Item-Level Profit Measures

The emphasis so far has been upon the evaluation of costs and profitability across the whole store or organization. In retailing, however, there are many decisions that require measures of profitability at the individual item, or product category, level. Buyers must be able to appraise the profitability of their individual buying decisions; pricing decisions also require this type of input, as do decisions on own-brand products, promotions and shelf/display space allocation. Traditionally, markups or gross margins have been at the core of the merchandise management function, serving as one indicator of relative performance within the assortment.

6.3.1 Margins and Markups

Given that markups and gross margins are such fundamental measures, it is unfortunate that confusion sometimes surrounds the use of the terms. Within this book, 'markup' is used to describe the difference between the buying and the selling price, expressed as a percentage of the former. The 'percentage gross margin' is the same quantity but expressed as a percentage of the selling price. To provide a simple example:

Cost of item to retailer	£40
Price at which item was sold	£50
Markup	25 per cent
Gross margin	£10
Percentage gross margin	20 per cent

In sectors such as clothing retailing, where it is quite common to reduce the price of items not sold by the end of a season, a distinction will usually be made between the 'initial' markup and the 'maintained' markup. The former is the percentage that would have been achieved at the price initially set, whereas the latter is the percentage realised after the price reduction. For example:

Cost of garment to retailer	£23
Price initially set	£49
Initial markup	113 per cent
Price after reduction	£39
Maintained markup	70 per cent

The reader, however, will probably encounter other definitions. Occasionally the expressions 'percentage markup on retail price' and 'percentage markup on cost' are used to describe percentage gross margins and markups, respectively. Sometimes the term 'markup' is reserved for the expression of profit on individual items, whereas the term 'margin' is used to describe profits on whole ranges of items. These inconsistencies arise partly from different sector or national conventions, but they can obviously cause difficulties when comparing sources. In some proprietary analyses, the definitions appear to be deliberately obscured. Profits expressed as markups may be warmly received by senior management or shareholders; in dealing with manufacturers, government or consumer groups, it may be tactful to express profits as percentage gross margins!

Quite apart from the problems of definitions, there has been a tendency to place too much emphasis upon markups and gross margins in merchandise management. Sweeney (1973) noted that the rate of return on equity achieved by department stores had seriously declined, while over the same period percentage gross margins had increased. The adverse practices arising from overdependence upon these ratios were summarized by Knee and Walters (1985):

1 A lack of attention to market-based pricing.
2 An assumption that all items had similar costs.
3 A disregard of possible elasticities of demand.
4 No distinctions being made between fixed and variable costs.
5 General acceptance of net sales as an appropriate basis of expense allocation.
6 Overconfidence in final department net profit percentages after expense allocation.
7 Frequent tie-in of the gross margin percentage with buyer's compensation.
8 The focus of attention on ratios of sales, rather than on 'dollars', and the use of convenient percentages to support a weak position.

Clearly, what is needed is a better measure of the contribution of an item to the firm's profits, although this is easier to say than to accomplish. Two measures of item profitability that have been highly influential in recent years are 'gross margin return on inventory investment' (GMROI) and 'direct product profitability' (DPP). The former approach was adapted to the product category level by Sweeney (1973), although he emphasized that it should be used exclusively for planning and controlling merchandising inventory investment. Gross margin return on inventory investment (GMROI) is defined as follows:

$$\text{GMROI} = \frac{\text{Gross margin dollars}}{\text{Average inventory investment}}$$

The following particular advantages of this measure, as a criterion for merchandising, were claimed by Sweeney (1973):

1 GMROI is a meaningful measure of the performance of buyers or other merchandising executives, measuring how well the major asset under his or her control, i.e., merchandising inventories, is being used to generate gross profit dollars.
2 At department level, GMROI goals can be set that have a clear and consistent relationship with the retailer's overall ROI goals.
3 The merchandising executive can define appropriate combinations of target gross margins and sales-to-inventory ratios to produce the target GMROI for the category or department.
4 GMROI offers a composite measure for comparing key performance characteristics between product categories.

5 GMROI is easily calculated from data that are routinely available within most retail companies.

Naturally, such a simple measure cannot accommodate the full complexity of retail cost structures. Serpkenci and Lusch (1983) particularly noted the limitation that GMROI does not take into account the costs of financing consumer credit or the benefits that a supplier may provide in the form of favourable credit terms. These particular costs and benefits can differ very considerably between product lines. They observed that:

> *In a capital-scarce environment, GMROI has become misdirectional because it focuses the retail manager's attention only on a portion of the total operating cycle. Inventory turnover is considered but not the actual or real investment in merchandise.*

Gilman (1988) argued that GMROI does not adequately consider the real profitability per square foot of selling space achieved by individual items. Some of the actions taken to improve margins have also tended to conflict with those taken to stimulate sales. He noted: 'A question was raised as to whether or not gross margin return on investment really equates with profitability.' Sanghavi (1988) also advocated a shift of emphasis from measures of sales per square foot to measures of profit per square foot.

> *Retailers have realised that it is very easy to give stuff away. The name of the game now is not the big bucks but the bottom line. Profit per square foot has now become the tool to judge the performance of these product categories.*

6.3.2 Direct Product Profitability

A measure that sets out to apportion all relevant costs, notably those of space and labour, is direct product profitability.

> *Direct product profitability (DPP) is a detailed measure of an individual item's actual profit contribution. In simple terms, the calculations involve adjusting the gross margin of a product to reflect allowances, payment discounts or any other form of 'income', and then subtracting any costs directly attributable to that product as it passes through the retail system (Pinnock, 1986).*

The DPP of an item is therefore the gross margin, after adjustments, minus direct product costs (DPCs). These direct product costs arise at the warehouse, in transport, in the store and in head office functions. The largest single element of DPC is likely to be incurred in the store. Here a cost is allocated for the labour involved in receiving, sorting, moving, price-marking (if needed), shelf-loading and checking out the item. A space cost is allocated, being a function of the linear, square or cubic space occupied and the rate of stockturn of the item. In other words, within the merchandise accounting system, the item is, in effect, charged a rent for the space/time occupied. Table 6.8 shows the DPP and DPC calculations for typical items within the frozen, dry grocery and refrigerated food categories.

Table 6.8 DPP and DPC: typical items in category

Note: [1] Cost of capital tied up in stock.

Source: Pinnock (1986).

	Frozen	Dry grocery	Refrigerated
Direct product profitability			
Adjusted gross margin %	30.0	20.6	26.4
Direct product cost %	17.8	10.6	8.9
Direct product profit %	12.2	10.0	17.5
DPP per item $	0.139	0.103	0.159
Direct product costs			
(a) Warehouse			
Labour $	0.0136	0.0124	0.0077
Space $	0.0130	0.0068	0.0038
(b) Transport	0.0125	0.0092	0.0058
(c) Store			
Labour $	0.0602	0.0437	0.0405
Space $	0.0914	0.0281	0.0186
(d) Head Office			
Warehouse $[1]	0.0043	0.0040	0.0024
Store $[1]	0.0041	0.0039	0.0014
Invoicing $	0.0005	0.0004	0.0005
Total DPC $	0.1996	0.1085	0.0807

Direct product profitability owes its early origins to the McKinsey Company in the USA (Retail and Distribution Management, 1987). However, before the advent of sophisticated retail information systems and PC-based DPP models, the measurements and calculations were too onerous to encourage widespread adoption. Furthermore, it was not until the 1990s that a unified European model of DPP was available and incorporated within space management software packages, such as Spaceman III by Logistics Data Systems International (Nelson and Pinnock, 1991). While DPP remains a somewhat data-demanding technique (Borin and Farris, 1990), it is a very powerful tool for the analysis of item profitability:

1 DPP attempts to consider all the revenue earned by the item.
2 It considers the cost of handling the item.
3 It can give some very different answers from those obtained using gross margin (Harris, 1987).

Table 6.9 provides examples of these very different results, for 12 product categories. Noticeably, bottled water and dried fruit achieve very similar levels of percentage gross margin, at just over 30 per cent. However, the dried fruit requires less labour and less space, so its percentage DPP is almost double that of bottled water. Three categories can be seen to be producing direct product losses, due to low gross margins and/or high labour costs. Had these items been peripheral to the retailer's product offering, they would be candidates for deletion: this is clearly not the case with these three products. The analysis may however suggest ways of reducing their DPCs, while retaining them within the assortment.

Table 6.9 Gross margins and DPP

Source: derived from Progressive Grocer (1992).

Product	% Gross margin	% DPP	$DPP per unit
Baby food	13.72	−10.30	−0.08
Bottled water	30.75	12.24	0.14
Flour	4.93	−11.08	−0.11
Dried fruit	30.45	23.35	0.38
Canned milk	13.63	3.68	0.03
Snacks	28.39	20.94	0.38
Paper goods	18.25	4.66	0.06
Soaps/detergents	18.25	11.68	0.31
Bakery	44.46	−27.25	−0.14
Prime meat	34.18	29.01	1.01
Fresh fruit	36.34	12.08	0.09
Frozen fruit	35.07	28.46	0.41

A study by Touche Ross (1990) found that 80 per cent of its retailer sample had used DPP in their decision-making, yet only 30 per cent of manufacturers had done so. Given the potential persuasive power of DPP analysis, it would be argued that DPP may be most beneficial to manufacturers (Bultez and Parsons, 1998), provided they offer products with high DPP. As with any profitability measure, it is of course important to recognize the limitations of DPP.

1 It is based around average costs, whereas marginal costs may be more relevant, if some retailing costs are fixed, at least in the medium term (Gardiner, 1993).
2 It does not deal with cross-elasticities, specifically, the impact of price adjustments or deletion upon the sales of other items in the category (Bultez and Parson, 1998).
3 It may encourage a perspective that is more product than customer oriented in its application (Davies and Rands, 1992).
4 It is still a relatively complex and expensive measure to apply (Borin and Farris, 1990).

Most of these criticisms imply excessive expectations of DPP, resulting in part from the 'hype' of some early advocates. It remains a useful tool but, in common with other profit measures, it is not a substitute for management judgement. Walters and Hanrahan (2000) report the successful use of DPP by Boots to evaluate its pet food offer. This was found to be unprofitable and, being peripheral to the company's core assortment, was not developed. Likewise, Woolworths found the 'Grobag' garden product to have high DPC at almost every stage in the process, being a bulky, low-price product.

Some retailers have shifted more towards the use of target costing models, although these can incorporate elements of the DPC calculations. The difference is as much in the orientation as in the calculation. Within the target costing approach, the selling prices are determined by the market and the retailer then determines the profit requirement. From this, the target buying prices are established, as well as the fixed and variable costs of selling the product/category. Another difference is that the analysis of direct costs may extend beyond those of the retailer, to include supplier costs and, in companies such as IKEA, the costs of customer relationships (Walters and Hanrahan, 2000). Target costing models have not, however, escaped criticism, notably that the existing required margin might become fixed in the minds of managers, rather than being a variable involved in assembling the optimal retail offer.

The concepts of DPP/DPC, while not always applied in their entirety, have encouraged retailers to look far more closely at costs involved in specific retail practices. Activity-based costing (ABC) studies at the product or category level tend to be very similar in approach to DPP analysis (e.g. Purpura, 1997). However, ABC can also be applied to a specific practice, such as home deliveries or night-time shelf-loading (Brown, 1997). It can also be applied to the costs of retailing to specific customers or segments, leading to a measure of 'direct customer profitability'. In any such analysis, the availability and cost of information remain an issue.

To recall a relevant adage:

> *'sometimes it is better to have approximate answers to the right questions than exact answers to the wrong questions'.*

SUMMARY

Few elements of retail strategy can be pursued without cost, so it is important to monitor the financial implications of strategic actions. The objective of cost minimization must be carefully balanced with the requirements of the company's intended positioning. This requires considerable clarity in understanding concepts of productivity, efficiency and effectiveness in retail organizations.

The evaluation of productivity has been fraught with problems, notably with defining the true 'output' of retail organizations. Relatively simple measures exist to assess the productivity of a specific 'input', for example sales per square metre of space, or sales per full-time (equivalent) employee. These provide useful benchmark figures for comparing retail companies or individual stores, provided that issues of comparability are properly accounted for. However, they are not measures of effectiveness in achieving the overall strategic goals of the retail organization.

Every retail company must have proper regard for its continued solvency. In the case of publicly owned companies, it must also consider its duties to shareholders and potential vulnerability to hostile takeover. Most of the standard accountancy measures can be applied to evaluate the financial health of a retail company, such as profitability, liquidity, leverage and activity ratios.

Profitability measures range from the relatively crude gross margin analyses to ratios of particular interest to shareholders and investors, such as return on equity and earnings per share. Liquidity ratios indicate the company's ability to meet its liabilities, notably the claims of creditors. Leverage ratios indicate the funding structure of the organization, whereas activity ratios reflect upon the management of the asset base.

In order to ensure continued survival and profitability, retailers must remain constantly vigilant in the areas of cost control. The concept of business process re-engineering has been applied to help eliminate costs that are not relevant to the production of the required retail 'outputs', for example, quality, choice, service and good value. Retailers need to audit each element of their financial structures, typically benchmarking their activities against external rivals or internal best practice.

For the vast majority of retailers, the cost of goods comprise the biggest single element of retail cost, emphasizing the key role of retail buyers in cost control. Among the operating expenses, labour usually represents between 7 per cent and 20 per cent of turnover. The costs of store space vary greatly, due mainly to differences in land costs, but construction, maintenance and energy costs also vary, according to the nature of the store. Space can be best utilized if high rates of stockturn are achieved; major UK retailers have generally been successful in this respect. At around 1 per cent of turnover, crime has now also become a significant area of retail cost.

Many types of retail marketing decision require the evaluation of profitability at the department, product category or individual item level. The simple measures of gross margin or markup provide a starting point, but only a limited period perspective on true profitability. The measure of gross margin return on inventory (GMROI) is a composite ratio, but fails to take into account many aspects of cost. Direct product profitability (DPP) offers a difficult but more thorough measure of the profitability of retailing specific items or categories. The concept of activity-based costing (ABC) can also be extended to help evaluate the profitability of retail practices, or even customer relationships.

REVIEW QUESTIONS

1 Distinguish between the terms 'productivity', 'efficiency' and 'effectiveness'. Give examples of measures of each that are relevant to the evaluation of retail performance.

2 Give two examples of each of the following, indicating how each ratio is calculated:

   a) profitability ratios

   b) liquidity ratios

   c) leverage ratios

   d) activity ratios.

What does each of these ratios tell retail management about the financial state of the company?

3 Distinguish between business process re-engineering and straightforward cost-cutting programmes. Illustrate how business process re-engineering might improve the effectiveness of:

a) the movement of goods from delivery vehicles to display fixtures

b) the checkout operation in a superstore.

4 Both internal and external benchmarking are used by retailers to evaluate their costs and productivity. What issues must be taken into account to ensure that the benchmarking is a valid exercise?

5 What are the main elements of cost within retail operations? With reference to a specific retailer, suggest the best options for cost reduction that may be available, without prejudicing the positioning of that company.

6 As larger stores are developed, it would be expected that economies of scale could be achieved, especially with regard to labour costs. Explain why economies of scale may be anticipated, yet do not always appear using measures of 'labour productivity'.

7 Why have many of the major retailers in the UK achieved favourable rates of stock turn, compared to international benchmarks? What are the benefits that arise from improving stock turn?

8 How does a retailer calculate GMROI? Discuss the scope, strengths and limitations of this measure.

9 How can DPP be applied to assist retail marketing decisions? What are the main difficulties in using DPP and how can these be overcome?

10 Activity-based costing (ABC) can be applied to many areas of retail activity. What elements would you include if applying ABC to:

a) an improved store security system

b) a customer loyalty programme.

REFERENCES

Achabal, D.D., J.M. Heineke and S.H. McIntyre (1984) 'Issues and perspectives on retail productivity', *Journal of Retailing*, **60** (3), 107–127.

Bamfield, J. (1996) *Retail Civil Recovery: Can Thieves Compensate Shopkeepers?* Nene College, Northampton.

Bansal, P. and W.E. Kilbourne (2001) 'The ecologically sustainable retailer', *Journal of Retailing and Consumer Services*, **8**, 139–146.

Bates, A.D. (1990) 'Pricing for profit', *Arthur Anderson Retail Issues Letters*, **2** (8), Center for Retailing Strategies, Texas A&M University.

Borin, N. and P. Farris (1990) 'An empirical comparison of direct product profit and existing measures of SKU productivity', *Journal of Retailing*, **66** (3), 297–314.

Brown, D. (1997) 'True cost: activity-based costing can expose costs and streamline the whole grocery value chain', *Progressive Grocer*, **76** (7), 17.

Bucklin, L.P. (1981) 'Growth and productivity change in retailing', in *Theory in Retailing: Traditional and Nontraditional Sources*, R.W. Stampfl and E.C. Hirschman (eds), AMA, Chicago.

Bultez, A. and L. Parsons (1998) 'Channel productivity: in the small and in the large', *International Journal of Research in Marketing*, **15**, 383–400.

Burt, S. and L. Sparks (1997) 'Performance in food retailing; a cross-national consideration and comparison of retail margins', *British Journal of Management*, **8** (2), 133–150.

Business Ratio Plus (1998) *The Retail Industry*, ICC Business Publications, London.

Caruana, A., B. Ramaseshan and M.T. Ewing (2001) 'Anomia and fraudulent behavior by retail customers: a study among employees', *Journal of Retailing and Consumer Services*, **8** (4), 181–187.

Competition Commission (2000) *Supermarkets: a Report on the Supply of Groceries from Multiple Stores in the United Kingdom*, HMSO, London.

Cotter, J. and R.W. Hutchinson (1999) 'The impact of accounting reporting techniques on earnings enhancement in the UK retailing sector', *International Review of Retail, Distribution and Consumer Research*, **9** (2), 147–162.

Cowton, C.J. and G. Pilz (1995) 'The investment appraisal procedures of UK retailers', *International Review of Retail, Distribution and Consumer Research*, **5** (4), 457–471.

Cox, A.D., D. Cox, R.D. Anderson and G.P. Moschis (1993) 'Social influences on adolescent shoplifting—theory, evidence, and implications for the retail industry', *Journal of Retailing*, **69** (2), 234–246.

Cox, R. (1948) 'The meaning and measurement of productivity in distribution', *Journal of Marketing*, **12** (2), 433–441.

Cronin, J.J. and S.J. Skinner (1984) 'Marketing outcomes, financial conditions and retail profit performance', *Journal of Retailing*, **60** (4), 9–22.

Davies, G. and T. Rands (1992) 'The strategic use of space by retailers: a perspective from operations management', *International Journal of Logistics Management*, **3** (2), 63–76.

Dawson, J.A. and D.A. Kirby (1977) 'Shop size and productivity in British retailing in the 1960s', *European Journal of Marketing*, **11** (4), 262–271.

Deloitte and Touche (1999) *Retail Benchmarking Survey*, Deloitte and Touche, London.

Doyle, P. and D. Cook (1985), 'Marketing strategies, financial structure and innovation in UK retailing', in *Insights into Strategic Retail Management*, J. Gattorna (ed.), MCB University Press, Bradford, 99. 75–88.

Egan, C. and C. Guilding (1994) 'Dimensions of brand performance: challenges for marketing management and managerial accountancy', *Journal of Marketing Management*, **10**, 449–472.

European Retail Digest (1996) 'European retail performance indicators', *European Retail Digest*, Spring, 65–71.

Gadrey, J. and F. Jany-Catrice (2000) 'The retail sector: why so many jobs in America and so few in France?', *The Service Industries Journal*, **20** (4), 21–32.

Gardiner, S.C. (1993) 'Measures of product attractiveness and the theory of constraints', *International Journal of Retail and Distribution Management*, **21** (7), 37–40.

Gilman, A.L. (1988) 'The benefits of looking below gross margin', *Retailing Issues Newsletter*, **1** (6), 1–4.

Gold, P. and L.H. Woodliffe (2000) 'Department stores in Spain: why El Corte Inglés succeeded where Galeriás Preciados failed', *International Journal of Retail & Distribution Management*, **28** (8), 333–340.

Goldman, A. (1992) 'Evaluating the performance of the Japanese distribution system', *Journal of Retailing*, **68** (1), 11–39.

Good, W.S. (1984) 'Productivity in the retail grocery trade', *Journal of Retailing*, **60** (3), 81–97.

Goodman, C.S. (1985) 'On output measures of retail performance', *Journal of Retailing*, **61** (3), 77–82.

Guy, C. (1995) 'Retail store development at the margin', *Journal of Retailing and Consumer Services*, **2** (1), 25–32.

Hall, M., J. Knapp and C. Winsten (1961) *Distribution in Great Britain and North America: A Study in Structure and Productivity*, Oxford University Press, Oxford.

Hamel, G. and C.K. Prahalad (1994) *Competing for the Future*, Harvard Business School Press, Boston, MA.

Hammer, M. and J. Champy (1993) *Re-engineering the Corporation*, Nicholas Brealey, London.

Harris, D. (1987) 'DPP takes off with new technology', *Retail & Distribution Management*, **15** (2).

Hutchinson, R.W, and R.L. Hunter (1995) 'Determinants of capital structure in the retailing sector in the UK', *International Review of Retail, Distribution and Consumer Research*, **5** (1), 63–78.

IGD (2000) *Non-Food Retailing 2000*, Institute of Grocery Distribution, Watford.

Kamakuwa, W.A., T. Lenartowicz and B.T. Ratchford (1996) 'Productivity assessment of multiple retail outlets', *Journal of Retailing*, **72** (4), 333–356.

Kaplan, R.S. and D.P. Norton (1996) 'Using the balanced scorecard as a strategic management system', *Harvard Business Review*, **74** (1), 75–85.

Keh, H.T. (1997) 'The classification of distribution channel output: a review', *International Review of Retail, Distribution and Consumer Research*, **7** (2), 145–156.

Knee, D. and D. Walters (1985) *Strategy in Retailing: Theory and Application*, Philip Allen, Oxford.

Knox, S. and S. Maklan (1998) *Competing on Value*, FT/Pitman, London.

Kuwahara, H. (1997) 'Concentration and productivity in the retail trade in Japan', *International Review of Retail Distribution and Consumer Research*, 7 (2), 109–124.

Leaver, D. (1993) 'Legal and social changes affecting UK retailers' response to consumer theft', *International Journal of Retail and Distribution Management*, 21 (8), 29–33.

Libre Service Actualités (1991) 'La situation chez les douze', *Libre Service Actualités*, **1263**, 98–99.

McCaffery, K., R. Hutchinson and R. Jackson (1997) 'Aspects of the finance function: a review and survey into the UK retailing sector', *International Review of Retail, Distribution and Consumer Research*, 7 (2), 125–144.

McGurr, P.T, and S.A. DeVaney (1998) 'Predicting business failure of retail firms: an analysis using mixed industry models', *Journal of Business Research*, **43**, 169–176.

Micklethwait, J. and A. Woolridge (1996) *The Witch Doctors*, Heinemann, London.

Moir, C.B. (1987) 'Research difficulties in the analysis of Sunday trading', *International Journal of Retailing*, 2 (1), 3–21.

Morgan Stanley Dean Witter (1999) *Pan-European Retailers: The Value Drivers*, MSDW, London.

Nelson, D. and A. Pinnock (1991) 'DPP: towards an efficient use of resources', *International Journal of Retail and Distribution Management*, 19 (5), 7–9.

Nooteboom, B. (1986) 'Costs, margins and competition: causes of structural change', in *Retail Strategies for Profit and Growth, ESOMAR (eds)*, ESOMAR, Amsterdam, pp. 186–198.

O'Riordan, D. (1993) 'Retail gross margins: some international comparisons', *International Journal of Retail and Distribution Management*, 21 (4), 33–39.

Pariente, S. (1994) 'Comparative profitability of large French and British retailers', *International Review of Retail, Distribution and Consumer Research*, 4 (2), 239–256.

Pinnock, A.K. (1986) *Direct Product Profitability: an Introduction for the Grocery Trade*, Institute of Grocery Distribution, Watford.

Progressive Grocer (1992) 'The Marsh super study', *Progressive Grocer*, 71 (12), 28–31.

Purpura, L. (1997) 'H.E. Butt is expanding curriculum for its ABC studies', *Supermarket News*, 1 September, 65–66.

Reardon, J. and I. Vida (1998) 'Measuring retail productivity: monetary vs. physical input measures', *International Review of Retail, Distribution and Consumer Research*, 8 (4), 399–413.

Reardon, J., R. Hasty and B. Coe (1996) 'The effect of information technology on productivity in retailing', *Journal of Retailing*, 72 (4), 445–461.

Retail and Distribution Management (1987) 'Curtain up for DPP', *Retail and Distribution Management*, 15 (2), 6–7.

Retail Review (1996) 'Progress in fight against crime—at a cost', *Retail Review*, February, 1–2.

Sanghavi, N. (1988) 'Space management in shops: a new initiative', *Retail and Distribution Management*, 16 (1), 14–18.

Santos-Requejo, L. (2001) 'A new approach to gross margin analysis for the Spanish retail sector', *International Review of Retail, Distribution and Consumer Research*, 11 (1), 39–47.

Serpkenci, R.R. and R.F. Lusch (1983) 'New model offers retailers a realistic estimate of gross margin return from merchandise lines', *Marketing News*, 18 February, 6.

Shaw, S.A., D.J. Nisbet and J.A. Dawson (1989) 'Economies of scale in UK retailing: some preliminary findings', *International Journal of Retailing*, 4 (5), 12–26.

Stern, L.W., A.I. El-Ansary and A.T. Coughlan (1996) *Marketing Channels*, Prentice-Hall, Englewood Cliffs, NJ.

Strutton, D., S.J. Vitell and L.E. Pelton (1994) 'How consumers may justify inappropriate behaviour in market settings: an application of the techniques of neutralization', *Journal of Business Research*, 30, 253–260.

Sweeney, D.J. (1973) 'Improving the profitability of retail merchandising decision', *Journal of Marketing*, 37 (1), 60–68.

Switzer, G.J. (1994) 'A modern approach to retail accounting', *Management Accounting*, 75 (8), 55–58.

The Times (1999) 'The disappearing hidden assets', *The Times*, 4 December, 31.

Thomas, R., M. Gable and R. Dickinson (1999) 'An application of the balanced scorecard in retailing', *International Review of Retail, Distribution and Consumer Research*, 9 (1), 41–67.

Thomas, R.R., R.S. Barr, W.L. Cron and J.W. Slocum (1998) 'A process for evaluating retail store efficiency: a restricted DEA approach', *International Journal of Research in Marketing*, 15, 487–503.

Thompson, A.A. and A.J. Strickland (1987) *Strategic Management: Concept and Cases*, Richard D. Irwin, Homewood, IL.

Touche Ross (1990) *Direct Product Profitability*, Touche Ross, London.

Treadgold, A. (1991) *The City View of Retailing*, Longman, Harrow.

Tucker, K.A. (1975) *Economies of Scale in Retailing*, Saxon House, Farnborough, Hants.

Walters, D. and J. Hanrahan (2000) *Retail Strategy: Planning and Control*, Macmillan, Basingstoke.

Walters, D. and D. Laffy (1996) *Managing Retail Productivity and Profitability*, Macmillan Business, Basingstoke.

Weinstein, S. (1993) 'The legacy of leverage', *Progressive Grocer*, 72 (6), 70–76.

Zimmerman, R.M., R.M. Kaufman, G.S. Finerty and J.O. Egan (1990) *Retail Accounting and Financial Control*, Wiley, New York.

PART TWO
THE RETAIL MARKETING MIX

CHAPTER

Seven

Retail Location

INTRODUCTION   Store location decisions are frequently considered to be the single most important elements of retail marketing. Although a good location is unlikely in itself to compensate for mediocre overall strategy, a poor location can be a deficit that is very difficult to overcome. Even very small physical differences between locations can exert a major influence upon the stores' accessibility and attractiveness to customers. As George Davies reflected:

> *you can be the best retailer in the world, but if you set up your shop in the wrong place, you'll never do much business. If you operate from the wrong properties, you start with your hands tied behind your back (Clarke and Rowley, 1995).*

The adage, that the three most important things in retailing are 'location, location and location', may be old but it is still frequently reiterated.

The implementation timescale also distinguishes location from other decision areas in retail marketing. Changes in merchandising or pricing, for example, can be administered almost immediately (although customer perceptions will of course change more slowly); the opening of a new store, on the other hand, is preceded by a planning and development process that can take years. The location decision represents a long-term investment and a very major investment, in the case of large, purpose-built outlets.

Rising property and land costs, coupled with competitive pressures to develop new store formats, have ensured that location decisions are also a major part of retailers' financial strategies. Estimates of Debenham's fixed asset values in 2004 place them at £1658 million (Cockrell et al., 1999). In the grocery sector, each square foot of superstore space is estimated to cost £500, assuming a 40 000 square foot store costs £20 million in the UK (Fowler et al., 1999). Such organizations are therefore not just in the retailing business, but are deeply involved in the property business too. Each store location decision is therefore a long-term financial commitment that will become either an asset or a liability.

This said, retailers should not throw refurbishment resources at locations that are manifestly unsuitable for current strategies, assuming that locations are 'too expensive to change'. Lusch (1992) points out that mutual fund managers quickly liquidate poor performing stocks and reinvest in ones with more potential: maybe retailers should view locations in a similar way. However, where good sites are scarce and expensive, the switching costs can be considerable.

In keeping with its importance within the strategic mix, the subject of store location has developed an extensive literature. The topic has been addressed from several perspectives, being of direct interest to researchers in geography, marketing, town planning, operations research and economics. It will not be possible within this chapter to do justice to each of these perspectives, or to explore fully all the related theoretical approaches. Specialist texts (e.g. Brown, 1992a; Davies and Rogers 1984; Guy, 1994; Jones and Simmons, 1990; Wrigley, 1988) are available to facilitate the exploration of specific topics in greater depth.

The first section of the chapter presents the techniques that may be used in identifying areas for geographical expansion and in evaluating specific sites. The section starts with a brief review of location practices, then presents a checklist of factors to be considered. While these checklists raise many relevant questions, some of the data to help answer these are provided by geographic information systems (GIS); some examples are presented. The use of analogues in site assessment is discussed as a precursor to multiple regression and other statistical forecasting techniques. Other models relevant to retail location are also considered, including central place, rent models and spatial interaction (gravity) models.

Up to this point, the influence of town planning is virtually ignored, although this represents a major constraint upon retail locations in most countries. The second section of the chapter therefore examines the planning framework and the procedures for obtaining planning permission. The key issues are discussed, notably those relating to land use, the environment, traffic, consumer welfare and impact on other traders.

7.1 Store Location Techniques and Models

This section will first examine the techniques most frequently used by retailers to help identify and evaluate potential new sites. Most of these techniques would serve equally well for the assessment of existing store performance, providing more objective performance yardsticks than those commonly used. The techniques are therefore used to guide decisions on:

- new store locations
- floor-space extensions
- chain rationalisation
- store repositioning
- localization of assortment, prices, etc.
- performance assessment.

Major distinctions are therefore not drawn here between techniques for store location and techniques for store assessment. Some of the more sophisticated modelling techniques are then discussed, representing the direction in which store location analysis is now moving.

7.1.1 Location Techniques in Practice

A number of researchers have suggested sequences that retail location decisions should follow, starting with the most general assessments of geographical areas, through to the detailed evaluation of specific site characteristics. Davies (1976) points out, however, that the need for quick decisions often prevents such systematic ordering of the location strategy process, a conclusion reaffirmed by Bennison et al. (1995). In general, retailers with a well-defined, medium- to long-term location strategy are more likely to be in a position to follow a logical decision sequence than retailers whose location decisions are mostly reactions to specific opportunities or threats. Bowlby et al. (1984) offer a sequence which could be considered part of an 'ideal' retail location strategy:

1 *Search*: the identification of geographical areas that may have potential for new outlet(s)
2 *Viability*: finding the best site(s) available within the given areas and forecasting the store turnover that may be derived from these
3 *Micro*: examination of all the detailed features of a specific site that are relevant to potential store performance

Figure 7.1 depicts the different geographical levels of retail location decisions. At the first level, the retailer has identified an urban area with potential, best represented in its south-eastern sector (level 2). Finally, specific sites are evaluated at the 'micro-scale' of analysis (Brown, 1992a).

The characteristics of each level in this decision hierachy clearly vary according to the nature of the retail company, in particular the level of product specialization and the importance of convenience in the strategic mix. It is therefore more difficult to classify rigidly the techniques that are appropriate to each stage of the decision. Many of

Figure 7.1 Homing in on retail sites

Source: Brown (1992, p. 17).

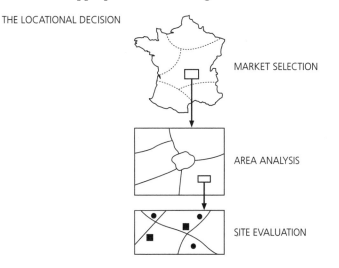

THE LOCATIONAL DECISION

MARKET SELECTION

AREA ANALYSIS

SITE EVALUATION

the techniques outlined in the following sections may assist at more than one stage of the location decision sequence.

Simkin et al. (1985) concluded that many of the more sophisticated techniques to be found with the literature are not used by retailers in general. It was also observed that the more financially successful retailers, do not necessarily undertake location research more thoroughly or to a higher quality. Bennison et al. (1995) note that those likely to use the most systematic location procedures are the major grocers, DIY retailers, some department and variety stores, larger financial services retailers and public house chains.

From a study of five retail organizations, Clarkson et al. (1996) found that all used checklists, at the initial screening stage, but that regression and other mathematical models are not universally applied. It is clear that checklists, comprising factors to be assessed, and analogues, based upon stores with comparable characteristics, are still the cornerstones of most retailers' locations research. Indeed, even as more sophisticated techniques gain wider utilization, they tend to complement rather than replace the use of checklists and analogues. Checklists also tend to be relatively cheap to administer and, while requiring experience, they do not need high levels of technical expertise (Beaumont, 1987).

Table 7.1 Store location techniques used

Note: in the sector comparison, High indicates use by over 50 per cent, Low indicates use by 25 per cent or less respondents in category.

Source: adapted from: Hernandes and Bennison (2000).

A major survey of location technique utilization was undertaken by Hernandez and Bennison (2000), involving nearly 100 retailers operating 55 000 outlets. Table 7.1 summarizes some of its findings, confirming the continued popularity of 'gut feel' and checklists, while also pointing to growth in the use of more sophisticated techniques. Over half of these retailers also use GIS, which can contribute data and/or visualization facilities when using any of the techniques listed in Table 7.1.

Technique	Cost factor	Retailers % use	Extent of use in sectors:			
			Variety/ department	Grocery	Home improvement	Fashion and accessories
Experience	Low	96	High	High	High	High
Checklists	Low	55	Med	High	Low	High
Analogues	Medium	39	High	High	Low	Med
Regression	Medium	40	High	High	Low	Med
Gravity models	High	39	High	High	Med	Low
Neural networks	High	16	Med	Low	Med	Low

The importance of managers' experience is also noticeable: location is indeed a retail function requiring extensive knowledge and expertise. Clarke et al. (2000) utilized cognitive mapping to analyse and structure the knowledge held by retail location decision makers. During in-depth interviews, 'laddering' was used to encourage managers to elaborate how each issue mentioned is influenced by other issues within the location decision. In this way, both individual and organizational cognitive maps could be produced, as a way of sharing experience and making assumptions more explicit.

7.1.2 Location Evaluation Checklists

Most major retailers have developed detailed checklists of the factors to be considered when evaluating potential new trading areas and sites. Some elements of these checklists will be common to all retail types, but each retailer's list is likely to contain elements reflecting that company's particular trading style. It is obvious that a petrol retailer will have a very different checklist from that of a fashion retailer. It comes as more of a surprise to learn the extent of differences in the checklists of more comparable retailers, reflecting important differences in their positioning strategies and trading strengths. The importance of integrating location decisions within the overall strategy of retail organizations was emphasized by Clarke et al. (1997). Figure 7.2 illustrates some of the linkages between strategic positioning, typical locations and major information requirements.

The checklist technique was developed over 40 years ago. Nelson (1958) presented one of the most detailed checklist evaluation formats, comprising eight major categories and 36 specific areas of evaluation. That checklist placed much emphasis upon changes in population and land use, reflecting a time of rapid building and growth. Rather more emphasis now tends to be placed upon the detailed characteristics of the population within the projected trading areas. A checklist primarily helps to avoid the danger of overlooking aspects of relevance to potential trading performance. You need only study a nearby shopping area to find

Figure 7.2 Locational positioning

Source: Davies and Clarke (1994, p. 7).

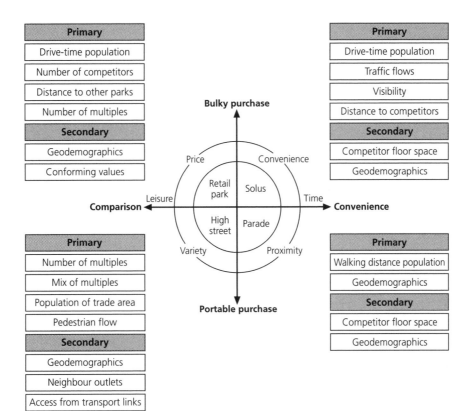

many outcomes of location decisions that appear to have ignored important checklist factors. This may or may not in fact be true. Retailers and developers are limited in their choice of site, and few locations are so good as to score highly on all elements of a checklist. If nothing else, at least a checklist may have served to highlight the deficits in order that these could be weighed in the decision, rather than ignored.

A checklist is only the starting point of an evaluation process; it essentially provides the questions, not the answers. Many of the techniques described in subsequent sections in fact build upon the checklist by providing detailed answers or estimates of specific elements. The checklist can also provide the framework of a strategic planning database, developed on a long-term rolling basis.

In that a checklist forms the starting point of most store location evaluations, it may be helpful at this stage to note the factors that could be examined under each major heading. Table 7.2 presents a very generalized checklist of the types of information that may be sought in order to estimate likely trading areas, forecast turnover and calculate the likely profitability of the proposed store. The issues relevant to obtaining planning permission, where this is required, are considered in Sec. 7.2.

Table 7.2 Location checklist factors

Population	Accessibility	Competition	Costs
Population size	Pedestrian flow	Existing retail activity	Purchase price
Age profile	Pedestrian entry routes	Direct competitors	Leasing terms
Household size	Public transport	Indirect competitors	Site preparation
Income levels	Types	Anchor stores	Building restrictions
Disposable income	Cost	Cumulative attraction	Development concessions
per capita	Ease of use	Compatibility	Rates payable
Occupation classifications	Potential	Existing retail specification	Refurbishment needs
Main employers	Car-ownership levels	Selling areas	Maintenance costs
Economic stability	Road network	Turnover estimates	Security needs
Unemployment levels	Conditions	Department/product	Staff availability/rates
Seasonal fluctuations	Driving speeds	analysis	Delivery costs
Housing density	Congestion	Trade areas	Promotional media/costs
Housing age/type	Restrictions	Age of outlets	Turnover loss/other
Neighbourhood	Plans	Standard of design	branches
classification	Parking	Car parking	
Home-ownership levels	Capacity	Saturation index	
Building/demolition plans	Convenience	Competitive potential	
Life-style measures	Cost	Outlet expansion	
Cultural/ethnic groupings	Potential	Refurbishment	
Current shopping patterns	Visibility	Vacant sites	
	Access for staff	Interception	
	Access for transport	Repositioning	
	and deliveries	Competitor policy	

Population

Fundamental to any evaluation is a detailed review of the population characteristics within the relevant zones. Not only is population the major determinant of store viability, it also suggests the store size best suited to the specific location (Lord and Lundregan, 1999). Many of the key statistics relating to population size, age profiles, household composition and occupations can be obtained through the decennial censuses. However, this information eventually becomes outdated and the statistics for small areas may prove awkward to aggregate for the area under investigation. Local authorities may be able to provide more current information but the GIS providers, such as Experian and CACI (see Sec. 7.1.4), are now the major providers of these data.

Several factors combine to indicate the present and potential spending power within an area. Income levels are a poor indication, unless linked to information about family and mortgage/housing commitments. Measures of disposable income and current spending propensities, if available, are therefore preferable. Local unemployment levels are now a key statistic, as broad regional data can disguise very major differences within smaller areas. The employment structure and stability of an area should be assessed. If for example a major car production plant closes, the effect on the local economy can be drastic; previously viable retail sites may lose most of their value.

The location analyst should also seek information on the existing housing density, age and type. Levels of house ownership may also be important, for example, in the evaluation of a DIY superstore site. Housing and neighbourhood types are increasingly used as segmentation bases, but other bases may also be utilized, such as lifestyle measures and cultural, religious and ethnic groupings. If such information about the population can be obtained, a more thorough assessment of viability can be undertaken. If the site is selected, the information can then provide an input to the store and merchandise planning process.

Accessibility

In spite of pressures to increase use of public transport (Ibrahim and McGoldrick, 2002), accessibility is still sometimes seen as synonymous with driving times and parking provision. These are indeed key variables in most retail location decisions, but a detailed assessment requires consideration of many other factors that may facilitate, or deter, journeys to and from the store. Care must also be taken to give appropriate weightings to the factors most salient to the particular type of outlet proposed. A free-standing superstore may represent the primary purpose of most customers' journeys; many smaller stores, however are part of a multipurpose journey, by car, on foot or by public transport. Very different criteria of accessibility are therefore implied (Hass-Klau et al., 1999; Kurose and Hagishimsa, 1995).

Within existing centres, the number of pedestrians moving past the proposed site is an essential measure. Even the most successful shopping centres have relative 'low spots', in spite of attempts by centre management to encourage circulation in all sections and levels. For example, the Meadowhall Centre designers managed to overcome the typical imbalance between ground-floor and upper-level pedestrian traffic flows. This was achieved by siting some of the major entrances, including the one from the train/tram/bus stations, at the upper level.

Many traditional centres are dependent upon public transport for a fairly high proportion of their customer traffic. Under such circumstances, the types currently and potentially available, and their costs, should be part of the site evaluation. Environmental considerations are leading many governments to promote the development and use of a wider range of public transport options. The Metro trams in cities such as Sheffield and Manchester are examples of heavily subsidized systems, designed to reduce the difficulty of using public transport for a range of travel purposes.

The same environmental concerns are leading to a range of measures to deter car usage, including bus priority lanes, high parking costs and possibly road use charging. In spite of these measures, most retailers must still pay the closest attention to their accessibility to car-borne shoppers. The overall level of car ownership continues to grow but local measures of ownership help to judge the likely balance of car/public transport/pedestrian shoppers. No two retail locations are quite alike in terms of the surrounding road conditions, so the most detailed study of these is warranted.

The problems that can be caused by traffic congestion, difficult manoeuvres, traffic signals (or lack of them) and turning restrictions have long been recognized. Cohen and Applebaum (1960) presented a series of detailed maps which vividly illustrated the outcome of such problems for retail sites. These old maps illustrate classic errors in accessibility judgements, errors that are still being replicated today. The site assessor is well advised to calculate or obtain micro-isochrones, which represent the driving time/distance 'contours' around a site. These can provide graphic illustration of the areas within 5, 10, 15, (etc.) minutes' driving distances. For a large shopping development, effects of the new shopper traffic must also be estimated and the plans for road development should be consulted. For example, one very large store lost 50 per cent of its existing customer traffic when a nearby motorway junction was closed during a three-year road improvement project.

The requirement for adequate car parking places a heavy additional demand upon space required for a new centre or free-standing store. Neafcy (1984) indicated that Asda consider 10 places per 1000 square feet as appropriate for their superstores, at the upper end of the norm of 6.5–10 places for UK superstores. This provision is more generous than that typical of North American centres (4–5 spaces/1000 square feet gross retail area) and far more generous than is usual in town centres (Guy, 1994).

The access routes to car parks require careful negotiation with local planners, to avoid the creation of congestion points and, preferably, to enable necessary modifications to be made to relevant junctions and feeder road. The site assessment must also weigh the potentials for ground-level and multi-level car parking. The former is usually preferred on cost and accessibility grounds, although an excessively large ground-level car park may be inconvenient to shoppers in bad weather and may also, at off-peak times, give the impression that the store is not popular.

The visibility of a store is an important facet of accessibility, plus a valuable measure of its ability to attract passing trade. In the case of new stores, the retailer's wish to maximize visibility is frequently at odds with the town planner's desire to blend or disguise new developments. An Asda superstore at Newport, for example, enjoyed convenient access to the M4 motorway but was rather less visible than the retailer would have preferred. Within the busy centre of Manchester's Piccadilly, a group of new shops failed, mainly because they were hardly visible from the outside and were accessible only by subways and escalators.

The checklist should also consider the accessibility of the store for staff; retail outlets situated on motorways or remote from public transport routes, for example, may incur the cost of transporting staff or be restricted in their recruitment scope. Within existing, congested centres, the access for delivery vehicles can be a major issue, particularly if loading times are restricted or if loading interferes with customer traffic.

Competition

If competition could be easily defined then it would be a simpler task to measure existing competition within an area. Very few retailers, however, trade within sectors that are not subject to a great deal of 'indirect' competition from other types of retailer. As competitors become less constrained and more aggressive in their diversification policies, this difficulty increases. A variety store or department store retailer may have to consider a very large number of indirect competitors in a new area; if only competitors of the same type were considered, serious deficiencies in the forecasts would result.

The evaluation must also weigh the positive effects of other retail activity in an area. The 'anchor stores' within a shopping centre may well offer competition to the proposed store, but they are crucial elements in maintaining the customer flow to and within the centre. Figure 7.3 shows the ground-floor layout of the Sheffield Meadowhall Centre, where the Sainsbury hypermarket, Marks & Spencer, House of Fraser and Debenhams stores provide the main anchors. Anderson (1985) demonstrated through regression analysis that anchor stores can be a powerful determinant of non-anchor stores' sales and profitability. This effect may however be most important when a centre is newly opened. McGoldrick and Thompson (1992) found that 47 per cent of users were attracted to the MetroCentre by a particular store, when the centre was only one year old. This proportion dropped to 36 per cent, three years later.

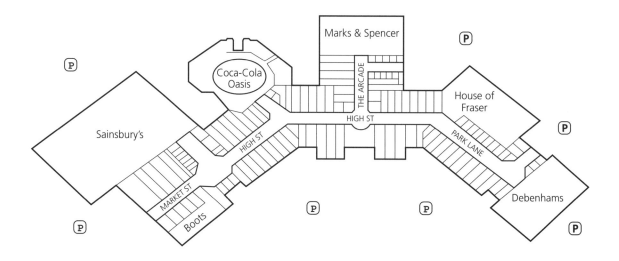

Figure 7.3 Meadowhall's ground-floor plan

Source: Meadowhall Centre.

A grouping of smaller, specialist outlets may also benefit from the concept of cumulative attraction, together providing a magnet that no one such store could have offered in isolation. The benefits of agglomerated centres are discussed in some detail by Ghosh (1986). Groupings may often be found of high-fashion stores, shoe shops or antique stalls, with the street or locality developing a favourable reputation for choice of products and stores. This form of agglomeration not only reduces the cost of doing business, through shared car parking, services, etc., it also reduces risk for individual vendors (Brown, 1989).

As shoppers frequently wish to visit several stores on one shopping trip, there has been some study of consumers' tendencies to link store visits (e.g. Brown, 1992b; Dellaert et al, 1998). Shoppers were over 35 per cent more likely to visit adjacent stores that were of similar, rather than dissimilar, type. This effect proved strong for comparison goods and convenience retailers but not for retail services (Brown, 1991). This linkage was especially strong in the case of clothing shops and department and variety stores, where comparison shopping is most likely to occur (Brown, 1987).

Having identified the relevant competition, an analysis of trading strengths and weaknesses should be conducted. Selling areas, if necessary broken down by product/department groupings, would be a basic element of this evaluation. Surveys may be undertaken to help estimate turnovers and calculate existing trade areas. The physical characteristics of the stores would also be assessed, including their age, standard of design and car-parking provision.

When comparing alternative possible trading areas, it is tempting to reduce the assessment of competition and potential to an index of retail saturation (La Londe, 1961). This can provide a useful comparative measure, provided that the relevant product/market competitive set(s) have been defined. This index may be calculated using the following formula.

$$IRS_{ji} = \frac{C_{ji} \times RE_{ji}}{RF_{ji}}$$

where

IRS_{ji} = index of retail saturation for product j in area i

C_{ji} = number of consumers in i who buy j

RE_{ji} = retail expenditure per consumer in i on j

RF_{ji} = total retail floorspace in i devoted to selling j

The concept of saturation however must be treated with great caution (Guy, 1996; O'Kelly, 2001), for a number of reasons.

1 Retailers may still wish to enter an area that is technically 'saturated', as new retail space tends to drive out old.
2 A large geographical area that is generally 'saturated' may include many pockets of opportunity in local areas.
3 UK superstores operators have created new formats to trade in these smaller catchment areas, also adapting the product/service mix to overcome the effects of superstore saturation.

It is clearly unrealistic to assume that competitors will not react to a new store opening or that they will not pursue their own development programmes. A study of the scope for outlet expansion or refurbishment may help to predict reactions. Other available sites should also be viewed as potential competition, presenting a particular concern if the site intercepts customers from the principal trading area. Some retailers scan press information and information on building contracts to gain early warning of new competition (Clarkson et al., 1996). Most try to maintain close contact with competitors' policies and plans, so as to predict changes in competition.

Costs

The evaluation of population, accessibility and competition attributes are combined to produce a forecast of the likely turnover that could be derived from a site. The calculation of profit potential then requires a detailed study of all the likely development and running costs that will be incurred. Most of the 'easy' sites, where a retailer could hardly fail to produce a profit, are long gone (Bowlby et al., 1984). Even a small outlet can cost over £500 000 to lease, equip and stock. As superstores are developed on more expensive land, especially in the South East of Britain, the development cost may be around £30 million for a superstore. In areas where good sites are especially scarce, retailers have paid nearly £20 million for superstore sites, resulting in an overall cost of £30 million for such stores (Guy, 1994).

These figures are difficult to reconcile with the assumptions of traditional 'rent bid theory', which places grocers at the low end of a hierarchy of willingness/ability to pay for best locations (Brown, 1993). The same theory suggests that variety stores and women's clothing stores are most willing to pay higher prices or rents. Because of the more widespread use of out-of-town locations, more complex accessibility issues and more varied site requirements, the 'best location' for one form of retailing may be less appropriate for others.

Many of the cost data emerge following negotiations with developers or lease owners and from detailed estimation of construction/refurbishment costs. In this respect, the figures are mostly derived from internal company sources, although many site-specific attributes must be taken into account. In comparing site cost/rental levels with national norms, Jones (1984) noted a paucity of data. A time-series analysis of shop rent levels is however provided by the *Investors Chronicle*, in conjunction with Hillier-Parker.

When a new site is developed, the cost of site preparation may be greater than the purchase price, especially if extensive demolition is needed or unsuitable land has to be converted. The initial site of the Gateshead MetroCentre, for example, was bought for a very modest £1 million, but a far larger investment was then required to remove the waterlogged ashpits from the site. Building restrictions relating to height, architectural requirements or landscaping can also greatly influence building costs. The rates payable are frequently an area of contention between retailers and local authorities; they may present a disincentive to develop inner-city sites, unless significant concessions are made.

The location, site and building design of a store greatly influence future running costs. A store requiring multi-level sales floors or car parking will have to cover the substantial maintenance costs of escalators of lifts. A location with a high crime rate, typically identified by adverse insurance ratings, is inevitably going to increase security costs and 'shrinkage' through theft. Retailers have been forced to close stores in some especially bad areas, when the theft of not only stock but also store equipment reached unacceptable levels. At the other end of the spectrum, an area with high employment and wage rates may bring problems of staff recruitment and retention.

Other cost factors include delivery costs; a site remote from the main distribution network may considerably increase such costs or require a major extension of the network. The costs of promoting the store locally could also be considered, although the proliferation of local media now provides suitable opportunities in most areas. Finally, and very importantly, the cost analysis must consider any possible impact of the new outlet on other branches. The higher the existing market share within an area, the greater the potential loss, although this has been accepted as a necessary trade-off by major grocery multiples expanding their superstore networks.

7.1.3 Mapping Techniques

The methods utilized to survey and map stores' trading areas and sites do not in themselves comprise forecasting techniques; they do, however, provide a valuable input. Surveys at equivalent stores can provide estimates of trade area density and also show the effects of competition within that area. Such surveys can also provide inputs to promotional strategy and can assist in the evaluation of store performance.

Many detailed examples, showing the several applications of mapping techniques, were presented by Cohen and Applebaum (1960) and Applebaum (1968). At the simplest level, a map can depict, with the use of dots, the home addresses of each customer interviewed at the store. In the USA, maps of this type have sometimes been constructed based upon the licence plates of cars entering the car park, but in the UK a customer survey is usually necessary. Alternatively, if a retailer has comprehensive customer information derived from loyalty cards, credit transactions, guarantee registrations, deliveries or service calls, this may provide the basis of a trade area map. Care must be taken, however, to ensure that the information is truly representative of the overall customers, not just of a specific subset.

When related to population data, a store survey can provide valuable estimates of market penetration within each part of the trading area. Figure 7.4 was based upon a survey (Thomas et al., 1977) at a Co-operative superstore to the north of Manchester. Data were obtained,

Figure 7.4 Mapping a superstore catchment area

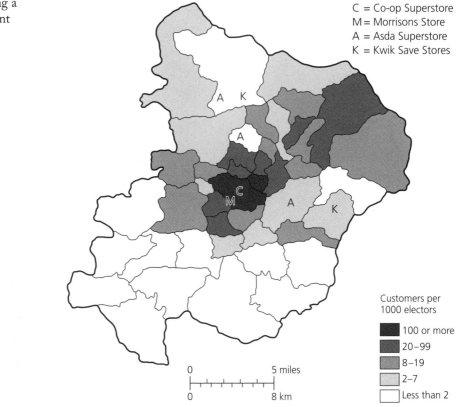

indicating the number of electors within 47 adjacent districts, which formed the basis of this map. A weighting system was applied to give less weight to the frequent users, who naturally tend to be overrepresented in a store-based sample (Blair, 1983).

Figure 7.4 illustrates that the trade area of this store could not have been estimated accurately using concentric circles or simple time/distance zones. Strong competition to the north creates a trough in the catchment area, whereas the primary area extends further to the north-east, assisted by good public and private transport accessibility, plus a relative lack of competition in that direction. In contrast, the trading area is truncated to the south by the city centre of Manchester.

Mapping techniques have been developed with three-dimensional representations of trade-area densities (Kohsaka, 1992). With improved flow of data, continuous mapping systems are also available, which can be interrogated to display origins of customers at different times, or to show trade areas for specific products and departments (Rust and Brown, 1986). Similarly, the effects of changes in competition, promotional strategies or access routes can be depicted, on a before and after basis.

Figure 7.5 Drive-time bands for a site

Source: Bowlby and Foot (1994).

At the location evaluation stage, micro-isochrones can be mapped around the prospective site, showing the relevant drive-time bounds. Figure 7.5 shows the drive times around a superstore site near the junction of the M4 and the A33, to the south of Reading. This illustrates

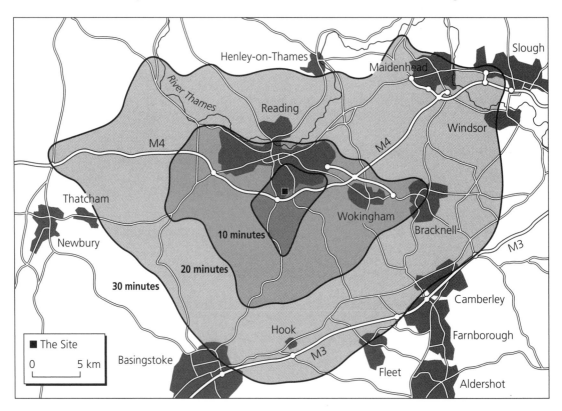

how the 30-minute drive-time zone extends furthest to the east and west, but does not include Henley-on-Thames to the north, due to congestion in and around Reading. This mapping technique can also highlight the effective proximity of major competitors. In this case, there were seven large grocery outlets within the 20-minute band, 12 within the 30-minute band.

Mapping also contributes to location decisions at the microscale. Goad plans show the detailed shape and locations of over 325 000 outlets in 1100 UK shopping areas, plus 5500 out-of-centre locations. The plans are updated by a team of surveyors every one or two years. They include the following information, of relevance to assessing adjacent tenant mix and traffic/pedestrian flows:

▶ trading fascias
▶ activity of each retailer
▶ street names and numbers
▶ pedestrian areas
▶ service roads and car parks
▶ bus stops
▶ location of services
▶ one-way streets
▶ pedestrian crossings
▶ new developments
▶ vacant properties and sites.

Figure 7.6 shows an example of a Goad map for Oxford. Now these maps have become digitized, joining the ever growing family of GIS data, discussed in the next section. Using these micro-location data, Webber (1997) has demonstrated how the attractiveness of areas can vary enormously, even within adjacent streets. The digitized plans facilitate the task of picking out the 'financial services ghettos' or streets with more vacancies and charity shops. In terms of retail compatibility, a new branch of a book chain may find attractive a site close to upmarket cafés, record shops and upmarket fashion shops.

7.1.4 Geographic Information Systems

For many years the retail location analyst in the UK suffered a paucity of basic marketing statistics (Jones, 1984). There was a heavy dependence upon government department data, although these tended to be less well co-ordinated than, for example, the population and expenditure data of the Bureau of Censuses in the USA. The supply of UK information grew considerably worse following a series of government cuts, including the mid-term sample population census and the detailed Censuses of Distribution (Guy, 1992). It became clear that the UK government was no longer prepared to finance retail statistics. Opportunities were therefore created for a new generation data providers, who harnessed the more accessible and faster information technologies to integrate a wide range of geographic data sources.

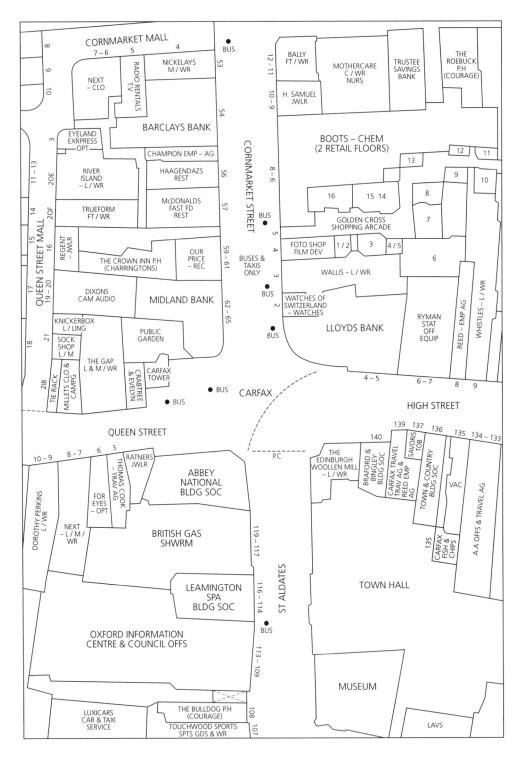

Figure 7.6 Goad plan of Oxford

Source: Greenland (1994).

Geographic information systems had their origins in the 1960s but their impact on retailing has been most apparent since the mid 1980s (Goodchild, 1991). Geographic information has been defined as information which can be related to a location (defined in terms of a point, area or volume) on the Earth, particularly information on natural phenomena, cultural or human resources (AGI, 1991). Utility companies were among the earliest users of GIS, providing them with information on the locations of underground systems. Now there has been a vast expansion in the range of GIS applications, as these spatial data can support a huge diversity of political, economic, commercial and scientific decision-making. Applications include goods delivery optimization programmes, traffic management systems and in-car real-time navigation (EGII, 1995).

A pioneer in developing a computerized database from the census was CACI, well known for its classification of residential neighbourhoods (ACORN), described in Chapter 3. Parts of the House of Fraser group have used CACI to analyse store catchment areas and to better define their key target groups. Because of their relatively upmarket profile, they found that market penetration was sometimes highest in areas some distance away from their stores, rather than in the immediate vicinity. This spelt a clear warning about the dangers of oversimplified trade area assumptions. Comet has also made extensive use of CACI services. From 150 000 customer addresses derived from product guarantee registrations, it was possible to develop a detailed profile of customer types and to model the effects of opening stores in new areas.

Among the services developed primarily for retail location analysis, CACI has assembled data files of road types and congestion levels. From this, a digitized isochrone system has been developed, which indicates drive-time bands for any site in the UK. Another enhancement is a system called 'Shopping Centre Planner', which identifies competition in an area. Table 7.3 shows an excerpt from these data, relating to Basildon. The index in the final column compares the proportion of outlets of each type with a national base of over 1000 centres and over 200 000 outlets. In this specific example, footwear shops are heavily represented, whereas florists have a low representation. A similar analysis can also be provided indicating relative proportions of floor space. Clearly, more needs to be known about the nature of outlets within an area, although this type of analysis provides a useful starting point in the identification of suitable areas for store development.

A company which has developed a prominent position in retail GIS is Experian, previously CCN, now operating in several different countries. Their MOSAIC system for classifying residential neighbourhoods represents a fusion of several different data sources (Table 7.4). This process helps to overcome many of the limitations of the UK census statistics. The census data are however the starting point for most of the UK geodemographic systems, as in the USA, where around 70 demographic and housing variables are collected during the Census of Population and Housing (Putler et al., 1996)

The MOSAIC system defines 12 broad groups and 52 more specific types of neighbourhood, as summarized in Table 7.5. These were derived

Distribution of outlets by activity type	Outlets		Base	
	N	%	%	Index
Convenience outlets				
1. Bakers	5	1.9	2.3	86
2. Butchers	6	2.3	2.4	96
3. Greengrocers and fishmongers	0	0.0	2.1	0
4. Grocers and provision dealers	4	1.5	3.3	47
5. Off-licences	1	0.4	1.2	33
6. Confectioners, tobacconists, newsagents	7	2.7	3.7	73
Total convenience outlets	23	8.9	14.9	60
Comparison outlets				
7. Footwear shops and repairs	21	8.1	4.0	201
8. Mens and boyswear	12	4.6	3.0	155
9. Ladies and girlswear/drapers/woolshops	33	12.7	9.0	142
10. Furniture, furnishings, carpets	10	3.9	5.2	75
11. Books, art, stationery, cards, printing	8	3.1	3.3	94
12. Gas, electrical, hi-fi, optical goods	22	8.5	7.4	115
13. Building, decorating, ironmongery	6	2.3	3.0	78
14. China, glassware, leather, fancy goods	3	0.8	3.1	37
15. Cycle, pram, motor accessory	2	0.8	1.3	59
16. Chemists, opticians and surgical suppliers	10	3.9	3.5	110
17. Variety, department and general household	11	4.2	2.1	201
18. Florists and horticultural	1	0.4	1.1	36
19. Hobby, craft, toys, sports shops	6	2.3	2.3	101
20. Jewellers, watchmakers, engravers	10	3.9	2.8	136
21. Petshops and petfood	1	0.4	0.6	67
22. Camping, gov't surplus, secondhand	1	0.4	0.7	54
Total comparison outlets	156	60.2	51.3	117
Services outlets (categories 23–29)				
30. Unclassified and misc.	6	2.3	2.6	88
31. Vacant and under construction	31	12.0	8.2	145
Car park spaces per outlet—12.2	Base = 3.9	Index = 312		

Table 7.3 Extract from shop count report (CACI Centre, Basildon, Essex)
Source: based upon information supplied by CACI Market Analysis Division.

Source	Type of data
Census statistics	Socio-economic data
Office of Population Censuses	Housing
and Surveys	Household and age
Demographic data	Age
Electoral registers	Household composition
	Population movement
Financial data	
Lord Chancellor's Office	County court judgements
Experian Credit Database	Consumer searches
Companies House	Directors
Housing data	Address types
Post Office	
Retail data	Accessibility
Experian	

Table 7.4 Sources of
MOSAIC data

Source: based upon
information supplied by
Experian.

Table 7.5 MOSAIC groups and types

Source: based on information supplied by Experian.

Group	Type	%
1. High income families (9.9%)	Clever capitalists	1.5
	Rising materialists	1.5
	Corporate careerists	2.4
	Ageing professionals	1.7
	Small-time business	2.7
2. Suburban semis (11.0%)	Green belt expansion	3.4
	Suburban mock tudor	3.2
	Pebble-dash subtopia	4.4
3. Blue-collar owners (13.0%)	Affluent blue collar	2.9
	30s industrial spec.	3.8
	Lo-rise right to buy	3.3
	Smokestack shiftwork	3.1
4. Low-rise council (14.4%)	Co-op club and colliery	3.4
	Better-off council	2.1
	Low-rise pensioners	3.2
	Low-rise subsistence	3.5
	Problem families	2.2
5. Council flats (6.8%)	Families in the sky	1.3
	Graffitied ghettos	0.3
	Small-town industry	1.4
	Mid-rise overspill	0.7
	Flats for the aged	1.4
	Inner-city towers	1.8
6. Victorian low status (9.4%)	Bohemian melting pot	2.3
	Victorian tenements	0.1
	Rootless renters	1.5
	Sweatshop sharers	1.1
	Depopulated terraces	0.8
	Rejuvenated terraces	3.5
7. Town houses and flats (9.4%)	Bijou homemakers	3.5
	Market town mixture	3.8
	Town centre singles	2.1
8. Stylish singles (5.2%)	Bedsits and shop flats	1.2
	Studio singles	1.7
	College and communal	0.5
	Chattering classes	1.9
9. Independent elders (7.4%)	Solo pensioners	1.9
	High-spending greys	1.3
	Aged owner-occupiers	2.7
	Elderly in own flats	1.5
10. Mortgaged families (6.2%)	Brand new areas	1.0
	Pre-nuptial owners	0.8
	Nest-making families	1.7
	Maturing mortgagers	2.7
11. Country dwellers (7.0%)	Gentrified villages	1.5
	Rural retirement mix	0.6
	Lowland agribusiness	1.8
	Rural disadvantage	1.2
	Tied/tenant farmers	0.6
	Upland and small farms	1.3
12. Institutional areas (0.3%)	Military bases	0.3
	Non-private housing	0.1

through cluster analysis, designed to achieve the maximum discrimination between types, in terms of the consumption, expenditure and credit behaviours of the residents. Every postcode is defined in terms of a MOSAIC group and type, a postcode covering on average 14.5 households. This is clearly a more precise definition than a census enumeration district, which averages 148 households. The GIS companies are however conscious that there is a demand for even more precision than is provided by groupings of, on average, 14.5 addresses.

As GIS systems evolve, both within specialist organizations and retailers' own databases, the individual household and the individual within the household become the target GIS units.

The applications of GIS data extend well beyond the area of location decision-making, potentially informing many interrelated decisions within retail marketing. Table 7.6 outlines some of these applications, all of which include spatial considerations. Retailers have become increasingly conscious of the need for, and gains from, local adaptation. This can include the design characteristics of the store, the services provided, the product range, displays, pricing and promotions. Another logical extension of GIS has been to assess international markets; major retailers have used MOSAIC to assist international market appraisals.

The benefits of GIS can be summarized in terms of speed, the comprehensive range of data available, the co-ordination of these data,

Table 7.6 Examples of GIS applications

Retail function	GIS information	Decision areas
Location	Neighbourhood profiles	Assess suitability for company's stores
	Drive-time boundaries	Estimate size of catchment areas
	Shopping area maps	Micro-location decisions on accessibility and adjacent outlets
	International data	Market entry decisions
		Site decisions
Design	Car ownership	Car-parking needs
	Household composition	Assess need for café, children's facilities
Promotion	Address files	Direct mail
	Media usage	Advertising mix decisions
Pricing	Income levels	Price levels
	Demographics	Types of offers
Merchandising	Product consumption	Local assortments
	Data	Space allocation and display decisions
Services	Credit data	Loans and special terms
	Age and employment structure:% students	Hours of opening
	Adjacent service providers	Demand for videos, dry cleaning, shoe repairs, etc.

quality controls and data continuity (Clarke and Rowley, 1995). It should also be added that a retailer without access to GIS is now at a severe competitive disadvantage. As most systems are now designed to run on PCs or laptops, the information is readily available to be interrogated with the specific questions of the retail analyst. Indeed, the systems allow 'all persons to become cartographers' (EGII, 1995), producing colourful maps which can be viewed at the scale of a whole city, or a specific high street. Both the method and the systems have acquired a certain glamour, heightened by menu and graphics-driven packages, which are increasingly user-friendly (Goss, 1995). Thus, the analyst can view the concentrations of, for example, affluent older couples or beer and lager drinkers in a defined area (Bennison and Clarke, 1994).

Naturally, GIS is not without its costs. In common with most areas of IT, the hardware costs have fallen but the data-sets remain expensive. Much of the cost is also incurred within the retail organization, if the maximum use is to be made of GIS. Organizational and decision-making systems need to change, and the expertise needed to integrate internal and external GIS data tends to be expensive (Clarke and Rowley, 1995). However, the GIS providers do face competition, which keeps pressure on costs (O'Malley et al., 1997).

Not only is competition provided by other large and niche GIS providers, the large retailers themselves are developing increasingly sophisticated databases, with loyalty cards providing household and address data. However, loyalty cards provide little information on what customers do with the rest of their time and money, nor do they pinpoint non-customers (Joyner, 2001). Consequently, GIS providers have evolved their databases from segments to fragments to individuals, in order to maintain their relevance to retailers' micro-marketing activities (Ziliani, 2000).

7.1.5 The Analogue Method

The discussion so far has focused mainly upon ways of identifying, obtaining and depicting information of relevance to store location and related decisions. Attention now turns to methods of combining information, with varying degrees of mathematical sophistication, to produce forecasts of turnover that could be achieved from a prospective site. The analogue method, although not using any advanced mathematics, is still fairly popular among retailers (Hernandes and Bennison, 2000). The analogue procedure is essentially as follows:

1 Identify other stores, preferably within the same chain, which have many essential features in common with the proposed store and location.
2 Quantify the key features of these stores and trading areas, then tabulate and summarize these data.
3 Extrapolate from these analogue stores to estimate the likely turnover and profitability of a store at the proposed location.

Extrapolations are sometimes made based upon broadly analogous competitors' stores from each time/distance zone, but this causes additional problems. Detailed turnover data are more difficult to obtain, and competitors' stores may be less truly analogous in terms of product ranges and overall images.

The analogue method therefore represents a systematic use of checklist data, which is designed to minimize the need for subjective judgement on the part of the analyst. Early examples of the method were presented by William Applebaum (1966), following its development as a forecasting technique with the Kroger Company. Retailers using the method now frequently update their analogue data and, in common with most other forecasting techniques, it is also a valuable method for evaluating existing stores. Table 7.7 presents a simple example of the analogue method, based on data for a medium-performing UK superstore chain. The first section of Table 7.7 shows the proportion of trade derived by four analogue stores.

The analyst then establishes the population living within each of these zones, then calculates the per capita sales for each analogue/zone. The final section of the table shows the extrapolation for the proposed store.

Table 7.7 Example of a superstore analogue

Driving time zones (mins)	Proportion of analogue stores' sales from zones (%)			
	A	B	C	D
0–4	7	5	7	6
5–9	27	22	24	24
10–14	26	30	33	30
15–19	18	19	14	17
20+	22	24	22	23
Zones (mins)	Per capita sales of analogues (£)			
	A	B	C	D
0–4	5.81	4.85	6.94	5.87
5–9	0.82	0.61	0.69	0.71
10–14	0.38	0.41	0.50	0.42
15–19	0.16	0.17	0.13	0.16

	Application of analogues A–D to the new location		
Zones (mins)	Population	Est. sales per capita (£)	Est. weekly sales (£000)
0–4	32.3	5.87	189.6
5–9	79.6	0.71	56.5
10–14	122.0	0.43	52.5
15–19	251.8	0.16	40.3
Estimate from four zones			338.9
Adjustment for estimated sales (21%) from outside zones			90.1
Estimated weekly sales			429.0

The estimates may not be based strictly upon the mean values for the analogue; the analyst is likely to exercise judgement as to likely deviations from the means. Typically, if the store is built, the realized sales/zones data will be collected in order that future forecasts can be further refined.

In that the analogue technique is based upon actual historical sales performances, it represents a considerable improvement upon generalizations such as the so-called 'share of space' method. This very crude rule of thumb was often used in the absence of systematic data. It worked on the assumption that the new store's share of sales within the likely trading area would be proportional to the store's share of selling space within that area. With the vast range of space productivities achieved, as an extreme comparison, by Tesco and the co-operatives, this is generally an unacceptable assumption.

It was never claimed that the analogue method would replace subjective judgement, rather, that it would both guide and limit it. As Drummey (1984) points out, subjective judgement inevitably has a role in evaluating new sites, as no two situations are ever exactly alike. The precision of the analogue can be further refined through the addition of survey data and information from GIS databases. Rogers and Green (1979) do, however, identify problems in using the analogue approach alone: essentially that the task of the analyst becomes extremely difficult as the database grows and more intricate causal relationships are identified. At that point it makes sense to start developing multivariate regression models, in order better to investigate the causal linkages.

7.1.6 Multiple-Regression Analysis

Given the increasingly complex array of data potentially available to the location analyst, there is a need to utilize more sophisticated procedures to identify the relationships between store sales and the various predictor variables. For example, measures of population, per capita income, competition and store size may each be known to relate to potential sales. Using multiple regression analysis, a model can be constructed which harnesses the predictive power of all, or the most appropriate subset, of the available predictor variables. Few applications of this technique have been published in detail, although Simkin et al. (1985) note that regression models are being used, particularly by major grocery retailers.

Davies (1973) presents an example based upon 72 analogous tailoring stores. Given the fairly large sample, he was able to enter several, potential predictor variables into the regression model. The following five variables explained 71 per cent of the variance in sales:

- gross selling area
- rent and rates
- distance to car park
- number of branches
- store accessibility.

Higher levels of explanation were achieved when subgroups of stores were analysed independently: 80 per cent of variance was explained in the case of corner-site stores. Drawing upon previous evidence, Moutinho et al. (1993) conclude that there are seven main factors relevant to location decisions:

- population in the surrounding area
- spending power of this population
- overall average spending on the product
- quality of transport links to site
- average distance from site to population
- competition
- average distance from competitors to population.

A regression analysis of this type requires a reasonable number of analogous stores. Bowlby et al. (1985) illustrate alternative regression strategies which can be used when few equivalent stores are available. Instead of making each store a unit of analysis, the trade areas of a few stores may be divided into grid squares, which become the units of analysis. The regression equation then estimates potential sales derived from each grid square within a new trade area. Clearly, this regression approach requires far more detailed surveys of the catchment and trade area characteristics of the analogous stores. Different regression equations can be derived for different types of grid square, for example those representing high-, medium- and low-status areas.

If information is limited or expensive, it is possible that just two or three key variables may provide a satisfactory level of prediction, at least for initial screening of sites. Table 7.8 shows an example based upon 25 analogous superstores, using just population and competition as predictor variables. While the 20 minutes drive time may appear a somewhat arbitrary cut-off point, Ghosh and Craig (1991) find considerable evidence of 'reservation distances', beyond which people are unwilling to travel. This equation explained 88 per cent of the variance in the sales of these 25 stores, giving reasonable confidence in the model's predictive power. As Table 7.8 illustrates, multiple regression requires some modest computing power to calculate the coefficients. However, the simplest of calculators is all that is required to apply these weights to the population and competition measures, in order to estimate total sales for the proposed site.

Regression analysis can also be applied to the estimation of market potential, as part of the broad scan of possible geographical areas for expansion. Ingene (1984) illustrates how the available expenditure per household for a number of store types can be predicted on the basis of several demographic and marketing variables. If sufficient data were available relating to the population and competition within an area, this approach could offer an improvement upon the rather basic index of retail saturation, described in Sec. 7.1.2.

Table 7.8 Example of regression equation

Source: Bowlby and Foot (1994, pp. 211–212).

Stage 1: establish co-efficients based on data from 25 analogue
        superstores, of similar size and in similar out-of-town locations.

$$Y = 186{,}835 + 0.7822P - 1.1381C$$
sales   (constant)   (population)   (competition)

where   Y = retail sales of proposed store

        P = population within 20 minutes drive time of proposed site

        C = competition: the floor space (m^2) of all stores over 1000 m^2
            within 20 minutes drive time of proposed site.

Stage 2: use co-efficients to estimate sales from the proposed store.

Population within 20 minutes   (   ) x   0.7822 =

Competition within 20 minutes   (   ) x –1.1381 =

Constant   = 186, 835

Total estimated sales   =

The main advantages of multiple regression, for the retail location analyst, are as follows.

1 Once the equation is developed, it is easy to use.
2 It provides an objective discipline for location evaluations by different market analysts.
3 It provides a purpose built equation for each retailer, not an 'off the peg' solution.
4 The range of potential error in the sales estimates can be determined statistically.
5 It has particular value to retailers that have a segmented customer appeal.
6 Through analysis of residuals, it provides also an evaluation of existing store performances (Rogers, 1992).

Inevitably, multiple-regression analysis has its dangers and drawbacks. It does require a large database; if each store is treated as a unit of analysis, each variable must equate to approximately six stores (Poyner 1984). A company with less than 15 analogous stores would therefore not be able fully to utilize this regression approach. Davies (1976) also points to the need to distinguish cause and effect clearly when selecting 'predictor' variables. For example, store size may, in some cases, be more a long-term effect than a cause of sales levels. Wilson (1984) also warns that the accuracy of the forecast deteriorates as the sites being evaluated become increasingly different from the types of store upon which the model was initially calibrated.

Where a number of interrelated variables are considered as possible predictors, the analyst must also avoid the dangers of multicollinearity. If two or more independent variables are strongly associated, the model will become less stable. One solution to this problem, especially where the number of variables is large, is to apply factor analysis in order to identify the common dimensions within the variables. In the study of 72 tailoring stores by Davies (1973), six factors emerged from a factor analysis of 43 variables. Ingene (1984) also utilized factor analysis, which provided the inputs to his regression model and avoided a severe multicollinearity problem.

The use of discriminant analysis has also be suggested as a technique to assist site selection. Like multiple regression, it constructs a model based upon a number of predictor variables. Unlike regression, it predicts category membership, rather than the actual expected sales or profits. Sands and Moore (1981) illustrate how discriminant analysis, using four demographic variables, predicted whether stores would fall into the break-even or non-break-even categories, achieving 72 per cent accuracy. This was advocated as an initial screening technique, although in this particular case multiple regression could have been used instead to forecast profit (or loss) on the basis of the same set of variables. Categorical response variables can also be accommodated using logistic, linear logit and long-linear models (Wrigley, 1985). Readers are referred to an appropriate statistical text for a fuller exposition of these techniques (e.g. Hair et al., 1998).

An interesting comparison between the forecasting performance of multiple regression and neural networks was reported by Coates et al. (1995). Neural networks try to represent the activities of the brain, in dealing with and processing large amounts of information. They are composed of an interconnected network of processing elements, each accepting a number of weighted inputs but producing one output. This output in turn either excites or inhibits the other processing elements to which it is connected. In this particular comparison, the neural network performed only marginally better than multiple regression, in spite of the latter being a relatively straightforward approach. However, as the software for neural networks becomes more powerful, user-friendly and familiar to location analysts, it is likely that this form of artificial intelligence will play an increasing role in location and choice modelling.

These multivariate techniques clearly demand a higher level of statistical sophistication than the more basic techniques, discussed earlier. However, they should not be seen as a 'packaged' solution to retail location problems or as likely to replace the judgement of the analyst. They are merely analytical tools, which help to understand and measure the influence of the predictor variables. As Jones and Mock (1984) point out, their success is dependent largely upon the quality of the initial data, the proper application of statistical procedures and the analyst's intuitive understanding of the problem. In the future, mathematical approaches that incorporate managerial judgements within the model building process are likely to play a more significant role in retail location. (e.g. Durvasula et al., 1992).

7.1.7 Spatial Interaction Models

This 'family' of models, also referred to as gravity models, has evolved as part of a major stream of development in retail location theory. A comprehensive discussion of the earlier model developments was provided by the National Economic Development Office (1970), and reviews of more recent developments by Craig et al. (1984) and Rogers (1992).

The basic principle of spatial interaction models is that the aggregate movements of shoppers are positively related to the attractiveness of a shop/centre and inversely related to the distance, or some other 'deterrence' measure. The basic principle of spatial interaction has been widely accepted and various forms of gravity model have been applied by more sophisticated retailers and database agencies. There is, however, considerable debate as to the most appropriate attraction and deterrance measures and as to the nature of the relationship between them.

One of the earliest models of this type was that of Reilly (1931). 'Reilly's Law' states that the frequency with which the residents of an intermediate settlement trade with two towns is directly proportional to the populations of the two towns and inversely proportional to the square of the distances from the two towns to the intermediate settlement. From this 'law' was derived a formula to describe the 'breaking-point' between two towns, defined as the point up to which one town dominates and beyond which the other is dominant. This is of the following form:

$$d_{01} = \frac{d_{12}}{1 + \sqrt{(A_2/A_1)}}$$

where

d_{01} = is the distance, or journey time, of the breaking point 0 from town 1

d_{12} = is the distance, or journey time, between towns 1 and 2

A_1. A_2 = are measures of the 'attractiveness' of towns 1 and 2.

This crude formulation, based upon an analogy with the physical laws of gravity, formed the basis of many subsequent models. The early gravity models suffered many serious limitations, as noted by Huff (1964):

1 The breaking-point formula provided no graduated estimates above or below the break-even position between two centres.
2 The model was ill-equipped to predict trade areas of more than two centres.
3 The form of the function will vary between types of shopping trip, and will not be a constant across all types.

In order to overcome these specific problems, Huff developed a model founded upon the 'utility' that a customer derives from shopping at a store or centre for a particular type of product. From this, the probabilities of patronizing each of a series of shops or centres could be calculated:

$$P_{ij} = \frac{F_j/t_{ij}b}{\sum F_j/t_{ij}b}$$

where

P_{ij} = is the probability of a consumer resident at i visiting centre j

F_j = is the floor space of centre j

t_{ij} = is the travel time from the consumer's residence i to centre j

b = is a parameter taking different values for different classes of goods.

Refinements upon the early gravity models include the work of Lakshmanan and Hansen (1965), who evolved a model to predict the effects of several existent and proposed centres in the Baltimore area. Their approach provided a basis for a model produced by Manchester University (1966), relating to the impact of a possible centre at Haydock. The Lakshmanan-Hansen model was also shown by Gilligan et al. (1974) to be reasonably effective in forecasting the impact of a large, individual retail outlet.

Although the concept of spatial interaction has retained its appeal, the extreme parsimony of some of the models has been criticized. Mason and Moore (1970) question the concepts of mass and distance as suitable delineators of trade areas in basic gravity models. It was pointed out that this assumes similar patronage decisions from various income, educational and occupational categories.

The calculation of 'deterrence' as a direct function of distance or journey time can also lead to serious oversimplifications (Ibrahim and McGoldrick, 1999). Whereas driving time has been found to be highly influential in patronage decisions in relatively simple retail networks, the relationship is less consistent in more complex, urban areas (Cox and Cooke, 1970). Bucklin (1971) notes that the propensity to search differs greatly between customers; 'travel sensitivity' is affected by perceptions of direct cost and opportunity time/cost. Another problem with most spatial interaction models is that the distance is assumed to relate to a single-stop shopping journey, whereas consumers often incorporate multiple stops on one journey (Dellaert et al., 1998).

It has also been found that shoppers' perceptions of store locations can differ considerably from their actual locations (Olshavsky et al., 1975). Naturally, the perceptions of location are more likely to be important determinants of patronage than the actual distances, although this is more difficult to research. The procedure of cognitive mapping could be used to measure these distance perceptions (MacKay and Olshavsky, 1975; Mazze, 1974). Differences between perceived and actual distances appear to relate to 'frictional' factors, such as volume of traffic or ease of parking, and aspects of store or centre attractiveness.

A more refined but data-demanding specification of deterrence has been suggested by Gautschi (1981). He included factors relating to transport costs, parking, travel atmosphere (clean, attractive environs), convenience, reliability, flexibility and safety (from accidents and vandalism). The model therefore sought to quantify and include many more of the 'accessibility' factors discussed in Sec. 7.1.2. Not all these factors contributed significantly to the explanation of retail patronage, although they demonstrate the diversity of factors associated with evaluations of 'distance' and 'convenience'.

Concern has also been expressed as to the adequacy of population, floor space or other crude measures of attractiveness in spatial interaction models. Cox and Cooke (1970) used measures of the size of department stores, supermarkets and car parks, in addition to total store space. In fact, presumably because of a high degree of correlation between these variables, they did not add significantly to the explanatory power of the model. As noted above, the Haydock shopping model contained a composite index of facilities. All such measures of attractiveness, however intricately constructed, are limited in that they relate to the physical properties of the shop or centre, ignoring the great diversity of image characteristics.

The realization that image factors represent significant determinants of attractiveness grew with the development of image research. Mason and Moore (1970) concluded that images of shopping centres significantly influence the shape of their trading area. Stanley and Sewall (1976; 1978) set out to integrate image components into spatial interaction models. Driving time, however, still accounted for more variation than did image. Nevin and Houston (1980) found that the inclusion of three image variables did not significantly improve the predictive power of the model although it was a major determinant of shopping centre preference.

Insights into the practical utilization by Tesco of an 'evolved' spatial interaction model were provided by Penny and Broom (1988). This model took the following form:

$$EXP_{is} = \beta_0 \left(\sum_k E_k H_{ik} \right) . \frac{W_s . e^{-\beta_1 t_{is}}}{\sum_m W_m . e^{-\beta_1 t_{im}}}$$

where

EXP_{is} is the expenditure from zone i to site s

β_0, β_1 are parameters

E_k is the mean food expenditure by household category k

H_{ik} is the number of households of category k located in zone i

W_s is a measure of attraction of the proposed store s

t_{is} is the travel time from zone i to the site at s

W_m is the attractiveness of competitor m

t_{im} is the travel time from zone i to competitor m.

This formulation recognizes the considerable differences between the expenditure potential of various household types, using the data now available to refine the model. It also incorporates an improved deterrence function, using the concept of 'generalized time'. This includes measures of local accessibility, size and type of car park, along with general customer convenience around the store, translated into 'travel time impedance'. The attractiveness measure is also a composite, based upon survey data indicating what attributes are most influential within customer's choices of stores. In other words, the above formulation represents only the final calculation from a number of empirically derived components: the total number of variables used within the overall process is quite large.

Other extensions upon the basic forms of spatial interaction models include the multiplicative competitive interaction model (MCI). This was considerably developed by Nakanishi and Cooper (1974), building upon the Huff model to include more explicitly the specific competitive situation. They also demonstrated that the parameters of the model could be effectively estimated using the least squares approach, as in multiple regression analysis. This development considerably increased the usefulness of the model as a practical tool. Nakanishi and Cooper did not relate the MCI model specifically to retail patronage forecasting, although Achabal et al. (1982) reported that several retailers in the USA have used such formulations in this context. The models can be expanded to include a wide range of attributes (e.g. Jain and Mahajan, 1979) and can cope with a number of shopping alternatives. Their explanatory power can also be improved if specific MCI models are estimated for each target segment of consumers (Frasquet et al., 2001).

There has been increased interest also in modelling the optimal location of multiple branches. Retailers moving into new areas often set out to establish a network of outlets in each area, thereby increasing the effectiveness of their advertising, management and distribution systems. Most models have addressed themselves to improving decisions on individual locations, which may not result in the best network overall. An exception is the MULTILOC model, presented by Achabal et al. (1982). This extends the MCI model to take into account effects upon other units with the same chain. Alternative approaches to assist in the development of a branch network have been suggested by Mahajan et al. (1985), Ghosh and Craig (1986, 1991) and Kaufmann et al. (2000).

Progress has also been made in the development of multinomial logit (MNL) models as an alternative to MCI. Again, this approach operates initially at the disaggregate level, i.e., predicting individual shopper choice behaviour. Such predictions can of course be combined to produce estimates of aggregate consumer behaviour. Weisbrod et al. (1984) provide an example of an MNL model, used to forecast aggregate travel patterns among major shopping centres. They illustrated that the approach could be useful in forecasting response to possible changes in population distribution, road and transport characteristics or changes in the competitive mix.

Ibrahim and McGoldrick (2002) utilized MNL models to test the relative importance of shopping centre and travel mode attributes, when a realistic choice of travel modes is available. As discussed in the following section, concern for the environment is increasing the pressure to provide public transport options for shopping purposes, and to locate new developments in locations with good public transport infrastructure. Most models of shopping centre choice have represented travel simply in terms of distance, time or cost. These will increasingly fail to represent the true significance of travel mode options, and their attributes, within consumers' choices of major stores and centres.

7.2 Town Planning and Retailing

So far, the emphasis has been upon the approaches, techniques and models that can assist the retailer in the tasks of site finding and site assessment. There are, however, many ways in which retail locations are influenced and constrained by local and central government planning policies. Even the change of use of an existing building may require planning permission, depending upon the building's previous purpose. Over the last 20 years, the major thrust of retail development has been of a far more radical nature, involving large stores and centres, often in locations not previously used for retail purposes.

The task of obtaining planning permission can easily consume more time and management resources than all the location evaluation procedures. Neafcy (1984) quotes the extreme example of the Brent Cross Centre in north London, which required 14 years of negotiation with local government and several revisions of the design. Owing to a major shift in government policy along the way, plus a protracted legal wrangle, nine years elapsed between application and permission being obtained in 1995 to proceed with the Trafford Centre near Manchester. These are, of course, not typical, although the total process of site negotiation, planning applications, appeal against refusal, and planning inquiry is still very protracted.

When a proposal becomes the subject of a planning inquiry, this alone tends to add 8–10 months from initiation to final decision. Success in obtaining planning permission is influenced by the judicious choice of the site, with regard to planning issues, and by the skilful preparation and pursuit of the application. Although an expensive and time-consuming procedure, public inquiry does provide the opportunity to sway opinions in favour of the development (Greed, 1996). The interface between town planning and retailing is therefore an integral element in the development of new retail locations.

7.2.1 The Framework

All governments in the Western industrial nations intervene in the retail sector (Dawson, 1980). The extent of this intervention does however differ considerably, as do the structures and processes of planning (Davies, 1995). In the UK and many European countries, retailers and developers have been more constrained than their counterparts in the USA. The modest number of major out-of-town shopping centres and the uneven distribution of large stores are indicative of these constraints.

The relaxing and tightening of planning policies towards retailing have occurred at different times across Europe (European Retail Digest, 1994). Belgium, France and Germany eased restrictions on out-of-town developments in the 1970s, resulting in many hypermarkets and regional centres. As these countries tightened their policies in the 1980s, the UK became more permissive of such developments, followed at a later stage by the Mediterranean countries.

The 1990s saw a tightening of planning controls upon retail developments in the UK and Mediterranean countries. By that stage, the European Commission had started to express views on large scale, out-of-town developments. The Directorate concerned with the urban environment, DG11, published a Green Paper in 1991 which pointed to the role of urban sprawl in increasing environmental pollution. DG23, which includes retailing within its remit, expressed concern about the effects on unemployment of a decline in the number of small shops (Davies, 1995; European Retail Digest, 1994).

An understanding of the planning framework in the UK requires a brief description of the respective roles of central and local government. Through the Town and Country Planning Act of 1971, local authorities were required to prepare plans, which would include provision for retail uses. These plans usually took some time to research, draft and debate before being submitted to central government for approval. The administration and consideration of individual planning applications is part of the local government role, but operating within central government guidelines. If an application is turned down at local level, the retailer or developer has the right to appeal to central government. For major appeals, the Department of the Environment would normally appoint an inspector to conduct a public inquiry into the case.

Table 7.9 shows the outcomes of 775 decisions by local planning authorities from mid-1996 until the analysis by the Competition

Table 7.9 Planning applications and appeals

Note: percentages based on the total number in category, i.e., the sum of columns 1 and 2.

Source: derived from Competition Commission (2000).

Type of location	Granted or resolution to grant	Refused or non-determination	Went to appeal	Allowed on appeal	Dismissed on appeal
Town centre n	144	17	13	4	1
(%)	(89)	(11)	(8)	(3)	(1)
Edge of centre n	169	42	34	11	11
(%)	(80)	(20)	(16)	(5)	(5)
Out of centre/ n	254	77	55	15	12
out of town (%)	(77)	(23)	(17)	(5)	(4)
District or n	58	14	10	3	2
local centre (%)	(81)	(19)	(14)	(4)	(3)

Commission (2000). In each of the four categories, the majority were granted, or given permission 'in principle', demonstrated by a 'resolution to grant' consent. Applications for town-centre sites incurred the lowest proportion of refusals or failures to determine the outcome within a reasonable time period. More than half of those refused or non-determined went to appeal, where more were allowed than dismissed. However, as appeal processes can continue for many years, some appeals fall by the wayside, due to mounting costs or changing circumstances. For comprehensive discussions of the planning process, see for example Davies (1995), Guy (1994) or Sparks and Findlay (1999).

As many major planning applications do go to appeal and public inquiry, the Department of the Environment is clearly able to exert a major influence at this stage. The final decision in such cases rests with the Secretary of State for the Environment, who usually follows the recommendation of the inspector appointed. This is not always the case, however, as RAM EuroCentres found to their cost, when a factory outlet permission near Tewkesbury was overruled by the Minister. The inquiry and appeals extended over two years and cost the company over £200 000 (Ruston, 1999). The actual planning inquiry can last several days, sometimes weeks. The retailer or developer's case is usually presented by a specialist barrister or Queen's Counsel, normally assisted by other lawyers or company personnel. The inquiry typically hears cases presented by various expert witnesses, trade representatives, vested interest groups and local authority officers. Naturally, the legal and other costs incurred by the retailer up to and including this stage are very considerable indeed, providing a major disincentive to make proposals with low probabilities of success.

It is obviously in the interests of a retailer to try to enhance its chances of success by favourably influencing the opinions of planners and the local community. This may be regarded as a special area of retail marketing, communicating the benefits of a proposed store to the relevant public. Asda has shown considerable flair in this area; Neafcy (1984) describes the inquiry at Rawtenstall, where the local community turned out in force, mostly to support the proposal. The inquiry was delayed while a larger hall was found to accommodate the crowds! Asda have used large advertisements in newspapers to convey specific messages. In one series, the benefits of superstores in transforming derelict land were illustrated by before and after pictures. Such 'brownfield' developments have found increasing favour among planners, as restrictions upon greenfield sites increased.

In the late 1980s the UK government was increasingly criticized for a lack of clarity in its guidance on retail development. In 1993, a revised version of the Planning Policy Guidance Note 6 (PPG6) was issued by the Department of the Environment and Welsh Office (1993). This confirmed a major shift in government attitutude, which had started to become evident in the refusal of recent out-of-town schemes

(Hallsworth, 1991). Howard (1994) sums up the advice of the revised PPG6 to local authority planners.

1 More priority should be given to the improvement of town centres and to ensuring the availability of a wide range of shopping opportunities for everyone.
2 Encouragement of the location of shopping facilities where they can be reached by a range of means of transport: in practice, in or next to existing town centres.
3 Consider the establishment of town centre managers (e.g. Tomalin and Pal, 1994).
4 Grant planning permission for large stores 'out of town' only where they would not adversely affect the vitality and viability of existing centres overall.
5 Refuse planning permission for large out-of-town regional shopping centres, except under very special circumstances.
6 Refer to the Department of the Environment, for further approval, any proposals for development of 20 000 square metres or more.

This PPG6 clearly shifted emphasis towards the preservation of existing town centres, making permissions for regional out-of-town centres far more unlikely. However, it did note that food superstores in free-standing positions had become generally accepted by local authorities (Davies, 1994), and it was not entirely negative towards out-of-centre developments. As well as the above points, it emphasized:

> *that the planning system should continue to facilitate competition between different types of shopping provision, by avoiding unnecessary regulation of shopping development.*

By the middle of 1996, a new version of PPG6 represented a bigger shift, because it put the emphasis upon:

- a plan-led approach, rather than the development-led approach of the previous decade
- a sequential approach to selecting sites for development.

Within this sequential approach, first preference should be given to town-centre sites, followed by edge-of-centre and, finally, out-of-centre sites which are accessible by a choice of transport means (Howard, 1998; National Retail Planning Forum, 2000). In the latter part of the 1990s, the failure rate of retailers' appeals against refusals for out-of-town schemes increased (Ruston, 1999). In spite of this, out-of-town turnover has continued to grow, and is expected to account for a third of retail sales by 2005 (Retail Review, 2001).

The timing of guidelines issued in Scotland differed from those in England and Wales but the policy directions now have much in common (Gotts, 1999). National Planning Policy Guidance, in the form of

NPPG8, places much emphasis upon sustainable development, the importance of the town centre and modes of transport other than the car. Succinct reviews of retailing planning environments elsewhere in Europe are provided by the European Retail Digest (1999).

Concern for the inner city is now not only a European phenomenon. Porter (1995) highlights the need for a coherent, commercially driven strategy to revitalize inner cities in the USA. He points out that small-scale, social developments rarely attract wider-scale economic activity. Whysall (1995) is also sceptical of the 'regeneration thesis', whereby a large new store is seen as a catalyst to wider shopping regeneration. Following the arrival of a large, modern store in New York's Harlem, Lavin (2000) notes the disruption to locally managed, existing outlets, that were well attuned to the cultural and product preferences of the local communities.

The 'pendulum swing' against large, out-of-town centres was further confirmed in PPG13, from the Department of the Environment and the Department of Transport, which placed much emphasis upon the use of non-car transport for shopping. Some of the suggestions of PPG13 have been heavily criticized (e.g. Spriddell, 1994), due to the strong preference of most car owners to shop by car. However, it did give a clear signal that environmental issues are now even higher on the agenda, when local authority planners consider retail applications.

7.2.2 The Issues

In Sec. 7.1.2 checklists were presented which could help in evaluating the economic viability of potential sites. Equivalent checklists could well be constructed to help appraise the planning viability of a location. In view of the importance of obtaining planning permission, the identification and understanding of the key issues is vital to success. Sites that are most unlikely to be acceptable in planning terms can be eliminated at an early stage in the screening process; in other cases, the most detailed attention can be directed to those issues that are likely to be foremost at the planning inquiry.

Table 7.10 summarizes the major advantages and problems that tend to be cited in relation to large new stores. These are often broadly classified as economic, environmental or social issues, although overlap obviously occurs. In the case of superstores, lower prices are usually cited as the major economic advantage from the consumer viewpoint. Taking the wider perspective, they also create new employment, generate rates, and may be used to enhance the appeal of the existing centre. Retailers and developers have also offered 'planning gains' to make their proposals more attractive to local planners and communities. Table 7.11 gives some examples of planning gains offered by retailers in the Plymouth area. These range from better access facilities to contributions towards art or community facilities.

On the environmental side, large new stores usually offer the advantage of safe and more comfortable shopping environment, free of traffic and not subject to the vagaries of the weather. In certain

Possible advantages	Possible problems
Economic	
Lower prices	Conflicts with existing hierarchy
Enhancement of centre (if integrated)	Affects other traders
New employment	Town centre viability/vitality
Generates rates and revenue	Depletion of other centres
Meets demand in growth area	Changes employment structure
'Planning gain'	Supply of employment land
	Extra infrastructure costs, e.g. roads
Environment	
Improvement of run-down areas	Visual intrusion
Reduction of congestion in existing centres	Air pollution from traffic
Safe, comfortable environment	Overloads motorway network
Innovation in retail formats	New congestion points
	Less character than old centres
	Inhibition of other development
Social	
Convenient shopping	Favour car-borne shoppers
Efficient shopping	Lack social role of small shops
Increases choice	May isolate elderly and immobile
Popular with majority	Local monopolies

Table 7.10 Large new stores: planning issues

Source: based upon Davies and Reynolds (1986); Guy (1994); Jones (1991).

circumstances, the environmental case may focus upon the improvement of a derelict/run-down area or on the reduction of congestion in existing centres. It tends to be assumed that other advantages will accrue to the shopper, notably more convenient and efficient shopping, provided that access and car parking are satisfactory. Greater choice of merchandise is also normally claimed, although one counter-argument is that large stores may lead to local monopolies and, ultimately, may reduce the real choice available.

Table 7.11 Examples of planning gain

Source: Planning (1993, p. 10).

Developer	Planning gain
Sainsbury	Provided alternative employment land
	Park and ride scheme
	Crèche facilities
	'Per cent for art' contribution
	Tourist information centre
	Associated highway works
Tesco	Crèche facilities
	Facilities for the disabled
	Nature conservation areas
	'Per cent for art' contribution
	Highway works
Co-op	Provided areas of open space
	Community buildings

Indeed, there are counter-arguments to most of the cited advantages, so most attention tends to be focused upon the reasons why planning permission is refused. Up to a dozen reasons may be given for refusal in any one case, although these are mostly centred around the themes of land use, traffic and impact.

Land use

Land use issues may be further classified into those relating to designation, intrusion or nuisance (Lee and Kent, 1978). When a site is within a designated green belt, in particular, the chances of success have tended to be low. In 1987 a draft Department of the Environment (DoE) circular ruled out further green belt developments and also indicated that other open countryside developments would generally be opposed. This presumption against greenfield development has been reinforced further in the latest version of PPG6. Sustainability is now a term much used in the planning system, defined as: 'development that meets the needs of the present generation without compromising the ability of future generations to meet their own needs' (Brundtland, 1987).

A more flexible attitude tends to be shown with regard to land designated for industrial use, provided that alternative industrial land is available. Objections to new stores simply on the grounds that land is not designated for retail use are rarely accepted, in that many designations were drawn up before the demand for new retail forms was fully recognized.

In cases where green belt designation does not apply, the objection of intrusion can still be a major reason for refusals. Numerous commercially attractive sites have been identified on the outskirts of towns and cities; many have been refused planning permission on the grounds of physical and visual intrusion. Retailers have submitted elaborate proposals for landscaping such sites in order to blend into the rural area, although such measures are usually considered unlikely to be effective. In Britain there is a general planning preference for urban containment and the prevention of scattered development. In contrast, the likelihood of nuisance to adjoining residents or other land users tends to be regarded as a lesser issue, unlikely to be the primary cause of refusal.

Traffic

Traffic issues generally relate to the immediate access to the proposed store or the increased load on surrounding roads. In some cases, the retailer or developer offers to finance the costs of junction modifications or even new roads, offering both better accessibility and 'planning gain'. For example, the A34 bypass in Cheshire was largely financed by the retailers obtaining adjacent sites, primarily Tesco, J. Sainsbury, Marks & Spencer and John Lewis.

In that traffic flows and road capacities can be estimated by established procedures, it is usually possible for retailers to anticipate objections on traffic grounds. For example, it was estimated that one development by J. Sainsbury would generate around 4320 vehicle trips per shopping day. The results of failing to anticipate traffic increases correctly were seen in some early cases. I can recall the opening of (arguably) Britain's first hypermarket at Caerphilly; the existing road network was quite inadequate to carry the extra load, and major traffic jams resulted. The store manager actually appeared on television asking people to stay away, with the inevitable effect that yet more came! Subsequently it was necessary for road schemes to be initiated or given higher priority to cope with the increased traffic.

Following the 1992 Earth Summit in Rio, and the commitment by the UK to reduce CO_2 emissions, more attention has been given to the issue of cars and pollution. By 1996, potential pollution had become a central issue in the initial refusal of permission for a superstore at Bath (Retail Review, 1996). The government's quest to develop a 'multi-model' integrated transport system will increasingly militate against development on sites which do not have a viable public transport option. The 1996 version of PPG6 emphasized the importance of transport issues:

> *Three key tests for assessing retail developments: impact on vitality and viability of town centres; accessibility by a choice of means of transport; and impact on overall travel and car use.*

Impact

Impact issues have been argued in terms of the likely adverse effects upon individual retailers or existing shopping centres. The former carries little weight per se at inquiries, unless the cumulative effect of such impacts would markedly jeopardize the viability of important existing shopping areas. The major impact issues therefore revolve around effects upon the shopping hierarchy, the consequences for inner cities, and the social effects of more car-oriented shopping provision.

The concept of a retail hierarchy has been developed from the 1930s, with the emergence of central place theory. An extensive body of literature has accumulated and the limitations of the theory are well documented (e.g. Craig et al., 1984; Huff, 1981). The essential postulates of the theory were summarized by the National Economic Development Office (1970):

> *for any given commodity there is a level of demand below which it will not be offered for sale. Dealers in commodities with a high (threshold) level of demand will be located in relatively few centres with large trade areas; businesses offering commodities with a low threshold demand level will be located in many more centres having small trade areas. Businesses with intermediate threshold demand level will be found in centres which lie between these extremes, both in number and in the size of the trade areas. On this basis, a stepped hierarchy of trading centres may be constructed.*

It is widely accepted that central place theory has provided a normative rather than a prescriptive model of the retail hierarchy. Nonetheless, there has been a tendency within town planning to defend the established hierarchy, whereby comparison shopping is grouped within larger centres and convenience shopping is more widely dispersed.

In the 1960s, a major challenge to this hierarchy would not be accepted; the proposal for a major centre at Haydock Park was turned down when the likely impact upon existing centres was demonstrated (Gayler, 1984). In the 1970s the rapid development of superstores challenged the hierarchy but their emphasis was initially upon convenience goods; comparison shopping remained essentially a town centre activity. Then specialist durable goods stores developed outside existing centres, notably electrical, carpet and furniture stores. Mainly in the 1990s, centres of regional proportions developed in fringe and out-of-town areas. It was therefore accepted by successive stages that impact upon the established heirarchy could not be avoided, while catering for the demand for new retail formats.

The fact that more shop vacancies will occur in an existing centre, as a consequence of a new proposal, was not usually adequate justification for refusal. However, impact upon existing centres was frequently underestimated. For example, the effects of the Merry Hill Centre on Dudley were described as devastating (Schiller, 1994). After the out-of-town centre opened, the main high street stores moved out of Dudley, increasing vacancy rates and dramatically lowering retail property values (Lee Donaldson Associates, 1995). Some commentators have been critical that government guidelines were slow to address the issues of 'vitality and viability' of town centres:

> *the policy guidance and the explanatory detail only catches up with the policy issue after the debate has moved on … shutting the garage doors after the Volvo and Micra have zoomed off to the nearest out-of-town shopping centre (Tomalin, 1999).*

Concern has also been expressed about the impact of large new developments upon consumer welfare (Davies and Reynolds, 1986). If such developments cause local shops and town centres to close, then older, poorer and less mobile shoppers are placed at an increased disadvantage. The effect may also be to create undesirable monopolies, at least for those shoppers without the mobility to get to competing stores some distance away.

A major problem in assessing impact is that of accurate quantification. Some of the modelling approaches discussed in Sec. 7.1 have been applied to impact estimation, although the task is more complex than that of potential turnover assessment. They are most likely to be of value where there is agreement on the basic assumptions underlying their use and where, if different models are used, any difference in results can be identified and explained. A comprehensive review of impact assessment procedures was presented by Wade (1983).

SUMMARY

Location decisions are among the most crucial and long-term elements of retail marketing strategy. Large new stores can now cost many millions of pounds to develop, so the consequences of poor location decisions are extremely serious in both marketing and financial terms. Major retailers are now using a range of techniques and expert assistance in order to reduce the risks. The relatively straightforward checklist and analogue approaches are still widely used, although computerized databases and mathematical modelling techniques have gained an important role in location decision-making.

A comprehensive checklist of factors is the starting point of most location evaluations. These may be considered under the general headings of population, accessibility, competition and costs. Population factors relate to the demographic, economic, lifestyle and behavioural characteristics of those resident within the catchment area. Accessibility measures require the detailed study of pedestrian flows, public transport, road access and car parking. The competition analysis should examine existing retail activity and specification, plus likely competitive reactions. The cost estimates will include all the store development costs and the running costs at a specific location.

The demand for comprehensive, local-area statistics to assist location decision-making is increasingly being met by providers of GIS data. Companies such as CACI and Experian have now accumulated very large, GIS databases, including detailed local information on population characteristics, existing retail activities and driving times. These databases continue to grow, while the agencies have become increasingly diverse and international in their range of services. Users are able to interrogate these databases to chart or map many facets of a proposed location.

The analogue method can be used if a number of existing stores and locations are analogous to the one proposed. Key features of their performance and trading areas can be tabulated; an extrapolation for the proposed store can then be made, based upon equivalent trading area data. Analogues are relatively straightforward and help forecast sales, based on drive times and population data. They do not, however, cope well with variations in other factors that can affect turnover.

More complex mathematical models have been extensively developed and reported within the academic literature. Approaches involving multiple-regression analysis and forms of spatial interaction modelling are gaining wider acceptance. Various other model forms, including neural networks, are also being developed as retail location decision aids. As the volume of data available to the decision-makers continues to grow, it is likely that such models will increasingly be required to cope systematically with the information. They are likely to complement, not replace, the checklists and the judgement of the analyst.

In most countries, retail locations are constrained to a greater or lesser degree by government regulations and planning restrictions. In Britain, the local authority is responsible initially for granting or refusing planning permissions, although appeal inquiries are administered through central government. The government also issues planning guideline notes, which are becoming increasingly opposed to out-of-town developments and reliance upon car transport for shopping.

At planning inquiries, a wide range of economic, environmental and social issues are debated. The reasons for refusals relate mostly to land use, traffic and impact on existing centres. Even the most sophisticated location procedures serve little purpose if planning permission cannot be obtained. An understanding of the relevant, national planning framework and local issues is a crucial part of the retail location process.

REVIEW QUESTIONS

1 What are the logical stages of the store location process? What circumstances may prevent a retailer from going through these stages in an ideal sequence?

2 Why do different types of retailer tend to utilize different combinations of store location techniques?

3 Illustrate how some store location techniques can also be used for the assessment of existing stores.

4 Select a specific retail type and strategic positioning: what would be the main considerations in locating additional branches for company of that type?

5 Using the example selected above, develop a checklist of factors to be evaluated and data to be collected in the location process.

6 In locating the store type of your choice, what assistance would be available from GIS providers? In addition to location, what other aspects of retail marketing decision making could be assisted by GIS data?

7 What is the analogue method? Discuss the limitations of the method and the problems that may be encountered in using it.

8 Illustrate how multiple-regression analysis can be used to assist location decisions. Taking a store type of your choice, what variables are likely to be most useful in predicting the turnover of a new branch?

9 What is the basic principle of spatial interaction (gravity) models? Outline the progress that has been made in defining the main functions within such models.

10 To what extent is the location decision constrained and influenced by:

a) local authorities?

b) central government?

11 Your bid to build a superstore on the fringe of a town has become the subject of a public inquiry. What would you expect to be the key issues at the inquiry, and what would be your strategy to maximize chances of success?

12 All forms of 'planning gain' are likely to benefit the local community, yet some may be ruled as unacceptable by the courts. Giving appropriate examples, explain why some forms of 'planning gain' are legitimate inducements to obtain planning permission, while others are not.

REFERENCES

Achabal, D.D., W.L. Gorr and V. Mahajan (1982) 'MULTILOC: a multiple store location decision model', *Journal of Retailing*, **58** (2), 5–25.

AGI (1991) *GIS Dictionary, version1.1 (STA/06/91)*, Association for Geographic Information, London.

Anderson, P.M. (1985) 'Association of shopping centre anchors with performance of a nonanchor speciality chain's stores', *Journal of Retailing*, **61** (2), 61–74.

Applebaum, W. (1966) 'Methods for determining store trade areas, market penetration, and potential sales', *Journal of Marketing Research*, **3** (2), 127–41.

Applebaum, W. (1968) *Store Location Strategy Cases*, Addison-Wesley, Reading, MA.

Beaumont, J.R. (1987) 'Retail location analysis: some management perspectives', *International Journal of Retailing*, **23**, 22–35.

Bennison, D. and I. Clarke (1994) 'Network effectiveness: making locations work better', in *Cases in Retail Management*, P. J. McGoldrick (ed.), Pitman, London, pp. 214–231.

Bennison, D., I. Clarke and J. Pal (1995) 'Locational decision making in retailing: an exploratory framework for analysis', *International Review of Retail, Distribution and Consumer Research*, **5** (January), 1–20.

Blair, E. (1983) 'Sampling issues in trade area maps drawn from shopper surveys', *Journal of Marketing*, **47** (1), 98–106.

Bowlby, S. and D. Foot (1994) 'Location techniques', in *Cases in Retail Management*, P.J. McGoldrick (ed.), Pitman, London, pp. 204–213.

Bowlby, S., M. Breheny and D. Foot (1984). 'Store location: problems and methods 1', *Retail & Distribution Management*, **12** (5), 31–33.

Bowlby, S., M. Breheny and D. Foot (1985), 'Store location: problems and methods 3', *Retail & Distribution Management*, **13** (1), 44–48.

Brown, S. (1987), 'Retailers and micro-retail location: a perceptual perspective', *International Journal of Retailing*, **2** (3) 3–21.

Brown, S. (1989) 'Retail location theory: the legacy of Harold Hotelling', *Journal of Retailing*, **65** (Winter), 450–470.

Brown, S. (1991) 'Shopper circulation in a planned shopping centre', *International Journal of Retail & Distribution Management*, **19** (1), 17–24.

Brown, S. (1992a) *Retail Location: A Micro-Scale Perspective*, Avebury, Aldershot.

Brown, S. (1992b) 'Tenant mix, tenant placement and shopper behaviour in a planned shopping centre', *Service Industries Journal*, **12** (3), 384–403.

Brown, S. (1993) 'Micro-scale retail location: Cinderella or ugly sister?', *International Journal of Retail and Distribution Management*, **27** (7), 10–19.

Brundtland (1987) *The Brundtland Report: Our Common Future*, World Commission on Environment and Development, Oxford University Press, Oxford.

Bucklin, L.P. (1971) 'Trade area boundaries: some issues in theory and methodology', *Journal of Marketing Research*, **81** (1), 30–37.

Clarke, I. and J. Rowley (1995) 'A case for spatial decision-support systems in retail location planning', *International Journal of Retail & Distribution Management*, **23** (3), 4–10.

Clarke, I., D. Bennison and J. Pal (1997) 'Towards a contemporary perspective of retail location', *International Journal of Retail & Distribution Management*, **25** (2), 59–69.

Clarke, I., M. Horita and W. Mackaness (2000) 'The spatial knowledge of retail decision makers: capturing and interpreting group insight using a composite cognitive map', *International Review of Retail, Distribution and Consumer Research*, **10** (3), 265–285.

Clarkson, R.M., C.M. Clarke-Hill and T. Robinson (1996) 'UK supermarket location assessment', *International Journal of Retail & Distribution Management*, **24** (6) 22–33.

Coates, D., N. Doherty, A. French and M. Kirkup (1995) 'Neural networks for store performance forecasting: an empirical comparison with regression techniques', *International Review of Retail, Distribution and Consumer Research*, **5** (4) 415–432.

Cockrell, N., J. Ramshaw and C. Mardones (1999) *Debenhams: Tarred with the Same Brush*, Morgan Stanley Dean Witter, London

Cohen, S.B. and W. Applebaum (1960) 'Evaluating store sites and determining store rents', *Economic Geography*, **36**, 1–35.

Competition Commission (2000) *Supermarkets: A Report on the Supply of Groceries from Multiple Stores in the United Kingdom*, The Stationery Office, Norwich.

Cox, W.E. and E.F. Cooke (1970) 'Other dimensions involved in shopping centre preference', *Journal of Marketing*, **34** (4), 12–17.

Craig, C.S., A. Ghosh and S. McLafferty (1984) 'Models of the retail location process: a review', *Journal of Retailing*, **60** (1), 5–35.

Davies, M. and I. Clarke (1994) 'A framework for network planning', *International Journal of Retail and Distribution Management*, **22** (6), 6–10.

Davies, R. (1994) 'Retail planning policy', in *Cases in Retail Management*, P.J. McGoldrick (ed.), Pitman, London, pp.230–240.

Davies, R. (1995) *Retail Planning Policies in Western Europe*, Routledge, London.

Davies, R.L. (1973) 'Evaluation of retail store attributes and sales performance', *European Journal of Marketing*, **7** (2), 89–102.

Davies, R.L. (1976) *Marketing Geography, with Special Reference to Retailing*, Retailing and Planning Associates, Corbridge.

Davies, R.L. and J. Reynolds (1986), 'Retail development pressures on Greater London', *Retail*, **3** (4), 42–44.

Davies, R.L. and D.S. Rogers (eds) (1984) *Store Location and Store Assessment Research*, Wiley, Chichester.

Dawson, J.A. (1980) *Retail Geography*, Croom Helm, London.

Dellaert, B., T. Arentze, M. Bierlaire, A. Borgers and H. Timmermans (1998) 'Investigating consumers' tendency to combine multiple shopping purposes and destinations', *Journal of Marketing Research*, **35** (May), 177–188.

Department of the Environment and Welsh Office (1993) 'Town centres and major retail development', *Planning Policy Guidance Note 6 (PPG6)*, HMSO, London.

Drummy, G.L. (1984) 'Traditional methods of sales forecasting', in *Store Location and Store Assessment Research*, R.L. Davies and D.S. Rogers (eds), Wiley, Chichester, pp. 279–299.

Durvasula, S., S. Sharma and J.C. Andrews (1992) 'STORELOC: a retail store location model based on managerial judgments', *Journal of Retailing*, **68** (4), 420–444.

EGII (1995) Towards a European Geographic Infrastructure, discussion document of EUROGI Group, December, Brussels.

European Retail Digest (1994) 'Prospects for retailing and public planning policies within Europe', *European Retail Digest*, **3** (Summer), 21–43.

European Retail Digest (1999) 'European regional review', *European Retail Digest*, **21**, (March), 19–33

Fowler, A., J. Pritchard, A. Gulati and J. Lovett-Turner (1999) *Safeway: Catch the Falling Knife*, Morgan Stanley Dean Witter, London.

Frasquet, M., Gil, I. and A. Molla (2001) 'Shopping-centre selection modelling: a segmentation approach', *International Review of Retail, Distribution and Consumer Research*, **11** (1), 23–38.

Gautschi, D.A. (1981), 'Specification of patronage models for retail centre choice', *Journal of Marketing Research*, **18** (2), 162–174.

Gayler, H.J. (1984) *Retail Innovation in Britain: The Problems of Out-of-Town Shopping Centre Development*, Gi Books, Norwich.

Ghosh, A. (1986) 'The value of a mall and other insights from a revised central place model'. *Journal of Retailing*, **61** (1), 79–97.

Ghosh, A. and C.S. Craig (1986) 'An approach to determining optimal locations for new services', *Journal of Marketing Research*, **23** (4), 354–362.

Ghosh, A. and C.S. Craig (1991) 'FRANSYS: a franchise distribution system location model', *Journal of Retailing*, **67** (4) 466–497.

Gilligan, C.T., P.M. Rainford and A.R. Thorne (1974) 'The impact of out-of-town shopping, a test of the Lakshmanan-Hansen model', *European Journal of Marketing*, **8** (1), 42–56.

Goodchild, M.F. (1991) 'Geographic information systems', *Journal of Retailing*, **67** (1), 3–15.

Goss, J. (1995) 'Marketing the new marketing: the strategic discourse of geodemographic information systems', in *Ground Truth: the Social Implications of Geographic Information Systems*, J. Pickes (ed.), Guilford Press, New York, pp. 130–170.

Gotts, I. (1999) 'The retail planning environment; Scotland', *European Retail Digest*, **21** (March), 21–22.

Greed, C. (1996) *Introducing Town Planning*, Longman, London.

Greenland, S.J. (1994) 'Branch location, network strategy and the high street', in *Retailing of Financial Services*, P.J. McGoldrick and S.J. Greenland (eds), McGraw-Hill, London, pp. 125–153.

Guy, C. (1992) 'Estimating shopping centre turnover: a review of survey methods'. *International Journal of Retail & Distribution Management*, **20** (4), 18–23.

Guy, C. (1994) *The Retail Development Process: Location, Property and Planning*, Routledge, London.

Guy, C. (1996) 'Grocery store saturation in the UK—the continuing debate', *International Journal of Retail & Distribution Management*, **24** (6), 3–10.

Hair, J. F., R.E. Anderson, R.L. Tatham and W.C. Black (1998) *Multivariate Data Analysis*, Prentice-Hall, Englewood Cliffs, NJ.

Hallsworth, A. (1991) 'Regional shopping centres: case-studies on recent policy decisions in Canada and the UK', *Service Industries Journal*, **11** (April), 219–232.

Hass-Klau, C., I. Mobbs and G. Crampton (1999) *Accessibility, Walking and Linked Trips*, National Retail Planning Forum, London.

Hernandez, T. and D. Bennison (2000) 'The art and science of retail location decisions', *International Journal of Retail & Distribution Management*, **28** (8), 357–367.

Howard, E. (1994) 'United Kingdom', *European Retail Digest*, **3** (Summer), 39–41.

Howard, E. (1998) 'Emerging conflicts in UK planning and competition policy', *European Retail Digest*, **20**, 50–51.

Huff. D.L. (1964) 'Defining and estimating a trading area', *Journal of Marketing*, **28** (3), 34–38.

Huff. D.L. (1981) 'Retail location theory' in *Theory in Retailing: Traditional and Nontraditional Sources*, R.W. Stampfl and E.C. Hirschman (eds), American Marketing Association, Chicago, pp. 108–121.

Ibrahim, M.F. and P.J. McGoldrick (1999) 'Transport mode attributes and shopping centre choice: exploratory qualitative research', in *Proceedings of the 10th International Conference on Research in the Distributive Trades*, A. Broadbridge (ed.), Institute for Retail Studies, Stirling, pp. 33–44.

Ibrahim, M.F. and P.J. McGoldrick (2002) *Shopping Choices with Public Transport Options*, Ashgate, Aldershot.

Ingene, C.A. (1984) 'Structural determinants of market potential', *Journal of Retailing*, **60** (1), 37–64.

Jain, A.K. and V. Mahajan (1979) 'Evaluating the competitive environment in retailing using multiplicative competitive interaction model', in *Research in Marketing*, J. Sheth (ed.), JAI Press, Greenwich, CT, pp. 217–235.

Jones, K. and J. Simmons (1990) *The Retail Environment*, Routledge, London.

Jones, K.G. and D.R. Mock (1984) 'Evaluating retail trading performances', in *Store Location and Store Assessment Research*, R.L Davies and D.S. Rogers (eds), Wiley, Chichester, pp. 333–360.

Jones, P. (1991) 'Regional shopping centres: the planning issues', *Service Industries Journal*, **11** (April), 171–178.

Jones, P.M. (1984) 'General sources of information', in *Store Location and Store Assessment Research*, R.L. Davies and D.S. Rogers (eds), Wiley, Chichester, pp. 139–162.

Joyner, P. (2001) 'Making CRM deliver its promise', *Vision*, Spring, 4–5.

Kaufmann, P.J., N. Donthu and C.M. Brooks (2000) 'Multi-unit retail site selection processes: incorporating opening delays and unidentified competition', *Journal of Retailing*, **76** (1), 113–127.

Kohsaka, H. (1992) 'Three-dimensional representation and estimation of retail store demand by bicubic splines', *Journal of Retailing*, **68** (2) 221–243.

Kurose, S. and S. Hagishimsa (1995) 'A method of identifying accessibility properties of pedestrian shopping networks', *Journal of Retailing and Consumer Services*, **2** (2), 111–118.

La Londe, B.J. (1961) 'The logistics of retail location', in *The Social Responsibilities of Marketing*, W.D. Stevens (ed.), American Marketing Association, Chicago, pp. 567–573.

Lakshmanan, T.R. and W.G. Hansen (1965) 'A retail market prediction model', *Journal of American Institute of Planners*, **31**, 134–143.

Lavin, M. (2000) 'Problems and opportunities of retailing in the US "inner city"', *Journal of Retailing and Consumer Services*, **7** (1), 47–57.

Lee Donaldson Associates (1995) 'Whatever happened to Dudley?' *Development Economics Bulletin*, **22** (June), 1–2.

Lee, M. and E. Kent (1978) *Planning Inquiry: Study Two*. Donaldsons Research Report 5, London.

Lord, J.D. and J. Lundregan (1999) 'A market-area approach to determining optimum store size', *International Review of Retail, Distribution and Consumer Research*, **9** (4) 339–348.

Lusch, R.F. (1992) 'Stuck in Mudville', *Retailing Issues Letter*, **4** (5), 4.

Mackay, D.B. and R.W. Olshavsky (1975) 'Cognitive maps of retail locations: an investigation of some basic issues', *Journal of Consumer Research*, **2** (3), 197–205.

Mahajan, V., S. Sharma and D. Srinivas (1985) 'An application of portfolio analysis for identifying attractive retail locations', *Journal of Retailing*, **61** (4), 19–34.

Manchester University (1966) *Regional Shopping Centres in North-West England Part 11: A Retail Shopping Model*, Department of Town Planning, University of Manchester, Manchester.

Mason, J.B. and C.T. Moore (1970) 'An empirical reappraisal of behaviouristic assumptions in trading area studies', *Journal of Retailing*, **46** (4), 31–37.

Mazze, E.M. (1974) 'Determining shopper movement problems by cognitive maps', *Journal of Retailing*, **50** (3), 43–44.

McGoldrick, P.J. and M.G. Thompson (1992) *Regional Shopping Centres*, Avebury, Aldershot.

Moutinho, L., B. Curry and F. Davies (1993) 'Comparative computer approaches to multi-outlet retail site location decisions', *Service Industries Journal*, **13** (4) 201–220.

Nakanishi, M. and L.G. Cooper (1974) 'Parameter estimation for a multiplicative interaction model-least squares approach', *Journal of Marketing Research*, **11** (3), 303–311.

National Economic Development Office (1970) *Urban Models in Shopping Studies*, HMSO, London.

National Retail Planning Forum (2000) *The Sequential Approach to Retail Development*, NRPF, London.

Neafcy, E. (1984) The impact of the development process', in *Store Location and Store Assessment Research*, R.L. Davies and D.S. Rogers (eds), Wiley, Chichester, pp. 99–115.

Nelson, R.L. (1958) *The Selection of Retail Locations*, Dodge (McGraw-Hill), New York.

Nevin, J.R. and M.J. Houston (1980) 'Image as a component of attraction to intra urban shopping areas', *Journal of Retailing*, **56** (1), 77–93.

O'Kelly, M. (2001) 'Retail market share and saturation', *Journal of Retailing and Consumer Services*, **8** (1), 37–45.

O'Malley, L., M. Patterson and M. Evans (1997) 'Retailer use of geodemographic and other data sources: an empirical investigation', *International Journal of Retail and Distribution Management*, **25** (6), 188–196.

Olshavsky, R.W., D.B. MacKay and G. Sentell (1975) 'Perceptual maps of supermarket locations', *Journal of Applied Psychology*, **60** (1), 80–86.

Penny, N.J. and D. Broom (1988) 'The Tesco approach to store location', in *Store Choice, Store Location and Market Analysis*, N. Wrigley (ed.), Routledge, London, pp.106–119.

Planning (1993) 'Gain package ruled lawful', *Planning*, **1006**, 10.

Porter, M. (1995) 'The competitive advantage of the inner city', *Harvard Business Review*, **95** (3), 55–71.

Poyner, M.W. (1984) Getting the shop in the right place', *Retail & Distribution Management*, **12** (4), 20–24.

Putler, D.S., K. Kalyanam and J.S. Hodges (1996) 'A Bayesian approach for estimating target market potential with limited geodemographic information', *Journal of Marketing Research*, **33** (2), 134–149.

Reilly, W.J. (1931) *The Law of Retail Gravitation*, Knickerbocker Press, New York.

Retail Review (1996) 'General retailing', *Retail Review*, **219**, 1.

Retail Review (2001) 'Out-of-town transcendent', *Retail Review*, **269** (March), 2–3.

Rogers, D. (1992) 'A review of sales forecasting models most commonly applied in retail site evaluation', *International Journal of Retail & Distribution Management*, **20** (4), 3–11.

Rogers, D.S. and H.L. Green (1979) 'A new perspective on forecasting store sales: applying statistical models and techniques in the analog approach', *Geographical Review*, **69** (4), 449–458.

Rust, R.T. and J.A.N. Brown (1986) 'Estimation and comparison of market area densities', *Journal of Retailing*, **62** (4), 410–430.

Ruston, P. (1999) *Out of Town Shopping: The Future of Retailing*, The British Library, London.

Sands, S. and P. Moore (1981) Store site selection by discriminant analysis', *Journal of the Market Research Society*, **23** (1), 40–51.

Schiller, R. (1994) 'Vitality and viability: challenge to the town centre', *International Journal of Retail & Distribution Management*, **22** (6), 46–50.

Simkin, L.P., P. Doyle and J. Saunders (1985) 'How retailers put site location techniques into operation', *Retail & Distribution Management*, **13** (3), 21–6.

Sparks, L. and A. Findlay (1999) *A Bibliography of Retail Planning*, National Retail Planning Forum, London.

Spriddell, P. (1994) 'Retail planning policies in the UK', *European Retail Digest*, **3**, 12–15.

Stanley, T.J. and M.A. Sewall (1976) 'Image inputs to a probabilistic model: predicting retail potential', *Journal of Marketing*, **40** (3), 48–53.

Stanley, T.J. and M.A. Sewall (1978) 'Predicting supermarket trade: implications for marketing management', *Journal of Retailing*, **54** (2), 13–22, 91, 92.

Thomas, C.J., D. Thorpe and P.J. McGoldrick (1977) *Co-operative Society Superstores*, RORU, Manchester Business School, Manchester.

Tomalin, C. (1999) 'Retail planning environment: England and Wales', *European Retail Digest*, **21** (March), 19–20.

Tomalin, C. and J. Pal (1994) 'Local authority responses to retail change', *International Journal of Retail & Distribution Management*, **22** (6), 51–56.

Wade, B. (1983) *Superstore Appeals—Alternative Impact Assessment Methods*, Unit for Retail Planning Information, Reading.

Webber, R. (1997) 'New techniques for comparing site quality within and across shopping centres', *European Retail Digest*, Summer, 4–6.

Weisbrod, G.E., R.J. Parcells and C. Kern (1984) 'A disaggregate model for predicting shopping area market attraction', *Journal of Retailing*, **60** (1), 65–83.

Whysall, P. (1995) 'Regenerating inner city shopping centres', *Journal of Retailing and Consumer Services*, **2** (1), 3–13.

Wilson, B.L. (1984) 'Modern methods of sales forecasting: regression models', in *Store Location and Store Assessment Research*, R.L. Davies and D.S. Rogers (eds), Wiley, Chichester, pp. 301–318.

Wrigley, N. (1985) *Categorical Data Analysis for Geographers and Environmental Scientists*, Longman, London.

Wrigley, N. (1988) *Store Choice, Store Location and Market Analysis*, Routledge, New York.

Ziliani, C. (2000) 'Retail micro-marketing: strategic advance or gimmick?', *International Review of Retail, Distribution and Consumer Research*, **10** (4), 355–368

Eight

Product Selection and Buying

INTRODUCTION

Buying represents the translation of a retailer's strategic positioning statement into the overall assortment and the specific products to support that statement. The retail buyer therefore holds a pivotal role in the implementation of retail strategy and, especially within smaller organizations, may be a principle architect of that strategy. Getting the product assortment right has been described as the 'engine of success' in retailing (Aufreiter et al., 1993). It would therefore be an understatement to say that buying is an important element within the retail mix; the work of the buyer largely underpins many of the pricing, merchandising and communications decisions that will be examined in later chapters.

This chapter first considers the nature of the buying function within retail organizations, including the role of the buyer, relationships with suppliers, category management and the supply chain. Important decision areas are then examined, starting with the character of the overall product mix. Decisions on quantity, specific products, suppliers and negotiated terms are then considered.

In spite of its pivotal role, buying was not an early focus of conceptual and empirical attention within the retailing literature (Ettenson and Wagner, 1986: Holm Hansen and Skytte, 1998). Major changes in supply chain relationships and technologies have however provoked increased attention (e.g. Hendry, 1996). The product mix was recently the focus of a special issue of the Journal of Retailing (Kahn, 1999), with a subsequent issue devoted to supply chain management (Grewal, 2000). Readers requiring detailed treatments of the operation of retail buying can also consult one of the specialist texts on the subject (Cash et al., 1995; Diamond and Pintel, 1997; Jackson and Shaw, 2001; Varley, 2001).

8.1 The Buying Function

This section focuses primarily upon buying *within* retail organizations, rather than the external purchasing channels that may be utilized. It should be recognized, however, that some retailers prefer to delegate part of their buying functions to brokers or to resident buying offices, possibly situated in major centres of supply in other countries (Diamond and Pintel, 1997). As noted in Chapter 2, retailers within voluntary groups also delegate most of the purchasing role to the group wholesalers or head office. There is, in fact, an enormous diversity of purchasing structures, and the same holds true of the internal organization of the retailers' buying functions.

8.1.1 The Role of the Retail Buyer

Within small retail companies, buying may be one of the numerous management roles undertaken by the individual owner or store manager. If a buyer is employed, he or she is likely to have a very extended role, which may include most of the pricing, merchandising and promotional functions. Within larger retail companies, a twofold change has occurred in the role of buyers. On the one hand, the importance and complexity of the buying task has become greater as organizations grow larger, product assortments expand and competition intensifies. It is now the responsibility of the buyers to utilize this purchasing power to the best possible advantage, and mistakes become increasingly costly. On the other hand, as companies become sufficiently large to justify, or realize the need for, specialist marketing management, some of the functions traditionally undertaken by buyers have been taken over by other managers.

There are arguments for and against the separation of buying and the other marketing functions. Possibly the most persuasive argument is that they are different jobs, requiring different types of ability, personality and training. Rosenbloom (1981) also noted the lack of effective integration within some retail organizations when marketing decisions are scattered between buying and other functional divisions. On the other hand, it is obviously essential for the buyer to be involved in, or closely aware of, the relevant promotional and merchandising decisions. Rapid feedback on customer reactions at store level is also essential.

Retailers with full point-of-sale (PoS) data capture systems can process all this information to provide buyers with a completely up-to-date picture of sales trends by item and by store. Not only does this enable immediate adjustments to be made to reorder levels, it also provides a formidable weapon in negotiating with suppliers. It would be quite wrong, however, to assume that this type of information, however comprehensive and rapidly available, is a complete substitute for liaison between buyers and store personnel. The buyer also needs to know about customer needs *not* satisfied by the product range. A detailed system of recording reasons for product returns is one approach, although this relates only to the existing range. When Nordstrom Inc. improved its management information systems, some managers feared that computers might shield buyers from having good access to the shopping pattern of the consumer.

The old school was to read it off the customer's face. The new school reads it off their volume purchases and makes sure they are adequately in stock.

They are continuing with the strategy that highlights attention to the consumer, but at the same time centralising some of the organisation in order to leverage technology (Johnson, 1998).

The responsibilities of retail buyers are still extremely diverse, although more of them tend to be shared with other areas of retail management. From a survey of 63 retail buyers in the grocery, clothing and footwear sectors, Swindley (1992) identified 34 areas for which some or all of the buyers had responsibility. Table 8.1 shows the strong role of buyers within decisions on the assortment mix, if not always within the strategic planning of the company.

Table 8.1
Responsibilities of retail buyers

Source: Swindley (1992).

Area of responsibility	Extent of responsibility		
	% sole	% shared	% none
Strategic planning	7	40	53
Market monitoring	34	58	8
Identifying market gaps	48	48	4
Proposing product areas	72	19	9
Deciding on product areas	44	43	13
Selecting products within area	86	14	0
Product design	19	67	14
Specifying formulations	18	67	16
Assessing product feasibility	58	40	2
Specifying packaging	19	73	8
Quality control	13	62	25
New product launches	41	57	2
Monitoring stock availability	32	55	13
Allocating stock to stores	33	25	42
Physical distribution	7	19	74
Liasing with stores	36	61	3
Space allocation and planning	7	64	29
In-store display	6	60	34
Selecting suppliers	86	13	1
Supplier appraised	71	28	1
Negotiating with suppliers	89	11	0
Progress chasing with suppliers	58	36	6
Sales forecasting	47	45	8
Monitoring product performance	60	40	0
Replenishment buying	31	34	35
Initiating sales promotions	53	42	5
Implementing sales promotions	29	50	21
Initiating advertising	19	53	28
Implementing advertising	5	36	60
Budgeting for purchasing	50	36	14
Direct product profitability	55	31	15
Pricing	82	18	0
Authorizing markdowns	45	34	21
Training junior buyers	50	44	7

The study also revealed the extent of involvement in product design, formulation, packaging and testing. While these functions may be among the traditional roles of manufacturers, they are likely to be among the retail buyer's responsibilities when purchasing own-brand groceries or apparel (Chapter 9). While few buyers may have direct responsibility for physical distribution, the effectiveness of that system influences their ability to maintain optimum stock levels in stores. Along with merchandising managers, many buyers have involvement in allocation and display decisions (Chapter 12).

Supplier selection, appraisal and negotiation are core responsibilities of retail buying departments, and their most time consuming activity. The majority claimed to spend at least half their time dealing with suppliers. Sales forecasting is especially important in apparel buying, where there may be long lead times between ordering and delivery. In larger grocery companies, electronic, sales-based ordering (SBO) has taken over much of the routine reordering task.

The buyers claimed considerable responsibility for decisions on pricing and markdowns (where applicable). Their involvement in sales promotions and advertising varied considerably between companies. The majority of buyers spend some of their time training junior buyers: when presented with the statement: 'Good buyers are born, not made', only 19 per cent agreed and 61 per cent disagreed. Forrester (1987) and Farrington and Waters (1995) have also helped to dispel the myth that 'flair' alone is sufficient to make an effective buyer. There are many skills that can be enhanced by an effective training programme.

This raises the question of what are the most important characteristics of a retail buyer. Jackson and Shaw (2001) identified eleven personal characteristics sought by retailers when recruiting buyers:

- commercial skills
- multi-tasking flexibility
- retentive memory
- mental agility
- energetic
- positive approach to problems/criticism
- self-motivated
- consistent temperament
- people/action oriented
- tough but fair
- creative flair.

Table 8.2 extends and quantifies this list, based upon a survey of buyers. The complexity of retail buying decisions places considerable demands on buyers. They need effectively to assimilate large volumes of information, be highly competent in the mathematical appraisal of suppliers' terms and also be effective communicators and negotiators. Buying offers a challenging and rewarding career for many graduates;

some large organizations are having to develop a specialist career track within the buying function.

The effectiveness of buyers has long been recognized as an important component in the performance of retail companies. An early study of this relationship, Martin (1973) compared the buyers of two stores, one highly successful and one with declining sales. From detailed interviews and systematic evaluations of the buyers, it was found that those of the successful store were more self-confident, more aggressive and more likely to show leadership in new product trends. It was held that a lack of these traits contributed to the other store's decline.

Table 8.2 Most important characteristics of a retail buyer

Note: All these are considered to be important: the percentages indicate how often they were mentioned as being a most important characteristic.

Source: Swindley (1992).

Characteristic	%	Characteristic	%
Negotiation skills	42	Self-confidence	10
Market awareness	35	Knowledge of customer	10
Commercial/financial awareness	26	Good with people	10
Communication skills	24	Strong/assertive personality	10
Commercial taste	19	Can work under pressure	8
Numeracy	19	Clear thinking	8
Product knowledge	18	Ambition/motivation	6
Good planning/organization	18	Decisiveness	6
Determination/tenacity	16	Experience	6
Imagination/innovation/creativity	16	Marketing skills	6
Common sense	15	Leadership	5
Integrity/fairness	13	Ability to listen	5
Flexible/open mind	13	Teamworking	3
Analytical mind	12	Knowledge of competition	2

8.1.2 Organization of Retail Buying

The organization of the buying function must be developed to suit the size and structure of the retail operation, the types and assortments of products sold and the strategic focus of the company. A chain of largely homogenous DIY stores may be best served by strongly centralized buying, whereas more diverse groupings of department stores, or stores at airports, may benefit from local buying decisions (Freathy and O'Connell, 1998; Holm Hansen and Skytte, 1998). Some retailers allow their specialist product buyers considerable individual autonomy, whereas others utilize buying committees to oversee a wide range of buying decisions. Companies heavily involved in own brands and product innovation, such as Marks & Spencer, require a major technical input in the buying process, whereas others see this as the domain of the manufacturer.

One characteristic that has been common across most large retail organizations has been the increased centralization of the buying function. Indeed, this may be seen as part of a general trend towards the separation of conception from execution in retailing (Dawson, 1995; Freathy and Sparks, 1995). In Swindley's (1992) survey of grocery and apparel buyers, 80 per cent stated that no buying took place at store level within their companies. Cash et al. (1995) examined in detail the advantages and disadvantages of this trend. In summary, the main advantages are:

1 More effective use of buying power in negotiation of supply prices and terms.
2 Specialist buyers can devote more time to the analysis of market trends and the identification of new product opportunities in their product or customer category.
3 Own-brand development is more cost-effective of undertaken centrally.
4 With access to more and aggregate sales data, forecasts are likely to be more accurate than those based on limited, localized observations.
5 The cost of the buying function is lower as economies of scale are obtained.
6 Better and more rapid quality control procedures can be implemented, either at the manufacturer/importer's distribution point or within the retailer's own warehouse; time-consuming returns and customer complaints are therefore minimized.
7 A more consistent assortment can be presented across all the stores to back up national promotions and image-building.
8 The quality of buying and stock control decisions is equalized across stores.
9 Store managers need not be selectors and negotiators; their time is freed to concentrate upon store organization and the motivation of sales personnel.

The trend towards fewer, larger retail companies has increased the benefits to be derived from central buying but has also highlighted some of the problems. Accordingly, various attempts have been made to increase sensitivity to local needs while retaining the advantages of central buying. With improved information systems, more analyses can be undertaken at store level to identify different demand patterns and/or performance levels. In companies with very large numbers of outlets, systems have been introduced to fit assortments to local conditions (e.g. Grewel et al., 1999), with flexibility also in space allocations (e.g. Desmet and Renaudin, 1998) and prices (e.g. Competition Commission, 2000). Approaches to the localization of the product mix are considered further in Sec. 8.2.1.

Given the diversity of buying organizations within retail companies, it is not considered meaningful to represent a 'typical' buying structure. Tse (1985) undertook a detailed examination of the Marks & Spencer buying structure and the activities normally involved in the procurement process. Of particular interest was the breakdown of the buying function into four major elements: those undertaken by selectors, merchandisers, technologists and quality controllers. The prominent role of the technologist in the buying function, not just as a 'back room' expert, was then unusual in retailing. The concept of specification buying, with a very close involvement with the manufacturer, was more characteristic of industrial than retail buying. As retailers have become more proactive in product development, this type of involvement has become more common (Varley, 2001).

Although buying is now a highly specialized role, buyers must liaise with a large number of departments within their organizations, as well as many outside suppliers and other agencies. Figure 8.1 offers a generic view of the many interactions and influences that characterize a large retail buying organization. The merchandisers, own-brand product managers, technologists (if any) and quality controllers tend to work most closely with the buying function. In some companies, they are considered to be part of the buying team, or members of the buying committee.

The number of interactions implied by Fig. 8.1 underlines the need for effective communications within the organization. Retailers have been urged to 'go horizontal' in their communications between functions. This way they avoid the delays and potential distortions of 'up, over and down' communications, whereby information is reported to a senior executive, who then passes it over to another function before it is passed down to the people who will use that information.

Figure 8.1 Buying units: interactions and influences

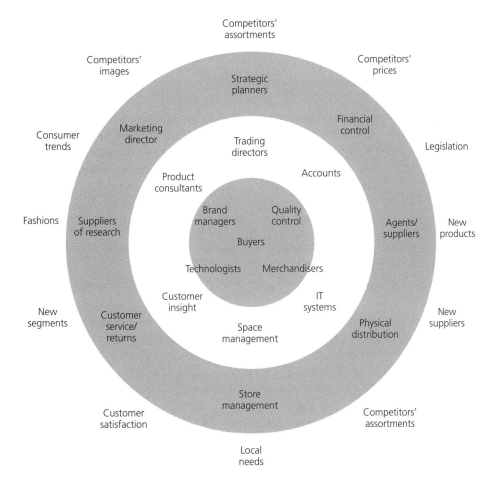

Information technology systems have made great progress towards the facilitation of horizontal communications, in order that the buyers and others can access information about a product's sales history, source, distribution, space allocation, promotions, current sales and returns. Likewise, the system can profile an individual supplier on its track record, delivery reliability, product quality and previous terms of trade. In addition, the buyer needs to be appraised of a great deal of information about market trends, fashions, competitor's products/prices and new product development.

While most large organizations have extensively deployed IT systems to improve information flow, the lines of responsibility differ greatly. *SuperMarketing* (1994) compared two multiples, one that gave its buyers extensive responsibility, yet major listing decisions had to be approved by a senior buyer. Its rival, on the other hand, held weekly committee meetings to hear arguments for new product listings, put forward by the buyers, not the suppliers. Although more time-consuming, buying committees do have some advantages:

1 A wider range of experience is applied to the decision-making process.
2 Decisions are made in a more scientific atmosphere.
3 The level of pressure in the buyer–salesperson relationship is lowered.

From a study of buying within one of Sweden's largest supermarket chains, Nilsson and Host (1987) identified the respective roles and orientations of individual buyers and the buying committee. The buyers receive tenders, gather information, negotiate and analyse the offers. Then they combine a number of facts on individual 'item sheets', which are then presented to a formal committee which meets once a month. The overall goals of the buyers and the committee members have much in common, although the different responsibilities and perspectives create the possibility of conflicts. Venkatesh et al. (1995) studied some of the power sources and influence strategies at work within buying centres, drawing upon the social power framework of French and Raven (1959):

1 *Referent power*: the person is held in high regard and others share his/her values.
2 *Information power*: the person has information and direct contact with suppliers.
3 *Expert power*: the person knows about the needs and the product and is competent to make the assessment.
4 *Reward power*: it is important to be recognized and approved of by him or her, for reasons of pay, promotions, etc.
5 *Coercive power*: the person could make life difficult, block promotions, assign unpleasant tasks, etc.
6 *Legitimate power*: the person has the authority, the right or a high stake in the outcome of the decision.

Within a retail buying committee, the buyer may well hold most of the information power, while the marketing or brand managers may have expert knowledge of market needs or product desirability. The trading director, on the other hand, may hold much of the reward or coercive power! In theory, the more effective sharing of information and greater clarity of goals should reduce the level of dysfunctional conflict within buying committees.

However, there is US evidence (Keaveney, 1992) that some good buyers leave committee-based buying situations to seek more autonomy, which has also been observed in the UK (SuperMarketing, 1994). The evidence would suggest that buyers generally have more autonomy in department store retailing (Fairhurst and Fiorito, 1990; Keaveney, 1995; Wagner et al., 1989). In the grocery sector, committees tend to be more common (Holm Hansen and Skytte, 1998; McGoldrick and Douglas, 1983; Nilsson and Host, 1987).

8.1.3 Buying Groups and Exchanges

Beyond the boundaries of the individual retail organization, there are also interorganizational groups, some formed primarily to strengthen the buying power of small-medium sized retail firms. The purpose of such alliances was summarized by Shaw and Dawson (1995): 'Co-operation between two or more retail companies, whereby each partner seeks to add to its competencies by combining some resources with those of its partners.'

Ansoff (1991) attributed the growth in alliance activity to turbulence in the retailing environment. In many countries, it is the growth in the power of the major chains that has induced the sometimes diverse groupings of smaller retailers to band together for survival. In so doing, they can achieve a number of benefits (Shaw et al., 1994):

1 *Economies of scale*: in buying, marketing, product testing, branding, operations, legal and personnel services.
2 *Economies of replication*: in operating systems, product assortments, designs and layouts.
3 *Economies of scope*: combining product ranges to achieve the optimum mix, and access to promotional vehicles beyond the scope of individual members.

The diversity of activities and obligations of buying group membership are illustrated by Table 8.3. This is based upon a survey of 37 groups, the majority of which provide purchasing services (Shaw and Dawson, 1995; Shaw et al., 1994). In addition, over half provided advertising and promotions, although only around one-third require participation. This is in contrast with the 'voluntary groups' (Chapter 2), which generally require greater participation by members. An example of a buying group is Associated Independent Stores, based in Solihull, which serves 300 independent stores. It imports and buys in the fashion, furniture and housewares categories, as well as providing marketing, quality control and statistical services (Retail Directory, 2000).

Table 8.3 Services of buying groups

Source: adapted from Shaw and Dawson, 1995; Shaw et al., 1994.

Function	% of groups offering (a)	% of (a) requiring participation
Advertising	57	33
Recommended prices	46	29
Price ticketing	32	17
Store layout advice	27	30
In-store promotion	57	33
Shelf layout advice	24	11
Stock management	22	13
Market research	24	22
Product catalogue	43	19
Own-brand provision	51	26
Product testing	16	17
Magazine	32	3
Social events	43	6
Political lobbying	22	25

Alliances are by no means confined to smaller retailers; many majors have developed power, as well as sharing expertise and sourcing opportunities (Robinson and Clarke-Hill, 1995). The European Marketing Distribution (EMD) alliance accounts for turnover of nearly 100 billion Euros, including chains from 13 European countries. Associated Marketing Services (AMS), which includes Safeway, follows closely behind (IGD, 2000). There are also alliances linking co-operatives internationally (NAF International and Intergroup): Spar International links Spar organizations from 28 countries. These international alliances are considered further in Chapter 14.

The Internet has facilitated the growth of a far more flexible form of buying relationship, the trading exchange:

> *The new exchanges are a little like an Internet chat room, allowing numerous players to exchange messages. Each participant can trade with as many or as few companies as they choose: retailers and suppliers can communicate electronically, negotiate deals, or invite tenders for particular contracts (Retail Intelligence, 2000).*

The World Wide Retail Exchanges (WWRE) was formed in 2000 by 11 of the world's major retailers, including Kingfisher, Tesco and Marks & Spencer. It rapidly grew to 55 retail members, with combined retail sales of $762 billion. The WWRE operates as an independent third party, focused purely on lowering costs and improving efficiency (IGD, 2001a). In the same year, Sears Roebuck and Carrefour formed the GlobalNetExchange (GNE), soon joined by Kroger, Sainsbury, Metro and Coles Myer. Wal-Mart, on the other hand, considered that it has less to gain from such an exchange, having already developed its own EDI and extranet system (Retail Link).

Trading on GlobalNetExchange was initially confined to goods not for resale, such as retailing and office equipment. However, its role was soon extended to goods for sale (Retail Intelligence, 2000). The networks provide scope for numerous, rapidly conducted auctions, which may be of the standard type (supplier led) or a reverse auction (buyer led) (Cuthbertson, 2000). Tesco was among the pioneers of WWRE electronic reverse auctions, conducting a three-hour auction for corned beef supplies. This attracted five bids, produced savings and trimmed purchase time down from three days to three hours (Retail Review, 2000).

Tesco is using such auctions to bring more continuity to its non-food assortments worldwide. Clothing, stationery and housewares in particular will be sourced this way (Retail Review, 2001). Ahold of Holland believes that it could be buying 30–50 per cent of its requirements from the World Wide Retail Exchange by 2010. However, the exchanges are not just about auctions, according to a review by the IGD (2001b) they are about:

▶ an on-line market place, i.e., matching buyers and sellers
▶ transaction processing, i.e., electronic data exchanges
▶ collaborative systems, i.e., sharing information and jointly co-ordinating logistics, promotions, etc.
▶ a club, i.e., a forum in which ideas can be aired and exchanged.

It remains to be seen whether the exchanges will lead to a fruitful harmonization of standards, a genuine rapport between retailers and suppliers, and low-cost entry for small players. The alternative scenario is that mutual distrust and opportunism may lead to their collapse (IGD, 2001b).

Indeed, when companies can form electronically enabled B2B alliances with increasing ease, the need for centralized exchanges comes into question (Harvard Business Review, 2000).

8.1.4 Relationships with Suppliers

The current emphasis upon relationship marketing has already been discussed in Chapter 3, with regard to retailer's efforts to build longer-term and better relationships with their customers. The same emphasis has also pervaded discussion of the supplier–retailer interaction, with the emergence or the reincarnation of terms such as 'partnering' and 'trade marketing'. It is appropriate now to consider how much of this emphasis reflects real change, wishful thinking on the part of suppliers, and/or enthusiasm to establish a 'new paradigm'.

Indeed, some of the most experienced of retailing academics have questioned the 'newness' of relationship marketing, in essence if not in terminologies. Roger Dickinson and Stanley Hollander are among those who pointed to interest in marketing relationships that spanned the last century (Keep et al., 1998). However, there have been changes in orientation, albeit more on the supplier side than the buying side. There have also been changes in the style and the technology of supplier–retailer interactions, both of which have changed the character of these relationships.

The expression 'trade marketing' (TM) conveys a supplier perspective upon how relationships with their (trade) customers can best be managed. It has not been consistently defined, as Dupuis and Tissier-Desbordes (1996) have observed. In Italy, it was defined as:

> *A series of actions, the purpose of which is to identify, plan and manage more effectively, in order to optimise the use of the company's resources and to obtain a lasting competitive advantage (Fornari, 1986).*

Fornari (1988) further specified the actions, which logically stem from a TM orientation, as:

1 Estimating the growth potential of each channel and member.
2 Measuring supplier–retailer power relations to identify negotiation issues.
3 Building a business plan with every client.
4 Increasing profitability for each channel/client by optimization of company investments.

Summarizing the emerging perspectives on the subject, Dupuis and Tissier-Desbordes (1996) offer a definition, which emphasizes the partnership aspect TM:

> *A methodical procedure carried out jointly by suppliers and retailers, whose objective is to better serve customers' needs and expectations, increase profitability and competitive position, while taking into account each other's constraints and specificity.*

Focusing upon the changing role of the trade marketer, Davies (1993) supports the view that TM is not an entirely new concept:

> *The trade marketing manager is not a totally new role: most sales forces have always had to recognise the significance of key accounts. What is new is its importance and professionalism. Trade marketers are now business managers, not just salespeople, advisers or planners, but people with an in depth knowledge of their customer.*

In the USA, the term 'partnering' tends to be used, generally implying a stronger relationship than TM (Mentzer et al., 2000). According to the *International Journal of Physical Distribution* (1990), the ultimate objective of partnering is 'the formulation of joint marketing plans and strategies between suppliers and retailers'. Indeed this comes closer to the objectives of 'category management' discussed in the following section.

In a study of retail buyers and their fresh-produce suppliers, Knox and White (1991) drew upon concepts of industrial marketing (e.g. Ford, 1990) to depict the development of the relationships:

1 *The pre-relationship stage*: during which an evaluation of a new supplier is made.

2 *The early stage*: in which negotiation of a sample delivery is made.

3 *The development stage*: where a contract is signed and deliveries begin.

4 *The long-term stage*: after several major purchases and large-scale deliveries have been made.

5 *The final stage*: when long-established stable markets have been achieved.

In spite of all the recent attention to relationships, a supplier would be ill advised to assume that all retailers necessarily want a long-term relationship. As the initiation and development stages can require much investment by the supplier, Ganesan (1994) suggested that they should first assess the time horizon of the retailer and direct their marketing effort accordingly. Smaller retailers (Chatterjee et al., 1995) or larger ones (Collins and Burt, 1999) may have good reasons to opt for a more balanced portfolio of sources, usually to reduce dependence upon one supplier for a particular product type.

There are, however, a number of reasons why even the most powerful of retailers may wish to focus their buying power around a small number of longer-term relationships:

1 The development and supply of own brand products usually involves a medium- to long-term relationship (Morelli, 1999).

2 Food retailers require consistent supplies of fresh foods to uphold their images, which favours longer-term contracts with growers (Knox and White, 1991). Examples are J. Sainsbury's 'Partnership in Livestock' and 'Partnership in Produce' schemes (Burt and Davis, 1999).

3 Joint development work often requires the expertise of both parties.

Partnership sourcing, our policy of establishing long-term, mutually beneficial partnerships with suppliers, brings great benefits to our customers through more vigorous product innovation and superior quality standards (Tesco Annual Report, quoted in Burt and Davis, 1999).

4 There is a limited number of manufacturers capable of supplying the volume and quality in some sectors, unless the retailer decides to use international sourcing (Bowlby and Foord, 1995).

5 Some manufacturer brands are almost essential to the assortment of a retailer wishing to offer good choice to its customers (Dawson and Shaw, 1989).

6 The development of trust in the supplier-retailer relationship can lead to cost-efficiencies and higher profits (Kumar, 1996; Nicholson et al., 2001).

An illustration of changing times was provided by the evolution of the relationship between the two giants, Procter & Gamble (P&G) and Wal-Mart. As the latter increased its power and refused to comply with the terms dictated by P&G, the two developed a notoriously adversarial relationship. As Sam Walton expressed the situation: 'We just let our buyers slug it out with their salesmen' (Walton and Huey, 1992).

Only when a mutual friend arranged a canoe trip for Sam Walton and Lou Pritchard, P&G's vice-president for sales, did things start to change. After that, senior members of both organizations met to re-examine the relationship between the two companies. Now the companies work far more closely together, using IT to increase sales and reduce costs for both parties (Kumar, 1996). In the words of one UK buyer, we must now: 'Change from being a Rottweiler to a St Bernard' (Loughlin, 1999).

If this starts to conjure a view of supplier–retailer relationships without tensions and conflict, then it is important to dispel this without delay. Corstjens and Corstjens (1995) emphasize the 'bottom line' of these relationships: 'Co-operation and partnerships can only be won from retailers by answering their needs better than the competition.' The Competition Commission (2000) referred to a 'climate of apprehension' among the suppliers of major grocery companies. Many refused to speak about the matter at all, others expressed varying levels of (dis)satisfaction:

> *They were satisfied with their overall relationships with the multiples they supplied, or had developed a modus vivendi in the interests of continuing business.*

> *Multiples talked about partnerships but these did not exist and multiples ruthlessly eroded suppliers' margins with no consideration to the damage they were doing to that company or its employees (Competition Commission, 2000).*

Retailers are well aware that, as their volume of trade with a supplier grows, the supplier will probably gain from 'experience curve' effects. If the supplier's costs per unit are falling, it is natural that the retailer will wish to revisit the issue of supply terms, from time to time. This creates one likely source of tension within longer-term relationships (Amirani and Dickenson, 1995).

In practice, it is unrealistic to assume that retailer–supplier relationships, however long-term, are likely to be free of conflict. Hughes (1996) argues that co-operation and adversarialism can and do coexist within such relationships. Further evidence of this was provided by Hogarth-Scott and Parkinson (1993): 'There is a confrontation, but there is also commitment. Both parties recognise how important they are to each other.'

In longer-term relationships, Ganesan (1993) concluded that the parties used problem-solving and 'passive-aggressive' strategies to resolve conflicts on major issues. Unlike the more bellicose, active-aggressive behaviours, passive-aggressive strategies tend to emerge when concern for own outcome (assertiveness) is combined with concern for the other party's outcome (co-operativeness). As mutual concern to maximize joint gain moves from being a short-term to a long-term feature of the relationship, the negotiating style is likely to shift from being simply co-operative to 'co-ordinative'. This is sometimes referred to as non-coercive influence strategy, usually involving extensive information sharing (Dabholkar et al., 1994).

From this brief overview of retailer–supplier relationships, it is clear that significant change has occurred on their operational characteristics. It is equally clear, however, that different levels of power and dependence produce enormous variations in the nature of individual relationships. From a study of supplier–retailer interactions in the bread and hosiery sectors, Bowlby and Foord (1995) identified many characteristics of the supplier and retailer that influence the relationship, these being summarized in Table 8.4. Generally, these identify specific elements of dependency, which in turn reflect the power of the other party.

Table 8.4 Influences upon the balance of the relationship

Source: Bowlby and Foord (1995).

Supplier characteristic	Examples and implications
Relative size and position in sector	Two largest suppliers in hosiery sector play major role in determining importance of hosiery in retailers' product mix, through advertisements and product presence
Size of product area in supplier's overall product range	Some hosiery firms increased bargaining power by diversifying into lingerie, decreasing their dependence on hosiery contracts
Sector organization and concentration	Competition between two main plant bakers weakened their bargaining power with retailers
Ownership of supplying firm	The corporate power of the two plant bakers allows them favourable access to materials supplies and to research
Balance of branded and retailer brand products in supplier's portfolio	Those producing only retailer brands are in a weaker position
Geographical location	Bakers who can supply all of a local or national retailer's stores are in a stronger position

Retailer characteristic	Examples and implications
Relative size and position of retailer	As major 'gatekeepers' to the consumer market, large grocery and variety store retailers are in a strong bargaining position
Volume of retailer's purchase	Retailers who purchase large volumes can demand lower prices from non-specialist suppliers
Significance of product area in retailer's mix	Hosiery is more significant to variety and department stores than to grocery retailers. The former are therefore more proactive in design, quality, etc.
Balance of manufacturer and retailer brands in retailer's mix	Growth in own brand sales increased retailer's bargaining power with producers of manufacturers brands

Figure 8.2 Dependence and power in relationships

Source: based upon Hogarth-Scott and Parkinson (1993); Kumar (1996).

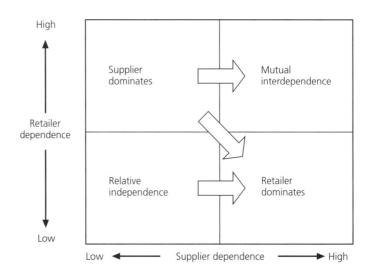

The importance of dependence has been widely recognized in the field of industrial purchasing (e.g. Cunningham and Homse, 1986) and is now acknowledged as being a key feature of retailer's relationships with their suppliers (e.g. Davies, 1990).

Figure 8.2 depicts the contrasting levels of mutual dependence, illustrating why such relationships can evoke so many different descriptions. The case of P&G and Wal-Mart mentioned earlier fits the category of high interdependence. Some of the cases reported by the Competition Commission (2000), on the other hand, suggest an imbalance of dependence, with the retailer holding the balance of power. With concentration of retailer buying power now being a feature in many countries, there is a general shift towards the right-hand side of the matrix in Fig. 8.2. Little wonder that manufacturers are keen to find other ways of trying to rebalance the relationship.

8.1.5 Category Management

The high-level meetings that occurred between Wal-Mart and Procter & Gamble have been attributed as being the origin of category management (Kumar, 1996; Management Horizons, 1999). The retailer moved on from those initial meetings to set up cross-functional teams, for specific categories, who interacted with their opposite numbers within the supplier organization. In common with most 'new concepts', category management has been the subject of varying definitions and interpretations.

Category Management is the strategic management of product groups through trade partnerships, which aims to maximise sales and profits by satisfying consumer needs (IGD, 1997).

Category management is a retailer/supplier process of managing categories as strategic business units, producing enhanced business results by focusing on delivering consumer value (ECR Europe, in IGD, 1999a).

The way some people talk, category management is just a fancy word for merchandising or ranging. For others, it's the key to the future (Management Horizons, 1999).

Many of the major suppliers and retailers in Europe are reported to have adopted, or at least experimented, with category management. The top four grocers in the UK, as well as Carrefour and Auchan in France, have used it. Boots, B & Q, Debenhams and Karstadt in Germany have also applied category management principles (Management Horizons, 1999). Some companies have fundamentally realigned their relationships with suppliers; others have simply allowed category management principles to influence the way they think about categories and their product assortments (Freedman et al., 1997).

Large-scale retailers, such as Boots and Debenhams, have had to compete increasingly with nimble and focused specialists. The application of category management is analogous in many ways to the use of shops-in-shops (Chapter 4), but without some of the drawbacks associated with using outside concessions. The category is run more like a strategic business unit, with the help or influence of suppliers' expertise, but the management of the point of sale is not delegated to another party (IGD, 1995).

A step-by-step approach is one way to illustrate the category management principle and how it works in practice. For detailed explanations, readers can consult Management Horizons (1999) which defines the major steps to create a category management structure. The IGD (1997) offers a detailed guide to the implementation of category management, when that structure is in place. The following overview focuses upon those elements which are particular, if not unique, features category management.

Cross-Functional Teamwork

Not all of the components of category management are new (Buckingham, 1994) including the idea of cross-functional involvement in product selection and buying. There has been a gradual movement in this direction, as retailers have become larger and the product management task more complex. Figure 8.3 illustrates this trend, as more specialists become involved in the management of the product mix.

On the face of it, this may appear to be a simple realignment of specialist functions that already exist within the organization. However, as Dettmann (1999) observes: 'The internal walls between departments or functions are often at least as high as those between suppliers and retailers.' As discussed in Sec. 8.1.2, IT systems have helped to overcome functional divisions, without a huge proliferation of internal meetings. Similarly, the cross-functional interactions between retailers and their suppliers can also be facilitated through information-sharing systems. In theory, when retailers and suppliers pool their information on consumer trends, they can achieve greater insight than when working alone.

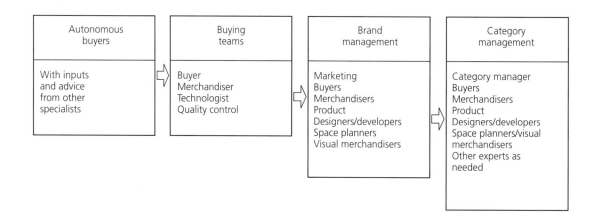

Autonomous buyers	Buying teams	Brand management	Category management
With inputs and advice from other specialists	Buyer Merchandiser Technologist Quality control	Marketing Buyers Merchandisers Product Designers/developers Space planners Visual merchandisers	Category manager Buyers Merchandisers Product Designers/developers Space planners/visual merchandisers Other experts as needed

Figure 8.3 The evolution of category responsibility

Source: adapted from Management Horizons (1999).

Figure 8.4 illustrates how the traditional buyer–account manager interaction could create a 'bottleneck' in the flow of information, and in the establishment of interorganizational working relationships. Under the category management model, more specialists interact, helping to find the best solutions to product development, marketing or supply chain issues. Clearly, if a retailer were to enter this form of relationship with large numbers of suppliers, it would become extremely time-consuming.

One answer to this is to appoint a major supplier as a 'category captain', a role that Procter & Gamble fulfils for Wal-Mart. Many Procter & Gamble executives are based at Wal-Mart's headquarters in Arkansas, running some categories on behalf of Wal-Mart, to agreed performance targets (Management Horizons, 1999). However, not all retailers agree with the idea of giving one supplier quite so much power in a category (Dettmann, 1999). The Competition Commission (2000) has also expressed concern about the potential barriers to smaller suppliers that are presented by category management in general, and the 'category captain' concept in particular

Category Definition

Traditionally, grocery retailers would see crisps, orange juice and sandwiches as items in different categories. Taking a view which aligns more closely with customer needs and perceptions, these could all be seen as part of a category called 'lunch-time snacks'. Varley (2000) illustrates how this category within Boots had been grouped to include also rolls/pastries, salads and desserts. Kroger supermarkets in the USA have created categories such as '15-minute meals', 'eating lite' and 'kids love this stuff'.

Almost inevitably, these category definitions lead to duplication of display, if an item logically exists within more than one category. The alternative is to risk confusing/alienating shoppers who are following the

Figure 8.4 Widening the retailer–supplier interface

Source: adapted from Management Horizons (1999).

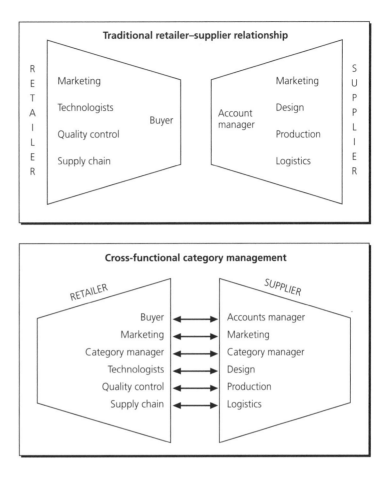

more conventional category logic. For example, if buying several dairy products, a shopper may be annoyed to find that his or her preferred type of plain yoghurt had been relocated to an 'organics' category, elsewhere in the store. If product displays are duplicated, this has implications for the size of the total assortment, and the replenishment of more, smaller display locations. The consumer perspective is however crucial:

> *A category is defined as a distinct, manageable group of products that consumers perceive as related and/or substitutable in meeting a consumer need (Gruen and Shah, 2000).*

There is no doubt that category redefinition can cause changes in buying patterns, sometimes not the ones anticipated (Areni et al., 1999). Needel (1998) presented a virtual-reality based simulation of the shopping environment to help predict consumer reactions to different display groupings. He also outlined techniques for producing 'behavioural maps' of consumers' cross-purchasing patterns, based upon panel data, to help identify category groupings for specific shoppers/segments. With loyalty card and EPoS data combined, some retailers are able to identify these purchase groupings themselves, from their own in-house data.

Category Planning and Implementation

Of course, customer-need based classification systems are not new to retailing; they have been used in retail store layouts for many years (e.g. Rosenbloom, 1981). Likewise, most of the prescribed tasks in the application of category management have earlier origins. The difference, however, is the focus upon the category as a strategic business unit, and the extent of supplier involvement in category planning.

Table 8.5 summarizes the recommended stages of category planning and implementation, once the intra-organizational and inter-organizational structures are in place. Having defined the category, its role(s) within the total assortment are established. It may be a 'destination' category, highly instrumental in creating visits to the outlet, or a 'core' category, the type of product that the outlet is expected to sell. Product category roles are considered further in Sec. 8.2.1, as these are not unique to category management.

Table 8.5 Category planning and implementation

Source: derived from IGD (1997).

1. *Define the category*: definition should be comprehensive and align with consumer needs and perceptions
2. *Set category role*: assigns the purpose of the category in helping to achieve business goals, taking into account customers, retail positioning, suppliers, category prospects and competition
3. *Category assessment*: identifies the performance gap between current and target performance, taking subcategories, segments, brands and individual skills
4. *Category strategy*: how to deliver the desired performance levels through effective use of available resources
5. *Category scorecard*: to measure performance improvement, taking into account the consumer, the retailer and supply chain efficiencies, making sure that targets in one area are not achieved at the expense of others
6. *Category tactics*: to convert the strategy into a series of specific measures, relating to range, pricing, promotion, space allocation and product availability
7. *Plan implementation*: gaining approval, allocating responsibilities, setting time frames
8. *Category review*: to measure, monitor and modify the category's progress on a regular basis

Having defined the category scope and role, targets may be set and strategies developed to close any performance gaps. Drawing upon the balanced scorecard principle (Chapter 4), strategies are evaluated to check that they do not achieve improvements in one area, at the expense of others. The implementation of the strategy will involve not only assortment planning but also the supply chain, pricing, promotions and space allocation. With clearly defined targets, progress can be monitored regularly. However, as emphasized in Chapter 5, it is important that monitoring is not limited to short-term sales and profit criteria. Customer satisfaction, the stated focus of category management, must also be evaluated, as the longer-term indicator of success.

Evaluations of Category Management

Freedman et al. (1997) estimated that category management *could* save suppliers the equivalent of 2 per cent of sales. However, they also point out that it would be naïve to assume that such benefits would be shared equally between powerful retailers and their suppliers:

> *Several retailers are already demanding an additional discount (sometimes 1–2 percent of turnover) simply for the 'privilege' of participating in their category management programme, regardless of the ultimate benefits.*

Table 8.6 Results from category management in Europe

Sources: Accenture (2000); IGD (1999a).

Measure of effect	% change (IGD)	% change (Accenture)
Sales	Up 5 ➔ 10%	Up to 10%
Return on inventory	Up 5 ➔ 10%	
Percentage gross margin		Up 3%
Inventory investment	Down 10 ➔ 20%	Down 15%
Store labour costs	Down 0.25%	

Pilot schemes in Europe have indicated benefits for retailers, including increased sales and profits, along with reduced inventories and store labour costs (Accenture, 2000; IGD, 1999a). Table 8.6 summarizes these benefits. In terms of the wider benefits of category management, the survey revealed notable differences between retailer and supplier perspectives. The main benefits for retailers are improved sales, allied with better understanding of customers and improved loyalty. For the suppliers, sales and improved relationships with retailers are the main benefits (Table 8.7).

Table 8.7 Key benefits of category management

Source: derived from IGD (1999a).

	% of respondents within:	
	Retailers	Suppliers
Sales/turnover	58	38
Consumer loyalty	8	2
Enhanced market share	—	3
Supply chain improvement	—	1
Customer service	—	3
Consumer understanding	33	13
Improved trading relationships	—	25
Profit margins	—	10
Consumer benefits	—	5

This contrast of perspectives is hardly surprising as, for suppliers such as Procter & Gamble, improved trading relationships were the main motive for what became known as category management. From a study of category management within the haircare product-supplier Bristol-Myers, Hogarth-Scott and Walters (2000) observed some evidence of these closer relationships:

> *We have a lot of influence with accounts where two years ago we did not. I guess it's sharing with the retailer our strategy and their sharing theirs with us. We are on the verge of developing what I would call true strategic alliances.*

However, some manufacturers are reported to be apprehensive about category management as retailers claim the lion's share of benefits. Some major retailers feel they can employ category management ideas without the help of manufacturers, and there have also been examples of 'pseudo category management', with limited information sharing between retailer and supplier (Freedman et al., 1997). Gruen and Shah (2000) summed up the main concerns of both parties:

1 A natural tension exists between manufacturers' brand focus and retailers' category focus.
2 Internally, manufacturer companies' brand management is likely to pressure the sales organization to favour their brands in category planning.
3 Retailers many not be able to recognize opportunism by the supplier in collaborative management relationships.
4 Suppliers that commit resources to category planning are vulnerable to inaction.

There is also the risk that full-blown partnerships could undermine the broader strategies of a branded manufacturer. A retailer might demand a measure of exclusivity within the relationship and other retailers may doubt the supplier's ability to maintain complete confidentiality between accounts. The manufacturer may also give away customer insights, which the retailer could exploit through its own-brands (Freedman et al., 1997). Skills in the design and evaluation of promotions could also be transferred to the retailer.

Another issue to arise in the evaluation of category management is the time involved in the planning stages. Clearly, this must be set against any improvements in sales and margins.

> *Many retailers and their supplier partners alike are becoming increasingly frustrated by lengthy category planning cycles. Too much emphasis is placed on planning and strategy, with not enough focus on implementation (Nicol, 2001).*

A risk confronting all parties is that category management may be further investigated by competition authorities, as another form of 'co-opetition' (Kim and Parker, 1999). Concerns have been expressed, notably about the barriers to the entry of smaller suppliers, as large suppliers and retailers develop closer supply chain and category management partnerships. The Competition Commission (2000) inquired about three practices in particular:

1 Payments being required from a supplier in return for it being appointed to manage a category.
2 Category managers (or captains) charging other suppliers to display their products in the retailer's stores.
3 Sales data provided to category captains but not to other suppliers.

It is difficult to pinpoint examples of 1 and 2 above as suppliers make many payments and concessions anyway to their principal retail clients. Asda did indicate that category captains received trading data free of charge, to compensate them for the cost of undertaking that role. However, the same data are available to other suppliers, in return for payment. Safeway was reported to have stopped using category management, but suggested that category captains did previously have access to data that were normally sold.

The main focus of the Competition Commission (2000) was upon competition between major grocery stores, rather than upon supply chain issues. However, it is clear that the evolving relationships along the supply chain have attracted interest in the UK and elsewhere in Europe:

> *Increased co-operation between suppliers, distributors and retailers, through the use of information technology and a close co-ordination of logistics, led to a greater investment between the parties concerned, but could act as a barrier to others wishing to enter the market (European Commission, 1997, reported in Competition Commission, 2000).*

8.1.6 Efficient Consumer Response

While some commentators are sceptical about the equality of partnerships within category management, the broader development of efficient consumer response (ECR) places considerable emphasis upon the supply chain and enabling technologies, notably electronic data interchange (EDI) (see Sec. 1.2). In the view of the Competition Commission (2000), the supply management and IT aspects of ECR are relatively uncontroversial. This is not least because the Web can also be used to stimulate competition between suppliers, for example, by facilitating reverse auctions on line (Retail Review, 2001).

As with most new terminologies, definitions of ECR vary, but to quote just two:

> *By focusing on the efficiency of the total supply system rather than on individual components, ECR helps to reduce total system costs, inventories and physical assets, while improving consumers' choice of high-quality, fresh products (Kurt Salmon Associates, 1993).*

ECR is about category management and co-managed inventory. That is the essence of ECR. Putting the two together successfully produces the benefits of ECR (Mintel, 1997).

The same Mintel report also quotes ECR-sceptics, who feel that ECR is just another new term, thrown around already existing practices. Indeed Rose (1994) observes that ECR grew out of the implementation of quick response supply chains in the textile industry, from the 1980s. However, to its credit, ECR has focused minds around an alternative supply-chain orientation: 'Reversal of the supply chain from "producer push" to "consumer pull"' (Cuthbertson, 1999).

The four main components of ECR are summarized in Fig. 8.5. 'Efficient store assortment' requires no further elaboration, having been discussed extensively in the previous section. It should be noted however, that ECR arrangements frequently stop short of the full-blown adoption of category management. 'Efficient replenishment' is the main component of ECR, incorporating a range of supply chain and IT developments. Consequently, this will be the main focus of this section, having firstly considered the other main components of ECR.

'Efficient promotion' essentially seeks to eliminate/reduce practices such as forward buying and diverting promotionally priced items to non-promotional periods (Kahn and McAlister, 1997). Procter & Gamble

Figure 8.5 Main components of ECR

Source: adapted from Kurt Salmon Associates (1993).

Efficient store assortment	Drawing upon or applying the principles of category management, determine the items within a category, the types, depth and breadth or assortment, then the prices and space allocations for those products.
Efficient replenishment	Obtain accurate PoS data, shorten order cycles, reduce stock holdings and eliminate unnecessary costs within the replenishment process. Likely to involve EDI or web-based links as well as logistical improvements, such as cross docking at warehouses.
Efficient promotions	Eradicate promotional activities, which increase costs, inflate inventories and do not in practice benefit consumers or influence their patronage decisions.
Efficient new product introduction	Reduce high failure rate for product innovation by accurately assessing demand, on the basis of well-instrumented, often localised, product trials.

found that 25 per cent of its sales peoples' time and 30 per cent of brand managers' time was spent designing, implementing and overseeing tactical promotions: often these cost more to run than they made in extra sales (Watson, 1996). Under the 'efficient promotion' regime, a retailer is rewarded on the basis of selling the promotional products, not on the quantity bought by the retailer (Rose, 1994). Under European Competition Law guidelines, a supplier is entitled to recommend the selling price, but no pressure or economic incentive may be used to make the retailer confirm to the recommended price (Competition Commission, 2000).

'Efficient new product introduction' is a response to the costs of a new product development, and the difficulties of obtaining full-scale adoption by retailers. In the USA, ECR companies that have introduced large numbers of new products have adopted quick response strategies to make major changes, as the product is trialled in a small number of stores. They have access to continuous PoS data, to evaluate these changes, and are guided by feedback from retailers and their customers. This should lead to more products being tested, at lower cost per test, an outcome that is favourable to all parties (Rose, 1994).

It is in the area of replenishment that ECR claims its greatest impact (e.g. de Wilt and Krishnan, 1995), although savings are likely to be greatest in countries that had not traditionally focused upon logistical issues. Fuller et al. (1993) described the low priority given to logistics by many companies in the USA:

> We often say 'that is just a logistical problem', as if certain vexing details of delivery may be left to relentless, mathematical people, long after 'creative' product designers and market strategists have had their say.

Fernie (1992) found that in continental Europe, too, logistics had not commanded a great deal of attention at board level, neglect that was reflected in the distribution networks of European retailers. By comparison, some of the major British retailers had already invested heavily in their distribution systems, well before ECR was coined as a phrase.

Centralization has been a notable feature of British retailers' distribution systems, although this does not mean one depot or one organization providing the logistics. Some use a mixture of their own facilities and those of third-party contractors, in part to learn and to benchmark their own performance (Fernie, 1998). However, the network of regional distribution centres (RDCs) is controlled centrally, virtually eliminating suppliers' direct influence upon store operations.

In France, too, deliveries are mostly consolidated at RDCs but extensive sales and merchandising by suppliers traditionally took place within the stores (Bell, 1996). In Sweden and in Germany, tension with suppliers has occurred as major retailers have re-engineered their supply chains, in the process reducing supplier influence at store level. The major German retailer Rewe also introduced a 1 per cent levy upon its

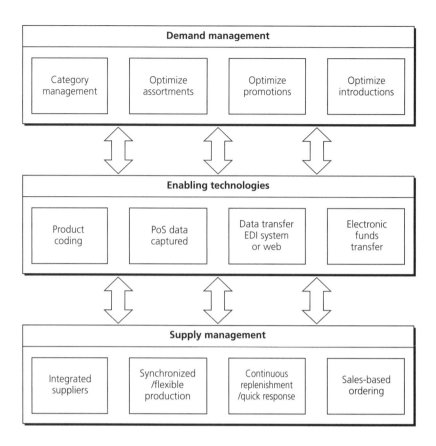

suppliers, creating further tensions: Rewe needed a major investment
programme to catch up with the logistics and IT requirements of ECR
(Retail Review, 1996). Having monitored developments in supply chains
in Europe and North America, Fernie and Staines (2001) illustrate how
logistical practices have been transferred across international markets.

A review of logistical and IT developments within the supply chain
would be beyond the scope of this book. This is the subject of other,
specialist texts (e.g. Gattorna, 1998). However, some of the key elements
of relevance to ECR are summarized in Fig. 8.6. The pivotal role of the
enabling technologies, already discussed in Chapter 1, cannot be
underestimated. Product codes, PoS data capture, electronic fund
transfer and EDI (electronic data interchange) and the Web provide the
information links within the system.

Although much of the early emphasis in ECR development has been
upon the grocery industry, its techniques and technologies can also be of
great value to clothing retailers (Chandra and Kumar, 2001; Riddle et al.,
1999). For fashion buyers, uncertainty is typically far higher and the risks
of purchase errors proportionally greater. Electronic data interchange
combined with flexible production techniques and distribution system
efficiencies can enable a fashion buyer to advance order as little as
20 per cent of the season's anticipated sales (Morgan Stanley Dean Witter,
2001). Figure 8.7 illustrates how this adds value, in terms of consumer

satisfaction, sales and cost reductions (Maltz and Srivastava, 1997).

The application of 'quick response' (QR) production and distribution techniques is a way of using the supply chain to increase *marketing effectiveness* as well as *efficiency* (Brockman and Morgan, 1999). With less stock held at stores, more space can be devoted to selling a larger assortment. Stock turns over much faster, so there is less old stock on display, also reducing the extent of markdowns at the season end. In spite of less stock being held, the systems should avoid stockouts through the rapid flow of information along the supply chain. Laura Ashley described the process as 'stock cleansing', moving the stock well before its target sell-by date is reached (Rich ard Bowley, 1996).

Quick response is often equated with the just-in-time (JIT) or just-about-zero (JAZ) inventory strategies of some manufacturers (e.g. Oliver, 1999). Under such arrangements, the supplier agrees to deliver goods to the customer, without fail, at the last possible moment, to a guaranteed quality level, such that the purchaser does not lose time inspecting large samples and returning many of them (Chatterjee et al., 1995). The parallels between JIT and QR are clear, yet there is an important difference. Whereas JIT minimizes the inventory required for production, QR maintains stock in stores, sufficient to met short-term demand fluctuations that are more difficult to predict (Fiorito et al., 1995).

While QR improves the flow of goods into the retailer's depots, the distribution system must continue that smooth flow through to the stores. Cross-docking is an approach which has turned old-style *warehouses* into *distribution centres*. Traditionally, goods were being received, then stored, then eventually picked from storage to fulfil orders for stores. With cross-docking, the goods flow directly from orders received to orders despatched (McKinnon, 1996). Clearly, this is feasible only if the right quantities are delivered to the distribution centres at the

Figure 8.7 Creating value from EDI and QR

Source: adapted from Maltz and Srivastava (1997).

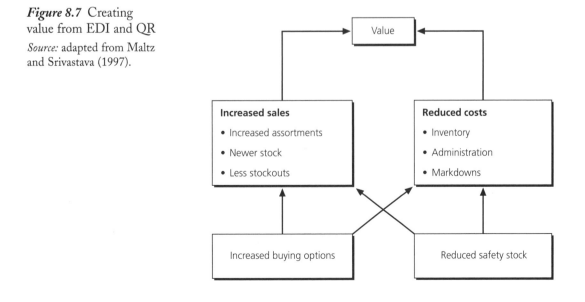

right time. Not all exporters find it easy to meet the logistical requirements of UK retailers (Collins et al., 2001).

Further enabling technologies help to ensure that the flow of goods continues, even after the goods are dispatched into the vagaries of the road system. For example, Safeway uses satellite positioning technology to monitor the progress of its trucks towards its stores, also saving money by reducing fuel-wasting driving habits. Vehicles can be warned of traffic congestion and rerouted. If one vehicle become seriously traffic-bound, another can be despatched from a different depot to minimize stockouts at the stores (Retail Review, 1997).

Without doubt, component parts of ECR are delivering real benefits in terms of reduced stock levels, combined with reduced stockouts (IGD, 1999b). Quick response was shown by Ko and Kincade (1997) to be producing various further benefits for clothing retailers, including availability of products that had been advertised, and better adaptation of assortments to market needs. Efficient consumer response as a whole, however, was seriously overhyped at the outset, with exaggerated claims as to its potential savings (de Wilt and Krishnan, 1995). In part this may reflect the greater scope for savings in US supply chains, compared with those in the UK, although it also has its critics within the USA: 'The perceived direct benefits of ECR have failed to trickle down through the industry, making ECR still more a matter of promise than performance' (Mathews, 1997).

Efficient consumer response has received only limited attention within the marketing literature, in spite of its potential importance in the delivery of service and value. Two studies (Brockman and Morgan, 1999; Lohtia and Murakoshi, 1999) have considered ECR within the diffusion of innovations framework (Rogers, 1995). It was noted that ECR is considerably more complex than EDI alone, and usually requires the changing of existing, non-compatible systems. In practice, it therefore tends to be trialled and adopted on a piecemeal basis, rather than introduced all at once.

In terms of payback, a period of about three years on ECR investments is to be expected (Lohtia and Murakoshi, 1999). As noted earlier, savings are unlikely to be enjoyed equally, if the power balance between suppliers and retailers is unequal. This in itself creates a diversity of view about the potential merits of ECR. However, a notable achievement of ECR has been to help make distribution systems more market oriented, and to raise the profile of the supply chain as an element of retail marketing.

8.2 Retail Buying Decisions

Retail buying decisions may be the responsibility of individual buyers or buying teams: sometimes they involve other organizations, as in buying alliances or within a category management framework. Whatever the structure and composition of the buying function, some key decision areas are common to virtually all retail organizations. These decisions are critical to achieving the broad strategic aims, discussed in Chapter 4.

As these strategic considerations represent the point of departure for specific buying decisions, it is worth reiterating some of the most relevant issues. Table 8.8 summarizes key strategic questions, which underpin the choices made by retail buyers.

Table 8.8 Strategic issues underpinning buying decisions

Key questions	Possible answers
Who are our target customers?	Old, young, affluent, bargain hunters, family, singles, time-poor, leisured, fashionable, down-to-earth
Which of their needs can we satisfy?	Foods, clothes, household goods, convenience, choice, value, solutions, need to impress
What are our competitors doing?	Product categories/brands/items that are essentials; gaps in their offers; customers' expectations
How can we do it differently and better?	Wider mix, deeper mix, designer brands, own brands, continuity, price, service, ambience

The target customers and their specific needs should be the focus of the buying task. However, competitors' assortments and moves must also be evaluated, both to identify gaps and to assess customers' expectations. From that point, the buying decisions are a major element in determining how to satisfy customer needs more effectively than the competition.

This section first considers the key question of the product mix, its breadth, depth, category roles and uniformity/localization within the chain. Decisions on quantity are then discussed, including the consequences of out-of-stock conditions. The criteria used and the decision process applied in selecting products and suppliers are then examined. Finally, terms of trade between retailers and suppliers are considered, illustrating the great diversity of issues upon which buyers can negotiate.

8.2.1 Assembling the Product Mix

A fundamental product strategy decision is whether to stock a wide or narrow range of product categories, then whether to offer a large (deep) or small (shallow) choice within each category. These basic choices are represented in Fig. 8.8, which also indicates some of the probable advantages and drawbacks of each choice combination. There are, of course, many other ways of combining these strategies. For example, superstores normally offer considerable depth of choice within their core food categories, but their assortments are relatively shallow in the clothing and household goods categories, if these are sold.

Few retailers are able to offer assortments that are both very wide and also deep. The great department stores traditionally fulfilled this role but even they have had to reduce category width, in the face of specialist competition. The format offers the potential of one-stop shopping and a

Narrow ◀———— **Number of categories** ————▶ Wide

Deep

e.g. Category Killer	e.g. Large Department Store
Focused market	Broad market appeal
Specialist image	Large choice overall
Good choice in category	One-stop shopping
Likely to meet needs of customers	Likely to meet needs of customers
Specialised staff	Customers may be loyal
Customers more loyal	High traffic potential
Susceptible to trends	*Large investment in stock*
No one-stop shopping	*More slow moving lines*
Less cross-selling	*Risk of obsolescence*
Consumer confusion	*Usually high service cost*
e.g. Convenience Store	**e.g. General Discounter**
Top-up of convenience market	General market appeal
High turnover of stock	Can focus on most profitable or
Concentrate on profitable items	cheapest items
Lower cost strategy	Some cross-selling
	High traffic potential
	Lower cost strategy
Little choice	*Low variety within category*
Unlikely to meet many needs	*Unlikely to meet all customer needs*
Weak assortment image	*Probably low loyalty*
Less cross-selling	*Weak image*

Items within each category (Deep ↑ / Shallow ↓)

Figure 8.8 Product assortment strategies

high probability that customers will find solutions to their needs. However, the complexity of managing wide and deep assortments has exposed some of the weaknesses of these generalists in the face of more focused competition. Another problem is that the shop premises most suitable for, say, fashion and cosmetics may be less suitable for heavier, more bulky goods.

Both a specialist tea shop and a large category killer, such as Toys 'R' Us, occupy the narrow, deep assortment position. Each has focused its buying and selling expertise on one or a few categories, albeit with some related products. These shops become a natural destination for people seeking the best variety available in their respective categories. Stores with deep assortments are of high utility to shoppers wanting to satisfy both immediate and future anticipated needs in that category (Lee and Stekel, 1999). For example, faced with a good choice, a shopper may stock up on gifts or greetings cards to reduce future acquisition costs.

Stores with narrow, deep assortments are however, more susceptible than the generalists to fluctuations in category sales, or direct category competition. They also offer more limited scope for cross-selling between categories. The depth of choice, while in one sense a virtue, may also cause customer confusion (Huffman and Kahn, 1998), thus increasing search costs (Bergen et al., 1996). As a response to this, it may be necessary to increase service levels and costs (Cadeaux, 1999). As

B & Q migrated from DIY superstores to giant warehouses, more specialist staff were introduced to assist shoppers and radio linked reception staff direct people to their required product categories.

Often a relatively shallow assortment is the outcome of physical site limitations, rather than limited buying scope. In Chapter 15, opportunities to overcome these limitations, through the 'bricks and clicks' model, are discussed. For example, Virgin's V Shops have a basic assortment of around 3000 CDs and DVDs. Through in-store Internet kiosks, however, this assortment is deepened to over 10 000 available disks (Retail Review, 2000a). Retailers may also use e-tailing to widen their assortment, for example, a widening range of housewares, clothing, books, and CDs through Tesco Direct (Retail Review, 2000b).

A shallow assortment may be the outcome of opportunistic buying of end of ranges, which combine both price and profit appeal. However, shoppers need to be flexible in the solutions that they find, as such stores offer little brand/item continuity. Where it is space that restricts the assortment, buyers must often select subsets of manufacturers' ranges. This is easier in categories of low 'volatility', i.e., subject to less additions and deletions, as retail buyers are better able to form their own judgements of product performance/suitability for target groups (Cadeaux, 1997). Alternatively, buyers may employ screen-based simulations to elicit customer reactions before finalizing their assortment and pricing decisions (McIntyre and Miller, 1999).

Having established the basic parameters of the product mix, a retailer needs to assess the instrumental roles of categories and individual products (Dhar et al., 2001). Table 8.9 identifies four basic roles, which are of relevance both to creating visits to the store, and to encouraging usage of each part of the store. Destination products are the prime reason

Table 8.9 Product category roles

Source: adapted from IGD (1999a).

Role	Examples of product categories	
	Superstore	**Forecourt**
Destination	Fresh produce Ready meals Bread Dairy products	Petrol
Core	Detergents Paper goods Coffee Deodorants	Motor oil Confectionery Magazines
Convenience	Magazines Greeting cards Cosmetics Cigarettes	Bread Sandwiches Flowers
Occasional/seasonal	Christmas cards Easter eggs Garden items Barbecue	Christmas trees Cool boxes BBQ charcoal

for many shoppers' visits at that specific time. Petrol is usually the main reason to visit a forecourt; fresh food requirements normally trigger a superstore visit. Consequently, although not all the products in this category yield high levels of direct product profitability (Chapter 6), they are important traffic builders.

To maintain that traffic, various core items are expected to be sold in any given type of outlet. Some of these are fundamental to the core purpose of the outlet, such as motor oil at the forecourt shop. Others arise through the actions of competitors, who create expectations that certain items will be sold. Consequently, many 'health and beauty' products are now core elements of a superstore assortment, which was not the case previously. Beyond these roles, there are the convenience items, which add to the shopper's utility from the shopping trip, while increasing the retailer's sales/customer. Many stores keep space available for 'seasonal' items: these may be offered by a wide diversity of competitors, but seasonal demand can be sufficient to merit their inclusion.

Retailers have a variety of ways to influence the linkages between product sales. Simonson (1999) argues that product differentiation is becoming more difficult, as competitors quickly adopt categories or items that are proving popular and profitable. It is suggested that retailers should focus upon the assortment subsets that specific customers or groups actually consider. This form of 'subcategory management' could lead to edited subsets of the assortment being displayed together to influence choices within that display.

Focusing on specific consumer needs can lead to profitable lifestyle groupings of products, such as the diverse range of accessories sold by Harley Davidson dealers (Grewal et al., 1999). Retailers can also deploy 'bundling' strategies, whereby linked products, perhaps services too, are offered as a single deal. This can increase spend/customer as well as simplifying the customer's choice task. Bundling is common in the selling of clothes and PCs with their accessories. An alternative mix strategy is 'scrambled merchandising', which presents consumers with a diverse mixture of items of great appeal to the variety seekers (Kahn and McAlister, 1997).

Another important issue in planning assortments is the local dimension. Ironically, many multiples have devoted extensive resources to achieving greater standardization across the chain. 'Price flexing' (Competition Commission, 2000) is commonly used to meet or beat local competition. Until recently, less attention has been given to local flexibility in the assortment (Stassen et al., 1999). Problems of control tended to limit retailers' enthusiasm for local assortment planning.

Two different organizational models, to achieve the best of centralization and localization, were suggested by Aufreiter et al. (1993). Figure 8.9 illustrates the different approaches towards the same goal. Wal-Mart is an example of the first, system-driven approach, using information technology to segment its far-flung store network. It starts

Assortment decisions	National discounter e.g. Wal-Mart	Department stores e.g. J C Penney
Assortment strategy	Centralised planning of assortment using market profiles	Centralised planning of assortment with local additions
Initial product allocations	System-driven allocation using market profiles	Store-level management of allocation and flow
Responsiveness to incremental local needs	Weekly store feedback: addition of some local items	Store-driven selection from central menu

Figure 8.9 Buy centrally, tailor locally

Source: adapted from Aufreiter et al. (1993).

with a database of more than 2500 variables, including demographics, climate and competitive intensity. From this, assortments are tailored to local conditions at very low cost, which is critical to its low-price strategy. The second approach gives more autonomy to the store managers but results are monitored centrally:

> *Headquarters buying staff typically have the most vendor leverage and this can most effectively source a majority of merchandise that meets consumer needs. But when individual stores have some purchasing flexibility, make sure that local purchases and inventories are visible in the corporate database, so results are known and actors accountable. Local assortment proficiency is primarily a function of better communications between local stores and corporate headquarters (Beninati et al., 1997).*

8.2.2 Quantity Decisions

At least part of the responsibility for sales forecasting and stock decisions usually rests with the retail buyer. In a small retail organization, the buyer might in fact have complete responsibility for these functions. In a large organization, merchandise managers and those responsible for physical distribution are also likely to be closely involved. For example, the merchandise manager may be responsible for estimating/forecasting sales and required stock levels within defined commodity groups, for example, men's raincoats. The buyer then translates these projections into actual purchases and may hold the responsibility for allocations between specific colours, styles and sizes. Until the item is delisted by the buyer or merchandise manager, the day-to-day control of stock levels and reorders may be delegated to store personnel, or virtually automated through a sales-based, rapid replenishment system (Sec. 8.1.5).

There is a considerable contrast between the tasks of estimating demand for staples and fashion goods (Cravens and Finn, 1983). For the latter, the forecast must be broken down into a very detailed specification of quantities required. Diamond and Pintel (1997) suggest the following breakdown:

1 *Classification*: the specific goods within a department, such as trousers, suits, shirts, ties, etc. Various information sources indicating trends and competition may be used to adjust quantity estimates between classifications.

2 *Style*: relating to skirt lengths, trouser widths, etc. Past sales may be a poor indicator of future needs, although buyers in many contexts will phase out old styles gradually to cater for more conservative customers.

3 *Price lines*: the price zones within which the items must be positioned. Few stores wish to offer an item and style within just one price zone.

4 *Sizes*: generally these can be determined from past records (e.g. Beazley, 1999), although particular styles may be manifestly unsuitable for certain sizes.

5 *Colour*: again, a decision requiring sensitivity to what is expected to be sought in the forthcoming season. There is also a need for co-ordination between classifications to encourage combined purchases.

The more accurately these elements can be estimated, the less chance there is of losing potential sales on the one hand, or having to mark down the prices of surplus stock on the other. It should be noted, however, that many buyers and merchandisers incorporate 'planned markdowns' within their purchasing plans, given the high volume of business conducted within 'sales' periods. Usually a number of items are bought primarily for selling within such periods.

There are several statistically based forecasting techniques, based either upon time-series projections from past sales trends or upon known correlations between sales and various independent variables. These techniques include:

1 *Moving averages*: item sales are recorded, for example weekly, and the forecast is based upon the average over the last four weeks. As each new weekly sales figure becomes available, it replaces the oldest sales figure in the calculation. This approach has the advantage of being easy to calculate, but forecasts are unresponsive to rapid change.

2 *Exponential smoothing*: each new forecast is a function of the last forecast, adjusted according to the accuracy of that forecast. The extent to which the forecast is adjusted is determined by setting the alpha factor in this equation:

$$F(t) = F(t-1) + x \{S(t-1) - F(t-1)\}$$

where

F	=	forecasted sales for time period
t	=	time period of constant duration
S	=	most recent actual sales
x	=	alpha factor

If an alpha factor of 1 is to set, the effect is to set the forecast equal to the most recent sales figure. A low alpha factor, such as 0.2, makes the forecasts less responsive to short-term changes; judgement is therefore required to establish the most appropriate alpha.

3 *Extended smoothing*: this entails a refinement of exponential smoothing to incorporate the overall sales trend and/or seasonality in

deriving the forecast. The technique may be referred to as double or triple exponential smoothing if one or both of these factors is included.

4 *Regression models*: instead of basing forecasts upon past sales trends, relationships between sales and other factors are determined by correlation analysis. For example, the sales of fur coats may be found to be sensitive to fashion trends, levels of disposable income and expectations of cold weather. A regression equation could then be constructed which produced a forecast based upon estimates of these three factors, plus any others that were found significantly to improve the forecast.

5 *Artificial neural networks*: an emerging technique which reflects the network processes of the human brain, avoiding the prior assumptions inherent in other techniques. They have been shown to perform well when demand conditions are unstable and/or seasonal (Alon et al., 2001).

Seasonality is just one of the retail buyer's forecasting challenges. In some areas, changes in fashion can cause sharp peaks in sales, followed by a steep drop. Product endorsements, for example, by pop stars or celebrity chefs, can also cause dramatic changes in demand. The effect of Delia Smith's recommendations is so strong that supermarkets are notified in advance of ingredients to be used, to enable greater quantities to be ordered (Varley, 2001).

Having estimated or forecasted sales levels, the economic order quantity (EOQ) must then be determined. This concept seeks to minimize total costs by establishing the optimum balance between ordering costs and stockholding costs. In many retail contexts, however, the order quantity is very tightly constrained by available shelf space, sometimes effectively the only storage space available to the retailer. Suppliers' or distributors' delivery cycles may also largely determine order quantities.

Stockholding costs can be estimated with reasonable accuracy and include the costs of rent, rates, energy, handling, administration, depreciation, insurance and interest charges. Costs of running out of stock, on the other hand, are rather more difficult to determine. Various studies have examined customers' substitution patterns when they encounter stockouts: most of this research has related to fast-moving consumer goods (e.g. Chetochin, 1992; Nielsen, 1975; Verbeke et al., 1998; 2000). The loss of goodwill (Hill, 1992) has not been as extensively measured, although Zinszer and Lesser (1980) demonstrated lower store image and less satisfaction, among shoppers who had experienced stockouts.

Shoppers may react in various ways under these circumstances. The following options identified by Schary and Christopher (1979), Emmethainz et al. (1991), Verbeke et al. (2000) and Campo et al. (2000) are not mutually exclusive:

> ▶ exiting the store, to seek the product elsewhere (brand loyal or highly specific product need)
> ▶ postponement of buying (low immediate need and/or high store loyalty)
> ▶ switch to another product
> ▶ switch to another brand
> ▶ switch to another size
> ▶ complain to retailer
> ▶ complain to peers.

While all stockouts can contribute to reduced satisfaction, maybe also undermining long-term loyalty (Fitzsimons, 2000), the greatest short-term effect arises from consumers transferring their purchase elsewhere. In 1975, Nielsen found that 39 per cent of stockouts led to a purchase at a different store. Table 8.10 would suggest that this proportion has decreased, based upon a study in the Netherlands (Verbeke et al., 1998). As stores have generally become much larger over the intervening years, the effort involved in making an extra store visit has increased. In spite of this, the proportion of sales lost after stockouts remains high in some categories.

Table 8.10 Consumer reactions to out-of-stock

Source: adapted from Verbeke et al. (1998).

Consumer response	Soft drink %	Cooking margarine %	Coffee creamer %	Rice %	Detergent %
Switched brand	65	47	62	50	31
Switched store	14	34	20	28	23
Postponed purchase	21	19	18	22	46

From one of the few studies in a non-grocery context, Kelly et al. (2000) found that 56.7 per cent of planned purchases were, in fact, not fulfilled. Not all of this was attributed to stockouts, as Table 8.11 illustrates, but assortment problems of one sort or another explained the majority of non-purchases. Limitations in the number of products stocked explained about one-third: out-of-stocks of the product or the required size explained a further 27.7 per cent.

Table 8.11 Purchases planned but not made

Source: adapted from Kelly et al. (2000).

Reason	%
Poor assortment, limited selection	24.3
Product not stocked	8.2
Out of stock	16.3
Size not available	11.4
Changed mind after seeing choices	17.0
Product quality lower than expected	5.5
Time pressure; had to leave	5.9
Could not find item	3.1
More expensive than expected	8.3

The accumulating evidence would suggest that retailers need to be especially careful to avoid stockouts of products with high brand loyalty or few substitutes in store. The likely urgency of need, reflecting consumers stocking habits at home, is also a factor. Ghosh (1994) suggested that retailers should have a 'never-out' list of such products. Chetochin (1992) showed that shoppers were very likely to switch to a different type/brand of pasta, but were much more brand loyal in the drinking chocolate category. Koelmeijer and Oppenwal (1999) demonstrated that different colours of tulips are readily substituted, but white and red roses are not substitutes at all.

Given the importance of maintaining variety and adequate stock levels, a major overhaul of buying and supply chain systems was long overdue. A traditional approach, still used by some companies, is the open-to-buy (OTB) system, wherein buyers are allocated a 'budget' for a given time period. From sales forecasts and the overall merchandise plan, the predicted sales within a commodity group are determined. The OTB amount equals these predicted sales, less the goods already bought.

While this is designed to inhibit overbuying or underbuying, in practice it has many limitations as a control system. Given their OTB limits on the menswear category, buyers may risk running short of some sizes of shirts, due to a surfeit of pyjamas in stock (Cash et al., 1995). In one of the few empirical studies of OTB effectiveness, Goodwin (1992) found that more successful departments purchased goods, even when there was no OTB allocation available. In contrast, less successful departments normally stayed within their limits.

The very concept of a sales period, be that a month or a week, has been called into question with the arrival of quick response and efficient consumer response. While forecasts are clearly still necessary for items with longer lead times, PoS data now inform quantity decisions on a day-by-day basis (see Sec. 8.1.5). Increasingly, retailers are looking for shorter lead times and greater supplier involvement in steering an accurate course between the dual hazards of stockouts and surplus stock, which may have to be marked down at the end of the season. Nordstrom is one of many retailers that has invested heavily in information systems, to try to achieve this (Johnson, 1998).

In the grocery sector in particular, most major retailers have gone a step further with model-driven sales-based ordering (SBO) systems (Achabal et al., 2000; Myers et al., 2000). On average, Tesco's automated ordering system is able to replenish the store in just 24 hours (Mintel, 1997). A detailed account of Safeway's SBO system is provided by Davison and Scouler-Davison (1997). In calculating the required quantity for each store, the system takes into account:

- stock level at store (based on PoS data, plus records of items not scanned, such as inter-store transfers, damaged goods, etc.)
- space allocated to each item

  ▶ shelf life of the products
  ▶ any outstanding deliveries
  ▶ expected sales
  ▶ business policies.

In commissioning SBO, Somerfield established in-stock targets of 98.5 per cent, gaining around 0.5 per cent of extra sales as a result, plus greater levels of customer satisfaction (SuperMarketing, 1996). In even the most advanced SBO system, however, differences eventually arise between the physical stock and the electronic record. Due to mis-scanning, theft and other forms of loss, these differences necessitate periodic stock checks (Sandoh and Shimamoto, 2001).

8.2.3 Selection and Delisting Criteria

A number of circumstances may precipitate a product selection decision, including the following:

1 New or different products/brands are offered to the buying unit.
2 A need is perceived to introduce new product lines.
3 A need is perceived to widen the choice of brands available.
4 A lack of satisfaction is noted with existing products/brands.
5 A routine review is undertaken of the existing assortment or category.

In practice, circumstances 1–3 can be classified simply as new product decisions, 4 and 5 as old product or rebuy decisions. Nilsson and Host (1987) have underlined the importance of this distinction between new and old product decisions, in terms of both the information used and the consequences of the decision. Figure 8.10 illustrates that the consequences of mistakenly accepting a new product are rather high, in terms of the costs of introduction, the costs of slow-moving stock, and the mark downs probably required to clear this stock. In general, the reverse is true of decisions relating to existing products, in that mistaken retention can soon be reversed with little loss. A mistaken delisting, on the other hand, may cause large sales losses, loss of customer goodwill, inappropriate markdowns and, possibly, the additional costs of reintroduction. Doyle and Weinberg (1973) suggested an approach by which supermarket buyers could quantify some of the opportunity costs of mistakes, as an aid to their *new* product decisions.

Figure 8.10
Consequences of buying errors

Source: adapted from Nilsson and Host (1987).

Existing products		New products	
Mistaken retention	**Mistaken delisting**	**Mistaken acceptance**	**Mistaken rejection**
Product can be deleted later with only minor losses arising from delay	Sales are lost, customer loyalty maybe reduced, possible costs of reintroduction	Costs of introduction, markdowns and/or excess inventory while selling outstock	Product can be accepted with only minor sales losses, due to delay
Mistake is easily discovered	Mistake more difficult/ slower to discover	Mistake is easily discovered later	Mistake is difficult to discover

Nilsson and Host (1987) point out that the contrasting consequences of old and new product decisions tend to lead to conservative decisions. In conditions of uncertainty, it is generally safer to retain the status quo. The situation is compounded by the fact that wrong decisions to reject new products, unlike other mistakes, may never be discovered by those responsible for evaluating the buyers' performance. Furthermore, buyers usually have extensive information about existing products, much of which is internally generated and therefore more likely to be trusted than information supplied in relation to new products. In theory, the concept of efficient new product introductions (Sec. 8.1.5) should reduce the imbalance between new and existing product decision risks. Among 2034 new product proposals studied by Rao and McLaughlin (1989), 68.1 per cent were rejected by retail buyers. The acceptance rate was noticeably higher for new products with high levels of marketing support.

In any selection decision it is likely that many different criteria will be considered, some relating to the product itself, others to characteristics of the supplier. It is of benefit to the consistency and objectivity of buying decisions if these can be identified and evaluated using a more specific framework. There are however a number of problems involved in researching these criteria, not least of which may be the difficulty/reluctance of buyers in articulating all the factors involved in their decision. It is also dangerous to generalize too widely from the factors identified in one particular country, store type or product area. In spite of these reservations, it is useful to examine briefly some of the evidence that has now emerged, indicating the wide diversity of criteria potentially relevant to retail buying decisions.

A major review was undertaken by Nilsson and Host (1987), who identified nearly 400 criteria in the studies reviewed. Clearly, many of these were closely related and Table 8.12 summarizes the main criteria to emerge. The percentages indicate the proportions of 'mentions' received by each criterion, or group of criteria. This provides some indication of relative importance but is not intended as a form of importance weighting. Given the wide diversity of retail buying situations, weightings will inevitably differ considerably.

This diversity has been demonstrated by several studies. For example, Hirschman (1983) compared the criteria cited by buyers for chain stores and department stores. McGoldrick and Douglas (1983) compared the importance ratings of factors considered by multiple and cash-and-carry buyers. Meidan and Tomes (1991) illustrated contrasts between the criteria of three different categories of cash-and-carry trade users. From a major survey of buyers, Shipley (1985) drew comparisons between several product fields and between samples in the USA and the UK. The differences between the two countries were not in fact great, although prices and delivery were more important criteria in the UK. In a study of the purchasing criteria of supermarket buyers in China, differences were identified between cities and types of company (Hansen, 2001).

Criteria	%	Criteria	%
Profitability and sales	13	**Supplier marketing**	13
Overall profitability	3	Introductory campaign	9
Rate of turnover	2	Continual marketing	4
Sales potential	8		
		Supplier characteristics	20
Financial terms	19	Supplier representative	1
Supplier's price	2	Reputation and reliability	8
Gross margin	4	Sales force organization	1
Allowances and rebates	4	Services and functions	8
Co-operative advertising	3	Other characteristics	2
Credit terms	2		
Other economic factors	5	**Competitive considerations**	3
Assortment considerations	5	**Distributive factors**	4
Existence of private brands	1	Transportation adaptations	1
Relation to other products	5	Flexibility to store needs	3
Consumer evaluation	19	**Tactical considerations**	1
Overall consumer value	5		
Retail price	3	**Sales person presentation**	2
Product's physical characteristics	5		
Product's psychological characteristics	3		
Packaging	3		

Table 8.12 Buyers' decision criteria

Source: Nilsson and Host (1987).

Even within a single company, buying criteria are likely to vary between individuals. Ettenson and Wagner (1986), comparing buyers with assistant buyers, found that the criteria were weighted differently by the two groups. Likewise, Marr and Thomas (1999) demonstrated criteria differences when buyers have complete autonomy, shared responsibility or work within a committee structure.

While accepting that criteria importance varies considerably, it is interesting to look further into one study, to illustrate the level of detail in buyers' evaluations. Table 8.13 is based upon a study of buyers in New Zealand, and includes only the 'top 20' among 41 identified criteria. The financial aspects were ranked highest, and these actually comprise numerous subcomponents: these are discussed further in the final section on terms of trade.

Numerous other studies have provided insights into the effects of specific influences upon retail buyers' decisions. Bronnenberg et al. (2000) demonstrate the importance of feedback on the brand/product's performance in other retailers' stores, illustrating the difficulty of gaining initial entry to provide that favourable feedback. Bergen et al. (1996) note that a greater number of variants within a brand (colours, designs, flavours, etc.) can favourably influence acceptance. Collins-Dodd and Louviere (1999) suggest that brand names, while important to independent buyers, do not influence their sensitivity to levels of consumer advertising, promotional allowances and supply.

Rank	Criteria	Rank	Criteria
1	The financial deal	11	Potential profitability of product
2	Retailer's profit and sales objectives	12	Initial visual appeal of product
3	Promotion and advertising commitment	13	Labelling and what is on it
4	Ability to maximize profit	14	Knowledgeable presenter
5	Likely consumer demand	15	Ability of presenter to make decisions
6	Supplier track record/performance	16	Promotional mix specification
7	Unique product benefits/features	17	Effects on the sales mix of product category
8	Potential growth in product category	18	Minimum purchase requirements
9	Availability of product	19	Likely slow/fast throughput at warehouse
10	Overall input of product within category	20	Regulations/legislation re product content

Table 8.13 Rankings of criteria in new product decisions

Note: a total of 41 criteria were identified in this study.

Source: Thomas and Marr (1993).

On the basis of this accumulating evidence, suppliers can clearly adapt their trade marketing strategies to the characteristics of the retailer and the buyers. However, much of the research in the area still places the emphasis upon 'supplier push', rather than 'retailer pull'. Walters and Hanrahan (2000), on the other hand, describe how some retailers, including IKEA, use target costing as a starting point in their product search. Suppliers are then sought who can meet their quality, price, margin and delivery specifications. In the following chapter, the proactivity of retailers in identifying own-brand product opportunities is discussed. In this context, it is interesting to observe why suppliers often *fail* to have their products accepted by Boots the Chemist:

> *If the product is not unique/innovative, value for money, of high quality, with good packaging.*

> *If the supplier demonstrates a lack of knowledge of the retail market, the retailers' requirement, or of their own company's operations and constraints, or if they lack ideas.*

> *To be successful, be prepared, visit some of our stores and share our vision to make our customers look good and feel good (William Reed, 1999).*

Delisting decisions have received rather less research attention than initial listing decisions. This is surprising, given the trend of supply chain rationalization, involving the delisting of many suppliers. Researchers have however examined the relative importance of good relationships and the 'harder', economic variables in delisting decisions. From a study of Norwegian buyers, Biong (1993) found that satisfaction with and loyalty to a supplier were based upon different factors. Good interpersonal relations, communication, co-operativeness, etc. were good predictors of satisfaction; however, loyalty also depended upon quality products, strong brands, product profitability and a unique product line. Among retail buyers of furniture in Spain, Ruiz (2000) found quality, design and price to be the best predictors of migration to different suppliers. Evidence from Australia (Davies and Treadgold, 1999) confirmed the importance of sales volume, sales potential and other economic variables in delisting decisions. The strength of the relationship with suppliers did, however, influence whether or how quickly disappointing sales led to a delisting position.

Davies (1994) had earlier shown that good relationships, described in terms such as 'business-like' and 'co-operative', were less likely to be severed completely, even if one of the supplier's products was delisted. In order to reduce the influence of interpersonal relationships with suppliers, many retail organizations move their buyers between categories, somewhat to the frustration of some suppliers (Competition Commission, 2000).

8.2.4 The Decision Process

Having identified the main criteria typically applied in product/supplier selection, the next stage is to develop an understanding of the actual decision process. A number of attempts have been made to model this process, using flow diagrams or a range of mathematical techniques. It has also been pointed out (e.g. Ettenson and Wagner, 1986) that retail buying has many characteristics in common with the more extensively researched area of industrial buying. Some of the early models developed in that context, including those of Webster (1965) and Sheth (1973), have therefore influenced the development of retail buying models.

With a wide diversity of buying structures, outlined in Sec. 8.1, no single model can fully describe all these buying functions. However, Fig. 8.11 attempts to incorporate elements and processes that are common to many retail buying situations. It is based upon an adaptation by Holm Hansen and Skytte (1998) of Sheth's (1981) 'theory of merchandise buying behaviour'. It has been further revised to incorporate terminologies used in this text. Most of its elements have already been discussed, but some now require further clarification.

Central to this model is the idea that the actual choice of product and supplier may not be 'ideal' choice, defined in terms of merchandise requirements and accessible/suitable suppliers. The actual choice may be influenced by the general business climate, for example, favouring the cheapest suppliers during recessionary times. Likewise, a retailer with cash flow problems may give priority to the supplier with the most favourable credit terms. Market disturbances, such as shortages, strikes or economic sanctions, can radically change the actual choice.

Although researchers differ in their views as to the influence of relationships on final decisions, there is sufficient evidence that they do play a role in many cases (e.g. Burt and Davis, 1999; Davies, 1994; Dawson and Shaw, 1989; Pellegrini and Zanderighi, 1991). The detailed negotiation of terms can also lead to outcomes, which would not have appeared optimal, purely from the viewpoint of merchandise requirements. It could be argued that the actual choice is therefore the ideal choice, given all the realities of the buying situation. It was originally argued that the 'ideal' choice is easier to model (Sheth, 1981), but that could suggest that models have not been sufficiently inclusive.

Figure 8.11 The buying decision process

Source: adapted from Holm Hansen and Skytte (1998).

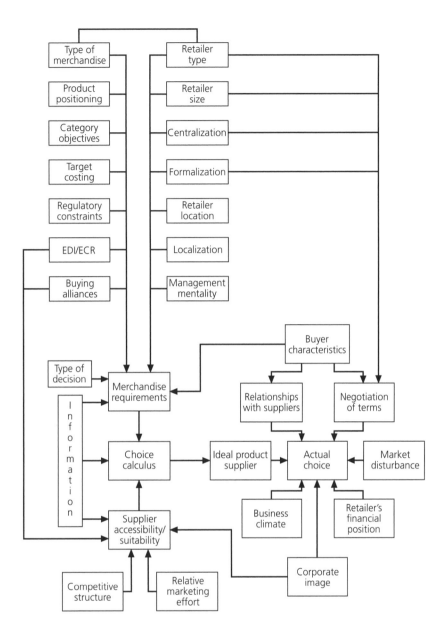

Evidence has emerged that buyer characteristics can influence the buying process. Runyan and Sternquist (1995) found that both experience and gender of the buyer influence negotiation behaviour. Male buyers were found to engage slightly more often in negotiation on terms of trade, a result consistent with the findings of Neu et al. (1998). Ettenson and Wagner (1986) found experienced buyers more likely to focus on margins and the supplier's product sales records. Fairhurst and Fiorito (1990) showed that experience has a positive effect upon the GMROI achieved.

Information is the lifeblood of buying decisions, and the quality/quantity of information is highly dependent upon the type of decision being made. When engaged in a periodic review of existing products or suppliers, major retailers have at their disposal 'warehouses' of PoS data, showing what was sold, when, where and, possibly, to whom. Products not currently sold may be tracked through AGB, GfK or Neilsen data on product/category sales. In addition, McGoldrick and Douglas (1983) found that multiple buyers kept in regular contact with all main suppliers in a category, including those not currently supplying.

Kline and Wagner (1994) found dominant information sources to be buyer's own knowledge, customer requests, consumer magazines, selling history, buyers from similar stores, sales representatives, reviews and the trade press. Where new products are offered to a retailer, the potential supplier must provide specific information to substantiate the proposal: Table 8.14 shows the standard information required by Boots the Chemist, under these circumstances.

Table 8.14 Information required from potential suppliers

Source: William Reed (1999).

Prior to first meeting with Boots the Chemist a supplier should send the following information:

Size and structure of supplier's company:
  ▶ Annual turnover
  ▶ Financing
  ▶ Nature of business
  ▶ Current customers of products
  ▶ Ability to produce own brand products

Market details:
  ▶ Market size and growth forecasts
  ▶ Market developments/new entrants

Why customers should want the product:
  ▶ Rationale behind proposal for Boots to stock the product
  ▶ Proposal for stocking: why the product is unique
  ▶ Number of products we should stock
  ▶ How many stores you want the product in

Cost price/pricing structure (including ex-works collection price)

Retail price

Marketing and advertising support

At the very core of any buying model is the process by which information on the many different attributes is combined and evaluated, in order to arrive at the final decision. If a systematic product-screening process is to be devised, it is essential to understand the 'decision rules' that are being used. Furthermore, the examination of these rules may lead to an improvement, or at least to a greater consistency, in the buying process. Three of the more frequently encountered examples of choice calculus are described as follows:

1 *Linear additive choice strategy*: by this method, a buyer assigns evaluative weights to each attribute of the brand, according to its perceived importance. Each brand under consideration then receives a

rating on each attribute dimension. These are combined linearly to form an overall judgement for each brand. The one selected would be the one with the highest 'global utility index'. This strategy is sometimes described as the compensatory model, as a high rating on one attribute may compensate for a low rating on another.

2 *Lexicographic choice strategy*: the buyer initially ranks the different attribute dimensions according to their importance. All the brands are then compared on the most important dimension and, if one offers a noticeably better outcome on that dimension, it is selected. If a choice cannot be made at this stage, the second most important dimension is considered. The process continues until the brand is selected.

3 *Conjunctive choice strategy*: the buyer establishes minimum cut-off values for each attribute dimension and then compares competing brands against these values. If any is rated below the cut-off values of any attribute, it is rejected as a choice possibility. This is an example of 'multiple cut-off' model.

Alternative terms may be encountered in describing these choice procedures. For example, Sheth (1981) cites three types of choice rule that may be applied, namely, trade-off choice calculus, dominant choice calculus and sequential choice calculus. These are broadly equivalent to choice strategies 1–3 respectively, as outlined above. There are many other variations upon these basic choice strategies. As described, they may sound too mechanistic really to describe the decision process of a buyer. The question that must be asked, however, is whether the models are too simplistic, or whether buyers are sometimes too erratic in their use of varying or undefined choice strategies. A decision aid for retail buyers that is frequently cited is the decision matrix approach (e.g. Ghosh, 1994). The matrix is constructed by:

1 Listing relevant selection criteria.
2 These are weighted according to their relative importance.
3 All suppliers under consideration are then rated on each individual criterion.
4 These supplier/criterion ratings are then multiplied by the criterion importance weights, to give each supplier a weighted score on each criterion.
5 These scores are then added to give each supplier an overall weighted score.

In effect, this procedure is assuming the 'linear additive' choice strategy, which is arithmetically convenient but not necessarily the most valid or appropriate strategy for all such decisions. In many instances a combination of choice strategies will be required. For example, the buyer or buying team may have established minimum cut-off points for quality, reliability of supply, etc. and maximum cut-off points for cost. Within these boundaries, trade-offs between criteria may determine which of the eligible products or brands is selected.

Given the complexity of this process, it is easy to understand manufacturers' enthusiasm for 'efficient new product introductions' (Sec. 8.1.5). However, even within an ECR regime, retailers still play a major 'gatekeeper' role with regard to product introductions.

8.2.5 Terms of Trade

Having considered many other factors of relevance to retail buying decisions, it would be incorrect to assume that the terms of trade are mostly fixed. There are in fact very few elements that cannot be the subject of negotiation. In the UK and some other countries, all elements of the supply price and discounts have been open to negotiation, as are delivery conditions, advertising allowances and many other elements of 'the deal'.

The value to retailers of effective negotiation can be very significant indeed. This is where the size and power of major retailers is translated into the tangible, detailed benefits that flow from that power. In Chapter 6 it was observed that a small multiple paid almost 9 per cent more for its goods than the largest chain, Tesco (Table 6.5). According to Morgan Stanley Dean Witter (1999), Tesco works constantly to improve buying terms and supply-chain efficiencies, unlocking around 0.2 per cent margin gain each year, in the UK alone.

Published terms of trade represent the starting point for negotiations. Along with the basic supply price, these terms sometimes include formalized scales of discounts, relating to one or more of the following:

1 Size of the overall order.
2 Size of orders at each delivery point.
3 Total purchases of the whole product range over a given period of time.
4 Period of credit given or taken.
5 Extent of promotional support by the retailer.
6 Compliance with specified stocking arrangements.

The unpublished terms are inevitably a good deal more complex and difficult to quantify, but they are a major element of buying. In 1981, the Monopolies and Mergers Commission estimated that special terms for the top four retailers cost manufacturers 9.2 per cent of sales: this had increased to 10.5 per cent by 1985 (Office of Fair Trading, 1985). Numerous types of special terms have been identified, for example:

1 Special prices, irrespective of published lists negotiated by large retailers.
2 Retrospective discounts or rebates, usually described as 'overriders', representing a reward given, or demanded, for reaching a sales target.
3 Favourable credit terms, agreed or taken by retailer, without imposition of published scale of penalties.
4 Special offers, usually linked to an agreed special price in the stores, which may or may not involve a reduction in the retailer's gross margin (Tyagi, 1999).

5 Disposal of seasonal lines or other surpluses, which may not be offered on equal terms to all retail customers.

6 Advertising support, a contribution to retailer advertising which, hopefully, benefits the supplier's products.

7 Promotional fees, to cover retailer's costs of participating in a joint promotion (Murray and Heide, 1998).

8 Coupons, representing a payment to participate in a coupon scheme.

9 Provision of training for sales staff.

10 Provision of shop equipment, such as refrigerated cabinets.

This list barely scratches the surface of this large and generally unpublished area of negotiation. The report of the Competition Commission (2000), weighing in at 1222 pages, does much more than that, providing unusual insights into unpublished terms of trade. Inevitably, it focuses upon the practices which have provoked complaints from suppliers or smaller retailers, providing therefore a rather dark view of retailer–supplier relationships. However, it is a useful antidote to some of the more rosy reports on category management and efficient consumer response!

The Commission's attempts to quantify various aggressive buying practices met with a number of problems. Suppliers were concerned about the consequences of being known to have complained. One said: 'It would be commercial suicide for any supplier to give a true and honest account of all aspects of relationships with retailers.' Major retailers also complained that they were being asked to comment on details of tens of thousands of negotiations, conducted over five years by numerous buyers, past and present. Given these caveats, it is likely that there was some degree of undercounting; Table 8.15 is based upon the survey of supplier's views. In total, 52 different practices are examined within the report. Table 8.15 looks at just 13 of these.

Table 8.15 Frequency of buying practices

Note: [1] The residual percentages represent the 'no answer' category.

Source: adapted from Competition Commission (2000).

Practice	Frequency % [1]			
	Never	**Rarely**	**Sometimes**	**Fairly often**
Delay payments by 15 days more than terms	44	33	18	4
Delay other amounts due	32	34	22	11
Break other contract terms	39	30	12	4
Change quality agreed without adequate notice	58	25	11	0
Change other agreed requirement	35	19	26	9
Threaten delisting without reasonable cause	21	42	32	2
Require contributions to charities	32	16	37	13
Require payments when product profit does not meet expectations	26	25	30	16
Require buyback of unsold goods	47	35	11	4
Make deductions to cover wastage	54	23	12	6
Impose slotting charges	44	11	18	21
Charge for any shelf space	49	19	18	11
Charge for listing	37	19	25	14

Delayed payments are a frequent source of tension, although retailers claimed that many of these are justified by order-delivery mismatch, or are simply oversights. United Kingdom retailers are by no means Europe's slowest payers (Burt and Sparks, 1997); in France, for example, Promodes obtained a 2.5 per cent discount for reducing its credit period from 57 days to 27 days. Changes in quantity or quality specifications are frequently requested, however, cases were identified of less than three days' notice being given.

Threats of delisting had been experienced by nearly 80 per cent of suppliers and are a common way of achieving better discounts. The different parties would argue the scope of 'reasonable cause'; the availability of a new and/or more profitable alternative may be seen as reasonable cause. Payments to compensate retailers for a product's underperformance are also quite common. The buyback of unsold goods may be a written term, as with Toys 'R' Us (Tordjman, 1994); it is sometimes required/requested of suppliers, even when it is not.

As the language of retailer–supplier terms evolves, the reader will meet some varied definitions. In the USA, White et al. (2000) refer to 'slotting fees' as upfront cash payments to retailers for accepting new products. In the UK, the term has been used to describe payments for preferred locations within the stores, for promotional or other reasons (Competition Commission, 2000). Listing fees/charges describe, in the UK, the increasingly prevalent practice of charging to stock new products, or even be on the list of suppliers. In the USA, Skinner et al. (1992) quote Safeway as demanding $25 000 before placing new products on their shelves.

Terminologies are not the only differences between countries; different legislative frameworks also apply. Figure 8.12 summarizes the most relevant aspects of these in just four countries. Since the 1930s, the Robinson-Patman Act in the USA has sought to limit the ability of large retailers to extract better terms, simply because they are large (Ingene and Parry, 2000). However, very large retailers, such as Wal-Mart, are able to offer provable cost savings to suppliers; own brands also offer a way to get better deals, while not breaching the Act. Early investigations by the Monopolies and Mergers Commission (1981) and Office of Fair Trading (1985) recommended against similar legislation in the UK.

Since that time, concern has increased in Europe, leading to restrictions and remedies being introduced in France, Germany and Ireland. Disputes had arisen in the Republic of Ireland about 'hello money', which a supplier might be invited to give in order to win shelf space, for example, on the occasion of a store opening or extension (Retail Review, 1999). Following the investigation of the Competition Commission (2000) in the UK, a binding Code of Practice has been suggested, covering many of the identified buying practices. This may inhibit some of the more aggressive manifestations of buying power, but is unlikely to substantially influence the overall balance of power.

United States *Robinson-Patman Act (1936)*	Germany *Gesetz gegen Wettbewerbsbechrankungen (1999)* *Act on Restraints on Competition (1999)*
Designed to protect smaller businesses by forbidding large competitors from using their size to gain lower supply prices. The law, however, permits price reductions in the following circumstances: 1. When the price reduction is made to meet the low price of a competitor. 2. When the lower cost price is based on cost savings in selling to the retailer (e.g. transport costs, genuine economies of scale, etc.). 3. When the price is reduced on goods that are (or about to be) obsolete, such as 'joblots'. The vendor must offer the discounts to all retailers that meet the same terms and conditions.	Similar in intention to the Loi Galland in France, seeking to shift the balance between larger retailers and their suppliers: 1. Retailers forbidden from setting prices permanently below purchase prices. 2. Firms can take action in courts against the abuse of a dominant position: they do not have to wait for the Cartel Office to act. 3. Suppliers may remain anonymous while complaining to the Cartel Office, but not before the court. 4. Some smaller retail buying groups have exemptions from the normal cartel laws
France *Loi Galland (1996)*	Ireland *Competition Act (1991, amended 1996)* *Restrictive Practicies (Grocery) Order (1987)*
Also designed to protect small shopkeepers and reduce perceived imbalance between suppliers and retailers: 1. Refunds must appear on bills: cannot be negotiated at the end of the year. 2. Selling at a loss is forbidden (a loss on cost price plus transport costs and taxes). 3. 'Excessively low prices' forbidden. 4. Refusal to supply is permitted. 5. Listing fees without any real benefits (e.g. retailer provided services) are not permitted. 6. Retailers asking for a listing fee must commit to a proportionate, minimum purchase. 7. To stop purchasing a particular product, a retailer must give prior written notice to a supplier.	1. Prohibits the selling or advertising for sale of grocery goods below cost price. 2 Prohibits payment or receipt of 'hello money'; cash or allowances offered by suppliers to gain preferential selling arrangements in particular stores. 3. Prohibits the imposition of resale price maintenance by suppliers/wholesalers. 4. Prohibits price fixing between suppliers, wholesalers or retailers. 5. Suppliers must keep copies of their standard terms and conditions available for inspection by Director of Consumer Affairs. 6. Suppliers must not discriminate against customers in applying their standard terms and conditions.

Figure 8.12 Legislation and buying terms

Sources: Berman and Evans (1998); Competition Commission (2000); NatWest Securities (1997).

SUMMARY

Buying plays a pivotal role in translating a retailer's positioning statement into the specific assortment to support that statement. Consequently, the effectiveness of buyers exerts a major influence upon the level of success enjoyed by the company. As firms have grown larger and more sophisticated, retail buying has become a more specialized function, while retaining close linkages with pricing, product development, advertising and in-store merchandising. Buyers now need excellent negotiation and communication skills, as well as strong awareness of market, commercial and financial issues.

A wide range of organizational structures exists to manage the buying function, depending upon the size, sector and objectives of the company. There has been a fairly consistent trend towards more centralized buying in large firms, in order to exploit specialization and economies of scale. The buying committee (or centre) has also increased in importance, which widens involvement in buying decisions but takes some responsibility from individual buyers.

In response to the buying power of large retailers, some smaller retailers have formed buying groups (or alliances), many of which also provide marketing services. Larger retailers too have banded together to form alliances to increase their international buying power, and to enhance the sharing of expertise. Internet-enabled exchanges have also developed, facilitating electronic reverse-auctions, where suppliers are invited to bid on-line to win a specified order.

As retailer power has increased in many countries, including the USA, much attention is now focused upon the changing relationship between suppliers and retailers. Previously dominant manufacturers have had to seek collaborative relationships with retailers, rather than dictating the terms. It is often in the interests of retailers to engage in fewer, more stable relationships, in order to facilitate innovation, quality, continuity and the effective flow of information. Such relationships are not without their tensions, but minor conflicts are less likely to lead to complete severance of the relationship.

Category management has emerged as a way in which these closer relationships can be utilized to co-manage product categories, sharing the expertise of both parties. By pooling information, the consumer can, in theory, be presented with an optimal assortment of products, prices and promotions, while both suppliers and retailers reduce costs. Category management principles have influenced the way retailers manage their product assortments, but often it is not implemented in its entirety. Category management has also attracted the attention of national and European competition authorities, especially the practice of nominating one supplier as the 'category captain' to manage the process.

The broader concept of efficient consumer response (ECR) advocates widespread collaboration within the supply chain, with the co-management of assortments, inventories, promotions and new product developments. The increased use of electronic data interchange (EDI) and quick response (QR) had already started to yield benefits to retailers, notably reduced inventories yet fewer stockouts. Stock at stores is newer, increasing its attractiveness and reducing wastage or markdowns. While some dispute the 'newness' of the ECR concept, it has helped to focus attention on the marketing effectiveness of supply chains, rather than just their efficiency.

Whatever the structure of the buying function, certain key decisions have to be made by all retail organizations. Strategies of specialization, category dominance, etc. are translated into specific assortment options, such as wide/narrow choice of categories, and shallow/deep choice within categories. The instrumental roles of products must also be clearly defined. Destination products promote visits to the store, core products establish authority in the class and other categories add value. Retailers can also link products in various different ways, including lifestyle categories, bundling and scrambled merchandising. As communication and control systems improve, there is increasing scope to vary these choices at local level.

Quantity decisions are a crucial aspect of buying, especially for products with long lead times for deliveries. Various statistical procedures are available to assist forecasting, including exponential smoothing and regression models. Some of these are now incorporated within sophisticated, sales-based ordering systems, which have reduced reliance upon longer-term estimates of likely sales. Although retailers try to reduce the cost and risks of surplus inventories, they also wish to avoid stockouts. In addition to the immediate loss of sales, stockouts can break patterns of store loyalty, reduce customer satisfaction and damage the retailer's image.

Buyers are faced with a constant stream of decisions on new products, and the retention of existing ones. The consequences of mistakenly rejecting a new product are generally lower and more easily reversed, than mistakenly delisting a good product. Buyers' criteria in selecting new products and suppliers have been extensively researched, relating to profitability and sales, category/assortment considerations, consumer evaluation, supplier's marketing, etc. The quality of the relationship with the supplier is rarely a main issue but it has been found to influence whether or how quickly underperforming products are delisted.

When deciding between products and/or suppliers, a wide range of financial, marketing and logistical factors enter the decision. Various attempts have been made to model how buyers evaluate the different combinations of attributes. In essence, attributes may be allowed to compensate for each other, choices may be made on basis of the most important attribute, or products may be judged against cut-off points on each attribute. Recognition of the most appropriate choice strategy can help to evolve a systematic and consistent screening process.

Terms of trade represent a major source of controversy, and of profit for larger retailers. In the UK, the value of special, unpublished buying terms secured by major retailers can greatly exceed the value of standard discounts. These special terms include overriders, favourable credit terms, advertising support, promotional payments, listing fees, slotting allowances, 'hello money' and many more. Measures to curb some of the more aggressive buying practices have been introduced within some countries, including a Code of Practice in the UK.

REVIEW QUESTIONS

1 Contrast the likely roles of the buyers in these three organizations:

a) an independent chain of six fashion stores

b) a chain of 20 department stores

c) a major grocery multiple.

2 Discuss the benefits and the drawbacks of centralized buying within large retail companies. What measures would you recommend to overcome the drawbacks?

3 Do you consider that buying committees represent an improvement upon individual buying? Justify your answer.

4 You are buying for a large retailer, in a market dominated by two main suppliers. What strategies are available to reduce dependence on those suppliers?

5 Do you anticipate that Internet-enabled networks and electronic auctions will play an increased role in retail buying? Justify your prediction.

6 In spite of their ability to engage in opportunistic purchasing, many major retailers have opted for fewer but longer-term relationships with suppliers. How do you explain this trend?

7 Category management has been variously described as 'the key to the future' and as 'a new label on an old bottle'. To which of these views do you subscribe, and why?

8 What are the advantages and possible problems of appointing one supplier as the 'category captain', from the viewpoint of the retailer and consumers?

9 Outline the main components and elements of efficient customer response (ECR).

10 Explain how the combination of electronic data interchange (EDI) and quick response (QR) can create value for retailers and their customers?

11 Give an example of a retailer that uses each of these product mix strategies:

a) narrow and deep

b) wide and shallow.

Discuss the merits and possible hazards of these two strategies, for the two retailers that you have chosen.

12 What are the advantages of varying the product mix of individual stores within the chain? How can a retailer ensure that decisions on local assortments are appropriate?

13 Identify the essential differences between exponential smoothing and regression models, as approaches to sales forecasting. For what types of commodity is each most suitable?

14 Why is it so important for retailers to avoid out-of-stock situations? What approaches are used to try to achieve this objective?

15 Wrong decisions regarding new products may bring very different consequences for the buyer, compared with wrong decisions regarding existing products. Discuss.

16 In selecting specific products and suppliers, what would be your 10 most important criteria if you were:

a) buying ladies fashion dresses for a department store

b) buying frozen ready meals for a superstore chain.

Justify the ranking of your criteria, in each of these two contexts.

17 Explain the distinctions between the 'linear additive', 'lexicographic' and 'conjunctive' choice strategies.

18 Why is the 'ideal' choice of product/supplier, in terms of merchandise requirements, not always the actual choice made?

19 In addition to normal quantity discounts, what other terms would you seek to negotiate if buying:

a) paper goods for a superstore chain

b) cosmetics for a voluntary group of pharmacies.

20 As more countries, including the UK, introduce measures to curb the more aggressive buying practices, how will larger retailers continue to benefit from their buying power?

REFERENCES

Accenture (2000) *ECR2000—Day-to-day Category Management Study*, Accenture, London.

Achabal, D.D., S.H. McIntyre, S.A. Smith and K. Kalyanam (2000) 'A decision support system for vendor managed inventory', *Journal of Retailing*, **76** (4), 430–454.

Alon, I., M. Qi and R.J. Sadowski (2001) 'Forecasting aggregate retail sales: a comparison of artificial neural networks and traditional methods', *Journal of Retailing and Consumer Services*, **8**, (3), 147–156.

Amirani, S. and R. Dickinson (1995) 'The experience curve and retail decision making', *Proceedings of the World Marketing Congress*, Melbourne, 8–80–8–85.

Ansoff, I. (1991) 'Strategic management in a historical perspective', *International Review of Strategic Management*, **1** (1), 3–69.

Areni, C.S., D.F. Duhan and P. Kiecker (1999) 'Point of purchase displays, product organisation, and brand purchase likelihoods', *Journal of the Academy of Marketing Science*, **27** (4), 428–454.

Aufreiter, N., N. Karch and C. Smith Shi (1993) 'The engine of success in retailing', *McKinsey Quarterly*, **3**, 101–116.

Beazley, A. (1999) 'Size and fit: the development of size charts for clothing—Part 3', *Journal of Fashion Marketing and Management*, **3** (1), 66–84.

Bell, D. (1996) 'The changing retailer-supplier relationship', in *The Outlook for West European Retail*, R. Davies (ed.), Financial Times Reports, London, pp. 46–67.

Beninati, M., P. Evans and J. McKinney (1997) 'A blueprint for local assortment management', *Chain Store Age*, February, 30.

Bergen, M. S. Dutta and S.M. Shugan (1996) 'Branded variants: a retail perspective', *Journal of Marketing Research*, **33** (1), 9–19.

Berman, B. and J. Evans (1998) *Retail Management: A Strategic Approach*, Prentice-Hall, Engelwood Cliffs, NJ.

Biong, H. (1993) 'Satisfaction and loyalty to suppliers within the grocery trade', *European Journal of Marketing*, **27** (7), 21–38.

Bowlby, S. and J. Foord (1995) 'Relational contracting between U.K. retailers and manufacturers', *International Review of Retail, Distribution and Consumer Research*, **5** (3), 333–360.

Brockman, B.K. and R.M. Morgan (1999) 'The evolution of managerial innovations in distribution: what prospects for ECR?', *International Journal of Retail & Distribution Management*, **27** (10), 397–408.

Bronnenberg, B.J., V. Mahajan and W.R. Vanhonacker (2000) 'The emergence of market structure in new repeat-purchase categories: the interplay of market share and retailer distribution', *Journal of Marketing Research*, **37** (1), 18–31.

Buckingham, C. (1994) 'Category management in Europe, from concept to reality', *European Retail Digest*, **1** (Winter), 4–9.

Burt, S. and S. Davis (1999) 'Follow my leader? Lookalike retailer brands in non-manufacturer-dominated product markets in the U.K.', *International Review of Retail, Distribution and Consumer Research*, **9** (2), 163–185.

Burt, S. and L. Sparks (1997) 'Performance in food retailing: a cross-national consideration and comparison of retail margins', *British Journal of Management*, **8** (2), 133–150.

Cadeaux, J.M. (1997) 'A closer look at the interface between the product lines of manufacturers and the assortments of retailers', *International Journal of Retail & Distribution Management*, **25** (6), 197–203.

Cadeaux, J.M. (1999) 'Category size and assortment in U.S. macro supermarkets', *International Review of Retail, Distribution and Consumer Research*, **9** (4), 367–377.

Campo, K., E. Gijsbrechts and P. Nisol (2000) 'Towards understanding consumer response to stock-outs', *Journal of Retailing*, **76** (2), 219–242.

Cash, R.P., J. Friedlander and J. Wingate (1995) *Management of Retail Buying*, Wiley, New York.

Chandra, C. and S. Kumar (2001) 'Taxonomy of inventory policies for supply chain effectiveness', *International Journal of Retail & Distribution Management*, **29** (4), 164–175.

Chatterjee, S.C., S. Hyvonen and E. Anderson (1995) 'Concentrated vs balanced sourcing: an examination of retailer purchasing decisions in closed markets', *Journal of Retailing*, **71** (1), 23–46.

Chetochin, G. (1992) *Marketing Strategique de la Distribution*, Editions Liaisons, Paris.

Collins, A. and S. Burt (1999) 'Dependency in manufacturer-retailer relationships: the potential implications of retail internationalisation for indigenous food manufacturers', *Journal of Marketing Management*, **15**, 673–693.

Collins, A., M. Henchion and P. O'Reilly (2001) 'Logistics customer service: performance of Irish food exporters', *International Journal of Retail & Distribution Management*, **29** (1), 6–15.

Collins-Dodd, C. and J.J. Louviere (1999) 'Brand equity and retailer acceptance of brand extensions', *Journal of Retailing and Consumer Services*, **6**, 1–13.

Competition Commission (2000) *Supermarkets: A Report on the Supply of Groceries from Multiple Stores in the United Kingdom*, The Stationery Office, Norwich.

Corstjens, J. and M. Corstjens (1995) *Store Wars: The Battle for Mindspace and Shelfspace*, Wiley, Chichester.

Cravens, D.W. and D.W. Finn (1983) 'Supplier selection by retailers: research progress and needs', in *Patronage Behaviour and Retail Management*, W.R. Darden and R.F. Lusch (eds), Elsevier-North Holland, New York, pp. 225–244.

Cunningham, M.T. and E. Homse (1986) 'Controlling the marketing-purchasing interface: resource development and organisational implications', *Industrial Marketing and Purchasing*, **1** (2), 3–25.

Cuthbertson, R. (1999) 'IT and future retailer-supplier relationships', *European Retail Digest*, **23** (September), 6–8.

Cuthbertson, R. (2000) '2 B or 2 B', *European Retail Digest*, **26** (June), 57–58.

Dabholkar, P.A., W.J. Johnston and A.S. Cathey (1994) 'The dynamics of long-term business-to-business exchange relationships', *Journal of the Academy of Marketing Science*, **22** (2), 130–145.

Davies, G. (1990) 'Marketing to retailers: a battle for distribution', *Long Range Planning*, **23** (6), 101–108.

Davies, G. (1993) *Trade Marketing Strategy*, Paul Chapman, London.

Davies, G. (1994) 'Maintaining relationships with retailers', *Journal of Strategic Marketing*, **2**, 189–210.

Davies, G and A. Treadgold (1999) 'Buyer attitudes and the continuity of manufacturer/retailer relationships', *Journal of Marketing Channels*, **7** (1/2), 79–94.

Davison, J. and S. Scouler-Davison (1997) 'Managing stock management III in Safeway stores', in *Cases in Retailing: Operational Perspectives*, C. Hart, M. Kirkup, D. Preston, M. Rafiq and P. Walley (eds), Blackwell, Oxford, pp. 97–105.

Dawson, J. (1995) 'Retail change in the European community', in *Retail Planning Policies in Western Europe*, R. Davies (ed.), Routledge, London.

Dawson, J.A. and S.A. Shaw (1989) 'The move to vertical marketing systems by British retailers', *European Journal of Marketing*, **23** (7), 42–52.

De Wilt, H.G.J. and T.V. Krishnan (1995) 'Supply chain management', *European Retail Digest*, **6** (Spring), 33–49.

Desmet, P. and V. Renaudin (1998) 'Estimation of product category sales responsiveness to allocated shelf space', *International Journal of Research in Marketing*, **15**, 443–457.

Dettmann, P. (1999) 'Reflections on category management and ECR at ICA', *European Retail Digest*, **23** (September), 15–17.

Dhar, S.K., S.J. Hoch and N. Kumar (2001), 'Effective category management depends on the role of the category', *Journal of Retailing*, **77** (1), 165–184.

Diamond, J. and G. Pintel (1997) *Retail Buying*, Prentice-Hall, Englewood Cliffs, NJ.

Doyle, P. and C.B. Weinberg (1973) 'Effective new product decisions for supermarkets'. *Operational Research Quarterly*, **24** (1), 45–54.

Dupuis, M. and E. Tissier-Desbordes (1996) 'Trade marketing and retailing: a European approach', *Journal of Retailing and Consumer Services*, **3** (1), 43–51.

Emmelhainz, M.A., J.R. Stock and L.W. Emmelhainz (1991) 'Consumer responses to retail stock-outs', *Journal of Retailing*, **67** (2), 138–147.

Ettenson, R. and J. Wagner (1986), 'Retail buyers' saleability judgements: a comparison of information use across three levels of experience', *Journal of Retailing*, **62** (1), 41–63.

European Commission (1997) *Green Paper on Vertical Restraints in EC Competition Policy*, European Commission, Brussels.

Fairhurst, A.E. and S.S. Fiorito (1990) 'Retail buyers' decision making process: an investigation of contributing variables', *International Review of Retail, Distribution and Consumer Research*, **1** (1), 87–100.

Farrington, B. and D. Waters (1995) *A Practical Guide to World Class Buying*, Thomson, London.

Fernie, J. (1992) 'Distribution strategies of European retailers', *European Journal of Marketing*, **26** (8/9), 35–47.

Fernie, J. (1998) 'Outsourcing distribution in U.K. retailing', *Institute for Retail Studies Research Papers in Retailing*, 9801, Stirling.

Fernie, J. and H. Staines (2001) 'Towards an understanding of European grocery supply chains', *Journal of Retailing and Consumer Services*, **8** (1), 29–36.

Fiorito, S.S., E.G. May and K. Straughn (1995) 'Quick response in retailing: components and implementation', *International Journal of Retail & Distribution Management*, **23** (5), 12–21.

Fitzsimons, G. J. (2000) 'Consumer response to stockouts', *Journal of Consumer Research*, **27** (2), 249–266.

Ford, D. (1990) *Understanding Business Markets: Interactions, Relationships and Networks*, Routledge, London.

Fornari, D. (1986) *Autonomia Imprenditoriale nel Commercio et Politiche de TM dei Produttori di Marca in Italia*, F Angeli, Milan.

Fornari, D. (1988) 'Metodologie e strumenti di planificazione per le strategie si TM dei produttori di marca', *Commercio*, **28**, 155–162.

Forrester, R.A. (1987) 'Buying for profitability', *Retail & Distribution Management*, **15** (3), 25–26.

Freathy, P. and F. O'Connell (1998) 'The role of the buying function in airport retailing', *International Journal of Retail Distribution Management*, **26** (6), 247–256.

Freathy, P. and L. Sparks (1995) 'Flexibility, labour segmentation and retail superstore managers: the effects on Sunday trading', *International Review of Retail, Distribution and Consumer Research*, **5**, 361–385.

Freedman, P.M., M. Reyner and T. Tochtermann (1997) 'European category management: look before you leap', *McKinsey Quarterly*, **1** (Winter), 156–164.

French, J.R.P. and B.H. Raven (1959) 'The bases of social power', in *Studies in Social Power*, D. Cartwright (ed.), University of Michigan Press, Ann Arbor, MI, pp. 150–167.

Fuller, J.B., J. O'Conor and R. Rawlinson (1993) 'Tailored logistics: the next advantage', *Harvard Business Review*, **93** (3), 87–98.

Ganesan, S. (1993) 'Negotiation strategies and the nature of channel relationships', *Journal of Marketing Research*, **30** (2), 183–203.

Ganesan, S. (1994) 'Determinants of long-term orientation in buyer–seller relationships', *Journal of Marketing*, **58** (2), 1–19.

Gattorna, J. (1998) *Strategic Supply Chain Alignment*, Gower, Aldershot.

Ghosh, A. (1994) *Retail Management*, Dryden Press, Fort Worth, TX.

Goodwin, D.R. (1992) 'The open-to-buy system and accurate performance measurement', *International Journal of Retail & Distribution Management*, **20** (2), 16–23.

Grewal, D. (2000) 'Supply chain management in a networked economy', *Journal of Retailing*, **76** (4), 415–429.

Grewal, D., M. Levy, A. Mehrotra and A. Sharma (1999) 'Planning merchandising decisions to account for regional and product assortment differences', *Journal of Retailing*, **75** (3), 405–424.

Gruen, T. W. and R. H. Shah (2000) 'Determinants and outcomes of plan objectivity and implementation in category management relationships', *Journal of Retailing*, **76** (4), 483–510.

Hansen, K. (2001) 'Purchase decision behaviour by Chinese supermarkets', *International Review of Retail, Distribution and Consumer Research*, **11** (2), 159–175.

Harvard Business Review (2000) 'The Napsterization of B2B', *Harvard Business Review*, **78** (6), 18–19.

Hendry, M. (1996) *Improving Retail Efficiency through EDI: Managing the Supply Chain*, FT/Reason Professional, London.

Hill, R.M. (1992) 'Using inter-branch stock transfers to meet demand during a stock-out', *International Journal of Retail Distribution Management*, **20** (3), 27–32.

Hirschman, E. (1983) 'An exploration comparison of decision criteria used by retail buyers', in *Retail Patronage Theory*, W.R. Darden and R.F. Lusch (eds), Elsevier-North Holland, New York, p. 5.

Hogarth-Scott, S. and S.T. Parkinson (1993) 'Retailer–supplier relationships in the food channel', *International Journal of Retail & Distribution Management*, **21** (8), 11–18.

Hogarth-Scott, S. and I. Walters (2000) 'The role of category management in hair colourants: Bristol Myers', in *Contemporary Cases in Retail Operations Management*, B.M. Oldfield, R.A. Schmidt, I. Clarke, C. Hart and M.H. Kirkup (eds), Macmillan, Basingstoke, pp. 154–169.

Holm Hansen, T. and H. Skytte (1998) 'Retailer buying behaviour: a review', *International Review of Retail Distribution and Consumer Research*, **8** (3), 279–301.

Huffman, C. and B.E. Kahn (1998) 'Variety for sale: mass customization or mass confusion', *Journal of Retailing*, **74** (4), 491–513.

Hughes, A (1996) 'Forging new cultures of food retailer-manufacturer relations?' in *Retailing, Consumption and Capital: Towards the New Retail Geography*, N. Wrigley and M. Lowe (eds), Longman, Harlow, pp.90–115.

IGD (1995), *The Category Management Revolution*, Institute of Grocery Distribution, Watford.

IGD (1997) *A Guide to Category Management*, Institute of Grocery Distribution, Watford.

IGD (1999a) *Category Management in Action*, Institute of Grocery Distribution, Watford.

IGD (1999b) *Retail Logistics 1999*, Institute of Grocery Distribution, Watford.

IGD (2000) *Grocery Retailing 2000*, Institute of Grocery Distribution, Watford.

IGD (2001a) *European Grocery Retailing*, Institute of Grocery Distribution, Watford.

IGD (2001b) *Guide to B2B Exchanges*, Institute of Grocery Distribution, Watford.

Ingene, C.A. and M.E. Parry (2000), 'Is channel coordination all it is cracked up to be?', *Journal of Retailing*, **76** (4), 511–547.

International Journal of Physical Distribution (1990) 'Developing a channels strategy and managing cultural change in logistics channels', *International Journal of Physical Distribution*, **20** (3), 45–60.

Jackson, T. and D. Shaw (2001) *Mastering Fashion Buying and Merchandising Management*, Macmillan, Basingstoke.

Johnson, R. (1998) 'Nationalizing Nordstrom', *Journal of Business Strategy*, **18** (5), 24–25.

Kahn, B.E. (1999) 'Introduction to the special issue: assortment planning', *Journal of Retailing*, **75** (3), 289–293.

Kahn, B.E. and L. McAlister (1997) *Grocery Revolution: The New Focus on the Consumer*, Addison-Wesley, Reading, MA.

Keaveney, S.M. (1992) 'An empirical investigation of dysfunctional organisational turnover among chain and non-chain store buyers', *Journal of Retailing*, **68** (2), 145–173.

Keaveney, S.M. (1995) 'Working smarter—the effects of motivational orientations on purchasing task selection', *Journal of Business and Psychology*, **9** (3), 253–271.

Keep, W.W., S.C. Hollander and R. Dickinson (1998) 'Forces impinging on long-term business-to-business relationships in the United States: an historical perspective', *Journal of Marketing*, **62** (2), 31–45.

Kelly, J.P., S.M. Smith and H.K. Hunt (2000) 'Fulfilment of planned and unplanned purchases of sale- and regular-price items: a benchmark study', *International Review of Retail, Distribution and Consumer Research*, **10** (3), 247–263.

Kim, N. and P.M. Parker (1999) 'Collusive conduct in private label markets', *International Journal of Research in Marketing*, **16** (3), 143–155.

Kline, B. and J. Wagner (1994) 'Information sources and retail buyer decision-making: the effect of product-specific buying experience', *Journal of Retailing*, **70** (1), 75–88.

Knox, S.D. and H.F.M. White (1991) 'Retail buyers and their fresh produce suppliers: a power of dependency scenario in the U.K.?', *European Journal of Marketing*, **25** (1), 40–52.

Ko, E. and D.H. Kincade (1997) 'The impact of quick response technologies on retail store attributes', *International Journal of Retail & Distribution Management*, **25** (2), 90–98.

Koelmeijer, K. and H. Oppenwal (1999) 'Assessing the effect of assortment and ambience: a choice experimental approach', *Journal of Retailing*, **75** (3), 319–345.

Kumar, N. (1996) 'The power of trust in manufacturer-retailer relationships', *Harvard Business Review*, **74** (6), 92–106.

Kurt Salmon Associates (1993) *Efficient Consumer Response: Enhancing Consumer Value in the Grocery Industry*, Food Marketing Institute, Washington, DC.

Lee, J.K.H. and J.H. Steckel (1999) 'Consumer strategies for purchasing assortments within a single product class', *Journal of Retailing*, **75** (3), 387–403.

Lohtia, R. and T. Murakoshi (1999) 'The adoption of efficient consumer response in Japan', *Journal of Marketing Channels*, **7** (1/2), 1–28.

Loughlin, P. (1999) 'Viewpoint: e-commerce strengthens suppliers' position', *International Journal of Retail & Distribution Management*, **27** (2), 69–71.

Maltz, E. and R.K. Srivastava (1997) 'Managing retailer–supplier partnerships with EDI: evaluation and implementation', *Long Range Planning*, **30** (6), 862–876.

Management Horizons (1999) *Profit from Category Management*, Management Horizons, London.

Marr, N.E. and W.A. Thomas (1999) 'The acceptance/rejection of new products in the retail grocery industry: the influence of background elements', *International Review of Retail, Distribution and Consumer Research*, **9** (2), 187–202.

Martin, C.R. (1973) 'The contribution of the professional buyer to a store's success or failure', *Journal of Retailing*, **49** (2), 69–80.

Mathews, R. (1997) 'ECR: more promise than performance', *Progressive Grocer Annual Report*, April, 26–28.

McGoldrick, P.J. and R.A. Douglas (1983) 'Factors influencing the choice of a supplier by grocery distributors', *European Journal of Marketing*, **17** (5), 13–27.

McIntyre, S.H. and C.M. Miller (1999) 'The selection and pricing of retail assortments: an empirical approach', *Journal of Retailing*, **75** (3), 295–318.

McKinnon, A. (1996) *The Development of Retail Logistics in the U.K.*, Technology Foresight, Retail and Distribution Panel, Office of Science and Technology, London.

Meidan, A. and A. Tomes (1991) 'Cash and carry customers' shopping habits and supplier choice criteria', *International Journal of Retail & Distribution Management*, **19** (5), 29–36.

Mentzer, J. T., S. Min and Z.G. Zacharia (2000) 'The nature of interfirm partnering in supply chain management', *Journal of Retailing*, **76** (4), 549–568.

Mintel (1997) *Efficient Consumer Response*, Mintel, London.

Monopolies and Mergers Commission (1981) *Discounts to Retailers*, HMSO, London.

Morelli, C. (1999) 'Information costs and information asymmetry in British food retailing', *Service Industries Journal*, **19** (3), 175–186.

Morgan Stanley Dean Witter (1999) 'It ain't half hot, mum', *UK Food Retailing*, 4 October.

Morgan Stanley Dean Witter (2001) *Minimising Risk in Fashion Retailing*, MSDW, London.

Murry, J.P. and J.B. Heide (1998) 'Managing promotion program participation within manufacturer-retailer relationships', *Journal of Marketing*, **62** (1), 58–68.

Myers, M.B., P.J. Daugherty and C.W. Autry (2000) 'The effectiveness of automatic inventory replenishment in supply chain operations: antecedent and outcomes', *Journal of Retailing*, **76** (4), 455–481.

NatWest Securities (1997) 'Relevant legislation', *European Food Retailing*, February, 5–9.

Needel, S.P. (1998) 'Understanding consumer response to category management through virtual reality', *Journal of Advertising Research*, **35** (4), 61–67.

Neu, J., J.L. Graham and M.C. Gilly (1988) 'The influence of gender on behaviours and outcomes in a retail buyer–seller negotiation simulation', *Journal of Retailing*, **64** (4), 427–450.

Nicholson, C.Y., L.D. Compeau and R. Sethi (2001) 'The role of interpersonal liking in building trust in long-term channel relationships', *Journal of the Academy of Marketing Science*, **29** (1) 3–15.

Nicol, I. (2001) 'The new rules of category management', *Supply Chain and Logistics Management*, **21** (3), 25–26.

Nielsen (1975), 'Distribution—a perennial problem', *Nielsen Researcher*, **3**, 1–6.

Nilsson, J. and V. Host (1987) *Reseller Assortment Decision Criteria*, Aarhus University Press, Aarhus.

Office of Fair Trading (1985) *Competition and Retailing*, OFT, London.

Oliver R.W. (1999) 'The end of inventory?', *Harvard Business Review*, **99** (1), 8–11.

Pellegrini, L. and L. Zanderighi (1991) 'New products: manufacturers' versus retailers' decision criteria', *International Review of Retail, Distribution and Consumer Research*, **1** (2), 149–174.

Rao, V.R. and E.W. McLaughlin (1989) 'Modelling the decision to add new products by channel intermediaries', *Journal of Marketing*, **53** (1), 80–88.

Retail Directory (2000) *Retail directory of the U.K. 2000*, Newman, London.

Retail Intelligence (2000) 'Expanding the trading exchange', *UK Retail Report*, **111** (June), 94–95.

Retail Review (1996) 'REWE 'slaps "1% ECR" levy on suppliers', *Retail Review*, **224** (July), 7.

Retail Review (1997) 'Safeway keeps satellite eye on trucks', *Retail Review*, **230** (March), 6.

Retail Review (1999) '"Hello money" row erupts in Irish Republic', *Retail Review*, **250** (March), 7–8.

Retail Review (2000a) 'Retail and online mix at V.Shop, son of Our Price', *Retail Review*, **266** (October), 22.

Retail Review (2000b) 'Tesco, the non-food merchant', *Retail Review*, **266** (October), 13.

Retail Review (2000c) 'Researchers forecast massive growth for Internet-based home shopping', *Retail Review*, **265** (August), 3.

Retail Review (2001) 'Tesco tuned in to non-food challenge, aided by B2B exchanges', *Retail Review*, **269** (March), 6.

Rich, M and G. Bowley (1996) 'Retailers aim to refill their shelves just in time', *Financial Times*, 12 February.

Riddle, E.J., D.A. Bradbard, J.B. Thomas and D.H. Kincade (1999) 'The role of electronic data interchange in quick response', *Journal of Fashion Marketing and Management*, **3** (2), 133–146.

Robinson, T. and C.M. Clarke-Hill (1995) 'International alliances in European retailing', *International Review of Retail, Distribution and Consumer Research*, **5** (2), 167–184.

Rogers, E.M. (1995) *Diffusion of Innovations*, 4th edn, Free Press, New York.

Rose, J.M. (1994) 'Spinning the ECR wheel in Europe', *European Retail Digest*, **4** (Autumn), 4–8.

Rosenbloom, B. (1981) *Retail Marketing*, Random House, New York.

Ruiz, F.J.M. (2000) 'The supplier-retailer relationship in the context of strategic groups', *International Journal of Retail & Distribution Management*, **28** (2), 93–106.

Runyan, R.C. and B. Stenquist (1995) 'Negotiations in retail-supplier channels', 8th International Conference on Research in the Distributive Trades, Milan, 1–2 September.

Sandoh, H. and H. Shimamoto (2001) 'A theoretical study on optimal inventory-taking frequency for retailing', *Journal of Retailing and Consumer Services*, **8** (1), 47–52.

Schary, P.B. and M. Christopher (1979) 'The anatomy of a stock-out', *Journal of Retailing*, **55** (Summer), 59–67.

Shaw S.A. and J.A. Dawson (1995) 'Organisation and control in retail buying groups', *Journal of Marketing Channels*, **4** (4), 89–103.

Shaw, S.A., J.A. Dawson and N. Harris (1994) 'The characteristics and functions of retail buying groups in the United Kingdom: results of a survey', *International Review of Retail, Distribution and Consumer Research*, **4** (1), 83–105.

Sheth, J.N. (1973) 'A model of industrial buyer behaviour', *Journal of Marketing*, **37** (4), 50–56.

Sheth, J.N. (1981) 'A theory of merchandise buying behaviour', in *Theory of Retailing*, R.W. Stampfl and E.C. Hirschman (eds), American Marketing Association, Chicago, pp. 180–189.

Shipley, D.D. (1985) 'Resellers' supplier selection criteria for different consumer products', *European Journal of Marketing*, **19** (7), 26–36.

Simonson, I. (1999) 'The effect of product assortment on buyer preferences', *Journal of Retailing*, **75** (3), 347–370.

Skinner, S.J., J.B. Gassenheimer and S.W. Kelley (1992) 'Co-operation in supplier–dealer relations', *Journal of Retailing*, **68** (2), 174–193.

Stassen, R.E., J.D. Mittelstaedt and R.A. Mittelstaedt (1999) 'Assortment overlap: its effect on shopping patterns in a retail market when the distributions of prices and goods are known', *Journal of Retailing*, **75** (3), 371–386.

SuperMarketing (1994) 'The balance of power', *SuperMarketing*, 15 April, 27–29.

SuperMarketing (1996) 'Somerfield takes its partners', *SuperMarketing*, 12 July, 22.

Swindley, D. (1992) 'Retail buying in the United Kingdom', *Service Industries Journal*, **12** (4), 533–544.

Thomas, W.A. and N.E. Marr (1993) 'Evaluation of new products by New Zealand supermarket retail grocery buyers', *International Journal of Retail & Distribution Management*, **21** (8), 19–28.

Tordjman, A. (1994) 'Toys 'R' Us', in *Cases in Retail Management*, P.J. McGoldrick (ed.), Pitman, London, pp. 165–183.

Tse, K.K. (1985) *Marks & Spencer: Anatomy of Britain's Most Efficiently Managed Company*, Pergamon Press, Oxford.

Tyagi, R.K. (1999) 'A characterization of retailer responses to manufacturer trade deals', *Journal of Marketing Research*, **36** (4), 510–516.

Varley, R. (2000) 'Buying operations at Boots the Chemist: the case of a product range update', in *Contemporary Cases in Retail Operations Management*, B.M. Oldfield, R.A. Schmidt, I. Clarke, C. Hart and M.H. Kirkup (eds), Macmillan, Basingstoke, pp. 104–114.

Varley, R. (2001), *Retail Product Management, Buying and Merchandising*, Routledge, London.

Venkatesh, R., A.K. Kohli and G. Zaltman (1995) 'Influence strategies in buying centres', *Journal of Marketing*, **59** (4), 71–82.

Verbeke, W., P. Farris and R. Thurik (1998) 'Consumer response to the preferred brand out-of-stock situation', *European Journal of Marketing*, **32** (11/12), 1008–1028.

Verbeke, W., X. Van Ginkel, S. Borghgraef and P. Farris (2000) 'An exploration of in-store brand-extension commitment efforts: or is brand loyalty always a good thing to have?', *International Review of Retail, Distribution and Consumer Research*, **10** (1), 23–39.

Wagner, J., R. Ettenson and J. Parrish (1989) 'Vendor selection among retail buyers: an analysis by merchandise division', *Journal of Retailing*, **65** (1), 58–79.

Walters, D. and J. Hanrahan (2000) *Retail Strategy, Planning and Control*, Macmillan, Basingstoke.

Walton, S. and J. Huey (1992) *Sam Walton, Made in America, My Story*, Doubleday, New York.

Watson, P. (1996) *Hypermarkets and Supermarkets in Europe: The End of Growth?* Financial Times Reports, London.

Webster, F.W. (1965) 'Modelling the industrial buying process', *Journal of Marketing Research*, **2** (4), 370–376.

White, J.C., L.C. Troy and R.N. Gerlich (2000) 'The role of slotting fees and introductory in retail buyers' new-product acceptance decisions', *Journal of the Academy of Marketing Science*, **28** (2), 291–298.

William Reed (1999) *Boots the Chemists Ltd*, William Reed Directories, London.

Zinszer, P.H. and J.A. Lesser (1980) 'An empirical evaluation of the role of stock-out on shopper patronage processes', in *Marketing in the 80s*, R.P Bagozzi et al. (eds), American Marketing Association, Chicago, pp. 221–224.

CHAPTER Nine
Retailers' Own Brands

INTRODUCTION   A major cornerstone of retail marketing has been the development of the retailer's name as a brand, rather than simply a name over the shop. We have now arrived at a situation where the names of major retailers are better known to customers than any but the biggest of the manufacturer brand names. Retailer brand equity was discussed in Chapter 5, as a measure of long-term market performance. For many retailers, own-brand products have played a key role in the development of this brand equity. Retailer own brands now account for over 40 per cent of grocery turnover in the UK (Mintel, 1998), 20 per cent in Europe as a whole, 16 per cent in the USA and 11 per cent in Australia (Euromonitor, 2000).

This represents just one reason why the topic of own brands merits individual consideration, rather than simply being treated as a special issue within retail buying and pricing. Own brands also tend to receive a higher proportion of management attention within retail companies than their turnover alone would indicate. Not only is the retailer typically more involved in product development or specification, the own brand also tends to receive special emphasis in space allocations and retailer advertising. A body of relevant literature has therefore developed, as the subject has attracted increased attention from practitioners and researchers.

The term 'own brand' is used as a collective term, in preference to 'own label', in spite of the fact that the latter is also commonly used in the UK. The term 'own *brand*' better depicts the actual, or potential, role of such product ranges in building consumer confidence and loyalty. There has, in fact, been a serious problem of terminology in the development of this subject. Martell (1986) referred to language that is 'vague, if not misleading' being used to describe own brands. In an early discussion of this problem, Schutte (1969) listed no less than 17 alternative terms that had been used to describe distributor-oriented brands; ironically, neither 'own label' or 'own brand' was among them!

Many different definitions of own brands are also to be found, although few adequately capture the diversity of retailer own brand activity today. For many years, a J. Walter Thompson definition served well:

'Products sold under a retail organization's house brand name, which are sold exclusively through that retail organization's outlets' (Rousell and White, 1970). However, some retailers and wholesalers now use more than one name to differentiate their various own brand ranges. Furthermore, the products may no longer be sold exclusively through the retailer's outlets. J. Sainsbury made its own brands available to small, primarily rural retailers to take its brand into areas some distance from one of its stores (McNair, 1999). Tesco has developed a thriving business exporting its own brands to non-competing retailers in Europe. The A.C. Nielsen definition now accommodates this greater diversity of branding and channels: 'a brand name owned by the retailer or a wholesaler for a line or variety of items under exclusive or controlled distribution' (Koskinen, 1999).

A number of different 'species' of retailer brands have been identified (e.g. Bhasin et al., 1995, Euromonitor, 1986; KPMG, 2000, Samways, 1995):

1 *Retailer name brands*: using the retailer's own name, such as Sainsbury's standard store brands.
2 *Store sub-brands*: carrying both the retailer's name and that of the sub-brand, such as Tesco's Finest range.
3 *Generic brands*: a plain-label variant upon the own brand concept, such as the Tesco Economy brand and Euroshopper's product range.
4 *Exclusive brands*: distributed exclusively by the retailer but packaged under various different names, as in the case of Tandil detergents in Aldi.
5 *Exclusive products*: not truly own brands but products exclusive to a retail chain: for example, Del Monte supplies exclusive products to Migros in Switzerland.

This chapter will first examine the development of own brands within different countries and specific retailers. Attention then turns to strategies of own-branding, retailers' costs/benefits, the branding of own brands and the supply of own brands. The final section considers consumer responses to own brands, purchase patterns and perceptions of price and quality.

9.1 Developments in Own Brands

This section first presents a summary of statistics that illustrate the widespread growth in own brand market share, in the UK and other European countries. Some of the reasons put forward to explain this growth are also examined. The own brand developments of specific companies are then considered, including leading own brands in Europe.

9.1.1 The Growth in Market Shares

In one sense, the history of own brands is as long as that of retailing itself, with tailors, shoemakers, bakers, etc., making and selling their own products. In another sense, own brands as we know them today are a more recent phenomenon, representing an integral component of retailers' increasing power and marketing sophistication. The late 1960s was when own brands started to be widely noted as a threat to manufacturers' brands, especially in packaged grocery markets. Surprisingly little attention was given to their growth in other markets; it tended to be taken for granted that many clothes were sold as own brands and that all of Marks & Spencer's sales were in own brands. This situation changed rapidly in the 1980s, when it was acknowledged that few categories had escaped significant inroads from retailers' own brands.

Table 9.1 represents a summary of own-brand growth across all retail product categories in the UK. As the data are based upon sales turnover, they understate the volume growth of own brands, with many own brands selling at lower retail prices. Because of the relative fragmentation of some non-food retail sectors, data are sparse outside of the categories normally sold by the grocery retailers. KPMG (2000) observed that statistics for overall retailer brand penetration are unavailable. However, Euromonitor (1998) is a good source of well-informed estimates, which suggest that retailer brands represented over 30 per cent of retail trade by 2000. Key Note (1997) estimates are based on different definitions and suggest a higher share, at around 37 per cent.

Although the UK saw some of the earliest growth of retailer own brands, the rate of growth has shown signs of slowing down. *The Grocer* (2000) went as far as to describe 'own label in the doldrums', pointing out that own-brand shares have decreased in some grocery categories. Some major grocery retailers, notably J. Sainsbury, have deliberately reduced their proportions of own brand products, in order to give their customers more choice of brands. However, it would be unwise to conclude that the progress of own brands has run its full course in the UK, for three main reasons.

Table 9.1 Growth in UK retailer brand shares

Sources: Euromonitor (1986; 1998).

Year	Retailer brand share %
1981	17.5
1986	22.3
1993	24.0
1997	28.6

1 Retailer concentration is lower in most sectors than in groceries, but it is rising. Although forms of own brands are stocked by some independents, own brand growth is generally linked to the advance of the multiples (e.g. Steenkamp and Dekimpe, 1997).
2 Retailer brands have reinvented themselves a number of times since an earlier lull in their progress in the late 1970s: no doubt new variants of retailer brand will continue to emerge, involving many different products and services.
3 Some of the most notable international competitors have strong commitments to own brands, including Aldi, IKEA and now Wal-Mart.

If own-brand growth is slowing in the UK, the pattern is not being replicated in most European countries. Retailer brands have advanced to

23 per cent of sales in Switzerland and around 14 per cent in France and Germany. The largest retail brand markets are Germany ($72 billion), the UK ($64 billion) and France ($47 billion). Although starting from lower shares, there has been especially vigorous growth of retailer own brands in Greece, Spain, Portugal, Finland and the Czech Republic (Euromonitor, 1996; 1998).

Own-brand shares in categories sold by grocery retailers are closely monitored in many countries by A.C. Nielsen. Table 9.2 compares own-brand penetration levels in four broad categories, within eight European countries. Switzerland now has the highest own brand share in each of these categories, Migros being a major own-brand retailer. Although the data are not precisely comparable, it is notable that the own-brand grocery volume share in Switzerland was only 10.1 per cent in the mid-1980s (Salimans, 1986). Germany has also experienced major expansion of own brands, from a mid-1980s grocery share of 9.7 per cent.

Table 9.2 Own brand shares in Europe

Source: KPMG (2000), based on Nielsen data.

Country	Volume / Sales	Volume/sales % shares of own brands			
		Food	Drink	Personal care	Household goods
Switzerland	V	59.6	45.9	44.0	58.0
	S	50.7	36.7	30.2	49.6
UK	V	42.0	34.2	22.2	47.4
	S	34.0	25.3	15.2	44.4
Belgium	V	34.5	35.3	28.5	48.6
	S	23.9	25.0	16.8	37.4
The Netherlands	V	25.3	16.6	16.7	34.8
	S	20.9	11.5	9.5	29.4
Spain	V	24.1	15.7	15.3	32.6
	S	17.6	10.5	8.7	28.0
France	V	20.0	15.4	12.1	33.3
	S	16.5	11.8	8.4	30.7
Germany	V	18.5	8.2	12.3	30.4
	S	12.2	5.8	7.0	20.3
Finland	V	9.7	2.1	7.5	15.1
	S	8.0	2.0	5.1	11.6

Table 9.2 also illustrates the importance of distinguishing between *volume* and *sales* data, the latter typically indicating lower shares. The difference between them offers an indication of the relative price gaps between manufacturer retailer brands. In Spain, for example, the volume share of drinks own brands is 47 per cent higher than the value share, indicating major price differences. In the household goods category, the difference between the share measures is only 10 per cent, pointing to smaller price gaps between manufacturer and retailer brands.

There are major contrasts between the penetration levels within the various categories of food. In the UK, for example, Nielsen (2000) recorded the following food category own brand shares:

Dry grocery	36.1 per cent
Dairy	65.4 per cent
Delicatessen	85.4 per cent
Frozen foods	48.6 per cent
Bakery	64.4 per cent
Confectionery	15.5 per cent
Petfood/care	19.6 per cent

At the subcategory level, differences become even more marked. For example, 95.1 per cent of chilled pizza is sold as own brands, compared with 12.1 per cent of instant coffee.

The growth of own brands has obviously been at the expense of manufacturer brands, but some have suffered far more than others. Drawing upon Datamonitor figures, Samways (1995) examined sectors in which retailer brands had grown significantly over a four-year period. In many cases, the brand leader had not lost share, although the cost of retaining that share may well have increased. The main damage had been inflicted upon shares of the third-ranked brand and other brands, many being delisted by retailers to accommodate own-brand expansion. Cullen and Whelan (1997) refer to 'trapped brands', squeezed between the dominant brand(s) and the swiftly rising retailer own brands.

Within the food sector, the difficulties of the marginal brands have been further compounded by the growing share of expenditure on eating out and takeaway food (Brady and Davis, 1993). The retailers have also kept watchful eyes on this trend, responding with salad bars, cafés and chilled, often healthier alternatives to takeaway foods.

A widespread pattern is therefore evident of increasingly powerful retailers expanding their own brands into many categories. Their motives are discussed in more detail in Sec. 9.2.1 but a number of researchers have explored the broader determinants of private-label growth. For example, Hoch and Banerji (1993) and Hoch (1996) identified six major factors that exerted positive or negative effects upon retailer brand shares; at the category level:

Consumer driven:	product quality (+ve)
	quality consistency (+ve).
Retailer driven:	category retail sales (+ve)
	category gross margin (+ve).
Manufacturer driven:	number of large manufacturers (-ve)
	national advertising per manufacturer (-ve).

Quelch and Harding (1996) assembled a list of factors that researchers had found to be associated with retail brand growth. As these studies span the decades of evolution of retailer branding, some of the

Table 9.3 Drivers of retail brand growth

Key: (V) Generally valid, but with exceptions.
(S) Valid in some situations.
(R) Reduced validity as retail brands evolve.

Source: adapted from: Quelch and Harding (1996).

generalizations are less valid now than in the earlier years of own-branding. For example, when retail own brands tended to be rather basic alternatives to manufacturer brands, their fastest growth was within low-price, low-risk product groups. Before many retailers became sophisticated in their sourcing, specification and product testing, it was also true that own brands tended to be easy to manufacture, using commodity ingredients.

Table 9.3 has therefore been annotated to indicate factors of reduced validity, or of limited applicability. The issue of few manufacturer-brand varieties, for example, may be valid in some categories, but is not valid in the bakery goods category, where own brand shares are high (Nielsen, 2000). Likewise, although the quality of own brands is generally improving, there are cases of successful generic and retailer brands where quality is variable.

1 Product category characteristics

- The product is an inexpensive, low-risk purchase (R)
- It is easy to make from commodity ingredients (R)
- It is perishable, favouring local suppliers (S)
- Product category sales are large and growing (V)
- Category dominated by a few major manufacturers, so retailers promote their brands to reduce dependency (V)

2 New product activity

- Manufacturer brands are offered in few varieties, so the retail brand offers clear alternatives (S)
- Manufacturer brand, new product introductions are infrequent or easy to copy (V)
- Consumers can easily make side-by-side comparisons of manufacturer and retailer brands (R)

3 Retailer brand characteristics

- Distribution is well managed (V)
- Variability in quality is low (S)
- Quality comparison with manufacturer brands is high and improving (S)
- Consumers have confidence in their ability to make comparisons about quality (R)

4 Price and promotion factors

- Retail margins in the category are relatively high (S)
- Price gaps between national brands and private labels are wide (R)
- Manufacturer brand expenditures on price promotions, as a percentage of sales, are high, raising price sensitivity and inducing switching (S)
- The credibility of manufacturer brand prices is low because of frequent and deep price promotions (S)
- Manufacturer brand expenditures on advertising as a percentage of sales are low (R)

5 Retailer characteristics

- The retailer is part of a stable oligopoly and therefore sells manufacturer brands at relatively high prices (S)
- The retailer has the size and resources to invest in high quality, own brand development (V)

A summary of driving forces could also include legislative issues, which have exerted significant influences in some countries. For example, the 'Loi Galland' in 1997 prevented French retailers from selling manufacturer brands at a loss (Puget, 1998). This prompted Carrefour and Promodes to compete more strongly with their own brands.

In the USA, the Robinson-Patman Act reduces the ability of powerful retailers to extract better supply prices for the same products. Retailer brands, if differentiated from the manufacturer brand equivalents, offer US retailers a way to avoid breaching this legislation (Bhasin et al., 1995). Excess capacity in manufacturing is also a major facilitator of own brand development, an issue discussed further in Sec. 9.2.2.

9.1.2 Retailers' Brand Developments

Table 9.4 Trends in retailers' own brand shares

Note: due to changes within some of the retail groups, plus changes in the data collection methods, the changes over time should be regarded only as indicative.

Sources: Barrett (1995) and Burt (1992), based on AGB Superpanel data; KPMG (2000), based on A.C. Nielsen data.

Long-term trends in the own-brand shares of six retail companies are summarized in Table 9.4. Among the leading UK grocery retailers, there has been considerable convergence in own brand policies, but from very different starting points. Tesco's own-brand share almost doubled through the 1980s and ended the 1990s well in excess of 50 per cent. Tesco has also internationalized its own brand, both by exporting to non-competitors and by introducing its no-frills range in its Eastern European stores.

Asda originally tended to limit its own brands to dairy goods, reflecting its origins as Associated Dairies. The 1990s however saw dramatic growth in virtually all categories, including the budget Farm Foods range, George clothing and other non-food items. In 2001, the influence of parent company Wal-Mart became apparent. The 'Smart Price' brand replaced the 'Farm Stores' budget range and, 'Asda Great Value' superseded the standard range. 'Sam's Choice', named after Wal-Mart founder Sam Walton, was introduced at the premium end of the range (Retail Review, 2000a)

Retailer	% own brand share of sales				
	1980	**1985**	**1990**	**1994**	**1998**
Tesco	20.8	36.2	39.4	50.0	55.2
J. Sainsbury	54.2	56.0	53.4	57.3	60.7
Asda (Wal-Mart)	6.4	7.6	30.6	35.5	57.9
Safeway	27.6	35.7	33.1	42.0	53.2
Somerfield:					
Gateway	18.0	16.7	24.4	33.6	50.3
Kwik Save	0.0	0.0	0.0	10.3	
Marks & Spencer	100.0	100.0	100.0	100.0	100.0

Kwik Save continued through its first 28 years as a strong advocate of manufacturer brands at discounted prices. However, the logic of own-branding can become overwhelming, so the company introduced 50 'No Frills', generic-style items in 1993. By 1997, the focus of their own-branding had shifted to a new, mainstream range of 1000 items (Retail Review, 1997a). Further development then followed, as own brands were harmonized under the Somerfield name (Nielsen, 2000).

In spite of some trading problems around the turn of the millennium, Marks & Spencer remains one of the UK's major own brands, achieving a UK turnover of £6.6 billion. This excludes a further £349 million in financial services, which are an important brand extension for the company (Nielsen, 2000). There have, however, been major changes. The 'St Michael' trademark, devised in the 1920s as a tribute to founder Michael Marks, appears now merely as a quality guarantee, rather than as the brand name. Interbrand Newell and Sorrell were appointed as consultants and advised harmonization of the Marks & Spencer logos, be they on products, the website, lorries or staff uniforms. A new 'Autograph' sub-brand was introduced, to promote exclusive ranges by designers, such as Betty Jackson and Timothy Everest.

J. Sainsbury was the first of the major grocers to pursue own branding across virtually all its product categories. The own-brand share was over 60 per cent in the 1970s but then fell slightly for two main reasons. First, the opening of more, larger stores brought the need and opportunity to stock more esoteric, manufacturer brand products. Second, the company introduced 'fighting brands', low-priced manufacturer items to help combat the discounters and other retailers' generic ranges. By the late 1990s, with many Sainsbury brand innovations and a generic-style range for the lowest price options, own-brand share again climbed beyond 60 per cent. However, it was suggested that J. Sainsbury lost market share as customers started to observe a lack of brand choice (Koskinen, 1999). Consequently, the company took steps to reduce the perceived dominance of its own brand (Key Note, 1998).

It would be incorrect to assume that own brands are restricted to large stores operated by multiple retailers. The symbol groups, such as Spar in the grocery sector and Numark in the chemists sector, have also been active in own-brand development. There may seem little scope for own brands to be sold in completely independent outlets, although those of cash-and-carry wholesalers may be sold. The wholesaler's name probably means little to the independent store's customers but some of the advantages of own brands can still be achieved through this channel (Simmons and Meredith, 1984).

For the cash-and-carry wholesaler, the brands help to increase the loyalty of independent retailers, as the own brands become established within their stores. In the case of the symbol groups, own brands offer an additional method of cohesion for stores that are typically more diverse than is ideal. Pan-European voluntary group Spar has introduced a range of Eurobrands, designed to be sold in several European countries. In its UK stores, 24 per cent of packaged groceries and toiletries are own branded (Burt and Davis, 1999).

The own brand shares of some leading retailers in the rest of Europe are shown in Table 9.5. Aldi stocks few manufacturer brands in its limited-line discount stores; only around 60 lines are well-known manufacturer brands. Its strategy is based around exclusive brands, using various different names (Samways, 1995):

- Albrecht—coffee
- Alpenmark—cheese
- Caribic—toiletries
- Gartenkrone—canned and bottled vegetables
- Sweet Valley—canned fruit
- Tandil—detergents.

Table 9.5 European retailers' own brand shares

Sources: Koskinen (1999); Samways (1995).

Retailer	Nationality	Retailer brand % share of sales
Aldi	Germany	99
Migros	Switzerland	95
Monoprix	France	35
Albert Heijn	The Netherlands	35
GB	Belgium	33
Delhaize 'Le Lion'	Belgium	28
Casino	France	25
Intermarche	France	20
Pryca	Spain	20
Carrefour	France	17
Rewe	Germany	14
Continent	France	12
Auchan	France	11
Leclerc	France	10
Systemell	France	10
Tengelmann	Germany	10
SMA	Italy	9

Aldi maintains flexibility in its product sourcing to obtain the best deals currently available, using large or small suppliers. As well as emphasizing low product prices, the company also seeks low process costs, through regular deliveries and labour-efficient packaging.

Migros, too, has a very high share of own brands. This can increase the challenge of expanding internationally, as consumers in the new country need to be persuaded to switch both store and brands (Kumar, 1997). Even the manufacturer brands stocked are largely exclusives. For example, Migros is the only retailer in Switzerland stocking Vittel mineral water and Del Monte juices (Koskinen, 1999). Many of its own brands are produced in its own factories, including items such as biscuits and detergents, where manufacturers are typically strong. Some parallels can be drawn with the development of the Co-op and Boots brands in the UK, both of which were originally produced largely in the organizations' own factories.

Although Carrefour has not got the highest own-brand share among French grocery retailers, their evolution forms an intriguing case study (Pellegrini, 1994). In response to strong competition from discounters and other hypermarkets, the company initially launched a range of plain label 'Produit Libres'. These were strongly advertised and of good quality but other retailers reacted with more basic generic ranges. The company reacted with its own 'Premiers Prix' generics range but this proved difficult to operate alongside Products Libres, being too closely positioned in consumers' minds. The company therefore moved towards a mainstream own brand, in the form of 'Produits Concertes'. Once again, Carrefour attracted publicity and goodwill, this time through the use of 500 panels of customers who tested the products. Each accepted product gained a label saying 'ce produit a reçu l'accord des clients de Carrefour' (this product has received the approval of Carrefour's customers).

9.2 Strategies of Own-Branding

From this brief account of own-brand developments, it will be apparent that different levels of success have been achieved by different retailers. In some cases, such as Marks & Spencer and J. Sainsbury, the own brand has been a major and integral part of the company's growth. In other cases, the own brands have required relaunched significant repositioning, typically if first introduced as a defensive rather than a positive strategy. The route to a successful own-branding strategy is first to determine the precise objectives to be fulfilled by the introduction/extension of the range(s). Then, appropriate sources of supply must be found that can deliver the required price–quality mix. Through their launch and development, the own brand(s) must be clearly differentiated both within the store's own assortment and within the retail sector as a whole.

9.2.1 Retailers' Objectives

The overall objective of own-branding must clearly be to achieve competitive advantage, although there are many forms that this may take. The potential advantages to the retailer can be broadly classified as relating to:

- store image/customer loyalty
- competitive edge/ turnover
- higher profits/better margins.

Using this framework, Table 9.7 summarizes the main possible advantages to retailers of own-branding. A successful own-brand range is likely to yield benefits under each of these three headings, although it is most unlikely that all the cited advantages will apply. It is difficult to quantify the relative importance of these advantages but Table 9.6 illustrates some contrasts from a survey of over 200 European retail/wholesale managers. Overall, better margins were the reason most often mentioned but, in Germany and Switzerland, issues of competitiveness predominate. Image-building was a more important factor for the UK managers than for the rest, at the time of the survey.

Most important reasons	UK %	France %	Germany %	Spain %	Switzerland %	Total %
Better margins	90	90	86	83	62	82
Lower price competitors to A-brands	83	36	91	83	78	68
Improves retailer competitiveness	79	51	82	50	78	65
Image-building	74	64	55	67	44	62

Table 9.6 Most important reasons to carry own brands

Source: adapted from The Grocer (1993), based on data from the Private Label Manufacturers' Association.

Table 9.7 Advantages of own brands for retailers

Sources: Bhasin et al. (1995); Euromonitor (1986, 1996); Harrison (1994); Laaksonen (1994); Webster (2000).

Store image/customer loyalty

1 Good value enhances store image
2 Build relationship of trust and credibility
3 Control over relationship with customer
4 Good value builds loyalty to the store and own brand
5 Increase loyalty, even if temporary stockout
6 Own brand may be perceived as equal to or better than manufacturers' brand
7 It is widely assumed that own brands are made by leading manufacturers
8 Own brands can give a distinctive corporate image
9 Own brands carry the retailer's name into the consumer's home
10 Retailer advertising can benefit both the stores and the own brand
11 Better design co-ordination can be achieved between the stores and the products

Competitive edge/extra turnover

1 Advantage over competitors with no own brand
2 Offer benefits distinct from competitors
3 More control of product specification and quality
4 Allows more retailer-led product innovation
5 More control over composition of product range
6 Can exploit gaps in the category
7 Imitation styles can be introduced quickly
8 Own-brand products cannot be obtained elsewhere
9 Can be sold at lower prices
10 More scope for differential pricing
11 Offer more price variety to the consumer
12 Inducement to use the store, leading to other purchases

Higher profits/better margins

1 Margins tend to be 5–20 per cent better
2 Manufacturers' promotional expenses are avoided
3 Display space can be manipulated for better returns
4 Sales can be promoted by placing own brands next to major brands
5 Tighter stock control is usually possible
6 There is more control over pricing
7 Exporting can increase buying power/economies of scale
8 Favourable buying terms occur where excess supply capacity exists
9 They can help to break down manufacturers' hold of certain markets

As own brands evolve, the objective of building customer loyalty and store image must be a major long-term consideration. Some of the most respected and sought after own brands are also those that have been longest established, such as the Sainsbury brand. It would be incorrect, however, to assume that own-brand longevity guarantees success, as the Co-op must be all too well aware. Neither is it impossible to develop own-brand strength more quickly. Asda, for example, has engaged in an extensive and aggressive development programme, although the cost of the necessary marketing support has been considerable.

The role of own brands in developing customer loyalty has been explored by several researchers. According to Steenkamp and Dekimpe (1997):

> *customers' loyalty is a fundamental reason for having own labels. If you have a nucleus of products which customers see as having a quality image, there is an inevitable dynamic created.*

It has been shown that customers buying primarily own brands are considerably less likely to shop at different stores to get the best prices (KPMG, 2000).

In the early stages of own-brand development, it was frequently claimed that they offered a means of avoiding the cost of advertising and promotion. This claim is now more difficult to sustain, in that much of that cost is now simply being borne by the retailers. However, a large retail organization can achieve considerable advertising 'efficiency', in that the company and own-brand name can be jointly promoted and the benefits spread over the whole product range. Key Note (1997) estimated that J. Sainsbury spent £8.0 million on own-brand advertising, 39 per cent of its total advertising spend. Boots, on the other hand, spent £0.5 million, just 6 per cent of their total spend.

The objective of achieving a competitive edge through own-branding can be pursued in various ways. The most common approach tended to be to present the own brands as a lower-price alternative. Unfortunately, this ceases to provide a competitive edge if most competitors are doing the same, and if leading brands are also being heavily discounted. Therefore more retailers have sought to follow the alternative methods of differentiation through quality, innovation and/or design. Tse (1985) describes in detail the product innovation role within Marks & Spencer; over 60 years ago, this company found that it could hardly obtain the products that it knew it could sell, often because they did not yet exist! A major product development function therefore developed within the company. J. Sainsbury also has a long history of close participation in product development, having established a food technology department in the 1920s. Each of the top five grocery multiples employs, on average, over 100 food technology staff, working in close collaboration with buyers (Omar, 1995).

Product innovation is certainly not limited to the food retailers. Body Shop, for example, developed a strongly innovative own-brand concept, based upon the 'healthy' and 'natural' properties of their hair and skin care preparations. In the fashion sector, Benetton and Laura Ashley have successfully developed a synergy between their store and product developments. Salmon and Cinar (1987) noted the competitive edge that can be achieved through greater cohesiveness between the merchandise and the retail presentation. However, the competitive edge can sometimes arise more through imitation than innovation. Some fashion retailers, including The Limited, spot trends early and respond quickly with lower price copies, sometimes known as 'knock-offs' (Bhasin et al., 1995).

Any retailer involved in own-branding is likely to see profit improvement as a major objective, although there are different routes to achieving this. In some cases an objective is to break down a monopoly/oligopoly position when strong manufacturers dominate specific markets (Simmons and Meredith 1984). At the very least, the existence of the private brand is likely to increase bargaining power, both with suppliers of the own brand and with those competing for the remaining shelf space.

Unlike the manufacturer, a retailer is able directly to control the selling environment of its brands so as to enhance their turnover and, hopefully, profitability. It is quite usual for leading brands to be displayed alongside the own-brand alternatives, to provide an attraction to the section and to emphasize own-brand advantages. Manufacturers often claim that retailers give a disproportionate amount of display space to their own brands. Some retailers can defend this in terms of the superior sales volume of their own brands, although excessive bias in space allocations can damage the retailer's image for product choice (Key Note, 1998).

Another way to enhance both bargaining power and economies of scale is to export the own brands to non-competing stores. This is a well-established practice for Marks & Spencer, which won an Export Award for its activities (Harrison, 1994). In 1986, Tesco set up an export department, selling the Tesco branded products to retailers in 45 countries. The Norwegian retailer Centre-Mat, for example, stocks 300 Tesco lines in its stores. Safeway branded products are to be found on the shelves of Casino stores in France, through a reciprocal arrangement within the European Retail Alliance.

In the final analysis, a most persuasive reason for most retailers to stock own brands is the ability to buy more cheaply and to sell at a higher margin. Table 9.8 combines UK and Spanish analyses to illustrate the basic economics of own branding. This example makes assumptions about cost structures that may not be valid in all cases. For instance, some retailers do participate in product research and development, (Birtwistle and Freathy, 1998). In the case of some Aldi products, savings are made on packaging. However, the example represents typical cost structures for own-brand grocery items.

Both KPMG (2000) and Mendez et al. (2000) agree on supply prices 21–25 per cent lower than for equivalent quality manufacturer brands. Table 9.8 then illustrates how retailers' gross margins can be enhanced at various different price points for the own brands (OBs). If the item is sold at a deeply discounted price, the margin will be lower but the price inducement for bargain-oriented shoppers will be very high. At the next price level, the margin will be about the same and the price discount to consumers still quite high. At the point at which the manufacturer brand price is 19 per cent higher, the retailers' margin is nearly nine percentage points higher than on the manufacturer brand. Mendez et al. (2000) use similar data to illustrate the enormous benefits of upgrading own-brand images, to the point that the products can be sold at or around the price of manufacturer brands.

Table 9.8 The economics of own brands

Source: adapted from KPMG (2000), based on OXRIM data, and Mendez et al. (2000).

Cost structures:	Manufacturer brands	Own brands
Raw materials	35	35
Packaging material	12	12
Manufacturing costs		
Variable	9	9
Fixed	5	—
Research and development	3	—
Sales force	4	—
Advertising and promotion	9	5
Transport and distribution	5	2
Other costs	10	10
Operating profit	8	2
Retail Buying Price	100	75
Price/margin levels:		
Manufacturer brand price	118	
retail margin	*15.3%*	
Very low OB price		79
(difference) margin	*(49.4%)*	*5.1%*
Low OB price		89
(difference) margin	*(32.6%)*	*15.7%*
Moderate OB price		99
(difference) margin	*(19.2%)*	*24.2%*
Premium OB price		118
(difference) margin	*(0.0%)*	*36.4%*

9.2.2 The Supply of Own Brands

With excess capacity in many areas of manufacturing within Europe (Corstjens and Corstjens, 1995), it may be assumed that the supply of own brands presents few problems for retailers. In fact, this is not entirely true, as there are still sectors within which manufacturers can inhibit the supply of own brands. Even within the grocery sector, problems can be encountered in securing reliable supplies to the required standards. As retailers become more demanding in their product specifications, and as sheer volume of own brands increases, the choice of suppliers with the required capability is very limited in certain categories.

Many manufacturers, including some of the biggest names, now operate 'mixed brand' policies, making both retailer and manufacturer branded products. Northern Foods is an example of a company which specializes in retailer brand production, Marks & Spencer and Tesco being the two largest of its several retail clients.

However, it also produces about a third of its output under the long established Fox's Biscuits and Bowyers brand names (Retail Review, 2000). For United Biscuits, on the other hand, retailer brands account for around 15 per cent of output. Even stalwart opponents of retail brands have waivered over recent years. Faced with overcapacity and falling volume, Heinz negotiated deals to supply Tesco, J. Sainsbury and Kwik Save (Bentley, 1996). More surprising was the decision by Kellogg's in 1999 to supply Aldi own-brand products, given the often repeated claim: 'If you don't see Kellogg's on the box, then it isn't Kellogg's in the box.' The deal with Aldi lasted less than one year but the episode was symptomatic of the pressures upon even the biggest of brand manufacturers.

Some suppliers are reluctant to disclose their retail brand customers, through fear of undermining consumer beliefs in their manufacturer brands (Mintel, 1998). *Which?* (1998) also found retailers generally reluctant to discuss their supply arrangements. Asda give the information to individual customers, if asked, but prefer not to publish the information, as suppliers 'change every so often'. With their 'right to know' policy towards product information, the Co-op has been the most open about its own-brand suppliers. These include Weetabix, Del Monte, Nestlé, KP, Baco, Ozram and Wilkinson Sword.

A variety of reasons have been cited by manufacturers for becoming involved in, or staying out of, own brands. Table 9.9 summarizes the main advantages and problems of supplying own brands, from the viewpoint of the manufacturers. The arguments most frequently given in favour of supplying own brands relate to the economic factors. When excess capacity exists, the production of own labels at least helps to absorb fixed costs. Greater economies of scale can also be achieved, an argument that may also be applied to distribution facilities. In this case, however, the strategy may backfire; for example, a frozen food manufacturer with a mixed-brand policy found that its expensive warehousing and transport system was increasingly difficult to sustain, as their own brands were mainly distributed by the retailers or their agency distributors.

Other cost savings may also be achieved by the own-brand supplier. In the electrical goods sector, some of the warranty liability normally accepted by the manufacturer may be transferred to the retailer (Monopolies and Mergers Commission, 1981). Unfortunately, this again may fail to yield real savings, if an existing repair network is then used less intensively. Where a manufacturer does not promote brands of its own, considerable savings in advertising costs will occur.

Advantages

1 Excess production capacity can be utilized
2 There is more efficient utilization of manufacturing and distribution facilities, exploiting economies of scale
3 Own brands help absorb fixed costs
4 Refusal to supply own brands may simply transfer more volume to competitors who will supply them
5 Own brands may provide a base for expansion
6 Small manufacturers can enter/stay in the market without incurring costs of branding
7 Some warranty liabilities may transfer to the retailers
8 Large manufacturers, using a mixed-brand policy, may retain more control and discriminate between product images, specifications and prices
9 Brand leaders may benefit as own brands have tended to compete more with minor brands
10 Retailers may refuse to stock manufacturer's brand unless it agrees to also produce own brands
11 Own-brand supply fosters a closer relationship with the retailers, increasing involvement in category management decisions
12 The retailer has an equal interest in selling the goods
13 'Co-opetition' rather than price wars

Problems

1 Advantages may be short-lived
2 It may be difficult to re-establish a manufacturer-brand position once promotion and advertising have been phased down
3 Long-term and major resources must be committed which do not benefit from or reinforce the manufacturer brand
4 Corporate schizophrenia, resulting from very contrasting brand policies, may undermine focus upon the main brand
5 Own brands may reduce sales of manufacturer's brands in the same store
6 Consumer beliefs in the added value of manufacturer brands may be undermined if they find out who makes the retailer brands
7 Retailers may restrict display and promotion of manufacturer brands to emphasize own brands
8 Own brands can lead to excessive reliance on a few customers (at worst, just one customer)
9 Bargaining power is lost as the retailer can usually switch to alternative channels of supply
10 Using own brands to recover overheads may simply postpone solving a problem of excessive overheads
11 Investment in technical development and competitive advantage is given away 'free' to own brands
12 Expensively developed expertise may in effect be handed over to rival domestic or foreign manufacturers, if retailer decides to switch suppliers
13 Margins can be 20 per cent less, and own-brand supply tends to achieve lower profitability

Table 9.9 Advantages and problems of supplying own brands for retailers

Sources: de Chernatony and McDonald (1992); Euromonitor (1986, 1998); Glemet and Mira (1995); Kim and Parker (1999); Mintel (1998); Samways (1995).

McKinsey analysed the costs of a large branded foods manufacturer and found that no less than 23 per cent of total costs were related, directly or indirectly, to the branding exercise (Caulkin 1987).

There could also be strategic considerations in the supply of own brands. Foremost among these may be the simple fact that a competitor will almost certainly supply them if you refuse. This not only leads to reduced economies of scale, it also further reduces control over the product market. Although retailers are becoming increasingly demanding in their product specifications, the own-brand supplier can at least retain some influence, if not control, over product images and prices. For example, the Wickes DIY chain was actually encouraged by

ICI to develop own-brand paints. The motive was to persuade Wickes to drop the Crown range of paints, the main rival of ICI's Dulux range. In this way, the manufacturer sought to increase control over this product category by supplying both the brand leader and the own brand (Ody, 1987). The development of surrogate brands, sometimes using old but respected brand names phased out after mergers, is another approach to retaining some control. Although these may be supplied exclusively to one retail group, the source of supply is far more difficult to switch.

The manufacture of retailer brands, alongside a leading manufacturer brand, may offer the opportunity for profitable price discrimination (Kim and Parker, 1999). Within any given category, there are likely to be consumers who are primarily manufacturer-brand buyers and those who prefer or accept retailer brands. Through strong brand advertising and other measures, the manufacturer is able to preserve a premium that the former group is willing to pay. It may not, therefore, be in the best interests of category management for the manufacturer brand prices to converge too closely upon those of the retailer brand. It is better to engage in short term price cuts, rather than a manufacturer–retailer brand war. Products that appear to compete may actually have a symbiotic relationship, of the sort referred to by Brandenburger and Nalebuff (1996) as 'co-opetition'.

There are, of course, major problems involved in supplying own brands, which have motivated some manufacturers to avoid them. At the most general level, own brands are likely to receive more emphasis in store and to take sales from the manufacturer's brands. This is, of course, no argument for staying out of own-brand supply, if rival companies could supply them equally well. Some leading brand manufacturers consider that own-brand production would be a 'downhill slope', with short-lived gains and very little chance of reverting to becoming a strong brand if promotional expenditure declines and management effort is diverted. There are also strong fears expressed that technical expertise, even 'trade secrets', may be transferred to another manufacturer, if the retailer changes its source of supply. Probably the most fundamental problem is the weak bargaining position of the manufacturer, most particularly if one retailer takes a high proportion of output. Some of Marks & Spencer's former UK suppliers encountered major problems, when the retailer switched to a far higher proportion of international sourcing (Retail Review, 2000b).

A number of strategies have been suggested for manufacturers that really want to keep out of own-brand production (e.g. Abe, 1995; Quelch and Harding, 1996). However, not all of this advice is equally applicable in very concentrated retail markets, where retail brands are highly evolved. It is generally agreed, however, that manufacturers adopting this position need to differentiate further their brands, through innovative product/packaging features and strong marketing support. Alternatively, or additionally, they may also try to narrow the price gap between their brands and retailer brands. The production of new and cheaper 'fighting brands', however, is not strongly recommended for major manufacturers, owing to the costs of establishing the brand name, and its low profit contribution. Proctor & Gamble deployed this strategy in the USA but subsequently phased out the White Cloud (toilet tissue) and Oxydol (laundry detergent) fighting brands.

For the retailer, the process of developing and sourcing own brands involves many stages and a great deal of management time. Temperley and Kirkup (2000) describe vividly the processes involved, as the Co-operative Group (CWS) developed a new own brand of fabric conditioner. Within the product development process, 122 stages could be identified as products and suppliers were evaluated. There are, however, contrasting approaches to managing the supply chain for own brands:

1 ***Retailer develops the specifications***: while using the manufacturing competence of their suppliers, Marks & Spencer set strict standards of specification, both of raw materials and finished product. Their level of involvement in both specification and quality control has earned them the title 'manufacturer without factories' (Tse, 1985).
2 ***Use third party intermediaries***: the Cott Corporation of Canada, for example, finds or buys producers of high-quality goods and sells a complete 'own brand' solution to retailers (Corstjens and Corstjens, 1995). In the fashion sector, manufacturing consultants are available to co-ordinate the specification, design and production of own brand products, usually those supplied by smaller manufacturers.
3 ***Buy from manufacturer specifications***: this passes the main burden of quality control, of ingredients and finished products, to the manufacturer: Aldi tend to adopt this approach (KPMG, 2000).

Within most major retail companies, however, there has been a trend towards more involvement in specification and quality control. Hazlewood Foods, a major own-brand supplier, has observed far greater attention by retailers to the specification of key points of product or package differentiation (Barnard, 2000). The food technology departments of major grocery chains have grown significantly in size and scope (Omar, 1995). J. Sainsbury have a programme known as 'search and reapply', which explores the world for new products and identifies benchmarks against which own brands can be specified and evaluated (McNair, 1999).

Although the power of major retailers is frequently manifested, the adoption of category management principles has shifted the supply relationship towards greater co-operation. In the 1980s, there were many quoted examples of suppliers being played off against each other (McMaster, 1987). As one manufacturer expressed the situation, 'when a supplier is asked to jump, his only response these days is, how high? More recently, the emphasis upon efficient customer response (ECR) has prompted a trend towards fewer suppliers, generally favouring larger ones (Clark, 1998). Burt and Davis (1999) quote several statements from annual reports, emphasizing the role of development-style partnerships with suppliers. However, as some of Marks & Spencer long-term suppliers discovered, it would be unwise for any manufacturer to assume continuation of such relationships, unless their quality and value continue to keep pace with market demands (Retail Review, 2000b).

9.2.3 Differentiating Own Brands

The majority of retailers have used prices as a major method of achieving competitive advantage for their own brands. As manufacturers have responded to the challenge, by paring down their own costs and margins, it has become increasingly difficult to achieve successful differentiation through price alone. Where own and and manufacturer brands compete directly, however, only a minority of own brands are being sold at the same or higher prices. It is normally assumed that the equivalent own brand will be noticeably cheaper. According to A.C. Nielsen, own brand prices are usually 20–40 per cent lower than manufacturers brand prices.

Evidence relating to the packaged grocery market supports this generalization. Table 9.10 compares four broad categories in four European countries. In the UK and France, both relatively evolved own-brand markets, the differences average around 30 per cent. In Germany, the mix of own brands is still weighted more towards generics and discount retailer brands; the difference is therefore rather greater at 43.4 per cent. Price comparisons in Tesco and Sainsbury stores found price differences averaged over two time periods, of 18 per cent (KPMG, 2000). Some of the budget-priced own brands, such as a 10p tin of beans, were excluded from this comparison. It does however demonstrate the strong position of the Tesco and Sainsbury mainstream brands, which generally do not need to be sold at a very deep discount.

Table 9.10 Own brand price differentials

Source: derived from KPMG (2000), based on Nielsen data.

Category	France %	Germany %	UK %	Switzerland %
Food	72.1	58.2	68.6	67.9
Drink	69.0	69.2	64.1	64.0
Household	83.4	55.8	86.9	69.3
Personal Care	58.4	43.0	60.0	51.2
Total	70.7	56.6	69.6	63.1

Table 9.10 also reveals contrasts in the relative price positioning within the different major categories. Noticeably, in the personal care category, own brands offered price savings averaging between 40 (UK) and 57 (Germany) per cent. This is an area in which margins have been traditionally high, therefore becoming a major focus for supermarket's own-brand development. Within the food area, there are many differences at individual category level. KPMG (2000) reported the following average price differences in Tesco and Sainsbury stores:

Frozen peas   4 per cent
Dog food   8 per cent
Toilet tissue   8.5 per cent
Cat food   9 per cent
Squash   11.5 per cent
Instant coffee   16 per cent
Baked beans   17 per cent
Fish fingers   22 per cent
Soft drinks   36.5 per cent

In some cases, price is the only real source of differentiation between the retailer and manufacturer brands. Corstjens and Corstjens (1995) list a long sequence of 'me too' own-brand introductions, seeking to mimic attributes of well-known manufacturer brands, at lower prices. In the mid-1990s, there was notable outbreak of 'lookalike' or 'copycat' own brand products, with retailers also mimicking the manufacturer brand packaging (Burt and Davis, 1999; Dennis, 1994). Retailers were accused of causing consumer confusion (Balabanis and Craven, 1997; Rafiq and Collins, 1996) and of stealing manufacturers' brand equity (Kapferer, 1995). There were a number of high-profile legal cases, including *United Biscuits* v. *Asda*, *Kelloggs* v. *Tesco* and *Coca-Cola* v. *J. Sainsbury* (Willock, 1996). Each led to the retailer making changes to the packaging of the offending own brands, but gaining much publicity in the process. Brand owners sued under the tort of 'passing off', defined by Drysdale and Silverleaf (1995) as:

a representation that a person's goods or business are connected with the goods or business of someone else.

an implied representation made by the use of a name, mark or some other idicia distinctive of someone else's business or goods.

The laws in Britain appeared to offer brand owners less protection than they enjoy elsewhere in Europe, or in Australia and New Zealand (Davies, 1998). However a more conciliatory tone then became apparent, more in keeping with the spirit of category management and efficient customer response. Tesco was said to be offering major manufacturers a voice in its own brand overhaul, in return for more contributions towards effective category management (Retail Review, 1997b).

The 'copycat' disputes drew much attention to own brands as imitators, rather than innovators. However, there has been innovation within own-brand ranges, both in terms of their positioning and their product attributes. A variety of positioning strategies may be employed in developing own brands. Three of these may be expressed in terms of consumers' motivations:

1 'Cheapest will do': motivated by economy or lack of pressure to select anything else. Shopping in this mood clearly favours budget own brands, including generics.

2 'Rational choice': a conscious quality/value judgement strongly associated with the store itself. This could favour mainstream or premium own brands, depending on the shopper's feelings about the store.

3 'Worth paying for quality': when there is some rejection of economy or even rationality, or when the shopper is under pressure to make an impression on others. This kind of motivation favours premium own brands or the own brands of upmarket stores, e.g. Harrods.

Indeterminacy in positioning is unlikely to result in success, in relation to either stores or own brands. Furthermore, the positioning does not have to be mainly price based. As Clark (1981) observed, the most successful own brands have been those with clearly differentiated 'product pluses' compared with existing branded products. These 'pluses' may relate to several factors, including quality, convenience, innovation, assortment and price. As noted earlier, Tesco, J. Sainsbury and Marks & Spencer, have made massive investments in the specification of quality products and the development of unusual additions to their assortments.

Helman and de Chernatony (1999) praise Marks & Spencer for 'widening customers' lifestyle horizons' with their ranges of prepared, ethnic foods. Casino launched France's first colourless Cola, ahead of major brands Coca-Cola and Pepsi. Delhaize 'Le Lion' has led the developments in the Belgian premium ready-meals market (Samways, 1995).

In other sectors, IKEA and MFI have achieved considerable success with their self-assembly furniture, which can usually be collected and transported immediately by the customers (Davies, 1994). This innovation incorported the major 'pluses' of convenience and price, relative to standard furniture. There are also many other examples of differentiation through product design, such as innovative safety features on Mothercare's products and the natural preparations developed by the Body Shop. In the clothing sector, fashion and design are major sources of differentiation. Next have expressed their product proposition as: 'an equation of style, quality and price … with a brand image that is acceptable and safe' (Birtwistle and Freathy, 1998).

In a study of own-brand development in 11 fashion chains, Moore (1995) found the retailers constantly searching for technological developments and styling improvements, as sources of competitive advantage. The successful fashion own brand, it was observed, has a powerful symbolic dimension, which conveys lifestyle messages to the consumer, who uses these as a mode of self-expression.

Own brands are therefore many and varied things, extending from 10p tins of generic beans, through to most exclusive, high-margin items in Harrods. This diversity has raised questions as to whether all these products truly qualify for the title 'brand', as opposed to simply a label (e.g. Davies, 1992).

There are, however, very many different definitions and interpretations of the 'brand' concept (e.g. de Chernatony and Dall'Olmo Riley, 1998a;

1998b; Feldwick and Bonnal, 1995). Doyle (1999) identifies sustainable differential advantage as the key property of successful brands, but also refers to neutral or negative brands that lack some or all of this ingredient.

If an own brand is differentiated only by its very low price, it may not be sustainable in the longer term. This proved to be the fate of a number of generic range, such as those of Euromarché and Carrefour (Pellegrini, 1994). However, if a budget own brand is backed by the buying power and low-cost structures of Aldi or Wal-Mart, differentiation mainly on price may prove entirely sustainable.

The budget brands of Tesco and J. Sainsbury, while not especially profitable individually, make important contributions to the price images and brand equity of those organizations. They also convey strong values of thrift and of avoiding the 'marketing surcharge' (McGoldrick, 1984), powerful messages for those who need or simply prefer to minimize their shopping bills.

9.3 Consumer Response to Own Brands

In common with any marketing strategy, own-branding requires the close monitoring of consumers' reactions, in terms of both perceptions and actual purchase patterns. It tends to be assumed, for example, that own brands are linked to loyalty, which may be a strong or a weak link, in relation to a particular retailer's brand. It may also be assumed that consumers perceive a particular range to represent high value, but these perceptions should be regularly checked. This section looks briefly at some of the studies undertaken to assess consumer reactions to own-brand ranges. From the earlier discussion, however, it will be recognized, that own brands have evolved into many different forms; the results of any one specific study, therefore, should not be assumed to apply to own brands in general.

9.3.1 Own-Brand Purchasers

There has been considerable research in identifying the types of consumer who are most prone to purchase own brands. Early studies in the UK generally confirmed a slightly higher propensity to purchase own brands among upmarket and young consumers (e.g. Mintel, 1976; 1985/86), a conclusion supported by some of the evidence from the USA (e.g. Murphy, 1978). This was attributed to the higher perceived risk in buying own brands, and the greater security of these upmarket consumers. This obviously cannot be generalized across all own brands; J. Sainsbury brand products, for example, have traditionally been regarded as extremely 'safe' purchases. Clearly, the extent of the perceived risk now depends upon the length of time that the own brand has been established, the marketing support invested by the retailer and consumers' perceptions of the retailer's overall reputation.

Insights into the purchasing patterns of a sample of UK consumers were provided by Key Note (1997). Table 9.11 summarizes the proportions within age and social-class categories who regularly buy retail brands within five product groups. The oldest repondents were generally less likely to prefer the retail brand options; however, the acceptability of retailer brands has spread into most of the other age categories. This seems to reflect the relative maturity of retailer brands in the UK, having been well established since the 1970s. Familiarity with retailer brands is a major determinant of their acceptance as a preferred brand (Richardson et al., 1996).

N = 1106	% regularly purchasing retail brand versions of				
	Frozen foods	**Canned foods**	**Soft drinks**	**Toiletries**	**Clothes**
All	55	57	40	49	20
Age:					
16–24	51	55	47	51	20
25–34	57	59	46	48	25
35–44	62	61	45	51	25
45–64	54	59	36	50	20
65+	52	50	29	43	10
Class:					
AB	47	52	43	44	19
C1	55	58	38	47	22
C2	54	54	35	49	21
DE	62	62	44	53	20

Table 9.11 Regular purchasers of retail brands

Source: adapted from Key Note (1997), based on Gallup survey.

The social-class breakdown does not support the evidence of the earlier studies. Although the differences are neither large nor consistent across product types, there is no longer a bias towards the upmarket shoppers. The same holds true of seven other product categories, not included in Table 9.11. In fact, the highest proportions of regular purchasers, in the majority of product categories, were in the DE social group (Key Note, 1997). This apparent change in the retail brand usage profile may be attributable to a number of causes:

1 *Reduction in perceived risk*: as retailer brands have become more widely accepted and trusted, less affluent shoppers no longer perceive significant performance risk in buying them.
2 *Budget own brands*: faced with discounter competition in the 1990s, many supermarkets introduced, or reintroduced, generic ranges at the lowest price points.
3 *Convergence of own-brand strategies*: when earlier studies were conducted, upmarket shoppers were far more likely to encounter retailer brands, if buying their food at Marks & Spencer, Waitrose or J. Sainsbury. As many other retailers have now developed extensive ranges, including Asda and Kwik Save, retailer brands are more accessible to all social groups.

Gordon (1994) was highly critical of attempts to rigidly classify consumers into retail brand buyers or non-buyers. Some studies depend excessively upon consumers' ability to recall past purchases and to classify accurately brand types. In fact, some loyal Marks & Spencer shoppers have claimed never to have bought a retailer own brand! The main problem, however, is the assumption that a shopper will have the same need states at all shopping occasions. For any consumer, the 'me-that-I-am' can vary considerably, according to the needs to be fulfilled by the purchase. Table 9.12 illustrates four possible 'me-that-I-am' conditions and the choice of biscuits that may result from those need states.

Table 9.12 Varying need states and product/brand choice

Source: derived from Gordon (1994).

'Me-that-I-am'	Product/brand choice
Need to shop in bulk for family fodder	Four-pack of standard own-brand digestives
Need a small treat for myself during week	Packet of Hob-Nobs
Need to impress others and show generosity	Packet of Boasters
Need to be good	Own-brand pack of low sugar biscuits

Examples of differential purchasing, according to need states, were encountered in studies of purchasers of generic grocery products (McGoldrick, 1984). Some people would buy the plain-label version for private use, but not to be offered to guests or taken for consumption at school by the children. From a meta-analysis of 24 earlier studies of generics purchasing, Szymanski and Busch (1987) concluded that:

> *marketing scholars have overemphasized the analysis of consumer descriptors while neglecting the study of the determinants of quality perceptions and their role in the decision-making process for generics.*

It is also important to try to measure the degree of loyalty engendered by the retailer brands. This should be assessed at two levels; loyalty to the retailer brands themselves and the beneficial effect of those brands, if any, upon store loyalty. KPMG (2000) cite Nielsen Homescan data, which showed higher store loyalty among those who tend to buy mostly retailer brands. However, East et al. (1995) demonstrated that store loyalty generally *leads to* more purchasing of the retailer's brands. They could find little evidence that store loyalty *is raised by* loyalty to retail brands.

At the product loyalty level, evidence from the UK and the USA suggests that retailer brands, in general, enjoy levels of loyalty similar to those of manufacturer brands (Ehrenberg et al., 1997). Uncles and Ellis (1989) also suggest that consumers appear to treat retailer brands just like any other brand. There are some loyal buyers but most people have a repertoire: they will buy other brands too. Table 9.13 illustrates that brand importance, whether manufacturer or retailer, does not always lead to single brand loyalty. In buying champagne, most people are concerned about the brand yet the majority have a repertoire of acceptable brands, between which they switch.

Table 9.13 Brand importance and buying patterns

Source: adapted from Cortsjens and Corstjens (1995); Kapferer and Laurent (1989).

Category	Brand importance	Buying pattern %		
		Loyal	Repertoire	Promiscuous
Coffee	High	52	41	7
Mineral water	High	44	37	19
Champagne	High	24	68	8
Washing-up liquid	Medium	54	39	7
Washing powder	Medium	45	40	15
Yoghurt	Low	23	49	28
Tights	Low	23	29	48
Dress	Low	4	33	63

Based on a study of Albert Heijn's brands in The Netherlands, Steenkamp and Dekimpe (1997) differentiated between two elements of a retailer brand's power:

1 *Intrinsic loyalty*: the ability of the brand to keep its existing customers.
2 *Conquesting power*: the brand's ability to attract a proportion of the market that is not loyal to any particular brand.

Using a model developed by Colombo and Morrison (1989), the products within the retailer brand portfolio were positioned on these two axes, as shown in Fig. 9.1. Decaffeinated coffee is an example of the 'giants' products, demonstrating both forms of power. Potato chips however are 'fighters', low on intrinsic loyalty but with some conquesting power. Steenkamp and Dekimpe (1997) suggested that retailers should regularly review their retail brand portfolios to identify underperforming items, with a view to withdrawal or repositioning.

9.3.2 Perceptions of Quality and Price

Laboratories undertake extensive product testing for retailers but only a few objective quality comparisons become available to consumers. *Which?* (1991), for example, found most own-brand baked beans to be ahead of the leading brand, on the basis of blind tasting. Also significant was the finding that a large number of retailer-branded tea bags and coffee granules equalled the taste of the leading manufacturer brands. *Which?* (1994) subsequently confirmed that retailer brands are often preferred in such tests. In a comparison of camera reliability, based upon user reports of breakdowns, the Boots APS camera was rated the best in its category (Which?, 2000).

Only a minority of consumers, however, consult these Consumer Association test reports. Perceptions of quality are, therefore, a key determinant of the positioning achieved by an own brand. Even when a product is preferred on the basis of a blind tasting, it may no longer be preferred when the package and brand name are revealed (e.g. Omar, 1994; Richardson et al., 1994). This illustrates why improvements in perceived quality can lag well behind improvements in actual quality.

In Chapter 5 we saw evidence that major retailers are now trusted more than many leading manufacturers, not to mention some national

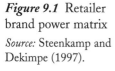

Figure 9.1 Retailer brand power matrix

Source: Steenkamp and Dekimpe (1997).

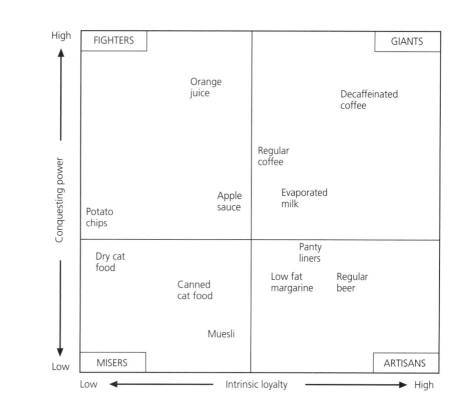

institutions (KPMG, 2000). It is clear that this trust also applies to retailer branded products, for many consumers. Mintel (1998) reported that 53 per cent of shoppers now consider own brands to be 'as good as' manufacturer branded foods. Noticeably, this belief was least likely to be held by the older shoppers, in line with the participation rates noted earlier.

While 'as good as' incorporates a bundle of attributes, on quality alone even more people believe own brands to be equivalent. Table 9.14 compares both price and quality perceptions in five European countries. Overall, 83 per cent consider own-brand quality to be the same or better than that of manufacturer brands. Perceptions in Germany are even more favourable on this measure, boosted no doubt by Aldi's long-running theme of quality at lower prices.

Table 9.14 Price/quality images of retail brands

Source: based upon Laaksonen and Reynolds (1994), data from Socodip, IGD and Europanel.

	Price %			Quality %		
	Lower	**Same**	**Higher**	**Lower**	**Same**	**Higher**
France	72	26	2	19	78	3
Germany	85	12	3	8	90	2
Italy	68	29	3	22	71	7
Spain	83	16	2	21	73	6
UK	86	13	1	18	77	4
All five	78	19	3	17	78	5

A study for the Private Label Manufacturers' Association, in five European countries, found that 68 per cent of consumers agreed that 'own brands are better value for money'. This increased belief in own-brand value is not just a European phenomenon. In the USA, only 37 per cent of respondents considered manufacturer brands to be worth the payment of a higher price, compared with 45 per cent five years earlier (Harvey and Kasulis, 1998; Harvey et al., 1999)

Perceptions of value are influenced by price perceptions, which may or may not reflect actual prices (e.g. de Chernatony et al., 1992). Consumers also have a tendency to impute a quality on the basis of price, an effect considered further in Chapter 10. Consequently, some shoppers may be difficult to convince that a cheaper own brand is of good quality, even if it does score top marks in laboratory tests. The strength of the price–perceived quality linkage varies between product categories. Buckley (1993), reported the percentages who say that highest prices equal highest quality, in five product categories.

Furniture	53 per cent
Shoes	49 per cent
Spirits	45 per cent
Wine	38 per cent
Cosmetics	30 per cent

Category differences in the extent of this belief were further illustrated by Sinha and Batra (1999). The belief was strong in the cases of frozen orange juice and ground coffee, less so for frozen vegetables and paper towels. Burton et al. (1998) confirmed the relevance of price-perceived quality beliefs, as a factor which deters some people from purchasing cheaper brands. On the other hand, value consciousness, deal proneness and 'smart-shopper' self-perceptions were positively correlated with own-brand buying.

Generics represent an interesting attempt to overcome the problem that low price may signal low quality. The essence of the generic concept is the communication to the consumer of a simple no-frills approach; the message implied is that they offer an escape route from the perceived 'marketing surcharge' commonly associated with leading brands. Early studies in the USA suggested that the approach was at least in part successful. Zybthiewski and Heller (1979) reported that most generics buyers attributed the lower prices to savings in advertising or packaging. Only 15 per cent of the buyers felt that lower quality was the reason, although this view was held by 38 per cent of the non-buyers.

A more recent study in New Zealand suggested that the generics concept worked better in some categories than in others (Prendergast and Marr, 1997). Five different scales were used, measuring perceptions of the products' value, quality, safety, freshness and package. Perceptions of these qualities of the rice and tissues were good, whereas the shampoo, soup and coffee received more muted approval.

A useful framework for examining the interplay between perceptions and purchases is that of perceived risk. This may be defined as the expected negative utility associated with the purchase of a particular product or brand. Sinha and Batra (1999) identified different levels of product category risk, high in the case of cold medicines, lower for paper towels. These risk perceptions influenced own-brand purchase properties. Dunn et al. (1986) looked at the types of perceived risk associated with buying national brands, own brands and generic brands. Not surprisingly, the greatest performance risk tended to be associated with generics, the greatest financial risk with national brands. In this particular study, social risk was not found to be a major issue, although this could be because the products studied were all fairly basic.

It is felt that social risk should not be eliminated as an issue in own-brand purchasing behaviour. McGoldrick (1984) found instances of leading brands being bought to offer to friends, whereas, generics were bought for own use. There was also some resistance to the purchase of own-brand wines for gifts or for serving to others, even wines that carried some of the most reputable retailer names. A combination of social and performance risk has also slowed the growth of own brands in some of the high-cost, high-prestige consumer durables sectors. However, the extent of perceived risk varies considerably between retailers and is prone to change over time.

A great deal of attention has, therefore, been given to monitoring the images of own brands. This is entirely appropriate, given their instrumental role within the overall images of retail companies. However, it is increasingly unwise to base strategy upon broad generalizations about own-brand images of prices, quality, risk, etc. These all vary considerably between countries, between retailers, between own-brand ranges and between product categories. Indeed, own brands are becoming at least as diverse as manufacturer brands in their relative positioning (Passingham, 1994).

The rapid evolution of own brands has also necessitated regular reappraisal of their performance and positioning. Retailers' names, and their own brands, gained much of the marketing support formerly given to manufacturer brands; by the same process, however, they lost much of the 'brand-free' appeal of their early phase. To a large extent, retailers' mainstream own brands, therefore, moved away from the position now adopted by the generic ranges in many countries. The gap between manufacturer and retailer brands has certainly diminished; both have shifted their positions. Manufacturers, for their part, have engaged in frequent promotions, discounting and cost reduction programmes (Feldwick and Bonnal, 1995).

Figure 9.2 offers a summary of the typical perceived positioning within a product category. The horizontal axis refers to qualities, in the plural, as differentiation may be achieved through innovative packaging, size differences, symbolic associations, etc., as well as product quality.

Figure 9.2 Perceived positioning within a category

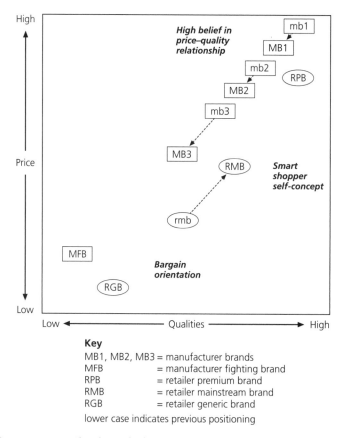

Figure 9.2 Perceived positioning within a category

Mainstream retailer brands have tended to trade up from their initial positions as lower-priced, lower (perceived) quality alternatives. The retailer brand portfolio is now likely also to include premium own brands and a generic, budget range. Among the manufacturer brands, the second and third brands have typically suffered more than the top brand, in terms of price and perceived quality, while lesser brands may have disappeared from the shelf completely.

SUMMARY

Many alternative terms are used to describe retailers' own brands, including 'private labels', 'own labels' and 'house brands'. These are all descriptions of brands owned by a retailer, or a wholesaler, for exclusive or controlled distribution. The range may carry the name of the retailer or a brand name specific to that retailer. There are also variants upon the own-brand concept, including generics, retailer 'exclusives' and surrogate brands.

Retailer own brands now account for over 30 per cent of retail trade in the UK. They are especially strong in clothing and in groceries, as well as in footwear and pharmacies. The UK and Switzerland saw some of the strongest, early development and retailer own brands but now they are a significant part of the retailing landscape in most parts of Western Europe, North America, Australia and New Zealand.

The major grocery chains in the UK have demonstrated convergent strategies, each now with over 50 per cent of sales in own brands. However, a 'glass ceiling' has been observed at around 60 per cent, beyond which shoppers may feel denied of adequate choice. Having said that, Marks & Spencer, Aldi and Migros have much higher levels at 100, 99 and 95 per cent respectively. Own brands are not unique to the multiple chains; they also exist in the symbol sector, to help maintain group cohesion, and by cash-and-carry outlets, to increase the loyalty of independent retailers.

Some own brands were introduced as defensive, 'me-too' ranges, simply copying characteristics of the leading manufacturer brands. Others, however, have demonstrated more positive approaches to gaining competitive advantage, reinforcing store image and increasing store loyalty. The ability to innovate and better control the product range can also help to create a competitive edge, while at the same time improving turnover. On the cost side, the stronger bargaining position with suppliers can lead both to better shelf prices and to considerably enhanced margins.

With excess capacity in most areas of manufacturing, it is usually possible to find one or more potential suppliers of own brands. Many retailers have exploited this opportunity to the full in order to gain maximum price advantage. As retailers increasingly recognize the need to innovate and maintain high quality in own brands, more care has to be given to establishing appropriate and reliable channels of supply. Buying specifications have tended to become more exacting, and some retailers established long-term working relationships with their best suppliers.

Where own brands are directly comparable with manufacturer brands, they tend to be 20–40 per cent cheaper. However, own brands now cover a wide spectrum of price points, from generics through to premium own brands. The continued vigour of own brands owes much an effective product differentiation, rather than simply imitation. Some of the most successful own-brand ranges are those that offer innovatory items or features not currently available elsewhere.

It is becoming increasingly difficult to characterize own brand purchasers, although there is tentative evidence that the oldest and wealthier groups are less likely to buy them. For many consumers, own brands form part of a repertoire of brands, the choice within which depends upon immediate needs, moods, etc. Own-brand purchasing appears to be linked to store loyalty, although there is conflicting evidence as to the direction of this link.

In the early development phase of most grocery own-brand ranges, they were often perceived as low-price, lower-quality alternatives. As own brands became better developed, more diverse and more vigorously advertised, perceived quality distinctions between them and manufacturers' brands became more blurred. In many cases, there is now less perceived risk in buying the retailer's brand. Own brands, therefore, build upon the consumer trust that many retailers have earned, at the same time as yielding superior gross margins in most cases.

1 What factors have influenced the pattern of growth in own-brand market share? Do you expect this growth to continue?

2 Explain why own-brands have achieved far more impact in some product sectors than in others.

3 'There is a "glass ceiling" for grocery own brand penetration at around the 60 per cent level, if the retailer is to maintain a large market share,' Discuss.

4 How would you define the role of own-brands in:

   a) a symbol group?

   b) a cash-and-carry group?

5 Reflecting upon the discussion of branding and brand equity in Chapter 5, do you consider that all retailers' own-brand ranges truly deserve to be called 'brands'? Justify your answer.

6 What would be the principal objectives in developing an own-brand range for:

   a) an established chain of department stores?

   b) an expanding chain of DIY superstores?

7 Identify the ways in which a grocery retailer may reduce costs and improve margins through own-brand development.

8 What factors could motivate a manufacturer of branded goods to also supply own brands? What risks are involved in this strategy?

9 Discuss the role of specification buying within retailers' own-brand programmes.

10 'The most successful own-brands have been those with clearly differentiated 'product pluses' compared with existing branded products.' Discuss.

11 Why do some own-brand positioning strategies fail to achieve high consumer loyalty?

12 What types of perceived risk should be taken into account in developing own-brand ranges of:

   a) women's blouses?

   b) washing machines?

   How would you overcome the problem of perceived risks in each case?

REFERENCES

Abe, M. (1995) 'Price and advertising strategy of a national brand against its private-label clone', *Journal of Business Research*, **33** (3), 241–250.

Balabanis, G. and S. Craven (1997) 'Consumer confusion from own brand lookalikes: an exploratory investigation', *Journal of Marketing Management*, **13**, 299–313.

Barnard, S. (2000) 'Own label', *The Grocer*, 22 April, 43–48.

Barrett, P. (1995) 'Pressure on brands as own-label share grows', *SuperMarketing*, 14 April, 2.

Bentley, S. (1996) 'Heinz own label hits supply snag', *Marketing Week*, 16 February, 9.

Bhasin, A., R. Dickinson and S. Nandan (1995) 'Retailer brands: a channel perspective: the United States', *Journal of Marketing Channels*, **4** (4), 17–36.

Birtwistle, G. and P. Freathy (1998) 'More than just a name over the shop: a comparison of the branding strategies of two UK fashion retailers', *International Journal of Retail & Distribution Management*, **26** (8), 318–323.

Brady, J. and I. Davis (1993) 'Marketing's mid-life crisis', *McKinsey Quarterly*, **2**, 17–28.

Brandenburger, A.M. and B.J. Nalebuff (1996) *Co-opetition*, Doubleday, New York.

Buckley, N. (1993) 'Cheap thrills are not enough', *Financial Times*, 11 September, 18.

Burt, S. (1992) 'Retailer brands in British grocery retailing: a review', *University of Stirling Working Paper Series*, 9204, Stirling.

Burt, S. and S. Davis (1999) 'Follow my leader? Lookalike retailer brands in non-manufacturer-dominated markets in the U.K.', *International Review of Retail, Distribution and Consumer Research*, **9** (2), 163–185.

Burton, S., D.R. Lichtenstein, R.G. Netemeyer and J.A. Garretson (1998) 'A scale for measuring attitude towards private label products and an examination of its psychological and behavioural correlates', *Journal of the Academy of Marketing Science*, **26** (4), 293–306.

Caulkin, S. (1987) 'The fall & rise of brands', *Management today*, July, 45–9, 104.

Clark, I.M. (1981) *Retailer Branding: Profit Improvement Opportunities*, Management Horizons, Richmond.

Clark, R. (1998) *Own Label in the U.K—the Grocery Trade Poised for Change*, Corporate Intelligence on Retailing, London.

Colombo, R.A. and D.G. Morrison (1989) 'A brand switching model with implications for marketing strategies', *Marketing Science*, **8** (1), 89–99.

Corstjens, J. and M. Corstjens (1995) *Store Wars: the Battle for Mindspace and Shelfspace*, Wiley, Chichester.

Cullen, B. and A. Whelan (1997) 'Concentration of the retail sector and trapped brands', *Long Range Planning*, **30** (6), 906–916.

Davies, G. (1992) 'The two ways in which retailers can be brands', *International Journal of Retail & Distribution Management*, **20** (2), 24–34.

Davies, G. (1994) 'Repositioning MFI' in *Cases in Retail Management*, P.J. McGoldrick (ed.), Pitman, London, pp. 42–55.

Davies, G. (1998) 'Retail brands and the theft of identity', *International Journal of Retail & Distribution Management*, **26** (4), 140–146.

De Chernatony, L. and F. Dall'Olmo Riley (1998a) 'Modelling the components of the brand', *European Journal of Marketing*, **32** (11.12), 1074–1090.

De Chernatony, L. and F. Dall'Olmo Riley (1998b) 'Defining a "brand": beyond the literature with experts' interpretations', *Journal of Marketing Management*, **14**, 417–443.

De Chernatony, L. and M.H.B. McDonald (1992) *Creating Powerful Brands*, Butterworth, London.

De Chernatony, L., S. Knox and M. Chedgey (1992) 'Brand pricing in a recession', *European Journal of Marketing*, **26** (2), 5–14.

Dennis, M. (1994) 'Classic incites cola war', *SuperMarketing*, 22 April, 5.

Doyle, P. (1999) 'Branding', in *The Marketing Book*, M.J. Baker (ed.), Butterworth-Heinemann, Oxford, pp. 364–378.

Drysdale, J. and M. Silverleaf (1995) *Passing Off, Law and Practice*, 2nd edn, Butterworth, London.

Dunn, M.G., P.E. Murphy and G.U. Skelly (1986) 'The influence of perceived risk on brand preference for supermarket products', *Journal of Retailing*, **62** (2), 204–216.

East, R., P. Harris, G. Willson and K. Hammond (1995) 'Correlates of first-brand loyalty', *Journal of Marketing Management*, **11**, 487–497.

Ehrenberg, A., J. Scriven and N. Barnard (1997) 'Advertising and price', *Journal of Advertising Research*, **37** (3), 27–35.

Euromonitor (1986) *The Own Brands Report*, Euromonitor, London.

Euromonitor (1996) *Private Label in Europe*, Euromonitor, London.

Euromonitor (1998; 2000) *Retail Trade International*, Euromonitor, London.

Feldwick, P. and F. Bonnal (1995) 'Reports on the death of brands have been greatly exaggerated', *Marketing and Research Today*, **23** (2), 86–95.

Glemet, F. and R. Mira (1995) 'To brand or not to brand', *Marketing Business*, September 20–21.

Gordon, W. (1994) 'Meeting the challenge of retailer brands', *Admap*, **338**, (March), 20–24.

Harrison, K. (1994) 'Success for UK own-label on international shelves', *SuperMarketing*, 29 April, 8.

Harvey, M. and J.J. Kasulis (1998) 'Retailer brands—the business of distinction', *Arthur Andersen Retailing Issues Letter*, **10** (1), 1–5.

Harvey, M., J.E. Rothe, J.J. Kasulis and L.A. Lucas (1999) 'Parallel brands: a strategic option for second-tier channel members', *Journal of Marketing Channels*, **7** (1/2), 53–78.

Helman, D. and L. de Chernatony (1999) 'Exploring the development of lifestyle retail brands', *Service Industries Journal*, **19** (2), 49–68.

Hoch, S.J. (1996) 'How should national brands think about private labels?', *Sloan Management Review*, Winter, 89–102.

Hoch, S.J. and S. Banerji (1993) 'When do private labels succeed?', *Sloan Management Review*, Summer, 57–67.

Kapferer, J.-N. (1995) 'Stealing brand equity: measuring perceptual confusion between national brands and 'copycat' own label products', *Marketing and Research Today*, **23** (2), 96–102.

Kapferer, J.-N. and G. Laurent (1989) *La Maque*, Ediscience International, Paris.

Key Note (1997) *Own Brands*, Key Note, London.

Key Note (1998) *Retailing in the UK*, Key Note, London.

Kim, N. and P.M. Parker (1999) 'Collusive conduct in private label markets', *International Journal of Research in Marketing*, **16** (3), 143–155.

Koskinen, S. (1999) 'UK private label: European brand leader?', *European Retail Digest*, **21**, 5–8.

KPMG (2000) *Customer Loyalty & Private Label Products*, KPMG, London.

Kumar, N. (1997) 'The revolution in retailing: from market driven to market driving', *Long Range Planning*, **30** (6), 830–835.

Laaksonen, H. (1994) *Own Brands in Food Retailing across Europe*, Oxford Institute of Retail Management, Oxford.

Laaksonen, H. and J. Reynolds (1994) 'Opportunities for own brands in European grocery retailing', *European Retail Digest*, **94** (3), 4–8.

Martell, D. (1986) 'Own labels: problem child or infant prodigy', *Quarterly Review of Marketing*, **11** (4), 7–12.

McGoldrick, P.J. (1984) 'Grocery generics—an extension of the private label concept', *European Journal of Marketing*, **18** (1), 5–24.

McMaster, D. (1987) 'Own brands and the cookware market', *European Journal of Marketing*, **21** (1), 83–94.

McNair, D. (1999) 'Retailer case study: taking the Sainsbury's brand forward', *European Retail Digest*, **21**, 12–13.

Mendez, J.L., J.O. Barbolla and M. R. Suplet (2000) 'Influencia de las marcas de distribuidor en las relaciones fabricante-distribuidor', *Distribución y Consumo*, **10** (53), 55–73.

Mintel (1976) 'Own labels', *Market Intelligence Reports*, **4** (10), 44–53.

Mintel (1985/86) 'Own labels', *Market Retail Intelligence*, Winter, 109–143.

Mintel (1998) 'Own label food', *Mintel Market Intelligence: Food & Drink*, November.

Monopolies and Mergers Commission (1981) *Discounts to Retailers*, HMSO, London.

Moore, C.M. (1995) 'From rags to riches—creating and benefiting from the fashion own brand', *International Journal of Retail & Distribution Management*, **23** (9), 19–27.

Murphy, P.E. (1978) 'The effect of social class on brand and price consciousness for supermarket products', *Journal of Retailing*, **54** (2), 33–42, 89, 90.

Nielsen (1998) *International Private Label Retailing: Indicators and Trends*, NTC Publications, Henley-on-Thames.

Nielsen (2000) *The Retail Pocket Book*, NTC Publications, Henley-on-Thames.

Ody, P. (1987) 'The growth in private brands', *Retail & Distribution Management*, **15** (3), 9–11.

Omar, O.E. (1994) 'Comparative product testing for own label marketing', *International Journal of Retail and Distribution Management*, **22** (2), 12–17.

Omar, O.E. (1995) 'Retail influence on food technology and innovation', *International Journal of Retail & Distribution Management*, **23** (3), 11–16.

Passingham, J. (1994) 'Own label and the store wars', *Admap*, **338** (March), 26–28.

Pellegrini, L. (1994) 'Carrefour: development of the retailer brand', in *Cases in Retail Management*, P.J. McGoldrick (ed.), Pitman, London, pp. 248–258.

Prendergast, G.P. and N.E. Marr (1997) 'Generic products: who buys them and how do they perform relative to each other?', *European Journal of Marketing*, **31** (2), 94–109.

Puget, Y. (1998) 'L'irresistible ascension des Marques de Distributeurs', *Libre Service Actualite* (LSA), 1605, 44–50.

Quelch, J.A. and D. Harding (1996) 'Brands versus private labels: fighting to win', *Harvard Business Review*, **74** (January/February), 99–109.

Rafiq, M. and R. Collins (1996) 'Lookalikes and customer confusion in the grocery sector: an exploratory survey', *International Review of Retail, Distribution and Consumer Research*, **6** (4), 329–350.

Retail Review (1997a) 'Supermarket lines—new own label launch at Kwik Save', *Retail Review*, **231** (April), 6.

Retail Review (1997b) 'Supermarkets moving away from cloned own labels', *Retail Review*, **232** (May), 5.

Retail Review (2000a) 'Asda develops new own label range via Wal-Mart connection', *Retail Review*, **263** (June), 8.

Retail Review (2000b) 'M&S supplier builds up Tesco side', *Retail Review*, **259** (February), 13.

Richardson, P.S., A.S. Dick and A.K. Jain (1994) 'Extrinsic and intrinsic cue effects on perceptions of store brand quality', *Journal of Marketing*, **58** (4), 28–36.

Richardson, P.S., A.J. Jain and A. Dick (1996) 'Household store brand proneness: a framework', *Journal of Retailing*, **72** (2), 159–185.

Rousell, D. and R. White (1970) *Private Label Reviewed*, J. Walter Thompson, London.

Salimans, R.W.J. (1986) 'Brands and own brands in Europe', in *Strategies for Retailer Growth*, ESOMAR (eds), ESOMAR, Amsterdam, pp. 125–151.

Salmon, W.J. and K.A. Cmar (1987) 'Private labels are back in fashion', *Harvard Business Review*, **87** (3), 99–106.

Samways, A (1995) *Private Label in Europe: Prospects and Opportunities for FMCG Retailers*, Pearson Professional, London.

Schutte, J.F. (1969) 'The semantics of branding', *Journal of Marketing*, **33** (2), 5–11.

Simmons, M. and B. Meredith (1984) 'Own label profile and purpose', *Journal of the Market Research Society*, **26** (1), 3–27.

Sinha, I. and R. Batra (1999) 'The effect of consumer price consciousness on private label purchase', *International Journal of Research in Marketing*, **16** (3), 237–251.

Steenkamp, J.E.M. and M.G. Dekimpe (1997) 'The increasing power of store brands: building loyalty and market share', *Long Range Planning*, **30** (6), 917–930.

Szymanski, D.M. and P.S. Busch (1987) 'Identifying the generics-prone consumer: a meta-analysis', *Journal of Marketing Research*, **24** (4), 425–431.

Temperley, J. and M. Kirkup (2000) 'CWS Retail: responsible product development', in *Contemporary Cases in Retail Operations Management*, B.M. Oldfield, R.A. Schmidt, I. Clarke, C. Hart and M.H. Kirkup (eds), Macmillan, Basingstoke, pp. 210–224.

The Grocer (1993) 'Profit and quality driving own labels', *The Grocer*, 2 October, 28.

The Grocer (2000) 'Own label in the doldrums', *The Grocer*, 8 July, 1.

Tse, K.K. (1985) *Marks & Spencer: Anatomy of Britain's Most Efficiently Managed Company*, Pergamon, Oxford.

Uncles, M.D. and K. Ellis (1989) 'The buying of own labels', *European Journal of Marketing*, **23** (3), 57–70.

Webster, F.E. (2000) 'Understanding the relationships among brands, consumers and resellers', *Journal of the Academy of Marketing Science*, **28** (1), 17–23.

Which? (1991) 'Own brand foods', *Which?* November, 629–632.

Which? (1994) 'Shopping for food', *Which?* January, 30–31.

Which? (1998) 'Brand surprise—an insider guide', *Which?* February, 18–20.

Which? (2000) 'Champion brands', *Which?* July, 34–35.

Willock, R. (1996) 'Tesco gains publicity in copycat dispute "defeat"', *SuperMarketing*, 23 August, 4.

Zbythiewski, J.A. and W.H. Heller (1979) 'Generics—who buys? Rich shopper, poor shopper, they're all trying generics', *Progressive Grocer*, March, 92–106.

Ten

Retail Pricing

INTRODUCTION   The role, complexity and importance of the retail pricing function varies enormously between different sectors and types of retailing institution. In the retailing of petrol cars or other major consumer durables, the task of retail pricing has much in common with that of manufacturer pricing, in that the transaction is typically the purchase of a specific product and the buyer is likely to be relatively well informed. These instances do not however represent the broad base of retailing, and accordingly will not be the main focus of this chapter. In department stores, grocery stores and other types of retailing characterized by large product assortments, pricing requires a very different approach from that implied within the conventional manufacturer-oriented view.

In most sectors of retailing, pricing decisions are regarded as being among the most crucial and difficult aspects of retail marketing. Whereas a range of 100 products may represent a fairly wide assortment for a manufacturer, it is not uncommon for a retailer to be responsible for the pricing of 10 000 or more items. Compounding upon this complexity is the fact that many multiple retailers differentiate at least some of their prices in response to different local markets. The assumption of well-informed customers, inherent in traditional pricing theory, clearly cannot be considered valid in relation to most retail markets. Neither can it be assumed that those responsible for the setting of the prices, or their competitors, are aware of all the relevant prevailing price levels.

Resale price maintenance (RPM) was abolished on all goods in the UK in 1964, with the exceptions of books and over-the-counter (OTC) medicines. This heralded a new wave of retail price competition, as retailers discovered their full power. Since that time, pricing techniques have become progressively more sophisticated as retailer explored the many dimensions of this pricing freedom. After intensive lobbying, especially by major supermarkets (Harrison, 2000), the last area of RPM in the UK was finally removed (Retail Review, 2001).

Ironically, the price function has tended to be somewhat fragmented within retail organizations, as in many other types of organization

(Engelson, 1995). It is not unusual for most day-to-day pricing decisions to be made by different groups of buyers, working within broad policy directives evolved by senior marketing and/or financial management. From elsewhere in the organization may be added various strategic or tactical overlays, such as the pricing decisions related to special offers, own-brand items or a newly opened store. However, the need to achieve greater co-ordination both within the pricing function and between different elements of the mix has been recognized by major retailers.

This evolving retail pricing function has not been especially well served by the existing literature. Having undertaken an extensive review of the models and approaches that exist to help or depict various types of pricing decision, Monroe and Della Bitta (1978) concluded that no greater deficiency existed in any other major decision area of marketing, a view largely confirmed by Greenley (1989). This problem is even more acute in relation to retail pricing, where the evidence is fragmented and the multidimensional nature of the function has not been fully explored. Various attempts have been made to extend the economist's theory of the firm to the retail case, including the early work of Holdren (1960). The rigidity of traditional microeconomic frameworks does, however, present problems in extending to the wide assortments typical in retailing (Den Hertog and Thurik, 1995).

This chapter will therefore present the many facets of retail pricing within a less conventional framework, which is considered better fitted to most retail applications. The relevance of traditional economic models to certain retail pricing decision is acknowledged, but the format adopted here underlines the multidimensional character of retail pricing. Having considered some of the basic terms and concepts of retail pricing, a framework is introduced which focuses upon the comparative, geographical, assortment and time dimensions. Relevant pricing strategies and research contributions are considered in relation to these major dimensions of retail pricing.

Having discussed the formulation of retail strategy within Part One of this volume, most of the pricing policies, strategies and tactics discussed in this chapter can be set within that overall context. It may be helpful, however, to summarize at this stage the objectives that tend to underlie most retail pricing decisions:

1 *Long-term profit maximization*: this is assumed to be the general goal of all retail companies, although shorter-term objectives frequently take precedence. Exceptions may include the co-operatives, which in their initial concept also pursued social policy goals, and some independent retailers, who may pursue a blend of personal, social and financial goals.

2 *Short-term profit maximization*: this may be pursued if maximum funds are required for new stores, major refurbishments, new systems, etc. Improved short term profits may also be required for tactical

reasons, to attract investment or to help ward off an unwelcome takeover bid. At such times managers are often instructed to achieve 'quick wins', which may not lead to the best long-term profits or image.

3 *Market penetration*: the need to establish a place in a market or to capture a better share may indicate pricing policies that are unlikely to yield the best short-term profits. This may be the objective of an entirely new retail organization, such as the hard-line discounters that have emerged in many sectors, or of specific stores sections. These discounters have had several knock-on effects, increasing consumer price sensitivity and putting pressure upon prices in most other stores (McGoldrick, 1993). Sometimes the penetration activity is focused upon specific departments or product groups. For example, Asda attracted much publicity for its discounting of books, contributing to the collapse of resale price maintenance on books in the UK (SuperMarketing, 1996).

4 *Market defence*: typically this follows the penetration activities of a competitor. Following the increase in grocery discounting, many established retailers introduced economy ranges and competed especially hard on 'known value items' (KVIs). Docters (1997) summarizes a range of strategies associated with market defence, including showing a willingness to compete on price, multi-level price schemes and loyalty programmes.

5 *Market stabilization*: this entails avoiding the use or provocation of aggressive price competition, which can lead to profit-damaging price wars (Heil and Helson, 2001). As Trout and Rivkin (1998) suggest 'don't train your customers to buy on price'. Market stabilization strategies help to shift consumer attention away from prices and usually leads to more profitable operations, if also pursued by major competitors (Fowler and Gulati, 2000). However, this can attract the attention of competition authorities if major retailers are accused of 'excess profitability' (Retail Review, 1999).

6 *Quality image*: an extensive literature has developed indicating a positive relationship between prices and perceptions of quality (e.g. Olshavsky et al. 1995; Riesz 1978). This serves as a warning against the use of certain price reduction activities, especially in exclusive markets and where quality and style are of paramount importance to shoppers.

7 *Pricing integrity*: this means being seen as fair by consumers. Excessive price fluctuations, because of special offers, for example, may suggest that the usual prices are not fair. Similarly, bargain offer claims that do not meet legal requirements (Berry, 1993) can bring adverse publicity. The claim by John Lewis, among others, of being 'never knowingly undersold' is a way of projecting fairness without undermining a quality image.

8 *Clearance pricing*: if a particular item or department is being phased out, the primary objective may be to clear stocks to make space for more profitable merchandise. If a store is to be sold, the retailer may

use low prices and 'spoil the market' to maximize turnover and get the best price for the business.

Some of these objectives are, of course, not mutually exclusive. Furthermore, a retailer may well pursue somewhat different pricing objectives at different points in time, in different outlets, or within different departments of the same store.

10.1 Price–Demand Relationships

In most retail settings, the objective of pricing is to maximize the overall profitability and/or sales within the total assortment. Models depicting the price–demand relationship for a single or just a few products are therefore of limited use to most retail price-makers. An understanding of the effects of price upon demand is, however, essential, in terms of both profit maximization and forecasting inventory requirements. A great deal of economic theory is centred upon the price–demand relationship, although traditional models fail adequately to depict the retail pricing function.

More recently there has been a growing interest in the psychological components of prices, which exert strong influences upon the price–demand relationship. The purpose of this section is to introduce briefly some of the basic concepts and terminology relevant to this relationship, including price elasticity, price sensitivity, price thresholds and reference prices.

10.1.1 Price Elasticity and Sensitivity

The elasticity of demand to changes in price is an expression of the extent to which the quantity sold changes as prices are increased or decreased. The measure represents the division of the percentage change in demand by the percentage change in price. Demand is said to be elastic if the percentage change in demand is greater than the percentage change in price; if the reverse is true, the demand is said to be inelastic. For example:

	Week 1	**Week 2**	**% change**
Price (£)	50	44	−12 (%p)
Demand (units)	450	531	18 (%q)

Elasticity = (%q)/(%p) = −1.5 (elastic)

Hoch et al. (1995) estimated elasticities for 18 product categories for a chain of 83 supermarkets. Although these elasticities varied across geographical areas, some examples of average category elasticities are shown in Table 10.1. Based upon previous evidence and the analysis of scanner data, Danaher and Brodie (2000) suggested three generalizations regarding the elasticities of frequently purchased goods:

1 Higher elasticities are observed in categories with lower competitive intensity.
2 Storable products usually have higher price elasticity.
3 Items with high market share tend to have lower price elasticity.

Table 10.1 Examples of product category elasticities

Source: derived from Hoch et al. (1995).

Category	Items in category	Items in calculation	Average elasticity
Soft drinks	619	10	–3.18
Bath tissue	57	9	–2.42
Canned soup	89	18	–1.62
Detergent	303	10	–1.58
Snack crackers	197	15	–0.86
Fabric softener	140	8	–0.79
Toothpaste	296	11	–0.45
Cereals	298	21	–0.20

The general concept of elasticity is of interest to the retailer in helping to assess likely responses to prices marked down for a seasonal sale, items used as special offers, or when a price is increased. In their most simple form, however, elasticity data may wrongly imply that the changes in demand will occur at an even rate across a wide range of price adjustments. Based upon scanner data, Mercer (1996) has provided evidence that elasticities rarely take the straight-line form suggested by many microeconomic models.

One interesting elaboration upon the basic elasticity concept was termed the 'kinked demand curve' (Hall and Hitch 1939). This suggests that increases in price may generate a more elastic response than decreases, thus the kink in the demand curve. The theory suggests that increases will cause a rapid loss of market share to competitors, whereas competitors will tend to follow decreases, thereby suppressing much of the additional demand that may otherwise have accrued to the individual company. Dickson and Urbany (1994) and Abe (1998) have provided empirical evidence that competitors are indeed more likely to 'follow down, not up'.

Aggregated elasticity data give little indication of the likely reactions of various types of competitor. Neither do they distinguish between the reactions of different shopper types. For example, a more affluent or brand-loyal shopper may be less prone to vary purchase levels in response to modest price changes. Furthermore, general product elasticity data do not necessarily reflect the demand functions of individual brands, sizes, flavour, styles or colours. Although scanner data provide the means to calculate elasticities at the store, category and item level, in practice this level of detail rarely enters pricing decisions (Bucklin and Lattin, 1992).

At first sight the concept of price sensitivity may appear directly analogous to that of price elasticity and, indeed, some authors use the terms interchangeably. There are, however, important differences. Gabor and Granger (1964) and Sampson (1964) were among the earlier writers to develop the concept of price sensitivity as distinct from traditional measurements of elasticity. In Sampson's view, the latter tend to oversimplify the price-demand relationship, to be too generalized, and also to lead managers to anticipate more sensitivity to price than usually exists. Among the many factors that may desensitize customers, at least to more modest price changes, are the following:

1 The effects of product differentiation.
2 Multiple dimensions of quality and preferences.
3 Consumer loyalty to products or stores.
4 Local competitive conditions.
5 A reduction in levels of price awareness.

In these respects, studies indicating sensitivity levels represent an improvement upon elasticity measures but many share the weakness of relating only to specific product demand functions, measured in isolation. Several methods have been used to obtain sensitivity estimates, including the use of somewhat subjective trade or consumer surveys. In-store experiments potentially provide more objective results, based upon scanner data. Such experiments are not, however, free of potentially serious pitfalls, especially when conducted without adequate controls for the impact of the numerous extraneous variables, such as competitors' strategies. It may also be considered unrealistic to measure reactions to price in isolation from other marketing variables, as interactions between price, display and/or advertising have been illustrated in multi-factor studies (e.g. Mulhern and Leone 1995; Wilkinson et al. 1982).

Some of the practical problems of in-store pricing experiments can be avoided by the use of approaches generally classified as 'hypothetical shopping situations'. These include simulations of the shopper's buying situation conducted in hall tests, at respondents' homes, at clubs, meeting places, etc. (e.g. Tinn, 1982). 'Laboratory' studies are also reported, sometimes based on computer simulations, but are subject to many limitations, including the possibility that subjects in this setting are likely to exhibit greater 'rationality' than they would within an actual store (Huber et al., 1986).

Price sensitivity can now be estimated with reasonable accuracy at the individual product level, but the existence of interrelated demand remains a complex issue in most sectors of retailing. For example, a price reduction on a suit may generate additional sales of that item, but can either positively or negatively influence the sales of other items in the store. Additional sales of shirts and ties may be generated, but the extra suits sold may cannibalize the demand for other suits. Conversely, the total store sales may be sufficiently boosted to increase the sales of all suits, whether or not their prices are reduced. These demand interrelationships, usually described as 'cross-elasticities' (e.g. Reibstein and Gatignon, 1984), are even more complex in a supermarket, within which a very large number of demand linkages exist (Bucklin and Lattin, 1992; Russell and Petersen, 2000).

Little and Shapiro (1980) noted that PoS scanners can facilitate the calculation of timely and more specific elasticity and cross-elasticity data. They also drew attention to the important distinctions between short-term product purchase decisions and longer-term store patronage decisions. More practical concepts and methodologies have therefore been developed which are of considerable potential use to retail price-makers. The necessity remains, however, to test for price sensitivity and price thresholds in relation to the products, market conditions and customer types of interest to the specific retailer.

10.1.2 Thresholds and Reference Prices

Within the general framework of price sensitivity, a number of early researchers suggested that there are certain ranges of prices that are 'acceptable' to consumers (e.g. Stoetzel, 1954). It is held that the consumer has two price limits in mind: an upper limit, beyond which the product is considered too expensive, and a lower limit, below which the quality would be suspect. This introduces two further departures from the basic elasticity concept: first, that demand responds more to price changes beyond a certain threshold and, second, that too low a price may cause doubts about quality and therefore may deter, rather than attract, purchases. There have been many studies demonstrating a price–perceived-quality relationship, although some of the study methods used are open to serious criticism. Reviews of this literature have been provided by Lichtenstein and Burton (1989) and Rao and Monroe (1989).

Evidence has continued to accumulate that prices can be set too low, as well as too high. Rao and Bergen (1992) suggest that this is especially true for experience products, i.e., products composed predominantly of attributes whose quality can be assessed only after purchase and use. During one price war in the UK, SuperMarketing (1994) found that a remarkably cheap tin of beans at 8p would be rejected as an option by 51 per cent of consumers. Naturally, the price acts along with brand and store image perceptions as quality indicators (Dodds et al., 1991). The way in which a price message is presented and the credibility of its source also affect the price–perceived-quality relationship (Grewal et al., 1994).

In a systematic breakdown of interpretations that consumers may place upon a price, Lichtenstein et al. (1993) observed that a high price may signal both higher product quality and high prestige for those able to buy at that price. Using a simulated store catalogue, Olshavsky et al. (1995) found a strong price–perceived-quality effect for purchases involving prestige or social risk. Brucks et al. (2000) warns that price may well influence consumers' perception of prestige, but not necessarily other dimensions of consumers' quality evaluations.

Some researchers do however warn against the generalization of these results to all countries and all economic conditions. Sjolander (1992) found little evidence of a price–perceived-quality relationship from his study in Sweden and Poland. Heenan (1993) noted that, even in the USA, there was a tendency towards 'inconspicuous consumption', i.e., turning away from prestige brands, during times of recession. He notes, however, that conspicuous consumption is alive and well among the *ya pi shi*, the yuppies of the People's Republic of China.

Whereas some of the earliest investigators of price thresholds used direct questions to establish upper and lower limits, Gabor and Ganger (1966) pointed out that this was an unrealistic task to request of consumers. In their research, they called out six different product prices to a large sample of respondents, who are simply asked to respond 'buy', 'no, too expensive' or 'no, too cheap'. By varying the prices called across the whole range of interest to management, they were able to plot 'buy response curves' for each product. These showed the percentage of respondents willing to buy at each price level. Buy response curves derived in this way can reveal the thresholds that appear to trigger greater changes in demand and can also illustrate when the price currently set is too high or too low.

Computer simulations offer an easier and lower-cost approach, especially when the subjects are college students! Using this approach, Kalwani and Yim (1992) identified regions of price insensitivity around expected prices. Likewise, Rao and Sieben (1992) investigated the effects of prior knowledge on acceptable price ranges.

The existence of price thresholds and ranges of acceptable prices imply the existence of internal price standards, or reference prices, within consumers' minds. Alba et al. (1994) point out that, although prices are 'concrete' relative to some other attributes, price perceptions are not. Price evaluations are based on comparisons to a reference point. Kalyanaram and Little (1994), using scanner data, found that consumers with higher reference prices tend to have wider ranges of acceptable prices. Janiszewski and Lichtenstein (1999) offer experimental evidence to demonstrate how adjustments in the range of comparison prices influence price-attractiveness judgements. However, implausible reference prices, which fall outside the credible range, have little or no effect on perceptions of value (Alford and Engelland, 2000).

Figure 10.1 Price thresholds and reference prices

Source: adapted from Lichtenstein and Bearden (1989).

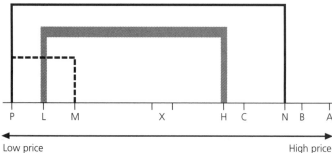

Key

— Range of expected prices (PN)
▓ Range of prices acceptable to consumer (LH)
‐ ‐ ‐ Perception of lowest prices available (PM)
LH Low, high price thresholds
X Internal reference price range
C Plausible but low external reference price
B Plausible but high external reference price
A Implausible high external reference price

Figure 10.1 summarizes many of the concepts and terms utilized in this section. It also introduces the terms internal and external reference prices. The former are the consumer's judgement of the normal price; the latter are retailer supplied reference prices, for example 'was £19.95' or 'Normal price £295'. Such external reference prices are common in seasonal 'sales' or with special offers (see Sec. 10.6).

10.2 The Dimensions of Retail Pricing

Retail pricing has received more research attention with the abundance of scanner data now available. Most studies, however, have taken only a partial view of this complex function. The microeconomic tradition has tended to focus largely upon the cost and competition elements, and has found difficulty in accommodating the wide assortments characteristic of most forms of retailing. Noteworthy attempts to overcome this particular problem have been made, and Nystrom (1970) made a significant conceptual contribution in exploring the assortment and time dimensions of retail pricing. Practising retail managers do, however, need to recognize and effectively control all the relevant dimensions of retail pricing; the further development of retail pricing theory also requires a more comprehensive and realistic framework.

A potentially helpful contribution, developed in relation to manufacturer pricing, was the 'differential pricing approach', expounded by Oxenfeldt (1979). This approach provides a view of pricing in terms of an interrelated network of differentials, applied to certain cost and competition bases. In particular, the potential use of geographical price differentials, ignored in many previous studies, is given explicit consideration. It is felt that this approach can be usefully adapted and extended to the retail case. The purpose of this section is to develop this framework, which will focus the attention of both researchers and decision-makers upon the several important dimensions of retail pricing. Some changes of terminology have been considered desirable, both to clarify meanings and to provide greater consistency with previous studies that have considered specific elements of retail pricing.

10.2.1 A Multidimensional Framework

Figure 10.2 illustrates, in necessarily simplified form, the major dimensions of the retail price decision. The core of the retail pricing function is seen as the establishment of different markup levels; each of these decisions, however, must have regard for the comparative prices in rival stores, previous prices, prevailing price levels in local areas and the numerous other prices within the product assortment. The sections that follow examine each of these in relation to conceptual insights available, and the pricing strategies most closely associated with each dimension.

The comparative dimension of retail pricing represents the many differences in price between those of the retailer and those of direct and indirect, local and national competitors. This dimension has been relatively well explored in early studies, although adequate recognition has not been given to the problems associated with gaining the necessary comparative information. The discussion of this

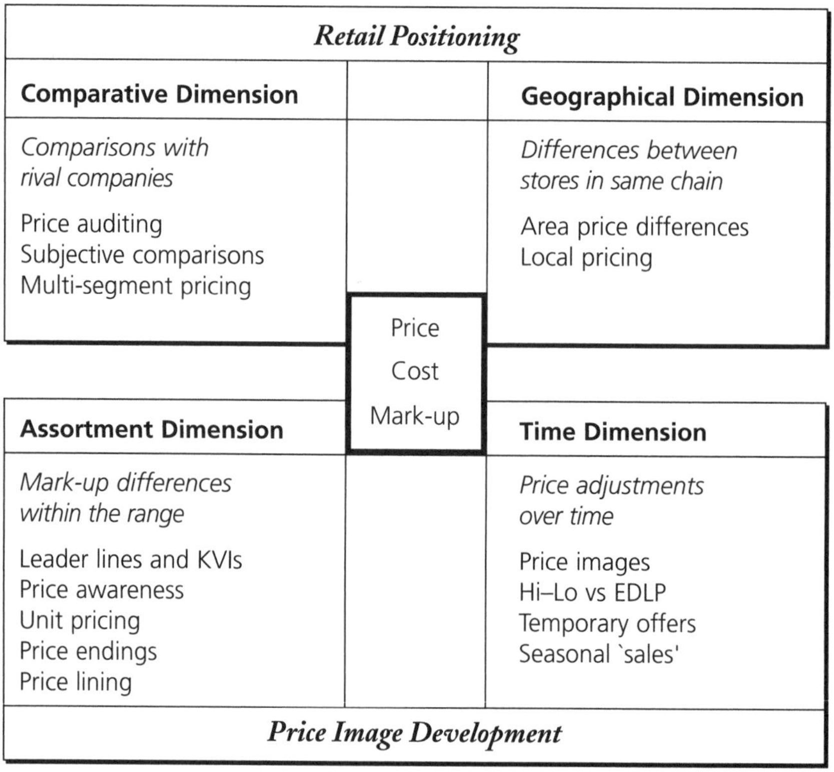

Figure 10.2 The dimensions of retail pricing

Source: adapted from McGoldrick (1987).

Retail Positioning		
Comparative Dimension		**Geographical Dimension**
Comparisons with rival companies Price auditing Subjective comparisons Multi-segment pricing	Price Cost Mark-up	*Differences between stores in same chain* Area price differences Local pricing
Assortment Dimension		**Time Dimension**
Mark-up differences within the range Leader lines and KVIs Price awareness Unit pricing Price endings Price lining		*Price adjustments over time* Price images Hi–Lo vs EDLP Temporary offers Seasonal 'sales'
Price Image Development		

dimension, therefore, includes a consideration of systems of retail price auditing and sources of such information.

The geographical dimension has increased in relevance as most retailing is undertaken by chain stores, rather than single-location independents. Even if a chain retailer decides to charge the same prices in all outlets, this dimension cannot be ignored, as this set of prices will be differently positioned in different locations. The practice of geographical differentiation has become an important element of major retailers' pricing strategies, albeit within the limits constrained by the price image of the company as a whole.

The assortment dimension has been the focus of considerable retail management attention. It has long been recognized that a fixed markup on all items in the range makes little sense either in terms of cost or competition factors, so varying markups between products tend to be the norm. It has also been increasingly recognized that certain items in the assortment are more powerful than others in the formation of price images; differential levels of item price awareness are therefore highly relevant in this context. As a further overlay to assortment pricing decisions, a number of concepts and strategies have been evolved with regard to the choice of specific price levels and endings.

The time dimension is also of great significance in retailing; in department stores, grocery and other wide-range retailing companies, it is not unusual for several hundred price adjustments to be administered each week. In addition, short-term pricing represents a major, if sometimes overworked, promotional tool, either in the form of seasonal 'sales' or temporary offers on a few items in the range. There has been considerable debate as to the relative merits of high–low ('Hi–Lo'), and everyday low prices (EDLP). In terms of consumer perceptions of store price levels, the time dimension is also relevant to the longer-term processes of favourably developing price images.

This framework, at least in this simplified form, is clearly not designed to supply precise answers to the many individual retail pricing decisions. It does, however, seek to draw attention to the essential complexity of this pricing function and to help the price-maker focus upon the dimensions that may be affected by the specific set of decisions. In the subsequent sections, pricing strategies and tactics are discussed in relation to the dimension primarily involved, although virtually all price actions influence some or all of the other dimensions.

10.3 The Comparative Dimension

All pricing decisions, whether long term or short term, item level or assortment level, local or national, must be taken with a view to the resulting comparative price position vis-à-vis competitors. The title 'competitive dimension' was considered for this element of the framework but was rejected on the grounds that it blurred the scope of this dimension. All the dimensions reflect part of the competitive pricing function; this dimension relates more specifically to the tasks of price comparison and positioning.

In numerous marketing and retailing texts, we are told that the price-maker faces the options of positioning prices below, at or above the market. Although this basic logic is difficult to refute, broad classifications of strategic options along these lines suggest a certain simplicity in retail marketing which is rarely encountered. In the first place, it is rather more difficult in retailing than in most forms of manufacturing to actually know what 'the market' is, in pricing terms. Large assortments of prices are typically competing with other large, but usually different, assortments; the bases of comparisons are therefore somewhat more complex. Given these uncertainties, both among retail price-makers and consumers, some stores offer price matching policies; they refund at least the difference if customers report a lower price, for the same product, in the area (Jain and Srivastava, 2000).

Rather than dwell upon the general issue of positioning, which has already been discussed in Chapter 4, this section will focus upon the specific issues of obtaining retail price comparisons. First, the techniques and problems of retail price auditing are discussed, then examples are presented to illustrate essential differences between objective and subjective comparison systems. Finally, audit data are utilized to illustrate how a retailer, even within the same store, can price at very different comparative levels.

10.3.1 Price Auditing

Although audits, or surveys of prices, are undertaken to report prices of particular products, in certain stores at particular points in time, these typically represent only a very small sample of the total. As in any sampling exercise, there is inevitably a trade-off between the sample size, and therefore the cost, and the reliability of the information produced. Some widely publicized audits take fairly small product samples. For example, *Which?* (1995) based its grocery price comparisons on 31 product prices, Verdict (1993) on 40. Some newspapers publish comparisons based on just 10–12 product prices, raising major questions about the typicality of those items within the overall profile of supermarket prices. Clearly, as the sample of products becomes large, it is increasingly difficult to undertake the audit without the knowledge of the store management.

Price audits exert an important influence upon retail pricing in a number of different ways:

1 Published audits that are available to consumers, such as those sometimes included in the *Which?* reports published by the Consumers' Association in the UK, may be very instrumental in the formation of price images by consumers who notice or seek this information. Accordingly, some retailers take a special interest in the sample of products audited to ensure that their price ratings emerge as favourably as possible.
2 Major 'trade-oriented' audits exist, such as those conducted on a continuous basis by Audits of Great Britain and A.C. Nielsen. These tend to identify a much wider range of product prices at individual store level, therefore providing retailers and manufacturers with a more comprehensive check upon the prices charged for those items by most major retailers.
3 Ad hoc price audits are regularly conducted by retailers to monitor competitor activities and, in some cases, to ensure that their own stores are complying with head office policy.

Table 10.2 Superstore pricing comparisons
Source: Fowler et al. (2000), based on www.tesco.com/whatsInStore/price_check.html.

Tesco commission regular price audits of over 1000 popular lines, both to check and to publicize their prices vis-à-vis those major rivals (Fowler et al., 2000). At the time of writing, these comparisons could be accessed through the company website on www.tesco.com/whatsInStore/price_check.html. Table 10.2 illustrates how the prices compared at one point in time.

Comparison	% Tesco cheaper	% Competitor cheaper	% Same price
Tesco/Safeway	84.3	6.0	9.7
Tesco/Sainsbury	61.3	3.9	34.8
Tesco/Asda	11.2	17.3	71.5

The validity of price comparisons derived through price auditing is highly dependent on the sampling and analytical methods employed. If a product sample is to be absolutely comparable between retailers, only

Figure 10.3 Issues in auditing retail prices

Objectives of Audit
Tracking price movements over time

Objectives of Audit

Tracking price movements over time
Comparisons between retailers/stores
Comparisons between regions/countries

Sampling Issues

Products: appropriate and widely available
Substitution for non-available items
Price levels may vary in different regions
Prices may differ by store size/type
Prices may differ by seasons

Procedural Issues

Record prices covertly or overtly
Direct observation, EPoS data or panel data
Weighted or unweighted indices

those items could be included that are widely available brands and sizes. This would, however, limit the scope of the audit and would concentrate too heavily upon more strongly promoted items. Many researchers have therefore accepted some variability in the product specification in order to include retailer brands, less popular sizes and/or fresh foods (e.g. Wood, 1976). Another decision is the extent to which observations are repeated over time. In comparing prices of women's clothing in discount and department stores, Hutchinson-Kirby and Dardis (1986) noted the prices every week for 13 weeks.

Having audited a selection of items, the construction of an index to represent comparative price levels requires a method of combining the item price observations. A commonly used approach is simply to add up the item prices, but this can overweight the importance of expensive items and/or items less frequently purchased. A somewhat better approach is to weight each item price statistically before combining them to form the price level index. Usually a weighting system is used that reflects 'average' allocations of expenditure to the various commodities, although it is recognized that difference weightings will be appropriate for different consumer groups. Figure 10.3 summarizes the main issues involved in constructing an audit of retail prices, noting that different purposes require different sampling and procedures

10.3.2 Objective and Subjective Comparisons

The problems outlined in attempting to gain measures of relative price levels clearly leaves some doubt as to whether such comparisons can be entirely objective. In evaluating the longer-term effects of pricing activities, the retailer is even more concerned to assess the entirely subjective evaluations of relative price levels formed by consumers. Relatively few studies have investigated consumer awareness of relative price levels, as opposed to awareness of individual item prices. A major study by Brown (1969) involved over 1000 shoppers in five different areas using 27 different stores. The prices of 80 items were audited twice in each store and then combined, using statistical weightings, to produce an index of price level for each store. Respondents were invited to rank up to four stores from the most to the least expensive; these rankings were then contrasted with the audit indices to produce 'perceptual validity' sources. Certain cues were important in the formation of price images, given that consumers could not really objectively compare price levels. A large shopping centre, heavy advertising or a wide assortment were signs of low prices, whereas extra services, late hours, expensive interiors and trading stamps conveyed the image of high prices. Major changes in retailing, notably the emergence of the narrow-range discounter, will probably have changed the effects of these cues, although the concept is still valid.

Table 10.3 offers similar comparisons, based upon audit comparisons and price image measures of 15 French supermarkets. The 'basket' price at the most expensive store (Suma) was 17 per cent higher than at the cheapest (Continent). As the image scale could not be directly compared, both scales have been converted to ranks, with the rank differences calculated. Positive signs indicate an image which is, based upon this evidence, better than the reality. According to Corstjens and Corstjens (1995), the favourable image of Leclerc owes much to the high profile, pro-consumer stance of Monsieur Leclerc. In contrast, Auchan, at number 2 on the 'objective' scale, lags well behind in terms of store price image. These data illustrate that it is not sufficient just to charge low prices. Prices must be carefully selected and aligned: they must also be supported by effective communication, which may or may not include advertising.

Table 10.3 Subjective and objective comparisons

Source: derived from Stoclet (1990), quoted in Corstjens and Corstjens (1995).

Company	Price image rank	Actual price rank (rank 1 is the cheapest)	Difference: actual – image
Leclerc	1	3=	+2
Intermarché	2	3=	+1
Continent	3	1	−2
Rallye	4	6=	+2
Euromarché	5	9	+4
Auchan	6	2	−4
Franprix	7	14	+7
Manmouth	8	8	0
Carrefour	9	5	−4
Lion	10	13	+3
Cora	11	11	0
Super U	12	10	−2
Champion	13	6=	−7
Geant Casino	14	12	−2
Suma	15	15	0

10.3.3 Multi-Segment Pricing

In comparisons of retail price positioning, a company or store is usually depicted as occupying just one position vis-à-vis its rivals. Increasingly, however, larger stores have been able to adopt multiple positions, by focusing different parts of their product range upon different customer segments. This is especially prevalent in large superstores, since the arrival of increased competition from limited range, hard discounters. *SuperMarketing* (1995) referred to 'two-tiered' pricing but that was somewhat of an understatement.

By way of an example, Table 10.4 was constructed by taking just eight products, for which at least three options were available for a given package size. The first column shows the leading brand prices, which may be paid by the least price sensitive segment. The second column shows mid-range prices, typically a follower brand or the store's own brand. These reflect the prices paid by those wishing to avoid premium prices, but avoid purchasing plain label economy items. The third column shows the cheapest available.

Table 10.4 Example of multi-segment prices

Source: based upon actual prices in one store, which may not be representative of those brand or retailer prices nationwide.

Product	Leading brand price (£) (1)	Follower or own brand price (£) (2)	Cheapest version price (£) (3)
Beans (420 g)	0.28	0.23	0.16
Tea bags (80s)	1.28	0.67	0.49
Dog food (400 g)	0.56	0.48	0.33
Lager (4 x 440 ml)	2.69	1.82	0.68
Tomato soup (430 g)	0.68	0.55	0.32
Frozen peas (2 lbs)	1.23	0.97	0.55
Fish fingers (20s)	1.98	1.55	0.69
Toilet rolls (4s)	1.24	0.88	0.62
Total (unweighted)	9.94	7.15	3.84

Table 10.4 illustrates a superstore's attempt to price for three segments:

1 Only the best will do: engage in few price comparisons and prefer the best brands; usually high disposable income.
2 Not convinced by leading brand advertising but suspicious of economy lines: typically more alert to prices in equivalent stores; probably lower-middle income.
3 Bargain seekers: highly price sensitive and more likely to be aware of comparisons with hard discount stores; usually but not invariably lower income.

If a shopper from each segment were to shop for just those eight items, 1 above would pay 159 per cent more than 3. In practice, this difference will be muted by the inclusion, in the shopping basket, of items on which there is far less price variation. Table 10.4 does, however, show how a superstore may try to position simultaneously at the premium level, competitive with similar rivals yet also competitive with discounters.

This practice is not exclusive to superstores, being common in other wide assortment formats. In Sec. 10.5, the approach of 'price lining' is illustrated as a possible mechanism for multi-segment pricing, even in smaller stores selling clothing or jewellery. In Chapter 9, the importance of retailer and 'generic' brands to multiple positioning strategies was also demonstrated.

10.4 The Geographical Dimension

Every retail store of a multiple chain operates within a local market that is at least slightly different from that experienced by other stores in the group. In spite of the rapid growth of the multiple chains in most sectors, this quite fundamental property of retail marketing has received little detailed attention from researchers. Within this section, a distinction is drawn between studies of price differences between areas, including whichever retailers are trading in those areas, and studies of geographical differentiation within the pricing strategies of individual companies. The former have received rather more attention, including comparisons of prices in urban and rural areas, the particular issues of prices in minority/poverty areas and studies of local prices in relation to levels of local concentration. This body of evidence will be summarized very briefly, then attention turns to the strategy of geographical differentiation from the viewpoint of the specific chain retailer.

10.4.1 Area Price Differences

The existence of area price differences has been firmly established from work undertaken in the USA, Europe and Australia. Naturally, such differences can emerge only when the geographical dimension is included within the study methodology; it represents a major weakness of many otherwise excellent studies of retail pricing that the spatial aspects were virtually ignored.

In an early study of prices in several Australian cities, Briggs and Smyth (1967) noted that an equivalent group of items in Hobart was 15.5 per cent more expensive than in Adelaide. More surprising was the finding that prices were lower in Perth than in Melbourne, in spite of the higher transport costs of many items to Perth. Clearly, the importance of competitive structure and style of retailing in each area outweighed transport cost considerations. Similarly, Murray (1977) noted major differences between grocery prices within England, with shoppers in Yorkshire being able to buy groceries for about 11 per cent less than their counterparts in (generally) less competitive Surrey.

Comparisons such as these may suggest that area price differences are to be found mainly where markets are a considerable distance apart. Some studies that have compared urban, suburban, and rural price levels have illustrated differences within smaller geographical areas. Campbell and Chisholm (1970) studied grocery prices in and around Swansea and found that they generally increased as one moved away from the centre, largely because of the mix of retailers then operating in these areas. Cultural factors can also influence price differences between adjacent areas. In a study of Chinese and American supermarkets in the Los Angeles area, the latter were charging 37 per cent more for packaged food, 100 per cent more for meats and seafood of the same type (Ackerman and Tellis, 2001).

Prices in poverty and/or racial minority areas have been the subject of more extensive, if not entirely conclusive, studies. Parker (1979) reviewed several of the early studies of price variation within North American cities and found some evidence of 'price-gouging' of lower-income consumers. Wilkinson et al. (1973) also found that the non-urban poor tended to be offered fewer special offers, thereby demonstrating that geographical price differentiation may be concentrated on temporary offers. A critical review of the early studies in this area was provided by Sexton (1974), who identified many methodological weaknesses. A study in New York could find no evidence of price differences between rich and poor areas, if similar store sizes are compared (Hayes, 2000). However, shoppers without cars may have greater difficulty accessing medium-large stores.

Bucklin (1972) briefly reviewed evidence suggesting associations between local concentration and retail prices. Clear indications had emerged that local concentration and prices are associated. Substantive data were subsequently presented by Marion et al. (1979; and Marion, 1989), illustrating relationships between local concentration and food prices. Based upon a study of supermarkets in local Vermont markets, Cotterill (1986) established that prices were significantly higher in more concentrated markets. Using data from geographically isolated markets. Bresnahan and Riess (1991) noted that competitive conduct changes quickly as the number of incumbents increased. Once the market had between three and five competitors, the next entrant had little effect upon competitive conduct. Dresdner Kleinwort Benson illustrated that prices in Cambridge, dominated by two chains, tended to be over 3 per cent higher than those in Peterborough and Huddersfield, where a third player (Asda) was also present (Retail Review, 2000).

A number of other variables, in addition to retailer concentration, have been found to relate to area price differences. From a series of audits of prices in areas of Florida, Simmons (1988) constructed a model to estimate price levels in areas not covered by the survey. The following variables were found to be good predictors:

- population growth rate (−ve)
- mean income (+ve)
- median gross rent (−ve)
- retail sales (−ve)
- population 45 year or over (+ve)

More recently, Binkley and Connor (1998) modelled relationships with food price levels, based upon data for 95 cities and a modest sized audit of 26 product prices. Neither the concentration levels, nor the extent of chain ownership of stores, proved to be significantly related to price levels. This could indicate that chain stores are starting to be more adaptive to local conditions, rather than invariably introducing lower prices. The proximity of fast-food restaurants did seem to exert downward pressure on packaged goods prices. The number of price changes were also linked with lower prices, suggesting that special offer activity increases price sensitivities.

10.4.2 Strategies of Localized Pricing

In that every local market is unique in terms of its level and type of competition, to exploit the potential fully a multiple retailer would need to charge different prices in each individual outlet. Until recently, the benefits to be gained from such a policy have been outweighed by the costs involved in collecting the necessary comparative information and in the administration of the system. Among the major retailers in the UK, it would appear that some large superstores operate with a degree of branch autonomy, to adapt to local conditions. At the other extreme, some of the hard discounters operate a more rigid pricing policy across their stores, taking the view that their prices are competitive in any location. Although this leads to more simple administration and control procedures, the weakness of the policy is clearly that the prices are only just competitive in some areas but almost too competitive in others.

So far, there is more evidence of general price differences between areas than of price differences between the different branches of the same chain. However, during a period of intensive price competition in Northern Ireland, Bell and Brown (1986) noted evidence of 'dual pricing' by an established chain which had decreased prices in some branches to meet local competition. The practice of 'price flexing' by UK supermarkets, according to local competitive conditions, was noted by the Competition Commission (2000) but was not thought sufficiently serious to justify official action. Safeway's use of local pricing and promotions was analysed by Morgan Stanley Dean Witter (2000), who estimated that the discounts, printing and administration cost around one percent of turnover.

Table 10.5 Within-company price level differences

Source: McGoldrick (1988).

Company	No. of stores sampled	Mean index level	Standard deviation	Range of store price indices	
				Lowest	Highest
A	40	104.1	159.7	98.4	106.5
B	40	103.2	316.2	94.9	107.3
C	40	100.5	92.5	97.3	102.5
D	40	93.4	75.9	91.6	95.6
E	10	92.3	15.3	92.1	92.5
F	10	95.5	29.9	94.8	95.8
G	10	102.0	59.2	100.8	103.1
H	10	105.3	119.5	102.9	107.0

As part of a study of geographical price differentiation, McGoldrick (1988) obtained 19 600 almost simultaneous price observations, comprising 98 item prices in each of 200 stores. A price index was constructed for each individual store, using a multi-level weighting system, adjusting for category consumption levels. Table 10.5 shows the dispersion of store price levels between the stores of the eight retailers involved, the levels being expressed relative to an overall mean index of 100. Very different policies towards geographical pricing may be implied from these analyses. The difference between the cheapest and most expensive stores in Company E was less than half of a percentage point; given that small time-lags can occur in the administration of price changes, this is indicative of no geographical differentiation by that company. In contrast, the most expensive store of Company B had a price level some 13 per cent higher than that of its cheapest store. These data illustrate both the extent of geographical pricing by some companies and also the fact that some hardly use the strategy at all.

The increased availability of EPoS data, plus GIS and other data relating to stores' catchment areas, has increased the interest of researchers in the potential of store level pricing. Having reviewed recent studies, Mulhern et al. (1998) questioned whether retailers should charge the same prices in all stores, or vary prices according to some specified price zones. However, the use of crude price-zoning arrangements, common among UK superstore operators for many years, has been questioned. Montgomery (1997) developed a model for the Dominick chain in the Chicago area, based upon 11 demographic and competitive variables. The chain previously adopted three price zones (high, medium and low); this improved gross profits by 0.66 per cent, compared with uniform pricing. The adoption of the store-level pricing model, however, improved gross margins by 2.74 per cent, translating into a 17 per cent to 25 per cent increase in operating profits (Matson, 1995).

So far, these models have been applied to limited geographical areas and limited parts of the product assortment. Their potential however will continue to provoke research and experimentation. Hoch et al. (1995) concluded that demographic variables are more influential than competitive variables in determining store-level price elasticities. They concluded:

1 More educated consumers are less price sensitive.
2 Large families are more price sensitive.
3 Households with expensive homes are less price sensitive.
4 Black and Hispanic consumer are more price sensitive.
5 Consumer self-select between stores that feature on lower prices or other attributes.
6 Isolated stores encounter less price sensitivity.

'Price customization' at store level is part of a wider interest in micromarketing and localization of the retail mix. Figure 10.4 summarizes some of the elements of this process. Given the blend of

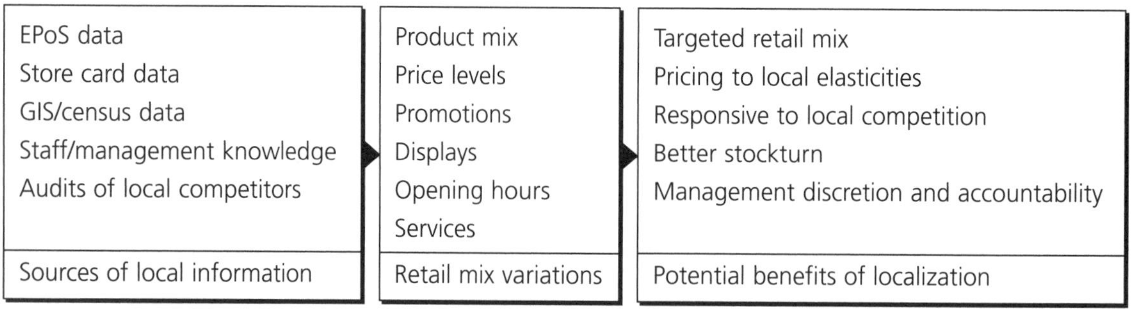

EPoS data	Product mix	Targeted retail mix
Store card data	Price levels	Pricing to local elasticities
GIS/census data	Promotions	Responsive to local competition
Staff/management knowledge	Displays	Better stockturn
Audits of local competitors	Opening hours	Management discretion and accountability
	Services	
Sources of local information	Retail mix variations	Potential benefits of localization

Figure 10.4 Localization of the retail mix

data and local knowledge, it is entirely logical to adjust the product mix to local preferences. The *New York Times Magazine* (1996) summarized a large number of local food preferences. In the UK, Sainsbury store managers have been given more local discretion to add up to 500 lines to their assortments (Retail Review, 1999a)

Other services may also be adopted or priced differently. For example, Basu and Mazumdar (1995) provide a convincing case for more differentiation in the pricing of delivery services by furniture and appliance retailers. In theory, the more precise local targeting of the mix can produce many benefits for customers, store operations and profitability. A question yet to be fully researched or resolved is the extent to which localization may blur images and/or alienate company-loyal customers who use different stores within the same chain (e.g. Retail Review, 1998).

10.5 The Assortment Dimension

With the exception of petrol stations, car dealers and other narrow-range retailers, most retail companies are concerned with the pricing of very large product assortments. A major problem arises therefore in setting markups for each item in the range that will maximize the overall company profitability. The practice of applying the same markup to every item in the range has long since been discredited (e.g. Holdren, 1960), being justified neither in cost nor in competition terms (Vilcassim and Chintagunta, 1995). Many systems of allocating item costs, as an aid to such decisions, have been offered to retailers. The concept of direct product profitability (see Chapter 6) has been advocated, and such approaches can provide useful inputs to many assortment decisions including pricing decisions, provided of course that the cost of the information does not outweigh the benefit derived.

While not ignoring these approaches to the analysis of item profitability, the discussion in this section will focus upon the strategies and concepts most relevant to the maximization of total assortment profitability. In the final analysis, the markup that can actually be achieved on each item is more a function of competitive prices, consumer awareness of specific item prices, their sensitivity to changes in those prices and the effect that an item price exerts upon the overall assortment price image. The 'leader line pricing' technique is described as an approach to selective discounting and favourable image formation.

The concept of item price awareness is explored as a major component of such strategies. Unit prices are then considered, in that many assortment pricing decisions relate to the different sizes of the same product. Finally, the tasks of setting the specific price points are examined, including the use of price lining and certain price endings. Price differentials between own brands and equivalent manufacturer brands are also highly relevant to the assortment dimensions; this topic was considered in detail in the previous chapter.

10.5.1 Leader Line Pricing with Known Value Items

The types of strategy that have generally come to be known as 'leader line pricing' represent an evolution of the temporary price-cutting strategies discussed in Sec. 10.6.2. The core concept is very similar, in that certain items within the assortment are made the subject of more competitive pricing, in order to convey a better price image which hopefully is generalized to the whole company or store. The difference is that these prices are usually not cut as deeply as in the case of short-term offers and there tend to be more items involved. Furthermore, the selectively discounted prices are held long term, apart from occasional fine-tuning of the leader line items. The logic of the approach is well established. In an early study by Parsons and Price (1972) they noted that even stores carrying the 'discount' title do not need to place low prices on every product in order to sustain that image. In other words, because of the processes by which consumer's form their overall price images, there is much to be gained by identifying the 'key indicators' within the assortment.

Several interesting case studies of leader line pricing were provided by the UK grocery retailers in the late 1970s. By 1977, the management of the Tesco chain had decided that their long-used mix of temporary price offers, trading stamps and only moderately competitive prices was not destined to keep them among the market leaders for many more years. Tesco's answer was a drastic and somewhat courageous alteration of their pricing and overall marketing policy, which was labelled 'Operation Checkout'. The most obvious manifestations were the dropping of trading stamps and a great deal of advertising. Less obvious but highly effective was a switch to a leader line pricing system, involving long-term reductions on approximately 150 lines. Although rapidly rationalizing its outlets, Tesco could not instantly transform its cost structure to allow truly 'across-the-board' discounting. The process was however highly successful in increasing turnover by 43 per cent in the first year alone. The approach was soon followed by several of the rival retailers, including at least one of the newer discounters.

The focus upon known value items (KVIs) has now become a major element of pricing strategy in grocery, DIY and other forms of wide assortment retailing. Anecdotal evidence points to such items as bread, fish fingers, washing powder, coffee and frozen chips as KVIs in supermarkets: one commentator described beans as the 'king KVI', during a price skirmish that brought prices of value packs down to just 7 pence. It seems that the range of KVIs is widening, Tesco having announced price reductions on over 400 items (Retail Review, 1999b). These are extending into household goods and health and beauty items. Reviewing evidence on the use of leader line pricing, Cox and Cox (1990) speculate that frequency of purchase is the key element of a KVI, consumers being more likely to remember prices of products bought frequently. Having surveyed the pricing practices of the major UK supermarkets, the Competition Commission (2000) referred to 'focused price competition'. This is clearly wider than competing primarily upon core KVIs. Taking the example of Sainsbury:

> *On its budget own-label range and KVIs, Sainsbury aims to match the strongest national competitors. On what it calls secondary value items (SVIs), prices must be close to the market leader, while on other background lines they must be reasonably close (Competition Commission, 2000).*

10.5.2 Consumer Awareness of Item Prices

With regard to assortment pricing decisions, studies that have examined awareness of specific prices, as opposed to overall store price, are especially relevant. An early Progressive Grocer (1964) study found a wide range of awareness levels; using a measure of recall within 5 per cent of the correct price, awareness levels varied between 12 and 91 per cent among the 59 products investigated. A follow-up study demonstrated considerably reduced awareness levels (Heller, 1974). McGoldrick and Marks (1987) found an 'average recall error' of 8.7 per cent in a 1980s study in two large supermarkets. In a later study, which included two superstores, the average recall errors were 11.9 and 12.9 per cent (McGoldrick et al., 1999). Factors contributing to this fall in price awareness include product range proliferation, greater price dispersion within the assortment (see Table 10.4) and a reduction of shopping around between the fewer, larger stores. Comparisons between different studies must however be treated with caution as different research designs produce different measures of recall accuracy (Estelami and Lehmann, 2001).

The study by McGoldrick and Marks (1987) produced indications of awareness levels in ten grocery product categories. These results are summarized within Table 10.6. Various measures of awareness were utilized, of which three are shown in Table 10.6. The level of exact recall is especially relevant when deciding upon the exact price point, whereas the measures of approximate recall are more appropriate to wider decisions on relative price positioning within the assortment. Using the mean percentage recall error measure, the products can be grouped into three significantly different groups, as shown in Table 10.6. Extensive proprietary research has been undertaken on behalf of specific retailers to measure item price awareness levels, from which leader line and other pricing strategies have been evolved. Clearly, far more detail is required than the general category means represented in Table 10.6.

Assortment pricing decisions must not only determine the markups on broad product categories but also establish prices for individual brands, varieties and sizes within each category. Under some circumstances, retailers must also decide whether to sell a 'package' of items at a composite price, or whether to partition the prices of each element. This is frequently an issue in the pricing of electrical goods and their accessories. While a keenly priced package can simplify the consumer's choice process, partitioned prices have been found to lower recalled prices (Morwitz et al., 1998).

Table 10.6 Levels of item price awareness (%)

Source: McGoldrick and Marks (1987).

Product	Exact recall	Recall + 5%	Recall error mean
Coffee	22	65	6.7
Beans	39	59	6.9
Fish fingers	25	69	6.9
Muesli	23	46	7.0
Canned soup	39	51	8.9
Flour	29	60	9.0
Sauces	20	52	9.5
Extracts	20	20	10.3
Vegetable oil	18	43	11.9
Digestives	23	46	12.0
All items	29	55	8.7

Some studies have investigated other correlates of price awareness. Goldman (1977) produced evidence that lower-income shoppers tend to be more price aware, a finding later supported by Wakefield and Inman (1993). Unfortunately, the evidence on relationships with other socio-economic variables tends to be patchy (McGoldrick et al., 1999). Berne et al. (1999; 2001), however, produce evidence that older shoppers seek price information more actively, as do 'market mavens', those who actively communicate their knowledge of prices, products, promotions, etc.

Dickson and Sawyer (1990) investigated the relationship between price search and price knowledge. In their study, only 58.9 per cent claimed to have checked the prices of grocery items: less than half could recall the price of items just placed in the shopping basket. Surprisingly low levels of price checking were also found in a study of durable goods purchasing decisions (Grewal and Marmorstein, 1994). From an experimental study, Mazumdar and Monroe (1992) suggested that inter-store price checking exerted a stronger influence on consumers' confidence in their price knowledge than upon their actual price knowledge. Figure 10.5 offers a summary of investigated influences upon price awareness, and the processes by which internal reference prices may be formed or modified.

10.5.3 Unit Prices

In many sectors of retailing, the price-makers must decide upon the relative prices of the different sizes or quantities of the same items. The term 'unit price' is used to denote the price expressed in relation to an

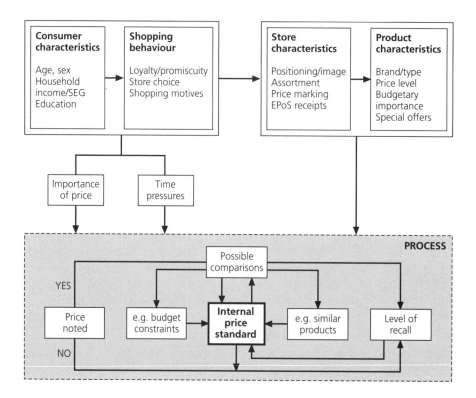

Figure 10.5 Price recall: determinants and process

Source: McGoldrick et al. (1999).

appropriate standard unit of measure, such as price per kilogram or price per litre. It would normally be assumed by consumers that larger sizes, or multipacks, cost less per unit than smaller sizes, although several studies have illustrated departures from this assumption.

A 'quantity surcharge' is said to exist when the larger size actually costs more per unit than the smaller size(s). Nason and Della Bitta (1983) found that 25 and 29 per cent of items in two price audits included at least one quantity surcharge in the various size comparisons. A similar investigation in supermarkets in Greece found quantity surcharges in 18 per cent of size–price comparisons, as high as 42 per cent in the chocolate bars category (Zotos and Lysonski, 1933). Only 9 per cent of those surcharges could be explained by promotions on smaller sizes.

Managers interviewed in the UK indicated that quantity surcharges are usually the result of errors or special offers on smaller sizes; they were less prepared to acknowledge that some may be the outcome of deliberate strategies, for example, leader line pricing featuring the smaller sizes (McGoldrick and Marks, 1985). It has been shown that price and promotion elasticities can vary significantly between the different sizes of the same brand (Kumar and Divakar, 1999). Whatever the reason, quantity surcharges, if noticed, clearly may alienate shoppers. Manning et al. (1998) claimed that consumers meeting quantity surcharges tend to feel more negative towards the brand manufacturer than towards the retailer. This result, however, may owe much to the limitations of the experimental design, which used known brands but an unknown retailer name.

The ability of consumers to compare unit prices both within and between brands is considerably hampered by the chaotic state of package sizes in the UK (Lennard et al., 2001). Although some products are sold in an orderly size progression, in others it is impossible to compare unit prices without an electronic calculator and conversion chart. In the USA it is common to find unit price information displayed either alongside the item price or on a composite list nearby (Aaker and Ford, 1983; Miyazaki et al., 2000). This practice has been resisted by many UK retailers, so unit prices tend to be displayed only where required by UK or European Union (EU) law (see O'Connor, 1995).

Most of the studies have been concerned with consumers' awareness of the information, its usage, and the reactions to different modes of information display. There is little direct evidence as to the effects of unit pricing upon price awareness in general. It could well be that unit pricing might reduce awareness of actual shelf prices, having given consumers an alternative yardstick by which to compare value. At the point of purchase, however, awareness of inter-product and inter-size differentials is likely to be increased, potentially increasing sensitivity to differentials within the retailer's assortment.

10.5.4 Price Endings

Various concepts and strategies have so far been examined which are relevant to the task of setting differential markups for items within the assortment. It would however be incorrect to assume that the specific price point chosen is an unimportant issue; there are firmly held beliefs that certain price endings are more effective than others, such as £9.95 or £9.99 rather than £10.00. Twedt (1965) suggested that this practice was originated by department stores to force cashiers to ring up sales and open the till to give change, thereby reducing cashier fraud. Whatever the origins, it has created customary prices in some product fields. When researching the buy-response curve (see Sec. 10.1.2), Gabor and Granger (1966) noticed sharp kinks in demand just below whole-number prices. Certain unaccustomed prices were simply not seen as 'real prices' by their respondents.

Following an elaborate study of odd price endings, Georgoff (1972) concluded that endings do appear to affect price illusions; direct effects upon sales could not, however, be detected. With the benefit of scanner data, Stiving and Winer (1997) were able to establish both sales effects and image effects, attributable to the right-hand digits within prices. Also using scanner data, Kalyanam and Shively (1998) identified major 'spikes' in the sales response function. Sales increases associated with odd prices were in the range 12 to 76 per cent, compared with the predictions of smooth response curves that eliminated the spikes. Based upon a catalogue experiment, Schindler and Kibarian (1996) also demonstrated major effects. A shift of just −0.03 per cent, from an even price to a 99 cent ending, brought an 8 per cent increase in sales.

Gendall et al. (1997) found little difference between the effects of 95 cent and 99 cent endings, implying that retailers should retain the extra

4 cents. Monroe and Lee (1999) provide further evidence that the left-most digit exerts most influence as consumers encode prices to memory. Another implication of this is that retailer stated reference prices should use higher left-most digits (e.g. £90 rather than £89), to maximize perceived savings with the special offer price. Schindler and Kirby (1997) refer to the 'cognitive accessibility' of certain round numbers that are highly accessible in memory. Using round numbers as internal reference points may lead consumers to conclude that, with the .99 ending, the retailer is giving a little back.

After many years of neglect by researchers, price endings have attracted increased attention in the last 10 years. Retailers have also experimented with the use of even prices to signal prestige and odd prices to signal that a price is more competitive (Gedenk and Sattler, 1999).

10.5.5 Price Lining

Another common approach in the setting of specific price points is the use of price lining, although there is little published evidence as to its effectiveness. Price lining implies the use of very few different price points for a range of items, rather than a wide variety of prices. Table 10.7 provides examples of different types of price lining, illustrating also the common use of odd endings through most of the scale, even endings at the upper, 'prestige' prices.

Table 10.7 Examples of price lining

Ties		Suits		Watches	
Price (£)	**Diff. (%)**	**Price (£)**	**Diff. (%)**	**Price (£)**	**Diff. (%)**
5.99		119.95		14.99	
	50.1		25.0		66.7
8.99		149.95		24.99	
	49.6		20.0		99.9
13.45		179.95		49.95	
	48.7		16.7		198.3
20.00		210.00		149.00	

One justification of price lining is that it simplifies the assortment pricing and, to an extent, the buying process. Having established price lines that appear appropriate to specific consumer segments and needs, the retailer can buy, or have produced, items that yield acceptable margins when sold at those price points. Gabor (1977) pointed to certain problems in using price lines, notably a reluctance to sell items that do not fit into the structure, even if they would be attractive to the consumer. Rigid price lines can also prove difficult to adjust in countries with rapid inflation. Rapid changes in technology, leading to falling prices in areas such as computers, digital cameras and mobile phone, can also be disruptive to price alignments within the product assortment (Shugan and Desiraju, 2001).

In spite of these problems, price lines are thought to have advantages in simplifying the consumer's choice, in some contexts. Particularly when purchasing clothing items, a consumer is typically faced with a wide choice of styles, colours, etc. in several different stores. If many different price levels within one store must also be evaluated within the complex choice process, the effect can be severe dissonance and an instinct to retreat from the store. When price lines are encountered, the consumer is likely to select from among the items at one or possibly two points, thereby considerably reducing the task of deciding upon the purchase.

Various alternative strategies may be employed in setting the differentials between price lines. In the first example in Table 10.7, the almost constant percentage differential is attempting to create an even spread across the mass market for ties. The second example, the diminishing percentage differential, may be used to encourage consumers to move up to the next price point above their intended purchase price for a suit. In the final example, a jeweller may be attempting to cater for a very diverse range of needs, from the basic utility watches to the more expensive fashion watches. Where very diverse segments are being catered for within one store, 'price clustering' may be used as a variant upon price lining. In such cases, prices are clustered around certain levels, rather than strictly adhering to specific price points. Among the elements of assortment pricing, the practice of price lining is the least well analysed within the published research literature.

10.6 The Time Dimension

This dimension first highlights the essential principal that pricing in retailing is not usually concerned simply with the maximization of individual product, short-term sales. A longer-term objective normally exists in attempting progressively to create the most favourable price image for the store or company. Approaches to this, which will be considered within this section, include the use of temporary special offers or more widespread seasonal 'sales'. These are clearly not the only routes towards the longer-term development of a lower-priced image, although they are ones that are widely used.

However, some retailers have turned away, wholly or in part, from these forms of temporal price differentiation, sometimes referred to as 'Hi–Lo' or high–low pricing (HLP). The section therefore concludes with consideration of the relative merits of 'everyday low pricing' (EDLP).

10.6.1 Formation of Price Images

The wider question of store images has already been considered in detail in Chapter 5. However, the specific issue of price images is highly relevant in this context, as retailer strategies and tactics are increasingly focused upon image formation. This facet of retail pricing was largely ignored within many early studies, but Nystrom (1970) effectively harnessed the concept within a simple model. The core of this was a recognition that consumers, even if they wish to be economically rational in their purchasing decisions, are prevented by lack of information and/or cognitive limitations. Accordingly, they are prone to generalize an image of the retailer's overall price level, which is based upon a relatively small number of (or maybe just one) individual price discrimination(s).

Figure 10.6
Generalization and
discrimination in retail
price evaluations

Source: adapted from
Nystrom (1970).

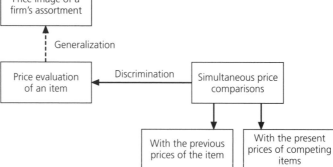

Case 1: Item specific price information dominates

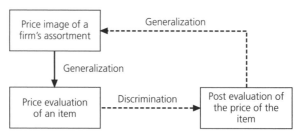

Case 2: Price image dominates

The process can also operate in a different order: the existing image held of the store prices may influence the customer's evaluation of a specific price offering. For example, a consumer patronizing a discount store may be easily convinced, because of store images held, that a sofa priced at £399 represents a good deal. If, on the one hand, it is later observed that the sofa is being sold for £450 elsewhere, that price image will be reinforced. If, on the other hand, the sofa is observed for sale at £349 elsewhere, this one discrimination may be generalized to modify considerably the image held, especially if the item was actually purchased at £399! Figure 10.6 illustrates the alternative processes of generalization and discrimination.

This concept of generalization on the basis of very limited discriminations is clearly valid in relation to the longer-term price images of retailers with large product assortments, such as variety stores or grocery stores. Fry and McDougall (1974) illustrated that the more traditional retailer may find it harder than a retailer with a discounter image to convince customers that a cut price is really the lowest in the area. However, the discounter may have more of a problem in terms of the credibility of its reference prices (Biswas and Blair, 1991). Gupta and Cooper (1992) expected to find consumers less likely to 'discount the discounts' claimed by high image stores but this did not prove to be the case; consumers were still sceptical.

10.6.2 Temporary Price Offers

As a device for conveying an image of competitive prices to the consumer, short-term price reductions have had a long history in most forms of retailing. Briggs and Smyth (1967) noted that they convey an 'image of cheapness' and also that more expensive firms often used the deepest cuts. Alderson (1963) summarized the process of heavily promoting a selection of special prices as the desire to 'minimize the cost of appearing competitive'. The advantages of temporary offers can be summarized:

1 Being short-term, they are less likely to provoke direct retaliation.
2 Concentration upon a few lines gives a flexibility in accordance with market conditions; special offers may be used to attract specific types of customers.
3 Special offers are likely to be heavily subsidized, perhaps paid for completely, by manufacturers.
4 From the consumer viewpoint, getting a bargain can contribute 'transaction utility' adding to the 'acquisition utility' of owning the item (Grewal et al., 1998). According to Thaler (1985), 'transaction utility' depends solely upon the merits of the deal, whereas 'acquisition utility' is derived from gaining the product's need-satisfying attributes.

The choice of products for temporary price offers represents a difficult task for retail price-makers. A retailer may be offered over 1000 promotions each month, yet may wish to feature only 30 items every two weeks. Various recommendations have emerged as to how a retailer should select special-offer items. It has been suggested that more expensive and/or bulky items should be used in order to inhibit stocking up by consumers. Litvack et al. (1985) explained widely varying levels of response to short-term price offers in terms of the 'stockability' of different products by consumers. As consumers become more knowledgeable of promotional schedules, this may affect purchase timings and stockpiling behaviour (Helsen and Schmittlein, 1992). Indeed, prolonged exposure to promotions can cause consumers to 'lie in wait' for especially good offers (Mela et al., 1998).

Holdren (1960) made a systematic attempt to identify the types of item with a strong 'transfer effect'; this denotes changes in the sales of a store resulting from the transfer of custom from one store to another, rather than from one product to another. Many retailers, however, have overestimated the size of the consumer segment that regularly switches stores for price specials (Urbany et al., 2000). Not surprisingly, this propensity is most notable among the less affluent shoppers (Laroche et al., 2001). From a study of panel data, Volle (2001) concluded: 'The short-term effect of store-level promotions on store choice is significant but weak: store choice is mainly driven by loyalty.'

The availability of scanner data makes it possible to study with more precision promotional cross-elasticities, i.e., the effects upon the non-promoted items. Walters (1991) found that promotions in one store significantly deceased sales of substitutes and complementary products in a competing store. Mulhern and Padgett (1995) used basket analysis to identify that most purchasers of promotions spend more, while in the store, on normally priced items. A series of guidelines on what, how and when to promote were developed by Karande and Kumar (1995), these varying according to the retailers' motive for the special offers.

Although retailers are becoming more discriminating in their choice of offers, in the UK grocery industry, for example, most cuts are 'subsidized' by at least 40 per cent by manufacturers; in some cases the manufacturer meets 100 per cent of the price cut, plus a contribution towards advertising and display costs. The chairman of one major grocery chain defined sales promotion as 'manufacturers' contribution to my profits'. Manufacturers generally agree that they require retailer assistance with promotions, although retailer's views are more varied. In a study of loss-leader promotions in Finland, Rinne et al. (1986) found that about half of them had a negative effect on store profits.

Increased attention has been given to the precise nature and framing of the special offer. Folkes and Wheat (1995) found that discounts paid as a rebate, rather than as an immediate discount, had less influence in lowering consumers' perceptions of the normal price. Chen et al. (1998) examined the use of percentage versus absolute discount statements. For high-priced products, the reduction framed in absolute, dollar terms proved preferable. Diamond (1992) found that, for higher-value promotions, consumers prefer discounts to free extra quantities of the product. Table 10.8 shows the deal-type preferences demonstrated for supermarket products, each of the alternatives offering essentially a half-price deal.

Table 10.8 Framing the price deal

Deal framing	% preferring
50% off	48.8
Buy one get one free (BOGOF)	20.9
Buy two get 50% off	4.0
All deals the same	18.1
Other deal combinations	8.2

Several studies have reported the short-term effects of price cuts coupled with increases in advertising and/or display (e.g. Bemmaor and Mouchoux, 1991; Wilkinson et al., 1982). Extravagant claims are often made by those with an interest in stimulating promotional activities; such claims may, however, make no reference to the demonstrated propensity of sales to fall away again to about the previous level after the temporary offer period (e.g. Van Heerde et al., 2000). In spite of these important qualifications, plus the somewhat uncertain impact of the offers upon the retailer's longer-term image, the lure of temporary price cuts remains strong.

10.6.3 Seasonal 'Sales'

The modern day 'sale' has been evolving for over a century under various social, economic and legal forces. Early department stores helped develop the notion of fashion and obsolescence, moulding tastes so that clothes, furniture, etc. were replaced when outdated, not when worn out. Shortening fashion cycles added urgency to clearing out slower-selling lines: the expanding range of styles increased the number of buying errors consigned to the reduced racks. The abolition of resales price maintenance meant that retailers were free to discount from 'normal' or recommended prices during their 'sales' (Betts and McGoldrick, 1995).

Figure 10.7 places seasonal 'sales' within the broader framework of the time dimension, as well as positioning variations upon the traditional 'sale'. These include the very short duration events, such as '12 Hour Spectaculars' (Burton Group) or 'Blue Cross Events' (House of Fraser). At the other extreme of the duration axis lie the 'perpetual sales' of stores that rarely take down the typically red 'sale' banners. The dotted line at the 10 per cent of lines level relates to a UK Code of Practice (DTI, 1988). Retailer should not display general 'sale' notices, unless at least 10 per cent of merchandise in the store complies with the stated discount (e.g. at least 25 per cent off) on the 'sale' notice.

Retailers try to contain the extent of seasonal markdowns, and models have been suggested to assist the planning of 26-week trading cycles (Smith et al., 1998). However, the factors that impact upon the need to

Figure 10.7 Positioning of price reduction activities

Source: Betts and McGoldrick (1995).

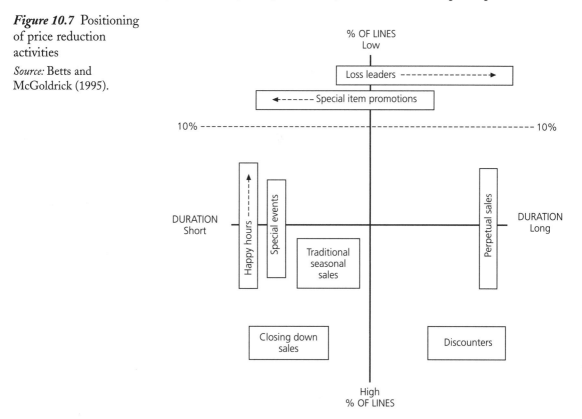

clear stock, including fashion, competitor action, consumer confidence and the weather, are not uniformly predictable. Bobinski et al. (1996) reported that over 60 per cent of US department store volume is sold at 'sale' prices. Hard evidence on the extent and depth of 'sale' markdowns is scarce but an audit of 21 women's wear chains, in the UK January 'sales' produced the following analysis:

▶ percentage of styles marked down (extent): 35.6 per cent
▶ mean percentage markdown (depth): 33.3 per cent
▶ margin impact (extent x depth): 11.8 per cent

The figure for 'margin impact' varied across categories from 15.5 per cent, in the case of outer overcoats, to just 3.5 per cent, in the case of the less seasonal jeans category (McGoldrick and Betts, 1997). Within fashion retailing in Europe, the industry norm is for 30–40 per cent of sales to be made not all full price (Morgan Stanley Dean Witter, 2001). Through improved communications, distribution and manufacturing arrangements, retailers such as Zara have been able to reduce this to 15–20 percent.

From the perspective of the economist (e.g. van Praag and Bode, 1992), seasonal 'sales' are one form of 'intertemporal price discrimination', serving purposes beyond simply clearance of stock. If goods are sold too cheaply too early in the season, some consumers are able to buy at less than their reservation (or 'willing to pay') prices. These differences in reservation prices, between different consumer segments, enhance the logic of discriminating prices over time.

For those consumers not inclined to pay new season, higher prices, the 'sales' provide a number of forms of satisfaction. (Betts and McGoldrick, 1996) interviewed a large number of 'sale' shoppers:

1 *Excitement*: 'I would love to go to the one in Harrods, it's not a matter of spending, it's just the madness of it, it's a dream.'
2 *Fear of missing out*: 'I'm going to make sure I get my fair share of whatever it is, presuming I want it.' Shorter time limits within which to respond and the apparent excess of shoppers over desirable items intensify the perceived urgency to act (Prus, 1986).
3 *Camaraderie*: sharing a common purpose and interest: 'You're with people like you, who are hunting for bargains, you can have a good laugh together.'
4 *Competition*: 'If someone finds something which someone else wants too, they'll tear it apart ... It's dog eat dog.' 'My husband says he has never seen women so violent in all his life. He said it was worse than a football match.' A competitive element arises between friends and family too: 'We all boast about our bargains, to your family, friends, anyone.' Some shoppers also enjoy 'Getting one up on the shop-keeper'.
5 *Guilt relief*: 'When I spend money I feel guilty, but when I get a bargain I don't.' Another 'sale' shopper suggested parallels with the

competitive element: 'If friends spend a fortune on a dress, they wouldn't tell you. But if it was a bargain, they would tell everyone.' Shoppers also felt less guilty if they bought for others too.

6 *Transaction and acquisition utility*: economy and self-satisfaction with getting a 'bargain'. Most shoppers touched upon the recurrent theme of 'feeling clever'.

10.6.4 Everyday Low Pricing

Marketing writers frequently intimate that a perpetual spotlight on reduced prices can damage store credibility and cheapen store images (e.g. Berry, 1986). 'Sales' also influence store positioning though dimensions other than price, including larger crowds, 'seconds' and 'end of lines', a change in ambience, poorer service, etc. The physical appearance and behaviour of a store's clientele also contribute to shaping its image, therefore 'meet(ing) a lower class of shopper in these sales' may also downgrade retailer's image (Prus, 1986).

Everyday low pricing	High–low pricing
Reduced price wars	Price discrimination: merchandise appeals to multiple market segments
Reduced promotional advertising	
More efficient use of store personnel	Creates excitement
Improved inventory management	All merchandise can be sold eventually
Increased profit margins	Price confusion reduces awareness of prices
The retailer can concentrate on being a seller, rather than a deal buyer	High initial prices guide customers' judgements of product and store quality
Less buyer time spent managing 'sale' events and more time merchandising the entire line	EDLP can be extremely difficult to maintain
More consumer appeal: price perceived as more honest	

Table 10.9 Relative merits of EDLP and high–low pricing

Source: McGoldrick and Betts (1997).

Concerns about the potentially damaging effects of excessive markdown activity has stimulated a debate on the relative merits of EDLP v. high–low pricing. Much has been said in support of the EDLP approach. The strengths of the opposing strategies are summarized in Table 10.9. However, despite the asymmetric column lengths and the implied superiority of EDLP, simple observation confirms that the high–low type stores (i.e., those using price promotions and 'sales') still greatly outnumber EDLP operators.

Sear's dramatic, widely publicized and costly switch to EDLP failed, partly because of consumer expectations about the Sears brand. They were conditioned to expect periodic 'sales' from the retailer. This, taken together with the fact that Sears actually continued to advertise some 'sales', left consumers extremely confused about Sears' pricing. The store subsequently resumed its high–low strategy, as Sears' prices were not sufficiently competitive to claim EDLP anyway. Kmart, too, failed on EDLP, owing to inappropriate infrastructures and high cost structures (e.g. Stockwell and Stockwell, 1992).

Only low-cost operators can maintain low and stable prices and few players can credibly maintain this position. Hoch et al. (1994) conducted a series of field experiments, finding that a switch to EDLP reduced a retailer's profits by 18 per cent. Wal-Mart is the most frequently cited example of a successful EDLP retailer, this being achieved through very strong buying and cost control. Electrical retailer Comet has also enjoyed growth in turnover and market share, through the pursuit of an EDLP strategy (Retail Review, 2001). For the majority, it would seem not to be the best strategy, high–low pricing offering more options to manipulate offers and price images. There are also hybrid solutions: B & Q proclaim an EDLP stance but do have end-of-session and other special offers. Alba et al. (1999) outlined the benefits of a strategy of many but shallow discounts:

> *Stores generally wish to create a low-price image. Conversely, brands may wish to be perceived as higher priced, should they desire to position themselves in a premium category.*

SUMMARY

Pricing is one of the most important decision areas of retail marketing. Until recently, however, it has not received the attention merited from either researchers or retail management. Specific decisions are still frequently made in isolation, and in many companies the pricing activities are dispersed between different parts of the organization. A clear and co-ordinated pricing function is required which recognizes the vital role of pricing within the marketing process and the important interrelationships between the various elements. The objectives of retail pricing must be set within the overall strategic plan but, equally, must be clearly defined to guide the choice of appropriate strategies and tactics.

Some of the basic concepts of pricing can be of assistance to the retailer, provided that their constraints are recognized. For example, elasticity of demand to price is a useful concept in making price adjustments, but the traditional assumptions are very rigid. A more flexible approach is to consider the sensitivity of customers to price, which may include reactions against prices that are too low or too high, and some degree of indifference to prices between certain thresholds. Such considerations can provide a valuable input to pricing decisions, particularly those of narrow-range retailers whose pricing decisions are focused upon one or just a few products. In the retailing of large product assortments in many different stores, as in the case of variety stores or grocery chains, rather more pricing dimensions need to be considered. Most of the strategies and concepts considered within this chapter are presented within a framework that draws attention to the multidimensional character of retail pricing, focusing upon the comparative, geographical, assortment and time dimensions.

All retail pricing decisions, whether long or short term, item specific or general to the range, local or company-wide, must be taken with regard to the resulting price positions vis-à-vis competitors. Techniques of price auditing are evolving, although serious errors of methods and/or interpretation are frequently encountered. With the development of large consumer panels, access to transaction data is improving. Comparisons are, however, complicated by some retailers' strategies for multi-segment prices, which can create very different price profiles within the same store. Although the surveys of comparative prices are important, it must be recognized that the consumers' subjective impressions of comparative prices are the essential indicator of the outcome of retail pricing activities.

The geographical dimension of pricing is salient to all multiple chains, in that each store trades under different market conditions. Some evidence has emerged that prices tend to be higher in more outlying areas, more downmarket areas and when a few major retailers hold a large local market share. Various strategies have been evolved to differentiate prices between stores to better exploit local conditions. With enhanced information on local markets, retailers are able increasingly to engage in localization of prices, as well as the product mix, services, hours of trading and promotions.

Some major retailers are trying now to take a more co-ordinated view of the task of pricing a large assortment of products. 'Leader line' pricing systems, whereby 'known value items' are selected for discounting to enhance the overall image, are increasingly used. Studies of consumers' price awareness have provided guidelines as to the products upon which such pricing tactics may be most effectively concentrated. The pricing of a large assortment involves other major decisions, such as the price differentials between different package sizes or between private and manufacturer brands. It is also necessary to consider the exact price points then to be used, and some sectors make extensive use of 'odd ending' prices and 'price lining'.

One essential property of retail pricing is that the effects are not only the immediate item sales. A longer-term process of price image formation is constantly in progress; as consumers are unable really to compare more than a handful of item prices, they naturally tend to generalize longer-term images from those few comparisons. A traditional approach in attracting customers to the stores is to offer short-term, price cuts on a few items. Several suggestions have been evolved as to how items should be selected to maximize overall sales improvement, rather than simply sell more of the offered items. 'Seasonal sales' are a major feature of pricing in clothing and some other forms of retailing, offering opportunities to clear stock and to differentiate prices over time periods. As a reaction against such 'high–low' strategies, some have tried everyday low pricing (EDLP) but only the lowest-cost operators have persisted.

REVIEW QUESTIONS

1 What considerations should be taken into account when allocating responsibility for the tasks of retail pricing within a large retail organization?

2 Under what circumstances would a retailer's pricing strategies be primarily oriented towards

a) market penetration?

b) market stabilization?

3 Compare and contrast the concepts of price elasticity and price sensitivity. Discuss the problems involved in deriving and using measures of each.

4 What particular facets of retail pricing make the function quite different to that of pricing by a manufacturer?

5 What problems may be encountered by a wide-range retailer in attempting objectively to compare store price levels with those of competitors?

6 How can a wide-range retailer adopt multiple positioning strategies within its stores? What are the benefits and possible drawbacks of such a strategy.

7 What factors tend to influence the prevailing retail price levels within different geographical areas?

8 Why would a multiple retailer consider charging different sets of prices in different stores within the chain? How could such a policy of geographical differentiation be best administered?

9 Why has the 'leader line' pricing strategy been adopted increasingly? How should a retailer select the products to be price discounted within such a strategy?

10 Define 'unit prices' and 'quantity surcharges'. What could a retailer gain by providing unit price information beyond that required by law?

11 Discuss the advantages and dangers of using

a) odd-ending prices

b) price lining.

12 Discuss the processes of discrimination and generalization in the formation of retail price images by consumers. With relevant examples, show how an understanding of these processes can assist retailers in setting prices within their product assortments.

13 Under what circumstances is the use of temporary price reductions an appropriate retail pricing strategy in the context of

a) grocery retailing?

b) department store retailing?

14 As a retail strategist within the clothing sector, you are concerned about the length and frequency of 'seasonal sales'. What factors would you take into account in undertaking a systematic evaluation of the costs and benefits of 'seasonal sales'?

15 Discuss the relative advantages of everyday low prices compared with high–low pricing. Which approach do you consider more appropriate for:

a) clothing boutiques?

b) DIY stores?

REFERENCES

Aaker, D.A. and G.T. Ford (1983) 'Unit pricing ten years later: a replication', *Journal of Marketing*, **47** (1), 118–122.

Abe, M. (1998) 'Measuring consumer, nonlinear brand choice response to price', *Journal of Retailing*, **74** (4), 541–568.

Ackerman, D. and G. Tellis (2001) 'Can culture affect prices? A cross-cultural study of shopping and retail prices', *Journal of Retailing*, **77** (1), 57–82.

Alba, J.A., S.M. Broniarczyk, T.A. Shimp and J.E. Urbany (1994) 'The influence of prior beliefs, frequency cues, and magnitude cues on consumers' perceptions of comparative drive data, *Journal of Consumer Research*, **21** (2), 219–235.

Alba, J.W., C.G. Melia, T A. Shimp and J.E. Urbany (1999) 'The effect of discount frequency and depth on consumer price judgements', *Journal of Consumer Research*, **26** (2), 99–114.

Alderson, W. (1963) 'Administered prices and retail grocery advertising', *Journal of Advertising Research*, (1), 2–6.

Alford, B.L. and B.T. Engelland (2000) 'Advertised reference price effects on consumer price estimates, value perception and search intention', *Journal of Business Research*, **48**, 93–100.

Basu, A.K. and T. Mazumdar (1995) 'Using a menu of geographic pricing plans: a theoretical investigation', *Journal of Retailing*, **71** (2) 173–202.

Bell, J. and S. Brown (1986) 'Anatomy of a supermarket price war', *Irish Marketing Review*, **1**, 109-117.

Bemmaor, A.C. and D. Mouchoux (1991) 'Measuring the short-term effect of in-store promotion and retail advertising on brand sales: a factorial experiment', *Journal of Marketing Research*, **28** (May), 202–214.

Berne, C., J.M. Múgica, M. Pedraja and P. Rivera (1999) 'The use of consumer's price information search behaviour for pricing differentiation in retailing', *International Review of Retail, Distribution and Consumer Research*, **92** (2), 127–146.

Berne, C., J.M. Múgica, M. Pedraja and P. Rivera (2001) 'Factors involved in price information-seeking behaviour', *Journal of Retailing and Consumer Services*, **8**, 71–84.

Berry, L. (1986) 'Multidimensional strategies combat price wars', *Marketing News*, **31** (January), 10.

Berry, L.L. (1993) 'Playing fair in retailing', *Retailing Issues Letter* (Arthur Anderson & Co.), **5** (2), 1–2.

Betts, E. and P.J. McGoldrick (1995) 'The strategy of the seasonal "sale": typology, review and synthesis', *International Review of Retail, Distribution and Consumer Research*, **5** (3), 303–331.

Betts, E. and P.J. McGoldrick (1996) 'Consumer behaviour and the retail "sales": modelling the development of an "attitude problem"', *European Journal of Marketing*, **30** (8), 40–58.

Binkley, J.K. and J.M. Connor (1998) 'Grocery market pricing and the new competitive environment', *Journal of Retailing*, **74** (2), 273–294.

Biswas, A. and Blair, E.A. (1991) 'Contextual effects of reference prices in retail advertisements', *Journal of Marketing*, **55** (3), 1–12.

Bobinski, G.S., D. Cox and A. Cox (1996) 'Retail "sales" advertising, perceived retailer credibility and price rationale', *Journal of Retailing*, **72** (3), 291–306.

Bresnahan, T.F. and P.C. Reiss (1991) 'Entry and competition in concentrated markets', *Journal of Political Economy*, **99** (5), 977–1009.

Briggs, D.H. and R.L. Smyth (1967) *Distribution of Groceries: Economic Aspects of the Distribution of Groceries with Special Reference to Western Australia*, University of Western Australia Press, Nedlands.

Brown, F.E. (1969) 'Price image versus price reality', *Journal of Marketing Research*, **6** (2), 185–191.

Brucks, M., V.A. Zeithaml and G. Naylor (2000) 'Price and brand name as indicators of quality dimensions for consumer durables', *Journal of the Academy of Marketing Science*, **28** (3), 359–374.

Bucklin, L.P. (1972) *Competition and Evolution in the Distributive Trades*, Prentice-Hall, Englewood Cliffs, NJ.

Bucklin, R.E. and J.M Lattin (1992) 'A model of product category competition among grocery retailers', *Journal of Retailing*, **68** (3), 271–293.

Campbell, W.J. and M. Chisholm (1970) 'Local variations in retail grocery prices', *Urban Studies*, **7**, 76–81.

Chen, S.S., K.B. Monroe and Y.-C. Lou (1998) 'The effects of framing price promotion messages on consumers' perceptions and purchase intentions', *Journal of Retailing*, **74** (3), 353–372.

Competition Commission (2000) *Supermarkets: A Report on the Supply of Groceries from Multiple Stores in the United Kingdom*, The Stationery Office, Norwich.

Corstjens, J. and M. Corstjens (1995) *Store Wars*, Wiley, Chichester.

Cotterill, R. (1986) 'Market power in the retail food industry: evidence from Vermont', *Review of Economics and Statistics*, **68**, 379–386.

Cox, A.D. and D. Cox (1990) 'Competing on price: the role of retail price advertisements in shaping store-price image', *Journal of Retailing*, **66**, 428–445.

Danaher, P.J. and R.J. Brodie (2000) 'Understanding the characteristics of price elasticities for frequently purchased packaged goods', *Journal of Marketing Management*, **16** (8), 917–936.

Den Hertog, R.G.J. and A.R. Thurik (1995) 'A comparison between Dutch and German retail pricing setting', *Service Industries Journal*, **15** (1), 66–73.

Diamond, W.D. (1992) 'Just what is a "dollar's worth"? Consumer reactions to price discounts vs. extra product promotions', *Journal of Retailing*, **68** (3), 254–270.

Dickson, P.R. and A.G. Sawyer (1990) 'The price knowledge and search of supermarket shoppers', *Journal of Marketing*, **54** (July), 42–53.

Dickson, P.R. and J.E. Urbany (1994) 'Retail reactions to competitive price changes', *Journal of Retailing*, **70** (1) 1–21.

Docters, R.G. (1997) 'Price strategy: time to choose your weapons', *Journal of Business Strategy*, **18** (5), 11–15.

Dodds, W.B., K.B. Monroe and D. Grewal (1991) 'Effects of price, brand and store information on buyers' product evaluations', *Journal of Marketing Research*, **28**, 307–319.

DTI (1988) *Code of Practice for Traders on Price Indications*, DTI/Pub 266/10K12/92/R, Department of Trade and Industry, London.

Engelson, M. (1995) *Pricing Strategy*, JMS, Portland.

Estelami, H. and D.R. Lehmann (2001) 'The impact of research design on consumer price recall accuracy: an integrative review', *Journal of the Academy of Marketing Science*, **29** (1), 36–49.

Folkes, V. and R.D. Wheat (1995) 'Consumers' price perceptions of promoted products', *Journal of Retailing*, **71** (3) 317–328.

Fowler, A. and A. Gulati (2000) *A New "Stability"? Don't Be too Sure*, Morgan Stanley Dean Witter, London.

Fowler, A., J. Pritchard and A. Gulati (2000) *Price: Who's Doing What to Whom?*, Morgan Stanley Dean Witter, London.

Fry, J.N. and G.H. McDougall (1974) 'Consumer appraisal of retail price advertisements', *Journal of Marketing*, **38** (3), 64–67.

Gabor, A. (1977) *Pricing, Principles and Practices*, Heinemann, London.

Gabor, A. and C.W.J. Granger (1964) 'Price sensitivity of the consumer', *Journal of Advertising Research*, **4** (4), 40–44.

Gabor, A. and C.W.J. Granger (1966) 'Price as an indicator of quality: report on an enquiry', *Economica*, **33**, 43–70.

Gedenk, K. and H. Sattler (1999) 'The impact of price thesholds on profit contribution—Should retailers set 9-ending prices?', *Journal of Retailing*, **75** (1), 33–57.

Gendall, P., J. Holdershaw and R. Garland (1997) 'The effect of odd pricing on demand', *European Journal of Marketing*, **31** (11), 799–813.

Georgoff, D.M. (1972) *Odd-Even Retail Price Endings*, MSU Business Studies, East Lansing, MI.

Goldman, A. (1977) 'Consumer knowledge of food prices as an indicator of shopping effectiveness', *Journal of Marketing*, **41** (4), 67–75.

Greenley, G.E. (1989) 'A managerial process for pricing decisions', *Quarterly Review of Marketing*, **14** (4), 1–9.

Grewal, D. and H. Marmorstein (1994) 'Market price variation, perceived price variation and consumers' price search decisions for durable goods', *Journal of Consumer Research* **21** (December), 453–460.

Grewal, D., J. Gotlieb and H. Marmorstein (1994) 'The moderating effects of message framing and source credibility on the price-perceived risk relationship', *Journal of Consumer Research*, **21** (June), 145–153.

Grewal, D., K.B. Monroe and R. Krishnan (1998) 'The effects of price-comparison advertising on buyers' perceptions of acquisition value, transaction value and behavioral intentions' *Journal of Marketing*, **62** (April), 46–59.

Gupta, S. and L.G. Cooper (1992) 'The discounting of discounts and promotional thresholds', *Journal of Consumer Research*, **19** (3), 401–411.

Hall, R.L. and C.J. Hitch (1939) 'Price theory and business behaviour', *Oxford Economic Papers*, **2**, 12–45.

Harrison, S. (2000) 'Shouts and whispers: the lobbying campaigns for and against resale price maintenance', *European Journal of Marketing*, **34** (1/2), 207–222.

Hayes, L.R. (2000), 'Are prices higher for the poor in New York City?', *Journal of Consumer Policy*, **23**, 127–152.

Heenan, D.A. (1993) 'Value pricing goes global', *Journal of Business Strategy*, **14** (6), 18–19.

Heil, O.P. and K. Helsen (2001) 'Towards an understanding of price wars: their nature and how they erupt', *International Journal of Research in Marketing*, **18**, 83–98.

Heller, W.H. (1974) 'What shoppers know and don't know about prices', *Progressive Grocer*, **53** (11), 39–41.

Helsen, K. and D.C. Schmittlein (1992) 'How does a product market's typical price-promotion pattern affect the timing of households' purchases? An empirical study using UPC scanner data', *Journal of Retailing*, **68** (3), 316–338.

Hoch, S.J., X. Dreze and M.E. Purk (1994) 'EDLP, Hi-Lo and margin arithmetic', *Journal of Marketing*, **58** (4), 16–27.

Hoch, S.J., B.-D. Kim, A.L. Montgomery and P.E. Rossi (1995) 'Determinants of store-level price elasticity', *Journal of Marketing Research*, **32** (February), 17–29.

Holdren, B.R. (1960) *The Structure of a Retail Market and the Market Behaviour of Retail Units*, Prentice-Hall, Englewood Cliffs, NJ.

Huber, J., M.B. Holbrook and B. Kahn (1986) 'Effects of competitive context and of additional information on price sensitivity', *Journal of Marketing Research*, **23** (3), 250–260.

Hutchinson-Kirby, G. and R. Dardis (1986) 'Research note: a pricing study of women's apparel in off-price and department stores', *Journal of Retailing*, **62** (3), 321–330.

Jain, S. and J. Srivastava (2000) 'An experimental and theoretical analysis of price-matching refund policies', *Journal of Marketing Research*, **37** (3), 351–362.

Janiszewski, C. and D.R. Lichtenstein (1999) 'A range theory account of price perception', *Journal of Consumer Research*, **25** (4), 353–368.

Kalwani, M. and C.K. Yim (1992) 'Consumer price and promotion expectations: an experimental study', *Journal of Marketing Research*, **29** (1), 90–100.

Kalyanaram G. and J.D.C. Little (1994) 'An empirical analysis of latitudes of price acceptance in consumer package goods', *Journal of Consumer Research*, **2** 408–418.

Kalyanam, R. and J.S. Shively (1998) 'Estimating irregular pricing effects: a stochastic spline regression approach', *Journal of Marketing Research*, **35** (February), 16–29.

Karande, K.W. and V. Kumar (1995) 'The effect of brand characteristics and retailer policies on response to retail price promotions: implications for retailers', *Journal of Retailing*, **71** (3), 249–278.

Kumar, P. and S. Divakar (1999) 'Size does matter: analyzing brand-size competition using store level scanner data', *Journal of Retailing*, **75** (1), 59–76,

Laroche, M., F. Pons, N. Zgolli and C. Kim (2001) 'Consumers' use of price promotions: a model and its potential moderators', *Journal of Retailing and Consumer Services*, **8**, 251–260.

Lennard, D., V.-W. Mitchell, P.J. McGoldrick and E.J. Betts (2001), 'Why consumer under-use food quantity indicators', *International Review of Retail, Distribution and Consumer Research*, **11** (2), 177–199.

Lichtenstein, D.R. and W.O. Bearden (1989) 'Contextual influences on perceptions of merchant-supplied reference prices', *Journal of Consumer Research*, **16** (1), 55–66.

Lichtenstein, D.R. and S. Burton (1989) 'The relationship between perceived and objective price-quality', *Journal of Marketing Research*, **26** (November), 429–443.

Lichtenstein, D.R., N.M. Ridgway and R.G. Netemeyer (1993) 'Price perceptions and consumer shopping behavior: a field study', *Journal of Marketing Research*, **30** (May), 234–245.

Little, J.D.C. and J.F. Shapiro (1980) 'A theory of pricing nonfeatured products in supermarkets', *Journal of Business*, **53** (3), pt 2, S199–S209.

Litvack, D.S., R.J. Calatone and P.R. Warshaw (1985) 'An examination of short-term retail grocery price effects', *Journal of Retailing*, **61** (3), 9–25.

Manning, K.C., D.E. Sprott and A.D. Miyazaki (1998) 'Consumer response to quantity surcharges: implications for retail price setters', *Journal of Retailing*, **74** (3), 373–399.

Marion, B.W. (1989) 'The concentration-price relationship in food retailing', in *Concentration and Price*, L.W. Weiss (ed.), MIT Press, Cambridge, MA, pp. 185–193.

Marion, B.W., W.F. Mueller, R.W. Colterill, F.E. Geithman and J.R. Smelzer (1979) *The Food Retailing Industry: Market Structure, Profits and Prices*, Praeger, New York.

Matson, E. (1995) 'Customizing prices', *Harvard Business Review*, **73** (6), 13–14.

Mazumdar, T. and K.B. Monroe (1992) 'Effects of inter-store and in-store price comparisons on price recall accuracy and confidence', *Journal of Retailing*, **68** (1), 66–89.

McGoldrick, P.J. (1987) 'A multi-dimensional framework for retail pricing', *International Journal of Retailing*, **2** (2), 3–26.

McGoldrick, P.J. (1988) 'Spatial price differentiation by chain store retailers', in *Transnational Retailing*, E. Kaynak (ed.), Walter de Gruyter, Berlin, pp. 167–180.

McGoldrick, P.J. (1993) 'Grocery pricing in the 1990s—war or peace?', *Irish Marketing Review*, **6**, 101–110.

McGoldrick, P.J. and E.J. Betts (1997) 'Seasonal markdown strategies of apparel retailers: audit evidence and consumer preferences', *Proceedings of the Academy of Marketing Science Annual Conference*, Miami, pp. 165–170.

McGoldrick, P.J. and H.J. Marks (1985) 'Price-size relationships and customer reactions to a limited unit pricing programme', *European Journal of Marketing*, **19** (1), 47–64.

McGoldrick, P.J. and H.J. Marks (1987) 'Shoppers' awareness of retail grocery prices', *European Journal of Marketing*, **21** (3), 63–76.

McGoldrick, P.J., E.J. Betts and A.F. Wilson (1999) 'Modelling consumer price cognition: evidence from discount and superstore sectors', *Service Industries Journal*, **19** (1), 171–193.

Mela, C.F., K. Jedidi and D. Bowman (1998) 'The long-term impact of promotions on consumer stockpiling behavior', *Journal of Marketing Research*, **35** (May), 250–262.

Mercer, A. (1996) 'Non-linear price effects', *Journal of the Market Research Society*, **38**, 227–233.

Miyazaki, A.D., D.E. Sprott and K.C. Manning (2000) 'Unit prices on retail shelf labels: an assessment of information prominence', *Journal of Retailing*, **76** (1), 93–112.

Monroe, K.B. and A.J. Della Bitta (1978) 'Models for pricing decisions', *Journal of Marketing Research*, **15** (3), 413–428.

Monroe, K.B. and A.Y Lee (1999) 'Remembering versus knowing: issues in buyers' processing of price information', *Journal of the Academy of Marketing Science*, **27** (2), 207–225.

Montgomery, A.L. (1997) 'Creating micro-marketing pricing strategies using supermarket scanner data', *Marketing Science*, **16** (4), 315–317.

Morgan Stanley Dean Witter (2000) *Safeway*, MSDW, London.

Morgan Stanley Dean Witter (2001) *Minimising Risk in Fashion Retailing*, MSDW, London.

Morwitz, V.G., E.A. Greenleaf and E.J. Johnson (1998) 'Divide and prosper: consumers' reactions to partitioned prices', *Journal of Marketing Research*, **35** (4), 453–463.

Mulhern, F.J. and R.P. Leone (1995) 'Measuring market response to price changes: a classification approach', *Journal of Business Research*, **33** (3), 197–205.

Mulhern, F.J. and D.T. Padgett (1995) 'The relationship between retail price promotions and regular price purchases', *Journal of Marketing*, **59** (October), 83–90.

Mulhern, F.J., J.D. Williams and R.F. Leone (1998) 'Variability of brand price elasticities across retail stores: ethnic, income and brand determinants', *Journal of Retailing*, **74** (3), 427–446.

Murray, I. (1977) 'Blazing the discount trail', *Campaign*, 18 November, 47.

Nason, R.W. and A.J. Della Bitta (1983) 'The incidence and consumer perceptions of quantity surcharges', *Journal of Retailing*, **59** (2), 40–54.

New York Times Magazine (1996) 'The geography of taste', *New York Times Magazine*, 10 March, 40–41, 104.

Nystrom, H. (1970) *Retail Pricing: An Integrated Economic and Psychological Approach*, Economic Research Unit, Stockholm School of Economics, Stockholm.

O'Connor, B. (1995) *A Business Guide to European Community Legislation*, Wiley, Chichester.

Olshavsky, R.W., A.B. Aylesworth and D.S. Kempt (1995) 'The price-choice relationship: a contingent processing approach', *Journal of Business Research*, **33**, 207–218.

Oxenfeldt, A.R. (1979) 'The differential method of pricing', *European Journal of Marketing*, **13** (4), 199–212.

Parker, A.J. (1979) 'A review and comparative analysis of retail grocery price variations', *Environment and Planning*, **11**, 1267–1288.

Parsons, L.J. and W.B. Price (1972) 'Adaptive pricing by a retailer', *Journal of Marketing Research*, **4** (2), 127–133.

Progressive Grocer (1964) 'How much do customers know about retail prices?' *Progressive Grocer*, **43** (2), 104–106.

Prus, R. (1986) 'It's on "sale": an examination of vendor perspectives, activities and dilemmas', *Canadian Review of Sociology and Anthropology*, **23** (1), 72–96.

Rao, A.R. and M.E. Bergen (1992) 'Price premium variations as a consequence of buyers' lack of information', *Journal of Consumer Research*, **19** (December), 412–423.

Rao, A.R. and K.B. Monroe (1989) 'The effect of price, brand name and store name on buyers' subjective product assessments: an integrative review', *Journal of Marketing Research*, **26** (3), 351–357.

Rao, A.R. and W.A. Sieben (1992) 'The effect of prior knowledge on price acceptability and the type of information examined', *Journal of Consumer Research*, **19** (September), 256–270.

Reibstein, D.J. and H. Gatignon (1984) 'Optimal product line pricing: the influence of elasticities and cross-elasticities', *Journal of Marketing Research*, **21** (3), 259–67.

Retail Review (1998) 'More experimentation with local pricing', *Retail Review*, **245** (August), 6.

Retail Review (1999a) 'The shape of things to come', *Retail Review*, **253** (June), 7.

Retail Review (1999b) 'Grocers referred to MMC—the official rationale', *Retail Review*, **251** (April) 4–5.

Retail Review (2000) 'Pricing—the local factor', *Retail Review*, **260**, 2–3.

Retail Review (2001) '2000—year of the Comet', *Retail Review*, **271**, 17.

Riesz, P.C. (1978) 'Price versus quality in the market place, 1961–1975', *Journal of Retailing*, **54** (4), 15–28.

Rinne, H.J., S.W. Bither and M.D. Henry (1986), 'The effect of price deals on retail store performance: an empirical investigation', *International Journal of Retailing*, **1** (3), 3–16.

Russell, G.J. and A. Petersen (2000) 'Analysis of cross category dependence in market basket selection', *Journal of Retailing*, **76** (3), 367–392.

Sampson, R.T. (1964) 'Sense and sensitivity in pricing', *Harvard Business Review*, **42** (6), 99–105.

Schindler, R.M. and T.M. Kibarian (1996) 'Increased consumer sales response through use of 99-ending prices', *Journal of Retailing*, **72** (2), 187–199.

Schindler, R.M. and P.N. Kirby (1997) 'Patterns of rightmost digits used in advertised prices: implications for nine-ending effects' *Journal of Consumer Research*, **24** (September) 192–201.

Sexton, D.E. (1974) 'Differences in food shopping habits by area of residence, race and income', *Journal of Retailing*, **50** (1), 37–48, 91.

Shugan, S.M. and R. Desiraju (2001) 'Retail product-line pricing strategy when costs and products change', *Journal of Retailing*, **77** (1), 17–38.

Simmons, J.C. (1988) 'The development of spatial price level comparison in the State of Florida', in *World Comparison of Incomes, Prices and Product*, J. Salazar-Carrillo and D.S. Prasada Rao (eds), North Holland, Amsterdam.

Sjolander, R. (1992) 'Cross-cultural effects of price on perceived product quality', *European Journal of Marketing*, **26** (7), 34–44.

Smith, M.F. and I. Sinha (2000) 'The impact of price and extra product promotions on store preference', *International Journal of Retail & Distribution Management*, **28** (2), 83–92.

Smith, S., N. Agrawal and S.H. McIntyre (1998) 'A discrete optimisation model for seasonal merchandising planning', *Journal of Retailing*, **74** (2), 193–221.

Stiving, M. and R.S. Winer (1997) 'An empirical analysis of price endings with scanner data', *Journal of Consumer Research*, **24** (June), 57–67.

Stockwell, D. and T. Stockwell (1992) 'EDLP—everyday low prices', *Office Products International*, December, 24–26.

Stoclet, D. (1990) 'Quelle politique de prix pour les grandes surfaces alimentaires', *Points de Vente*, **380** (15 Feburary) 34.

Stoetzel, J. (1954), 'Le prix comme limite', in *La Psychologie Economique*, P.L. Reynaud (ed.), Librarie Marcel Riviere et Cie, Paris, pp.184–188.

SuperMarketing (1994) 'How low can you go?', *SuperMarketing*, 19 August, 15–18.

SuperMarketing (1995) 'Two-tiered pricing inside the chiller', *SuperMarketing*, 12 May, 15.

SuperMarketing (1996) 'Advantage ASDA', *SuperMarketing*, 28 June, 22–24.

Thaler, R. (1985) 'Mental accounting and consumer choice', *Marketing Science*, **4** (3), 199–214.

Tinn, I. (1982) 'Some problems with pricing research', *Journal of the Market Research Society*, **24** (4), 317–34.

Trout, J. and S. Rivkin (1998) 'Prices: simple guidelines to get them right', *Journal of Business Strategy*, **18** (6), 13–16.

Twedt, D.W. (1965) 'Does the "9 fixation" in retail pricing really promote sales?', *Journal of Marketing*, **29** (4), 54–55.

Urbany, J. E., P. R. Dickson and A. G. Sawyer (2000) 'Insights into cross- and within-store price search: retailer estimates vs. consumer self reports', *Journal of Retailing*, **76** (2), 243–258.

Van Heerde, H.J., P.S.H. Leeflang and D.R. Wittink (2000) 'The estimation of pre- and post promotion dips with store-level scanner data', *Journal of Marketing Research*, **37** (3), 383–395.

Van Praag, B. and B. Bode (1992) 'Retail pricing and the costs of clearance sales: the formalisation of a rule of thumb', *European Economic Review*, **36** (4), 945–962.

Verdict (1993) *Food Pricing Survey*, Verdict Research, London.

Vilcassim, N.J. and P.K. Chintagunta (1995) 'Investigating retailer product category pricing from household scanner panel data', *Journal of Retailing*, **71** (2), 103–128.

Volle, P. (2001) 'The short-term effect of store-level promotions on store choice, and the moderating role of individual variables', *Journal of Business Research*, **53**, 63–73.

Wakefield, K.L. and J.J. Inman (1993) 'Who are the price vigilantes? An investigation of the differentiating characteristics influencing price information processing', *Journal of Retailing*, **69** (2), 216–233.

Walters, R.G. (1991) 'Assessing the impact of retail price promotions on product substitution, complementary purchase and interstore sales displacement', *Journal of Marketing*, **55** (April), 17–28.

Which? (1995) 'Save on shopping', *Which?*, **38** (January), 14-18.

Wilkinson, J.B., J.B. Mason and C.H. Paksoy (1982) 'Assessing the impact of short-term supermarket strategy variables', *Journal of Marketing Research*, **19** (1), 72–86.

Wilkinson, J.B., E.M. Smith and J.B. Mason (1973) 'Number and value of food specials in different socioeconomic areas', *Journal of Retailing*, **49** (3), 34–41.

Wood, D. (1976) *Food Prices near Three Superstores*, Social and Community Planning Research, London.

Zotos, Y. and S. Lysonski (1993) 'An exploration of the quantity surcharge concept in Greece', *European Journal of Marketing*, **27** (10), 5–18.

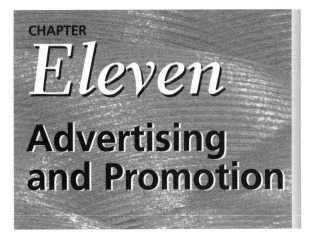

CHAPTER

Eleven

Advertising and Promotion

INTRODUCTION Advertising has become a major area of marketing expenditure and a key element of the marketing mix for most large-scale retailers. Several companies now spend over £20 million annually on media advertising, in addition to their expenditures on other forms of promotional activity. Advertising is usually defined as non-personal or one-way form of communication conducted through paid media under clear sponsorship. Advertising has a number of distinctive characteristics, notably:

- presenting a totally controllable message
- delivering messages to large numbers of people at low cost per 'contact'
- communicating rapidly with many people at the same time (Wilmshurst and Mackay, 1999).

In most retail marketing contexts, the store itself also provides many forms of non-personal communications, such as displays, design and the overall ambience; these store-based influences are the subject of the next chapter. The main focus of this chapter is on media advertising decisions, although consideration is also given to sales promotion, sponsorship and other forms of public relations activity.

It would appear obvious that retail advertising must be an integral component of overall marketing strategy. There have, however, been many instances of advertising being pursued almost independently of, or as a substitute for, an adequate retail strategy; under such circumstances, any benefits gained through the expenditure on advertising are likely to be very short-lived. There is little point in making specific claims or attempting to build images that are not reinforced by the product-service mix of the stores themselves. It is important therefore that the communication objectives be clearly defined, whether these be strategic or short-term tactical; for example:

1 *To win new customers*: the emphasis may be upon customers entering the geographical area or the relevant age category for the first time; in most cases, however, new customers must be won from competitors by

communicating the differential advantages of the store. When a new store is opened, an intensive local campaign is usually launched to create an awareness among target groups. In forms of non-store retailing, the advertising objective may be to attract initial enquiries from potential new customers.

2 *To increase expenditure by existing customers*: by increasing awareness of new departments or products, the variety and volume of sales to existing customers may increase. Some campaigns have as a primary objective the promotion of store credit card usage, to increase loyalty and provide better communications with customers. With more customer-specific information, subsequent campaigns can be targeted at specific market segments or may seek to increase the visit frequency of irregular shoppers.

3 *To increase store traffic*: special sales are frequently promoted to increase traffic during the dull periods. Alternatively, the promotion may seek to capture the maximum share of peak-season traffic by emphasizing particular advantages. In that many stores operate within shopping centres, such traffic-building promotions are sometimes conducted in co-operation with other retailers or shopping centre management.

4 *To increase product sales*: the emphasis may be upon specific products, to clear particular lines of merchandise or to utilize opportunities for co-operative advertising with manufacturers. A campaign may seek to establish association with well-known branded products or be used to announce the arrival of new lines. Alternatively, the focus may be upon promoting the quality, value and/or uniqueness of the retailer's own-brand products.

5 *To develop the store image*: all advertising is likely to influence image, but some campaigns are primarily image oriented. These usually seek to build the longer-term reputation and increase consumer confidence in the retailer's product and service expertise. Advertising may be used to increase awareness of the retailer's positive attributes and to communicate store policies; a secondary objective may also be to build the loyalty and confidence of staff. A campaign may be linked to specific public relations efforts to create goodwill for the retailer.

Retail advertising may therefore have many different primary and secondary goals, which require the use of different creative and media treatments. Some retailers, including J. Sainsbury, have used more than one agency to deal with their different advertising requirements. Sometimes different promotional objectives are pursued in different areas, according to local competitive and market conditions. While some of the objectives summarized above are quite compatible, others clearly are not. In defining the communication objectives, the retail advertiser must therefore ensure that local or short-term expedients are not in conflict with overall image requirements.

The need for integration across a company's marketing communications is paramount. Various terms have been coined by promotional agencies to emphasize this imperative:

'New advertising', 'orchestration', 'whole-egg', 'seamless communication', 'integrated marketing communications'. The integration of specialised communications functions that previously have operated with varying degrees of autonomy (Duncan and Everett, 1993).

11.1 Trends in Retail Advertising and Promotion

This section looks at five elements of retail advertising and promotion. First, the growth in expenditure on media advertising and the major differences that exist between companies are summarized. Second, the importance of co-operative advertising is considered, notably advertising that is financed at least partially by the manufacturers. Third, the growth in the utilization of sales promotions is reviewed, noting the wide range of techniques, retailers' preferences and international restrictions. Fourth, the developing role of public relations within the retail communications mix is assessed. Finally, the section looks at the use of sponsorship to reinforce corporate image.

11.1.1 Advertising Expenditures

Summaries of retail advertising expenditures say little about the effectiveness of this advertising, but they do indicate the strong commitment to media advertising of many major retailers.

Talk of the 'death of advertising' (e.g. Rust and Oliver, 1994) is, to say the least, premature as far as retailers are concerned. True, growth in the 1980s and early 1990s was sluggish, compared with the phenomenal growth in retail advertising in the 1970s. However, through the 1990s, retail advertising expenditure more than doubled from £423 million in 1991 to £1034 million in 2000 (Nielsen 1996; 2001). By that stage, the top 25 retailers accounted for over half of all UK advertising (Mintel, 1999).

This growth was in spite of the fact that retailers became well equipped to circumnavigate traditional media advertising, through direct marketing to loyalty card customers. Indeed, this has become an important part of the communications mix for many retailers. Such marketing activities do not, however, have the scope of television, radio, press, outdoor and cinema to reach customers of rival organizations, the primary targets of many marketing communications.

Table 11.1 shows the estimated expenditures of selected retail advertisers in 1996 and 2000. This list excludes the fast-food restaurants, such as McDonald's, which spent over £42 million in 2000. Even excluding such major spenders, there are now many retail companies in the UK which allocate over £10 million a year to media advertising. J. Sainsbury more than doubled its advertising spend through the 1990s from £15.5 million in 1991 to £33.3 million in 2000. Tesco reduced its advertising in the mid-1990s, from £20.3 million in 1994 to £15.0 million in 1996, increased spending levels to £27.8 million in 1999, cutting back to £19.5 million by 2000 (Nielsen, 2001).

Retailer	1996 £000s	2000 £000s
J. Sainsbury	20 669	33 293
B & Q	12 073	29 374
PC World	15 850	27 860
Currys	24 073	27 239
DFS Northern Upholstery	14 666	26 279
Homebase	6 100	25 074
Comet	19 334	20 066
Tesco	15 006	19 532
Asda	14 253	17 787
Dixons	13 527	15 266
Iceland	10 680	14 784
Woolworths	9 483	13 550
Boots the Chemist	8 271	12 483

The estimates within Table 11.1 also reveal the advertising costs associated with operating more than one retail name. The combined expenditures of Dixons, Currys and PC World amounted to £70.4 million, making the group collectively the largest retail advertiser. Likewise, J. Sainsbury and Homebase spent £58.4 million on advertising these two retail brands. Although there are many good reasons why sections of the Kingfisher Group retain their separate identities, it is notable that B & Q, Comet and Woolworths advertising cost around £63 million. The cost of rebranding Presto stores under the Safeway banner, estimated at between £5 million and £7 million, seems modest by comparison (SuperMarketing, 1996).

To place such data in context, Table 11.2 provides estimates of the advertising to sales ratios of six leading retailers. This illustrates the benefits of economies of scale in retail advertising. In the mid-1980s, Asda was spending around 0.5 per cent of sales on advertising. As the chain expanded and significantly increased market share, a similar level of advertising expenditure (in real terms) in 2000 represented just 0.21 per cent of sales.

Retailer	1986 %	2000 %
Asda	0.51	0.21
Boots The Chemist	0.50	0.31
B & Q	2.16	1.31
Marks & Spencer	—	0.07
J. Sainsbury	0.20	0.25
Tesco	0.29	0.11

Similarly, B & Q has been able to increase the strength of its advertising while reducing the advertising/sales ratio. Marks & Spencer, which hardly employed media advertising in the 1980s, was spending nearly £5 million by 2000. However, this still comprised only 0.07 per cent of sales. These ratios appear modest when compared with those of some consumer product manufacturers. Nielsen (2001) estimates typical advertising/sales ratios in the following sectors:

Soups	4.33 per cent
Shavers	6.07 per cent
Cereals	8.75 per cent
Toys, games	10.45 per cent
Nail-care products	16.47 per cent
Indigestion remedies	20.92 per cent
Hair colourants	34.53 per cent

11.1.2 Co-operative Advertising

Co-operative advertising occurs when two or more organizations sponsor an advertisement to promote their goods/services jointly. It is necessary to distinguish between horizontal and vertical co-operative advertising. In the former case, two or more retailers may get together to promote their advantages in common or to build traffic in their shopping centre. Vertical co-operative advertising, on the other hand, signifies agreements between suppliers and retailers to promote the product(s) and the stores jointly. Horizontal and vertical arrangements sometimes operate together, for example when a specific product or range is advertised and a number of retailers are listed or mentioned within the advertisement.

Vertical co-operative advertising can result in many different formats. Where the manufacturer is the dominant partner and the retailer or dealer is a small independent, the format may essentially be a product advertisement with the retailer's name inserted within the copy or at the end of the soundtrack (Marken, 1992). Where the retailer holds the balance of power and is in control of the advertising programme, the manufacturer's product may simply be one of many that are listed, pictured or mentioned within the advertisement. In that neither of these extremes provides a 'fair' balance of exposure, formats have been developed which give more equal emphasis to both parties. For example, some television commercials feature a specific well-known product for the first half, then switch to promoting the attributes of the store.

In the UK, advertising allowances have tended to become just another element within the negotiations between major retail buyers and their suppliers. Manufacturers often complain that such allowances are simply treated as a further price reduction or contribution to the retailer's gross margin. One industry commentator described major retailers' co-operative advertising policies as 'sheer blackmail'. Many manufacturers feel that the advertising appropriation is simply being used to develop retailers' images (Mintel, 1988). Even when the product is given reasonable exposure within the advertisement, manufacturers often feel that they have lost full control of the copy, placement, timing and media, possibly to the detriment of their promotional objectives.

In spite of these major reservations, there are reasons why manufacturers continue to offer co-operative advertising allowances. Curhan and Kopp (1987/88) noted that packaged goods manufacturers in the USA offer around twenty times more promotions than can be adequately supported by the retail trade; a similar 'promotional overload' exists in many other countries. In a largely theoretical study, Jorgensen et al. (2000) provided some evidence of a win–win situation, when manufacturers and retailers get together to advertise.

Advertising allowances may be a requirement for obtaining retailer support, or even retail listing. There are, however, some positive benefits for the manufacturer. Linkages with retail advertising can achieve greater local penetration of message and can stress local availability (Young and Greyser, 1983). The advertisements may also spur other retailers to promote or at least stock the product. In some cases, the image of the product may also be enhanced if linked to the name of a prestigious store. Small retailers should be rewarded appropriately if the co-operative campaign benefits other retailers' sales (Bergen and John, 1997).

Given the widespread availability of co-operative advertising allowances, the benefits and drawbacks of such advertising must be carefully evaluated by the retailer. Advantages may be summarized in the following terms, although some of these factors are clearly more applicable to smaller retail firms.

1 Advertising funds are increased, which in turn may lead to better discounts on media costs or agency commissions.
2 The increased funds may provide access to more diverse and/or powerful media than the retailer alone would have wished to finance.
3 A judicious selection of co-operative advertising partnerships can bring additional profits and prestige to the retailer.
4 A tie-up to a manufacturer's major advertising campaign can bring benefits beyond those yielded directly by the co-operative advertisements themselves.
5 Smaller retailers, without their own advertising staff or agency resources, can benefit from the quality of more professionally prepared copy.
6 Similarly, the retailer can benefit from the manufacturer's research into the best focus, timing, etc. for the advertisements.
7 If a retailer is not in a powerful bargaining position, the costs of such allowances may in any event be 'built into' the supply prices offered by the manufacturer.

There are, however, major drawbacks associated with co-operative advertising, which have caused some major retailers to limit such activities. The main drawbacks can be summarized as follows:

1 The products with the best advertising allowances may not offer the best short- or long-term profitability to the store; buyers should therefore take care to buy the products, not the allowances.

2 Excessive promotion of specific items may reduce the stores' perceived integrity as the provider of product choice and impartial advice; largely for this reason, the Neiman-Marcus chain formerly specified that no more than 20 per cent of advertising could be run with co-operative funds (Spitzer and Schwartz, 1982).

3 Too great a proportion of co-operative advertising may limit the scope for the retailer's own local or seasonal promotions.

4 The image of the products may not be consistent with the retailer's image-building requirements; for example, the co-operative allowances offered to promote a packaged 'junk food' may be excellent, but this could be in total conflict with a strategy of promoting the retailer as a supplier of fresh and healthy foods.

5 Co-operative advertising may lead to a 'sameness' if the emphasis is upon products and prices; this is in conflict with most retailers' need to differentiate themselves using more theme or institutional advertising.

6 Unless handled professionally, some forms of co-operative advertising for small stores can create ambiguity; for example, a glossy product advertisement shown in a cinema with a badly recorded retail announcement at the end can provoke entirely the wrong reaction from the audience!

7 The task of obtaining or supplying evidence of advertising exposure may prove a burden to the smaller retailer and may also lead to disputes with suppliers (Wilcox and Szathmary, 1991), although some third party agencies are available to assist with documentation.

In spite of these major reservations, co-operative advertising was estimated to be worth around £50 million in the UK (Mintel, 1988). As discussed in Chapter 8, much secrecy surrounds terms of trade, so it is not possible to quantify co-operative advertising deals precisely. From a study of 381 contracts in the USA, Haight (1976) found the following breakdown of manufacturer contributions:

Proportion of advertising cost paid by manufacturer	*Proportion of contracts in the survey*
Below 50 per cent	1.3 per cent
Around 50 per cent	61.9 per cent
60–80 per cent	15.7 per cent
100 per cent	21.0 per cent

One of the most systematic studies of co-operative advertising was undertaken, also in the USA, by Young and Greyser (1983). They considered the 'dual-signature' problem, the question of just whose name is primarily associated with the advertisement by consumers. One manufacturer was quoted as saying:

'Co-op is by definition a program of conflict. Two organisations, which by their very nature have different objectives, are sharing the cost of a common effort'.

On a more positive note, from a study of a furniture manufacturer's advertising programme, Somers et al. (1990) conclude:

'Co-operative advertising represents a blending of the resources of two organisations, each with different goals but both with certain common goals'.

It should be borne in mind, however, that advertising and promotional allowances are subject to many federal and local regulations in the USA, including the Robinson-Patman Act (Edwards and Lebowitz, 1981). In the UK, there are few external regulations upon the retail buyers' ability to demand advertising allowances, or upon the use that is made of these. Extensive allowances therefore continue to be paid to the more powerful retailers, even though there has been a marked decline in the product and specific price emphasis within their retail advertisements.

11.1.3 Sales Promotions

Increasing levels of advertising clutter, along with increases in many media costs, have led to some shifting of promotional budgets away from conventional advertising and towards sales promotion activities (Lichtenstein et al., 1995). Expenditures on sales promotion activities are much harder to estimate than advertising expenditures, given the wide diversity of activities, plus the lack of formal audit mechanisms for most of these. In the USA, Papatla and Krishnamurthi (1996) suggest that expenditure on sales promotions has grown to approximately double that on advertising. Advertising Association data for the UK suggest more modest growth but problems of definition hinder such comparisons (Wilmshurst and Mackay, 1999).

Sales promotions comprise a major part of what agencies often call 'below-the-line' expenditure, i.e., expenditure upon which the agency would not normally obtain a percentage commission. This contrasts with 'above-the-line', a term describing expenditures on various commissionable media. The growth of power of major retailers has played an instrumental role in diverting manufacturer expenditures from 'above-' to 'below-the-line' activities. (Laspadakis, 1999). Not only must manufacturers help major retailers with their advertising costs, they must also contribute to their sales promotion activities.

Based upon a survey of 44 food retailers in South Africa, Table 11.3 summarizes the relative popularity of various sales promotion types, both for the promotion of national and own brands. Price-off promotions, coupons, in-store demonstrators, sampling, on-pack competitions, special display placements and point-of-sale material are used by over 80 per cent of the sample. Most of the sales promotion types play a greater role in the promotion of national brands, possibly reflecting manufacturer contributions towards the costs. An exception is the

Table 11.3 Retailer use of sales promotion techniques

Source: derived from Abratt et al. (1995, p. 450).

Sales promotion technique	% of retailers using to:	
	Promote national brands	Promote own brands
Price-off promotions	80	87
Coupons	89	43
Refunds for multiple purchase	32	20
Bonus packs	64	37
In-store demonstrators	98	60
On-pack premiums	73	27
Continuity coupons	41	13
Sampling	89	54
In-store competitions	61	40
Mail-in competitions	61	30
On-pack competitions	87	27
Special display positions	96	90
Merchandising stands	75	40
Point-of-sale material	91	73

price-off category, a form of promotion towards which a sample of manufacturers expressed less positive attitudes (Abratt et al., 1995).

Coupons have proved to be a powerful inducement for consumers to switch brand (e.g. Lichtenstein et al., 1990). However, there is evidence that consumers tend to revert to pre-coupon choice behaviour after redemption (e.g. Kahn and Louie, 1990). As retailers tend to stock many brands, this switching back may be of less significance to them. Indeed, coupons are now used extensively within the mail-outs to retailers' loyalty card customers. Competitions, not limited to the on-pack variety, are also increasingly popular among retailers. From a three-year study of 2646 sales promotion competitions, Peattie and Peattie (1993) found that 47 per cent were sponsored by retailers.

Sales promotion activity may be driven by a number of different objectives, which can influence the choice of sales promotion vehicle. From their retailer sample, Abratt et al. (1995) identified 10 major objectives, listed below in descending order of rated importance:

1 To encourage more frequent or multiple purchases.
2 To counter competitive promotional activity.
3 To build trial among non-users.
4 To introduce new or improved products or services.
5 To capitalize on seasonal, geographic or creative advantages.
6 To encourage repeat usage.
7 To stimulate unplanned purchase.
8 To attract switching to own brand.
9 To fight competitors' advertising.
10 To induce trade-ups to larger sizes.

Promotion technique	UK	NL	B	SP	IR	IT	F	G	DK
On-pack promotions	✔	✔	?	✔	✔	✔	?	✔	✔
Branded offers	✔	?	?	✔	✔	✔	?	✔	✔
In-pack premiums	✔	?	?	✔	✔	✔	?	?	?
Multi-purchase offers	✔	?	?	✔	✔	✔	?	✔	✔
Extra product	✔	✔	✔	✔	✔	✔	?	✘	✔
Free product	✔	?	✔	✔	✔	✔	✔	✘	?
Reusable/other use packs	✔	✔	✔	✔	✔	✔	✔	?	✔
Free mail-ins	✔	✔	?	✔	✔	✔	?	✔	✔
With purchase premiums	✔	?	✔	✔	✔	✔	?	✘	?
Cross-product offers	✔	✔	✘	✔	✔	✔	✔	✔	✔
Collector offers	✔	✔	✔	✔	✔	✔	✔	✔	✔
Competitions	✔	?	?	✔	✔	?	✔	✔	?
Self-liquidating promotions	✔	✔	✔	✔	✔	✔	✔	✔	✔
Free draws	✔	✘	?	✔	✔	✔	✔	✔	✔
Share outs	✔	✔	?	✔	✔	?	?	✔	✘
Sweepstake/lottery	?	✘	?	✔	✘	?	?	?	✘
Money-off vouchers	✔	✔	✔	✔	✔	✔	✔	✔	✔
Money off next purchase	✔	✔	✔	✔	✔	✔	✔	✘	✔
Cashbacks	✔	✔	✔	✔	✔	✘	✔	✘	✔
In-store demos	✔	✔	✔	✔	✔	✔	✔	✔	✔

Table 11.4 Regulation of sales promotion techniques

Key: ✔ = permitted
✘ = not permitted
? = restrictions.

Source: Vantagepoint (2000), based upon information supplied by the Institute of Sales Promotion.

As in the case of seasonal sales (Chapter 10), the use of sales promotions is governed by a number of country-specific regulations. Table 11.4 summarizes the techniques that are allowed, not permitted or subject to some restrictions in nine European countries. From this analysis, it is clear that Spain, Ireland and the UK are relatively permissive, with regard to sales promotions, compared with many of their European neighbours. Money-off vouchers are permitted in most countries, as are self-liquidating promotions, i.e., those that pay for themselves through consumer participation. Other popular devices, such as competitions and multi-purchase offers, are generally allowed but are subject to restrictions in some countries.

11.1.4 Public Relations

With the rising cost of media advertising, increased attention is now being paid to other forms of publicity. This, too, has been stimulated by the advertising 'clutter' that exists in many traditional media and the problems therefore of conveying a clear and distinctive message within those media. The trend towards more powerful retailer branding has also favoured the use of longer-term publicity devices, such as sponsorships. Used judiciously, publicity may also achieve higher credibility than conventional advertising, in that the communication usually reaches the consumer through an impartial intermediary, such as a journalist or a television commentator.

Retailing has always had its share of entrepreneurs with a flair for publicity, but few retail organizations now leave this to chance. Even modest-sized companies tend to have a press officer or a member of the sales promotion staff nominated for press liaison. Most larger companies now have public relations sections and/or utilize the services of specialist PR agencies. It is not sufficient just to do things that are 'newsworthy'; a professional approach is required to ensure that press notices reach the right people in the right format and at the right time. Given the appropriate written and pictorial material, journalists and editors may be highly receptive, as it it 'easy' news and it satisfies a demand for local, consumer-oriented information.

The relationship between public relations (PR) and marketing within organizations has been the subject of some debate. Grunig and Grunig (1998) conclude that PR is most excellent when it is strategic, but when marketing does not dominate PR: the activities of PR and marketing have many distinctive features (Kitchen, 1997). However, the emergence of the term 'marketing public relations' (MPR) is indicative of the potential for PR to add a strong voice to a company's marketing communications mix (Kitchen and Papsolomou, 1999).

While consumers remain a major focus of PR activites, retail organizations also have other important 'publics' that they need to influence:

- shareholders and the city
- central and local government
- local communities
- the media
- opinion leaders
- employees and their families
- trade unions
- suppliers.

Given the influence of retail analysts upon share prices, good corporate PR (CPR) with the city can help avert hostile takeovers. In Chapter 7, we have already seen how PR activities can help win the support of local communities and local government, when planning permission is sought for new stores. High profile employment policies, such as B & Q's positive approach to employing the over 50s, can win the approval of government, the unions and employees, while also influencing an important customer segment. Gray (1998) quotes a number of PR activities of major UK multiples:

1 Tesco/BBC documentary 'superstore': as well as demonstrating a degree of openness, this communicated an efficient and innovative image, along with a caring attitude towards employees and customers.
2 Tesco campaign against (arguably) overpriced branded products: among much publicity, Levi, Calvin Klein, Adidas, Nike, Sony and others were sold at discounted prices.

3 Sainsbury's campaign to help village shops: they were allowed to sell Sainsbury own labels to help them ward off superstore competition in nearby towns.

4 Asda campaigns against resale price (RPM) on books and pharmaceutical products.

Timing can be crucially important, being seen as a prime mover for a particular cause. Consumers seem especially well disposed towards retailers who step in quickly, for example, to offer aid following floods, tornadoes or other disasters (Ellen et al., 2000). Retailers that are quick to assert their corporate social responsibility positions can also achieve greater advantage than those that follow later. For example, Iceland's position on genetically modified (GM) foods and B & Q's green purchasing and supply policies attracted much positive PR (Piacentini et al., 2000). However, the long-term, socially responsible stances of Body Shop and Benetton raise consumer expectations, leaving the companies vulnerable to a wide range of potential criticisms.

One measure of effectiveness of PR is the number of articles written in newspapers and magazines. Press Watch monitors material written about over 1000 companies, classifying it into favourable and

Table 11.5 The PR mix

Source: adapted from Smith (1993); Vantagepoint (2000).

Products and services	
Quality matches promise	Customer relations
Quality assurance	Courtesy magazines
Third party endorsement	Information services
Customer services	Complaints
Ethics and social responsibility	
Employee relations	Issue management
Internal communications	Environment
Community relations	Education
Community involvement	Employment
Open days	Health
Crisis management	Safety
Dealing with disasters	
Corporate image	
Communications audit	Design management
Corporate communications	Logo, letterhead, reports,
Corporate advertising	Signage, buildings, etc.
Publicity	
Public speaking	Media relations
Lectures	Press conferences
Conferences	Interviews
Events	Photocalls
News event management	Press releases
Sponsorship	
Choice of event, sport, team,	Event management
player, activity, charity	Supporting advertising
	Image monitoring

unfavourable comment, then reports quarterly. In a series of five reports in 1997/98, Tesco was consistently within the top six, achieving at times first or second place. Commenting on this success, Gray (1998) quotes the corporate communications manager of Tesco: 'It's about doing what is right for the customer ... It's about business strategy. It's not about positioning.'

Table 11.5 summarizes the diverse elements of the 'PR mix'. Clearly, not all the activities can be carefully scheduled and stage-managed. Some of the work of PR/corporate communications is about damage limitation, reacting quickly to the potential for bad news. The sequence of health-related issues that has hit the food industry has been a major test of the integration between strategy, marketing and PR. Companies that have got this act together are able to respond quickly, decisively and publicly, for example, in eliminating GM ingredients from their own products.

11.1.5 Sponsorships

Sponsorship has been a part of retailers' PR mix for many years but the emerging 'science' of sponsorship is of recent origin. The objectives and target audiences of a sponsorship activity should be clear, and defined criteria applied in the choice of sponsorship. In common with all forms of promotion, efforts should be made to assess the extent to which objectives have been met. Figure 11.1 summarizes possible objectives and the audiences typically targetted by the sponsorship.

Logically, these and other, more specific objectives translate into a number of criteria that can be applied when evaluating sponsorship opportunities. The following list of criteria is derived from Thwaites (1994) and Quester et al. (1998):

▶ naming of event
▶ name linked to event
▶ exclusivity
▶ low risk of ambush
▶ long-term association

Figure 11.1 Sponsorship objectives and audiences

Source: adapted from Hoek (1999).

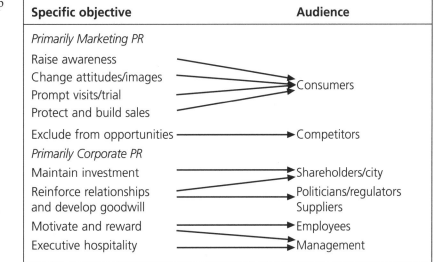

- good fit with image
- clean image/lower risk
- opportunity for differentiation
- new event
- can be incorporated into advertising and promotions
- media coverage available
- audience profile measurable
- audience size measurable
- cost/budget constraints
- executive personal preferences
- employee morale
- executive entertainment.

The term 'ambush marketing' has entered the sponsorship vocabulary to refer to an organization that claims association with an event, without incurring the costs of official sponsorship. When McDonald's were sponsoring the Winter Olympics, Wendy's used ski-racing posters and printed Olympic stories on their tray liners (Quester, 1997). Meenaghan (1998) has proposed a number of anti-ambushing measures, ranging from more rigorous contractual arrangements through to increased expenditure on advertising and promotion of the sponsorship. Indeed, it has been suggested that this related expenditure should equal or exceed the actual cost of the sponsorship.

In attempting to understand better the potential effects of sponsorship, Crimmins and Horn (1996) have suggested a 'persuasive impact equation', wherein the persuasive impact is a function of four main variables:

1 Strength of the link with sponsor.
2 Duration of this link.
3 Gratitude felt due to the link.
4 Perceptual change due to the link.

Numerous examples illustrate how the strength of the link may fail to meet sponsors' expectation. Pope and Voges (1999) found little evidence of increased awareness that could be firmly attributable to sponsorship, rather than to the strength of the brand name or prior usage. As a previous Olympic sponsor, the retailer J.C. Penney enjoyed only short duration awareness, lasting little longer than the games themselves. Marks & Spencer, Wal-Mart and other sponsors of local good causes, however, enjoy a high level of gratitude within the relevant communities (Arnold et al., 1996). Marks & Spencer and Littlewoods were also among the five official sponsors of England's campaign to host the football World Cup in 2006 (MAI, 2000).

A qualitative approach to sponsorship evaluation was employed by d'Astous and Bitz (1995), who classified 2499 sentences from respondents exposed to sponsorship scenarios into four main categories:

1 *Event related*: exposure, overall evaluation, specific evaluation, size, interest felt.
2 *Sponsor related*: image, image modification, support of the event, involvement in the sponsorship, organization/creation, objectives.
3 *Sponsorship related*: sponsor/event link, nature (commercial/ philanthropic), commercial impact, costs for the public, effectiveness.
4 *Other comments*.

In a quantitative study of sports sponsorship response, Speed and Thompson (2000) utilized three main measures of effect, namely, favourability, interest and intention to use. They also constructed measures for many of the potential influences upon these outcomes. Harvey (2001) observes that sponsorship changes attitudes towards the sponsor, while advertising changes attitudes towards the product. In that retailer product and store brands are now closely interlinked, this suggests that retail sponsorship can be effective at both levels.

In an experimental study, Hoek et al. (1997) identified some attitude changes but no increases in patronage probabilities among those exposed to information about the company's sponsorship activity. Javalgi et al. (1994) used six image measures to assess differences between those who were aware and not aware of a retailer's sponsorship of a marathon race; however, only two of the six were in the predicted direction. Sponsorship has therefore become established as a significant part of the promotional mix, in pursuit of a variety of marketing and corporate objectives. However, the tools for evaluating effects are only just starting to catch up with the increased expenditure on sponsorship activities.

11.2 Advertising Decisions

This section considers five of the major decision areas facing the retail advertiser. First, alternative approaches to establishing the level of advertising expenditure are compared. The choice of an advertising agency is next considered, in that most major retailers use the service of at least one agency. Attention then turns to the creation of advertisements, specifically ways of establishing the most appropriate advertising content and message. The relative merits of television, press and other available advertising media are then compared. The final part of this section examines approaches to the timing of advertisements, including considerations of seasonality.

11.2.1 Determining Expenditure Levels

The opportunities to advertise are almost without limit, and retailers are constantly under pressure to increase their advertising expenditures. Media owners naturally have a vested interest in advocating increased advertising, and agencies too are likely to benefit from larger expenditures. Pressure from the retailers' own branch and merchandise management, plus manufacturers' co-operative deals, may also contribute to an upwards drift in advertising expenditures. An objective approach to the task of establishing budgets is therefore required, in order to resist these pressures and to impose a financial discipline upon advertising managers and the agency. The budgets also form the framework within which the details of creative treatment and media schedules can be planned. Most companies do, however, allow a modest contingency fund, in order to allow reaction to unexpected opportunities or threats.

There are several different approaches that may be taken to establishing budgets, with varying degrees of merit. Among the least meritorious are the 'historical' methods, whereby budgets are simply an adjustment of previous years' budgets; obviously, the approach has little logic, in terms of either financial or marketing objectives. The 'arbitrary' or 'affordable' method bases allocations upon the level that controllers feel could be met that year, based upon financial estimates. This ignores the effects of advertising upon sales, introduces instability in the advertising programme from year to year and also tends to reduce advertising when it may be most needed. Elements of these approaches are still found within the budget planning of some retailers, although most major retailers now use one or a combination of the following methods.

Percentage-of-Sales Method

Using this method, the advertising budget is set as a percentage of recent or expected sales. The advertising expenditures of some of the UK's major retailer advertisers are expressed in Table 11.2 as a percentage of their sales. A merit of the approach is that advertising tends to remain within the affordable range; it may also encourage competitive stability within a sector if most other retailers use the same method. The approach may be useful for a wide-assortment retailer in allocation of advertising funds between departments, in that the industry norms in each product sector can be used as a guide (Kaufman, 1980). In a survey of 126 retailers by Ramaseshan (1990), including many smaller companies, the percentage-of-sales method was the most frequently used approach.

The drawbacks are that sales are allowed to determine advertising levels, whereas advertising should be regarded as a determinant of sales. The approach also tends to inhibit flexibility and experimentation with different inputs of advertising. It is not based upon a systematic analysis of the cost-effectiveness of advertising in achieving the various national and local, long-term and short-term goals of the company. White and Miles (1996) argue strongly that the long-term effects of advertising are neglected within most budgeting approaches: 'advertising is indeed a strategic investment in the organisation's stock of intangible assets, future cash flows and market value'.

Competitive Parity Method

The retailer establishes a budget equal to or above that of competitors. Typically, this would be based upon competitors' recent expenditures, as published by Media Expenditure Analysis Ltd or the Media Register. It is claimed that the competitive parity approach draws upon the collective wisdom of the sector and also tends to inhibit promotion wars, although neither claim is entirely valid. In that each company has different strategic objectives and is faced with different problems and opportunities, there is no reason why advertising expenditures should equate with those of competitors.

In a simulation exercise, Corfman and Lehmann (1994) found that competitive issues predominated among the considerations, namely:

▶ what they expected their opponents to do
▶ what their opponents did last time
▶ whether the competitive relationship was expected to continue market shares
▶ whether profit objectives were short or long term.

Danaher and Rust (1994) reviewed a number of variations upon the competitive parity method, including the use of advertising intensiveness curves (Jones, 1992). These plot competitors' market shares against their shares of voice, often leading to the conclusion that larger firms, which benefit from economies of scale, should spend a smaller percentage of their sales.

Objective and Task Method

Using this approach, the retail marketer is required to define detailed objectives, establish the tasks required to achieve these, and then estimate the costs of undertaking the tasks. The total of these costs forms the basis of the advertising budget. The method imposes a useful discipline, in that managers must more precisely define objectives and assumptions about relationships between advertising and sales, new customers, store image and/or customer loyalty. It also permits more systematic evaluations of the effects of the advertising in relation to each objective.

Of these three methods, the objective and task method clearly offers the most rigorous but difficult approach to determining advertising expenditure levels. Fulop (1988) described the specific objectives of Sainsbury in increasing its expenditure. Research had indicated a need to improve price perceptions; awareness of the company had to be built in new geographical areas and awareness needed to be developed of the wider product ranges in their newer, larger stores. From a study of a clothing retailer in the USA, D'Souza and Allaway (1995) concluded that budget allocation decisions (Sec. 11.2.5) across media and featured products are probably more important than decisions on the total budget.

It is also necessary to view the advertising budget as a part, albeit perhaps a major part, of the sales promotion budget. Intended allocations should also therefore be evaluated in terms of alternative uses for those funds, such as special events, publicity, displays or simply price cuts. In many companies this concept is taken a logical stage further, advertising expenditures being seen as an element of an overall 'strategic mix budget' or the 'customer motivation budget'. This philosophy encourages a more demanding and critical approach to advertising budgets, evaluating them against the effectiveness of other expenditures, such as store developments, refurbishments, product developments or additional customer services.

11.2.2 Selecting an Agency

The choice of an advertising agency can exert a major influence upon the results achieved from a given level of advertising expenditure. Retailers are faced with a wide choice of agencies, from the large, international organizations to the very small, often regionally based agencies. Some provide a full range of advertising and marketing services; others are specialists in specific functions, such as a creative work or media buying. A major retailer may decide to use different agencies to service its different advertising needs. A high-profile agency may be used for creativity, corporate identity and major initiatives, with one or more smaller, possibly cheaper agencies, used for local implementation (Vantagepoint, 2000).

Some retailers prefer to undertake all or part of their advertising work 'in-house'; for example, Next refused to use an agency for the initial launch of the 'Next Directory' home-shopping catalogue, declaring that agencies were too expensive (Britton, 1988). Most major retailers could develop the resources and media buying power to advertise without the help of agencies, but few elect to take this approach. Although a retailer would be unwise to delegate its strategic thinking to an agency, the input and stimulus provided by the agency can be a valuable contribution to its strategic planning. The creative and media buying services of an agency involve a range of specialist skills; to develop these in-house could reduce their flexibility in advertising approach. At the end of the day, the ability of clients to switch agencies imposes a continuous pressure to produce results.

The precise range and balance of services provided to retailers by their agencies differs in every case, depending upon the resources of each party and the specific needs of the retailer. The services are likely to include some or all of the following activities:

1 To assess the strengths and weaknesses of the client's stores, merchandise and image, vis-à-vis those of competitors.
2 To analyse the characteristics of the present and potential market, and of the client's competitive position.
3 In collaboration with the client, to determine the strategic plan, including relationships between advertising and other elements of the mix.
4 To define the specific objectives to be achieved by advertising.
5 To evolve a creative and media plan for presentation to the client.
6 To create and produce advertising copy, illustrations, soundtrack and television/film material for commercials.
7 To buy media space and time that will reach the maximum number of target customers at the lowest costs.
8 To evaluate the effectiveness of the advertising through both pre- and post-testing procedures.

Table 11.6
Considerations in
selecting an agency

Source: derived from Henke
(1995); Michell and
Sanders (1995);
Wilmshurst and Mackay
(1999); Woonbong et al.
(1999).

General reputation:	Proven track record Well known in the industry Large agency, or part of one Wins awards for its work
Skills base:	Creative skills Media planning and buying Marketing skills/consultancy Strategic planning capabilities Promotion/PR skills Direct marketing skills Electronic media experience Research facilities
People issues:	Access to senior managers Personal chemistry Low staff turnover Quality of account managers
Specific to client:	Relative size of client/agency Location and accessibility Retail sector experience No conflicts of interest Full service or specialist agency

Table 11.6 draws upon a number of sources to review typical considerations in selecting an advertising agency. The relative importance of these criteria varies from retailer to retailer. Whether or not the agency has a national or international reputation may be important to a large retailer, seeking major strategic and creative inputs. The considerations and priorities of smaller retailers are likely to be different (Fam and Merrilees, 1997). Collins (1992) suggests that a client should aim to represent between 5 and 20 per cent of an agency's business: below that range, the retailer may not receive the best service or value from the agency.

Compared with most other types of clients, retailers tend to be very demanding of their agencies. Although there has been a shift towards more theme advertising, many retailers still make extensive use of press and offer-based advertising. An agency therefore may produce 10 000 advertisements in a year, requiring swift movement from the brief to the finished art. Not surprisingly, the major retailers also wield their buying power, obtaining discounts an agency commissions.

Long-term loyalty to an agency is relatively uncommon. Henke (1995) reported that US agencies can expect to lose 67 per cent of existing accounts over the following five year period. Wilmshurst and Mackay (1999) recall an old agency saying: 'accounts are won by creativity but lost by administration'. A number of studies (e.g. Gofton, 1988; Henke, 1995; Michell et al., 1992) have examined factors lending to a client–agency split, which include:

> results not meeting expectations
> needed new ideas
> poor client service
> poor value for money
> not understanding client's problems
> agency in decline
> outgrown the agency
> need to rationalize agencies.

The early reluctance of some agencies to develop Internet expertise in-house has also been shown to put a strain upon client–agency relationships. In that good websites require frequent updating, and should co-ordinate with the other aspects of company communications, outsourcing this role both increases cost and potentially undermines loyalty (Durkin and Lawlor, 2001).

11.2.3 Content and Message

Because many retailers have shifted away from price as the major theme within their advertising, the selection of appropriate content and message formats has become a major decision area for retailers and their agencies. Although creativity has a major role to play in the production of advertisements, decisions on advertising content should be based upon sound research into consumers' motivations and the images held of the relevant stores. For example, Sainsbury's research indicated that it had acquired an austere and authoritarian image. Advertising therefore sought to portray a friendlier face and to create more of a relationship with the store's customers. Similarly, the image of Halfords was found to be solid, dependable and reliable; it was however perceived as a little boring, an impression that the company set out to overcome.

Based upon a technique developed by QED Research Ltd, Walters and White (1987) suggested a stage-by-stage route to the appropriate creative solution, which is summarized as follows:

1 Identify the store attributes and requirements that consumers consider to be most important when shopping in the particular retail sector.
2 Promotional emphasis should be reduced on attributes and requirements of low importance, as these are likely to be least effective in improving overall image.
3 Based upon the important factors, the store should be evaluated against competition to establish relevant strengths and weaknesses.
4 By reference to those with experience and greatest familiarity with the store, these strengths and weaknesses should be subdivided into those that are real and those that are 'illusory'
5 Serious consideration should be given to changing the store's actual attributes to correct real weaknesses and give substance to perceived strengths which are currently merely illusory.
6 The advertising strategy and creative solution is then formulated on the bases of (a) maintaining perceptions of real strengths,

(b) correcting perceptions of illusory weaknesses and (c) promoting any real improvements made to the store package.

7 The process of assessment and monitoring should continue, so as to provide inputs to retail strategy and advertising decisions.

There are, of course, significant methodological difficulties in ranking the importance of store attributes and in rating store images, as discussed in Chapters 3 and 5. This approach does, however, offer a systematic route between the consumer research and the creative solution. It can provide guidance on the general content of the advertisements, although decisions on how best to convey that content remain. Kapferer (1986) pointed out:

> *Traditionally, strategic communication platforms were only concerned by 'what to say'. Nowadays 'how to say it' is as important. It just cannot be abandoned to the hazards of mere creativity.*

In order to provide a framework for the creation of retail advertising, Kapferer presented the concept of an 'identity prism', illustrated in Fig. 11.2. The 'constructed sender' represents the physical and personality facets of the retail communicator; the 'constructed receiver' is the person to whom the advertising message is addressed. The six interrelated facets of the identity prism are as follows:

1 ***The physical facet***: the basic characteristic of the store, including prices, assortment, services, etc.; these are the traditional content of retail communications.

2 ***The personality facet***: the intangible personality characteristics ascribed to the store, such as the elitist store or the pioneering store; various projective techniques have been used to identify customers' symbolic images of stores.

Figure 11.2 The identity prism: facets of identity

Source: Kapferer (1986).

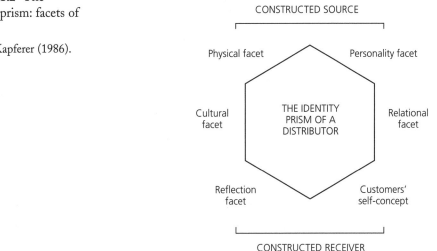

3 *The relational facet*: all retail activities involve a relationship between company and customers; this can be projected, for example, as a protection relationship, fighting against high prices, or as a guidance relationship, helping the customer through complex choices.

4 *The cultural facet*: particularly in the more specialized trades, stores may have cultural roots which can be utilized; for example, IKEA projects its Scandinavian origins, and their associations with good living, affluence and style; associations with various forms of popular culture may be projected by record and teenage fashion stores.

5 *The reflection facet*: the image of the customers that the store wishes to convey, which may not be a description of the target customers: this can be particularly important if research indicates that a low opinion is held of a store's customers. The choice of actors and models in advertisements make a strong statement about this facet.

6 *The self-concept facet*: the instrumental role of the store for customers' self-images; for example, in using a particular store a customer may feel himself or herself to be an astute shopper, a person 'in' fashion or a member of a restricted circle.

These six facets of the store identity provide useful direction for advertising research and creative solutions. They also draw attention to the dangers of creating a confused identity or ambiguity in advertisements if the facets are dissonant.

Other studies have stressed the importance of the people featured in advertisements, their body types, ethnicity (Jackson and Ross, 1997) and age (Carrigan and Szmigin, 1998). Among other aspects of style and content, the level of arousal caused by the pace of television commercials has been found to affect liking and believability. Yoon et al. (1998) provide compelling evidence of the power of well-chosen words, drawing parallels with Dostoevsky and other great works of literature. Among the many detailed aspects of an advertisement, the presence of a brand differentiating message is one of the most persuasive (Stewart and Furse, 2000).

The study of semiotics is of great relevance to advertising content, focusing upon the meanings and interpretations of signs (Hackley, 1999). In this context, the signs are likely to be verbal or visual but could also include tactile elements. Thus, logos, locations, actors' clothing, hairstyles, etc. can all communicate meanings and values to the viewer. Likewise, postures, facial expressions, accents and the tone/pace/volume of delivery will all supplement the words used (if any) in communicating an advertising message. Wal-Mart has considered carefully the semiotics of its advertising fliers:

> *They emphasise low prices, not sales. Unlike competitive fliers, which use professional models, they present 'plain folks', apparently ordinary people including Wal–Mart 'associates', spouses, children, parents, pets, suppliers and customers (Arnold et al., 2001).*

Quantitative approaches to the selection of advertising components have also been suggested. Green et al. (1984) presented the BENEMAX decision support system to assist in identifying sets of product features, benefits and image components for retail advertisements. Inputs to the system would comprise routinely collected survey data on consumers' store-feature and retail-feature preferences; background variables regarding store store usage, psychographics and demographics would also be input. The initial BENEMAX programmes develop a set of optimum advertising claims, i.e., the features, benefits and image components; further sub-routines develop perceptual/preference maps and identify the characteristics of potential buyers that are most highly associated with the 'feature package'.

In the more limited context of weekly special offer advertising, McCann et al. (1990) have devised a system which virtually automates the choice of products and prices. Based upon scanner data, plus the knowledge of experienced merchandisers, it achieves targets for discount levels, margins and variety in the use of products.

Although many retailers have moved away from the routine of numerous, short-term offers (see Chapter 10), comparative advertising is still utilized, often to strong effect. A recent Tesco advertisement, prepared for the tabloid newspapers, showed an Aldi and a Tesco till receipt. On a small basket of goods, the Tesco value lines worked out significantly cheaper. The real punchline of the comparison, however, was a list of nine additional free services at Tesco, all listed as 'not available' at the competitor's stores. Comparative advertisements do provide the consumer with more information but they also risk the 'boomerang effect', i.e, the precipitation of open media warfare (Barry, 1993).

The appropriate balance between pictures and words in retail communications was studied by Gardner and Houston (1986). Their evidence suggested that pictures retain their effects on memory and evaluations rather more than verbal material. This points to the need to pay great attention to the pictorial aspects of the store itself. The results suggest that, when using media with less exposure time, such as television, pictorial messages should be emphasized; verbal portrayal of store features should be given more emphasis when the consumer has adequate time to examine the advertisement, for example in a newspaper.

11.2.4 Evaluating Media Alternatives

The retail advertiser is faced with a wide choice of media, including television, radio, newspapers, magazines, direct mail, posters and electronic media. The choice of specific media vehicles is quite vast, especially in the printed media, where new magazine titles continue to proliferate. Each has its particular advantages and its limitations, which should be evaluated in relation to the retailer's communication requirements.

Table 11.7 offers generalized ratings of the performance of nine media categories, based upon 11 criteria. While most of these are self-explanatory. immediacy represents the medium's ability to present a newsworthy or timely message. Flexibility represents the number of different things that the retailer can do with the medium. Radio can deliver only sound, whereas direct mail can include gifts, coupons, catalogues, etc. The attribute 'interactivity' is included, primarily to reflect a key characteristic of many electronic media: other media can, however, stimulate almost immediate telephone responses. Clearly there is much variation in performance along these criteria, depending upon the specific media vehicle.

Attribute	TV	News-papers	Magazines	Cinema	Radio	Outdoor	In-store	Direct mail	Internet
Cost	H	M	M	H	L	L	L	M	L
Coverage	H	H	M	L	L	L	L	L	L
Selectivity	M	M	H	H	M	M	H	H	M
Impact	H	M	H	H	M	M	L	M	L
Image	H	M	H	H	M	H	M	M	M
Information	L	H	H	L	L	L	M	H	H
Immediacy	M	H	L	L	H	L	H	M	H
Interactivity	M	M	M	L	L	L	H	M	H
Flexibility	M	M	H	M	L	L	H	H	M
Lifespan	L	M	H	L	L	H	H	M	H
Clutter	M	H	H	L	M	H	H	M	H

Table 11.7
Characteristics of advertising media

Key: H = High, M = Moderate, L = Low.

Source: developed from several sources, including Leong et al. (1998) and Wilmshurst and Mackay (1999).

Newspapers

These vary in their degree of selectivity; local newspapers have a clearly defined geographical circulation, allowing retailers to advertise with minimum waste circulation. Nationals usually do not have this advantage, but detailed data are available relating to reader characteristics, allowing some selectivity by market segments. Although advertising rates vary enormously between newspapers, the 'cost per thousand' tends to be lower than television and the costs of producing the adverts is usually considerably lower. The advertiser also enjoys some flexibility of format in newspapers, and the lead time for preparing and inserting advertisements is very short.

From a study of newspaper advertising styles, Shipley et al. (1995) report preferences for straightforward messages, statements of benefits, facts and logical argument.

Some newspapers offer rather poor print and paper quality, whereas others provide some colour in advertisements. In that newspapers carry a large volume of advertisements, there is also a problem of 'clutter', which may limit impact unless the creative treatment is particularly effective. Daily newspapers have a very short life and little additional 'pass-on' exposure. By no means all newspaper buyers actually read the advertisements, although the proportion can be increased by careful positioning within the paper (Soley and James, 1982).

Television

In combining sight, sound and movement, television may achieve greater impact than most other media; it also allows a very wide range of creative treatments, regarded by many as the 'ideal medium' for promoting brand images. Television advertising therefore should make the most effective use of its special advantages, and not convey dull or detailed information that would be better and more economically communicated in print form. Also, the use of television may in itself bring some prestige to the advertiser.

Television tends to be expensive: a 30-second peak spot across a main network costs over £20 000 (Wilmshurst and Mackay, 1999). The proliferation of channels has offered a little more selectivity by time and programme, and some lower rates. However, this has contributed further to the competitive clutter in television advertising (Kent, 1995)

There are other problems too. Television lacks geographical selectivity, which means much wasted advertising unless a retailer has a high density of stores in a television area. Although special rates may be available to reach limited trading areas, these are unlikely to be available for more desirable time slots. Furthermore, the message time for television adverts is fleeting; the more widespread use of television and video remote controls is also leading to more people switching off the sound, switching channels or fast-winding tapes during commercial breaks (Yorke and Kitchen, 1985). Another drawback is that the production of high-quality television advertising is very expensive and relatively slow; promotional lead times are therefore much longer.

Magazines

These are now a very important medium for some retail advertisers. Given the very wide range of titles, advertising can be closely targeted on specific demographic or lifestyle segments, for example *Amateur Photographer*, *Mother & Baby*, *Practical Householder* and *Fitness* (D'Amico, 1999). Although some 'magazines' are closer to newspapers in their print and paper quality, the majority offer excellent reproduction quality; this allows the use of highly coloured and glossy creative treatment. Magazines tend to be kept around longer for reading at leisure and also are more likely to be passed on to others. Sainsbury has used advertisements containing recipe suggestions, printed on very stiff paper; these are designed to be pulled out of the magazine and retained.

Magazines have not escaped the problems of clutter. Ha (1996) defines three main elements of magazine advertising clutter:

- quantity (overload)
- competitiveness (interference as others target the same readers)
- intrusiveness (negative reactions if adverts interfere with the flow of the magazine features).

Furthermore, it costs more to produce an effective advertisement for a magazine than for a newspaper. This is a particular problem if different advertisements are designed with highly selective appeals for each magazine audience. Most magazines have a relatively small circulation, although this is less of a problem if it closely matches the target group. Production lead times tend to be considerably longer than those of newspapers.

Direct Mail

These communications range from basic leaflets to full-colour catalogues; some companies mail promotional information or store magazines directly to their customers on a regular basis. Factors that have stimulated the greater use of direct mail, along with direct marketing in general, include increased media costs, diminishing audiences and advertising clutter (Evans et al., 1996). In addition, retailers have access to their own 'warehouses' of loyalty card and EPoS data, as well as the more generally available GIS data (see Sec. 7.1.2).

The main advantage of direct mail is the minimal wastage of circulation; every recipient can be selected to be an actual or potential cusomer. Letters can be personalized by name and the message or contents adjusted to the known characteristics or spending habits of the recipient. The opportunities to experiment are also numerous, especially if store card usage allows a precise monitoring of specific customers' reactions.

Inevitably, direct mail involves a higher cost per recipient than other media. In those terms, the costs of production can also be relatively high, especially some of the more elaborate catalogues. Given the rapid proliferation of direct mail, it may also be treated as junk mail and quickly discarded, possibly not even opened. This problem may be partially overcome by enclosing direct mail advertising with credit statements or by incorporating a consumer competition to stimulate interest and retention of the material.

Outdoor

The poster industry claims to offer a far lower 'cost per thousand' than the other main media and also claims the highest coverage of the adult population. Posters have been used to particularly good effect by retailers to announce new store openings and to provide direction signs to the store. Posters also offer scope for dramatic creative effects, and impact can be further increased with lighting, mobile effects or three-dimensional displays. On the negative side, the audience selectivity of posters is low and the clutter of outdoor advertising is high in some areas.

The message content of the poster must also be brief; it should be designed to be completely understood within five seconds, if observed mainly from passing vehicles. Fast-food retailer Chick-fil-A has chosen to dominate poster advertising in its local areas, rather than spread its budget thinly across several media. Its various adverts feature two cows urging people to eat more chicken, creating impact and swift recognition (Berry, 2000).

Posters are just one form of 'ambient media', others include advertising on windows, doors, floors, stairs, washrooms, trolleys, balloons, waste bins, petrol pump nozzles and many other possibilities (Admap, 2001).

Internal

Retailers have numerous potential advertising opportunities within their own stores. These include posters, carrier bags, packages, leaflets or catalogues given away at the checkout, messages on sales receipts, etc. In-store advertising may also include audio announcements, videos or slide presentations promoting specific products or store benefits. The video concept has been taken much further by Asda, who use large videowalls in some of their stores (Paton, 1996). In-store kiosks are now extensively used, as information points and often to issue special offer vouchers. A store can therefore provide many opportunities to reinforce the retailer's 'brand image' and stimulate further impulse purchases, the limit is imposed by the need to avoid excessive clutter and confusion. The weakness of most in-store advertising is that it only reaches existing customers. However, packages and carrier bags take the name of the retailer beyond the store, while window displays may entice people to enter.

Internet

A basic website is relatively inexpensive to develop and maintain, thus providing a more 'level playing field' for advertisers of all sizes (Hamill and Kitchen, 1999). The website can also convey a great deal of information yet allow the consumer to select what is required. Internet adverts can be changed very quickly, in response to changing needs or market conditions (Ducoffe, 1996). Transactions can also be executed directly by consumers, providing convenience and the opportunity for impulse purchasing in the home. Morgan Stanley Dean Witter (1999) estimated an annual growth rate of Internet advertising of nearly 140 per cent between 1998 and 2002 and the UK has become Europe's largest Internet advertising market (Forrester, 2001).

However, the interactive characteristics of the Internet have been found to interrupt the process of persuasion by web adverts (Bezjian-Avery et al., 1998). There are also problems of limited production quality, sometimes relating to a propensity to develop sites in-house (Forrester, 1997). Sites can be excessively complex, with too many competing sights and sounds (Bruner and Kumar, 2000). Often elements of traditional media advertising transfer badly to the Internet and the medium has so far shown limited attention-getting potential (Leong et al., 1998; Preston, 2000). Further attention is given to the Internet and related technologies in Chapter 15.

Other Media

There are many other communication methods that may form part of the retailer's media mix. Local commercial radio channels provide reasonable selectivity and flexibility, at relatively low cost. 'Transit' advertising, on buses or underground trains, can deliver a timely message, just before a potential customer reaches a store. Cinema screen or theatre programme adverts tend to reach relatively small audiences, but this may not be a problem if the audience is particularly appropriate. Cinema admissions rose from a low of 80 million in the 1980s to 139 million in the late 1990s, increasing the attractiveness of this advertising medium (Mintel, 1999)

Local 'Shopper guides' or 'free sheets' have also proliferated, in some areas presenting a real challenge to the local newspapers. The telephone *Yellow Pages* can provide a valuable source of new customers, especially for goods and services required less frequently. Some retailers have employed leaflet distributors to target specific customer types within shopping centres or car parks.

Press advertising has traditionally been the highest area of retail expenditure. As Table 11.8 shows, its dominance has declined, although it still accounts for half of retail advertising. Television advertising takes nearly 40 per cent of retail spend and radio advertising has increased to take nearly 8 per cent (Mintel, 1999). While still less than 1 per cent, it is indicative that cinema advertising has started to interest some retailers, especially those targeting young adults (Ewing et al., 2000).

Table 11.8 Retail advertising by media type

Source: derived from Mintel (1999).

	Retailers only		All advertisers
	1994 %	1998 %	1998 %
Television	36.3	39.1	47.5
Press	59.6	50.2	37.4
Outdoor	1.8	2.4	7.2
Radio	2.2	7.8	6.9
Cinema	0.1	0.5	1.0

11.2.5 Media Planning

The choice between the alternative media must depend upon several factors, including the detailed objectives of the campaign(s), the type of message to be conveyed, the products (if any) to be featured, the media habits of target customers, and the costs of specific media in relation to the total budget. The previous section has illustrated that each media type has its particular strengths and its problems. There is no simple formula for determining the appropriate media mix, although Fam and Merrilees (1996) found strong relationships between strategic positioning and promotional tools used. Table 11.9 illustrates the media mix of three contrasting retailers. Each has shifted more emphasis to television and radio. The Gap has a relatively high participation in cinema advertising, finding both the style and the viewer age profiles to be a good fit with its positioning.

Media	The Gap		B & Q		Tesco	
	1994 %	1998 %	1994 %	1998 %	1994 %	1998 %
Press	100	7	85	46	50	24
Television	—	85	10	51	46	64
Radio	—	1	1	3	1	9
Outdoor	—	1	4	—	3	3
Cinema	—	6	—	—	—	—
Spend (£ million)	0.1	9.4	13.5	17.5	26.0	23.7

Table 11.9 Examples of media allocations

Source: derived from Mintel (1999).

The first stage in the media selection process is obviously to eliminate alternatives that are unavailable in the relevant areas or that are completely beyond the budget constraints. This is still likely to leave a wide choice of media and media vehicles, so a number of criteria may then be used to assist in the choice.

Cost per Thousand

Sometimes abbreviated CPT or CPM, this is simply an expression of the cost of reaching each 1000 households or people, using a specific media vehicle. For example, a half-page display in a major regional newspaper may cost £2300 and reach a circulation of 350 000; the cost per thousand would therefore be 657p. The calculation can be modified to reflect 'audience' rather than circulation, if audience is larger because of pass-on readership. Alternatively, the 'effective audience' may be the criterion, this being the people within the retailers' target groups who are exposed to the media vehicle. Further refinements to the calculation may be made to reflect the fact that some of the effective audience would not actually see the advertisement.

Cost per thousand measures can be a useful starting point in choosing between media of similar type. Comparisons between different media are fraught with difficulties but are sometimes encountered. For example, Poster Scene (1987) cited a comparison of major media on the basis of costs per thousand, compiled by Saatchi & Saatchi Compton:

- Cinema — 1830p
- Television — 322p
- National newspaper — 295p
- Colour supplements — 137p
- Radio — 81p
- Outdoor — 31p.

This was based upon a 30-second cinema, television or radio commercial, a full-page monochrome newspaper advertisement, a colour page in supplements and a weighted average of large and small outdoor posters. In attempting such intermedia comparisons, it is essential to recognize the very different levels of audience attention and impact achieved by these different media.

Impact

Certain media have inherent advantages in achieving impact, notably cinema and television, although impact also depends upon characteristics of the message and the target audience. A relatively complex series of price comparisons or technical specifications of particular products would clearly require the opportunity to be read carefully; newspapers or magazines would therefore achieve the highest impact. For other creative treatments, the availability of colour is essential, in which case television or magazines are likely to be preferred.

Analysis of the media habits of the target consumers also provides guidelines in choosing between media vehicles. Many magazines are very closely targeted upon specific groups, whereas television and national newspapers have somewhat wider appeal. The choice of specific television programme slots or locations within newspapers can however improve the impact. Higie et al. (1987) suggested that particular attention should be paid to the media habits of 'market mavens', defined as:

> *individuals who have information about many kinds of products, places to shop, and other facets of markets, and initiate discussions with consumers and respond to requests from consumers for market information (Feick and Price 1987).*

They suggest that direct mail and women's homemaking magazines are useful vehicles for targeting this group. In so doing, the retail advertiser may most favourably influence the frequent word-of-mouth communications, in which this type of consumer is likely to be involved.

Exposure

Exposures, sometimes referred to as 'impressions', are the number of times that an advert is seen by the media audience. Inevitably, exposure (E) is a function of reach (R) and frequency (F):

$$E = R \times F$$

For example, 12 million exposures could be achieved by reaching 4 million people an average of three times during the campaign period, or 2 million people an average of six times. If a well-known retailer is concerned primarily with expanding territory or announcing the arrival of a new product range, the emphasis could be on achieving a wide reach. A retailer as yet unknown in the area, on the other hand, might wish to achieve a higher frequency of exposure. Although this sounds like a fairly straightforward principle, media directors have expressed great concern about how estimates of reach and frequency are derived (Leckenby and Kim, 1994).

Gross rating points (GRPs) are a measure of frequency, times the percentage of the audience reached (R%):

$$GRP = R\% \times F$$

A schedule that reached 80 per cent of the audience an average of four times each would therefore have a GRP of 320. The appropriate number of exposures varies according to the communication objectives of the retailer. From a review of previous research, Teel and Bearden (1980) noted:

> *Although there is disagreement on the precise values of the upper and lower limits of the 'optimal effect' range, fewer than three message exposures are likely to fail to register, and more than ten exposures are probably unnecessary, for products advertised on broadcast media.*

It should be noted that an exposure does not necessarily occur every time a person reads a newspaper or watches television at a specific time. Less than half the people who had 'vehicle exposure' may have had 'actual exposure' to the advertisement, particularly with the relatively low-involvement media, such as television and radio (Krugman, 1975). To achieve high 'cumulative reach' (cume) over a series of advertisements in order to reach a high proportion of the target audience, the media planner may have to accept that many customers will have an excessive exposure frequency. This may be partially overcome by selecting different media vehicles with low audience duplication, for example, two daily papers with very little reader overlap.

Media selection sets out to find the most cost effective media to deliver the desired number of exposures to the target audience. However, the media planner is also concerned with the timing of the advertisements, in terms of both the overall seasonality (if any) in the advertising and the precise timing within the campaign. These two aspects of media planning are 'macroscheduling' and 'microscheduling' problems.

Macroscheduling

At this level, the planner may decide to maintain a fairly constant level of advertising over the whole year, to concentrate advertising in seasons with high expected sales levels, or use advertising to stimulate sales during the normally quiet seasons. In the grocery, department store and mail order retail categories, there is a strong bias towards the final quarter; even much of the post-Christmas sales advertising falls within the last part of this quarter. In some specific sectors, the bias may be even more pronounced. Ward (1985) reported that 54 per cent of advertising by the jewellery sector occurs in that final quarter. Not surprisingly, film process advertising is heavily concentrated around the main holiday months.

In contrast, the direct response mail order companies adopt an even pattern of expenditure over the year; in their case, the advertising is in a sense the store. The product emphasis within this advertising, however, is highly seasonal. The timing of advertising, to gain maximum awareness at peak seasons, depends upon the degree of advertising carryover, i.e. the extent to which the effect of the advertising continues or wears out over time. If carryover is high, the campaign may be initiated some time before the peak demand period. There are of course arguments against concentrating advertising at peak seasons. At such times, advertising clutter in the media can be high and the discounts obtainable by media buyers are likely to be low.

The cheapest months in which to advertise tend to be January, February, July and August. Because many retailing costs are fixed, it also makes sense to attract customers at times that some types of stores would be underutilized. The emphasis on long-term image-building, as opposed to short-term sales promotion, also suggests a more even pattern of advertising. Few retailers, however, can afford to ignore the sales opportunities provided by peak demand seasons, not least because competitors are likely to be promoting hard to gain maximum share of the temporarily increased market.

Microscheduling

At this level, the objective is to allocate the exposure within short time periods in order to achieve the highest impact. Advertising may be concentrated in a 'burst' pattern over a period of a few days, for example, in order to announce the start of a major 'sale'. Other objectives may call for a more continuous 'drip' pattern, for example, to maintain awareness of an everyday low pricing (EDLP) strategy.

Some schedules use an intermittent pattern, possibly concentrating the advertising around the most popular shopping days. DFS/Northern Upholstery, for example, concentrate 60 per cent of their television and press advertising on Fridays and Saturdays (Admap, 2000a). The company also targets its television advertising around popular 'soaps', spending £3 million on adverts adjacent to Coronation Street and Emmerdale Farm. Consistent with this profile, the company's two main press vehicles are the *Sun* and *Daily Mirror* newspapers. It also makes extensive use of local free sheets and regional papers (Admap, 2000b).

A number of computer-based decision support models have now been developed to assist in the selection and scheduling of the promotion mix. Based upon three years of sales and promotion expenditure data for a large speciality store, Allaway et al. (1987) developed a series of equations relating overall and department sales to promotional variables. These included the number of newspaper column inches, the contents of the adverts, the rates paid, whether a coupon was used, the price discount (if any), the timing and content of radio and television adverts, the size and content of billboards, and other variables. Optimal control modelling was used to derive the most cost-effective mix of media and the size, timing and promotional content of the adverts. Given the widespread availability of detailed and timely point-of-sale data, the scope for developing and using such models is now extensive.

11.3 Advertising Effects

Having considered some of the major decision areas facing the retail advertiser, it is appropriate to conclude with a brief look at the ways in which advertising effects can be monitored. In that several retailers now spend over £20 million annually on media advertising, the need to assess performance is very strong. For some major retailers, their only test of advertising effectiveness has been 'general intuition' (Nowak et al., 1996)

Less than half the retailers surveyed by Ody (1987) attempted to relate advertising to improvements in sales or profits, only 15 per cent to improvements in customer flow. A third of the sample estimated that more than half of their advertising expenditure was wasted; one even admitted: 'Seventy-five per cent is wasted, but I haven't the nerve to give it up completely.'

These findings suggested that much retail advertising has been prompted by the perceived need to match competitors' advertising, not by a scientific assessment of its cost-effectiveness as a marketing tool. In many cases, it is clear that increased expenditure on media advertising has not been accompanied by the necessary investment in performance evaluation research. The problems associated with advertising assessment have increased with the growth of theme or image-based advertising. The effects of this type of advertising are assumed to be longer term and therefore more difficult to measure in terms of immediate sales response. This section will look at some of the main approaches to evaluating advertising performance. First, however, we will consider some of the theories and models that have attempted to answer that perennial question: how does advertising work?

11.3.1 Models of Advertising Effects

Extensive expenditures on advertising, plus a thriving advertising industry, point to strong belief that advertising exerts effects upon consumers' beliefs, behaviours and/or expenditures. Explaining just how these effects may occur has proved problematic. Even those with closest responsibility for the creation and implementation of advertising campaigns rarely articulate, the 'mental models' that guide their work (Broadbent, 1995). This section summarizes a few of the more frequently cited models, while accepting that they all fall far short of providing a complete explanation.

Many of the earliest models posit a sequence or hierachy of responses by the consumer, on being exposed to advertising messages. The AIDA model, which had its origins in the 1920s, posits that the consumer will move through the stages of awareness, interest, desire, then action. The appeal of the model is that it suggests advertising priorities to influence each stage of this progression. The 1960s saw the emergence of a variation upon the hierarchy concept, the DAGMAR model (defining advertising goals for measured advertising results). This suggests that awareness is followed by increased knowledge, the development of liking, then a preference for the store/product/service.

These models share some of the characteristics of the C-A-C model (cognitive-affective-conative), widely used to explain human responses to various stimuli (Crosier, 1999). These stages are often paraphrased as 'think-feel-do', although 'intention to do' may be a more accurate interpretation of the last component. While this sequence may fit well with concepts of learning, there are other types of purchase situation. For example, during an impulsive purchase, a consumer may 'do-feel-think'; in many low-involvement purchases, a consumer may 'think-do-feel'.

Ehrenberg (1988) presented extensive empirical support for an ATR model (attention-trial-reinforcement). He maintains that advertising plays a relatively minor role in gaining attention and that trial is the main source of feelings about the product/store/service. However, advertising may play a significant role in helping to reinforce feelings and purchase patterns.

At the level of the individual advertisement, it is likely that a degree of interest must precede attention. Ducolfe and Curlo (2000) found that consumers tend to form almost instantaneous judgements on whether an advertisement is of interest or value to them; only then do they devote additional processing effort to its detailed elements.

Figure 11.3 summarizes these 'hierarchy' models, illustrating some of the differences. Although such models have continued to attract extensive criticism (e.g. Schultz and Schultz, 1998), it is also argued that they are preferable to no framework at all, in helping to understand advertising effects. Some of the differences between the models can be equated with contrasting purchase situations, e.g. choice of main grocery store, purchase of an expensive item of furniture or in-store decisions between competing grocery products.

A significant departure from the hierarchy of effects theories was King's (1975) 'scale of immediacy'. This suggested alternative roles that advertising could play in helping to stimulate action. His scale of immediacy suggested six levels of effect:

1 *Direct response*: on seeing the advertisement, the customer buys straight off the page (or screen).
2 *Seek information*: the customer is stimulated to find out more about the store or product.
3 *Relate to needs/desires*: advertising that provokes the 'what a good idea' response.
4 *Reminder role*: the customer is reminded of previous satisfaction with store/product and is prompted to patronize again.
5 *Modify attitudes*: possibly addressing an image weakness identified by research.
6 *Reinforce attitudes*: helping prevent fade out of positive attitudes towards a popular store/product.

Founded upon the research of J. Walter Thompson, this scale helps to clarify the aims of the advertising strategy. It also points to the dangers of using measures of effectiveness that are not appropriate to the specific aims of the campaign.

Most of the established models of advertising effect tend to regard consumer behaviour as 'rational, highly cognitive, systematic and reasoned' (Shimp, 1997). In contrast, the 'hedonic, experiential model' (HEM) focuses upon the pursuit of 'fantasies, feelings and fun'. As Hirschman and Holbrook (1982) pointed out, researchers have paid

Figure 11.3 Hierarchy of effects models

AIDA	DAGMAR	C-A-C	ATR
	Unawareness		
Awareness	Awareness	Cognitive	Attention
Interest	Comprehension	Affective	Reinforcement
Desire	Conviction	Conative	Trial
Action			

little attention to fun and playful activities, even though these are important components of consumers' lives. Some advertisements appeal primarily to reason, whereas others work more directly on the emotions. A prosaic list of prices charged by a discount retailer represents one extreme; some of Benetton poster advertisements illustrate the other.

Hedonic appeals can fulfil the functions identified in the earlier models, capturing attention, creating interest and influencing feelings. Entering the realm of semiotics, the signs and symbols utilized in hedonic appeals are 'decoded' quickly by consumers into impressions and feelings (Dermody, 1999). This contrast in advertising styles, and persuasion mechanisms, again highlights the need to utilize the most appropriate techniques to evaluate advertising effectiveness. As discussed in Chapter 5, images can be formed and stored as pictures, without necessarily generating a verbal elaboration: 'The left-brain reads, the right-brain scans images. This helps account for memory without recall, exposure without perception' (Krugman, 2000).

11.3.2 Evaluating Advertising Performance

There is no single method or technique that is most appropriate for the evaluation of all aspects of advertising performance. Some would argue that the overall cost-effectiveness of the advertising is, at the end of the day, the only relevant criterion, and that this is best assessed through the detailed analysis of sales/profit results and advertising costs. While this may be viable where the objective is simply to generate short-term sales response (Burton et al., 1999), the problems of isolating the effects of advertising on long-term sales and profits are far greater (Tellis et al., 2000).

The specific objectives of the advertisement or campaign must therefore guide the choice of method used to assess the extent to which these have been met (Britt, 2000). In the development of the campaign, techniques generally classified as 'pre-testing' can also be used to increase the probability that the advertisements achieve their objectives (Wells, 2000). Twyman (1986) provided a succinct review of general approaches to the monitoring of advertising performance; Table 11.10 summarizes the appropriateness of each of these for assessing specific aspects of the advertising. More detailed discussions of advertising evaluation methods can be found in Broadbent (1997), Duckworth (1995) and Admap (2000b).

Aspect of advertising to be assessed	Appropriateness of approach				
	Pre-testing	Day-after recall	Tracking	Area experiments	Sales analysis
Diagnostic information about advertisement	High	Low	Low	Low	No
Differences between alternative advertisements	Medium	Low	High	High	High
Achievement of impact	Low	High	High	Maybe	Low
Meeting communication objectives	High	Low	Low	Maybe	Low
Overall effectiveness	Low	No	No	High	High

Table 11.10 Approaches to advertising assessment

Source: adapted from Twyman (1986).

Pre-testing

Unlike all the forms of post-testing, pre-testing enables the advertiser to assess some aspects of the advertising before any media time or space is purchased; it therefore has the ability to avoid some expensive errors. Approaches include focus group sessions, at which shoppers are shown plans of the campaign in embryonic form or completed advertisements prior to broadcast or publication; alternatively, the plan can be exposed to larger samples of shoppers to obtain more quantitative assessments. Pre-testing methods can help to estimate the likelihood of attracting attention and the effects upon feelings and beliefs about the retailer. Alternative creative treatments or advertising formats can be compared and diagnostic information obtained.

The range of available techniques is impressive, including scales to measure the mental imagery evoked by adverts (e.g. Miller et al., 2000; Zaltman and Coulter, 1995). Pre-testing has also sought to measure emotional responses, through such techniques as the Facial Action Coding System (FACS) or electromyography (EMG), used to measure minute changes in the electrical activity of facial muscles (Hazlett and Hazlett, 1999). However, laboratory style pretests continue to attract the criticisms that the adverts are tested in isolation, therefore performance in the real marketplace cannot be accurately predicted (McQuarrie, 1998).

Day-After Recall

Tests of advertising recall shortly after the publication or broadcast provide a measure of impact vis-à-vis other current advertisements. Although recall tests measure consumers' propensity to remember the advertisement, there is some doubt as to whether recall is a good measure of advertising effectiveness (e.g. O'Guinn et al., 1998). A high level of attention and recall can be obtained, while not necessarily achieving the required influence upon shoppers' feelings and beliefs about the retailer. Day-after recall testing is less common in Europe than in the USA, although other recall tests are commonly applied.

In the *Marketing* magazine 10-year review of advertising awareness, McDonald's claimed the number two position, Asda the number six. The success of the latter has been attributed to its consistency in the use of price and value themes, including 'Asda price', with its jingle and 'pocket tap', and the 'Rollback prices' message. Safeway achieved number nine position, attributed to the memorable 'lightening the load' theme, using toddlers with voice-overs by famous adult actors (Marketing, 1999)

Advertising Tracking

Some of the limitations of the short-term recall measures can be overcome with regular or continuous measurement of advertising awareness and attitudes towards the retailer. Some of the specific techniques available for this purpose have already been discussed in the context of image measurement in Chapter 5. Tracking studies have the advantage of recording changes over time, rather than levels of awareness/belief at a specific point in time. They also record the effects of the total advertising input and other market influences, yet can estimate the relative effects of specific advertisements or campaigns within the overall time period (Admap, 1999)

Area Experimentation

This type of approach involves the administration of different advertising levels and/or content in different areas; this provides a good assessment of overall effectiveness and also enables comparisons to be made between different advertising treatments. Using the split-run facilities offered by some newspapers, different versions of an advertisement are given an identical position within the newspaper but are distributed to different sectors of the circulation. Coupons also provide a convenient way of monitoring the effects of newspaper, magazine or direct mail advertisements, using split-run or area experimentation (e.g. Chapman 1986).

The split-run approach requires careful experimental design to match the households receiving the different advertising messages. Cable television has provided a precise mechanism to deliver alternative messages to groups of households, matched for their locations, exposure to other advertising, retail environments, etc. Lodish et al. (1995) utilized the results of nearly 400 split cable television advertising experiments. In these, the data also include sales effectiveness, as the purchases of the household panels were monitored through scanner data.

Sales Analysis

As sales are normally the ultimate objective of advertising, their analysis would appear to provide the strongest measure of advertising effectiveness. However, numerous other marketing inputs, competitor activities and changes in the market can also influence sales; the problems of isolating advertising effects are therefore considerable, even in the analysis of short-term effects. Point-of-sale scanners have enhanced the opportunities for monitoring short-term sales effects by providing timely and product-specific data, although the problems of monitoring longer-term and more general effects remain. Information derived from scanners and customer identification devices, such as loyalty cards can, however, assist in estimating the longer-term sales effects of a campaign targeted at specific customer segments.

Another fundamental weakness of the sales analysis approach is that only the overall relationship between advertising and sales is estimated. Unless supplemented with other research approaches, nothing may be learnt of the intermediary processes by which those additional sales may have been stimulated. Specifically, if the strengths and weaknesses of the advertisements are not isolated, the wrong elements may be developed or deleted as the campaign is evolved.

SUMMARY

For most major retailers, advertising provides the main channel of communication with existing and potential customers, outside the store itself. The specific objectives of advertising should be carefully defined. These objectives may include various approaches to attracting new customers, increasing the expenditure of existing customers, building store traffic, increasing product sales or enhancing the store image. It is essential that all advertising and promotional activities be used as part of an overall strategy, not run in isolation or as a substitute for an adequate strategy.

Retailers continue to be among the major media advertisers, with an overall expenditure in 1999 of £955 million. In spite of the fact that retailers have developed more ways to communicate with their customers, notably through loyalty schemes, expenditure on conventional advertising media doubled through the 1990s. Among the major superstore companies, advertising to sales ratios are around a 0.25 to 0.5 of a per cent. In other retail sectors, ratios of 2 per cent or higher are not uncommon.

Part of the high expenditure on advertising has been supported by manufacturers' advertising allowances, i.e., 'vertical co-operative advertising'. For the largest retailers, these have tended to become just another discount, without which the manufacturer's products would not be promoted or maybe not even stocked. For small to medium-sized retailers, co-operative advertising can provide access to more powerful media, bring additional prestige and create profitable linkages to manufacturer campaigns. However, co-operative advertising has tended to give retail advertising an excessive product/price emphasis and often has led to the promotion of inappropriate products, in terms of the retailer's image and profitability.

Sales promotions play a major role in most retailers' communications mix, in spite of the shift by some towards everyday low pricing (EDLP, Chapter 10). Money-off promotions remain popular and coupons have found a new role within the packages mailed out to loyalty card customers. Competitions, either within the store or mailed out, have also gained in popularity. Across the countries of Europe, different laws on price claims, commercial communications and competitions restrict the use of some techniques in certain countries.

Because of the high cost and advertising 'clutter' in many established media, some retailers have become increasingly skilled at other forms of publicity. Public relations, often subsumed under the broader title of corporate communications, has developed a significant role for major retailers. Customers are a major focus of PR activities, such as the superstore documentaries and high-profile campaigns against manufacturers' high prices. However, the PR function also seeks to influence the views of shareholders, city institutions, the government, employees and suppliers.

Sponsorships have been a part of retail PR for many years but the 'science' of sponsorship is of recent origin. By creating or sponsoring newsworthy events, high attention and credibility can be achieved, as well as possibly media coverage at low cost. Social events, fashion shows and spectacular store openings are now among the ways of attracting publicity. Sponsorship of many different types has also been used, partly for the publicity benefits and partly in pursuit of personnel or welfare policies; sports sponsorship in particular has attracted major expenditure and interest.

Decisions on how much to spend on media advertising must be set within the retailer's promotional mix and overall strategic objectives. A number of approaches are adopted in setting advertising budgets, with varying degrees of merit. Some see a given percentage of sales as a rule of thumb, whereas others perceive a need to achieve a competitive parity in advertising expenditures. The more logical approach is to define the precise objectives, then determine the specific advertising tasks and costs required to achieve these.

Although many major retailers have extensive marketing departments, most use the services of one or more advertising agency. The agency can provide an outside perspective upon the characteristics of the market and the retailer's competitive position. Inputs can also be provided to strategic planning and in the formulation of advertising objectives. The agency also provides or obtains specialist creative and media planning services. While there are notable exceptions, the agency–retailer relationship is usually not in excess of five years. The main reasons for leaving an agency are disappointing results, poor service or the need for new ideas.

Determining the appropriate content and message of retail advertisements requires both creativity and a systematic appraisal of the company's strengths and weaknesses, both real and perceived. If an adequate volume and quality of consumer research data are available, computerized decision support systems have been developed which seek to maximize the advertising appeal to specific target groups. Detailed attention must also be paid to each precise element of the advertising content; the words, print faces, pictures, actors and the semiotics (signs and symbols) all communicate impressions of the retailer and store.

The choice of media types and specific media vehicles is very large indeed. Newspapers continue to attract a large proportion of retail advertising expenditure; local newspapers in particular provide relatively good geographical selectivity and low wastage. Television provides high impact but usually at high cost with waste circulation. Magazines have been adopted by some as major vehicles for image-building campaigns; the vast range of titles achieves high selectivity. Direct mail, although expensive, has become an increasingly popular means of communication, assisted by loyalty card records and other GIS data. The Internet, although low on impact, has high potential to convey detailed information at low cost, making it a feasible medium for retailers large or small.

In planning the media mix, the advertiser must compare the costs of each available media vehicle, relative to the number of exposures and the impact achieved. Clearly, the number of effective exposures is not equal to the total circulation or audience. The impact achieved in a given media vehicle depends upon the advertising message and characteristics of the target audience. In producing the detailed schedule of media use, the retailer may be influenced by strong seasonality in the sales of many product categories. A number of computer-based models have been evolved to assist in media mix and scheduling decisions.

Both the tasks of designing a campaign, then evaluating its effectiveness, require some 'mental model' of how advertising works to influence customer behaviour. Traditional models have depicted a sequence or hierarchy of effects, such as awareness, interest, desire, action. Not all purchase or patronage decisions follow this sequence: sometimes attitude formation mostly follows patronage, rather than vice versa. Such models also tend to overlook the opportunities for advertising to appeal more directly to emotions; using hedonistic images can often influence feelings more directly than 'rational' appeals.

In spite of their large expenditures, many retailers have not systematically monitored its effects. Changes in sales or store traffic may be caused by many other factors; rigorous experimental and/or statistical methods are therefore required to estimate the advertising effects. Prior to the campaign launch, pre-testing facilities can be used to minimize risk of failure; area experiments may then be used to test the effectiveness of alternative creative/media treatments. Campaign effectiveness can be fully measured only through a series of pre- and post-testing procedures.

REVIEW QUESTIONS

1 Taking a retail company of your choice, how should that company define its specific advertising objectives?

2 Explain why many retailers are among the major spenders on media advertising. Why do you think that advertising to sales ratios have declined in some cases?

3 How would you evaluate the advantages and drawbacks of vertical co-operative advertising arrangements if you were advising:

a) an independent electrical goods retailer?

b) a large grocery chain?

4 In designing a mail-out to send to loyalty card customers, how can the effectiveness of this be enhanced by the use of sales promotions techniques?

5 You have been appointed to a senior position in a retail company with a poor record for handling its public relations. How would you reorganise the PR function to communicate more effectively on behalf of the business?

6 How should a retailer decide between the many opportunities to engage in sponsorship? What specific benefits may be reasonably anticipated?

7 In establishing retail advertising budgets, compare the benefits and limitations of:

a) the percentage of sales method

b) the competitive parity method

c) the objective and task method.

8 Describe the role of advertising agencies in relation to retail clients. If you were an account director in an agency, how would you set about attracting and retaining a major retail client?

9 Explain the concept of the 'identity prism'. How could this assist in determining the content of advertisements for:

a) teenage fashion boutiques?

b) exclusive furniture stores?

10 'Price as a platform can only ever be your tactical weapon – it can never be your strategy'. Discuss the validity of this statement in relation to the advertising emphasis of three or more retailers.

11 Evaluate the strengths and limitations of (a) television and (b) newspapers as media for retail advertising. To what extent can internet advertising (a) supplement, and (b) replace these traditional media?

12 Discuss the importance of seasonality in the scheduling of media advertising. Under what circumstances is a continuous or a concentrated schedule of advertising more appropriate?

13 The models to help explain advertising effects have evolved from the early, sequential concepts, such as AIDA. Discuss how well these models can be related to various types of retail patronage decisions.

14 Compare and contrast the following approaches to the assessment of advertising effectiveness:

a) pre-testing

b) advertising recall tests

c) area experimentation.

REFERENCES

Abratt, R., M. Bendixen and A. du Plessis (1995) 'Manufacturer and retailer perceptions of in-store promotions in South Africa', *Journal of Marketing Management*, **11**, 443–468.

Admap (1999) 'Keep on tracking', *Admap*, **400** (November), 17–27.

Admap (2000a) 'Adstats: a good year for advertising', *Admap*, **404**, S1–S8.

Admap (2000b) *Statistics for Advertising Decision Making*, NTC Publications, Oxford.

Admap (2001) *WARC/ Admap Conference on Exploring Ambient Media*, Admap, London.

Allaway, A., J.B. Mason and G. Brown (1987) 'An optimal decision support model for department-level promotion mix planning', *Journal of Retailing*, **63** (3), 215–242.

Arnold, S., J. Handelman and D. Tigert (1996) 'Organizational legitimacy and retail store patronage', *Journal of Business Research*, **35**, 229–239.

Arnold, S.J., R.V. Kozinets and J.M. Handelman (2001) 'Hometown ideology and retailer legitimation: the institutional semiotics of Wal-Mart fliers', *Journal of Retailing*, **77** (2), 243–271.

Barry, T.E. (1993) 'Comparative advertising: what have we learned in two decades?', *Journal of Advertising Research*, **33** (2), 19–29.

Bergen, M. and G. John (1997) 'Understanding co-operative advertising participation rates in conventional channels', *Journal of Marketing Research*, **34** (3), 357–369.

Berry, L.L. (2000) 'Cultivating service brand equity', *Journal of the Academy of Marketing Science*, **28** (1), 128–137.

Bezjian-Avery, A., B. Calder and D. Iacobucci (1998) 'New media interactive advertising vs traditional advertising', *Journal of Advertising Research*, **38** (4), 23–32.

Britt, S.H. (2000) 'Are so-called successful advertising campaigns really successful?', *Journal of Advertising Research*, **40** (6), 25–31.

Britton, N. (1988) 'Next puts its fashions on the screen', *Marketing*, 14 January, 1.

Broadbent, S. (1995) *Best Practice in Campaign Evaluation*, Institute of Practitioners in Advertising, London.

Broadbent, S. (1997) *Acountable Advertising*, Admap Publications, London.

Bruner, G.C. and A. Kumar (2000) 'Web commercials and advertising hierarchy-of-effects', *Journal of Advertising Research*, **40** (1/2), 35–42.

Burton, S., D.R. Lichtenstein and R.G. Netemeyer (1999) 'Exposure to sales flyers and increased purchases in retail supermarkets', *Journal of Advertising Research*, **39** (5), 7–14.

Carrigan, M. and I. Szmigin (1998) 'Usage and portrayal of older models in contemporary consumer advertising', *Journal of Marketing Practice: Applied Marketing Science*, **4** (8), 231–248.

Chapman, R.G. (1986) 'Assessing the profitability of retailer couponing with a low-cost field experiment', *Journal of Retailing*, **62** (1), 19–40.

Collins, A. (1992) *Competitive Retail Marketing*, McGraw-Hill, Maidenhead.

Corfman, K.P. and D.R. Lehmann (1994) 'The prisoner's dilemma and the role of information in setting advertising budgets', *Journal of Advertising*, **23** (2), 35–48.

Crimmins, J. and M. Horn (1996) 'Sponsorship: from management ego trip to marketing success', *Journal of Advertising Research*, **36** (4), 11–21.

Crosier, K. (1999) 'Advertising', in *Marketing Communications: Principles and Practice*, P.J. Kitchen (ed.), Thomson Business Press, London, pp. 264–288.

Curhan, R.C. and R.J. Kopp (1987/88) 'Obtaining retailer support for trade deals; key success factors', *Journal of Advertising Research*, **27** (6), 51–60.

D'Amico, T. F. (1999) 'Magazines' secret weapon: media selection on the basis of behavior, as opposed to demography', *Journal of Advertising Research*, **39** (6), 53–60.

D'Astous, A. and P. Bitz (1995) 'Consumer evaluations of sponsorship programmes', *European Journal of Marketing*, **29** (12), 6–22.

D'Souza, G. and A. Allaway (1995) 'An empirical investigation of the advertising spending decisions of a multiproduct retailer', *Journal of Retailing*, **71** (3), 279–296.

Danaher, P.J. and R.T. Rust (1994) 'Determining the optimal level of media spending' *Journal of Advertising Research*, **34** (1), 28–34.

Dermody, J. (1999) 'CPM/HEM models of information processing'. in *Marketing Communications: Principles and Practice*, P.J. Kitchen (ed.), Thomson Business Press, London, pp. 156–171.

Duckworth, G. (1995) 'How advertising works, the universe and everything', *Admap*, **347** (January), 41–43.

Ducoffe, R. (1996) 'Advertising value and advertising on the web', *Journal of Advertising Research*, **36** (5), 21–35.

Ducoffe, R.H. and E. Curlo (2000) 'Advertising value and advertising processing', *Journal of Marketing Communications*, **6**, 247–262.

Duncan, T.R. and S.E. Everett (1993) 'Client perceptions of integrated marketing communications', *Journal of Advertising Research*, **33** (3), 30–39.

Durkin, M. and M.-A. Lawlor (2001) 'The implications of the Internet on the advertising-client relationship', *Service Industries Journal*, **21** (2), 175–190.

Edwards, C.M. and C.F. Lebowitz (1981) *Retail Advertising and Sales Promotion*, Prentice-Hall, Englewood Cliffs, NJ.

Ehrenberg, A.S.C. (1988) *Repeat Buying: Facts, Theory and Applications*, Charles Grifin, London.

Ellen, P.S., L.A. Mohr and D.J. Webb (2000) 'Charitable programs and the retailer: do they mix?', *Journal of Retailing*, **76** (3), 393–406.

Evans, M., L. O'Malley and M. Patterson (1996) 'Direct marketing communications in the UK: a study of growth, past, present and future', *Journal of Marketing Communications*, **2** (1), 51–65.

Ewing, M.T., E. du Plessis and C. Foster (2001) 'Cinema advertising re-considered', *Journal of Advertising Research*, **41** (1), 78–85.

Fam, K.S. and B. Merrilees (1996) 'Determinants of shoe retailers' perceptions of promotion tools', *Journal of Retailing and Consumer Services*, **3** (3), 155–162.

Fam, K.S. and B Merrilees (1997) 'Strategic promotion alignment among small New Zealand retailers', *New Zealand Journal of Business*, **19**, 53–61

Feick, L.F. and L.L. Price (1987) 'The market maven: a diffuser of marketplace information', *Journal of Marketing*, **51** (1), 83–97.

Forrester (1997) *Media and Technology Strategies: Internet Advertising*, Forrester Research, http://www.forester.com.

Forrester (2001) *German Online Ad Market Trails UK*, Forrester Research, http://www.forester.com.

Fulop, C. (1988) 'The role of advertising in the retail marketing mix', *International Journal of Advertising*, **7** (2), 99–117.

Gardner, M.P. and M.J. Houston (1986) 'The effects of verbal and visual components of retail communications', *Journal of Retailing*, **62** (1), 64–78.

Gofton, K. (1988) 'Hiring and firing', *Marketing*, 7 January, 31–32.

Gray, R. (1998) 'PR: The new retail battle ground', *Marketing*, 3 September, 18–19.

Green, P.E., V. Mahajan, S.M. Goldberg and P.K. Kedia (1984) 'A decision-support system for developing retail promotional strategy', *Journal of Retailing*, 53 (3), 116–143.

Grunig, J.E. and L.A. Grunig (1998) 'The relationship between public relations and marketing in excellent organisations: evidence from the IABC study', *Journal of Marketing Communications*, 4 (3), 141–162.

Ha, L.(1996) 'Advertising clutter in consumer magazines: dimensions and effects', *Journal of Advertising Research*, 36 (4), 77–84.

Hackley, C. (1999) 'The communication process and the semiotic boundary', in *Marketing Communications: Principles and Practice*, P.J. Kitchen (ed.), Thomson Business Press, London, pp. 135–155.

Haight, W. (1976) *Retail Advertising: Management and Technique*, General Learning Press, Morristown, NJ.

Hamill, J. and P. Kitchen (1999) 'The Internet: international context', in *Marketing Communications: Principles and Practice*, P.J. Kitchen (ed.), Thomson Business Press, London, pp. 381–402.

Harvey, B. (2001) 'Measuring the effects of sponsorships', *Journal of Advertising Research*, 41 (1), 59–65.

Hazlett, R.L. and S.Y. Hazlett (1999) 'Emotional response to television commercials: facial EMG vs self-report', *Journal of Advertising Research*, 39 (2), 7–23.

Henke,L.L. (1995) 'A longitudinal analysis of the ad agency-client relationship: predictors of an agency switch', *Journal of Advertising Research*, 35 (2), 24–30.

Higie, R.A., L.F. Feick and L.L. Price (1987) 'Types and amount of word-of-mouth communications about retailers', *Journal of Retailing*, 63 (3), 260–278.

Hirschman, E.C. and M.B. Holbrook (1982) 'Hedonic consumption: emerging concepts, methods and propositions', *Journal of Marketing*, 46 (3), 92–101.

Hoek, J. (1999) 'Sponsorship', in *Marketing Communications: Principles and Practice*, P.J. Kitchen (ed.), Thomson Business Press, London, pp. 361–380.

Hoek, J., P. Gendall, M. Jeffcoat and D. Orsman (1997) 'Sponsorship and advertising: a comparison of their effects', *Journal of Marketing Communications*, 3 (1), 21–32.

Jackson, H.O. and N. Ross (1997) 'Fashion advertising: does age, body type or ethnicity influence consumers' perceptions?', *Journal of Fashion Marketing and Management*, 1 (4), 322–332.

Javalgi, R.G., M.B. Traylor, A.C. Gross and E. Lampman (1994) 'Awareness of sponsorship and corporate image: an empirical investigation', *Journal of Advertising*, 23 (4), 47–58.

Jones, J.P. (1992) *How Much Is Enough? Getting the Most from your Advertising Dollar*, Lexington Books, New York.

Jorgensen, S., S.P. Sigue and G. Zaccour (2000) 'Dynamic co-operative advertising in a channel', *Journal of Retailing*, 76 (1), 71–92.

Kahn, B.E. and T.A. Louie (1990) 'Effects of retraction of price promotions on brand choice behaviour for variety-seeking and last-purchase-loyal consumers', *Journal of Marketing Research*, 18 (3), 279–289.

Kapferer, J.-N. (1996) 'Beyond positioning: retailer's identity', in *Retail Strategies for Profit and Growth*, ESOMAR (ed.), ESOMAR, Amsterdam, pp. 167–175.

Kaufman, L. (1980) *Essentials of Advertising*, Harcourt, Brace Jovanovich, New York

Kent, R.J. (1995) 'Competitive clutter in network television advertising: current levels and advertiser responses', *Journal of Advertising Research*, 35 (1), 49–57.

King, S. (1975) 'Practical progress from a theory of advertisements' *Admap*, 11 (10), 338–343.

Kitchen, P.J. (1997) *Public Relations: Principles and Practice*, Thomson Business Press, London.

Kitchen, P.J. and I. Papasolomou (1999) 'Marketing public relations', in *Marketing Communications: Principles and Practice*, P.J. Kitchen (ed.), Thomson Business Press, London, pp. 340–360.

Krugman, H.E. (1975) 'What makes advertising effective', *Harvard Business Review*, 53 (2), 96–103.

Krugman, H.E. (2000) 'Memory without recall, exposure without perception', *Journal of Advertising Research*, 40 (6), 49–54.

Laspadakis, A (1999) 'The dynamic role of sales promotion', in *Marketing Communications: Principles and Practice*, P.J. Kitchen (ed.), Thomson Business Press, London, pp. 289–308.

Leckenby, J.D. and H. Kim (1994) 'How media directors view reach/frequency estimation: now and a decade ago', *Journal of Advertising Research*, 34 (5), 9–21.

Leong, E.K.F., X. Huang and P.J. Stanners (1998) 'Comparing the effectiveness of the web site with traditional media', *Journal of Advertising Research*, 38 (5), 44–51.

Lichtenstein, D.R., R.G. Netemeyer and S. Burton (1990) 'Distinguishing coupon proneness from value consciousness: an acquisition-transaction utility theory perspective', *Journal of Marketing*, 54 (3), 54–67.

Lichtenstein, D.R., R.G. Netemeyer and S. Burton (1995) 'Assessing the domain specificity of deal proneness: a field study', *Journal of Consumer Research*, 22 (3), 314–327.

Lodish, L.M., M. Abraham, S. Kalmenson, J. Livelsberger, B. Lubetkin, B. Richardson and M.E. Stevens (1995) 'How TV advertising works: a meta-analysis of 389 real world split cable TV advertising experiments', *Journal of Marketing Research*, 32 (2), 125–139.

MAI (2000) *Sponsorship 2000*, Market Assessment International, London.

Marken, G.A. (1992) 'Firms can maintain control over creative co-op programs', *Marketing News*, 28 September, 7–9.

Marketing (1999) 'Adwatch of the decade', *Marketing*, 16 December, 20–23.

McCann, J., A. Tadlaoui and J. Gallagher (1990) 'Knowledge systems in merchandising: advertising design', *Journal of Retailing*, 66 (3), 257–277.

McQuarrie, E.F. (1998) 'Have laboratory experiments become detached from advertiser goals? A meta-analysis', *Journal of Advertising Research*, 38 (6), 15–25.

Meenaghan, T. (1998) 'Current developments and future directions in sponsorship', *International Journal of Advertising*, 17 (1), 3–28.

Michell, P.C.N. and N.H. Sanders (1995) 'Loyalty in agency-client relations: the impact of the organisational context', *Journal of Advertising Research*, 35 (2), 9–21.

Michell, P.C.N., H. Cataquet and S. Hague (1992) 'Establishing the causes of disaffection in agency-client relations', *Journal of Advertising Research*, 32 (4), 41–48.

Miller, D.W., J. Hadjimarcon and A. Miciak (2000) 'A scale for measuring advertisement-evoked mental imagery', *Journal of Marketing Communications*, 6 (1), 1–20.

Mintel (1988) 'Retail advertising its place in the marketing mix', *Retail Intelligence*, 1, 4.1–4.27.

Mintel (1999) *Retail Advertising*, Mintel Special Report, London

Morgan Stanley Dean Witter (1999) *The European Internet Report*, Morgan Stanley Dean Witter, London.

Nielsen (1996) *The Retail Pocket Book 1996*, NTC Publications, Henley-on-Thames.

Nielsen (2001) *The Retail Pocket Book 2001*, NTC Publications, Henley-on-Thames.

Nowak, G. J., G.T. Cameron and D. Delorme (1996) 'Beyond the world of packaged goods: assessing the relevance of integrated marketing communications for retail and consumer service marketing', *Journal of Marketing Communications*, **2** (3), 173–190.

Ody, P. (1987) 'How effective is your advertising?', *Retail & Distribution Management*, **15** (1), 9–12, 60.

O'Guinn, T., C.T. Allen and R.J, Semenik (1998) *Advertising*, Southwestern Publishing, Cincinnati, OH.

Papatla, P. and L. Krishnamurthi (1996) 'Measuring the dynamic effects of promotions on brand choice', *Journal of Marketing Research*, **33** (1), 20–36.

Paton, N. (1996) 'Asda goes live on "videowall" plans', *SuperMarketing*, 2 August, 10.

Peattie, S. and K. Peattie (1993) 'Sales promotion competitions—a survey', *Journal of Marketing Management*, **9**, 271–286.

Piacentini, M., L. MacFadyen and D. Eadie (2000) 'Corporate social responsibility in food retailing', *International Journal of Retail & Distribution Management*, **28** (11), 459–469.

Pope, N.K.L. and K.E. Voges (1999) 'Sponsorship and image: a replication and extension', *Journal of Marketing Communications*, **5** (1), 17–28.

Poster Scene (1987) 'Posters make the advertising £ go further', *Poster Scene*, **2**, 22–23.

Preston, C. (2000) 'The problem with micro-marketing', *Journal of Advertising Research*, **40** (4), 55–58.

Quester, P.G. (1997) 'Awareness as a measure of sponsorship effectiveness: the Adelaide Formula One Grand Prix and evidence of incidental ambush effects', *Journal of Marketing Communications*, **3** (1), 1–20.

Quester, P.G., F. Farrelly and R. Burton (1998) 'Sports sponsorship management: a multinational comparative study', *Journal of Marketing Communications*, **4** (2), 115–128.

Ramaseshan, B. (1990) 'Research note: marketing budgeting practices of retailers', *European Journal of Marketing*, **24** (8), 40–45.

Rust, R.T. and R.W. Oliver (1994) 'The death of advertising', *Journal of Advertising*, **4** (December), 71–77.

Schultz, D.E. and H.F. Schultz (1998) 'Transitioning marcoms into the twenty-first century', *Journal of Marketing Communications*, **4** (1), 9–26.

Shimp, T.E. (1997) *Advertising, Promotion and Supplemented Aspects of Integrated Marketing Communications*, Harcourt Brace, Fort Worth, TX.

Shipley, D., J. Fahy, C. Egan and T. Haugen (1995) 'Perceptions of agency executives on dimensions of press advertisement effectiveness', *Journal of Marketing Communications*, **1** (2), 91–104.

Smith, P.R. (1993) *Marketing Communications: An Integrated Approach*, Kogan Page, London.

Soley, L.C. and W.L. James (1982) 'Estimating the readership of retail newspaper advertising', *Journal of Retailing*, **58** (3), 59–75.

Somers, T.M., Y.P. Gupta and S.R. Herriott (1990) 'Analysis of co-operative advertising expenditures: a transfer-function modeling approach', *Journal of Advertising Research*, **30** (5), 35–49.

Speed, R. and P. Thompson (2000) 'Determinants of sports sponsorship response', *Journal of the Academy of Marketing Science*, **28** (2), 226–238.

Spitzer, H. and F.R. Schwartz (1982) *Inside Retail Sales Promotion and Advertising*, Harper & Row, New York.

Stewart, D.W. and D.H. Furse (2000) 'Analysis of the impact of executional factors on advertising performance', *Journal of Advertising Research*, **40** (6), 85–88.

SuperMarketing (1996) 'Argyll rebrands Safeway', *SuperMarketing*, 17 May, 3.

Teel, J.E. and W.O. Bearden (1980) 'A media planning algorithm for retail advertisers', *Journal of Retailing*, **56** (4), 23–39.

Tellis, G.J., R.K. Chandy and P. Thaivanich (2000) 'Which ad works, when, where and how often? Modeling the effects of direct television advertising', *Journal of Marketing Research*, **37** (1), 32–51.

Thwaites, D. (1994) 'Corporate sponsorship by the financial services industry', *Journal of Marketing Management*, **10**, 743–763.

Twyman, A. (1986) 'Monitoring advertising performance: a canter round the field', *Admap*, **250**, 131–135.

Vantagepoint (2000) *Overview of the Marketing Communications Sector*, Vantagepoint Management Consultants, London.

Walters, D. and D. White (1987), *Retail Marketing Management*, Macmillan, Basingstoke.

Ward, J. (1985) 'Retailers and advertising: who's changing who?', *Retail*, **3** (3), 8–9.

Wells, W.D. (2000), 'Recognition, recall and rating scales', *Journal of Advertising Research*, **4** (6), 14–20.

White, J.B. and M.P. Miles (1996) 'The financial implications of advertising as an investment', *Journal of Advertising Research*, **36** (4), 43–52.

Wilcox, D.R. and R. Szathmary (1991) 'Getting your money's worth: third party documentation agencies are trying hard to make co-op reimbursement as painless as possible', *Sales and Marketing Management*, **143** (5), 64.

Wilmshurst, J. and A. Mackay (1999) *The Fundamentals of Advertising*, Butterworth-Heinemann, Oxford.

Woonbong, N.A., R. Marshall and Y. Sou (1999) 'An assessment of advertising agency service quality', *Journal of Advertising Research*, **39** (3), 33–41.

Yoon, K., P. Bolls and A. Lang (1998) 'The effects of arousal on liking and believability of commercials', *Journal of Marketing Communications*, **4**, 101–114.

Yorke, D.A. and P.J. Kitchen (1985) 'Channel flickers and video speeders', *Journal of Advertising Research*, **25** (2), 21–25.

Young, R.F. and S.A. Greyser (1983) *Managing Co-operative Advertising: A Strategic Approach*, D.C. Heath, Lexington, MA.

Zaltman, G. and R.H. Coulter (1995) 'Seeing the voice of the customer: metaphor-based advertising research', *Journal of Advertising Research*, **35** (4) 35–52.

Twelve

The Selling Environment

INTRODUCTION In all forms of store-based retailing, decisions relating to the design and arrangement of the store environment are key elements of the retail market mix. The early spread of self-service retailing into many sectors emphasized the need to make the most cost-effective use of in-store selling space. The rapid development of large new stores from the 1970s drew attention to the need to consider the store selling environment as a whole, to ensure that the shopping experience is convenient and attractive. In the 1980s and 1990s, there was much emphasis upon store design, used as a powerful weapon in the quest to achieve image differentiation. In the 2000s, store environments are now also a key element in the competition between physical and electronic shopping alternatives.

Indeed, e-tailing competition has focused the minds of store-based retailers upon consumers' experiential motives for shopping (Sec. 3.1). While the potential of stores to provide pleasure and theatre has long been acknowledged, retailers increasingly find themselves within an 'experience economy' (Pine and Gilmore, 1999). As people spend more time within their homes, they have a greater appetite for 'experiential retailing' when they do go out (Kim, 2001). Consequently, retailers are redefining themselves as a source of memories, rather than simply goods, as an 'experience stage' (Mathwick et al., 2001). Stores are therefore being transformed into 'retail interactive theatre', offering cooking lessons, beauty makeovers, fashion shows and much more (Mahler, 2000).

This chapter considers several elements in creating the store environment, starting with the overall design of stores, which could be seen as an extension of retail advertising and promotion. The concept of atmospherics is explored, as are elements of environmental psychology which are relevant to the design of the retail environment. Decisions regarding store layout and product display are then considered, including measures of display effectiveness. Attention then turns to the detailed allocation of display space, the concept of space elasticity, and systems for allocating space between categories and individual products.

Finally, concepts and measures of unplanned purchasing are examined, this representing one of the main effects of a well-designed selling environment. The focus is therefore upon the store itself and on its multiple roles in attracting customers, contributing towards an enjoyable/stimulating experience and maximizing their purchases within the store.

It is relevant at this stage to comment on the term 'merchandising', in order to avoid ambiguities. To manufacturers, the scope of merchandising may be almost as wide as that of retailing itself. In the USA, retailers also tend to adopt a broad definition of the term; for example:

> *merchandising consists of the activities involved in acquiring particular goods and/or services and making them available at the places, times and prices, and in the quantity that will enable a retailer to reach its goals (Berman and Evans, 1995).*

In the UK, retailers usually ascribe a more specific meaning to the term. Rogers (1985) lists the merchandise mix, space allocation and product placement as being the primary scope of merchandising. The role of 'merchandising managers' does however vary enormously between companies. Because of its many different definitions and connotations, the term 'merchandising' is used sparingly.

12.1 Design and Atmosphere

Throughout the last two decades, there has been enormous investment by retailers and shopping centre developers in new store designs and refurbishments. Accordingly, a major industry has developed, as design companies have focused their attention on the design of retail selling environments. Mintel (1999) estimated shopfitting projects to have an annual worth of £1.5 billion, with the design work valued at around £70 million per year. As yet, a strong conceptual framework for retail design has not been developed, although promising contributions have been made in the study of retail 'atmospherics'. This section first looks at the current role, scope and effectiveness of retail design, and then considers some of the conceptual and empirical research findings that are relevant to this function.

12.1.1 Store Design

The design function has become one of the most visible elements of retail positioning strategy. Although not a panacea for strategy problems, the importance of retail design is now widely acknowledged. According to leading designer Rodney Fitch: 'only one company in any market can be the cheapest: all the others have to add value and the most effective way of doing that is by design'. This could be regarded as a partisan view, although it is backed up in large measure by Anita Roddick of the Body Shop: 'Design is a matter of survival. In the cacophony of the High Street, you need to set yourself apart to survive' (Design Council, 1997).

Indicative of the enhanced stature of design is the number of potential roles that the store design may now be seen to fulfil. It can be assumed that the design will seek to achieve basic, functional requirements, while providing a pleasant shopping experience, conducive to making purchases. In addition, a number of authors have suggested other objectives that the retail environment may be designed to achieve:

▶ The store provides information value, attracting shoppers requiring such comparative information (Baker, 1998).
▶ The exterior and interior design convey messages to passers-by about the likely prices, quality, service levels, etc. of the store (Ward et al., 1992).
▶ Designs can reinforce or expand upon the values associated with a specific brand name (Gottdiener, 1998).
▶ The store can enhance consumer judgements about the qualities of the products and brands sold (Akhter et al., 1994).
▶ The store can create an experience that is an embodiment of a strong brand identity, such as Nike Town Chicago (Sherry, 1998).
▶ The store may aim to lower customers psychological defences, encouraging them to spend more time and maybe invite salesperson assistance (Green, 1986).
▶ The store design creates a stage upon which lifestyle roles are acted out, as in some of the finest Japanese stores (Creighton, 1998).
▶ The uniforms and neatness of the staff, along with corresponding consumer reactions, enhance the experience in the retail environment (Solomon, 1998).
▶ The store is designed to reflect the particular values of the locality, requiring design differentiation within the chain of stores (Wallendorf et al., 1998).
▶ 'Retailing theatre' and 'store theatrics' are terms coined to reflect the convergence of retailing and theatre, for example in music shops with live appearances by artists (Newcomb, 1999).
▶ Experiential retailing is especially conspicuous at the stores of Walt Disney, Warner Brothers, Niketown, Rainforest Cafes and Planet Hollywood restaurants (Kim, 2001).

The demand for more exciting store designs is largely consumer led. Expectations have been widened by increased travel, highly developed media and a greater diversity of leisure activities. There is also a growing need to establish some degree of individuality, which is particularly manifest in the purchasing of furniture and fashion goods. The selling environment should therefore make a positive statement about what the products can do to make the shopper a more interesting individual (Calcott, 1980). The role of the retail designer has progressed from shopfitting to the provision of entertainment and inspiration to customers, thus creating added value in using the store (Mintel, 1999).

Having defined the target customer segments, retail design can assist in focusing the store upon their needs, while also 'getting away from the curse of the average'. Thomas (1987) pointed out that there are other reasons, good and not so good, for implementing design changes. Some retailers have refurbished stores simply because the competition has done so; others have tried design as a last resort when everything else has failed. Practical reasons may dictate the need for design changes, such as changing product assortments or the need to make better use of space. Whatever the motives, the use of design is unlikely to be successful unless it is integrated with merchandise policy, pricing, advertising and other elements of the strategic mix.

The scope of a store design project depends upon the existing conditions and limitations, the marketing strategy of the retailer and, of course, the available budget. In the case of new stores and centres, where few prior limitations exist, the potential scope of the design function is very wide indeed. It could encompass all facets of internal and external design, fixtures, fittings and forms of communications with the customer. Table 12.1 summarizes the 'total visual merchandising process', as defined by Management Horizons (UK). In practice, a retailer may define a far more restricted design brief, although the designer should ensure that these elements are harmonized in order to avoid incongruity.

Table 12.1 Total visual merchandising process

Source: adapted from Management Horizons.

Store environment design	Merchandise presentation	In-store customer communications	Consumer senses appeal
Store façade	Major trends	Signs	Sight
Decor	Store layout	Tickets	Hearing
Walls	Presentation methods	Product information	Smell
Floors	Assortment	Graphics	Taste
Ceilings			
Lighting	Category co-ordination	Sound	Touch
Atmosphere			
Design integrity	Sample displays	Textures	Concept
		Entertainment	– ideas
Fixtures	Feature	Education	– images
Communications	Lighting	Active	
Heating and ventilation	Colours	Promotions	
		Personal	
Services	Window displays	Services	
Interior		Cash points	
Partitioning			
Modular systems		Interactive kiosks	

For example, when redesigning the exclusive Dunhill Shop in the St James area of London, Landor Associates moved the entrance to a corner position and made it somewhat less intimidating to customers. Overall, the store moved from a 'clubby' and traditional atmosphere to one of elegance and leisure. A new design for Greggs bakeries was developed by Crabtree Hall. Here again, attention was given to softening the entrance and removing the barrier that traditional shop doorways represent. In this case, it was achieved by a special counter which curves round in line with the store frontage. The Greggs redesign took care not to give the impression of moving upmarket, as the company wished to retain its successful mass market position.

Designers of new stores in the UK are more restricted by planning regulations than their counterparts in some other countries (see Chapter 7). Some of the more bizarre and eye-catching exteriors to be found in the USA cannot therefore be emulated. However, there has been a movement towards more distinctive and attractive exteriors, which can actually help in obtaining permission to build. The architects of Asda's Harrogate store set out to reflect the Edwardian character of the neighbourhood, using a design that incorporated gables and turrets, with decorative stone, slate and ironwork (Sharples, 1986). The Homebase DIY warehouse at Catford adopts the theme of a Victorian greenhouse, with extensive use of plate glass and PVC-domed roofs. Situated next to an existing pond, this offers an eye-catching design, elements of which have since been copied in many other new store exteriors.

Design has also become a major competitive weapon for shopping centres, as they too seek new ways of establishing their competitive differentials. Marking (1986) described the additional problems involved in designing attractive and effective shopping centres:

> *In motivating consumers through a building, the desire for visual variety can play a large part. Retailers use it in the same way that classical gardens were designed—to provide surprise and delight: each new entrance reveals a new vista with its own special atmosphere and treasures beyond. Shopping centres have great trouble duplicating this come-on factor. Unexpectedness is rare because each floor or area is created to be a matching part of the whole complex.*

Very large new centres, such as the Trafford and Bluewater Centres, have sought to overcome this problem by a diversity of materials and design within the different malls. Other, older centres have sought to increase diversity within their refurbishment programmes. Some are rumoured to have consulted experts in the Chinese art of Feng Sui, meaning literally 'wind and water'. Feng Sui does indeed include principles similar to those commonly applied in shopping centres:

- Walkways should be cleared of obstructions to develop a free traffic flow and open mindset.
- Mirrors and seating arrangements enhance feelings of spaciousness and allow for greater awareness of surroundings.
- Crystals, art and bright colours add vibrancy and reflectivity.
- Wind chimes and mobiles develop sounds and movement that stimulates attention: water soothes.
- Plants produce oxygen; ideal for clear thinking.
- Pillars and statues represent stability and being grounded.
- Full-spectrum lighting adds brightness and increases energy levels (Greco, 1999).

Design consultants now play a major role in most major projects. Even the superstore operators, which traditionally preferred to use in-house expertise, are often utilizing outside designers at the concept stage. For example, J. Sainsbury utilized the 20/20 Design & Strategy Consultants to develop new store formats and vehicle liveries. The project management remains in-house, yet the consultants were retained to evaluate the four-year roll out to all stores by 2003. Mintel (1999) lists a number of consultancies specializing in retailing interiors: many are increasingly exporting their expertise with design projects in Europe and elsewhere. Four of the largest design consultancies are:

	Turnover from retail interiors (£000)
Checkland Kindleysides	11 300
Fitch	5 596
BDG McColl	4 593
Conran	2 596

The majority of design projects do meet their objectives, including typically a change of image, an increase in store traffic and/or an increase in average spend. However, the briefing process can be a source of conflict, for a number of reasons. For example, Woodger (1997) describes the retail 'client from hell':

> *A retail strategy may be driven initially by the marketing department but then the trading, merchandising and property departments must be rightly consulted. Unfortunately, our 'client from hell' will have all these departments as clear cut power bases and empires who vigorously defend their areas of interest, too often to the detriment of an idea which needed a creative approach between divisions.*

Sometimes the problems arise because the design concept is communicated in rather a vague way to the retail client:

> *design has been described as a 'complex act of faith'—a design is only a representation of a plan and reality can often be disappointingly different, particularly if managers are not sufficiently informed and aware at the design stage (Lochhead and Moore, 1999).*

To an extent, this problem of 'design communication' will be overcome with increased use of three-dimensional and virtual reality images.

Mintel (1999) set out a number of elements which should be considered within a comprehensive design brief:

1 *Branding and positioning*: the importance of co-ordinating the many elements of design (see Table 12.1) to focus upon the values and preferences of the target market.
2 *Customer flow and space utilization*: retailers need to make the most productive use of space and customers do not like environments which impede their shopping activity, either through confusion or bottlenecks.

3 *Flexibility*: seasonality and local preferences are among the reasons why a design needs to incorporate scope for variations.

4 *Security and safety*: retailers owe a duty of care to shoppers but will also wish to protect themselves against theft by shoppers, estimated at around £1 billion per year (Bamfield, 1994).

5 *Accessibility to all*: this includes those with prams, those using wheelchairs and those with restricted vision. Kaufman-Scarborough (1999) identified many accessibility problems, inspite of legislation in the USA and Europe.

6 *Infrastructure*: wiring for IT, lighting, etc., as well as climate control and other services, impose constraints but the maximum flexibility should be planned within these.

7 *Quantitative analysis*: many 'measures of effect' can be quantified, including customer flow, unit sales and direct product profitability.

8 *Mood and emotions*: the subject matter of the next section, it is becoming increasingly valuable and viable also to measure impacts on customer mood states.

These issues received further elaboration from research by Doyle and Broadbridge (1999). They developed 10 design principles to guide the formulation and implementation of a retail design project.

In addition to the above issues, particular attention is given to the need to change and evolve designs, in the light of experience, new competition and changing customer needs/expectations. Issues of resource are also highlighted, these including money, time, expertise and creativity. In common with all other areas of the retail mix, design must be cost-effective. Among talk of 'store theatrics' it is easy to forget one of the simplest of design principles: 'Shops are designed for one purpose, to generate profits for the companies owning them by performing as effective selling environments' (Mintel, 1999).

12.1.2 Atmospherics in Retailing

The high cost of retail design programmes and, in some cases, their lack of commercial success should underline the need for a scientific approach to the design of retail environments. In some cases, the designs have done no more than imitate others, have been based upon 'packaged concepts', or have simply been aesthetically pleasing. However, major design companies have now developed research functions and the science of 'atmospherics' is developing rapidly. Kotler (1973) defined atmospherics as:

> *The conscious designing of space to create certain effects in buyers. More specifically, atmospherics is the effort to design buying environments to produce specific emotional effects in the buyer that enhance his purchase probability.*

Markin et al. (1976) were among the earliest researchers to focus upon the social psychology of store environments: They concluded:

Retail space, i.e. the proximate environment that surrounds the retail shopper, is never neutral. The retail store is a bundle of cues, messages and suggestions which communicate to shoppers. Retail store designers, planners and merchandisers shape space but that space in turn affects and shapes customer behaviour. The retail store is not an exact parallel to a Skinner box but it does create mood, activate intentions and generally affect customer reactions.

Kotler maintained that the atmosphere of a particular environment could be described in terms of the sensory channels through which the atmosphere is apprehended. The four main dimensions of atmosphere, in the retail context, are therefore:

1 **Visual (sight)**
   Colour
   Brightness
   Size
   Shapes

2 **Aural (sound)**
   Volume
   Pitch
   Tempo

3 **Olfactory (smell)**
   Scent
   Freshness

4 **Tactile (touch)**
   Softness
   Smoothness
   Temperature

This typology does not include impressions gained through the sense of taste, nor have these been the subject of systematic research in the context of retail environments. However, the serving of coffee or wine to browsers in Waterstone's bookshops undoubtedly adds to the store visit experience. Likewise, food samples produced by a chef in Sainsbury's London Colney store add excitement and interest for shoppers. Not only is the work of the chef projected onto videowalls inside the store, it is also accessible on the company website, forming a link with the 'Naked Chef' television advertisements.

More extensive typologies of atmospheric elements have subsequently been developed. For example, Turley and Milliman (2000) identified 57 specific elements, including aspects of the store exterior, as well as 'human variables', such as crowding, privacy and employee characteristics. However, most atmospheric research has focused upon visual, aural and/or olfactory elements, or their cumulative effects.

Visual Components

The visual dimension has been the subject of more scientific investigation, particularly in relation to the use of colours. Bellizzi et al. (1983) undertook a laboratory-based experiment which indicated the effects of colours upon attraction to displays and upon store image. Warm colours would appear appear to be appropriate for store windows, for entrances and for situations associated with unplanned purchases. On the other hand, where a more difficult and prolonged buying decision is usual, warm tense colours may make shopping unpleasant and cause the shopping trip to be more rapidly terminated; cool colours may be more appropriate in such circumstances. The authors pointed out however that, because of the visual overstimulation in many shopping environments, reactions in stores will not exactly correspond with those observed in laboratory settings. The psychological, temperature and distance effects generally associated with different colours are summarized in Table 12.2.

Table 12.2 Effects of different colours in a retail store

Source: Hayne (1981).

Colour	Psychological effect	Temperature effect	Distance effect
Violet	Aggressive and tiring	Cold	Very close
Blue	Restful	Cold	Further away
Brown	Exciting	Neutral	Claustrophobic
Green	Very restful	Cold-neutral	Further away
Yellow	Exciting	Very warm	Close
Orange	Exciting	Warm	Close
Red	Very stimulating	Warm	Close

The implications of colour for retailers are also discussed within a wide-ranging treatment of colour by Rossotti (1983). She noted that different colour schemes can be used to emphasize the uniqueness of departments but that the colour change between departments should not be too abrupt, otherwise customers may feel that they are being 'pushed' through the stores. Bright, primary colours are recommended to create a mood of excitement in the toy department, whereas neutral colours are likely to be more appropriate in the women's clothing departments to avoid clashing with the colourful merchandise. Although some of the effects of colours remain long term, fashions in colours do change. Dalke (1997) observes how orange, unpopular after the 1970s, then made a comeback. Mauve, from being unpopular as a colour in the UK, more recently found a role in association with sports and 'masculine' products.

The technology of store lighting has also responded to the demand for truer colour rendition, combined with the ability to highlight specific merchandise. In this context, the very compact, low-voltage tungsten halogen lights have gained great popularity, with 1750 of them in use within Debenham's refurbished Oxford Street store in London. This was subsequently outshone by the rebuilt Grace Bros department store in Sydney, which now boasts 17 500 light fittings (Hogan, 1998).

The research in this area is still patchy but Rook (1987) recommended bright lighting to facilitate impulse purchases. On the other hand, softer lighting may induce patrons to peruse the merchandise at greater length (Markin et al., 1976). Areni and Kim (1994), on the other hand, found that brighter lights encouraged more examination of products in a wine store; sales, however, were not affected by the lighting level.

Aural Components

A director of a large retail chain asked me about research into the effects of music upon shoppers. It was surprising to learn that the company had not based their use of music upon any systematic research, in spite of running some of the noisiest stores in the UK! Milliman (1982) studied the effects of music tempo upon shopper behaviour. Slow tempo music was found to reduce the pace of traffic flow in-store, compared with fast music or no music at all; the slow music also achieved the best effect upon sales volume. Milliman did warn against excessive generalization of these findings, in that the study was limited to a supermarket setting.

However, the practice of varying music tempo in restaurants has been widely reported (e.g. Yalch and Spangenberg, 1990). Fast tempo music may be used to speed the reuse of tables during the busy lunch period. During quieter evening times, slower music may encourage customers to linger and order high-margin desserts and cocktails. In the store context, it has been found that people shop for longer when exposed to unfamiliar music, but *feel* they are shopping longer when the music is familiar (Yalch and Spangenberg, 2000).

Research sponsored by the Musak Corporation reported higher sales per customer when Musak was played, compared with no music or radio music (Ware and Patrick, 1984). The right choice of music can also improve customers' disposition towards waiting for service. However, the type of music that provokes the most favourable attitude towards the organization may actually increase the perceived duration of the wait (Hui et al., 1997). Perhaps music cannot be a substitute for good service!

The Musak Corporation, based on Seattle, is by no means alone in the provision of music for atmosphere. Muzicord in the UK have supplied 'bespoke' music backgrounds for Laura Ashley, Richards and Toys 'R' Us. Some chains have their own, in-house 'radio stations' (Mintel, 1999). In Sydney, Satellite Music Australia (SMA) broadcasts on 10 channels to over 2000 stores, restaurants and clubs (Walters and Hanrahan, 2000). The style and tempo varies by day and by time. Thursday is a day when many pensioners shop, so the music is chosen accordingly. After 11 p.m., a faster tempo lifts the spirits of late-night shoppers, as well as the night shift of shelf stackers.

Some retail environments, including many UK supermarkets, do not use background music. However, some shoppers find quiet stores intimidating. In the banking context too, silence can detract from the privacy of conversations (Greenland and McGoldrick, 1994). For such circumstances, UK supplier Retail Dynamics can provide 'white noise', a hum which is barely discernible but which reduces feelings of awkwardness (Jones, 1996).

Olfactory Components

Aromatherapists have been exploiting the mood-altering powers of fragrances for very many years. It is claimed that Marcel Proust was prompted to write his epic *A La Recherche Du Temps Perdu* by the aroma of madeleines dipped in tea (Abrahams, 1994). Systematic research into the role of scents in retail environments is of more recent origin. Although limited evidence of measured effects is available, little is known about the ways in which aromas influence moods and behaviour (Bone and Ellen, 1999). There are, however, numerous reported uses of scents in retailing and service environments.

- Aromas chosen to increase optimism, therefore larger bets, in Las Vegas casinos.
- The smell of pot-pourri to contribute to the particular identity of the Victoria Secret lingerie store (Grewel and Baker, 1994).
- Essence of leather to enhance the perception of luxury in car showrooms.
- The smell of coconuts or rum punch in travel agents, to induce purchase of more exotic holidays (Jones, 1996)
- Air smelling of pine trees in the Denver Park Meadows shopping centre, an ambiance supported by security guards dressed as park rangers (Wakefield and Baker, 1998).
- Aroma of baking bread to convey the image of freshly produced food, even if most is pre-packaged.

The technology of using olfactory devices has moved on in recent years, particularly in terms of achieving more even circulation. The BOC Group, a major supplier of oxygen and other gasses, now supplies a system called Aroma Gas, with many available varieties (Jones, 1996). Senta Aromatic Marketing, based in The Netherlands, specializes in the use of scents in retail stores and other marketing contexts.

Table 12.3 lists the aromas tested by Spangenberg et al. (1996), while investigating relationships with attraction and stimulation. The science however is still at an early stage. Scents clearly need to be congruent with target customer preferences/experiences, as well as with the merchandise and brands being sold (Mitchell et al., 1995; Morrin and Ratneshwar, 2000). It is also important to recognize the notion of Gestalt, as consumers perceive environments holistically, not in terms of each individual element. For example, a more pleasurable experience is enjoyed if scents and music are perceived to match, rather than mismatch (Mattila and Wirtz, 2001).

Table 12.3 Examples of scents tested

Source: derived from Spangenberg et al. (1996).

Category	Scent tested	Category	Scent tested
Florals:	Lavender Ylang ylang Blue chamomile Geranium	Woods:	Spruce Sandalwood Cedarwood Birch
Spices:	Cinnamon leaf Nutmeg Clove buds Sage Cardamon Rosemary Marjoram Ginger	Citrus: Mints:	Lemon Bergamot Orange Peppermint Pennyroyal Spearmint

Tactile Components

The tactile elements of a retail environment are numerous and comparatively obvious, although most have not been systematically researched. Modest experiments have shown predictable relationships between heat levels and soft drink sales (Jones, 1996) but the precise effects of temperature and air condition in stores awaits fuller investigation. Assumptions are clearly made, such as the attractiveness of a hot air curtain at the store entrance, on a cold winter's day. Likewise, a cool interior can be a major attraction to visit and to linger, in the heat of an Australian or South European Summer.

Baker (1986) and Mintel (1999) list many store design elements that impact upon the sense of touch. Flooring, such as carpets or cushion tiles, can increase shopper's walking comfort but harder surfaces, such as marble or wood, may be used to signal luxury, style or warmth. Shoppers also touch shopping trolleys, baskets and counter surfaces, each of which communicates impressions of the store. Information technology may also have tactile appeal, with touchscreen kiosks providing information on product locations, stock levels, bargain offers, etc.

The ability to touch merchandise can be a major step towards buying, moving the shopper a step towards possessing, as well as providing reassurance about texture, quality, etc. According to Underhill (2000):

> *We live in a tactile-deprived society, and shopping is one of our few chances to freely experience the material world firsthand. Almost all unplanned buying is a result of touching, hearing, smelling or tasting something on the premises of a store.*

Although not part of the designed environment as such, people clearly play a part in retail atmospherics. Chapter 5 has already looked at how other shoppers influence the images of stores. Store staff and shoppers are both influenced by the store ambiance, and also contribute towards it (Bitner, 1992). In tests of environmental effects, Baker et al.

(1992; 1994) examined social factors, specifically the number and friendliness of employees, alongside non-personal factors, such as lighting and music. Both sets of factors influenced the levels of pleasure and arousal of shoppers.

The conceptual framework that has become most influential in the study of atmospherics was suggested by Donovan and Rossiter (1982), based upon an environment psychology approach. Their study suggested that: 'store atmosphere, engendered by the usual myriad of in-store variables, is represented psychologically by consumers in terms of two major emotional states—pleasure and arousal'. These two emotional states are held to be important mediators between in-store stimuli and shopper behaviour. Behavioural responses were classified into a series of approach or avoidance outcomes, including whether or not the shopper wished to stay in the store and whether or not a desire to explore the store was generated. The study concluded:

> *arousal, or store induced feelings of alertness and excitement, can increase time in the stores and also willingness to interact with sales personnel. In-store stimuli that induce arousal are fairly easy to identify and almost certainly include bright lighting and upbeat music. Inducement of arousal works positively only in store environments that are already pleasant; arousal inducement may have no influence (or even negative influence) in unpleasant store environments.*

While some would argue the ease with which the key stimuli can be identified, the framework as a whole has received extensive support from later research. McGoldrick and Pieros (1998) demonstrated linkages between three environmental variables and measures of pleasure and arousal. Others have focused upon the latter part of the framework, i.e., the effects of pleasure and arousal upon behavioural intentions (e.g. Babin and Darden, 1996; Van Kenhove and Desrumaux, 1997).

The impact of pleasure and arousal upon time spent in the store, and incremental spending, has been further validated (Donovan et al., 1994). However, most of the store environment elements that can induce pleasure and arousal can also produce irritation, if of the wrong type or of the wrong intensity (D'Astous, 2000). Optimal arousal theories suggest the existence of target-arousal levels to achieve maximum satisfaction levels (Wirtz et al., 2000). Clearly, the optimal level of any environmental stimulus will vary, according to the characteristics and self-images of the target clientele (Sirgy et al., 2000).

The emphasis upon two mood states, pleasure and arousal, has led to the neglect of other emotions potentially engendered by in-store environments (Machleit and Eroglu, 2000). Based upon ethnographic interviews, Yoo et al. (1998) suggested a wider range of emotional factors:

Positive feelings	*Negative feelings*
Pleased	Ignored
Attractive	Anxious
Excited	Nullified
Contented	Displeased
Proud	Angry
Satisfied	

Of course, environments can affect behaviour in a number of different ways, not just through mood states (Greenland and McGoldrick, 1994). For example, aspects of the efficiency of the environment, such as layout and information availability, also directly influence shopper behaviours. Other elements impact upon consumers' images of the store (e.g. Baker et al., 1994), thereby influencing future patronage decisions and word-of-mouth communications. Atmospherics have also been found to affect shoppers' perceptions of salespeople, thereby influencing their ability to sell effectively (Sharma and Stafford, 2000).

Figure 12.1 draws together some of these themes, offering a model of how retail environments may influence short and long-term shopping outcomes. This also incorporates Tai and Fung's (1997) observation that in-store behaviour can influence mood states, rejecting the notion that the causal link is normally the other way around.

Another concept of relevance to the store environment is that of 'hedonic consumption' (Hirschman and Holbrook, 1982). Hedonism

Figure 12.1 A model of retail environments' influences on shopping outcomes

Source: derived from Baker et al. (1994): Greenland and McGoldrick (1994); Tai and Fung (1997).

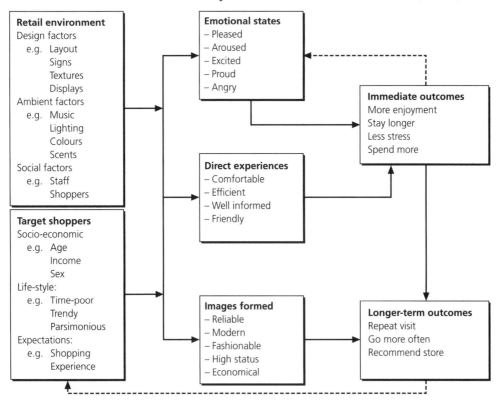

has been variously defined as the pursuit of pleasure, or a lifestyle devoted to pleasure-seeking. While few are able to devote themselves entirely to pleasure, the quest for hedonic experience is widespread (Hopkinson and Pujari, 1999). According to Campbell (1987), through hedonism we create enchantment or endow the world with magic. Hirschman and Holbrook (1982) defined hedonic consumption as 'those facets of consumer behaviour that relate to the multisensory, fantasy and emotive aspects of product usage experience'.

'Multisensory' indicates the receipt of experience through multiple senses, such as sounds, scents and visual images. The hedonic perspective suggests that consumers not only respond to multisensory imagery from external stimuli but also generate multisensory images within themselves. These may represent historic imagery, recalling past events on the basis of the stimuli, or fantasy imagery, where an imaginary experience is constructed in the mind of the consumer. The visual effects, aromas and sounds of a specialist delicatessen, for example, may evoke historic images of enjoyable foreign holidays. The multisensory stimuli of the boutique or the cosmetics department may be designed to evoke fantasy imagery of a rather different kind!

The concept of 'experiential marketing' has gained increased recognition, as so many services, like goods before them, become commoditized (Chebat and Dubé, 2000). According to Pine and Gilmore (1998), the next competitive battlefield lies in staging experiences, a trend in which some retailers and shopping centres are well ahead of the field. As Tauber observed in 1972, shopping can provide immediate personal gratification, a form of experiential value, in addition to the utilitarian value of obtaining goods, services, information, etc. (Babin and Attaway, 2000). Schmitt (1999) refers to five 'strategic experiential modules':

1 *Sense*: various sensory experiences.
2 *Feel*: appeals to inner feelings and emotions.
3 *Think*: creating problem-solving experiences that engage customers creatively.
4 *Act*: inducements to act spontaneously, rather than through elaborate reasoning, for example, in making impulse purchases.
5 *Relate*: appeals that identify with a peer group, or perhaps a sports team.

The potential for stores to engage in experiential marketing has long been recognized, at least implicitly, but enormous scope exists for scientific investigation. Some of the qualitative techniques utilized in advertising research, such as the Metaphor Elicitation Technique (Zaltman and Coulter, 1995), could well be adapted and deployed in the context of atmospherics research. Likewise, techniques based upon neuro-linguistic programming could help capture the experiences that people associate with a store (Drummond, 1995).

12.2 Store Layout and Display

Having considered the effects of the overall store design and atmosphere on shopper behaviour, this section examines the more direct approaches to maximizing sales through the arrangement of the store environment. Through careful design of the store layout, a retailer can make the best use of available space and also manipulate traffic flow within the store to maximize exposure to the merchandise. Through the selective use of special displays, that exposure can be further increased to assist in the promotion of specific products or to provide an additional attraction to the stores as a whole. Displays also form an important part of the 'information environment' which should assist shoppers in their decision-making processes (Fletcher, 1987).

12.2.1 Store Layouts

Many different types of layout option are available to retailers, and the choice is likely to be determined by market positioning, merchandise type, size of store cost, and security considerations. Most layout patterns contain elements of one or more of the following:

1 *Grid pattern layout*: this is characterized by long rows of parallel fixtures, with straight aisles and little or no opportunity to pass between aisles, other than by going to the end of the aisle. Grid patterns are common in supermarkets and have also been adopted in some non-food contexts, especially where there is a desire to convey an image of cheapness. The grid gives the maximum exposure to merchandise by encouraging circulation around the whole store. Little space is wasted, and it is usually economical to install and maintain. On the other hand, the overall effect can be rather dull, and shoppers may become alienated by having to walk down long aisles, if the concept is pursued to extremes.

2 *Free-flow layout*: here the shopper is allowed considerably more freedom to move in any direction between fixtures, which are arranged in more irregular patterns. Many fashion stores use a free-flow layout, which encourages browsing and can be visually appealing. On the other hand, less intensive use is made of floor space, costs are usually higher and, unless carefully co-ordinated, the overall effect may be one of confusion.

3 *Boutique layout*: this is a variation of the free-flow layout, but the departments or sections are arranged in the form of individual speciality shops, targeted at specific market segments (Rosenbloom, 1981). The boutique layout may be a result of using concessions (shops within shops), but its use is by no means confined to that situation. This layout does not usually offer an economical use of space but it does allow more complete orientation of design towards the target group.

4 *Guided shopper flows*: less common than the above variants, this approach is used in particular by IKEA. Termed the 'yellow brick road' by some (e.g. Which?, 1989), this long path takes shoppers through almost every section of its 200 000 square foot stores.

Although giving massive exposure to the store's many themed areas, the approach has exhausted the patience of some users of its stores (Retail Review, 2000a).

Whatever system, or combination of systems, is adopted, the effects of the layout upon shopper circulation should be carefully evaluated. Rogers (1985) outlined the procedure adopted in tracking studies, starting with a diagram of the store or section of the store. The path taken through the store by a sample of customers is then observed and recorded on the diagram. Tracking can be useful too in observing shopper movements within shopping centres (Brown, 1988; 1992), demonstrating how shoppers combine visits to different stores. It has also been used to produce detailed insights into the role of young children within the purchase decisions of family groups in stores (Rust, 1993).

Shopper tracking was a labour-intensive process and it was often difficult to do it covertly, so as not to interfere with the behaviour being studied. A number of largely automated systems are now available, such as Datatec's infrared movement detectors at entrances to stores or departments (Mandeville, 1994). More sophisticated systems use ceiling sensors to detect unique signals from each shopping trolley, mapping the route and timing of progress through the store. To an extent, self-scanning, as offered by Safeway and some other European retailers, can also provide this information (Harrison, 1995). Reliance Electronics offer a system called SensUs, based upon small cameras around the store, which can automatically produce movement maps, as well as visual images of shopper behaviour. Systems like these offer many benefits to retailers:

- More checkouts can be opened or more deli staff can be provided before the queues build up. System provider Schedule Works claims it can give 15 minutes warning of the need for more checkout staff.
- Knowing the number of browsers in an area helps gauge rates of conversion from browsers to buyers. While EPoS data give precise measures of what is bought, tracking can help to gauge what is not being bought (Kirkup, 1999).
- Group influences can be monitored. National Opinion Poll (NOP) Research Group termed the person–spouse interaction in store 'the elastic band effect'. As one member of the couple stopped to browse, the body language or remarks of the other often exerted a pull upon the browser, causing the browsing to cease (Langton, 1995).
- Another measure is provided, in addition to sales, to assess effectiveness of displays and promotions.
- Customer waiting times can be monitored.
- 'Flat spots' in the layout can be detected and more traffic builders introduced.
- Congestion points are identified and possibly eradicated.

Buttle (1984a) reported increases in sales of 11 per cent, mostly attributable to layout changes following a tracking study. However, as privacy becomes a matter of increased concern among consumers, retailers must beware of a privacy backlash. There are few guidelines on the ethical use of video surveillance by retailers (Kirkup and Carrigan, 2000).

The results of most tracking studies remain confidential but one classic study was published by *Progressive Grocer* (1975). Table 12.4 shows a few of the results from that study. It provides many insights into the workings of the grid pattern layout of a typical supermarket. 95 per cent of shoppers passed through aisle 1, most making a purchase. By aisles 4, 5 and 6, the proportions of shoppers visiting had fallen to around 60 per cent. This rose again to 80 per cent in aisle 7, due to the items in that aisle that are regularly purchased by most shoppers.

Table 12.4 also shows the prevailing directions of travel, most walking inwards in aisle 1, outwards in aisle 2. This zigzag pattern prevailed throughout all 14 aisles of the store, although the effect became more muted as shoppers skipped aisles later in their journeys. Knowledge of the direction of flow can be valuable when making decisions on special display locations, or the location of especially profitable items.

Aisle	Main categories	% shoppers who pass	% passers who buy	% with the flow[1]	% against the flow
1	Fresh fruit, meat, vegetables	95	93	93	0[2]
2	Sauces, charcoal, baby foods	77	90	73	11
3	Soap, health and beauty aids	69	68	80	10
4	Household goods and cleansers	59	59	75	20
5	Detergents, hosiery, sewing	63	83	75	19
6	Kitchen, auto, paint, toilet rolls	58	78	81	14
7[3]	Paper towels, tea, coffee, milk, petfoods	80	88	58	33

Table 12.4 Results from a tracking study

Notes: 1 The flow is the prevailing direction, inwards for aisle 1, outwards for aisle 2, etc.
    2 The residual percentage represents the passers who moved in both directions while in the aisles.
    3 The store had a total of 14 main aisles.

Source: derived from Progressive Grocer (1975).

In multi-level stores, it is a major challenge to stimulate circulation in the higher floors; cafés and other customer services are sometimes used as an attraction to these areas. There has been a great deal of investment by department stores in lifts and escalators that are both attractive and efficient, to try to lessen the perceived barriers between floors, but the costs can be formidable (Woodger, 1997). Even in single-floor layouts, it is a considerable challenge to try to equalize traffic flow in all areas. In a study of mental mapping of two supermarkets, Sommer and Aitkins

(1982) found that the locations of items in peripheral aisles were recalled more frequently and accurately than those of items in central aisles.

In some non-food stores, the front third of the store, nearest the entrance, has more than three times the selling power of the back third of the store. Department and variety stores with food areas often site these centrally or in basement areas, in order to draw regular shoppers through the other departments. Some have had to modify this approach in the case of sandwiches and other snacks, especially if competitors are offering more convenient access.

A battery of supermarket layout techniques has been developed to help maximize circulation and sales (Buttle, 1984b). For example, retailers often place high-demand items close to the entrance, in order to quickly overcome buyer inertia and inhibitions that the customer may have about spending money. The entrance areas are also typically used to create an impression of the store, regardless of the practicality of buying those items at the start of the shopping journey. Easily damaged fresh fruit and flowers are often found on entering supermarkets. In department stores, shoppers have been observed trying to avoid the cosmetics sale staff, who tend to be in abundance around the entry zones (Davies and Rands, 1992).

Within the main gondola areas, high-demand items are placed at regular intervals in order to 'pull' the customer through the aisles. Sometimes these are alternated between the two sides of the aisle to create a 'bounce' pattern, as the customer moves from side to side, gaining maximum exposure to all the displays. Other experiments have shown that, as a trolley is turned one way, the shopper tends to look the other way, into the 'strong side' of the turn. Items displayed on that side therefore have a much better chance of being noticed (Hitt, 1996).

It is also thought that the more difficult, main meal decisions should be encouraged in the first few aisles, allowing shoppers to relax more for the remainder of the shopping trip. 'Impulse' items are typically situated between regular purchase items, sometimes being complementary to the adjacent high-demand items, such as toppings situated near to the desserts. Dreze and Hoch (1998) also suggested that retailers should use their data mines to identify products for which customers are loyal to them, and those they would buy anywhere. Sales of the latter category can then be improved by cross promotions and by placing them close to the high-loyalty items.

With all layout techniques, a delicate balance must be struck between the manipulation of traffic flow and ensuring that the shopping experience is as convenient and enjoyable as possible. Some retailers have learnt this to their cost: displays blocking the aisles, product categories scattered around the stores and frequent, unnecessary changes to product locations are all likely to give the impression of a chaotic or, worse, a conniving store. A layout needs to achieve 'environmental legibility' to avoid causing anger and frustration among shoppers (Titus and Everett,

1995). Some retailers succeed in maintaining a convenient and orderly store, while still encouraging thorough traffic flow. Perhaps the acid test should be the question, 'Am I inviting or am I forcing the customer to be in this part of the store?' From a series of regular surveys, Mintel (2000) found increasing numbers of shoppers who felt that retailers should address issues of layout and design.

A similar balance of considerations must be applied to the width of aisles and the space allowed around checkouts or payment points. Wide aisles run the risk that shoppers will ignore the surrounding displays, but congestion inevitably loses sales (Buttle, 1984a). In the layout of shopping centres, too, the problem exists of trying to maximize exposure to the store frontages without inducing the feeling in shoppers that the centre is dangerous or claustrophobic (Marking, 1986). Both for commercial reasons and because of stronger legislation, retailers are now giving more attention to keeping aisles clear for disabled access (Kaufman-Scarborough, 1999).

The concept of 'retail crowding' is highly relevant to the design of layouts. Eroglu and Harrell (1986) found that customers' perceptions of density in a retail environment are affected by their motives, constraints and expectations. Density could be functional under some circumstances, for example where a low price image has attracted price-sensitive shopper segments. In this situation, the crowds actually reinforce the image and the decision to patronize the store. In an exclusive boutique, however, or where the convenience of shopping is of primary importance, crowding (or dysfunctional density) will deter shoppers. Some 83 per cent of shoppers interviewed by Aylott and Mitchell (1998) mentioned crowding as a cause of stress while shopping. The potentially dysfunctional role of crowding was also confirmed by Hui and Bateson (1991).

Taking a rather different approach, Grossbart et al. (1990) looked for relationships between environmental dispositions and tolerance for crowding in stores. It may be expected that those tending towards pastoralism, antiquarianism and/or the need for privacy would have low tolerance. Those more prone to urbanism, environmental adaptation, environmental trust and/or stimulus seeking may be more tolerant, even attracted, towards crowds. Such esoteric forms of segmentation may be difficult to apply in mass-market environments but could have a role in planning the layout of more focused, niche outlets.

12.2.2 Display Techniques

This section considers the way in which merchandise is presented within stores; the amount of space allocated to each product and category is discussed in the following section. A distinction is usually drawn between 'normal' displays, which include every shelf or grouping of merchandise that is visible to the customers, and 'special' or 'off-shelf' displays. Special display have tended to receive more attention both from retail management and from researchers; some of the studies of display effectiveness are considered here. It should be remembered, however, that the design of every area of display within the store exerts an influence upon product sales, the overall image of the store and the efficiency with which available space can be utilized. There are several different approaches to display which represent developments upon the more basic styles of product presentation:

1 *Open displays*: these set out to create involvement by surrounding the shopper with merchandise, rather than distancing the shopper from the display. This approach is used extensively in department and fashion stores. The shopper is more likely to stop and touch the merchandise; the propensity to purchase then tends to increase (Rosenbloom, 1981).

2 *Theme displays*: the choice of themes is very wide, including local or national events, festivals, or specific international themes. The theme may be devised by the store, possibly to suit a particular season or an activity relevant to the clientele, such as support of a local football team.

3 *Lifestyle displays*: in these, the presentation is likely to include pictures and other 'display props' designed to suggest the appropriateness of the store and the merchandise displayed to a specific target segment. These are widely used in clothing retailing, sports goods shops and many other sectors. Marks & Spencer adopted lifestyle displays in its store redesigns, a departure from displaying all clothes alongside these of similar type (Retail Review, 2001).

4 *Co-ordinated displays*: these follow the logic that items, if normally used together, should be displayed together. Clothing retailers, such as Jaegar, therefore display co-ordinated outfits; (Buttle, 1994). Furniture retailers, such as IKEA, create many complete room settings within their stores. This approach presents items within the best context; it tends to be more reasssuring to customers and also stimulates sales of related items.

5 *Category dominance displays*: these are designed to suggest that the retailer offers a great width or depth of assortment in a particular class of merchandise. This may be achieved by displaying together every size, colour or type of a specific product. Tordjman (1994) refers to category dominance displays at Toys 'R' Us, reinforcing the message that the choice is vast.

6 *Power aisles*: a large quantity of a few items is displayed in a power aisle, to give the impression that the prices are low (Smith and Burns, 1996). The approach is characteristic of large, discount operations, such as warehouse clubs, but has been tried out in some superstores.

7 *Names or concessions*: these offer collections of products linked to a specific brand name (Hart and Davies, 1996). The name may be that of an external brand, as in the case of most department store concessions, or an 'internal brand', such as Per Una at Marks & Spencer.

Indeed, there are numerous different approaches to the question of how to group product displays. On the one hand, there is the aim of making the store navigable for shoppers, in terms of being able to find the required items. On the other hand, displays offer much scope for suggestion selling by appropriate positioning of related items. In the case of Jaeger (Buttle, 1994), merchandise is displayed in four main categories:

▶ evening wear
▶ business wear
▶ occasion wear
▶ casual wear.

The proportions of these categories vary by location. Cheltenham, for example, places more display emphasis upon evening wear than casual wear. Detailed decisions on displays and their positions are the responsibility of the company's VM (visual merchandising) department.

The adoption of category management principles (see Chapter 8) by many retailers has stimulated much rethinking of display logic (e.g. IGD, 1997; Varley, 2000). For example, Marks & Spencer improved sales of sandwiches and other lunch snacks by 30 per cent by bringing them together, closer to the entrances. Jones (1996) also reports sales increases in supermarkets of 15 to 20 per cent, when fresh, tinned and dried fruit were grouped together.

Although there are examples of successful regroupings, display rearrangements can add to consumer confusion and time spent searching for goods. If a shopper normally visits most or all of the aisles of the store, the regrouping probably offers no time saving. In fact, the order of the mental or written shopping 'list' is likely to reflect the recalled sequence of products in the store.

Areni et al. (1999) report on a regrouping of wine displays by region of origin, rather than colour or variety. The new arrangement did not lead to the predicted effect. Sales of wines from less preferred regions decreased, compared with when they were grouped by colour and variety. It was concluded that the grouping had increased the salience of the region criterion within consumers' choices.

As superstores become increasingly involved in selling categories of non-foods, it raises the question of how best to locate the displays of these items. Hart and Davies (1996) addressed this question with regard to six categories, as shown in Table 12.5. Consumer preferences clearly reflect familiarity with various types of product display but clear patterns emerge. Aisles are not the most favoured display locations in supermarkets for clothes, but they are acceptable for household goods and health and beauty products. Displays on separate fixtures or floors, but within the main shop, are preferred for stationery and items for the home. The separate 'boutique' areas for clothes and entertainment also offer better security with these easily stolen items.

Displays are not confined to the immediate selling areas of the store. For many years, department stores have practised the art of elaborate window displays (Lea-Greenwood, 1998) and, at the more basic level,

Table 12.5 Consumer preferences for display locations

Note: scores closer to 100 indicate high preference for that type of display location, closer to zero indicates low preference.

Source: derived from Hart and Davies (1996).

Non-food item in supermarkets	Type of display location			
	Aisle	**Fixturing**	**Boutique**	**Name or concession**
Clothes	30.0	59.7	63.4	48.3
Household	93.2	94.6	8.1	4.2
Home	58.4	71.0	44.1	27.0
Health and beauty	87.5	91.8	13.2	7.8
Stationery	54.9	66.1	45.8	34.4
Entertainment	32.7	51.8	64.8	51.6

windows are used extensively for price announcements by many discount stores. Although window displays can provide a powerful attraction to the store, they are now being given less emphasis in some retail contexts. One reason is that the more elaborate window displays are expensive and require specialist skills if they are to be effective. Another is that designers often try to lessen the perceived barriers between the outside and inside of the store. An open view into the store or, in enclosed shopping malls, an entirely open frontage can achieve this. More attention is now being given to the total store's display potential. Walls or support pillars are more attractive and useful if adorned with displays relevant to the adjacent products; similarly, high ceilings can offer scope for suspended display material, which may also help to create a more intimate and exciting atmosphere.

Display techniques appropriate to supermarket-type settings were discussed in detail by Buttle (1984a; 1984b). In some cases the most orderly displays do not achieve the best effects, at least not in terms of immediate product sales. In fact, 'starter-gaps' are sometimes left in newly constructed displays to suggest that the product is selling rapidly; there may also be some inhibition about disturbing orderly displays. Dump bins and cut case displays can also achieve the dual benefits of making products easy to pick up and also conveying the impression of bargains. The objectives of 'off-shelf' displays include the following:

1 Meeting consumer demand, if normal shelf space does not allow sufficient stock to be displayed at peak season or during promotions.
2 Creating consumer demand, by attracting consumers' attention in order to increase sales of high-margin lines, bulk puchases or excess stock.
3 Reminder displays for items required with low frequency but by most shoppers, such as holiday needs (Fader and Lodish, 1990).
4 Suggesting gift ideas, bought by people who do not tend to browse the usual display location for the products.
5 Enhancing store image, by conveying impressions of bargain prices, exclusive merchandise or extensive assortments.

6 Controlling traffic movement, acting either as barriers, to widen circulation, or as attractions to otherwise rather quiet areas of the store.

Some research attention has been given to the short-term effectiveness of displays. Table 12.6 shows the effects achieved by displays positioned in four different types of location within the store (Dyer, 1980). Clearly, those situated at the entrance of the first aisle tend to achieve considerably more effect. In a study of displays of a pharmacy product, Gagnon and Osterhaus (1985) also found that effectiveness varied significantly between different positions within the stores.

Table 12.6 Effectiveness of display locations
Source: Dyer (1980), © Progressive Grocer 1980.

	Increase upon normal sales %
On back of store gondola end	110
Mid-aisle in front of checkouts	262
On front of store gondola end	153
At entrance to first aisle	363

The measurement of display effects is made more complex by the fact that changes in display are usually accompanied by changes in price, advertising and/or space allocation. Characteristics of the product and its market are also likely to exert an influence upon the effects on display. Based upon eight product categories, Chevalier (1975a) investigated the effects of market growth, competitive structure, market share, price cuts and advertising-to-sales ratio upon the impact of display.

Display proved to be most effective for mature products and for those product groups within which no one brand has a clear market advantage. The combination of display and a special price cut appeared to be especially effective where products had a close competitive structure and a low advertising-to-sales ratio. For some commodities, a special display can move the item into the consideration set of shoppers, and possibly reduce price sensitivity for the promoted item. Consequently, a special display can increase sales, even at normal prices.

In a further multiple-factor experiment, Wilkinson et al. (1981; 1982) studied the short-term effects of price reductions, display alternatives and newspaper advertising on the sales of four supermarket products. Three display levels, three price levels and two advertising levels were incorporated within a factorial design which, with replication and alternating non-experimental weeks, was administered over an 80-week period. It was concluded that, 'Price reductions and changes in display appear to offer a greater opportunity for temporarily increasing unit sales'.

The effects of display and advertising upon the price–sales relationship for each product were also investigated, and the conclusion reached that: 'The effect of increasing shelf space was negligible compared to the sales effect of building a special display' (Wilkinson et al., 1981). This also underlines one of the problems in attempting to compare and generalize from the experimental studies conducted. The actual 'quality' and type of display changes administered varies considerably between the studies, and the distinction between display and in-store advertising becomes somewhat blurred.

The combined effects of display signs and price reductions were investigated by Woodside and Waddle (1975) in a rather smaller-scale experiment, which included two price levels, two price signs and one product (instant coffee). They found that the display sign without a price cut produced more additional sales than a 20 per cent price cut with no special display sign. When both treatments were applied, a synergism was found to exist in that additional sales greatly exceeded the sum of those produced by each treatment used independently.

In a study based upon department store products, McKinnon et al. (1981) distinguished between the types of display sign used and their interactions with price. Signs that indicated both the price and some product benefits were more effective than 'price only' signs in stimulating sales when the price was reduced. In fact, they were effective even at normal prices! Although many display signs, particularly in supermarkets, tend to be of the 'price only' type, considerable scope exists for combining price and benefit information.

Studies of display effects have concentrated mainly on the direct effects upon product sales, many studies having been sponsored by manufacturers. A major problem for the retailer in researching display effects is to measure also the longer-term effects on store image and patronage. A store that contains many individual displays, each achieving improvements in short-term product sales, may actually be building an image of an uncoordinated, even chaotic environment, which may inhibit patronage in the longer term. Alternatively, the displays may be helping to reinforce an image of the store as an exciting environment or one with many bargains. These longer-term effects are more difficult to measure, but certainly should be a major consideration in display decisions.

12.3 Allocating Display Space

With the long-term trend towards larger stores, it may be tempting to assume that the problems of allocating space are becoming less acute. In fact, this is far from true, and space remains a scarce and valuable resource for retailers. Consumers' demand for more choice, and extensive product developments to satisfy that demand, have ensured that space continues to be under pressure. Retailers' strategies of specialization and/or diversification have also created the need for more space to display deeper or wider product assortments.

12.3.1 Space Elasticity

There has been a tendency in many approaches to space allocation to ignore the influence of space upon sales or, alternatively, to assume that it is equal across all products. This possibly stems from the artificial distinction that is often drawn between 'special' and 'normal' displays.

Few people would expect all products to respond equally to special displays, yet it is sometimes assumed that this is the case with normal displays. However, Phillips and Bradshaw (1993) have shown that shoppers have a flattened cone of peripheral vision, through which they automatically and subconsciously scan the shelves that they pass. A product allocated more space is therefore more likely to be visually perceived, sifted out from the surrounding mass of detail, and therefore more likely chosen.

A number of researchers have set out to prove that 'space elasticity' differs considerably between products. Space elasticity has been defined as: 'the ratio of relative change in unit sales to relative change in shelf space' (Curhan, 1973). Attempts to measure space elasticity have generally adopted either experimental or cross-sectional approaches. Experimentation allows the manipulation of a real situation and the observation of the results, set against a control situation. There are, however, some difficulties:

1 The scope of the experiment is usually limited to a few products, stores and/or points in time.
2 Only the short-term results are usually observed, whereas space allocations also affect longer term images and patronage decisions.
3 It is difficult to exclude bias from the experiment, for example, the propensity of staff to keep displays unusually tidy when they are known to be under observation.

These problems are difficult to overcome, as retailers are understandably reluctant to risk major disruption of store operations and customer goodwill in order to co-operate with large-scale experiments. Cross-sectional approaches overcome these problems by statistically deriving the space–sales relationship from observations of space allocations and sales results in many different stores. The approach therefore permits the calculation of space elasticities for many, even all, products or categories within the assortment. The cross-sectional approaches unfortunately are not without their problems, either:

1 The relationships are only inferred; it cannot therefore be firmly established that the space is the cause and the sales are the effect, as the reverse may be true.
2 The available sample of stores may be too heterogeneous for the space–sales records to be truly comparable.
3 The approach is effective only if a range of space allocations exists between the stores; if they are standardized, then it is not possible to judge the effects of different allocations.

Among the early experimental approaches, Kotzan and Evanson (1969) found significant responses to increased space allocations for three of the four drug store products that they tested. That type of experimental design gave no indication of the extent of inter-brand or size substitution. In order to overcome this limitation, Chevalier (1975b) adopted a more comprehensive measurement system in a study in four supermarkets and concluded that only a modest proportion of sales increase resulted from substitution within the store; most of the increase was therefore assumed to be gained at the expense of other stores.

From a review of several earlier experiments, Dreze et al. (1994) report typical space elasticities of around 0.2. In other words, the effect of doubling the facing would be to increase sales by 20 per cent. Desmet and Renaudin (1998) estimated space elasticities for 24 product categories in a chain of variety stores. Table 12.7 shows some of these elasticities. These range from high levels of 0.57, in the case of costume jewellery, fruit and vegetables, down to −0.13 in the case of fashion. In the latter case, increases in space may reduce sales, possibly by undermining the image of exclusivity (*Which?*, 1989). At the high end of the scale, it is likely that some individual products have elasticities far in excess of the category average of 0.57.

Table 12.7 Product category space elasticities

Source: Desmet and Renaudin (1998).

Category	Elasticity	Category	Elasticity
Costume jewellery	0.57	Household	0.17
Fruit and vegetables	0.57	Frozen food	0.17
Underwear	0.55	Table items	0.16
Shoes	0.50	Household linen	0.16
Haberdashery	0.49	Home	0.11
Perfumery	0.39	Kitchen	0.06
Drinks	0.39	Men's wear	0.05
Meat	0.33	Baby clothes	0.03
Dairy	0.23	Do-it-yourself	0.02
Grocery	0.22	Ladies' wear	0.01
Delicatessen	0.22	Children's wear	−0.10
Recording/books	0.18	Fashion	−0.13

Curhan (1972) set out to establish the effects of several independent variables upon space elasticity, based on a study of nearly 500 grocery products under actual operating conditions. The changes in space allocations were those suggested by store management and a computerized management information system. Elasticity proved to be higher for retailer brands than for manufacturer brands and, not surprisingly, higher for 'impulse' items. Unfortunately, from the regression analysis it proved possible to explain only a very small proportion of the variance in space elasticity. From a review of space elasticity studies, Curhan (1973) subsequently concluded that:

> *There is a small, positive relationship between shelf space and unit sales. This relationship, however, is uniform neither among products nor across stores or intra-store locations. A curvilinear model of declining marginal return probably holds; although for specific changes implemented, curvilinear, linear and indeterminate relationships are reported.*

The likely existence of non-linear space–sales relationships had previously been hypothesized by Brown and Tucker (1961). Writing at a time when products tended to be crudely dichotomized as being 'staple' or 'impulse', they suggested that there are at least three broad categories of response:

1 *Unresponsive products*: such as salt, for which increases/decreases in space would be unlikely to cause significant increases/decreases, provided that out-of-stock situations are avoided.
2 *General use products*: such as breakfast foods, for which the effects of increasing space are fairly strong from minimum levels but the point of diminishing returns is reached fairly quickly.
3 *Occasional purchase products*: such as peanuts, which are 'unlooked for' by most shoppers. Sales are likely to respond slowly to shelf space increases until the display is large enough to force its attention on the shopper, at which point the sales curve might rise steeply. This implies the existence of a step function or a threshold effect for some products.

It is intuitively reasonable to assume that space-sales relationships will frequently be non-linear and that thresholds and/or diminishing returns will occur in many cases. Figure 12.2 illustrates the importance of these concepts. Simple, linear elasticity measures can underestimate the potential for improving sales, if the space changes are applied at the right point in the response curve.

Based upon a cross-sectional study of 57 products categories in over 100 supermarkets, McGoldrick and Thorpe (1977) used curve-fitting procedures to identify relationships between space and sales. In only 9 per cent of sales did a linear relationship provide the 'best fit'. Using the equations derived from this procedure, an optimization process was undertaken which, within given boundaries, reallocated space between

Figure 12.2 Alternative space–sales relationships

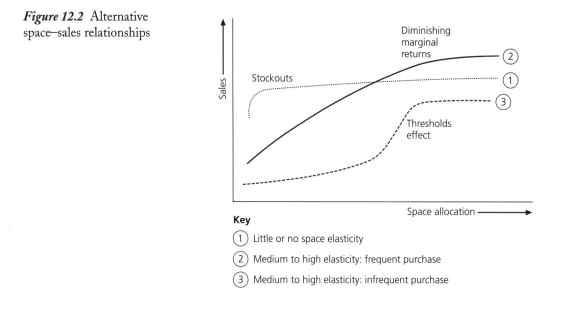

Key
(1) Little or no space elasticity
(2) Medium to high elasticity: frequent purchase
(3) Medium to high elasticity: infrequent purchase

product categories. After a large number of iterations, a solution was produced that suggested an increase in sales of 11.2 per cent.

A major problem in the empirical work is to separate the relatively modest effects of space allocation changes from other more dramatic effects, such as those caused by changes in price, advertising and competitor activity. However, it must be remembered that sales improvements through space allocation changes can be achieved at relatively low cost. This is rarely true of price cuts or increased advertising.

12.3.2 Space Management

Retailers face numerous space allocation decisions at various different levels, i.e., between major departments, between categories, between products and between individual stock-keeping units (SKUs). The broader, category allocation decisions of 14 food retailers were analysed by Verdict (2000). This showed, for example, that Netto allocates nearly 50 per cent of store space to packaged groceries, compared with 27.7 per cent at Tesco and 23.2 per cent at Asda. These allocations reflect different levels of participation in fresh foods and non-food ranges. From a detailed case study in the clothing sector, Kirkup and Moirano (1997) show the minimum space allocations needed to display main lines of clothing within 13 broad categories.

Because these decisions are so numerous, especially in grocery retailing, there has been a tendency to rely upon relatively simple approaches which use readily available data. One doctrine frequently cited is that the space allocated should be directly proportional to the market share of each product. This has been termed the 'share-of-shelf = share-of-market rule' (Borin and Faris, 1995). Some retailers describe the approach as the 'level rundown principle', denoting that the stocks of every item on display run down at approximately the same rate. In situations where the display areas carry all the stocks held by the store and where deliveries to the store are not frequent, the space allocation plan is likely to adopt the principle to some extent.

The manufacturers of leading brands are also enthusiastic advocates of the practice of relating space allocations to current market shares, as this helps to reinforce their market position and to exclude, or at least reduce, potential threats to their position. There are however several reasons why a retailer should not adhere to the principle of relating space allocations directly to sales:

1 It ignores the differential effects of display space in stimulating product sales (space elasticities).
2 Fast-moving lines and market leaders may not produce the best profit for the retailer.
3 Some speciality products may be excluded or may receive negligible display space.
4 Displays dominated by fast-moving lines can give the impression of a narrow and/or mundane assortment.

5 The progress and potential of new products may not be effectively exploited.

Most major retailers have therefore sought to incorporate a wider range of factors in their space management systems. Some of the earlier, 'packaged' systems to emerge included SLIM (store labour and inventory management) and COSMOS (computer optimization and simulation modelling for supermarkets). COSMOS included the DPP (direct product profitability; see Chapter 6) of items. However, Corstjens and Doyle (1981) found many limitations of the early models:

> *The drawback of all these systems stems from their failure to incorporate demand effects. Being limited to data normally on-hand to retailers, they focus essentially on cost and static margin considerations. All have the unrealistic assumption that products have uniform space elasticities and that zero cross elasticities exist among products. As such, none can be considered seriously as optimisation models.*

Corstjens and Doyle (1981; 1983) developed models that recognized both the cost and the demand effects of space allocations. A particular feature of these was the inclusion of cross-elasticities, in addition to space elasticities. The parameters were estimated from a case study, which included 140 stores and five product groups; the cross-sectional approach was used to derive the elasticities. Table 12.8 shows the changes in percentage space allocations suggested by the model for small and for large stores within the chain. When the model was run without the inclusion of cross-elasticities, the implied profit improvement was $128 000 less across the 140 shops. The researchers concluded that:

> *Very significant profit improvements can be expected from an allocation procedure which optimally balances, on the cost side, product gross margins and handling costs and, on the demand side, space elasticities and cross elasticities among items in the store.*

Product	Small stores		Large stores	
	Model % space	**Existing % space**	**Model % space**	**Existing % space**
1	26	30	46	35
2	20	30	25	32
3	7	12	6	12
4	22	18	17	10
5	25	10	6	10
Profit ($)	37 680	31 436	46 530	45 011

Table 12.8 Model and existing space allocations

Source: Reprinted by permission of M. Corstjens and P. Doyle (1981) 'A model for optimizing retail space allocations', *Management Science*, **27**, 7, Copyright © 1981 The Institute of Management Sciences.

Inevitably, as models become more comprehensive, they also tend to become more demanding of data and less readily understood by the majority of retail managers. In order to try to overcome both of these problems, a number of models have been suggested which require the input of management judgements. Singh et al. (1988) suggested a decision support system that used a combination of 'hard' data and management judgements. Rinne et al. (1987) presented an approach to the allocation of space for departments within department stores. Again, management judgements provided an important input, and the model suggested both the specific location and the space for each department for each month.

Even the most sophisticated models may be subject to errors at the estimation stage. However, Borin and Farris (1995) show that a model can significantly outperform the 'level rundown principle', even if subject to error in parameter estimation.

Recent years have, therefore, seen an abundance of new systems and software products, all designed to provide more user-friendly interfaces and outputs for category managers (Buckingham, 1994). In the USA, systems include SpaceMax, Spacemaster and, from the Nielson Retail Information Group, Spaceman (Pearson, 1993). In the UK, Birtwistle (2000) describes how the space management system at Safeway answers numerous 'what if' questions, invaluable if space is to be diverted to other categories.

Most modern systems are able to provide planograms, i.e., plans that allow the retailer to picture the horizontal and vertical layout of the display (Steinhagen, 1990). This brings together many of the tasks of 'numeric' and 'visual' merchandising, reducing the trial and error needed to develop the 'look' of a display. Two-dimensional representation may be sufficient to envisage most supermarket displays. For fashion retailers, however, systems such as Fashion Yield have been developed, which provide three-dimensional images of product layouts (Lea-Greenwood, 1998). A major advantage of such visual images is that they can be downloaded to stores, which can replicate the layout or display.

Planograms also draw attention to the importance of space quality, rather than just quantity. Section 12.2.1 illustrated how different parts of stores can attract very different levels of footfall. Arnold (1996) reports on the intensive use now being made of the front parts of superstores, selling many high margin and impulse prone items. Even at the microlevel of a display close to a till, Pickersgill (1991) shows how sales could improve by 70 per cent, if the product is moved from the worst to the best location within the display.

Dreze et al. (1994) also concluded that space quality effects could be much greater than space quantity (elasticity) effects. Moving an item from the worst to the best *horizontal* position within a display yielded an average improvement of 15 per cent. Movement from the worst to best *vertical* position improved sales, on average, by 39 per cent.

The old retail adage that 'eye level is buy level' has therefore been substantially validated.

Hitt (1996) reports that the optimum position on a shelf is 51 to 53 inches (130 to 135 cm) off the floor. This is based upon standard ergonomic tables of U.S. adult sizes, plus the finding that the best viewing angle is 15 degrees below the horizontal. However, as the average heights of men and women differ by 5 inches (12.5 cm), there is clearly scope for some differentiation (Dreze et al., 1994). There are also significant national differences in average heights; furthermore, child-oriented products, such as certain cereals, will clearly benefit from much lower shelf positions. A very large number of factors should therefore be considered in developing a space plan; Fig. 12.3 outlines some of the major issues. Market share and space elasticity have already been discussed but the space planner must also have regard for the following:

1 ***Avoidance of out-of-stock***: Mintel (2000) report increased numbers of shoppers wanting better stock availability. With smaller space allocations in particular, retailers depend on the supply chain to provide swift replenishments to help avoid stockouts. Not all stockouts lead to the buying of a substitute product in the same store

Figure 12.3 The space plan: influences and consequences

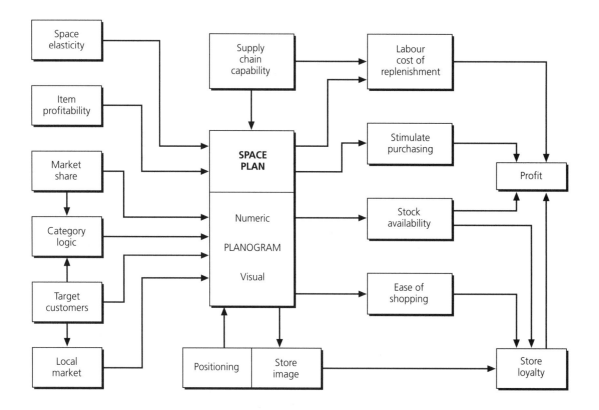

(Koelemeijer and Oppewal, 1999; Verbeke et al., 1998). Not only are sales directly lost to competitors, customers are inconvenienced and their loyalty potentially undermined.

2 *Store image and positioning*: Aldi, for example, devotes just 1.9 per cent of space to chilled provisions, compared to 18.0 per cent for this category at Marks & Spencer (Verdict, 2000). Space allocation both reflects market positioning and contributes to image. Kirkup and Moirano (1997) discuss a menswear store that set out to avoid a 'Jack of all trades' image in its space planning.

3 *Local market needs*: examples of local adaptation of space plans have been reported in the UK (Retail Review, 2000b), France (Desmet and Renaudin, 1998), Belgium (Campo et al., 2000) and The Netherlands (Borren et al., 1995). The *New York Times* (1996) offered many examples of how food preferences differ across the regions of the USA. Armed with GIS data (see Chapter 7), plus their own EPoS data and management knowledge, retailers are well able to adapt to local market needs.

4 *Product profitability*: measures such as GMROI (gross margin return on investment) and DPP (direct product profitability) (see Chapter 6) are commonly used to allocate space between categories. However, retailers have been warned against reverting to a profit push, rather than consumer demand pull, approach to space management (Sanghavi, 1988). The deletion of a line, because its DPP is low, would clearly be ill advised if this caused more people to shop elsewhere (Davies and Rands, 1992).

5 *Category management*: in theory, category management should define the logic of what comprises a category from a consumer perspective (Hogarth-Scott and Walters, 2000; IGD, 1997). The space plan must also have regard for the overall objectives established for the product category. However, excessive tinkering with displays and the locations of products within stores can increase the time, effort and stress of shopping, thereby undermining store loyalty.

It will be apparent from the above that space management requires a balance of strong quantitative techniques and sound judgement. There is little point in creating the ideal store design and atmosphere, if the space plan fails to maintain stock, makes shopping unnecessarily difficult and/or conveys the wrong image.

12.4 Impulse Purchasing

A major objective in designing and arranging the retail environment is to maximize the extent of impulse or unplanned purchasing within the store. It is generally accepted that impulse purchasing has now become a prevalent feature of shopper behaviour in most retail settings. Clearly, the attributes of the retail environment are not the only factors that precipitate impulse purchasing; prices, product characteristics and packaging, point-of-purchase advertising and sales personnel can all contribute to the process. Impulse purchasing may therefore be regarded as a cumulative effect of the many in-store marketing variables.

Impulse purchasing has traditionally been defined in terms of the rapidity of the buying decision. For example, Davidson and Doody (1966) defined it as '*an unplanned, spur of the moment decision to purchase a product*'. For Rook (1987), impulse buying is when '*a consumer experiences a sudden, often powerful and persistent urge to buy something immediately*'. These definitions do not limit impulse purchasing to in-store decisions. For example, D'Antoni and Shenson (1973) pointed out that a rapid or impulsive buying decision could also be made at home, possibly in response to a television commercial. Conversely, a decision made entirely within the store may be the subject of extensive comparison and deliberation. This extension of the concept is of considerable interest to companies involved in direct selling or home shopping. From the viewpoint of store-based retailer, however, the essence of impulse purchasing is the location at which the decision is made. A definition proposed by Engel and Blackwell (1982) is therefore more appropriate in this context:

> *A buying action undertaken without a problem previously having been consciously recognised or a buying intention formed prior to entering the store.*

12.4.1 Measures of Unplanned Purchasing

Although the concept of impulse purchasing is of immense importance in both retail and product marketing, it is difficult to form generalizations as to its extent. The available evidence spans a period of over 50 years, but few of the published studies are truly comparable. This problem arises from inconsistency in the definitions used and from fundamental differences between the methods adopted in measuring impulse purchasing. With this necessary caveat, a useful summary of research findings, compiled by Cobb and Hoyer (1986), is presented in Table 12.9.

The series of studies undertaken by the du Pont company between 1945 and 1965 illustrated a general increase in the extent of impulse purchasing. This was attributed both to changing customer characteristics and to changes in store environments. Time pressures arising from two-career families, geographical mobility and competing leisure-time opportunities reduce the opportunity for detailed pre-planning; increases in discretionary income may also reduce the inclination for such planning (Williams and Dardis, 1972). The spread of self-service, increased product assortments and increased point-of-purchase promotion have also contributed to a tendency to transfer actual buying decisions to within the store. Cobb and Hoyer (1986) cited some evidence that impulse purchasing may have declined somewhat in the early 1980s, owing to recessionary conditions at that time; the long-term trend, however, appears to remain upward.

Table 12.9 Incidence of unplanned purchasing by type of product and outlet: summary of findings

Source: Cobb and Hoyer (1986).

More recent work has focused upon explaining rather than measuring impulse purchasing (e.g. Beatty and Ferrell, 1998; Rook, 1987: Rook and Fisher, 1995). An exception is the study by Kelly et al. (2000). Their main focus was upon the extent to which planned purchases were actually fulfilled, rather than the extent to which purchases were/were not planned. However, some 64 per cent of their sample made one or more unplanned purchase while in the store.

Source	Year	Type of product	Rate of unplanned purchasing (%)	Type of outlet	Rate of unplanned purchasing (%)
Du Pont	1945	Grocery product categories		Grocery	38.2
	1949				38.4
	1954				48.0
	1959				50.9
	1965				50.0
Clover	1950	n.a.	n.a.	19 types incl.	
				Variety	60.5
				Grocery	26.0
				Service station	14.8
				Book	14.7
				Department	14.5
				Furniture	3.8
West	1951	14 categories, incl.			
		Candy	65.8	Grocery	43.5
		Bakery goods	70.1	Drug	26.6
		Cosmetics	41.8	Variety	41.5
		Jewellery	49.5	Department	33.6
		Wearing apparel	24.1		
Point-of Purchase Advertising Institute	1963	50 categories, incl.		3 styles of drug stores:	
		Prescriptions	0.0	Clerk-assisting	11.0
		Camera supplies	10.0	Self-service	22.0
		Cosmetics	23.0	Super drug	30.0
		Candy	48.0		
Kollat and Willett	1967	64 grocery categories		Grocery	50.5
Williams and Dardis	1972	Women's outerwear	46.0	Speciality	33.0
		Women's underwear	30.0	Department	37.0
		Menswear	32.0	Discount/	
		Household textiles	24.0	variety	31.0
Prasad	1975	Various non-food Categories		Department	39.3
				Discount	62.4
Bellenger, Robertson and Hirschman	1978	20 categories, inc.			
		Lingerie	27.0	Department	38.7
		Cosmetics	33.0		
		Men's apparel and furnishings	40.0		
		Bakery goods	50.0		
		Costume jewellery	62.0		

Table 12.9 also illustrates that the extent of impulse purchasing differs very significantly between types of product and between retail settings. For example, Bellenger et al. (1978) found that 62 per cent of costume jewellery purchases in a department store were essentially unplanned, compared with only 27 per cent of women's lingerie purchases. In the study by Prasad (1975), 62.4 per cent of discount shoppers bought at least one item on an unplanned basis, compared with 39.3 per cent of department store shoppers.

Various researchers have examined factors that may contribute to impulse purchasing. Naturally, these include many aspects of the retail store environment. As these have been discussed in previous sections of this chapter, no further elaboration is needed here. Other factors relate to the product, the shopper and aspects of the shopping trip:

1 *Product characteristics*: lower purchase frequency was found to be related to the higher incidence of impulse purchasing (Kollat and Willett, 1967). Results regarding price levels are not in agreement (e.g. Bellenger et al., 1978; Stern, 1962). Small, lightweight and easy to store products may be more likely to be impulse purchased.

2 *Household structure*: Kollat and Willett (1967) found that couples married within the last ten years were less likely to buy on impulse.

3 *Use of shopping lists*: *Progressive Grocer* (1993) reported that 73 per cent of supermarket shoppers almost always make a list. Thomas and Garland (1993) found that people shopping without lists spend a similar amount of time in store but spent more.

4 *Time pressure*: using structural equation modelling, Beatty and Ferrell (1998) demonstrated that time pressure reduces the propensity to browse and, thus, the likelihood of impulse purchasing.

5 *Money available*: a feeling of having more money available is linked with more impulse purchasing, both directly and by means of facilitating more positive mood states (Beatty and Ferrell, 1998).

6 *Impulse buying tendency*: this has been researched as a general trait among some shoppers (Rook, 1987). Rook and Gardner (1993) found that 75 per cent of their sample reported feeling better after a recent impulse purchase. However, normative beliefs that impulse buying is, for example, wasteful, silly or unacceptable tend to reduce the extent to which impulse buying tendency (IBT) actually leads to impulse purchasing.

There is no general agreement on 'the best' way of measuring impulse purchasing. The problem is essentially to determine when and where the decision to purchase an item was formed. Every methodology used runs the risk of biasing the results in some way. Four main types of approach have been adopted:

1 Shoppers are asked what they intend to purchase on entering the store; actual purchases are then recorded as they leave the store. The

difference between intentions and outcomes are deemed to be impulse purchases (e.g. Du Pont, 1965; Kelly et al., 2000; Kollat and Willett, 1967; Prasad, 1975). One problem with this approach is that, having been asked to articulate their purchase intentions, shoppers may become more committed to fulfilling them (Pollay, 1968). This would have the effect of reducing impulse purchasing. Furthermore, the shopper may be unable and/or unwilling to itemize all purchase intentions at the start of the shopping trip (Kollat and Willett, 1969). An incomplete recording of intentions would then result in the overstatement of impulse purchasing, using this method.

2   Shoppers are questioned on leaving the store about the time and place of the purchase decision for specific item(s) bought (e.g. Bellenger et al., 1978; Deshpande and Krishnan, 1980; McGoldrick, 1982). The major problem with this approach is that respondents may tend to overstate their extent of pre-purchase planning, if they have a negative attitude towards impulsiveness in shopping (Rook and Fisher, 1995). The extent of impulse purchasing may therefore be underrecorded by this method.

3   Direct observation of shoppers' behaviour within this store (e.g. Cobb and Hoyer, 1986; Davidson, 1981; Wells and Lo Sciuto, 1966). Unless undertaken very discreetly, however, this will almost certainly affect shopping behaviour. Direct observation cannot alone determine whether or not a purchase was planned but it can provide insight into browsing/decision times. In the supermarket setting, 75 per cent of product purchase decisions are made in 15 seconds or less (Dickson and Sawyer, 1990). Accompanied shopping (Otnes et al., 1995) is a way to both observe and to question shoppers' decisions, but may well affect the behaviour of the accompanied shopper.

4   Combination methodologies (e.g. Langton, 1995). With the sophisticated range of tracking devices now available (Sec. 12.2.1), plus EPoS and loyalty card purchase records, there is extensive scope to monitor what causes changes in purchase patterns. However, some form of survey is still required to ascertain which items the shoppers intended to buy, at that store, on that day.

Some studies of impulse purchasing have dichotomized the recorded purchases into those that were planned or unplanned. In fact, there are various different levels of purchase planning, so it may be more appropriate to identify different degrees of impulse purchasing. Stern (1962) suggested four broad classifications of impulse purchasing:

1   *Pure impulse*: a novelty or escape-type purchase which breaks a normal buying pattern.

2   *Reminder impulse buying*: when a shopper sees an item and remembers that the stock at home is low, or recalls an advertisement or other information and a previous decision to buy.

3 *Suggestion impulse*: when a shopper sees a product for the first time and visualizes a need for it; such purchases can be entirely rational or functional, unlike pure impulse purchases, which are sparked by emotional appeal.

4 *Planned impulse*: when a shopper enters the store with some specific purchases in mind but with the expectations and intention of making other purchases, depending on price specials, etc.

Table 12.10 Extent of purchase planning
Source: McGoldrick (1982).

Product group	% of purchases that were:			
	Specifically planned	Generally planned	Reminder	Entirely unplanned
Toothpaste	45	32	21	2
Soap, shampoo, bath products	57	25	13	5
Cosmetics	54	25	7	14
Baby products	73	11	8	8
Medicines, surgical	77	14	8	1
Food and drinks	40	26	22	12
Optical and photographic	76	12	12	0
Household, garden, electrical	48	26	13	13

Stern's classification has however proved difficult to operationalize, particularly the distinction between categories 1 and 3. A more straightforward classification system was adopted in a study by McGoldrick (1982), summarized in Table 12.10. This was based upon post-purchase interviews with 449 shoppers at six pharmacy stores. Their purchases were classified as follows:

1 *Specifically planned purchases* (57 per cent): the need was recognized on entering the store and the shopper bought the exact item planned.
2 *Generally planned purchases* (23 per cent): the need was recognized but the shopper decided in the store upon the item to satisfy the need.
3 *Reminder purchases* (13 per cent): the shopper was reminded of the need by some influence within the store.
4 *Entirely unplanned purchases* (7 per cent): the need has been recognized neither on entering the store nor prior to that.

Three of these categories therefore represent degrees of in-store decision-making, comprising 43 per cent of all the purchases. The results summarized in Table 12.9 would also suggest that rates of unplanned purchasing would be higher in many other types of retail store. The simple division of purchases into 'impulse' and 'planned' has inevitably tended to underestimate the effects of the store environment. From the retail marketing perspective, the identification of different levels of unplanned purchasing also provides the basis for a more thorough analysis of in-store effects.

SUMMARY

The retail store environment exerts an influence upon shopper behaviour at several different levels, including the overall design of the store, its atmosphere, the arrangement of its layout, the displays and the allocation of space between departments and between products. At each of these levels, the decisions taken are likely to influence both the in-store purchasing behaviour of consumers and their longer-term patronage decisions. Store-based retailers therefore face numerous options and a complex network of decisions in attempting to achieve optimum results from the store environment.

Retail design has now become a very prominent element of retail marketing, as retailers have sought new forms of differentiation. The scope of design and refurbishment is very wide, potentially including most facets of the store's external and internal appearance. A major new retail design industry has developed, and most major retailers have employed consultants for at least part of their design programmes. Naturally, design changes are likely to be effective, only if they are part of a co-ordinated marketing strategy. Retailers are also accepting that format life cycles are getting shorter, so flexibility and change are becoming an important design principle.

More systematic attention is now being given to 'atmospherics', which describes the conscious designing of space to create certain effects on buyers. Visual, aural, olfactory and tactile dimensions may all be utilized to create a favourable atmosphere. Considerable evidence is available of the effects of music tempo, colours, light and scents on shoppers' perceptions and in-store behaviour. It is important that the effects induced by atmospherics are compatible with the type of store and shopping experience.

The design of the store layout contributes to the image created and can also be used to manipulate traffic flow. Many supermarkets use a grid pattern layout, which encourages circulation within all parts of the store. High-demand items are typically placed near the entrance, to initiate purchasing, and at appropriate points within each aisle. Free-flow or boutique-type layouts are usually favoured by department and fashion stores, making less intensive use of space but conveying an appropriate image. Tracking methods are extensively utilized to study shopper movements within the layout, identifying areas of congestion, areas of poor circulation, and centres of attraction within the store.

Special displays can provide interest and attraction, as well as stimulating the sales of the products featured. Displays may be centred on a specific theme or consumer lifestyle. Co-ordinated displays can link items that are normally used together, or classification-dominance displays can emphasize the strength of the assortment in a specific category. Power aisles can convey a strong price message. The evaluation of a display should consider both long- and short-term effects; in many cases, the effects of the display must also be separated from the effects of changes in prices or advertising.

The growth of product assortments has increased the pressure to optimize the use of space in most retail settings. Space elasticity is a measure of the reaction of sales to changes in space allocated. Several experimental and cross-sectional approaches have been utilized to estimate space elasticity; some products are clearly more responsive than others to changes in space allocations. Studies have also shown that height and position within a display can exert a strong influence upon sales.

Space management systems have evolved a great deal over the last 30 years, most now being both comprehensive and user-friendly. They have become important tools for category managers, enabling them to utilize a wide range of data to produce planograms. These simulated displays combine both the numerical and the visual aspects of space planning, and can be easily communicated to stores for implementation.

The extent of impulse or unplanned purchasing has tended to increase, partly because of greater time pressures upon consumers but also because of more effective store environments. Studies of the extent of impulse purchasing have illustrated major differences between products and between retail store types. Various methodologies have been used to measure impulse purchasing; each has its limitations because of the problems in identifying the time and place of the purchase decision. Measures of unplanned purchasing do however provide valuable insights into the overall effects of in-store marketing variables.

REVIEW QUESTIONS

1 'Only one company in any market can be the cheapest: all the others have to add value and the most effective way of doing that is by design'. Do you agree?

2 How would you ensure that your design programme for a chain of menswear stores is cost-effective? What criteria would you use to evaluate the success of the programme?

3 'Atmospherics becomes a more relevant marketing tool as the number of competitive outlets increases'. Discuss.

4 What would be your specific objectives when selecting the in-store colour schemes and the background music for:

   a) a discount clothing store?

   b) a department store?

5 Discuss how the concept of 'hedonic consumption' can contribute in the designing of store environments.

6 Compare the advantages and disadvantages of:

   a) the 'grid pattern' layout

   b) the 'free-flow' layout.

7 What methods are available to track shoppers' movements within the store? How could such tracking studies contribute to the redesign of your store layout?

8 Compare the objectives and techniques of:

a) lifestyle displays

b) co-ordinated displays

c) classification dominance displays.

9 How would you evaluate the effectiveness of special, off-shelf displays in a supermarket?

10 Define space elasticity. What approaches are available for the measurement of space elasticity, and what problems are likely to be encountered?

11 What factors should be taken into account by category managers when allocating space between products? In what ways can the space plan influence the profitability of the category and the store?

12 Explain how the planogram has contributed towards the effective management of space.

13 Define an impulse purchase. To what extent is the concept of impulse purchasing relevant to the design of the retail environment?

14 Compare and evaluate the alternative approaches to the measurement of impulse purchasing.

REFERENCES

Abrahams, C. (1994) 'The smell-good factor', *Sainsbury's Magazine*, November, 64–66.

Akhter, S.H., J.C. Andrews and S. Durvasula (1994) 'The influence of retail store environment on brand-related judgements', *Journal of Retailing and Consumer Services*, **1** (2), 67–76.

Areni, C.S. and D. Kim (1994) 'The influence of in-store lighting on consumers' examination of merchandise in a wine store', *International Journal of Research in Marketing*, **11**, 117–125.

Areni, C.S., D.F. Duhan and P. Kiecker (1999) 'Point-of-purchase displays, product organisation and brand purchase likelihoods', *Journal of the Academy of Marketing Science*, **27** (4), 428–441.

Arnold, H. (1996) 'Multiples launch a full frontal assault', *SuperMarketing*, 22 November, 24–26.

Aylott, R. and V.-W. Mitchell (1998) 'An exploratory study of grocery shopping stressors', *International Journal of Retail & Distribution Management*, **26** (9), 362–373.

Babin, B.J. and J.S. Attaway (2000) 'Atmospheric affect as a tool for creating value and gaining share of customer', *Journal of Business Research*, **49**, 91–99.

Babin, B.J. and W.R. Darden (1996) 'Good and bad shopping vibes: spending and patronage satisfaction', *Journal of Business Research*, **35**, 201–206.

Baker, J. (1986) 'The role of the environment in marketing services: the consumer perspective', in *The Services Challenge: Integrating for Competitive Advantage*, J.A. Czepiel, C.A. Congram and J. Shanahan (eds), American Marketing Association, Chicago, pp. 79–84.

Baker, J. (1998) 'Examining the informational value of store environments' in *Servicescapes: The Concept of Place in Contemporary Markets*, J.F. Sherry (ed.), NTC Business Books, Chicago, pp. 29–54.

Baker, J., D. Grewal and A. Parasuraman (1994) 'The influence of store environment on quality inferences and store image', *Journal of the Academy of Marketing Science*, **22** (4), 328–339.

Baker, J., M. Levy and D. Grewal (1992) 'An experimental approach to making retail store environment decisions', *Journal of Retailing*, **68** (4), 445–460.

Bamfield, J. (1994) *National Survey of Retail Theft and Security*, Nene College, Northampton.

Beatty, S.E. and M.E. Ferrell (1998) 'Impulse buying: modelling its precursors', *Journal of Retailing*, **74** (2), 169–191.

Bellenger, D., D. Robertson and E. Hirschman (1978) 'Impulse buying varies by product', *Journal of Advertising Research*, **18** (6), 15–18.

Bellizzi, J.A., A.E. Crowley and R.W. Hasty (1983) 'The effects of color in store design', *Journal of Retailing*, **59** (1), 21–45.

Berman, B. and J.R. Evans (1995) *Retail Management: A Strategic Approach*, Prentice-Hall, Englewood Cliffs, NJ.

Birtwistle, G. (2000) 'Store merchandising and effective use of space: the Safeway experience of in-store pharmacies' in *Contemporary Cases in Retail Operations Management*, B.M. Oldfield, R.A. Schmidt, I. Clarke, C. Hart and M.H. Kirkup (eds), Macmillan, Basingstoke, pp. 125–134.

Bitner, M.J. (1992) 'Servicescapes: the impact of physical surroundings on customers and employees', *Journal of Marketing*, **56** (April), 57–71.

Bone, P.F. and P.S. Ellen (1999) 'Scents in the marketplace: explaining a fraction of olfaction', *Journal of Retailing*, **75** (2), 243–262.

Borin, N. and P. Farris (1995) 'A sensitivity analysis of retailer shelf management models', *Journal of Retailing*, **71** (2), 153–171.

Borren, C., O. Bakker and W. Mensing (1995) 'Local FMCG marketing and merchandising in The Netherlands', *European Retail Digest*, **5** (Winter), 4–12.

Brown, S. (1988) 'Shopper movement in a planned shopping centre', *Retail & Distribution Management*, **16** (1), 30–34.

Brown, S. (1992) *Retail Location: A Micro-Scale Perspective*, Avebury, Aldershot.

Brown, W.M. and W.T. Tucker (1961) 'Vanishing shelf space', *Altanta Economic Review*, **9**, 9–16, 23.

Buckingham, C. (1994) 'Category management in Europe: from concept to reality', *European Retail Digest*, **1** (Winter), 4–9.

Buttle, F. (1984a) 'Retail space allocation', *International Journal of Physical Distribution & Materials Management*, **14** (4), 3–23.

Buttle, F. (1984b) 'Merchandising', *European Journal of Marketing*, **18** (6/7), 104–123.

Buttle, F. (1994), 'Jaeger ladies', in *Cases in Retail Management*, P.J. McGoldrick (ed.), Pitman, London, pp. 259–277.

Calcott, D. (1980) 'Sell more and sell better with good design', *Retail & Distribution Management*, **8** (3), 45–47.

Campbell, C. (1987), *The Romantic Ethic and the Spirit of Capitalism*, Blackwell, Oxford.

Campo, K., E. Gijzbrechts, T. Goossens and A. Verhetsel (2000) 'The impact of location factors on the attractiveness and optimal space shares of product categories', *International Journal of Research in Marketing*, **17**, 255–279.

Chebat, J.-C. and L. Dubé (2000), 'Evolution and challenges facing retail atmospherics', *Journal of Business Research*, **49**, 89–90.

Chevalier, M. (1975a) 'Increase in sales due to in-store display', *Journal of Marketing Research*, **12** (4), 426–31.

Chevalier, M. (1975b) 'Substitution patterns as a result of display in the product category', *Journal of Retailing*, **50** (4), 65–72, 88.

Clover, V.T. (1950) 'Relative importance of impulse buying in retail stores', *Journal of Marketing*, **15** (1), 66–70.

Cobb, C.J. and W.D. Hoyer (1986) 'Planned versus impulse purchase behaviour', *Journal of Retailing*, **62** (4), 384–409.

Corstjens, M. and P. Doyle (1981) 'A model for optimizing retail space allocations', *Management Science*, **27** (7), 822–833.

Corstjens, M. and P. Doyle (1983) 'A dynamic model for strategically allocating retail space', *Journal of the Operational Research Society*, **34** (10), 943–951.

Creighton, M. (1998) 'The seed of creative lifestyle shopping: wrapping consumerism in Japanese store layouts' in *Servicescapes: The Concept of Place in Contemporary Markets*, J.F Sherry (ed.), NTC Business Books, Chicago, pp. 199–228.

Curhan, R.C. (1972) 'The relationship between shelf space and unit sales in supermarkets', *Journal of Marketing Research*, **9** (4), 406–412.

Curhan, R.C. (1973) 'Shelf space allocation and profit maximisation in mass retailing', *Journal of Marketing*, **37** (3), 54–60.

D'Antoni, J.S. and H.L. Shenson (1973) 'Impulse buying revisited: a behavioural typology'. *Journal of Retailing*, **49** (1), 63–76.

D'Astous, A. (2000) 'Irritating aspects of the shopping environment', *Journal of Business Research*, **49**, 149–156.

Dalke, H. (1997) 'Showing your true colours' in *The BPMA Yearbook 1996–1997*, BPMA (ed.), Promotions News, Byfleet, pp. 77–80.

Davidson, H. (1981) 'How and why shoppers buy', *Marketing*, 28 October, 18–20.

Davidson, W.R. and A. Doody (1966) *Retailing Management*, Ronald Press, New York.

Davies, G. and T. Rands (1992) 'The strategic use of space by retailers: a perspective from operations management', *International Journal of Logistics Management*, **3** (2), 63–76.

Deshpande, R. and S. Krishnan (1980) 'Consumer impulse purchase and credit card usage: an empirical examination using the log linear model', in *Advances in Consumer Research*, J.C. Olson (ed.), Association for Consumer Research, Ann Arbor, MI, pp. 792–795.

Design Council (1997) *Design in Britain 1997–98*, Design Council, London.

Desmet, P. and V. Renaudin (1998) 'Estimation of product category sales responsiveness to allocated shelf space', *International Journal of Research in Marketing*, **15**, 443–457

Dickson, P and A. Sawyer (1990) 'Price knowledge and search of supermarket shoppers', *Journal of Marketing*, **54** (3), 42–53.

Donovan, R.J. and J.R. Rossiter (1982) 'Store atmosphere: an environment psychology approach', *Journal of Retailing*, **58** (1), 34–57.

Donovan, R.J., J.R. Rossiter, G. Marcoolyn and A. Nesdale (1994) 'Store atmosphere and purchasing behavior', *Journal of Retailing*, **70** (3), 283–294.

Doyle, S.A. and A. Broadbridge (1999) 'Differentiation by design: the importance of design in retailer repositioning and differentiation', *International Journal of Retail & Distribution Management*, **27** (2), 72–82.

Dreze, X. and S.J. Hoch (1998), 'Exploiting the installed base using cross-merchandising and category destination programs', *International Journal of Research in Marketing*, **15**, 459–471.

Dreze, X., S.J. Hoch and M.E. Purk (1994) 'Shelf management and space elasticity', *Journal of Retailing*, **70** (4), 301–326.

Drummond, G. (1995) 'Making sense of research', *SuperMarketing*, 24 March, 17.

Du Pont (1945, 1949, 1954, 1959, 1965) *Consumer Buying Habits Studies*, Du Pont de Nemours, Wilmington, DE.

Dyer, L.W. (1980) In-store research at Publix', *Progressive Grocer*, **59** (12), 98–106.

Engel, J. and R. Blackwell (1982) *Consumer Behaviour*, Dryden Press, Chicago.

Eroglu, S. and G.D. Harrell (1986) 'Retail crowding theoretical and strategic implications', *Journal of Retailing*, **62** (4), 346–363.

Fader, P.S. and L.M. Lodish (1990) 'A cross-category analysis of category structure and promotional activity for grocery products', *Journal of Marketing*, **54** (October), 52–65.

Fletcher, K. (1987) 'Consumers' use and perceptions of retailer controlled information sources', *International Journal of Retailing*, **2** (3), 59–66.

Gagnon, J.P. and J.T. Osterhaus (1985) 'Effectiveness of floor displays on the sales of retail products', *Journal of Retailing*, **61** (1), 104–116.

Gottdiener, M. (1998) 'The semiotics of consumer spaces: the growing importance of themed environment', in *Servicescapes: The Concept of Place in Contemporary Markets*, J.F. Sherry (ed.), NTC Business Books, Chicago, pp. 29–54.

Greco, J.-A. (1999) 'Multiple spaces for multiple tasks', *Journal of Business Strategy*, **20** (5), 11–15.

Green, W.R. (1986) *The Retail Store: Design and Construction*, Van Nostrand Reinhold, New York.

Greenland, S.J. and P.J. McGoldrick (1994) 'Atmospherics, attitudes and behaviour: modelling the impact of designed space', *International Review of Retail, Distribution and Consumer Research*, **4** (1), 1–16.

Grewal, D. and J. Baker (1994) 'Do retail store environmental factors affect consumers' price acceptability? An empirical examination', *International Journal of Research in Marketing*, **11**, 107–115.

Grossbart, S., R. Hampton, B. Rammohan and R.S. Lapidus (1990) 'Environmental dispositions and customer response to store atmospherics', *Journal of Business Research*, **21**, 225–241.

Harrison, K. (1995) 'The naked ape', *SuperMarketing*, 24 March, 16–18.

Hart, C. and M. Davies (1996) 'The location and merchandising of non-food in supermarkets', *International Journal of Retail & Distribution Management*, **24** (2), 17–25.

Hayne, C. (1981) 'Light and colour', *Occupational Health*, **33** (4), 198–205.

Hirschman, E.C. and M.B. Holbrook (1982) 'Hedonic consumption: emerging concepts, methods and propositions', *Journal of Marketing*, **46** (3), 92–101.

Hitt, J. (1996) 'The theory of supermarkets', *New York Times Magazine*, 10 March, 56–61, 94–98.

Hogan, C. (1998) 'Store wars: retail giants strike back', *Sun Herald*, 15 November.

Hogarth-Scott, S. and I. Walters (2000) 'The role of category management in hair colourants: Bristol-Myers', in *Contemporary Cases in Retail Operations Management*, B.M. Oldfield, R.A. Schmidt, I. Clarke, C. Hart and M.H. Kirkup (eds), Macmillan, Basingstoke, pp. 154–169.

Hopkinson, G.C. and D. Pujari (1999) 'A factor analytic study of the sources and meaning of hedonic consumption', *European Journal of Marketing*, **33** (3/4), 273–290.

Hui, M.K. and J.E.G. Bateson (1991) 'Perceived control and the effects of crowding and consumer choice on the service experience', *Journal of Consumer Research*, **18** (2), 174–184.

Hui, M.K., L. Dubé and J.C. Chebat (1997) 'The impact of music on consumers' reactions to waiting for services', *Journal of Retailing*, **73** (1), 87–104.

IGD (1997) *A Guide to Category Management*, Institute of Grocery Distribution, Watford.

Jones, H. (1996) 'Psychological warfare', *Marketing Week*, 2 February, 32–35.

Kaufman-Scarborough, C. (1999) 'Reasonable access for mobility-disabled persons is more than widening the door', *Journal of Retailing*, **75** (4), 479–508.

Kelly, P.P., S.M. Smith and H.K. Hunt (2000) 'Fulfilment of planned and unplanned purchases of sale- and regular-price items: a benchmark study', *International Review of Retail, Distribution and Consumer Research*, **10** (3), 247–263.

Kim, Y.-K. (2001) 'Experiential retailing: an interdisciplinary approach to success in domestic and international retailing', *Journal of Retailing and Consumer Services*, **8** (5), 287–289.

Kirkup, M. (1999) 'Electronic footfall monitoring: experiences among UK clothing multiples', *International Journal of Retail Distribution Management*, **27** (4), 166–173.

Kirkup, M. and M. Carrigan (2000) 'Video surveillance research in retailing: ethical issues', *International Journal of Retail & Distribution Management*, **28** (11), 470–480.

Kirkup, M. and L. Moirano (1997) 'Store layout and merchandising in fashion retailing', in *Cases in Retailing: Operational Perspectives*, C. Hart, M. Kirkup, D. Preston, M. Rafiq and P. Walley (eds), Blackwell, Oxford, pp. 12–25.

Koelemeijer, K. and H. Oppewal (1999) 'Assessing the effects of assortment and ambience: a choice experimental approach', *Journal of Retailing*, **75** (3), 319–345.

Kollat, D.T. and R.P. Willett (1967) 'Consumer impulse purchasing behaviour', *Journal of Marketing Research*, **4** (1), 21–31.

Kollat, D.T. and R.P. Willett (1969) 'Is impulse purchasing really a useful concept for marketing decisions?' *Journal of Marketing*, **33** (1), 79–83.

Kotler, P. (1973) 'Atmospherics as a marketing tool', *Journal of Retailing*, **49** (4), 48–64.

Kotzan, J.A., and R.V. Evanson (1969) 'Responsiveness of drug store sales to shelf space allocations', *Journal of Marketing Research*, **6** (4), 465–469.

Langton, J. (1995) 'The unseen eye keeping watch over shop flaws', *Sunday Telegraph*, 22 January, 11

Lea-Greenwood, G. (1998) 'Visual merchandising: a neglected area in U.K. fashion marketing', *International Journal of Retail & Distribution Management*, **26** (8), 324–329.

Lochhead, M. and C.M. Moore (1999) 'A Christmas fit for a Princes' Square: the role of strategic design in shopping centre positioning', in *European Cases in Retailing*, M. Dupuis and J. Dawson (eds), Blackwell, Oxford, pp. 247–256.

Machleit, K.A. and S.A. Eroglu (2000) 'Describing and measuring emotional response to shopping experience', *Journal of Business Research*, **49**, 101–111.

Mahler, D.Q. (2000) 'An American century of retailing', *Chain Store Age*, April, S44.

Mandeville, E. (1994) *Customer Tracking Systems*, RMDP, Hove.

Markin, R.J., C.M. Lillis and C.L. Narayana (1976) 'Social-psychological significance of store space', *Journal of Retailing*, **52** (1), 43–54, 94, 95.

Marking, G. (1986) 'Design for shopping', *Survey*, **3** (3), 9–11.

Mathwick, C., N. Malhotra and E. Rigdon (2001) 'Experiential value: conceptualization, measurement and application in the catalog and Internet shopping environment', *Journal of Retailing*, **77** (1), 39–56.

Mattila, A.S. and J. Wirtz (2001) 'Congruency of scent and music as a driver of in-store evaluations and behavior', *Journal of Retailing*, **77**, 273–289.

McGoldrick, P.J. (1982) 'How unplanned are impulse purchases?' *Retail & Distribution Management*, **10** (1), 27–32

McGoldrick, P.J. and C.P. Pieros (1998) 'Atmospherics, pleasure and arousal: the influences of response moderators', *Journal of Marketing Management*, **14**, 173–197.

McGoldrick, P.J. and D. Thorpe (1977) *Shelf Space Allocation in Supermarkets*, RORU, Manchester Business School, Manchester.

McKinnon, G.F., J.P. Kelly and E.D. Robinson (1981) 'Sales effects of point-of-purchase in-store signing', *Journal of Retailing*, **57** (2), 49–63.

Milliman, R.E. (1982), 'Using background music to affect the behaviour of supermarket shoppers', *Journal of Marketing*, **46** (3), 86–91.

Mintel (1999) 'Retail store design', *Retail Intelligence*, August, 1–112.

Mintel (2000) *Retail Review*, Mintel, London.

Mitchell, D.J., B.E. Kahn and S.C. Knasko (1995) 'There's something in the air: effect of congruent or incongruent ambient odor on consumer decision making', *Journal of Consumer Research*, **22** (September), 229–238.

Morrin, M. and S. Ratneshwar (2000) 'The impact of ambient scent on evaluation, attention, and memory for familiar and unfamiliar brands', *Journal of Business Research*, **49**, 157–165.

New York Times (1996) 'The geography of taste', *New York Times*, 10 March, 40–41.

Newcomb, P. (1999) 'I heard it at the record store', *Forbes*, 8 July, 88.

Otnes, C., M.A. McGrath and T.M. Lowrey (1995) 'Shopping with consumers', *Journal of Retailing and Consumer Services*, **2** (2), 97–110.

Pearson, R. (1993) 'Space management: from product to store', *Progressive Grocer*, **72** (December), 31–32.

Phillips, H. and R. Bradshaw (1993) 'How customers actually shop: customer interaction with the point of sale', *Journal of the Market Research Society*, **35** (1), 51–62.

Pickersgill, P.R. (1991) 'How research helped to measure the effects of display and assess the contribution of salesmen and merchandisers', *Journal of Market Research Society*, **33** (3), 153–162.

Pine, B.J. and J.H. Gilmore (1998) 'Welcome to the experience economy', *Harvard Business Review*, **76** (4), 97–105.

Pine, B.J. and J.H. Gilmore (1999) *The Experience Economy: Work Is Theatre and Every Business a State*, Harvard Business Press, Boston, MA.

Point-of-Purchase Advertising Institute (1963) *Drugstore Brand Switching and Impulse Buying*, POPI, New York.

Pollay, R. (1968) 'Customer impulse purchasing behaviour: a re-examination', *Journal of Marketing Research*, **5** (3), 323–325.

Prasad, V.K. (1975) 'Unplanned buying in two retail settings', *Journal of Retailing*, **51** (3), 3–12.

Progressive Grocer (1975) 'Consumer behaviour in a supermarket', *Progressive Grocer*, **54** (10), 36–59.

Progressive Grocer (1993) 'Shoppers are making lists, scrutinizing coupons', *Progressive Grocer*, **72** (4), 92.

Retail Review (2000a) 'IKEA under fire', *Retail Review*, **260** (March), 23.

Retail Review (2000b) 'M & S puts more staff into customer services and more resources into local choice', *Retail Review*, **259** (February), 22–23.

Retail Review (2001) 'M&S cuts back world wide to make UK retail its sole concern: some of the detail', *Retail Review*, **270** (April), 20–21.

Rinne, H., M. Guerts and J.P. Kelly (1987) 'An approach to allocating space to departments in a retail store', *International Journal of Retailing*, **2** (2), 27–41.

Rogers, D. (1985) 'Research tools for better merchandising', *Retail & Distribution Management*, **13** (6), 42–44.

Rook, D.W. (1987) 'The buying impulse', *Journal of Consumer Research*, **14** (2), 189–199.

Rook, D.W. and R.J. Fisher (1995) 'Normative influences on impulsive buying behaviour'. *Journal of Consumer Research*, **22** (December), 305–313.

Rook, D.W. and M.P. Gardner (1993) 'In the mood: impulse buying's affective antecedents', in *Research in Consumer Behaviour (vol 6)*, J. Arnold-Costa and R.W. Belk (eds), JAI Press, Greenwich, CT, pp. 1–28.

Rosenbloom, B. (1981) *Retail Marketing*, Random House, New York.

Rossotti, H. (1983) *Colour*, Princeton University Press, Princeton, NJ.

Rust, L. (1993) 'Observations: how to reach children in stores: marketing tactics grounded in observational research', *Journal of Advertising Research*, **33** (6), 67–72.

Sanghavi, N. (1988) 'Space management in shops: a new initiative', *Retail & Distribution Management*, **16** (1), 14–17.

Schmitt, B. (1999) 'Experiential marketing', *Journal of Marketing Management*, **15**, 53–67.

Sharma, A. and T.F. Stafford (2000) 'The effect of retail atmospherics on customers' perceptions of salespeople and customer persuasion', *Journal of Business Research*, **49**, 183–191.

Sharples, S. (1986) 'Asda's "gables": merging the old and new', *Retail & Distribution Management*, **14** (6), 22–23.

Sherry, J.F. (1998) 'The soul of the company store: Nike Town Chicago and the emplaced brandscape' in *Servicescapes: The Concept of Place in Contemporary Markets*, J.F. Sherry (ed.), NTC Business Books, Chicago, pp. 109–146.

Singh, M.G., R. Cook and M. Corstjens (1988) 'A hybrid knowledge-based system for allocating retail space and for other allocation problems', *Interfaces*, **18** (5), 13–22.

Sirgy, M.J., D. Grewal and T. Mangleburg (2000) 'Retail environment, self-congruity, and retail patronage: an integrative model and a research agenda', *Journal of Business Research*, **49**, 127–138.

Smith, P. and D.J. Burns (1996) 'Atmospherics and retail environments: the case of the "power aisle"', *International Journal of Retail & Distribution Management*, **24** (1), 7–14.

Solomon, M. (1998) 'Dressing for the part: the role of the consumer in the staging of the servicescape', in *Servicescapes: The Concept of Place in Contemporary Markets*, J.F. Sherry (ed.), NTC Business Books, Chicago, pp. 81–108.

Sommer, R. and S. Aitkens (1982) 'Mental mapping of two supermarkets', *Journal of Consumer Research*, **9** (2), 211–215.

Spangenberg, E.R., A.E. Crowley and P.W. Henderson (1996) 'Improving the store environment: do olfactory cues affect evaluations and behaviours', *Journal of Marketing*, **60** (April), 67–80.

Steinhagen, T. (1990) 'Space management shapes up with planograms', *Marketing News*, 12 November, 7.

Stern, H. (1962) 'The significance of impulse buying today', *Journal of Marketing*, **26** (2), 59–62.

Tai, S.H.C. and A.M.C. Fung (1997) 'Application of an environmental psychology model to in-store buying behaviour', *International Review of Retail, Distribution and Consumer Research*, **7** (4), 311–337.

Tauber, E.M. (1972) 'Why do people shop?', *Journal of Marketing*, **36** (4), 46–49.

Thomas, A. and R. Garland (1993) 'Supermarket shopping lists', *International Journal of Retail & Distribution Management*, **21** (2), 8–14.

Thomas, H. (1987) 'The design dilemma', *Marketing*, 5 November, 24–27.

Titus, P.A. and P.B. Everett (1995) 'The consumer retail search process: a conceptual model and research agenda', *Journal of the Academy of Marketing Science*, **23** (2), 106–119.

Tordjman, A. (1994) 'Toys R Us', in *Cases in Retail Management*, P.J. McGoldrick (ed), Pitman, London, pp. 165–183.

Turley, L.W. and R.E. Milliman (2000) 'Atmospheric effects on shopping behavior: a review of the experimental evidence', *Journal of Business Research*, **49**, 193–211.

Underhhill, P. (2000) *Why We Buy: The Science of Shopping*, Texere, London.

Van Kenhove, P. and P. Desrumaux (1997) 'The relationship between emotional states and approach or avoidance responses in a retail environment', *International Journal of Retail, Distribution and Consumer Research*, **7** (4), 351–368.

Varley, R. (2000) 'Buying operations at Boots The Chemist: the case of a product range update', in *Contemporary Cases in Retail Operations Management*, B.M. Oldfield, R.A. Schmidt, I. Clarke, C. Hart and M.H. Kirkup (eds), Macmillan, Basingstoke, pp. 286–289.

Verbeke, W., P. Farris and R. Thurik (1998) 'Consumer response to the preferred brand out-of-stock situation', *European Journal of Marketing*, **32** (11/12), 1008–1028.

Verdict (2000) *Grocers and Supermarkets 2000*, Verdict, London.

Wakefield, K.L. and J. Baker (1998) 'Excitement at the mall: determinants and effects on shopping response', *Journal of Retailing*, **74** (4), 515–539.

Wallendorf, M., J. Lindsey-Mullikin and R. Pimentel (1998) 'Gorilla marketing: customer animation and regional embeddedness of a toy store servicescape', in *Servicescapes: The Concept of Place in Contemporary Markets*, J.F. Sherry (ed.), NTC Business Book, Chicago, pp. 151–198.

Walters, D. and J. Hanrahan (2000) *Retail Strategy, Planning and Control*, Macmillan, Basingstoke.

Ward, J.C., M.J. Bitner and J. Barnes (1992) 'Measuring the prototypicality and meaning of retail environments', *Journal of Retailing*, **68** (2), 194–220.

Ware, J. and G.L. Patrick (1984) 'Gelson's supermarkets: effects of Musak music on the purchasing behaviour of supermarket shoppers', *Musak Research Report*, Musak, Seattle.

Wells, W.D. and L.A. Lo Sciuto (1966) 'Direct observation of purchasing behaviour', *Journal of Marketing Research*, **3** (3), 227–233.

West, C.J. (1951) 'Results of two years of study into impulse buying', *Journal of Marketing*, **15** (3), 362–363.

Which? (1989) 'Talking shop', *Which?* August, 404–406.

Wilkinson, J.B. J.B. Mason and C.H. Paksoy (1981) A demand analysis for newspaper advertising and changes in space allocation', *Journal of Retailing*, **57** (2), 30–48.

Wilkinson, J.B., J.B. Mason and C.H. Paksoy (1982) 'Assessing the impact of short-term supermarket strategy variables', *Journal of Marketing Research*, **19** (1), 72–86.

Williams, J. and R. Dardis (1972) 'Shopping behaviour for soft goods and marketing strategies', *Journal of Retailing*, **48** (3), 32–41.

Wirtz, J., A.S. Mattila and R.L.P. Tan (2000) 'The moderating role of target-arousal on the impact of affect on satisfaction: an examination in the context of service experiences', *Journal of Retailing*, **76** (3), 347–365.

Woodger, C. (1997) 'The role of strategic design in retail', *European Retail Digest*, Winter, 15–17.

Woodside, A.G. and G.L. Waddle (1975) 'Sales effects of in-store advertising', *Journal of Advertising Research*, **15** (3), 29–34.

Yalch, R. and E. Spangenberg (1990) 'Effects of store music on shopping behaviour', *Journal of Consumer Marketing*, **7** (2), 55–63.

Yalch, R.F. and E.R. Spangenberg (2000) 'The effects of music in a retail setting on real and perceived shopping times', *Journal of Business Research*, **49**, 139–147.

Yoo, C., J. Park and D.J. MacInnis (1998) 'Effects of store characteristics and in-store emotional experiences on store attitude', *Journal of Business Research*, **42**, 253–263.

Zaltman, G. and R.H. Coulter (1995) 'Seeing the voice of the customer: metaphor-based advertising research', *Journal of Advertising Research*, **35** (4), 35–52.

CHAPTER

Thirteen

Retail Service

INTRODUCTION   The last decade has seen major improvements in the understanding, delivery and measurement of retail service. As Sparks pointed out in 1992, customers could be forgiven for believing that retailers understood only lip-service, rather than customer service. From a practitioner perspective, Norman (1999) observed:

> *People behave as if service has been discovered within the last four years. It was not a way of competing. It had all been done on advertising, product development and on pricing.*

Of course, there have been examples of excellent retail service stretching back through centuries. Its focal position within the retail strategies of mainstream retailers is, however, of more recent origin. This heightened interest in service has been mirrored in the academic literature. From an analysis of over 1 million business and management articles, 21 per cent refer to service (Johns, 1999).

In part, this prolific use of the word reflects the several meanings of service(s). Figure 13.1 illustrates how the term can be used on at least five different levels in the context of retailing. Retailing has usually been classified as a 'service industry', and most aspects of the retailing mix represent a form of service. For example, the buying and merchandising functions assemble and present an assortment to the customer, at competitive prices. The location function seeks to ensure that this value and choice is conveniently accessible. This chapter adopts more specific connotations of service, focusing upon personal service, financial services and other elements to reduce risks, make shopping easier, more efficient and more pleasant.

The potential scope of retailer's service mix is very wide indeed. Within the domain of personal service, there is a great deal of opportunity to enhance the shopping experience through appropriate staff management and training. The efficiency, appearance, attitude, availability and product knowledge of store personnel are important issues for many shoppers. Among the financial services, store cards and

Figure 13.1 Service: what does it mean?

many other forms of credit have contributed both to transaction efficiency and to marketing effectiveness. Times of opening have also become an important form of differentiation, as retailers must increasingly cater for those unable to shop at 'normal' times. Some services aim to reduce the perceived risks of product purchases, such as changing rooms, favourable returns policies and extended warranties. Others aim to enhance convenience, such as free bagging and carry-out services.

It is essential that a retailer should develop an integrated services policy, based upon a clear understanding of the needs and preferences of the target segments. A service of great appeal to some types of shopper may convey altogether the wrong image for others. For example, the acceptance of credit cards for grocery purchases may be perceived as highly convenient, or as adding to cost; the provision of a service delicatessen may be regarded as adding to choice and human contact, or as an additional inconvenience and delay.

At the very core of service policy, a retailer must have the right mechanisms in place if 'satisfaction guaranteed' is to move from rhetoric to reality. Customers enter a store with expectations, some created by the retailer, others founded upon competitors' offerings and past experience. If the retailer fails to meet expectations, this 'gap' needs to be detected and remedied promptly, otherwise even loyal customers will eventually defect. This requires the development of monitoring and problem-solving procedures that are both effective and timely.

13.1 Personal Service

Many of the developments in retail outlets, discussed in Chapter 2, involved increased levels of self-service and reduced levels of staffing. The supermarket represented the first major shift, and then self-service spread into most retail sectors. This trend was fuelled by the desire to minimize labour costs, which are still the largest category of retail cost, in most cases. Although the quest for greater operational efficiency continues, it is recognized that services, including elements of personal service, can be important routes to competitive advantage. An acute need therefore exists to differentiate clearly between those activities that represent avoidable costs and those that truly provide a service and an attraction to customers.

This section first considers the role of personal service in retail, including evidence of consumer preferences for personal service levels. Attention then turns to the personal selling function, the requirements of effective selling personnel and the stages in the selling process. A detailed examination of human resource management issues in retailing would be beyond the scope of this text, although the reader can consult reviews by Marchington (1995), Samli and Ongan (1996) and Broadbridge et al. (1999). The effectiveness of human resource management (HRM) functions in retailing are major determinants of the quality of personal service provided in the store.

13.1.1 The Role of Personal Service

Even in settings dominated by self-service, the services provided by the store staff can exert a major influence upon retail images and patronage decisions: 'Contact employees deliver the promises of the firm, create an image for the firm and sell the firm's services' (Bettencourt and Brown, 1997).

When asked about areas in which service improvements would be welcomed, the three issues mentioned most frequently by UK customers all related to personnel-provided services. As Table 13.1 shows, faster service at checkouts/pay desks was mentioned by almost half, staff to help with queries and staff knowledge by around a third (Mintel, 2000). Clearly, these issues relate to the number of staff, effectiveness of deployment, training and technological support, as well as the quality of staff recruited and retained. Sam Walton of Wal-Mart established a vigorous staff motivation and customer care programme (Aldred, 1989). To quote from the 'gospel according to Sam': 'I solemnly promise and declare that every customer that comes within 10ft of me I will smile, look them in the eye and greet them, so help me Sam.'

Wal-Mart are not alone in setting such service standards. Houston-based clothing retailer Palais Royal specifies that every customer should be greeted or acknowledged within 30 seconds of entering a department (Sparks, 1992). Other specifications cover each aspect of the service encounter, right through to the writing of 'thank you' cards to some customers.

With the pressure to drive up sales per employee ratios, it is essential to remember that store staff are not just shelf packers and till operators.

Table 13.1 Service
improvements sought

Source: derived from Mintel
(2000).

Faster service at pay desk/checkout	46%
More staff to help with queries	35%
Better product knowledge among staff	33%
More choice of sizes/styles	31%
Better price information	29%
Better product availability	25%
Rapid order system for unavailable items	22%
Better store layout and design	19%
Delivery of goods ordered from home	18%
Longer opening hours	16%
24-hour shopping (groceries)	15%
Self-scanning in-store	14%

They are the human face of the retail operation, so warmth during 'non-productive' retail encounters is an essential input to the production of a favourable service encounter (Lemmink and Mattsson, 1998). Social interchange is an important element in the remembered role of the retail store (Baron et al., 1996): 'People make a visible difference in the average Wal-Mart. They treat their customers like neighbours—which is what they are in many cases.'

While many elements of personal service can be prescribed within staff training manuals, staff that help customers 'beyond the call of duty' are particular assets to the retail organization (Bettencourt and Brown, 1997). Tesco have empowered staff at all levels to solve customers' problems; without this ability to exercise discretion, staff are limited in their scope to deliver excellent service (Kelley, 1993). The ability to listen effectively is a major prerequisite, both in the diagnosis and immediate solution of the problem, also in capturing the information for the benefit of the whole company (Jones and Sasser, 1995). The mood of staff is another important element, as happy staff are far more likely to provide a good service encounter (Kelley and Hoffman, 1997). Many aspects of the working environment, as well as the retailer's service culture, can influence staff moods and motivation (Norman, 1999). However, recruiters should also look for appropriate mood traits when appointing front-line staff.

The importance of relationships in sustaining customer loyalty was emphasized in Chapter 3, and personal service can play a major part in such relationships. Even when a customer deals with several different store employees, their actions can be highly instrumental in building loyalty to the store (Macintosh and Lockshin, 1997). Building relationships with customers can increase satisfaction and loyalty, generate positive word of mouth and also increase purchases (Reynolds and Beatty, 1999a). Figure 13.2 summarizes key elements and stages within the formation and enhancement of such relationships.

Figure 13.2
Relationship formation
and enhancement

Source: adapted from Beatty
et al. (1996).

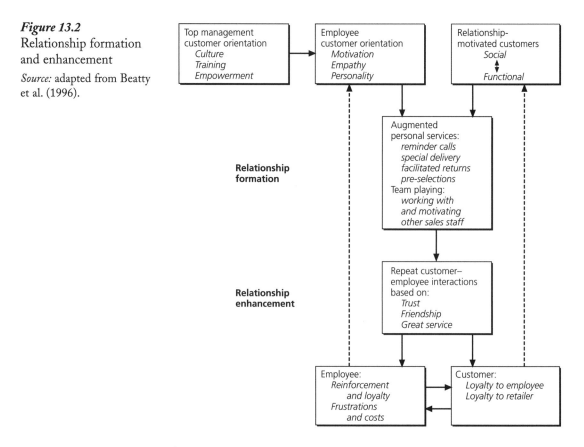

A strong customer orientation at top management level creates the culture and environment within which employees are encouraged, then rewarded, for developing effective customer relationships. In the study by Beatty et al. (1996), highly capable and motivated employees provided some unusual augmented services for their customers/clients. These included visiting the office of an especially busy lawyer with a selection of shoes, following an 'emergency' call from the lawyer's wife. Through repeated good experiences, friendship and trust lead to increased loyalty, both to employee and store. Of course, not all customers need or seek social (or parasocial) relationships with retailers. Reynolds and Beatty (1999b) suggest a typology of relationship preferences, helping retailers and their employees to develop relationship types, targeted to each of these identified segments.

Bateson (1985) found very different levels of preference for personal service and self-service. Many customers prefer the self-service option, even when it does not save money, effort or time. To an extent, this was attributed to a greater degree of control, and lower levels of dependence on others, when using the self-service option. Control and enjoyment were also found to influence consumers' propensity to adopt self-service through touchscreen ordering devices (Dabholkar, 1996). Others, however, prefer the human contact involved in personal service and, in many cases, the lower risk. This underlines the need to identify correctly those elements of service that are really important to targeted customers, as opposed to those that are simply the usual way of delivering the service. Whatever the balance between personal and self-service, the attitude, manner and appearance of staff remain key elements of customers' store images.

While the personal element in service delivery is normally associated with store staff, the role of other shoppers should not be overlooked. Especially within self-service environments, shoppers may interact with others about such issues as product performance or suitability (Baron et al., 1996). McGrath and Otnes (1995) identified several ways in which a purchase may be influenced by other shoppers, who may admire a particular article, helping promote purchase, or 'spoil' the purchase through words or actions. It is also well established that a customer's level of co-operation during a service encounter contributes to his or her own and others' satisfaction with service quality (e.g. Bettencourt, 1997). While retailers cannot directly control these personal interactions between customers, those with whom a good relationship is formed are likely to be positive advocates for the store.

13.1.2 Personal Selling

Personal selling remains a very important element of the retail marketing mix in some sectors, especially where products are relatively complex, expensive and/or infrequently purchased. Even in predominantly self-service stores, well-trained staff with high levels of product knowledge can be a major asset. Consequently, B & Q employs gardeners, plumbers, electricians, builders and decorators to advise their customers, and some sports shops look for staff with capability in relevant sports (Retail Review, 1996). In the supermarket environment, it may well be recently recruited shelf-fillers who are called upon to find items, comment on availability or give opinions on product suitability. These may not be sales people in the traditional sense but they are performing crucial selling roles.

The competence and actions of salespeople can exert strong influence upon the likelihood that a customer will make a purchase (e.g. Babin et al., 1999). Much evidence has accumulated to indicate the determinants of good or poor salespeople performance. From a meta-analysis of over 100 articles, Churchill et al. (1985) concluded that the top six factors are:

1 Personal characteristics
2 Skills
3 Role perceptions
4 Aptitude
5 Motivation
6 Organizational/environmental factors.

While many studies have focused upon just one of these elements, this overview analysis underlines the need to organize the selling function appropriately, recruit the right people *and* train them well. Researchers disagree as to the importance of personality in the recruitment of frontline sales personnel but Hurley (1998) provides a convincing case for seeking salespeople with *extroversion, adjustment* and *agreeableness*. According to Mittal and Lassar (1996), staff who: 'Exude enthusiasm and send out warmth in service encounters offer their customers a personally rewarding shopping and service experience'.

At the most complex level of personnel selling, the process is often depicted as following a number of stages. For detailed descriptions of the selling process, readers can consult specialist texts, such as Rogers (1988) or Anderson (1995). However, many descriptions of personal selling portray a situation in which the salesperson engages a series of tactics to 'win' the sale. This selling orientation contrasts with a customer orientation, that is more consistent with the relationship marketing ethos. According to Goff et al. (1997), customer oriented selling requires a: 'salesperson to engage in behaviors that increase long-term customer satisfaction and avoid behaviors leading to customer dissatisfaction'.

Using the SOCO scale (selling orientation–customer orientation) (Saxe and Weitz, 1982), it has been found that the customer-oriented approach can increase satisfaction with the salesperson, the product, the retailer and the manufacturer (Goff et al., 1997). However, this should not be taken to mean that persuasion, even a little pressure, are now absent from the selling process. The point is that the customer's needs should be central to the process and the salesperson should focus on the long-term value of the customer relationship, not just the value of today's transaction. Shoppers are most likely to repatronize a store if the sales staff show respect for the customer, knowledge and responsiveness (Darian et al., 2001).

The stages suggested below reflect the crucial balance that must be achieved between achieving the sale, and developing the relationship.

Preparation

Before any contact is made with the customer, the salesperson needs to be fully informed of product features, benefits, options, prices, stock levels, delivery schedules, guarantees, returns policies, etc. According to Berry (1993), retailers should:

> *Encourage salesperson professionalism through ongoing skill and knowledge development, and incorporate customer satisfaction measures into salesperson compensation.*

> *Firms that reward only selling behavior and ignore serving behavior are asking for trouble.*

Prior to any selling activity, the appropriate reward structure should be in place and appropriate training given. Uncles (1995) describes the virtuous circle achieved through investment in training, shown in Fig. 13.3. Where complex selling activities are required, retailers also have to

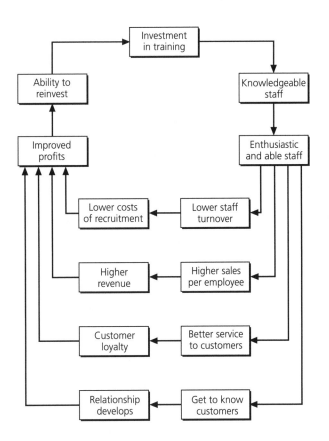

Figure 13.3 Benefits of training

Source: adapted from Uncles (1995).

accept the necessity of selling specialization, i.e., the mobility between product categories may be limited.

Opening the Conversation

It is sometimes argued that more potential sales are lost at the initial contact stage than at any other. Many shoppers prefer to avoid engaging in discussion with sales staff when they are in the browsing or 'window-shopping' phase in their purchase decision (Fletcher, 1987). The opening remarks of sales people often fail to initiate a conversation: questions like 'can I help you?' almost invite the answer 'no thank you, I'm just looking'. Sometimes a warm smile and general greeting are more effective in lowering the barriers to a conversation. Researchers have also explored the effect of touch in the initial encounter, providing some evidence of increased warmth and co-operation (Hornik, 1992). Obviously discretion is required in applying this technique, which could create offence within some cultures or circumstances.

At busy times, or where stores are understaffed, it may be the customer who has difficulty in opening the discussion. Table 13.2 shows the general ratings given by a team of mystery shoppers visiting stores to purchase electrical goods. In many cases, especially of the department stores, it proved difficult to get the attention of a salesperson in under five minutes. Reports included the following comments:

There were plenty of staff on duty but they all seemed to be running around with sheets of paper and disappearing into the back somewhere.

The shop was virtually empty and the staff were chatting together.

Failings in recruitment, training and/or store management are sometimes all too obvious to customers.

Chain	Service within 5 minutes	Helpfulness	Demonstrations	Advice
Comet	Med	Med	Med	Med
Currys	Med	Good	Med	Med
Dixons	Med	Med	Med	Med
Granada	Good	Good	Good	Good
House of Fraser	Poor	Med	Med	Good
John Lewis	Poor	Med	Med	Med
Independents	Med	Good	Med	Med

Table 13.2 Four measures of personal service

Note: mystery shoppers visited at least six stores of each chain and 12 independents.

Source: adapted from Which? (1996a).

Listening to the Customer

Having opened the conversation, the traditional, selling oriented approach is to launch into a set-piece presentation of the product's potential benefits to the consumer. While it is still important to sell the product's benefits, it is clearly better to find out first what benefits are sought by the customer. Ramsey and Sohi (1997) note that poor listening costs US businesses billions of dollars, and is one of the primary causes of salesperson failure. Fortunately, good listening is a trainable skill and it can also be measured (Churchill et al., 1985).

Of course, while listening, a salesperson is expected to react not only to the words, but also to the emotions of the shopper. Menon and Dube (2000) experimented with various shopper emotional states, illustrating the benefits of the appropriate reactions from the salesperson. It is feasible to plan a wide variety of interpersonal strategies, in order to engineer satisfaction-inducing responses from selling staff.

Understanding the Customer's Needs

Typically salespeople classify their customers, according to their level of purchase intention and the amount of assistance needed (Sharma et al., 2000). In many cases, these classifications are made on the basis of first impressions, which may actually hinder the salesperson's efforts (Evans et al., 2000). Having listened to the customer, an astute salesperson should not only be able to identify the customer's needs, but also the decision style and criteria to be used in making the final choice (Sharma and Levy, 1995).

Presenting Solutions

Some customers enter a store with fixed or highly specific ideas of what they want. The salesperson's challenge is then to meet this requirement as precisely and quickly as possible, maybe involving special delivery or inter-branch transfers if the item is not currently in stock.

In other cases, the customers' criteria are ill-defined, maybe in conflict, so the maximum skill is required in understanding and helping to solve such dilemmas. Customers should be encouraged to use, try on or touch the products to increase involvement and assist the decision. A common error is to confuse the consumer with too many possible solutions: a better strategy is to withdraw items that are obviously of less appeal, to reduce the decision to a manageable subset of the available choice.

Handling Objections

At some stages in the conversation a customer is likely to express 'objections', reasons not to make the purchase. The intention may be to delay the purchase decision, to seek reassurance and/or to express strongly felt doubts. These typically relate to the product itself, the store, the after-sales service or the price.

Skill is required to identify the motive and nature of the 'objection', in order to respond appropriately. Engaging in a direct argument with the customer is rarely the most appropriate approach; clearly, the customer must be correctly informed and reassured, without giving offence. Here the credibility of the salesperson is of particular importance in reassuring the customer (Swinyard, 1995); instances have been cited where sales assistant's advice has carried little credibility (e.g. Harris et al., 1997). This highlights another advantage of developing trust within a longer-term customer–salesperson relationship (Reynolds and Beatty, 1999a).

Closing the Sale

Even the most successful sales conversation usually requires a positive effort to close the sale effectively. Some car dealerships have tarnished their reputations through the use of high-pressure tactics to close the sale, including some unethical practices (Honeycutt, 1993), such as telling lies about the interest of other customers.

However, there are many closure techniques that are entirely ethical and which assist the consumer's choice. For example, the salesperson may summarize the benefits of two or more solutions to the customers needs; alternatively, an additional inducement, such as gift wrapping or free delivery, may clinch the sale and add value for the customer. Timing of closure is critically important. Attempts to rush closure, possibly because other customers are waiting, may leave major objections and doubts outstanding. Excessive delay, on the other hand, may leave the customer weary and confused, becoming more likely to leave without buying.

Companion or Suggestion Selling

At the conclusion of an order or a sale, it is not unusual for the salesperson to ask if the customer requires complementary items. For example, ties may be suggested to complement a particular shirt or suit, or the customer may be offered batteries needed with an electrical item.

In some cases, the point of sale computer prompts the salesperson with possible suggestions, linked to the purchase just entered.

Polonsky et al. (2000) recorded mixed reactions from customers to this practice. If the suggestion is well tuned to the shopper's needs, and might save time and effort in future shopping, the practice can enhance the purchase encounter. If, on the other hand, the salesperson is seen to be pressuring for more sales, or simply acting out a set routine, the effect can be more detrimental to goodwill. The Consumers' Association has published a number of reports on the hard selling of over-priced extended warranties by electrical retailers (e.g. Which?, 1998).

Post-Purchase Activities

As the salesperson is the company representative, in the context of a specific purchase, it makes sense to ensure personally that all follow-up activities are completed to the customer's satisfaction. A salesperson who simply blames the fitters or delivery staff for promises that are subsequently broken is not likely to build up sustained or profitable relationships with customers (Reynolds and Beatty, 1999b).

Longer-term follow-up activities can also be productive and, if not seen as high-pressure tactics, add to customer satisfaction. For example, the salesperson may advise the customer of the arrival of new items that are likely to be of interest (Beatty et al., 1996). Within the customer-oriented model of personal selling, the process should not be an isolated series of events, rather a part of the relationship building cycle (Fig. 13.2).

13.2 Financial Services

The ease with which customers can pay, both in terms of efficiency and available credit, is an important influence upon store patronage and transaction size. Retailers have a long history of providing credit for regular customers, a practice that evolved into store cards, now full-scale banking services. For many years, credit tended to be associated with more expensive purchases; the spread of credit cards and the tendency towards fewer, larger shopping trips has brought credit usage into virtually all sectors of retailing.

This section first examines the changing trends in transaction modes, with cash and cheque use giving way to credit and debit cards. The prospects for smart cards and the 'electronic wallet' are also considered. The development of store cards opened up many marketing opportunities for retailers, offering many of the benefits of a loyalty programme, providing also for some a route into other financial services. Strategic alliances with banks have provided another means by which some retailers have moved into banking and a wide range of financial services.

13.2.1 Transaction Services

Methods of payment in stores need to be quick and cost-effective for both consumers and retailers, if service is to be of high standard, without damaging profitability. The cashless society remains a tantalising prospect but is still a long way off (Worthington, 1995). The movement of cash around the banking system costs the UK banks around £2 billion each year. For retailers too, accepting payment by cash can be a costly and time-consuming process. Costs are associated with robberies, cash losses and counterfeits, as well as costs of collection, counting, carrying and insurance (Table 13.3). Nevertheless, cash is still a very popular form of payment, especially among the poorer groups, with less access to more sophisticated payment methods (Mintel, 1998).

Table 13.3 Costs of cash to UK retailers

Source: Retail Consortium, quoted in Worthington (1996).

Annual costs	£ millions
Cash protection equipment	21
External cash collection	83
Cash security staff	33
Cost of robberies/till snatches	12
Cash losses	16
Counterfeit	2
Total	**167**

The introduction of the Euro created many costs and issues for those involved in this currency change (Vissol, 1999). It was estimated to cost European retailers between 1.3 and 2.6 per cent of turnover (IGD, 2001). Deloitte & Touche identified the following areas of changeover cost:

1 *Handling two currencies*: extra capital costs, more bank charges, security costs, more errors.
2 *Dual display of prices*: shelf edge/product labels.
3 *IT modifications*: hardware and software updates to make systems Euro-compatible.
4 *Store layout modification*: changes to tills, scales, counting devices, cash carriers.
5 *Personnel/training*: staff time in training, staff to cover, external trainers.
6 *Communication*: point-of-sale and advertising/promotion.

Cheques represent a rather slow and expensive form of transaction, leading some retailers to set a minimum payment value for the use of cheques. The payment of cheques into a business account can cost between 25p and 60p per transaction. The writing and acceptance of a cheque adds around 40 seconds to the transaction, adding time-cost for both consumer and retailer, as well as frustration for those waiting to be served. The need to write down the amount paid can also have a muting effect on spending behaviour, likewise, the fact that the consumer's wealth is depleted almost immediately (Soman, 2001). The Association for Payment Clearing Services (APACS) estimates that personal cheque transactions will have fallen by around a half between 1992 and 2006 (Mintel, 1998).

Table 13.4 Credit card penetration

Source: adapted from Morgan Stanley Dean Witter (2000), based on NOP Financial Research Survey.

Group		1996 %	2000 %
Socio-economic	AB	66	73
	C1	48	55
	C2	32	41
	DE	13	19
Age	18–24	18	29
	25–34	37	45
	35–44	46	53
	45–54	49	55
	55–64	41	45
	65+	24	29
All (over 17)		36	43

Credit cards, on the other hand, continue to grow, with over 40 per cent of adults holding at least one credit card by 2000 (Morgan Stanley Dean Witter, 2000). Table 13.4 illustrates the far higher penetration among the affluent socio-economic groups, and the lower penetration among the youngest and oldest groups. Compared with many other countries in Europe, credit card take-up in the UK has been strong, but is still well behind in the USA (Antonides et al., 1999). There are estimated to be 1.26 credit cards per person in the USA.

When credit card payments involved the completion of a multi-copy voucher by the retailer, they were a slower form of transaction than cheques, taking an average 75 seconds (Mintel, 1987). However, this comes down to 22 seconds when used without vouchers and with on-line authorization. This has created a willingness among UK consumers to use credit cards even for small transactions. For example, 17 per cent of UK card holders will use them for payments under £5, compared with only 1 per cent of Germans (Mintel, 1998).

Because credit cards offer interest-free periods, if the monthly account is settled in full, various different patterns of usage have evolved. Szmigin and Foxall (1999) identified four categories of card users:

1 *Controllers*: careful planners, with a favoured form of payment, used for most transactions. The credit card is normally used as charge card, i.e., the account is paid in full, with no interest incurred.
2 *Finessers*: use a wide range of payment methods to obtain the best value in terms of payment dates, interest-free periods, time before reaching account, etc. They generally seek to pay no interest, or as little as possible.
3 *Money managers*: often senior managers or self-employed, tend to be confident in their dealings and juggle between a range of accounts. Tend to view interest charges as an inevitable by-product of operating a range of payment methods.

4 *Product enthusiasts*: the card conveys emotional benefits, the pleasure of being able to spend. They are likely to have a wide range of cards and accept that paying interest is often a necessity.

A further, small category of debt incurring shoppers were termed 'addictive consumers' by Elliott et al. (1996). While the shopping experience and buying of goods brings pleasure to many people, for these consumers it has become an addiction. The consequences can include huge levels of personal debt and the breakdown of relationships.

While both credit cards and store cards offer consumer benefits/risks of credit, debit cards offer a more direct alternative to cash or cheques. In theory, electronic funds transfer at the point of sale (EFTPoS) can occur almost immediately (Kirk, 2001); in practice, many transactions occur off-line but the funds do then move quickly between accounts. Debit cards, such as Switch, also serve as cheque guarantee cards and can be used in automated teller machines (ATMs) to obtain cash. Their versatility was also extended through the introduction of 'cash-back' by many stores, such that shoppers can have up to £50 added to the bill and paid to them in cash (Worthington, 1998). This arrangement is mutually beneficial, in that it reduces the retailer's cash handling costs.

Figure 13.4 illustrates the rapid growth in debit card use, compared with the decline in the use of personal cheques. By 1997, debit card transactions also exceeded those of credit cards, at 4.3 million and 3.0 million respectively per day. However, the average transaction size is higher for credit cards, at £49 compared with £29 (Mintel, 1998). Debit card adoption progressed at differing rates throughout Europe (Antonides et al., 1999) but they have now achieved widespread acceptance, including within the USA. Like all other transaction modes, debit cards are not free of costs to the retailers, including hardware, communications and merchant service charges (MSCs). These MSCs

Figure 13.4 Cheque and debit card payment volumes

Source: based upon Mintel (1998) estimates.

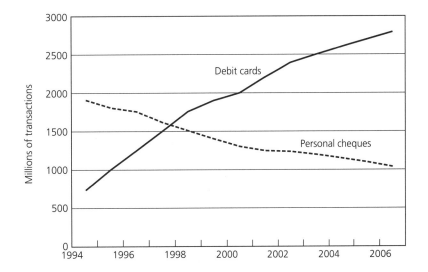

could vary between 5p and 70p per transaction, depending upon the bargaining power of, and amount of processing performed by, the retailer (Worthington, 1996).

Most credit, debt and store cards store their machine-readable information on a simple magnetic strip. However, 'smart cards', including their own computer chip, have been in use in France since the 1970s and are now becoming an affordable alternative. Although sometimes described as 'technology looking for a use' (Mintel, 1998), smart cards do offer a number of advantages which could ensure their widespread adoption. With a read-and-write memory facility, they are able to convey the updated account details, reducing the need for on-line authorization networks. They also provide enhanced security through encrypted codes or digital signature, which uniquely identifies the card, helping to combat card fraud (Ody, 1997).

From the consumer viewpoint, a major advantage ultimately could be the versatility of the smart card. It could in theory become the one card carried, incorporating all debit, credit, ATM and loyalty programme functions. They could also largely eliminate the remaining uses of cash for small transaction, by carrying a prepaid electronic float, transferred to the card from the customer's account (Worthington, 1996). This prepaid float can be enlarged from the main account via the telephone, Internet or in-store terminals. The 'electronic wallet' is capable of moving money between smart cards, for example, to pay children's spending money or to pay a local shop that does not have EFTPoS equipment. Consequently, electronic cash can circulate between cards, without the need to route each transaction through complex communications networks (Weber et al., 1995).

Extensive trials of the 'electronic wallet/purse' have occurred, such as the Mondex scheme in Swindon and 'Visa Cash' in Leeds (Worthington, 1996). However, without almost universal acceptance by retailers and other service providers, it becomes just another card to carry around. Given their heavy investment in EFTPoS and loyalty programmes, many retailers have been reluctant to invest in further upgrades of point of sale equipment. Boots and Shell have however opted for smartcard-based loyalty schemes, facilitating a possible move to such payment systems in the future (Baxter, 1998).

13.2.2 Retailers' Financial Services

Retailers are certainly not newcomers to financial services, having provided credit to regular customers over the centuries. As Italian writer Rossi commented in the 1800s: 'It is the baker who acts as banker to the common man.' As credit arrangements became more formalized within the multiple chains, a range of charge accounts, budget accounts and longer-term credit plans developed. More recently, the growth in popularity of credit cards prompted some retailers to introduce their own store cards, gaining more control over costs and the relationship with customers (Alexander and Colgate, 1998; 2000).

Store cards are, in effect, credit cards that can be used to make purchases only in a certain store, or group of stores (Which?, 2000). For many years, neither John Lewis nor Marks & Spencer would accept any other form of credit card, although by the year 2000, both had bowed to the inevitable.

By no means do store cards offer the customer cheaper credit than Visa or Mastercard. The notable exception is the John Lewis card, which has consistently offered a cheaper annual percentage rate (APR). Table 13.5 contrasts the APR of 10 retailer-issued store cards, most of which offer a slightly better rate, if the account is settled by direct debit.

Table 13.5 Store cards: annual percentage rates

Source: adapted from Which? (2000).

Store/group	Other stores accepting	APR (direct debit)	APR (other methods)
Allders	Arding & Hobbs	26.8	29.8
BhS/Mothercare		26.0	29.0
Burton/Debenhams	Dorothy Perkins, Evans, Principles, Topshop	28.0	29.9
Duet Network	Adams, Fosters, Miss Selfridge, Richards, Wallis	27.8	30.9
Etam		28.0	29.9
Frasercard	House of Fraser Group	27.5	29.3
John Lewis/Waitrose	Peter Jones, Bainbridge, Jessops, Tyrrell & Green	16.0	16.0
Marks & Spencer		25.1	25.7
Owen Owen		28.7	30.7
River Island		28.0	29.9

No transaction system is cost-free to the retailer: cheques incur bank charges, cash creates handling costs, credit cards incur merchant service charges (Alexander et al., 1992). Store cards too create overhead costs in running the system, as well as bad debts, collections, credit scoring and funding (Worthington, 1994). However, as Table 13.5 illustrates, most store cards do attract high rates of interest from accounts not cleared in full. Store cards also have many of the advantages to the retailer of loyalty cards, discussed in Sec. 3.5.2. The main benefit of running a store card include:

1 Larger transaction sizes, with more unplanned purchasing.
2 Loyalty to the store can be nurtured through targeted communication and the feeling of exclusiveness.
3 Detailed information is gained about customer characteristics and spending patterns.
4 The effects of promotions can be more precisely monitored.
5 Costs may be lower than those incurred on Visa or Mastercard transactions.
6 Other financial services can be developed and promoted.

Table 13.6 Retailers and
financial services

Source: adapted from
Alexander and Pollard
(2000).

Marks & Spencer was highly successful in using its store card to promote
a wider range of financial services. As Table 13.6 illustrates, these now
include a range of savings accounts, investments, insurances and
pensions. While Cornhill Insurance underwrite some of these products,
all the administration is conducted through Marks & Spencer Financial
Services. Along with price, service features and the quality of advice, the
corporate brand is a major, value-adding feature in financial services
(Devlin, 2001). Consumer trust in the Marks & Spencer brand was
highly influential in the development of these financial services, which
have become significant profit contributors for the company (Morgan
Stanley Dean Witter, 2001a).

Retailer	Financial services	Providers
Marks & Spencer	Savings accounts Personal loans Home and contents insurance Life insurance Pensions Mortgage protection PEPs, ISAs, unit trusts	Marks & Spencer Financial Services Cornhill Insurance
Tesco	Instant access savings account Credit card Travel insurance, currency Life insurance Motor insurance Pet care insurance ISAs (individual savings account) Mortgage finder (on line)	Royal Bank of Scotland Scottish Widows Direct Line
Sainsbury	Instant access savings account Credit cards Travel insurance Home insurance Pet care insurance Car loans Mortgages ISAs	Bank of Scotland Royal and Sun Alliance
Safeway	Instant access account Deposit account	Abbey National
Morrisons	Savings account	HSBC

Based on a survey of retailers in Australia, Ireland, New Zealand and the
UK, Alexander and Colgate (2000) identified six main benefits in
developing financial services:

1 Financial services provide marketing information.
2 Financial services make direct contributions to profits.
3 Financial services develop closer relationships with customers.

4 Financial services build on the trust already created.

5 Financial services support sales growth in core product markets.

6 Financial services are a natural extension of service activity at the point of sale.

Figure 13.5 depicts how the acceptance of various payment systems have facilitated the adoption of subsequent financial innovations. Through the analysis of adoption rates in ten European countries, Antonides et al. (1999) demonstrated how the acceptance of cheques weaned customers away from cash, paving the way for credit cards, then ATM/credit cards. In parallel to this, retailers have been developing consumer acceptance of their store cards and loyalty cards, facilitating their diversification into other banking and financial services.

Most of the earlier store card activities were among the clothing retailers and variety stores, but grocery retailers too were making steps into the banks' domain. The installation of ATMs at large stores, then the introduction of cash-back on debit cards, made superstores a natural place to obtain cash. As the loyalty programmes of Tesco and Sainsbury became well established, these retailers in particular had the databases, communication channels and customer relationships to facilitate the marketing of a wider range of financial services.

Conscious of the potential hazards of running very diverse business operations (The Economist, 1997), the major grocers formed alliances with banks and other financial institutions. Tesco initially allied with the NatWest Bank but this relationship was short-lived (Graham, 1997). The bank was concerned about Tesco's power within this partnership, and the dangers of cannibalizing its own market (Alexander and Colgate, 1998). The latter issues was less of a concern for Tesco's next partner, the Royal Bank of Scotland (RBS), which at that stage had less geographical coverage south of the border. Ironically, NatWest was

Figure 13.5 Influences on adoption of financial services

Source: adapted from Antonides et al. (1999).

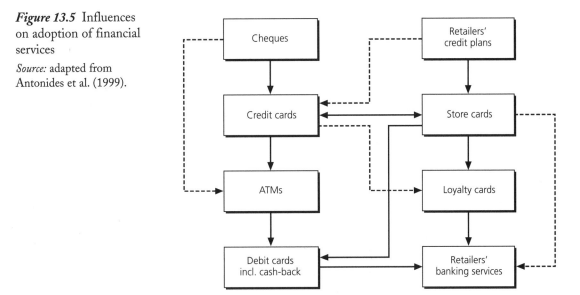

Benefits to retailers	Benefits to financial service provider
Extends relationship with customers	Extend geographical coverage
Extends retail brand	Compensates for branch closures
Promote via loyalty programme	Increase economies of scale
Savings may be spent at store	Regain share lost to 'new' competitors
Can cherry-pick services	Learn retail and customer relationship skills
Prospects to extend profits	Long opening hours
Most technology already there	Co-promotion with retailer
Synergy with international activities	
Hazards for retailers	**Hazards for financial service provider**
Distraction from core business	Loss of brand identity
Offends customers turned down after credit scoring	Bank visibility diminishes sharply as e-banking prevails
Blame for errors/computer problems	Lower margin services remain
Bad publicity/compensation	Loss of privileged access to customer information
Can overload service capacity	Cannibalise own customer base
Exposure to bad debts	Retailer dictates terms
Initial losses	Adverse reactions to more branch closures

Figure 13.6
Benefits/hazards for retailers and providers

Source: derived mainly from Alexander and Pollard (2000).

subsequently taken over by RBS in 2000. Geographical expansion was also a strong motivation for the Bank of Scotland to work with Sainsbury in developing its range of financial services.

The alliances between these banks and insurance companies have enabled both Tesco and Sainsbury to expand quickly their financial service offerings, as Table 13.6 illustrates. Noticeably, the branding of these activities tends to be in the name of the retailer, rather than the bank, which represents a long-term hazard for the banks (Alexander and Pollard, 2000). As more financial business is conducted at stores, over the telephone or through the Internet, opportunities for banks to reinforce their brands will become more limited.

Ironically, the strong retail branding of financial services also has its risks. When errors occur, or when service centres become overloaded, adverse publicity can damage the brand (e.g. Bibby, 1997; Lumsden, 1997). The retailers may also damage relationships with regular store users by turning down their loan applications. Balancing customer service and risk management is not familiar ground for most retailers, and Sainsbury turned down around 50 per cent of loan applications in the first year of operation (Hilton, 1997). As with all diversifications and strategic alliances, each party has to weigh carefully the many potential benefits and hazards; Fig. 13.6 provides a summary of these from both perspectives.

13.3 Other Elements of Service

Having now examined the major elements of personal and financial services, this section moves on to look at some of the other ways in which retailers try to serve their customers better. Chapter 3 underlined the benefits of minimizing shoppers' time, effort, stress and risk: many services set out to fulfil one or more of these objectives. In that 'time poverty' is widely reported, especially among some of the more affluent shoppers, retailers have addressed this issue in a number of ways, notably in reduction of waiting times and increasing the choice of shopping hours.

Various other services have also been introduced to 'lighten the load' and increase the pleasure and/or efficiency of the customer's shopping visit. However, while a smile costs nothing and rapid payment systems may actually save money, many other augmented services do add to operating costs. Retailers therefore need to plan the service mix carefully to ensure that it is really attuned to the needs of their target customers.

13.3.1 Time-Saving Service

When Leo Burnett (1987) surveyed shoppers' complaints about service, not enough tills at busy time (44 per cent) and queues (40 per cent) were the two most common areas of dissatisfaction. Since that time, service has become a major preoccupation among superstores and other retailers (Norman, 1999), with numerous initiatives to ease the process of getting out of the store (Drummond, 1995). However, Mintel (2000) still identified speed of service at the checkout or pay desk as the biggest single service deficit, as Table 13.1 demonstrates.

The two surveys are not directly comparable in their wording, but the fact remains that nearly half of shoppers still express dissatisfaction about this element of service. Of course, the high profile given to service over recent years may have increased expectations, partly negating the effects of some real improvements in service levels. It is also apparent that waiting times differ between companies, as Table 13.7 shows. A third of the visits to Asda involved a queue of over 5 minutes, compared with less than 10 per cent at Waitrose (Which?, 2001a). Table 13.2 also suggests that the problem of slow service is not unique in supermarkets, with many shoppers waiting over 5 minutes to be served in electrical goods shops/departments (Which?, 1996a).

Table 13.7 Time spent queuing

Note: based upon timings during the next visit after receiving the questionnaire.

Source: Which? (2001a).

Retailer	% queuing more than 5 minutes
Waitrose	9
Tesco	17
Somerfield	18
Safeway	20
Sainsbury	25
Asda	33

The Superquinn chain in Ireland and Tesco in the UK were early adopters of the 'one in front', policy (Drummond, 1995), whereby more checkouts (if available) are opened when queue lengths reach three people or more. This involves a combination of good planning, flexible staffing roles and, in some cases, tracking technology. While customer flows can be predicted to an extent from previous experience, the weather, traffic conditions, special television programmes, etc. are among the factors that can cause significant variations. The ability to monitor the flow of customers into a store enables retailers to model far more precisely the demand for checkout services, when those shoppers are ready to leave the store.

While faster service should be the ultimate objective, it is unlikely that waiting time in stores will be entirely eliminated. Customer perceptions of waiting time can, however, be reduced if that time is filled pleasantly or usefully (Pruyn and Smidts, 1998; Taylor, 1995). One approach is to have videos showing a combination of information features and commercials; another is to offer the chance of other incidental purchases, such as lottery tickets, while waiting (Dennis and Arnold, 1996). The unfairness of the wait also influences the extent of customer dissatisfaction, for example, when people use express checkouts with too many items (Bell et al., 1997). It can also be beneficial to advise customers of the expected duration of the wait (Hui and Tse, 1996), a practice now adopted through information screens at collection points in Argos stores.

Not all shoppers are 'time poor' and East et al. (1994) found a sizeable minority (32 per cent) that did not mind queuing at checkouts. For some, it becomes part of the social element of shopping, while others see it as confirmation that they have chosen a popular store. Crowding has been found to be a positive attribute under some circumstances (Hui and Bateson, 1991) and a virtually empty store can be off-putting. However, crowd avoidance was the main reason given by those choosing to shop early in the week or at quieter times of day (East et al., 1994).

13.3.2 Hours of Trading

As large supermarkets and convenience stores are now open most evenings in the week, grocery shopping is no longer so heavily concentrated into Fridays and Saturdays. These do, however, remain the most popular shopping days, as Table 13.8 shows. It also illustrates the growing popularity of Sunday shopping, in spite of most larger shops (in excess of 280 m²) being limited to six hours of opening on Sundays. Prior to the Sunday Trading Act of 1994, most large stores in England and Wales were breaking the law if they opened on Sundays (Rowell, 1994).

Retailers in the UK now have considerable flexibility to use trading hours as a competitive service. This is in contrast with many other part of the European Union, where opening times are more severely restricted (Grünhagen and Mittelstaedt, 2001; NatWest Securities, 1997).

Table 13.8 Expenditure by day of week

Source: derived from Nielsen (2000), based on A.C. Nielsen Homescan.

Day	% of grocery expenditure	Average spend per visit £
Monday	11.0	10.1
Tuesday	11.5	10.3
Wednesday	12.2	11.0
Thursday	16.7	13.3
Friday	21.0	13.8
Saturday	20.2	13.3
Sunday	7.3	16.4

Sunday opening in particular has been opposed by a number of pressure groups, including staff unions (Freathy and Sparks, 1993) and religious interests. Small shopkeepers, who were allowed to open anyway, also opposed Sunday opening by the larger stores, as it undermined a major element of their competitive advantage.

For UK retailers, the choice of opening hours is now a balance of economics, competitive considerations and service expectations within specific areas. The economics of longer opening hours and Sunday trading have been the subject of detailed analyses (e.g. Moir, 1987; Thurik, 1987) but the optimum hours appear to be location specific. Some have opted for 24-hour opening, notably superstores on busy urban/suburban commuting routes, including over 300 Tesco Stores (Morgan Stanley Dean Witter, 2001b). To comply with the law in England and Wales, however, they must open only for 6 hours on Sundays. This restriction does not apply to convenience stores of less than 280 m^2: some in city areas do open for all 168 hours of the week. Not that 24-hour opening is limited to food stores, as Borders bookshop in Charing Cross Road demonstrated (Retail Review, 1999).

There are a number of arguments in favour of longer opening hours:

1 Some staff are in-store around the clock anyway, for stocking and security purposes.
2 Longer hours may spread the peak loads.
3 They provide a service of great value to some customers.
4 Better utilization of assets and fixed costs may be achieved.
5 Previously loyal customers may be lost if competitors' hours are longer.

There are also potential disadvantages:

1 Labour costs will be increased, especially where higher rates are paid for Sunday working (Freathy and Sparks, 1993).
2 Additional revenues may not be sufficient to offset these costs.
3 Late-evening, night-time and Sunday working are not popular with some staff, including many store managers (Freathy and Sparks, 1995).
4 The atmosphere of the store may be difficult to maintain when customers are outnumbered by shelf-fillers, especially in 24-hour stores.
5 Pressures to reduce wastage may lead to diminished displays of perishable goods at quiet times.

Table 13.9 illustrates typical opening times for different organization types, but the variations within organization can be considerable.

While recent trends have been towards increased trading hours, some have been reluctant to follow. For example, many discounters operate on shorter hours, in order to minimize labour costs. The opening times of clothing specialists are often limited by the shopping centre, or by the common practice among neighbouring stores. John Lewis, although now trading on Sundays, does not usually open most of its stores on

Table 13.9 Typical hours open/week

Source: adapted from IGD (2000).

		Hours	Typical times
Symbol groups		105	0700–2200
Co-operatives	Large	84	0800–2100
	Small	98	0800–2200
Convenience multiples	Normal	112	0700–2300
	24 hours	168	All day, everyday
Major multiples	Normal	96	0700–2200
	'24 Hours'	140	All day: 6 hours Sunday
Forecourts	Normal	126	0600–2400
	24 hours	168	All day, everyday

Mondays. They argue that this is necessary to maintain a consistently high standard of personal service.

13.3.3 Planning the Service Mix

The range of other services that a retailer may consider offering is almost without limit. Services include the most basic, such as free parking or free carrier bags, to the most specific services, such as engraving or gift wrapping. Some facilities, such as in-store pharmacies or petrol stations, can provide valuable services to customers, while also comprising potentially profitable areas of diversification. Other services, such as customer toilets, may be expensive in terms of space and maintenance, yet have become an expectation in larger stores.

Table 3.10 summarizes the proportions of major grocery stores offering service counters. These not only increase customers' choice, particularly in terms of quantity purchased, they also enhance the image of the store, and the likelihood of positive interactions. Bakeries have almost become the norm in larger supermarkets, contributing also to the atmospherics of the stores. Among the other facilities, petrol stations would be more ubiquitous, but for the size constraints of sites and planning restrictions.

Retailers offering a wide range of services have used these to emphasize competitive advantage. For example, Tesco's newspaper adverts have published price and service comparisons with Aldi and other 'hard' discounters. These illustrate that a basket of goods can be cheaper in Tesco, and that the discounters provide none of the listed services.

Pledges and guarantees have also played a part in retailers' efforts to communicate their service levels, and to help in their maintenance. Figure 13.7 lists some of Sainsbury's customer commitments, based upon the company's research into how customers judge service delivery (Bell et al., 1997). Shopping centres have also established detailed service standards for various categories of shoppers. For example, the Meadowhall Centre near Sheffield published lists of specific guarantees for the disabled, families with young children, motorists and customers

Table 13.10 Service
facilities provided

Source: adapted from IGD
(2000).

	% stores providing the facility			
	Tesco	**Sainsbury**	**Asda**	**Safeway**
Service counters:				
Fresh fish	56	50	47	18
Fresh meat	33	44	19	25
Delicatessen	79	44	97	94
Bakery	87	87	93	83
Hot food	33	98	83	46
Pizza bar	4	0	95	0
Other facilities:				
Crèche	0	0	13	20
Dry cleaner	4	21	17	20
Petrol station	48	47	59	33
Coffee shop	50	44	0	44
Post office	2	0	6	6
Pharmacy	33	19	33	21
Lottery terminals	77	n/a	84	63

in general. To show that these were not empty promises, Meadowhall offered compensation if any of its many guarantees was breached.

These few examples have illustrated the range of services offered to enhance convenience or make shopping more interesting. However, a retailer must evaluate each service possibility with care, in relation to expectations, feasibility and cost-effectiveness. A number of factors need to be taken into account when deciding the service, or the level of a service, to offer:

1 *Positioning*: is it a prestige store, where high service levels are typically offered, or a discounter, where basic services are the norm?
2 *Competition*: it is important to be aware of competitors' service propositions, not necessarily to follow them.

Figure 13.7 Some of
Sainsbury's service
pledges

Sources: Barrett (1995); Bell
et al. (1997).

- Extra bag packers at peak times
- Assistants to carry groceries to cars on request
- AA service if car breaks down in car park
- Parent and child parking spaces
- Free nappies in baby 'changing room'
- Milk/baby food warming service
- Complimentary wheelchairs
- Guidance for the visually impaired
- Staff 'go-for' policy if customer at checkout has forgotten an item
- Staff 'follow-me' policy if product cannot be found
- Voucher if promoted product is out of stock
- No quibble refund policy

3 *Target market*: this indicates likely service preferences, willingness to pay, experience of using specific competitors, etc.

4 *Expectations*: these can be at the level of what the retailer will offer, should offer or could ideally offer (Taher et al., 1996). Input by customers to the service innovation process increases the likelihood of success (Martin, 1996).

5 *Store size*: this determines the likely utilization and the viability of space-demanding services (Tax and Stuart, 1997).

6 *Location*: a cafeteria and children's play area, for example, may be more important if the store is self-standing and remote from other such facilities.

7 *Product types*: are they heavy or bulky? Are the perceived risks high?

8 *Cost-effectiveness of service*: service expenditures are not equally effective in attracting and retaining customer, although the longer-term benefits can be difficult to estimate (Rust et al., 1995; Zeithaml, 2000).

9 *Image of cost*: would the service be viewed as an unnecessary elaboration, catering for a minority but adding to prices?

10 *Promotion*: services that are more distinctive, apt and interesting are easier to promote to attract new customers.

These criteria should not only be applied to new service decisions: existing services too should be frequently re-evaluated.

Some of the more basic services, such as free car parking, become expected and could not easily be withdrawn by retailers. Other 'supplementary services' appear to go through a form of life cycle, an appreciation of which may assist decisions to retain or withdraw the service (James et al., 1981).

1 *Introduction*: a new service is introduced, giving differential advantage to a specific retailer.

2 *Duplication*: if the service is popular and viable, it will be copied, to neutralize the competitive advantage.

3 *Stalemate*: all retailers in the sector offer the service, so it becomes just an added cost; elimination of the service by just one retailer would however create differential disadvantage (Martin, 1996).

4 *Institutionalization*: over time, the service is taken for granted by consumers and becomes a basic part of the retail sector's offering.

5 *Replacement*: some services never disappear, whereas others may diminish in need and importance. Shopping patterns change, different market segments may be targeted, and some functions are taken over by other types of business. This may signal the need to delete, replace or introduce/increase charges for a service currently offered.

Bates and Didion (1985) suggested a matrix approach to the development of service strategies. Each service should be evaluated according to whether its costs are high or low and whether its value to the customer is high or low. Low-cost, high-value services (patronage builders) are obviously attractive from the retailer's viewpoint: high-cost, low-value services (disappointers), on the other hand, are clear candidates for elimination. The evaluation of service cost-effectiveness is not an easy task, however, as a wide range of direct and indirect costs and benefits much be carefully weighed. The retailer must also judge the competitive advantage that is achieved and the congruence of the service with overall strategy and positioning.

13.4 Customer Satisfaction

Having looked at some of the numerous specific services that retailers can provide, it is appropriate now to return to a broader connotation of service, the achievement of customer satisfaction. The recent emphasis upon customer relationship management (CRM), discussed in Chapter 3, has drawn attention to the importance of retaining existing customers. Traditionally, a great deal of marketing effort and expenditure was devoted to attracting new customers, often with insufficient attention to existing ones. It is now generally accepted that the retention of good customers is less expensive than the attraction of new customers of similar value (e.g. Chenet and Johansen, 1999).

While customer satisfaction may not alone be sufficient to ensure loyalty (Rust and Oliver, 2000), it is usually a necessary first step. Retailers require effective problem-solving mechanisms to deal with a wide variety of product-related and service-related dissatisfiers. Product complaints are usually referred to the retailer, rather than the manufacturer, especially in the case of clothing (Kincade et al., 1992); an appropriate returns policy is therefore essential. Most dissatisfaction does not, however, lead to complaints, so retailers much proactively monitor customer satisfaction levels. The SERVQUAL framework can be valuable in detecting and diagnosing gaps between perceived performance and customers' expectations.

13.4.1 Problem-Solving

The minimum requirement in dealing with product-related problems is, of course, compliance with relevant legislation. In the UK, the Sale and Supply of Goods Act 1994 specifies that goods must be of *satisfactory quality* and, if not, that they should be returned within a *reasonable amount of time* after purchase (Which?, 1996b). In practice, many retailers operate returns policies that go beyond the requirements of the law, accepting the return of goods simply because they are not wanted. Under these circumstances, the retailer may stipulate a time limit for the return of unwanted goods, such as 16 days at Argos, 28 days at B & Q.

Davis et al. (1995) identified four main factors that influence the profitability of money-back guarantees:

1 The salvage values of returned merchandise.
2 Transaction costs of returning merchandise.
3 Probability of mismatching product to consumer.
4 Consumer value of product trial.

A fifth factor could well be added, i.e., ability to inspect before purchase. In the e-tailing or catalogue showroom contexts, this may be extremely limited. Similarly, if a clothing retailer does not offer adequate changing room facilities, a more liberal returns policy would be required.

In spite of the costs involved in accepting the return of unwanted goods, these policies greatly reduce customers' purchase risk perceptions. Neo (1993) observed how the very liberate exchange and money-back policies in Singapore encourage customers to shop more frequently and with greater confidence. Once the items are tried at home, the chances that they will be retained are far greater. However, very liberal returns policies can produce a torrent of returns, between 30–50 per cent in some cases (Meyer, 1999).

There are also dangers that the returns procedures can add to customer dissatisfaction, if not handled efficiently. Sherry et al. (1992) encountered many negative descriptors as consumers discuss their experience of returning unwanted gifts, including troublesome, uncomfortable, awkward, time-consuming, boring, a 'hassle'. Where gifts are bought in the knowledge that the recipient may well return the item, the difficulties of returning the item may negatively influence feelings towards the giver.

Another hazard for the retailer is that some customers will engage in 'retail borrowing', defined by Piron and Young (2001) as: 'The purchase of an item with the intent to return the same item for refund once the item has been used, with satisfaction, for a specific purpose.' The full extent of the practice is difficult to estimate, with studies reporting between 8 and 22 per cent of returns being fraudulent (Piron and Young, 2000). In some cases, the garment is 'borrowed' for a job interview or a special date. In other cases, notably CDs or fashion items, the item may be 'borrowed' with a view to illicit copying (Schmidt et al., 1999). While a retailer may develop a database of frequent returners, it is clearly a challenge to balance the control of fraud and cost with the operation of an efficient and courteous returns system.

Product-related issues are not the only problems that may lead to complaints and/or customer dissatisfaction. Using the Critical Incident Technique, Rudolph et al. (2000) examined the negative buying experiences of over 400 food shoppers. Table 13.11 classifies these into 12 groups, the first seven being failures of the retailers' service systems, the rest being people related. Apart from product defects, the largest category of failures relates to slow or unavailable service, including unacceptable waiting times at checkouts. The failure type with the highest importance rating was where embarrassment is caused by an employee. Failures involving bad information, while fewer in number, appear especially damaging to customer retention.

Whether or not the problem leads to a loss of patronage depends largely upon the way in which a complaint is handled. Blodgett et al. (1997) have examined the effects of three aspects of service recovery:

Failure type	Frequency %	Failure rating [1]	Retention % [2]
Service system failures			
Policy failures	7	6.3	64
Slow/unavailable service	15	6.9	66
Pricing failures	2	6.4	63
Packaging errors	5	5.3	86
Out of stock	10	6.1	80
Product defects	34	6.6	68
Bad information	2	7.1	25
People failures			
Failures with special requests	2	5.9	77
Mischarging	4	6.6	87
Employee causes embarrassment	5	7.5	60
Attention failures	6	7.0	55
Customer's error	8	6.3	97

Table 13.11 Negative shopping experiences

Notes: 1 Failures rated on scale from 1 (very low importance) to 10 (very high importance).
2 Retention indicates the percentage who shop at the store with the same or greater frequency since the incident occurred.

Source: adapted from Rudolph et al. (2000).

1 The perceived fairness of the remedy offered by the retailer.
2 The perceived fairness of the policies and procedures used to deal with the complaint.
3 How the complainant was treated, e.g., courteously or rudely.

Courteous treatment proved especially instrumental towards achieving effective service recovery. Indeed, when a customer receives an unfriendly reaction to a complaint, it can lead to serious 'failure escalation' (Rudolph et al., 2000). Timing is also of critical importance; most customers tend to return if the complaint is dealt with quickly (Mitchell and Critchlow, 1993; Swanson and Kelley, 2001).

Unfortunately, many companies commit the 'dual sins' of understaffing customer service departments and/or staffing them with underqualified personnel (Horovitz, 1997). Not only should staff be well versed in the company's procedures and policies, they should also be empowered to make adaptive reactions to particular problems. While some personalities are better suited than others to complaint-handling, Menon and Dube (2000) argue that personnel can be trained to display appropriate emotional responses to customers' anger or anxiety. According to Chenet and Johansen (1999), complaint-handling should aspire to more than just problem solving:

A complaint is primarily a possibility to create a memorable experience.
According to research, one of the main reasons for losing customers is
complaint handling. Nobody knows what failure and complaints costs to

the company because we only monitor the Complaint Department's budget ... We contend that the highest cost is losing the customer because the firm has failed to create a unique experience (unique recovery).

They prescribe steps that a company or employee can take to achieve effective complaint handling:

1 Take full responsibility.
2 Apologize for the occurrence and thank the customer for complaining.
3 Understand the customer and the problem.
4 Create a unique solution.
5 Act quickly and conclusively.
6 Strengthen and confirm the experience by means of an 'economic' compensation and a surprise.
7 Ensure that the organization learns from the complaint.

A complaint is therefore an important opportunity to diagnose a problem, as well as a chance to effect a positive service recovery. When dissatisfied, by no means all shoppers complain. In the context of grocery shopping, 70 per cent of shoppers did not complain; 30 per cent took no action in the case of durable goods (Broadbridge and Marshall, 1995). Reasons given for not complaining include time pressures and a feeling that it would not change anything (Which?, 2001b).

Even when no action is taken, it cannot be assured that the incident will be forgotten and that the retailer's image will not be damaged. Figure 13.8 summarizes outcomes of dissatisfaction, illustrating that actions may be either public or private in nature.

Public actions include complaints to the retailer, to agencies such as the Trading Standards Authority, or direct legal action. Failures in primary complaint handling can trigger an escalation through these options. Private actions include negative comments to friends and family, as well as the loss of some or all of the customer's own patronage. Being less assertive in

Figure 13.8 Consumer complaint behaviour

Source: adapted from Broadbridge and Marshall (1995).

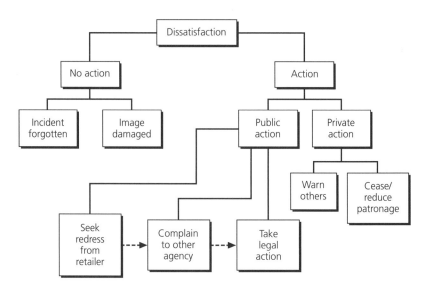

nature, there has been a tendency for companies to overlook these private actions, in spite of their importance as indicators, and influencers, of customer satisfaction (Williams et al., 1993).

13.4.2 Service Quality and Satisfaction

The linkages between customers' perceptions of service quality and satisfaction levels have been extensively investigated. Some researchers have questioned (e.g. Dabholkar, 1993) whether customer satisfaction and service quality are essentially the same construct, although most regard them as different but related (e.g. Spreng and Mackoy, 1996). Definitions that attempt to distinguish between the concepts also vary; to give an example:

> *Satisfaction is a 'post consumption' experience which compares perceived quality with expected quality, whereas (perceived) service quality refers to a global evaluation of a firm's service delivery system (Sivadas and Baker-Prewitt, 2000).*

Difficulties in distinguishing the two concepts relate in part to the many meanings of 'service' (Fig. 13.1), plus the fact that much satisfaction research has been conducted in service settings.

From a multi-company study, Zeithaml et al. (1996) produced strong evidence that service quality influenced consumers' return intentions. Jones et al. (2000) confirmed this relationship but found that it declined when switching barriers are high. Hence, even if customers are inclined to move to another service provider, they may not do so if it 'costs' them time, effort, stress or money.

Cronin et al. (2000) identified both direct and indirect relationships between service quality and (re)patronage intentions. Dabholkar et al. (2000) emphasize the mediating role of satisfaction in this relationship, highlighting the importance of achieving service quality that is relevant to consumers' needs.

Customers' expectations play a major part in determining satisfaction levels. Szymanski and Henard (2001) point to the dual role of expectations, both influencing satisfaction directly and creating reference levels, against which future service encounters are judged. A number of different types of service expectations have been identified, for example:

Desired service	*Ideal* service level
↓	↓
Adequate service	Level that *should* be provided
↓	↓
Predicted service	Anticipation of what *will* be provided
(Zeithaml et al., 1993)	(Taher et al., 1996)

Although these typologies of expectations differ slightly, they both point to the different levels at which expectations can be expressed and measured. If a service experience falls below the level that a customer expects, or regards as adequate, a threshold effect is likely to be

Figure 13.9 Satisfaction and return intentions

Source: Swinyard and Whitlark (1994).

encountered, and return intentions will decline sharply (Murphy and Suntook, 1998). An understanding of expectations is therefore crucial in identifying these critical threshold levels.

A negative service experience may have a proportionately larger effect upon return intentions that the equivalent positive experience. In this context, Swinyard and Whitlark (1994) applied prospect theory, described as: 'A theory of asymmetry which argues that dissatisfaction has a much greater negative effect than satisfaction's positive effect.' Using experimental scenarios to depict negative and positive experiences of equivalent magnitude, they produced measures of satisfaction and return intentions, shown in Fig. 13.9. This suggests asymmetry in the return intentions, rather than in the recorded satisfaction levels. In fact, the drop in return intentions, due to the negative experience, was almost double the gain, in response to the positive experience.

This raises questions about the sustainability of strategies that seek to delight, rather than simply satisfy, customers. Deming (1986) was among those who exhorted higher and higher levels of quality: 'It will not suffice to have customers that are merely satisfied.' However, if a customer is delighted, does this simply 'raise the bar', creating expectations that are hard to meet on future occasions (Rust and Oliver, 2000)? The concept of 'customer delight' has been defined as: 'A profoundly positive emotional state, generally resulting from having one's expectations exceeded to a surprising degree' (Oliver et al., 1997).

It has even been suggested that companies should manage expectations by promising less than they can actually deliver. However, given the direct influence that expectations can have upon satisfaction, lowering expectations could easily lead to lower satisfaction (Spreng and Dröge, 2001).

In practice, the relationship between service quality and satisfaction varies according to the type of service attribute. As discussed in Chapter 3, some attributes, such as security, come to be regarded as 'essentials', for which a high level of performance is seen as norm. Any lapses on such attributes, however, can lead to serious dissatisfaction, as Fig. 13.10 illustrates. Other 'basics', such as speed of service, can lead either to satisfaction or dissatisfaction, although individual customers will have their own tolerance thresholds. By virtue of being unexpected, 'delights' can create high satisfaction. However, if they become institutionalized as part of the store's (or sector's) service offering, their removal may subsequently result in dissatisfaction (Rust and Oliver, 2000).

13.4.3 Service Quality Measurement

The concept of service quality 'gaps' has been a notable feature in the development of the SERVQUAL scale by Parasuraman et al. (1988). Figure 13.11 illustrates how such gaps can arise, starting with the creation of consumer expectations through word of mouth communications, the shopper's needs, previous experience and/or competitors' actions.

Gap 1: retail managers may not be fully aware of what is expected from the company: this can often be remedied by more/better market research and improved internal communications between 'front line' staff and strategists.

Gap 2: even if expectations are properly understood, they may not be translated into the appropriate service specifications: this may be due to lack of resources, leadership or service culture (Lewis, 1994).

Gap 3: if employees are not willing or able to perform at the specified level, or if systems are inadequate, then the service level actually delivered will not meet that specified by management (Chenet et al., 1999).

Figure 13.10 Service quality and satisfaction

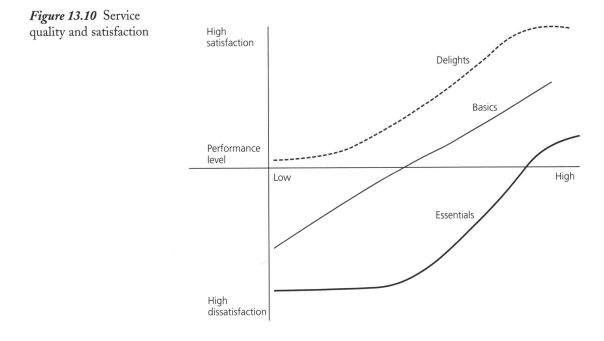

Gap 4: service(s) claimed or promised in advertisements or other external communications will contribute to expectations but may not match the service levels that are delivered.

Gap 5: differences between what is expected and what is perceived, the focus of the SERVQUAL scale.

Gap 6: noted but not originally included by Zeithaml et al. (1988), it is worthy of consideration none the less. In Chapter 5, many examples were observed of (subjective) images not accurately reflecting objective measures. In Sec. 13.3.1, it was noted that a 5-minute wait to be served may be perceived as a long wait or a reasonable one, depending upon surrounding conditions. Retailers are sometimes, therefore able to influence how a given level of service is perceived.

SERVQUAL offers a 22-item instrument, within which expectations of each of the 22 service attributes are measured first, followed by perceptions of the same 22 attributes. These items were delivered from a much larger battery of 97 service attributes, reduced down to minimise overlaps and to make the scales more manageable (Parasuraman et al., 1988). The 22 attributes represent five major service dimensions:

Figure 13.11 Gaps model of service quality

Source: adapted from Zeithaml et al. (1988).

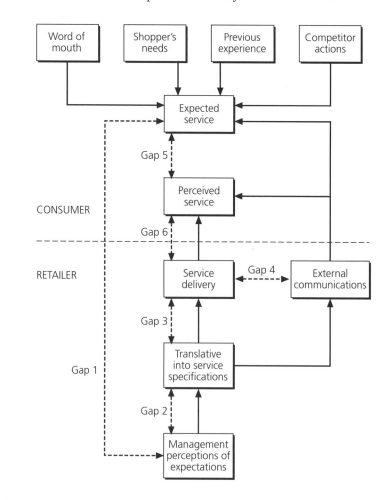

1 *Tangibles*: physical facilities, equipment and appearance of personnel.
2 *Reliability*: ability to perform the promised service dependably and accurately.
3 *Responsiveness*: willingness to help customers and provide prompt service.
4 *Assurance*: knowledge and courtesy of employees and their ability to inspire trust and confidence.
5 *Empathy*: caring, individualized attention for customers.

Over the years, SERVQUAL has been subject to several refinements (e.g. Parasuraman, 1991; 1994), as well as criticisms (e.g. Babukus and Boller, 1992; Cronin and Taylor, 1994). In particular, some have argued against the use of calculated difference (gap) scores, on statistical grounds (e.g. Brown et al., 1993). A comprehensive review of this extensive literature is provided by Buttle (1996). In spite of its critics, SERVQUAL has been very widely used, in original or modified form, since its inception. For example, Hussey (1999) demonstrated how the performance of SERVQUAL can be improved through the use of weightings, and by focusing upon the negative gaps, i.e., customers' disappointments with service.

A limitation of SERVQUAL in the retailing context is that its scale items have been developed and tested mainly in 'pure' service settings, such as banking and credit card services. It does not therefore fully reflect the product–service mix of most retail stores. Dabholkar et al. (1996) made modifications and additions to the scales to produce the 28-item Retail Service Quality (RSQ) scale, as summarized in Table 13.12. Eleven of these items are not represented in SERVQUAL, and five items from SERVQUAL were excluded from this scale.

Dabholkar et al. (1996) conclude that a measure of service quality across all industries is not feasible. Indeed, Mehta et al. (2000) found differences between sectors, the perceptions part of SERVQUAL performing better in the electronic goods sector, while the Retail Service Quality scale worked well in a 'more goods and less services' sector, i.e., a supermarket. Service attribute salience and expectations are also likely to vary between national markets. Different service factor structures have been reported from studies in Spain (Vazquez et al., 2000) and in Singapore (Teo and Lim, 2001).

SERVQUAL has therefore been the subject of extensive technical criticism, but both satisfaction and service quality measurement have raised wider concerns:

> *Satisfaction scores have become an end in themselves at many companies, but scores mean nothing unless the satisfaction they purport to measure translates into purchases and profit (Reichheld, 1996).*

Rust and Zahorik (1993) also urged that benefits to bottom-line profitability should be clearly demonstrated. Mägi and Julander (1996) found perceptions of service quality to be related to loyalty, but not

Retail Service Quality dimension	RSQ subdimension	Scale item (abbreviated)
Physical aspects	Appearance	Store has modern-looking equipment and fixtures
		The physical facilities are visually appealing
		Materials associated with service (e.g. carrier bags) are visually appealing
		Store has clean, attractive and convenient public areas (ns)
	Convenience	Store layout makes it easy to find what is needed (ns)
		Store layout easy to move around (ns)
Reliability	Promises	Meets promises on time
		Provides services at time promised
	Doing it right	Performs service right first time
		Merchandise available when needed (ns)
		Insists on error-free sales transactions and records
Personal interaction	Inspiring confidence	Staff have knowledge to answer questions
		Behaviour instils confidence
		Feel safe in transactions in this store
	Courteousness/ helpfulness	Give prompt service to customers
		Tell exactly when services will be performed
		Never too busy to respond to requests
		Store gives customers individual attention
		Consistently courteous with customers
		Treat customers courteously on the telephone (ns)
Problem-solving		Willingly handles returns and exchanges (ns)
		Shows sincere interest in solving problems if they arise
		Staff can handle complaints directly and immediately (ns)
Policy		Store offers high quality merchandise (ns)
		Plenty of convenient parking (ns)
		Hours convenient for all customers
		Accepts most major credit cards (ns)
		Offers its own credit card (ns)

Table 13.12
Components of the Retail Service Quality scale

Note: ns indicates that the scale item is not included in SERVQUAL.

Source: based upon Dabholkar et al. (1996).

linked to profitability. In part, this was because labour productivity, conventionally defined, tended to decline as service quality increased. An extensive review of work on service quality and profitability is provided by Zeithaml (2000).

The emphasis upon customer perception scales has also deflected attention away from important issues in how service is delivered. Drawing upon organizational theory and other disciplines, Mishra (2000) highlights a number of existing and potential contributions to the understanding of service delivery. In particular, a need is perceived to integrate issues of employee training, reward, communication and motivation in the delivery of service. Lytle et al. (1998) propose an organizational service orientation scale (SERV*OR), measuring the extent to which the company has embraced polices, practices and procedures that represent an organizational service orientation.

Of course, scales are not the only way to measure customers' quality perceptions. Keaveney (1995) demonstrated the power of the critical incident technique, especially when focusing upon why customers switch service providers. Hundreds of individuals, who had left a service provider recently, were asked to tell stories about the events leading to the switch. Judges pinpointed and classified the critical incidents, the largest categories being core-service failures (44 per cent) and personal interaction failures (34 per cent). A particular strength of this technique, however, is its ability to capture critical issues that may fall outside the scope of established scales, however comprehensive and well tested those scales may be.

Mystery shoppers, also referred to as secret, phantom or anonymous consumer shoppers, may also be deployed to assess service quality. Buttle (1994) reported how Jaeger recruited 58 mystery shoppers, demographically matched to the Jaeger Lady profile. They visited stores and performed a selection of other tasks, such as applying for an account and returning some items. They provided Jaeger management with a wealth of numerical and qualitative feedback on a large number of merchandise and service issues.

Although a mystery shopping report can cost about ten times more to obtain than a completed customer survey, Finn and Kayandé (1999) claim that they can represent better value. The mystery shoppers are trained in the relevant observation and evaluation techniques, and can judge according to the same standards across several stores. Their evaluations may be closer to objective measurements of service attributes, for example, the actual rather than perceived speed of service. As such, they may also provide valuable insights into 'gap 6' within Fig. 13.11.

These observations can therefore provide a sharp focus upon specific service issues, highlight contrasts between employees and stores, and also point to service delivery improvements. However, a retailer should be wary of depending entirely upon this data source. In the final analysis, a retailer ignores the perceptions of actual customers, and potential customers, at its peril. It is these perceptions that measure the strength of the brand, and provide early warnings of disappointments that may lead to defections.

SUMMARY

Retailing has traditionally been classified as a 'service industry' but, for most retailers, the preoccupation with service quality and services offered is of more recent origin. At the broadest level, most of a retailer's activities deliver a form of service to the consumer, creating assortments at competitive prices in accessible locations. These activities therefore all play major roles in creating customer satisfaction. A more specific connotation of the term service points to the many specific services that a retailer may, or may not, decide to offer. In general, these services set out to make shopping more enjoyable, more convenient and/or less worrying for the customers.

Even in self-service settings, store personnel play a crucial role in forming retail images and patronage intentions. Enlightened retailers encourage staff to give time and help when needed to customers, and allow discretion in how problems are solved. It has been found that good relationships between store staff and customers improve loyalty, word-of-mouth recommendations and expenditure levels. However, not all customers seek social-type relationships, and some prefer self-service options, when available. This can arise from the desire to maintain control and avoid dependence on store personnel. Other customers within the store can also exert a strong influence upon purchase intentions and the service encounter.

The effectiveness of selling staff depends upon success in recruitment, organization and training. Extrovert and enthusiastic staff are particular assets to the company. However, the high-pressure, sales orientation has given way to customer-oriented selling, designed to identify needs and provide the best solutions to these. While traditional selling skills are by no means obsolete, the need to create long-term satisfaction should take precedence over the desire to win a specific sale. Retailers are encouraged to reward sales staff for the service they provide and the satisfaction they create, not just for sales achieved.

Transaction services also play a significant part in customer satisfaction, both in terms of efficiency and the availability of credit. All forms of transaction incur costs for the retailer, notably handling and security in the case of cash, bank charges for cheques and merchant service charges for credit cards. Some predict that smart cards, incorporating computer chips, will take over most or all card functions, providing a comprehensive but compact 'electronic wallet'. This would incorporate credit, debit, loyalty cards and stored 'cash', as well as facilitating electronic 'cash' transfers to the smart cards of other people or companies.

Some retailers now operate their own store cards, partly to reduce certain elements of cost but mainly to facilitate relationship marketing activities. Store cards bring most of the advantages of loyalty programmes, such as better knowledge of customers and their purchase patterns. Store cards and loyalty programmes have paved the way for retailers to widen their financial services range, some including savings accounts, loans, mortgages, insurance products and pensions. Some of the most rapid developments have involved alliances with banks. While financial service diversifications extend the retail brands, they also risk alienating customers when errors occur, or when customers are refused.

An aspect of service which receives many complaints is the waiting time at checkouts or pay desks. In spite of many service improvements, this is still perceived to be the worst element of service in many stores. Some have introduced explicit service standards, such as Tesco's 'only one in front' queue policy. These involve staff flexibility, good forecasting and possibly tracking numbers entering the store. When waiting is inevitable, retailers are advised to make the wait as pleasant as possible and to ensure 'fair play' in the queuing arrangements.

Some shoppers target quieter days and times in order to avoid queues and congestion. Trading hours have tended to increase, with Sunday trading now being common in the UK, some stores staying open for 24 hours on other days. Whether or not extended hours are beneficial depends upon the cost structure of the company, competitive pressures and the extent to which the service is valued by some customers; this tends to vary by locality. If a store does open for long hours, it is important to ensure that standards of personal service, stock availability, ambience, etc. are maintained.

Given the vast choice of service options, a retailer must very carefully evaluate the costs and benefits, both direct and indirect, of providing a service. The appropriateness of a service depends on the positioning, size and location of a store, the product types sold, competitors' services, the target clientele and their expectations. Many supplementary services display a form of life cycle, whereby the differential advantage is lost as the service is copied, then eventually taken for granted. All existing services should periodically be re-evaluated in terms of their costs and real value to customers.

At the core of retailers' service strategies is the need to ensure high levels of customer satisfaction. Generous returns policies incur cost and can encourage illicit 'borrowing' of items by customers; however, they do reduce purchase risks and encourage greater patronage. Even the best of retailers encounter product and service delivery problems, so the ways in which these are solved are critical. A complaint handled quickly and effectively can turn into a positive service encounter for the customer. However, many instances of dissatisfaction do not lead to a complaint, yet may result in negative word of mouth or reduced patronage.

Service quality has been shown to influence repatronage intentions, both directly and through varying satisfaction levels. Customers' expectations of service are fundamental to whether or not an encounter leads to satisfaction. Consistent with prospect theory, when an experience falls short of expectations, repatronage intentions decline sharply. The strategy of trying to 'delight' customers, by greatly exceeding expectations, can therefore be dangerous, if the same is always expected in future. It also warns against inflating expectations beyond a level that can reliably be met.

Various scales have been developed to measure and compare service quality, most notably SERVQUAL. This 22-item scale can be used simply to measure perceptions or to identify 'gaps' between expectations and perceptions. These gaps can arise through poor analysis, implementation or communication strategies. SERVQUAL has been much used, modified and criticised; an alternative scale, focused upon retail stores, is the Retail Service Quality scale. Among the available open-ended techniques, critical incident analysis has been applied to the study of service disappointments and failures. Mystery shoppers have also been deployed by some retailers to obtain comparative assessments of store, and employee, performance.

REVIEW QUESTIONS

1 'Customers may be forgiven for believing that retailers understand only lip-service, rather than customer service'. Do you agree?

2 How would you define the role of personal service in:

a) a fashion boutique?

b) a superstore?

c) a DIY warehouse?

3 Discuss the ways in which personal service can contribute to increased customer loyalty.

4 Is self-service simply a lack of service?

5 What are the differences between selling orientation and customer orientation in the retail selling context?

6 What measures could salespeople in a carpet shop take to improve their performance at each stage of the selling process?

7 Even though debit cards incur merchant service charges and involve investment in further point-of-scale technology, these cards are now accepted by major retailers. Why?

8 Some commentators see the 'electronic purse/wallet' as the next major step towards the cashless society. Do you share this view, and why?

9 Certain retailers and groups issue their own store cards, offering facilities similar to those of the major credit cards. What are the main benefits of this strategy?

10 What are the major hazards facing retailers as they expand their ranges of financial services?

11 Your research for a major retailer has shown its customers to be dissatisfied with waiting times at the tills. What measures would you suggest to alleviate this situation, bearing in mind that staffing is already the largest area of cost for most retailers?

12 How would you evaluate the advantages and disadvantages of extending opening hours to the maximum allowed by law?

13 You are considering the option of introducing staff to greet each customer as he or she enters the store. What factors should you consider before reaching your decision?

14 Explain the concept of the service life cycle. Give an example of a retail service at each stage of this life cycle.

15 What factors may motivate a clothing retailer to offer a liberal returns policy, well in excess of the basic legal requirements? What are the major costs and risks of such a policy?

16 You have been assigned the task of overhauling the complaints handling procedures of a retail company. How would you undertake this task?

17 Explain how an understanding of prospect theory can provide insights into the relationship between service quality and repatronage intentions.

18 Outline the main features of the 'gaps' model. Explain why the various gaps arise, and how retail managers should seek to minimise/eliminate the gaps.

19 Compare and contrast the main features of SERVQUAL and the Retail Service Quality scale. If evaluating service in store of your choice, which would you use, and why?

20 Your senior manager has recently heard a consultant's presentation on the merits of using mystery shoppers to monitor service quality. You have been asked to prepare an independent brief on the benefits and limitations of this approach.

REFERENCES

Aldred, G. (1989) 'Service with a sneer', *Retail*, **6** (4), 6–7.

Alexander, A. and J. Pollard (2000) 'Banks, grocers and the changing retailing of financial services in Britain', *Journal of Retailing and Consumer Services*, **7** (3), 137–147.

Alexander, N. and M. Colgate (1998) 'The evolution of retailer, banker and customer relationships: a conceptual framework', *International Journal of Retail & Distribution Management*, **26** (6), 225–236.

Alexander, N. and M. Colgate (2000) 'Retail financial service: transaction to relationship marketing', *European Journal of Marketing*, **34** (8), 938–953.

Alexander, N., J. Howells and J. Hine (1992) 'EFTPoS: impact on channel relationships', *International Journal of Bank Marketing*, **10** (6), 38–44.

Anderson, R. (1995) *Essentials of Personal Selling: The New Professionalism*, Prentice-Hall, Englewood Cliffs, NJ.

Antonides, G., H.B. Amesz and I.C. Hulscher (1999) 'Adoption of payment systems in ten countries—a case study of diffusion of innovations', *European Journal of Marketing*, **33** (11/12), 1123–1135.

Babakus, E. and G.W. Boller (1992) 'An empirical assessment of the SERVQUAL scale', *Journal of Business Research*, **24** (3), 253–268.

Babin, L.A., B.J. Babin. and J.S. Boles (1999) 'The effects of consumer perceptions of the salesperson, product and dealer on purchase intentions', *Journal of Retailing and Consumer Services*, **6**, 91–97.

Baron, S., K. Harris and B.J. Davies (1996) 'Oral participation in retail service delivery: a comparison of the roles of contact personnel and customers', *European Journal of Marketing*, **30** (9), 75–90.

Barrett, P. (1995) 'JS serves up a pledge', *SuperMarketing*, 16 June, 5.

Bates, A.D. and J.G. Didion (1985) 'Special services can personalise retail environment', *Marketing News*, 12 April, 13.

Bateson, J.E.G. (1985) 'Self-service consumer: an exploratory study', *Journal of Retailing*, **61** (3), 49–76.

Baxter, A. (1998) 'Retailer case study: Boots the Chemists—Advantage Card scheme', *European Retail Digest*, **20**, 14–17.

Beatty, S.E., M. Mayer, J.E. Coleman, K.E. Reynolds and J. Lee (1996) 'Customer–sales associate retail relationships', *Journal of Retailing*, **72** (3), 223–247.

Bell, J., D. Gilbert and A. Lockwood (1997) 'Service quality in food retailing operations: a critical incident analysis', *International Review of Retail, Distribution and Consumer Research*, **7** (4), 405–423.

Berry, L.L. (1993) 'Playing fair in retailing', *Retail Issues Letter*, **5** (2), 1–5.

Bettencourt, L.A. (1997) 'Customer voluntary performance: customers as partners in service delivery', *Journal of Retailing*, **73** (3), 383–406.

Bettencourt, L.A. and S.W. Brown (1997) 'Contact employees: relationships among workplace fairness, job satisfaction and prosocial service behaviors', *Journal of Retailing*, **73** (1), 39–61.

Bibby, A. (1997) 'Honey, Sainsbury's bank shrunk our £10,000 quid', *Observer*, 23 November, 16.

Blodgett, J.G., D.J. Hill and S.S. Tax (1997) 'The effects of distributive, procedural and interactional justice on postcomplaint behaviour', *Journal of Retailing*, **73** (2), 185–210.

Broadbridge, A. and J. Marshall (1995) 'Consumer complaint behaviour: the case of electrical goods', *International Journal of Retail & Distribution Management*, **23** (9), 8–18.

Broadbridge, A., V. Swanson and C. Taylor (1999) 'The implications of retail changes on employees' job demands, satisfactions and the work/home interface', *Research Papers in Retailing*, 9903, University of Stirling, Stirling.

Brown, T.J., G.A. Churchill and J.P. Peter (1993) 'Improving the measurement of service quality', *Journal of Retailing*, **69** (1), 127–139.

Burnett, L. (1987), *Are You Being Served?* Leo Burnett, London.

Buttle, F. (1994) 'Jaeger ladies', in *Cases in Retail Management*, P.J. McGoldrick (ed), Pitman, London, pp. 259–277.

Buttle, F. (1996) 'SERVQUAL: review, critique, research agenda', *European Journal of Marketing*, **30** (1), 8–32.

Chenet, P. and J.I. Johansen (1999) *Beyond Loyalty: The Next Generation of Strategic Customer Relationship Management*, Oak Tree Press, Dublin.

Chenet, P., C. Tynan and A. Money (1999) 'Service performance gap: re-evaluation and redevelopment', *Journal of Business Research*, **46**, 133–147.

Churchill, G.A., N.M. Ford, S.W. Hartley and O.C. Walker (1985) 'The determinants of salesperson performance: a meta-analysis', *Journal of Marketing Research*, **22** (2), 103–118.

Cronin, J.J. and S.A. Taylor (1994) 'SERVPERF versus SERVQUAL: reconciling performance-based and perceptions-minus-expectations measurement of service quality', *Journal of Marketing*, **58** (1), 125–131.

Cronin, J.J., M.K. Brady and G.T.M. Hult (2000) 'Assessing the effects of quality, value and customer satisfaction on consumer behavioral intentions in service environments', *Journal of Retailing*, **76** (2), 193–218.

Dabholkar, P.A. (1993) 'Customer satisfaction and service quality: two constructs or one?' in D.W. Cravens and P.R. Dickson (eds), *Enhancing Knowledge Development in Marketing*, vol. 4, AMA, Chicago, pp. 10–18.

Dabholkar, P.A. (1996) 'Consumer evaluations of new technology-based self-service options: an investigation of alternative models of service quality', *International Journal of Research in Marketing*, **13**, 29–51.

Dabholkar, P.A., C.D. Shepherd and D.I. Thorpe (2000) 'A comprehensive framework for service quality: an investigation of critical conceptual and measurement issues through a longitudinal study', *Journal of Retailing*, **76** (2), 139–173.

Dabholkar, P.A., D.I. Thorpe and J.O. Rentz (1996) 'A measure of service quality for retail stores: scale development and validation', *Journal of the Academy of Marketing Science*, **24** (1), 3–16.

Darian, J.C., L.A. Tucci and A.R. Wiman (2001) 'Perceived salesperson service attributes and retail patronage intentions', *International Journal of Retail & Distribution Management*, **29** (5), 205–213.

Davis, S., E. Gerstner and M. Hagerty (1995) 'Money back guarantees in retailing: matching products to consumer tastes', *Journal of Retailing*, **71** (1), 7–22.

Deming, W.E. (1986) *Out of the Crisis*, MIT Center for Advanced Engineering Study, Boston, MA.

Dennis, M. and H. Arnold (1996) 'Keeping the customer satisfied', *SuperMarketing*, 25 October, 16–17.

Devlin, J.F. (2001) 'Consumer evaluation and competitive advantage in retail financial services', *European Journal of Marketing*, **35** (5/6), 639–660.

Drummond, G. (1995) 'Are they being served?', *SuperMarketing*, 23 June, 42–44.

East, R., W. Lomax, G. Willson and P. Harris (1994) 'Decision making and habit in shopping times', *European Journal of Marketing*, **28** (4), 56–71.

Elliot, R., S. Eccles and K. Gournay (1996) 'Man management? Women and the use of debt to control personal relationships', *Journal of Marketing Management*, **12**, 657–669.

Evans, K.R, R.E. Kleine, T.D. Landry and L.A. Crosby (2000) 'How first impressions of a customer impact effectiveness in an initial encounter', *Journal of the Academy of Marketing Science*, **28** (4), 512–526.

Finn, A. and U. Kayandé (1999) 'Unmasking a phantom: a psychometric assessment of mystery shopping', *Journal of Retailing*, **75** (2), 195–217.

Fletcher, K. (1987) 'Consumers' use and perceptions of retailer-controlled information sources', *International Journal of Retailing*, **2** (3), 59–66.

Freathy, P. and L. Sparks (1993) 'Sunday working in the retail trade', *International Journal of Retail & Distribution Management*, **21** (7), 3–9.

Freathy, P. and L. Sparks (1995) 'Flexibility, labour segmentation and retail superstore managers: the effects of Sunday trading', *International Review of Retail, Distribution and Consumer Research*, **5** (3), 361–385.

Goff, B.G., J.S. Boles, D.N. Bellenger and C. Stojack (1997) 'The influence of salesperson selling behaviors on customer satisfaction with products', *Journal of Retailing*, **73** (2), 171–183.

Graham, G. (1997) 'Supermarkets risk biting hand that feeds them', *Financial Times*, 14 February.

Grünhagen, M. and R.A. Mittelstaedt (2001) 'The impact of store hours and redistributive income effects on the retail industry: some projections for Germany', *International Review of Retail, Distribution and Consumer Research*, **11** (1), 49–62.

Harris, K., B. J. Davies and S. Baron (1997) 'Conversations during purchase consideration: sales and assistants and customers', *International Review of Retail, Distribution and Consumer Research*, **7** (3), 173–190.

Hilton, A. (1997) 'Loan stars', *Evening Standard*, 18 August, 33.

Honeycutt, E. D. (1993) 'Ethical dilemmas in the automotive industry', in AMA Educators' Proceedings, American Marketing Association (ed.), AMA, Chicago, pp. 352–358.

Hornik, J. (1992) 'Tactile stimulation and consumer response', *Journal of Consumer Research*, **19** (4), 449–458.

Horovitz, J. (1997) 'Effective management of customer complaints', *International Journal of Retail & Distribution Management*, **25** (7), 235–236.

Hui, M.K. and J.E.G. Bateson (1991) 'Perceived control and the effects of crowding and consumer choice on the service encounter', *Journal of Consumer Research*, **18** (2), 174–184.

Hui, M.K. and D.K. Tse (1996) 'What to tell consumers in waits of different lengths: an integrative model of service evaluation', *Journal of Marketing*, **60** (2), 81–90.

Hurley, R. F. (1998) 'Customer service behavior in retail settings: a study of the effect of service provider personality', *Journal of the Academy of Marketing Science*, **26** (2), 115–127.

Hussey, M.K. (1999) 'Using the concept of loss: an alternative SERVQUAL measure', *Service Industries Journal*, **19** (4), 89–101.

IGD (2000) *Grocery Retailing 2000*, Institute of Grocery Distribution, Watford.

IGD (2001) *European Grocery Retailing 2001*, Institute of Grocery Retailing, Watford.

James, D.L., B.J. Walker and M.J. Etzel (1981) *Retailing Today*, Harcourt Brace Jovanovich, New York.

Johns, N. (1999) 'What is this thing called service?', *European Journal of Marketing*, **33** (9/10), 958–973.

Jones, M.A., D.L. Mothersbaugh and S.E. Beatty (2000) 'Switching barriers and repurchase intentions in services', *Journal of Retailing*, **76** (2), 259–274.

Jones, T.O. and W.E. Sasser (1995) 'Why satisfied customers defect', *Harvard Business Review*, **73** (6), 88–99.

Keaveney, S.M. (1995) 'Customer switching behavior in service industries: an exploratory study', *Journal of Marketing*, **59** (2), 71–82.

Kelley, S.W. (1993) 'Discretion and the service employee', *Journal of Retailing*, **69** (1), 104–126.

Kelley, S.W. and K.D. Hoffman (1997) 'An investigation of positive affect, prosocial behaviors and service quality', *Journal of Retailing*, **73** (3), 407–427.

Kincade, D.H., A. Redwine and G.R. Hancock (1992) 'Apparel product dissatisfaction and the post–complaint process', *International Journal of Retail & Distribution Management*, **20** (5), 15–22.

Kirk, V. (2001) 'Unravelling EFT', *Retail Automation*, **21** (3), 18–19.

Lemmink, J. and J. Mattsson (1998) 'Warmth during non-productive retail encounters: the hidden side of productivity', *International Journal of Research in Marketing*, **15**, 505–517.

Lewis, B.R. (1994) 'Customer service and quality', in *Retailing of Financial Services*, P.J. McGoldrick and S.J. Greenland (eds), McGraw-Hill, Maidenhead, pp. 266–288.

Lumsden, G. (1997) 'Tesco's savers lose interest', *The Times*, 15 November, 64.

Lytle, R.S., P.W. Hom and M.P. Mokwa (1998) 'SERV*OR: a managerial measure of organizational service-orientation', *Journal of Retailing*, **74** (4), 455–489.

Macintosh, G. and L.S. Lockshin (1997) Retail relationships and store loyalty: a multi-level perspective', *International Journal of Research in Marketing*, **14** (5), 487–497.

Mägi, A. and C.-R. Julander (1996) 'Perceived service quality and customer satisfaction in a store performance framework', *Journal of Retailing and Consumer Services*, **3** (1), 33–41.

Marchington, M. (1995) 'Shopping down different aisles: a review of the literature on human resource management in food retailing', *Journal of Retailing and Consumer Services*, **3** (1), 21–32.

Martin, C.R. (1996) 'Retail service innovations', *Journal of Retailing and Consumer Services*, **3** (2), 63–71.

McGrath, M.A. and C. Otnes (1995) 'Unacquainted influences: when strangers interact in the retail setting', *Journal of Business Research*, **32** (3), 261–272.

Mehta, S.C., A.K. Lalwani and S.L. Han (2000) 'Service quality in retailing: relative efficiency of alternative measurement scales for different product-service environments', *International Journal of Retail & Distribution Management*, **28** (2), 62–72.

Menon, K. and L. Dube (2000) 'Ensuring greater satisfaction by engineering salesperson response to customer emotions', *Journal of Retailing*, **76** (3), 285–307.

Meyer, H. (1999) 'Many happy returns', *Journal of Business Strategy*, **20** (4), 27–31.

Mintel (1987) 'Electronic funds transfer at the point of sale', *Retail Intelligence*, **1**, 157–165.

Mintel (1998) *Retail Payment Methods in Europe*, Mintel, London.

Mintel (2000) *Retail Review*, Mintel, London.

Mishra, D.P. (2000) 'Interdisciplinary contributions in retail service delivery: review and future directions', *Journal of Retailing and Consumer Services*, **7** (2), 101–118.

Mitchell, V.-W. and C. Critchlow (1993) 'Dealing with complaints', *International Journal of Retail & Distribution Management*, **21** (2), 15–22.

Mittal, B. and W. M. Lassar (1996) 'The role of personalization in service encounters', *Journal of Retailing*, **72** (1), 95–109.

Moir, C.B. (1987) 'Research difficulties in the analysis of Sunday trading', *International Journal of Retailing*, **2** (1), 3–21.

Morgan Stanley Dean Witter (2000) *Great Universal Stores*, MSDW, London.

Morgan Stanley Dean Witter (2001a) *Marks & Spencer: Coming Home*, MSDW, London.

Morgan Stanley Dean Witter (2001b) *Tesco: We Have Lift Off!*, MSDW, London.

Murphy, J. and F. Suntook (1998) 'Keeping the satisfied customer', *Mastering Management Review*, **11** (April), 32–35.

NatWest Securities (1997) *European Food Retailing*, Natwest Securities, London.

Neo, L.C.-W.K. (1993) 'Customer service in Singapore: luxury or necessity?', *International Journal of Retail & Distribution Management*, **21** (1), 21–25.

Nielson, A.C. (2000) *The Retail Pocket Book*, NTC Publications, Henley-on-Thames.

Norman, A. (1999) 'The ASDA service reality', *Journal of Marketing Management*, **15**, 107–116.

Ody, P. (1997) 'Smart moves', *The Grocer*, **220** (7331), 36–37.

Oliver, R.L., R.T. Rust and S. Varki (1997) 'Customer delight: foundations, findings and managerial insight', *Journal of Retailing*, **73** (3), 311–336.

Parasuraman, A., V.A. Zeithaml and L.L. Berry (1988) 'SERVQUAL: a multi-item scale for measuring consumer perceptions of service quality', *Journal of Retailing*, **64** (1), 12–40.

Parasuraman, A., V.A. Zeithaml and L.L. Berry (1991) 'Refinement and reassessment of the SERVQUAL scale', *Journal of Retailing*, **67** (4), 420–450.

Parasuraman, A., V.A. Zeithaml and L.L. Berry (1994) 'Alternative scales for measuring service quality: a comparative assessment based on psychometric and diagnostic criteria', *Journal of Retailing*, **70** (3), 201–230.

Piron, F. and M. Young (2000) 'Retail borrowing: insights and implications on returning used merchandise', *International Journal of Retail & Distribution Management*, **28** (1), 27–36.

Piron, F. and M. Young (2001) 'Retail borrowing: definition and retailing implications', *Journal of Retailing and Consumer Services*, **8** (1), 121–125.

Polonsky, M.J., H. Cameron, S. Halstead, A. Ratcliffe, P. Stilo and G. Watt (2000) 'Exploring companion selling: does the situation affect customers' perceptions?', *International Journal of Retail & Distribution Management*, **28** (1), 37–45.

Pruyn, A. and A. Smidts (1998) 'Effects of waiting on the satisfaction with service: beyond objective time measures', *International Journal of Research in Marketing*, **15**, 321–334.

Ramsey, R.P. and R.S. Sohi (1997) 'Listening to your customers: the impact of perceived salesperson listening behavior on relationship outcomes', *Journal of the Academy of Marketing Science*, **25** (2), 127–137.

Reichheld, F.F. (1996) 'Learning from customer defections', *Harvard Business Review*, **74** (2), 56–62.

Retail Review (1996) 'What is a "category killer"?', *Retail Review*, **222** (May), 18–19.

Retail Review (1999) 'Borders opens 24–hour bookshop', *Retail Review*, **256** (October), 25.

Reynolds, K.E. and S.E. Beatty (1999a) 'Customer benefits and company consequences of customer–salesperson relationships in retailing', *Journal of Retailing*, **75** (1), 11–32.

Reynolds, K.E. and S.E. Beatty (1999b) 'A relationship customer typology', *Journal of Retailing*, **75** (4), 509–523.

Rogers, L. (1988) *Retail Selling: A Practical Guide for Sales Staff*, Kogan Page, London.

Rowell, R. (1994) 'Open all hours?', *Marketing Business*, November, 35.

Rudolph, T., A. Busch and S. Busch (2000) 'Retail food failures and recovery strategies in Switzerland', *Journal of Marketing Channels*, **7** (3), 69–91.

Rust, R.T. and R.L. Oliver (2000) 'Should we delight the customer?', *Journal of the Academy of Marketing Science*, **28** (1), 86–94.

Rust, R.T. and A.J. Zahorik (1993) 'Customer satisfaction, customer retention and market share', *Journal of Retailing*, **69** (2), 193–215.

Rust, R.T., A.J. Zahorik and T.L. Keiningham (1995) 'Return on quality (ROQ): making service quality financially accountable', *Journal of Marketing*, **59** (2), 58–70.

Samli, A.C. and M. Ongan (1996) 'The gaps in retail human resource management: the key to developing competitive advantage', *Journal of Marketing Channels*, **5** (2), 81–99.

Saxe, R. and B. A. Weitz (1982) 'The SOCO scale: a measure of the customer orientation of salespeople', *Journal of Marketing Research*, **19** (3), 343–351.

Schmidt, R.A., F. Sturrock, P. Ward and G. Lea-Greenwood (1999) 'Deshopping—the art of illicit consumption', *International Journal of Retail & Distribution Management*, **27** (8), 290–301.

Sharma, A. and M. Levy (1995) 'Categorization of customers by retail salesperson', *Journal of Retailing*, **71** (1), 71–81.

Sharma, A, M. Levy and A. Kumar (2000) 'Knowledge structures and retail sales performance: an empirical examination', *Journal of Retailing*, **76** (1), 53–69.

Sherry, J.F., M.A. McGrath and S.J. Levy (1992) 'The disposition of the gift and many unhappy returns', *Journal of Retailing*, **68** (1), 40–65.

Sivadas, E. and J.L. Baker-Prewitt (2000) 'An examination of the relationship between service quality, customer satisfaction and store loyalty', *International Journal of Retail & Distribution Management*, **28** (2), 73–82.

Soman, D. (2001) 'Effects of payment mechanism on spending behavior: the role of rehearsal and immediacy of payments', *Journal of Consumer Research*, **27** (4), 460–474.

Sparks, L. (1992) 'Customer service in retailing—the next leap forward', *Service Industries Journal*, **12** (2), 165–184.

Spreng, R.A. and C. Dröge (2001) 'The impact on satisfaction of managing attribution expectations: should performance claims be understated or overstated?', *Journal of Retailing and Consumer Services*, **8**, 261–274.

Spreng, R.A. and R.D. Mackoy (1996) 'An empirical examination of a model of perceived service quality and satisfaction', *Journal of Retailing*, **72** (2), 201–214.

Swanson, S.R. and S.W. Kelley (2001) 'Service recovery attributions and word-of-mouth intentions', *European Journal of Marketing*, **35** (1/2), 194–211.

Swinyard, W.R. (1995) 'The impact of shopper mood and retail salesperson credibility on shopper attitudes and behaviour', *International Review of Retail, Distribution and Consumer Research*, **54** (4), 488–503.

Swinyard, W.R. and D.B. Whitlark (1994) 'The effect of customer dissatisfaction on store repurchase intentions: a little goes a long way', *International Review of Retail, Distribution and Consumer Research*, **4** (3), 329–344.

Szmigin, I. and G. Foxall (1999) 'Styles of cashless consumption', *International Review of Retail, Distribution and Consumer Research*, **9** (4), 349–365.

Szymanski, D.M. and D.H. Henard (2001) 'Customer satisfaction: a meta-analysis of the empirical evidence', *Journal of the Academy of Marketing Science*, **29** (1), 16–35.

Taher, A., T.W. Leigh and W.A. French (1996) 'Augmented retail services: the lifetime value of affection', *Journal of Business Research*, **35**, 217–228.

Tax, S.S. and I. Stuart (1997) 'Designing and implementing new services: the challenges of integrating service systems', *Journal of Retailing*, **73** (1), 105–134.

Taylor, S. (1995) 'The effects of filled waiting time and service provider control over the delay on evaluations of service', *Journal of the Academy of Marketing Science*, **23** (1), 38–48.

Teo, T.S.H. and V.K.G. Lim (2001) 'The effects of perceived justice on satisfaction and behavioral intentions: the case of computer purchase', *International Journal of Retail & Distribution Management*, **29** (2), 109–124.

The Economist (1997) 'Checkout accounts', *The Economist*, 4 January, 70–72.

Thurik, A.R. (1987) 'Optimal trading hours in retailing', *International Journal of Retailing*, **2** (1) 22–30.

Uncles, M. (1995) 'Securing competitive advantage through progressive staffing policies', *International Journal of Retail & Distribution Management*, **23** (7), 4–6.

Vazquez, R., I.A. Rodriguez-Del Bosque, A.M. Diaz and A.V Ruiz (2001) 'Service quality in supermarket retailing: identifying critical service experiences', *Journal of Retailing and Consumer Services*, **8**, 1–14.

Vissol, T. (1999) 'Introduction to special issue on the Euro: consequences for the consumer and the citizen', *Journal of Consumer Policy*, **22** (1/2), 1–6.

Weber. A., B. Carter, B. Pfitzmann, M. Schunter, C. Stanford and M. Waidner (1995) *Secure International Payment and Information Transfer*, Institut für Sozialforschung, Frankfurt.

Which? (1996a) 'Buying electrical goods: standards of service compared', *Which?* June, 22–25.

Which? (1996b) 'Shopping rights', *Which?* January, 14–17.

Which? (1998) 'Extended warranties', *Which?* February, 12–13.

Which? (2000) 'Storing up trouble', *Which?* January, 46–48.

Which? (2001a) 'Supermarkets—how they stack up', *Which?* January, 30–31.

Which? (2001b) 'I wish to register a complaint ...', *Which?* March, 6–8.

Williams, T.D., M.F. Drake and J.D. Moran (1993) 'Complaint behaviour, price paid and store patronized', *International Journal of Retail & Distribution Management*, **21** (5), 3–9.

Worthington, S. (1994) 'Retailer aspirations in plastic cards and payment systems', *Journal of Retailing and Consumer Services*, **1** (1), 30–39.

Worthington, S. (1995) 'The cashless society', *International Journal of Retail & Distribution Management*, **24** (9), 27–34.

Worthington, S. (1996) Smart cards and retailers—who stands to benefit?', *International Journal of Retail & Distribution Management*, **24** (9), 27–34.

Worthington, S. (1998) 'The card centric distribution of financial services: a comparison of Japan and the UK', *International Journal of Bank Marketing*, **16** (5), 211–220.

Zeithaml, V.A. (2000) 'Service quality, profitability, and the economic worth of customers: what we know and what we need to learn', *Journal of the Academy of Marketing Science*, **28** (1), 67–85.

Zeithaml, V.A., L.L. Berry and A. Parasuraman (1988) 'Communication and control processes in the delivery of service quality', *Journal of Marketing*, **52** (2), 35–48.

Zeithaml, V.A., L.L. Berry and A. Parasuraman (1993) 'The nature and determinants of customer expectations of service', *Journal of the Academy of Marketing Science*, **21** (1), 1–12.

Zeithaml, V.A., L.L. Berry and A. Parasuraman (1996) 'The behavioural consequences of service quality', *Journal of Marketing*, **60** (2), 31–46.

PART THREE
RETAILING SANS FRONTIÈRES

INTRODUCTION

Like many industrial sectors the retail industry is becoming increasingly internationalized. As we visit shopping centres or high streets in any part of the world we recognize trade names and fascias which are familiar to us. Although attention is often focused on the largest players, such as Wal-Mart, Tesco, IKEA or Kingfisher, retail organizations of all shapes and sizes, and operating in all retail sectors, appear to be moving inexorably into non-domestic markets. The scale and importance of international activities varies from company to company and sector to sector. The proportion of sales accounted for by international retail operations is generally highest in the non-food sectors, particularly among the niche clothing retailers, although when measured in absolute value the large, food based companies dominate. What is clear, when one examines the world's largest retailers (Table 14.1), is that non-domestic

Table 14.1 The world's largest retailers and their international involvement, 2000

Source:
PricewaterhouseCoopers (2001).

Company	Domestic base	Main activity	Sales million Euro	Number of countries	% foreign sales
Wal-Mart	USA	Discount Stores	194 290.2	9	17.2
Carrefour	France	Hypermarkets/grocery	65 609.8	27	47.5
Kroger	USA	Supermarkets	52 659.9	1	0.0
Ahold	The Netherlands	Supermarkets	49 170.4	24	80.8
Home Depot	USA	DIY	49 154.2	4	5.5
Metro	Germany	Diversified	47 489.9	22	42.1
Kmart	USA	USA	39 793.7	1	0.0
Sears, Roebuck	USA	Department stores	39 573.3	2	11.6.
Albertson's	USA	Supermarkets	39 507.8	1	0.0
Target	USA	Discount Stores	39 077.9	1	0.0
ITM Enterprises	France	Supermarkets	36 272.1	8	36.0
Safeway	USA	Supermarkets	34 365.3	3	10.8
JC Penney	USA	Department stores	34 224.6	3	0.5
Costco	USA	Warehouse clubs	33 982.5	7	18.7
Tesco	UK	Supermarkets	33 680.3	10	12.5

operations are a common feature of their operations, and one is left with the impression that an international dimension to strategy is inevitable.

The high-profile market entry (and exit) of leading national chains increases the visibility of international retailing. Although we are often led to believe that this internationalization is a relatively new phenomenon, one could argue that it is simply a function of a greater awareness of what is happening, fuelled by improved information sources in the trade press and from market research agencies. We tend to forget that many major retailers (of the time) stepped outside their own national borders at the start of the last century. Hollander (1970) produced a seminal piece of work, which charted international moves in a range of retail sectors. Among those companies with an established international presence before 1914 are familiar names such as F.W. Woolworth, C&A and W.H. Smith. In similar vein, Godley and Fletcher (2000) have examined the level of foreign investment in British retailing since 1850. Their work shows that, although the major surge in international activity took place in the last 20 years, there were significant levels of inward investment in the first 30 years of the last century.

Various studies exist at a macrolevel which monitor specific geographical flows in investment and record the experiences of individual companies. Trends on transatlantic activity have proved popular with several authors (Hamill and Crosbie, 1990; Kacker, 1985; Muniz-Martinez, 1998; Wrigley, 1989) and others have examined events in the Association of South East Asian Nations (ASEAN) region (Alexander and Myers, 1999; Davies 1994; Davies and Fergusson, 1995; Davies and Jones, 1993) or specific retail sectors such as grocery (Burt, 1991) and fashion clothing (Moore et al., 2000). All of these studies note particular upsurges in activity as conditions within the international environment change. The strength of sterling against the dollar and the general buoyancy of the UK retail sector in the 1980s, for example, led to a growth in British investment in the USA during this period. In the 1990s, the liberalization of former Eastern Bloc economies led to a similar growth of regional investment, and the recent economic crisis in the ASEAN region has stimulated a series of investments in food retailing by major European companies who have brought stores and companies while prices are low.

Retail internationalization is also recorded in a range of studies looking at the activities of individual companies. These range from studies of companies in mass-market sectors, such as Carrefour (Burt, 1986), Daimaru (Clarke and Rimmer, 1997), Sears Roebuck and Co. (Truitt, 1984), and J. Sainsbury (Wrigley 1997a; 1997b; 2000) to cases from more specialist retail sectors, for example, Laura Ashley and Dixons (Treadgold, 1991), Hennes and Mauritz, Toys 'R' Us and IKEA (Laulajainen, 1991a; 1991b), 7-Eleven (Sparks, 1995) and Kookai and Morgan (Moore, 1998). All these studies tend to dissect motives for internationalization, market entry choice and methods, and basic operational issues.

Despite the apparent surge in international activity, the trials and tribulations of a number of leading retailers suggest that internationalization is a risky strategic option. We often point to the close relationship between retailing and culture. Local culture, both consumer and business, affects the how and wherefore of retailing. If this is the case, how then can retailing be international? How can a retail idea or format successfully transcend culture? Many retailers have tried the international route to expansion. Only a few have succeeded. Somewhat naively, retail internationalization it is often thought to be seductively simple.

This chapter looks at the different forms that retail internationalization might take, explores the motives which encourage retailers to move into foreign markets and considers how retailers try to minimize some of the risks involved through choice of entry strategy, country selection, and experience. The need to understand the macro, task and organizational environments of host nations is then discussed, and finally implementation strategies are reviewed.

14.1 Forms of Retail Internationalization

One issue which has troubled academics for decades has been a clear definition of 'retail internationalization' (Dawson, 1994). This debate has been hindered by attempts to 'squeeze' retailing into definitions and explanations of the internationalization process developed for manufacturing or consumer goods industries, rather than to consider if retailing per se exhibits characteristics which make such adaptations fruitless. There are many ways of classifying international retailing (Helfferich et al., 1997), although generally we identify with various forms of operational involvement. Other forms of internationalization may involve the transfer of retail concepts, the transfer of management functions and, in some areas of the world, the transfer of consumer spending.

14.1.1 Internationalization of Consumer Spending

In areas close to national political borders a considerable amount of cross-border shopping may take place, as consumers deliberately move to other countries for the purchase of products. Differences in product prices, usually arising from different rates of indirect taxation, such as excise duty and sales taxes, provide the main stimulus. Such transfer of consumer spending, in effect internationalization of the consumer, creates problems for local traders in the 'expensive' market and represents a loss of taxation revenue for national governments. Examples of areas in which cross-border trading has been identified as an issue include the USA–Canadian border, the German–Danish border, and the Republic of Ireland–UK (Northern Ireland) border.

Some retailers have responded to this transfer of spending by adjusting their offer to non-domestic consumers. In effect, they internationalize by adjusting a domestic offer to suit foreign nationals. For several years Ahold operated a chain, Ter Huurne, on the Dutch–German border which was deliberately targeted at and merchandised for German consumers. Signs in English in French hypermarkets near the channel ports are designed to cater for the cross-channel consumer, while in Singapore retailers train staff in the Japanese language and customs to take advantage of tourist traffic which traditionally accounts for a third of retail sales. The proposed standardization of indirect taxation in the single market is, on the one hand, expected to reduce the 'pull' of cross-border shopping, although, on the other hand, the adoption of the Euro highlights price differentials across national boundaries. This factor, plus the growth of Internet shopping, suggest that for 'standardized' products such as books, audio-visual equipment and CDs, cross-border price comparisons and the attraction for consumers of shopping (or, rather, spending) overseas may well increase.

14.1.2 Internationalization of Management Functions

The internationalization of a retail management function may be primarily undertaken to develop or assist the domestic business. International sourcing and buying, recruitment, the use of managerial and technology consultancy, and the raising of financial capital on international money markets would fall into this category. The most common form is the international sourcing of products (Liu and McGoldrick, 1996), which has increased considerably as a result of factors such as:

1 *Global divisions of labour*: providing low-cost manufacture and assembly in certain parts of the globe, which offset higher distribution costs.
2 *Improved international transport and physical distribution*: which reduce transport costs but more significantly improve transport efficiency, allowing a faster time to market and acceptable standards of quality control. The internationalization of logistics support companies alongside retail organizations often enables domestic support mechanisms to be maintained.
3 *Retail buyers search for new product*: the continual search for new and innovative product takes buyers further afield as they seek to satisfy an increasingly world-aware and world-travelled consumer market.
4 *Widening of consumer demand*: whether one accepts Levitt's globalization thesis or not, travel and media expose consumers to new products, lifestyles and cultures at an increasing rate.

As a consequence, retailers set up buying offices in product source areas: southern Spain for fruit and vegetables, Hong Kong, New York and, for non British retailers for fashion items, London, and increasingly China for low-cost production of basics. The impact of this form of retail internationalization is seen in former bastions of domestic purchasing switching buying to other geographic locations. For example in 1999, Marks & Spencer, once a champion of UK production, announced that 35 per cent of products were bought outside the UK. A second area in which domestic retailers feel the impact of international sourcing is in the use of the grey market to source products which were not part of the original retail offer, albeit often for a short period of time. The appearance of Levi jeans in Tesco stores is an example.

Again, international sourcing is not new. Although the formation of international buying groups or alliances has increased in recent years, they are by no means a new phenomenon. The consumer co-operatives have had buying links via Euroco-op, Interco-op and NAF since 1957, 1971 and 1918 respectively, while the International Spar Group, the forerunners of BIGS, was formed in the 1940s. The significance of the new grocery-based groups formed since the late 1980s is that they include multiple chains (e.g. the membership of AMS, Sedd, Eurogroupe and, until recently, Deuro), and national buying groups (e.g. EMD). These groups and alliances now wield massive buying power potential, as measured through member company turnover (Table 14.2).

Table 14.2 Major grocery buying groups and alliances in Europe
Source: IGD(2001a).

Group/alliance	Member companies/groups	Turnover Euro million
EMD	Axford; Cactus; Elos; Eurolec; Euromadi; Markant; Musgrave; Nisa Today's; ORS; Selex: Unil/KK; KEV Markant	101 658
AMS	Ahold; Dansk Supermarked; Edeka; Jeronimo Martins; Kesko; Mercadonna; Opera; Safeway; Superquinn	100 197
Eurogroupe	Co-op Schweitz; Laurus; Rewe	45 987
NAF International	Co-op Italia; CWS; FDB; INEX ; KF Konsum;NKL	41 657
SED	Delhaize le Lion; Esselunga; Sainsbury	29 287
Lucie	Leclerc; System U	32 500
Opera	Cora; Casino; Monoprix; Match; Louis Delhaize	27 693
Intergroup	Co-op Italia; Co-op Hungary; FDB; Eroski; KF Konsum; NKL; Tradeka	26 494
BIGS	Spar Austria; Axford; BWG; Dadrofa; Despar; Spar Finland; Spar Schweitz; Veropoulos Brothers	23 155
Europartners	Somerfield; Superunie; Colruyt	14 796

Perhaps more significantly in the long term, a number of these alliances go beyond simply buying to include a wider range of management functions associated with supply chain management, such as distribution co-ordination, stock-handling, own-brand development and co-ordinated marketing. Bailey et al. (1995) devised a taxonomy of international retail alliances which takes into account the evolution of these groupings from simple exchange mechanisms. While most press attention has focused upon developments in the grocery market, similar groupings exist in other non-food sectors, e.g., Intersport (sports goods), Expert (electrical goods) and Euro-Active (photographic equipment).

In addition to product sourcing, other general retail management functions which have seen increasing internationalization include:

1 *The recruitment of senior management*: Laura Ashley, Arcadia, Safeway and Marks & Spencer are examples of British companies which have been or which are currently led by non-UK nationals.

2 *The adoption of management technology*: stimulated through growing use of international consultants, technology hardware and solutions suppliers, which lead to the presentation of global solutions to generic issues.

3 *The sourcing of finance on international stock exchanges*: a growing number of retailers are now quoted on more than one exchange. Benetton, for example, is now listed on the Milan, London, Frankfurt, New York and Toyko exchanges.

14.1.3 Internationalization of Retail Concepts

The internationalization of retail concepts includes the diffusion of a particular retail format (e.g. department store or convenience store) or an approach to retailing (e.g. self-service) to a foreign market. This type of internationalization is closely associated with the internationalization of operations, as generally a concept is brought into a country by a foreign retailer, who becomes the pioneer for that concept within the market. Once the concept or innovation has arrived, it may be adopted by domestic retailers, or alternatively a domestic retailer may assume the role of innovator by 'importing' and reproducing a concept observed abroad.

Kacker (1988) illustrates a range of retail 'technologies' (or concepts) which can be said to have transferred from one environment to another. His definition of 'technology' as having a management and technical dimension provides a useful distinction. The managerial dimension includes retailing concepts and philosophies, retail policies and strategies, systems and controls, while the technical dimension encompasses operational issues such as location and site selection, layout and atmospherics, communications, and credit appraisal systems. He further distinguishes between diffusion or unplanned and incidental flows, which may arise from observation or conference attendance, and the purposive or planned transfer of ideas, more closely associated with investments in foreign markets.

Often the transfer of retail concepts is associated with a transfer from countries with 'developed' retail systems to those with less developed systems. Goldman (1981; 2001) examines the case of the supermarket in less developed countries, and format transfer into China. Ho and Sin (1987) have examined the concept of the convenience store format and its adoption in Hong Kong. Examples of concept transfer may be found in both food and non-food sectors. An example of this kind of format transfer within Europe would be the hypermarket, which was 'exported' from France to Spain and other Mediterranean markets. Originally introduced by French companies, domestic organizations have since adopted the format. A further example of format transfer in the food sector would be the limited-line hard discount store or boxstore, introduced into many European countries by Aldi. In non-foods, large store toy retailing has arrived from the USA via Toys 'R' Us. These latter illustrations show that concept transfer also occurs between countries with 'developed' retail systems.

Technology transfer of this type, however, is not easy and while there may be benefits for the efficiency of the retail or wholesale sector in the host country, there may be cultural influences which can nullify improvements in efficiency and make a nonsense of the introduction of 'more efficient' management methods (Goldman, 1981). Retail and wholesale technology transfer to the developing world is a potentially interesting, and perhaps even profitable activity, but one not to be entered upon without considerable preparation. For those companies who can scan the environment and adapt a Western method of selling to the cultural conditions of a developing country, and then start that innovative selling method on its life cycle, there are potentially large profits to be earned as well as the possibility of influencing economic development. The pitfalls in introducing innovation in that way are numerous however.

The internationalization of retail concepts is not even a straightforward process in 'developed' conditions. As we shall discuss later, the local environment, with its cultural and social influences and range of existing retail institutions, may force adaptation and change in the original concept. Although the French-style hypermarket has found success in Latin America, attempts to develop in North America have failed. Tordjman (1988) identified a range of contributing factors to this failure:

1 *Lack of innovation*: the basic trading proposition of the hypermarket (vast food and non-food ranges under one roof) was not innovative in this market, as similar large-scale mixed merchandise formats existed.
2 *Existing competition*: intra-type (concept) competition existed. There was a range of store types in the American market offering options to the consumers.
3 *Lack of power*: small-scale entry from internal growth (i.e., opening own stores) did not provide scale or leverage with suppliers, particularly in the food market.
4 *Customer preferences*: the 'one-stop-shop' behaviour more familiar to Europe, was less prevalent in the USA. Perceptions of distances and other shopping criteria also varied.
5 *Management culture*: the traditional hypermarket as developed in France was heavily dependent on a decentralized management culture: this was generally an alien concept in the USA and indeed provided a major obstacle to Carrefour's attempts to enter the UK in the early 1980s.

14.1.4 Internationalization of Retail Operations

It is the internationalization of retail operations that most of us think of when we consider retail internationalization. This takes many forms and has attracted much attention. It may range from a token store, owing to historical legacy, for example Safeway's presence in Gibraltar dating from Lipton days, or a prestige presence such as Mitsukoshi in London,

Mechanism	Advantages	Disadvantages
Internal expansion	Can be undertaken by any size of firm; experimental openings are possible with modest risk and often modest cost; ability to adapt operation with each subsequent opening; exit is easy (at least in early stages); allows rapid prototyping	Takes a long time to establish a substantial presence; may be seen by top management as a minor diversion; requirement to undertake full locational assessment; more difficult if host market is distant from home market; requires firm to become familiar with host country property market
Merger or takeover	Substantial market presence quickly achieved; management already in place; cash flow is immediate; possibility of technology transfer to the home firm; may be used as a way to obtain locations quickly for conversion to the chosen format	Difficult to exit if mistake is made; evaluation of takeover target is difficult and takes time; suitable firms may not be available; substantial top management commitment necessary; management of acquired firm may be unsuited to new operation
Franchise-type agreements	Rapid expansion of presence possible; low cost to franchisor; marginal markets can be addressed; local management may be used; wide range of forms of agreement available	Possible complex legal requirements; necessary to recruit suitable franchisees; difficult to control foreign franchisees; may become locked into an unsatisfactory relationship
Joint ventures	Possible to link with form already in the market; help available to climb learning curve and to overcome non-tariff barriers; possible to move later to either exit or make full entry into the market; share entry costs with other entrant	Necessary to share benefits; difficulties in finding a suitable partner
Non-controlling interest	Find out about market with minimal risk; allows those who know the market to manage the operation	Passive position; investment made over which little influence

Figure 14.1 Advantages and disadvantages of alternative mechanisms to establish retail international operations
Source: Dawson (1994).

to the development of a major chain in several countries. From a managerial perspective, involvement may take the form of foreign investment in a company primarily for financial return, in which case the management and operation is left to the domestic operation, or the foreign retailer may assume full management control over the international operation. It has been shown that such decisions can have a long-term effect upon sales and efficiency, which at least in part: 'Depend on the strategic choices made at the time of entry, as they shape the platform from which competitive advantages can be gained' (Gielens and Dekimpe, 2001).

There are several methods of international expansion open to retailers, these have been summarized by Dawson (1994) and are shown in Fig. 14.1. These different options require different levels of resource commitment, allow different rates (i.e., speed) of market entry, involve different degrees of local market knowledge and provide varying degrees of domestic control.

Companies may have a preferred entry mechanism, but it is not uncommon for a company to internationalize via a combination of the above routes. Marks & Spencer used a combination of acquisition of existing chains in North America, internal expansion in core European markets, and franchise in European and other world markets.

The choice of entry mechanisms may be affected by the country of origin, country of destination, and the retail sector involved. In his study of the internationalization of grocery retailers in Europe, Burt (1991) found some evidence of preferred entry mechanisms by retailers from different domestic markets. There appeared to be a higher propensity on the part of French grocery retailers to develop internationally by operational joint ventures, in contrast to the British grocery retailers who preferred to acquire existing companies. This pattern was explained by a replication of preferred growth mechanisms in the domestic market (i.e., acquisition was the normal method of expansion in the British retail sector) and by the characteristics of the destination market. For example, early British expansion took place in the USA and Ireland, where acquisition targets were available, whereas the French moves into Mediterranean Europe, particularly Spain, involved investment in a market with limited acquisition opportunities, so internal growth or joint venture arrangements prevailed.

The characteristics of the retail sector in which the company operates also seems to have an influence on choice of entry mechanisms. In some sectors, such as grocery, operating scale at the local level is important. Despite a growing number of international food brands, the bulk of the grocery offer will remain national. This implies that local market scale is important to compete with local competition. Therefore acquisition is a more plausible means of market entry, particularly in 'developed' markets such as the USA or in markets with a limited number of established indigenous operators (e.g. Eastern Europe and ASEAN markets). Acquisition, where possible, allows rapid development of scale and may present a barrier to market entry for other competitors. However, in some less developed markets, lacking takeover targets, internal growth may be the only option.

In other sectors, such as fashion, and where niche segments of markets are the target, internal growth, franchising and concessions provide for an approach more suitable to market skimming. In the clothing market, which is fashion oriented, generally highly competitive and made up of a series of niches or segments, retaining corporate control over any particular source of competitive advantage (fashion, design, style, brandname, etc.) is important. Entry is often into established markets with existing local competition. As such, a 'test market' approach of slow growth, often preceded by in-store concessions or wholesaling of product ranges, seems logical to lower risk. Petersen and Welch (2000) provide an overview of internationalization in the Danish clothing and footwear industry, with case studies of the InWear and Carli Gry chains, which follow this sequence of entry mechanisms. Franchising in particular is attracting attention as an entry mode in these 'specialist' and niche sectors (Doherty, 2000; Quinn, 1998), although like all entry mechanisms it is not without issues of management control (Quinn and Doherty, 2000). The expansion of Body Shop (Table 14.3), which is now trading from over 1300 franchised outlets plus nearly 500 company-owned stores in almost 50 countries, provides a further example of the geographical spread achievable through low-cost entry mechanisms.

Table 14.3 The geographical spread of Body Shop, 2001

Source: Body Shop Annual Report.

Region/country	Number of shops (company owned)	Region/country	Number of shops (company owned)
UK and Republic of Ireland	*315*	*Europe and Middle East*	*684*
UK	294 (159)	Austria	11 (2)
Republic of Ireland	21	Bahrain	6
		Belgium	19
Americas	*413*	Cyprus	3
Antigua	1	Denmark	18
Bahamas	3	Finland	29
Bermuda	1	France	20 (16)
Canada	122	Germany	87 (37)
Cayman Islands	1	Gibraltar	1
Mexico	4 (4)	Greece	56
USA	281 (250)	Holland	47
		Iceland	3
Asia Pacific	*429*	Italy	60
Australia	68	Kuwait	11
Brunei	4	Lebanon	3
Hong Kong	22	Luxembourg	2
Indonesia	21	Malta	4
Japan	116	Norway	35
Korea	39	Oman	4
Macau	2	Portugal	16
Malaysia	33	Qatar	1
New Zealand	16	Romania	2
Philippines	16	Saudi Arabia	55
Singapore	20 (20)	Spain	82
Taiwan	54	Sweden	59
Thailand	18	Switzerland	43
		UAE	7
Number of countries	*49*	*Number of stores*	*1 841 (488)*

14.2 Motives and Movements

Internationalization as a strategic option is clearly further up the business agenda for retail companies of all sizes and in all sectors. Consideration of the motives and drivers for internationalization, and the way management interprets and responds to these stimuli, provides an understanding of how the process starts to be managed.

14.2.1 Motives for Retail Internationalization

Like many business decisions, trying to disentangle the motives behind retail internationalization is difficult. Post hoc rationalization of decision processes suggests a much more structured assessment of the decision than is often the case in reality. In 1976, in one of the first British PhDs to look at retail internationalization, Jackson (1976) commented: 'The motives were a combination of gradually felt pressures, some rational self analysis, subjective feelings in some executives and systematic planning.' This mix of factors is probably just as applicable today. Although more information on international markets is available, temporal expediency often lies behind many moves into non-domestic markets. While we tend to look for patterns and rationalization in decision-making, and usually believe strategies (whether they work or not) are well thought through and planned, Dawson (2002) has begun to question whether the final move is driven by textbook planned approaches or expediency.

There have been several studies ranging from the 1960s (Yoshino, 1966) to the 1990s (e.g. Alexander, 1990; 1995; Quinn 1999; Williams, 1991; 1992) which have attempted to identify and rank the relative importance of the motives stimulating international activity. A number of factors are recognized in these studies. These have commonly been classified as push and pull factors, supported by a group of enabling factors which further stimulate the motives.

Push Factors

Push factors are those which pressure the organization into actively seeking international moves. Typically these would include negative factors such as mature or saturated domestic markets, adverse demographic or economic conditions and legislative constraints in the domestic market, or more positive issues such the belief that an innovative trading format or style is internationally transferable. Usually further market share gains in the domestic market are restricted by format saturation or competition. In both The Netherlands and Belgium a combination of the small size of the domestic market, saturation and, in the latter case, legislative constraints on large store development have lead to the leading grocery chains, Ahold and Delhaize, seeking opportunities elsewhere, with the domestic market now contributing a minority of sales and profits (see Table 14.4)

Pull Factors

In contrast, pull factors are commonly associated with a more proactive search for market opportunity. In these cases perceived growth opportunities arise from either favourable economic and demographic

	Ahold (2000)				Delhaize le Lion (1999)		
Country	**Sales (%)**	**Profit (%)**	**Outlets (%)**	**Countries**	**Sales (%)**	**Profit (%)**	**Outlets[1] (%)**
USA	*57.9*	*63.2*	*1313*	*USA*	*73.3*	*80.4*	*1382*
Europe	*31.6*	*28.9*	*6102*	*Europe*	*25.8*	*22.3*	*846*
The Netherlands	17.5		2203	Belgium	19.5	20.8	609
Scandinavia	8.9		3124	Czech Republic	2.2	−1.0	101
Portugal	2.5		198	Slovakia			19
Spain	0.9		241	Greece	3.0	1.3	54
Czech Republic	1.1		190	France	1.1	1.2	55
Poland	0.7		146	Romania			8
Latin America[2]	*9.7*	*8.8*	*567*	*Latin America*			
Brazil	2.9		106				
Argentina	4.1		235				
Chile	1.5		96				
Guatemala	1.2		130				
Asia	*0.8*	*−0.9*	*80*	*Asia*	*0.8*	*0.1*	*71*
Thailand	0.6		41	Singapore			30
Malaysia	0.2		39	Indonesia			20
				Thailand			21

Table 14.4 International activities of Ahold and Delhaize le Lion

Notes: 1 Projected stores for 2000.
       2 Ahold's Latin American interests also have stores in Peru, Paraguay, El Salvador and Honduras.
Source: derived from Ahold and Delhaize le Lion Annual Reports.

conditions, an apparently attractive business environment (few legislative constraints, low operating costs) or where indigenous competition is believed to be weak. These factors are amplified if potential (good value) acquisition targets exist or where economies of scale and scope may yield rewards. A final factor often included in this category, which should not be discounted, is managerial ego and a 'follow my leader' mentality when others, particularly domestic rivals, begin to move.

Enabling Factors

A third group of factors which are believed to amplify the above drivers and reduce perceived barriers to movement are the enabling factors or facilitators. In this category we include various information based technologies which allow control over greater geographical distance, the growing internationalization of the supply base, the existence of support agencies in the form of international consultancies, the removal of traditional political barriers, whether real or perceived, and favourable exchange rates. All of these may ease the internationalization decision.

McGoldrick (1995) summarizes these and other factors influencing the decision to internationalize in Fig. 14.2. Although we seek to categorize factors as one or the other, in reality the decision to move overseas will be driven by a combination of these motives and facilitating agents.

14.2.2 Experience Curve Effects

Like all new business ventures, the internationalization of retailing is affected by experience curve effects. Studies in the field of international and export marketing suggest that internationalization increases in intensity over time, and that culturally or geographically close countries provide the first experiences. The logic is that these countries are more similar in terms of culture and behaviour or are easier to monitor and manage, owing to physical proximity. International retailing brings us into contact with macro, task and operational environments which may be different to those experienced at home. While general market conditions and an environmental scan of business opportunities at the macrolevel may suggest similarities, there are often differences at the task and operational level. Given these dangers, one way of reducing risk is to gain experience in culturally or geographically similar markets first. When one examines flows of international activity over time, evidence of this behaviour can be observed. Early British moves seem to favour English-speaking markets, such as North America and Ireland, or The Netherlands, which has a retail structure and task environment similar to the UK. In contrast, French retailers are initially drawn to culturally similar Mediterranean markets, the Dutch towards Belgium and the Germans towards Austria. Over time, with experience, companies then move on to more culturally and geographically distant markets.

As companies become more familiar with international markets and the operational issues that arise, they become more ambitious in choice of markets entering culturally and geographically more distant markets. Vida and Fairhurst (1998), drawing on behavioural work in international marketing, suggest that the initial decision to enter a market will be based upon company capacity (firm characteristics) and management

Figure 14.2 Driving forces of retail internationalization
Source: McGoldrick (1995).

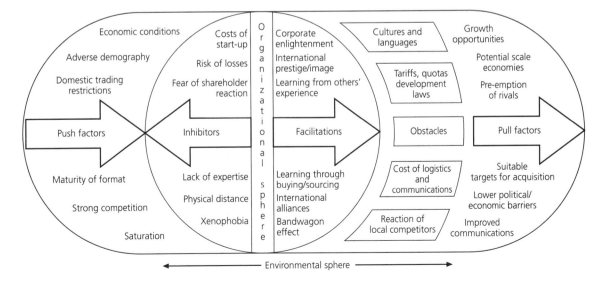

Figure 14.2 Driving forces of retail internationalization

perceptions (decision-maker characteristics, such as knowledge, experience and attitudes). These antecedents promote or inhibit the decision to move internationally or divest, which then leads to two outcomes: entry methods and market selection. They conclude that with experience retailers become more ambitious.

> *In the initial cycles, it appears reasonable to believe that inhibiting factors which stem primarily from the internal climate of the firm will influence the decision to enter more similar countries. In the subsequent cycles of the process, these decisions may increasingly become a function of the external environment and cautious planning (Vida and Fairhurst, 1998).*

The significance of management perceptions and experiences appears crucial in determining the response to international opportunity and the approach taken. Opportunities and motives are judged through personal experiences and corporate ambition. Alexander and Myers (2000) provide a matrix which combines market considerations, represented by market coverage, and corporate perspectives to provide four types of international companies: proximal, multinational, transnational and global (Fig. 14.3).

Treadgold (1990) also integrates the idea of the experience curve and management ambition in a model which identified three stages of development. These stages can be used to place the activities of companies or individual retailers in context. The three stages are defined as:

1 *Reluctance*: the company is primarily domestic in outlook and begins to look overseas only because it can see no similar opportunities at home.
2 *Caution*: is reflected in the geographical direction of investment with the early stages of internationalization characterized by investment in geographically or culturally close markets.
3 *Ambition*: the company will grow in ambition as experience is gained. The emphasis switches from expansion into 'safer' similar markets to 'attractive' markets, irrespective of cultural or geographical proximity.

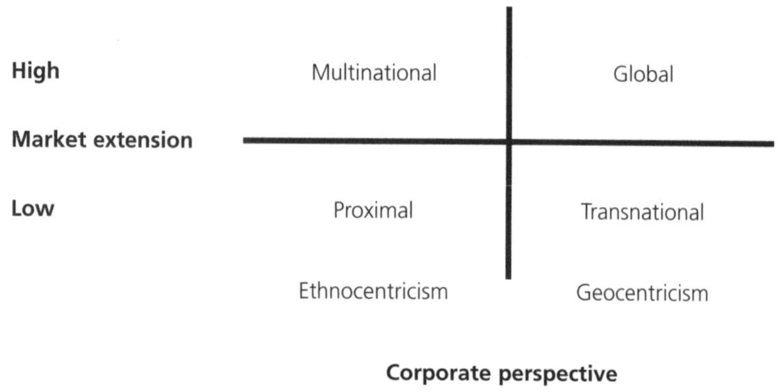

Figure 14.3 Classifying international retail approaches: market and operational considerations

Source: Alexander and Myers (2000).

The choice of entry method, the initial preference for culturally or geographically close countries and the growth of ambition and experience over time, all represent a means of reducing, or at least managing, the risk of international market entry. The high-cost, but high-control method of internal growth appears to be favoured in the lowest risk markets. On the other hand, culturally or geographically distant markets (which provide a higher perceived risk) may create a preference for franchising or joint ventures as an entry method.

The trade-off between geographical and cultural risk, experience and control are reflected in Treadgold's (1988) scheme, which combined the dimensions of entry and operating strategy, represented as high, medium, and low levels of cost (and control), with the extent of geographical coverage to classify internationalization strategies into four groups. These are:

1 *Cautious internationalists*: companies who have used a high-cost entry mechanism (internal growth or acquisition) to develop a limited international presence, seen as entering only one or two markets.
2 *Emboldened internationalists*: companies who, although still using high-cost entry mechanisms, are established in a wider range of geographical markets.
3 *Aggressive internationalists*: entry method is still high cost (usually internal growth), but these retailers have established international ambitions illustrated by a trading presence in a wide range of geographical markets.
4 *World powers*: this group is different, using low-cost entry methods (franchising) to establish a large international presence in terms of the number of markets entered.

It is clear from the preceding discussion that there is no one 'best' way of entering international markets, but by understanding the different influences upon market entry decisions we may start to put in place a strategy which can reduce the basic risks involved.

14.3 Understanding International Retail Markets

It has already been said that retail internationalization is a strategic option which carries a great deal of risk. It can bring retailers into contact with consumers, retailers and suppliers who are different from those found at home and who may behave and react in ways alien to domestic business practice. We are dealing with customers, public policy agents, suppliers and competitors who we do not always understand and, perhaps just as important, who do not fully understand us. Apparent similarities in the macro environment between countries may be offset by differences in the task and operational environments. The problem for retail organizations is that identifying these differences is often difficult and some differences (e.g. those in the macro environment) are more visible than others (e.g. differences in the task and organizational environments).

As in all location decisions (Chapter 7), a checklist can be helpful in addressing the many detailed issues of relevance to a potential market entry. Table 14.5 is a checklist developed by McGoldrick and Blair (1995), which includes nearly 100 factors that can influence the viability/profitability of an international market. While not providing the answers, such checklists have helped to provoke the questions that should be asked during a market evaluation. They have helped retailers to avoid expensive, potentially disastrous, pitfalls in their expansion programmes. They have also helped to identify information gaps to be filled by the various international data providers.

14.3.1 The Macroenvironment

Our first assessment of any retail market focuses on the macroenvironment. This provides broad scale opportunities and threats to the organization. As far as the impact of the macroenvironment on retail internationalization is concerned, retailers must consider potential differences in consumer characteristics and behaviour, government attitudes to distribution, and business structure in the retail sector.

Table 14.5 International market appraisal checklist

Based on: McGoldrick and Blair (1995).

Spending power	Barriers and risks
Total GDP	
Disposable incomes:	Entry barriers:
▸ spending patterns	▸ tariffs
▸ spending improvements	▸ quotas
▸ seasonal fluctuations	▸ development restrictions
▸ employment structure	▸ competition laws
▸ taxes on incomes	▸ barriers to foreign entry
▸ taxes on spending	▸ religious/cultural barriers
▸ savings ratios	
	Political risks:
Population:	▸ change of government
▸ size/growth projections	▸ nationalization or controls
▸ age profile	▸ war or riot
▸ cultural/ethnic groupings	▸ international embargoes
▸ expatriates and tourists	
▸ lifestyles	Civil risks:
▸ religion	▸ effectiveness of policing
	▸ rate of theft
Residential structure:	▸ rate of murder/violence
▸ urban v. rural	▸ level of organized crime
▸ housing density	
▸ ownership levels	Economic risks:
▸ household structures	▸ inflation
	▸ exchange rate fluctuations
Adjacent markets:	▸ employment structure and stability
▸ cornerstone status	▸ taxes on business
▸ market proximities	
▸ market similarities	Other risks:
▸ market accessibilities	▸ geological
	▸ climatic

Table 14.5 Continued.

Costs and communications	Competition
Factor costs: ▶ land availability and costs ▶ costs of acquisition targets ▶ taxes on business ▶ energy costs ▶ labour availability costs ▶ training costs ▶ development costs	Existing retailers, competition: ▶ same or similar formats ▶ indirect competition ▶ specialist retailers ▶ other marketing channels ▶ price competitiveness ▶ extent of differentiation
Logistics and costs: ▶ road networks ▶ rail transport ▶ air freight ▶ sea freight ▶ available carriers ▶ distances between markets ▶ transport safety ▶ transport reliability	Existing retailers, co-operation: ▶ synergies from partnerships ▶ international alliances ▶ franchising activities ▶ cumulative attraction ▶ acceptance of format Saturation levels: ▶ structure of outlets by sector ▶ concentration levels ▶ primary/secondary markets
Communications and costs: ▶ telephone/fax/Internet connections ▶ automatic international dialling ▶ available international lines ▶ costs of calls	Gap analysis: ▶ positioning of competitors ▶ viability/size of gaps ▶ reasons for gaps ▶ age of existing stores
Marketing communications: ▶ television/radio advertising ▶ direct mail agencies ▶ outdoor advertising ▶ print/magazine advertising ▶ cable television penetration	Competitive potential: ▶ site availability ▶ financial strength of home retailers ▶ attractions to international retailers ▶ opportunities to reposition

Consumer Characteristics and Behaviour

As consumer businesses, retailers clearly have to understand the basic parameters surrounding consumer structures and behaviours in the markets that they operate in. While broad trends can be found in all markets, the pace at which these changes have taken place and their impact upon consumer markets, varies from country to country. A scan of key demographic and socio-economic indicators from official national statistics may illustrate simple variations. To take Western Europe as an example, Eurostat statistics show:

1 *Different rates of population growth*: between 2000 and 2010 the Italian population is projected to remain stable, whereas The Netherlands is expected to grow by 5.1 per cent, Norway by 4.4 per cent and France by 3.9 per cent.

2 *Differences in population age structures*: in 2010 it is expected that 12.6 per cent of the Irish population will be over 65 years of age,

compared with 19.3 per cent in Italy, 18.9 per cent in Greece and 18.1 per cent in Sweden.

3 *Differences in household structure*: in 1995/96 only 12.7 per cent of households in Spain and 13.7 per cent in Portugal were classified as one-person households, compared to over 35 per cent in Germany, Finland and Denmark and around 40 per cent in Sweden.

4 *Differences in employment structures*: in 1991 less than 50 per cent of civilian employment was in the service sector in Portugal and Greece, compared with over 70 per cent in the UK and Norway. Similarly, female involvement in the formal labour force was under 35 per cent in Ireland and Spain, but over 44 per cent in the UK and Denmark.

At a macrolevel these characteristics will determine market size, market segments and labour force availability. When combined with differences in lifestyle attitudes, consumer beliefs and preferences, we are faced with a consumer market that is generally different from that encountered at home. Although common trends in demographic, socio-economic and political thought can be observed, we are still a long way from a 'United States of Europe'. There are important differences not only between nations but also within nations. Demographic and socio-economic trends and consumer behaviour in Milan and Barcelona may be closer to those found in Paris, Copenhagen and Cologne than in the south of Italy or North Western Spain.

Government Attitudes to Distribution

In the previous discussion of motives for internationalization, a favourable legislative environment was considered important. Government intervention, whether aimed directly or indirectly at the sector, can have a major impact upon market opportunities and restraints, as well as how retail markets behave. Indirectly, economic and fiscal policy influences the economic environment and consumer confidence. Interest rate policy, income tax levels, sales tax, and wage controls all affect consumers propensity to spend and retailer attitudes to investment. In more direct relation to retailing, the extent of change over the last 30 years has created concern over whether the speed or direction of change should be controlled by government. Within most European countries governments have considered the various issues and debated whether to intervene or whether to allow the processes of structural change to run their course.

There are several areas in which government legislation directly impacts upon retailing. The most significant areas as far as internationalizing retailers are concerned are:

1 *Rules on competition and trading practices*: these exist in most countries to prevent excessive concentration of market power, the creation of monopolies and 'unfair competition'. The recent

Carrefour-Promodes merger required approval from the European Union, and in some markets, such as Spain, fell foul of national competition policy, requiring the disposal of certain stores to prevent regional monopolies. Similarly in the USA, the Federal Trade Commission has often forced store disposals when companies such as Ahold and Delhaize have acquired existing operations. At the operational level, rules on competition affect specific aspects of trading which are felt to prejudice 'fair trading'. Legislation relating to advertising, loss leading, refusal to supply and shop hours are common examples. Until recent changes, German opening-hour legislation caused problems for many potential entrants into the market, while below-cost selling legislation has caused problems for Wal-Mart in Germany and Tesco in the Republic of Ireland.

2 *Building controls*: these influence the construction or renting of specific types of stores, and ultimately will effect expansion plans. Davies (1989; 1995) has edited overviews of policy, in this area which is typically referred to as 'retail planning' (see Chapter 7). Control of this type may fall under the auspices of general land use planning regulation as in the UK and The Netherlands, or specific permission may be required for certain types of stores (usually large area stores). For example, several governments observed the growth in market power of hypermarkets and the decline in independent, traditional retailing, and jumped to the conclusion that in these two changes there is direct cause and effect. Often in response to independent shopkeeper lobbies, which in some markets have an important and influential political voice, several European governments for example have introduced legislation to control hypermarkets and other large unit retailing. Legislation has been introduced in Italy (1971), France (1973; 1996), Belgium (1975) and Germany (1978). Similarly in Japan, legislation to control large-store openings has been regarded as an entry barrier (Dawson and Sato, 1983; Kaikati, 2000). Such legislation increases the costs and complexities of store openings.

3 *Rules on the ownership and establishment of enterprises*: this represent a third area of legislation which can impact upon retailers. Rules on the foreign ownership of companies may influence the entry mechanisms available. In the ASEAN region this has often provided a barrier to market entry (Davies, 1993). Elsewhere while legislation may not control ownership it may inhibit operations through controls over product ranges. Licences may be required for specific product groups, often those deemed to be detrimental to public health. For example, alcohol is sold through state-owned companies in Canada and Sweden, and therefore is unavailable in supermarkets, and licences are required for pharmacy products in most countries. In many Mediterranean markets, licences to trade are required for many general product groups.

Business Structure in the Retail Sector

Over the last 40 years, enormous structural adjustments have taken place within retailing. In the case of Europe, Burt (1989), Dawson (1982), Dawson and Burt (1998) and Jefferys and Knee (1962) provide overviews of these broad changes. Small firms, operating often only a single shop, have lost competitive position to large firms operating many shops, often in several different countries. While most apparent in the food sector, the same pattern runs through the retail trade in general (see Chapter 2).

This growth of large firms has led to an increasing concentration in retail sales. From a UK perspective we tend to assume that all retail markets and sectors are dominated by highly centralized corporate chains. This is not always the case. The dominant organizations may be consumer co-operatives or buying groups, such as in the Nordic grocery market. These differences in organizational form may influence market behaviours, perceptions of strategic priorities and the skills base available in the market. The legacy of state-controlled retail enterprises in the former Eastern Europe have posed many problems for retailers entering these markets. The skills base, attitude to initiative and reaction to change have not always dovetailed with the requirements of the new arrivals.

As well as differences in retail market structure at the organizational level, there are also differences in selling technique or retail format. For example, in the UK, we have not yet been fully exposed to the hypermarket, a common trading format in most of continental Europe, and it was only in the 1990s that British grocery retailers faced competition from limited-line discounters such as Aldi, Netto and Lidl. Warehouse Clubs, which developed market share strongly in the USA, have had less success in being culturally accepted in the European market, while the tobacconist kiosk prevalent throughout most of Europe is unseen in the UK, where we frequent confectioners, tobacconists and newsagents (CTNs). Similarly, wet markets in Singapore make interesting tourist trips for photo opportunities, but more importantly these places are where local consumers shop for fresh produce. These apparently small differences in shop type impact upon the acceptance of innovations which either conform to or disrupt the norm.

The outcome of these structural differences is that the source and nature of competition, the range of retail formats and selling techniques (and the associated customer reaction and loyalty to them) may present us with a very different competitive landscape than that which we are used to at home. Johnson and Allen (1994) explain the research process that Adams, the childrenswear retailer, went through before entering Spain. The environmental scanning exercise highlighted several differences in the macrolevel business structure. Entry into the Spanish market would bring Adams into competition with different organizational forms and trading formats. They discovered that there were few multiple childrenswear specialists, the traditional source of childrenswear was department stores and the hypermarket represented a new format for Adams to compete against. In addition the lack of suburban shopping centres meant that they had no locations equivalent to those in the domestic market from which to trade.

14.3.2 The Task Environment

The individual retail firm has little control over macroenvironmental considerations. However, on the whole, these macroissues are visible and, with improving information sources, basic information on consumer and retail markets is available. An environmental scan of these factors will often lead to a decision on whether entry into a market is viable.

Less visible, but of crucial importance to the success of an international venture, are task environment considerations. The task environment comprises the business environments within which retail and other organizations operate. It consists of factors external to an individual organization, but which affect relationships with other organizations. In short, this involves the 'norms' of business behaviour or how retail markets work. This can be illustrated by reference to the following behavioural norms and cultures, and relationships between institutions.

Behavioural Norms and Cultures

If we are considering investment in an international market where language differences exist, we are at least alerted to the fact that the people we are dealing with (whether customers, staff or suppliers) might be different. However, cultural and behavioural influences on how people and institutions work and interact go deeper than language. O'Grady and Lane (1997) examined how 'unnoticed' differences between the Canadian and USA markets hindered retail internationalization. In their study they found Americans to be different from Canadians in respect of their competitiveness, work ethic, aggressiveness, attitudes to risk-taking, individualism, action orientation and sense of mastery. These cultural differences meant that, despite apparent market similarities, the 'norms' of business behaviour between the two markets were very different and this was reflected in a number of aspects of retail behaviour. Consumer expectations of product ranges, locations, price, service and convenience differed between the two markets and business relationships were characterized by a shorter-term view of suppliers, staff and customers in the USA. Managerially the strong performance ethos in the USA saw a greater emphasis upon targets, performance, and productivity measures, with reward systems and incentives reinforcing this ethos, and the competitive nature of Americans was reflected in tactical retaliation via price cuts, and advertising.

One of the most substantial studies of national cultures was undertaken by Hofstede (1980), based on the values and beliefs of IBM employees in 40 countries. From the many facets of cultural difference, four major dimensions were identified, as summarized in Fig. 14.4. Scales were devised to rate each country on the four dimensions, such that countries could be 'positioned' on their cultural attributes. Thus,

1. Individualism	
COLLECTIVIST *e.g. Venezuela* 'We' consciousness dominant Identity based on social system Value standards differ for in-groups and out-groups (particularism)	**INDIVIDUALIST** *e.g. Australia* 'I' consciousness dominant Identity is based on the individual Value standards should apply to all (universalism)
2. Uncertainty avoidance	
LOW UNCERTAINTY AVOIDANCE *e.g. Denmark* Time is free Acceptance of dissent Belief in generalists and common sense	**HIGH UNCERTAINTY AVOIDANCE** *e.g. Japan* Time is money Strong need for consensus Belief in experts and their knowledge
3. Power distance	
SMALL POWER DISTANCE *e.g. Australia* Inequality in society should be minimized Superiors accessible All should have equal rights	**LONG POWER DISTANCE** *e.g. Philippines* Everyone has a rightful place, high or low Superiors inaccessible Power holders entitled to privileges
4. Masculinity/femininity	
FEMININE *e.g. Sweden* Should be equality of sexes Sex roles fluid Quality of life important	**MASCULINE** *e.g. Japan* Men should dominate Sex roles differentiated Performance is what counts

Figure 14.4 Hofstede's dimensions of cultural difference

Source: derived from Hofstede (1980; 1992).

Australia was rated low on the power–distance dimension yet high on the individualist scale. Venezuela, on the other hand, is seen as a collectivist society with fairly high power distance.

Stenquist (1998) identified many linkages between these attributes and the management of international retail organizations. For example, in a collectivist society, governments may be more protective of small businesses. In a country with small power distance, customers may be less prone to conspicuous consumption and the flaunting of wealth. Typologies such as Hofstede's have helped to understand the properties of national cultures, yet should not be generalized to all companies and consumers within a given market. It should also be recognized, as noted in Sec. 2.1, that national values have been seen to shift over time.

Relationships between Institutions

Returning to differences in the task environment in Europe, one area which clearly illustrates differences in business practices is that of supplier–retailer relationships in the grocery market. Broad trends indicate a general move to a more collaborative approach, viewing the channel and all its constituents as a vertical market system. However, the pace and extent to which this view has been adopted varies. The impact of past practice and existing modes of behaviour can be reflected in logistics practices and product brand decisions.

Despite the general move to ECR type initiatives (see Chapter 8), logistics practices still vary with a consequent impact upon measurable variables such as stock levels, the location of stock, the degree of third party involvement and the centralization of distribution systems. The GEA (1994) report showed that typical inventory levels in a number of European grocery markets varied from 28 days in the UK, to 42 or 43 days in France, Italy and Spain, and 50 days in Germany. These figures clearly showed that practices in the UK provided markedly different stock levels (measured in days) in both the retail warehouse and in stores, than was found in other European markets. Fernie (1995) suggests that national differences in logistics practices arise from a range of factors, including attitudes to collaboration with suppliers and logistics providers, the nature of competition in the market, adoption and use of information technology, particularly EDI usage, and local market cost structures, e.g., variations in land, labour, capital and transport costs.

The outcome is that when entering international markets, even within Europe, the grocery retailer will be faced with a supply chain that may operate in a very different way from that found at home. The GEA (1994) report places the larger European markets in a sequence, arguing that an Efficient Consumer Response-type approach to supply chain management is most developed in the UK and least developed in Spain. In the case of UK companies, differences in logistics practices have often provided a constraint to international expansion, but one which is often not apparent until experienced.

Differences in the nature of competition and attitudes to supplier–retailer relationships in the grocery market are commonly reflected in product and brand range decisions. In markets where price competition is keen, the practice of speculative inventory is common: Paché (1995) illustrates this in the case of France. He argues that the historical development of the French grocery market over the past 20 years has encouraged bulk buying of very large quantities of branded product to be stored and sold at a later date, rather than regular restock purchases. Regional distribution centres in France are built to hold such speculative inventory, rather than to provide centralized distribution facilities, as in the UK. He estimated that in the early 1990s, up to 60 per cent of retail stock was speculative inventory, although this has now slowly declined to around 40 per cent. As a consequence, the emphasis within the grocery sector in France has been on volume discounts with retailers 'feverishly looking for the lowest purchase prices'. This price-focused approach, coupled with long payment delays, leads towards a more confrontational, conflict-based type of supplier–retailer relationship.

A further difference in approach to product and brand management in the grocery sector is found in the type and nature of retail brands.

There are a number of reports available that comment upon retail grocery brands in Europe (e.g. Laaksonen, 1994; Martensen 1992). Most of these recognize that there are different types or generations of retailer brand, ranging from the low-price/acceptable-quality position of generics to the high-price/high value-added retail brand common in the UK. Throughout Europe, the position of the retail grocery brand within both retail marketing strategies, and the minds of consumers varies. The historical development of the retail brand, the competitive context and the nature of retail-supplier relationships all contribute to this situation. In the case of France, Pellegrini (1994) has charted the development of different types of retail brand, while Fernie and Pierrel (1996) have considered the potential for the French retail grocery brand to evolve into the 'British' model and concluded that:

> *although both markets are highly concentrated, the organisational structure of French grocery businesses and the highly competitive market environment and regulatory controls over the distribution sector combine to inhibit the development of store brands in France, compared with the situation in the UK (Fernie and Pierrel, 1996).*

A further illustration of these differences is provided by Hughes (1996), who contrasts the development of retail brands in the UK with the USA. Figure 14.5 summarizes her findings.

Figure 14.5 Differences in retail brand management and perceptions in the UK and USA

Source: derived from Hughes (1996).

Issue	UK	USA
Role of own brand in the retail marketing mix	Own brand central to retail positioning; move to high-margins/high-value products showing innovation	Own brand part of a product range; quality improving but essentially follower/me too products; often not branded with retailer name
Supply chain relationships and management	Proactive search for appropriate suppliers; collaborative approach to product development; frequent retailer–supplier contact	Manufacturer brand still the key innovator; frequent use of third party 'brokers'; arms-length governance; less collaboration and little joint development
Competitive structure and features of the retail sector	National-level concentration; high investment in capital and IT; centralization on national level; limited price competition, emphasis on added value/service differentiation	Regional concentration (reinforced by Robinson Patman Act); price orientated market with brand choice in categories; less IT and capital investment
Consumer perceptions of own brand	Trust own brand; recognized as good quality product and innovative product market	Quality perception rising but still low; view own brand as copy-cat, low/average quality alternative

One major problem faced by J. Sainsbury in the American market is that attempts to introduce a 'British-Style' own-brand, central to domestic retail strategy, have been inhibited by supplier and consumer perceptions of own brand.

These differences in how the market 'works', in the sense of normal business practices and attitudes, can create major barriers to retail internationalization. It is a natural reaction for us to assume that how we work is the 'norm' or the best. To quote O'Grady and Lane (1997):

> *executives were limited by their own culture, because it created mental models that prevented them from perceiving differences. The mental models appropriate for the Canadian market led top management teams to make decisions as they would for that market, such as selecting the wrong strategy for the USA, as well as making numerous other operating decisions that were inappropriate.*

14.3.3 The Organizational Environment

It may well be that 'our way' is more efficient or productive, but the factors that allow us to work in this way may not exist in the international marketplace. This may arise because macroenvironment factors create a different task environment within which to compete or that the way we organize ourselves is not appropriate (or allowed) in a non-domestic market. This leads to consideration of differences in the organizational environment. Again, while on the surface retail sectors or companies may look similar, often they operate differently because of differences in cost structures, and management styles and corporate culture.

Cost Structures

The organization of any retail activity must ultimately pay some homage to cost structures. Differences in macroenvironment considerations and business behaviour all combine to influence cost structures. In any retail organization, buying and distribution costs (costs of goods sold) are the most important element of cost structures. The importance of buying power, but more importantly how this buying power can be leveraged and used, can vary from domestic to international markets. The differences in logistics practices and stockholding discussed above have implications for, and reflect, cost considerations.

The importance of people in retailing is recognized. However, labour costs and employment structures vary considerably internationally. Britain has traditionally had the lowest labour costs in retailing and wholesaling in Western Europe. A French survey in 1987 showed that the average hourly cost per employee in distribution in Britain was 52–54 per cent that of Belgium, The Netherlands and Germany, and 71 per cent that found in France. These differences in costs reflect labour structures, which in the British case are dominated by part-time labour. Only in the Netherlands is part-time employment as widespread as in the UK (over 40 per cent). In Germany and France 26–28 per cent of wage and salary earners in retailing are part-time; in Belgium the figure is around 18 per cent while in Spain, Portugal and Greece under 7 per cent is the norm. In the UK we have developed very flexible labour structures in multiple retailing, an organizational feature which is not always replicated elsewhere.

Baret et al. (1999) contrasted employment practices in large stores in France, Germany and the UK, and noted differences in approach in respect of the motives for introducing part-time labour, the legal definitions of part-time labour, the use of overtime, and labour scheduling procedures and contractual arrangements. These differences have an impact not just upon cost structure but on how labour within stores is organized and managed. The way labour is deployed in turn reflects market practice and consumer expectations. Gadry and Jany-Catrice (2000) attempt to explain differences in labour levels in the USA and France and conclude:

> *about 22 per cent more hours' work are used in the American retail trade (for the same basket of groceries in France) and if labour productivity is the same or even a little higher, it is because, on average, American stores offer more services (particularly labour intensive ones) and, to this end, place more staff at the disposal of customers.*

These labour-intensive services were seen as 24-hour opening, customer care, assistance on the shop floor and at checkouts, and security staff.

Management Styles and Corporate Culture

The organization and implementation of retail activity will also reflect management styles and cultures. Throughout the retail world certain contrasts arise in management styles, owing to historical reasons, regional trading differences and corporate philosophy. Management roles and responsibilities, the skills base and expectations within the workplace can vary significantly. This has implications in the international arena for the transferability of operational and management practices.

In many grocery chains the management mantra during the 1980s and 1990s was centralization. The desire to leverage economies of scale and replication saw most operational decisions transferred from the store to the corporate centre. One well-documented exception to this was the French hypermarket, which operated under a more decentralized management style. Various market-related decisions such as product ranging, pricing and promotions were taken at the store, and even product department level. Regional and national management tiers retained control over strategic decision-making, but performed a more supportive rather than command role for many day-to-day operational decisions. Companies, such as Carrefour, which champion decentralized management systems, argued that staff were more motivated and that the company was more responsive to local market conditions.

A lack of understanding of the existing corporate philosophy or approach can cause problems when entering the international market, particularly if the venture is achieved through acquisition. The corporate culture and internal work practices of one retailer may not fit those of another. We are aware of some of these issues in the domestic market when acquisition takes place, but these issues are magnified when the acquisition is across national boundaries.

Shackleton (1996) provides evidence of this in her study of Sainsbury's acquisition of Shaw's in the USA. The 'Sainsburyization' of Shaw's caused great resentment within the American company. Existing employees felt there was a 'loss of family atmosphere', with Sainsbury's 'big capital' ethics. The belief was that Sainsbury was focused on the bottom line, therefore was less caring about employees, and that existing management was being sidelined or removed. On the shop floor resentment focused around what was seen as a casualization of the labour force, with a move to part-time employment and a disregard for unions. In essence, all Sainsbury were doing were bringing existing 'British' work practices to bear, but in many areas these conflicted with the established way of operation.

These differences in the organizational environment are clearly linked to the changes in the macro and task environments, but again the key issue for an internationalizing retailer is to understand fully how retailing operates in the target market. Existing perceptions of tasks, responsibilities, skills and rewards may need just as much adaptation as product range or prices.

An initial environmental scan of an international market may suggest great opportunity, but the key to success is to understand how that market works. For example, the apparently high retail margins in British grocery market have been looked at with envy by many operators from other parts of the world. However, as Burt and Sparks (1995) argue in their comparison of Britain and France, simplistic price and margin comparisons between countries, which may make one market look more attractive than the other at a macrolevel, fail to recognize that these differences are derived from different market conditions and practices at the task and organizational level. The markets operate differently and this needs to be understood before internationalization occurs.

14.4 Implementing Internationalization

Whatever the motives for pursuing a retail internationalization strategy, the methods of entry chosen, or the awareness and appreciation of similarities and differences in the way host markets operate, the ultimate test of any strategy is implementation.

14.4.1 Is Retailing Different?

In the search for an understanding of how the internationalization process works on the ground, the natural inclination is to explore theories and models developed in other business sectors. Most concepts have been developed in relation to manufacturing industry and the exportation of consumer products. A key question is whether these concepts can be applied to the case of retailing (Davies and Fergusson, 1995). Of particular interest to studies of retail internationalization have been the stages theories of international expansion, the eclectic paradigm of internationlization and the value chain and network theory.

The Stages Theories of International Expansion

The apparent attempts by internationalizing retailers to minimize risk by choosing geographical markets which are perceived as being physically or culturally close has drawn attention to a series of papers commonly termed 'stages theory'. This body of work, attributed primarily to the 'Uppsala School' in Sweden (Johanson and Vahlne, 1977; 1990; Johanson and Wiedersheim-Paul, 1975) and related American work on exporting (Bilkey and Tesar, 1977; Cavusgil, 1980; 1984), takes a behavioural approach to the internationalization process.

In essence, stages theory sees knowledge and experience, allied to certain firm characteristics, as the key to explaining international expansion. Uncertainty and lack of knowledge means that internationalization starts with small, tentative, steps into local markets. As experience is gained, companies successively enter more distant markets. In a manufacturing context this increase in experience and commitment leads from indirect exporting, to the establishment of sales subsidiaries and, finally, overseas production. Although initially derived from small-scale studies of small firms, the authors acknowledge that larger companies with more resources may be able to take larger steps, even in the first stages of internationalization. The apparent patterns of expansion seen in retailing and discussed earlier would seem to fit with these ideas.

The Eclectic Paradigm of Internationalization

One of the most widely recognized models of internationalization is the eclectic paradigm devised by Dunning (1981; 1988; 1993). This model suggests that the extent, form and pattern of international expansion, and in particular the decision to invest directly in an overseas operation, is a function of:

1 *Ownership-specific advantages*: an innovative product, or production process which gives the firm a unique source of competitive advantage.
2 *Location-specific advantages*: the host country has cost or market opportunities not available at home (lower land or labour costs are common examples).
3 *Internalization advantages*: organizational ownership of corporate 'secrets' or mechanisms is crucial to success.

Again in the context of manufacturing, the basic argument of Dunning's paradigm is that, when all three types of advantage are important, then foreign direct investment will be preferred to other forms of indirect internationalization. In a retail context the idea of ownership specific advantages (a retail brand in the fashion sector or an innovative sales method such as fast food) in retailing is appealing. Similarly, market and cost differentials between countries (possibly reflected in differences in operating margins) may provide evidence of location-specific advantages. Finally, a desire to internalize operating procedures by internal expansion is also evident in retailing.

The Value Chain and Network Theory

A third area of conceptual work, borrowed from manufacturing theory to explain retail internationalization, is the value chain and network theory. The value chain (Porter, 1985) is a means of achieving competitive advantage through a transactionally linked sequence of activities, each of which adds to the total 'added value' presented to the customer (see Sec. 4.2.2). Management of each of the activities and relationships in the value chain provides a basis for unique competitive advantage. The idea of a business activity as comprising a series of stages or activities involving relationships, often with other institutions, has drawn attention to network theory (Hakansson, 1982). Networks provide the potential for flexibility in delivering a specific business activity and may provide competitive advantage through an organization's ability to create and organize a coherent network, and to manage that network towards a common competitive goal.

The increasing emphasis placed upon managing the whole value/distribution chain as a single entry within retailing is clear. Therefore, a focus upon value chain and network considerations may provide explanations for international sourcing, increases in the use of franchising as a means of international expansion, and the growth and rapid international expansion of Benetton.

Figure 14.6 The Strategic International Retail Expansion (SIRE) model

Source: Sternquist (1997).

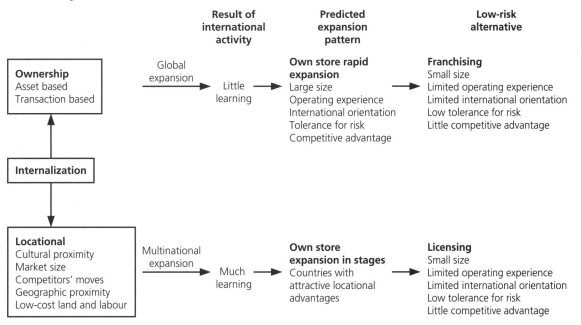

Sternquist (1997), attempts to integrate four different models of internationalization, including some of the above, into a single model. She draws on various concepts within existing theory, such as locational and ownership advantages and internalization, global and multinational approaches to markets, expansion stages, and risk in her Strategic International Retail Expansion (SIRE) model (Fig. 14.6).

Although authors such as Sternquist (1997) clearly believe that these models developed for manufacturing have some explanatory value in respect to retail internationalization, others, notably Dawson (1993), argue that retailing exhibits a number of characteristics which limit the applicability of these models:

> *The balance between centralised and decentralised decision-making, the relative importance of organisation and establishment scale economies, the degree of spatial dispersion in the multi-establishment enterprise, the relative size of establishment to the size of the firm, the relative exit costs if decisions are reversed, the speed with which an income stream can be generated after an investment decision has been made, different cash flow characteristics, the relative value of stock and hence importance of sourcing; all these items, and others, serve to differentiate the manufacturing firm and the retail firm not least in respect of the internationalisation process (Dawson 1993).*

Do the characteristics of retailing as an industry mean that it faces unique issues when it moves outside its domestic environment?

14.4.2 The Process of Retail Internationalization

One of the models which Sternquist (1997) includes is that of Salmon and Tordjman (1989). This is one of the few academic papers which attempts to tackle the question of how retail companies might implement internationalization. They identify three potential approaches to operating in international markets, once the entry decision had been made. The first of these, the investment strategy, is purely a financial investment in a retail operation in a foreign country. It may entail little involvement in the day to day operation of that business, and is often seen as a precursor to more direct involvement through either a global or multinational strategy.

The Salmon and Tordjman schema draws on a long-established debate in international marketing literature. Central to this is Levitt's (1983) proposition that telecommunication technology, consumer change and the behaviour of transnational corporations were leading inexorably to a 'global village', with a convergence of consumer needs, values and behaviour. This debate focuses on whether the marketing response of the consumer goods industry should be one of a standardized or global offer, or a differentiated offer, adapted for local market conditions. The rationale for globalization, the implications of such an approach and the barriers to achieving full standardization has formed an ongoing debate in marketing (e.g. Buzzell, 1968; Quelch and Hoff, 1986; Sorenson and Wiechmann, 1975).

While this discussion has focused almost exclusively on consumer goods, the growth of apparently 'globalized' retail chains in fast-food and specialist niche markets allows immediate parallels to be made in retailing. As discussed above, Treadgold (1988) named one of his categories 'world powers' and allocated retailers normally associated with a global approach to this category. The Salmon and Tordjman framework considers two key strategic options: global strategy and multinational strategy.

Global Strategy

In a global strategy the store network is not a collection of domestic operations but a series of linked stores. There is a high level of standardization in marketing strategy, with the assumption that the target consumers are homogenous. Thus, in several different countries similar product lines, price level, distribution system, communication, service level and store design and decor are used. This allows the firm to take advantage of economies of scale, particularly in purchasing or product procurement, and economies of replication. Typically, it is the speciality retailers who adopt this strategy. Often, vertical integration is strong with a unique or distinctive product range or brand central to the strategy. Thus, the high-fashion retailers use this strategy as do specialist retailers such as Body Shop, Benetton, Laura Ashley, Lush, Zara, IKEA and Toys 'R' Us. Such a strategy, with economies of scale at a global level, allows expansion based on a form of market skimming i.e., entry into a large number of markets with relatively few stores in each.

Examples of the global approach tend to come from the non-food sector. Benetton, the Italian casual clothing/knitwear chain has over 7000 stores in 110 countries. Approximately 70 per cent of sales are now generated overseas with 39 per cent from other European (not Italy) markets, 10 per cent from the Americas and 20 per cent from the rest of the world. It opened its first stores in Italy in 1968, and then its first overseas store in Paris the following year. Expansion has been mainly by a form of franchise with a standard package involved and, most important, a requirement to purchase only Benetton-supplied products (Fréry 1987). IKEA, the Swedish-based furniture chain, began as a mail order operation in 1947, issued its first catalogue in 1950, and opened its first store in 1958. Since the 1960s, international expansion has been rapid. Catalogues have been widely used to increase market penetration once a country has been entered. Product design and sourcing is handled by the Swedish head office, with the company using 2500 suppliers in 70 countries, and there is a considerable degree of central control over the standardized marketing approach in all countries (Martenson, 1987). In both of these cases (and that of Body Shop, as shown in Table 14.3) the speed and spread of international store networks is impressive.

Multinational Strategy

In a multinational strategy, the store networks are adjusted to national conditions in a multi-domestic approach. International activities are managed on a portfolio basis. Concepts and marketing strategies are modified for each country and a distinct competitive position is sought in the country. There are no substantial cost savings by replication of units in different countries, but multiplication of units in each country results in domestic scale and replication economies, and a market penetration strategy occurs. The marketing strategy involves the tailoring of the offering, i.e., assortment, price, promotions, service level, format design, distribution etc. to the local conditions. When expansion takes place by acquisition, it is usual to respect the internal corporate culture of the acquired company and not to impose control from headquarters. In effect, the acquirer is buying local market knowledge.

This type of strategy has typically been implemented by companies in the grocery sector, such as Ahold, and Carrefour, and by highly diversified companies. For both Ahold and Carrefour, the initial policy was to increase their presence, and thus market share, in a few countries, rather than to seek a global presence. Although in the past decade the global spread of both companies has expanded dramatically, the same approach is seen in attempts to become the dominant player in 'developing' markets. If one considers the case of Carrefour (Table 14.6), the range of markets is balanced by an attempt to build market share and become a leading retailer in each market.

One problem with such intuitively simple frameworks as the global versus multinational approach is that we tend to regard it as two discrete options and search for retailers which 'fit' either of these options. Many companies exhibit characteristics of both approaches and cannot be neatly categorized as a global or multinational retailer. Most companies have some multinational features, with operations in individual countries having a considerable degree of managerial autonomy. Although operations may be highly standardized at the national level, internationally the different subsidiaries represent autonomous SBUs.

Goldman (2001) argues that, rather than the simplistic either/or option, format transfers should consider the specific factors driving change. He suggests six format transfer strategies:

1 *Global niche promotion strategy*: the aim is to protect and retain the company's global niche position in a global segment. A purist global replication strategy is the outcome.
2 *Opportunism strategy*: the goal is to exploit opportunities in the host country. Numerous format adaptations occur in order to pursue these opportunities. A virtually new format may be created.
3 *Format pioneering opportunity strategy*: driven by a global strategic vision, if success occurs in the host market transfer elsewhere in the region is the aim. Adaptation occurs to develop a format which will fit host country/region conditions and can then be transferred.

Region/country	% share	Rank	Stores	Market leader	% share
Western Europe			4874		
France	26	1	1726	Carrefour	26
Spain	26	1	1939	Carrefour	26
Portugal	6	5	277	Modelo Continente	24
Italy	6	2	413	Co-op Italia	9
Greece	6	1	323	Carrefour	6
Turkey	1	5	46	Migros	6
Switzerland	2	6	10 (JV)	Migros	39
Belgium	19	1	140	Carrefour	19
Eastern Europe			31		
Poland	3	3	23	Metro	11
Czech Republic	1	10	6	Metro	8
Slovakia	under 1	11	2	Tesco	4
Americas			574		
Mexico	5	5	18	Walmex	10
Columbia	3	5	3	Casino	34
Chile	1	9	3	D&S	11
Argentina	9	1	361	Carrefour/Norte	9
Brazil	12	1	189	Carrefour	12
Asia			94		
China	n.a.	1	24	Carrefour	n.a.
Thailand	2	6	11	SHV Makro	19
Malaysia	2	3	6	The Store	5
Indonesia	1	3	7	Hero	3
Taiwan	7	1	24	Carrefour	7
Korea	5	2	20	Carrefour	5
Japan	under 1	15	1	Daiei	5

Table 14.6 Carrefour's international market shares

Source: IGD (2001b); Carrefour Annual Reports.

4 *Format-extension compatible country of origin*: involves formats transferred from highly compatible home countries. The home-country format is replicated with few changes.

5 *Portfolio-based format extension*: formats are transferred from compatible countries which are not the format's original home. A format exists developed for a specific market and this can be transferred. This strategy may evolve from a format pioneering strategy.

6 *Competitive-positioning orientated*: if the host country has strong local retailers operating the same format, the strengths of the format must be maximized at least cost. Elements which will make limited contributions to the competitive position in the host market or which are costly will be dropped.

14.4.3 Understanding Retail Competitive Advantage: What Is Being Internationalized?

The crux of Salmon and Tordjman's scheme and the issues surrounding format transfer is that for some retailers, or perhaps some retail sectors, the transferability of the domestic operation into non-domestic markets is more desirable and plausible than others. In most cases one would assume that the operating approach taken to international markets would seek to replicate the competitive or differential advantage achieved in the home market. In order to achieve this, the internationalizing retailer needs a clear view of what is the source of competitive or differential advantage. In other words not only should the retailer understand the host environment which they wish to enter and how it operates, but also what they intend to take into that market.

> *What do retailers actually internationalise? Is it management expertise and management systems? Innovative forms of trading? Or unique retail brands? ... [this] ... will allow us to assess whether retailing faces genuinely unique problems or whether it simply faces the same problems as other industrial sectors which internationalise (Brown and Burt, 1992).*

Image or Technique?

In a sense, this brings us back to the issues of definition with which we started this chapter. For many retailers competitive advantage is tied up in all these dimensions: management systems, format and brand. All of these contribute to a unique 'added value' package which is presented to consumers and forms the retail offer. As retailers in virtually all product sectors become brands in their own right, the overall image (and consumer perception of that image) provides the source of differentiation in the domestic marketplace. In this situation, the issue then becomes one of assessing how transferable is this overall image.

In the case of speciality retailers, Simpson and Thorpe (1995; 1999) provide a framework for assessing the differential advantage and consequent global opportunities for retailers. They claim that their PLIN model is based on four elements which are unique and common to speciality retailers who have succeeded overseas. These elements comprise:

- *Product*: a category or mix of unique merchandise which differentiates a retailer from competitors.
- *Lifestyle*: a match between the retailer's unique retail mix and the lifestyle and behaviour patterns of target consumers.
- *Image*: the composite picture of the strengths and personality of the retailer which is found in the mind of consumers.
- *Niche*: a position in the marketplace which fills a gap or avoids competitors.

These elements are seen as interdependent and as 'a precondition ... to create a differential advantage for speciality retailers in the market place'.

While such characteristics or features as 'niche' or 'lifestyle' can readily be associated with a global approach to retail internationalization, in particular, speciality markets, they are less easy to relate to retailers dealing in mass markets such as grocery. In these sectors, competitive advantage is more likely to be immediately 'hidden' from consumers' eyes and take the form of management systems which provide greater efficiencies than existing operators. Only if these factors are accompanied by an innovative trading format, such as the hypermarket or limited-line discount store, which is new to the host market will such differentiation be immediately visible to consumers. The distinction between customization of the 'front store' and standardization of the 'back room' is clear in Ahold's approach:

> *we achieve synergies by localizing everything the customer sees and enjoys, and globalizing back room activities, thus making the local experience affordable. By maintaining local identities, our stores ensure their local brands remain highly popular among local customers who feel at home in their store (Ahold Annual Report, 2000).*

Environmental Fit

Even if we have a clear understanding of our source of competitive advantage, we still face the issue of environmental fit. Earlier in this chapter we discussed potential differences in the macro, task and organizational environments, of which internationalizing retailers must be aware. It is these factors which will ultimately determine if competitive advantage can be transferred and if a global or standardized approach to international markets is feasible.

Ultimately, a pure global approach to retail internationalization is rare. Commonly, some form of adaptation is needed, even in very niche/lifestyle-based markets. Moore (1998) assesses the entry of Kookai and Morgan into the UK. Even in this sector, which would appear to exhibit all the characteristics necessary for a global approach, he noted the need for adaptation in:

1 *Product range*: British customers were more adventurous and experimental than their French counterparts, particularly in terms of innovative styles and colour. Product ranges had to be widened and adapted.
2 *Communication*: French personalities, cultural references and 'straplines' were not understood by the British consumer. 'British' reference points (e.g. David Ginola) were used in adverts.
3 *Services*: discount cards and credit cards were introduced as these were the norm in the UK fashion sector.
4 *Shopfitting*: the original French shop fit was perceived as too 'downmarket'. A new shop fit with timber floors and pale stone was introduced.

Examples such as this again suggest that the interpretation of the global or multinational approach to retail internationalization as two totally independent options is naïve. We are often told that 'retail is detail'; if so, then local market detail may be the key to success.

Another illustration of the problems of transferring an established position to non-domestic markets is provided by the case of Marks & Spencer. The trials and tribulations of Marks & Spencer's international expansion are well known. It could be argued that these problems arise (paradoxically) from the source of competitive advantage in the domestic

Figure 14.7
Determinants of
international image
Source: McGoldrick (1998).

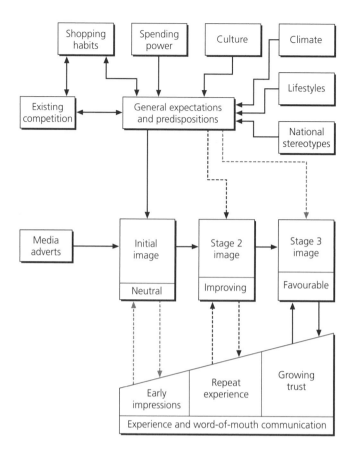

Figure 14.7
Determinants of
international image
Source: McGoldrick (1998).

market. In the UK, we attribute a series of values to Marks & Spencer
built up through (literally) generations of exposure to the company. This
provides the company with an overall image, which is composed of
intangible as well as tangible dimensions. When moving overseas this
poses particular problems; while the tangible elements of image can be
recognized by non-British customers, it is more difficult for them to
relate to the intangible elements. In short, they do not understand or
appreciate Marks & Spencer in the same way as the British. What they
'see' is a variety store selling a range of clothing and food. The levels of
trust or faith that British customers traditionally place in Marks &
Spencer do not immediately travel.

In three separate studies, McGoldrick and Ho (1992), McGoldrick
(1998) and Burt and Carralero-Encinas (2000), the image and position
of Marks & Spencer in the UK, Hong Kong, France and Spain is
considered. Although not directly comparable, these studies have similar
findings. The most positive perceptions of store image are found in the
home market, as is the recognition that both time in the market (i.e.,
exposure to the company) and relative competition (i.e., reference points
for consumers) determine image and position. McGoldrick (1998)
suggests a model for new market entrants for how image will change
over time (Fig. 14.7).

Business distance in ...	USA	Taiwan
Retail mix/ retail format	HRM practices more centralized than in France; different product range; aspects of format (car park/opening hours) not innovative; price competition already strong	Locations very different (in-town/ catchment areas); high cost of land so smaller stores; staff culture different (issues of responsibility and control)
Channel management	Relationships with local retail management/partners a problem (e.g. Leclerc); no scale in the buying process; shorter payment delays	90% local suppliers but very passive, no brand advertising; scope to develop retail brands limited; unorganized but flexible suppliers
Consumer environment	One stop for food/non-food not an issue; use shopping centre not stand-alone locations; 'buy American' campaigns	Different local tastes (e.g. ice cream flavour); limited competition; travel by scooter not car; price advantage a key factor

Figure 14.8 Impact of business distance upon Carrefour's entry to Taiwan and the USA

Source: derived from Dupuis and Prime (1996).

The environmental-fit theme is further explored by Dupuis and Prime (1996), who introduced the idea of a prism effect of 'business distance' which has implications for the original source of competitive advantage. Business distance is created through many of the factors discussed in the macro, task and organizational environments, and may affect the initial competitive advantage in three ways: transparency (no influence), amplification and reduction. In contrasting the failure of the French hypermarket format in the USA with its initial success in Taiwan, they illustrate how business distance has impacted upon the original source of competitive advantage (Fig. 14.8).

An important point made by Dupuis and Prime (1996) is that all retail formats (or companies) have a grounded history, built up over years of operation in the home environment, and the 'fit' with the host environment needs to be understood otherwise 'the decision to export a retail format to another cultural environment may drastically modify its initial competitive advantage'.

SUMMARY

Retailing as an industry is becoming more and more international in its outlook and operations. For companies of all sizes and in all sectors, and at different stages in their corporate histories, internationalization is a strategic option on the agenda. Although we focus primarily on operational internationalization, we should not forget that internationalization takes many forms; consumer spending, specific management functions and retail concept are commonly involved. The increased awareness of internationalization, the highly visible moves of major players and niche operators, and experience of the processes involved provide a stimulus to the traditional push and pull motives for internationalization.

Depending upon their available resources, characteristics of the target markets and the desired speed of expansion, retailers have a number of possible entry modes. Franchising, concessions and licensing represent lower-cost options, but with less overall control. Acquisition and self-start entry offer greater control but at higher cost, with joint ventures representing a 'middle course'. Once in the market, strategic positioning may adopt a global stance, or the more adaptive multinational approach.

The lure of foreign markets is attractive. However, implicit in this chapter and in the experiences of several leading domestic chains, is a 'health warning', that retail internationalization is risky. The basic assumption is often what works at home should/will work overseas. It is not as simple as that. Sometimes the increased complexity overextends the company's financial and managerial resources, making it less reactive to local conditions. The underperformance in the new markets and the drain on resources leads to the loss of shareholder value. Figure 14.9 illustrates how retail internationalization can result in either a viscious or a virtuous spiral of events.

In order to reduce the risks of failure in international markets, it is imperative that retailers have a clear understanding of what it is that they are internationalizing, and how the market which they are entering works. Market conditions, market and organizational behaviours can vary quite markedly from country to country. Without this awareness and understanding, many companies will join the long list of major domestic retailers who have failed overseas.

Figure 14.9 Vicious or virtuous spirals

Source: adapted from IGD (2000).

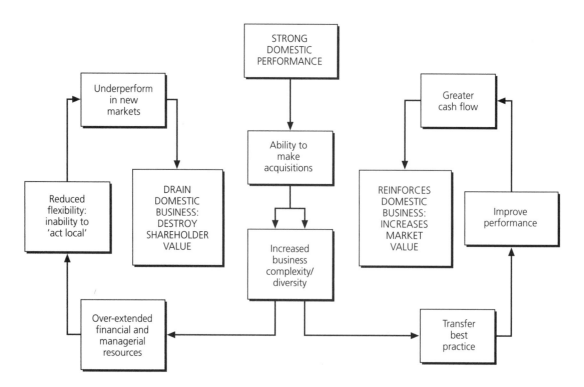

REVIEW QUESTIONS

1 For a retailer of your choice, identify what its competitive advantage would be if it internationalized. Is this suited to a global or multinational approach?

2 Distinguish between the internationalization of retail concepts and the internationalization of retail operations. Provide examples from food and non-food sectors.

3 Is retail internationalization inevitable? Justify your answer.

4 Consider the motives for retail internationalization. Reclassify these as proactive or reactive. What are the implications of such a distinction?

5 Critically assess Treadgold's (1988) classification. Are his categories of cautious internationalists, emboldened internationalists, aggressive internationalists and world powers applicable today?

6 Illustrate how Hofstede's dimensions of cultural difference can assist in the understanding of international retail markets. What are the limitations of these measures?

7 Why do retail markets operate differently in different countries? What are the implications for internationalizing retailers?

8 Can models developed for the manufacturing sector be used to explain the internationalization of retailing? Justify your answer.

9 As well as in the USA, the French hypermarket failed in the UK during the early 1980s. Why?

10 Why do successful domestic retailers fail overseas? Select a case of international failure/withdrawal to illustrate your argument.

11 For an international retailer of your choice, identify the sequence and patterns of international market entry. How do these relate to the theories of minimizing risk.

12 How does retail internationalization relate to the corporate strategy options for growth, discussion in Sect. 4.3?

REFERENCES

Alexander, N. (1990) 'Retailers and international markets: motives for expansion', *International Marketing Review*, **7** (4), 75–85.

Alexander, N. (1995) 'UK retail expansion in North America and Europe: a strategic dilemma', *Journal of Retailing and Consumer Services*, **2** (2), 75–82.

Alexander, N. and H. Myers (1999) 'European retail expansion in South East Asia', *European Business Review*, **99** (2), 91–104.

Alexander, N. and H. Myers (2000) 'The retail internationalisation process', *International Marketing Review*, **17** (4/5), 334–353.

Bailey, J., C. Clarke-Hill and T. Robinson (1995) 'Towards a taxonomy of international retail alliances', *Service Industries Journal*, **15** (4), 25–41.

Baret, C., J. Gadrey and C. Gallouj (1999) 'France, Germany, Great Britain: the organisation of working time in large retail stores', *European Journal of Industrial Relations*, **5** (1), 27–48.

Bilkey, W.J. and G. Tesar (1997) 'The export behaviour of smaller-sized Wisconsin manufacturing firms', *Journal of International Business Studies*, **8** (1), 209–231.

Brown, S. and S. Burt (1992) 'Conclusion—retail internationalisation: past imperfect, future imperative', *European Journal of Marketing*, **26** (8/9), 80–87.

Burt, S. (1986) 'The Carrefour Group—the first 25 years', *International Journal of Retailing*, **1** (3), 54–78.

Burt, S. (1989) 'Trends and management issues in European retailing', *International Journal of Retailing*, **4** (4), 1–97.

Burt, S. (1991) 'Trends in the internationalisation of grocery retailing: the European experience', *International Review of Retail, Distribution and Consumer Research*, **1** (4), 487–515.

Burt, S. and J. Carralero-Encinas (2000) 'The role of store image in retail internationalisation', *International Marketing Review*, **17** (4/5), 433–453.

Burt, S. and L. Sparks (1995) 'Performance in food retailing: a cross-national consideration and comparison of retail margins', *British Journal of Management*, **8**, 138–150.

Buzzell, R.D. (1968) 'Can you standardise international marketing?', *Harvard Business Review*, **46** (6), 102–123.

Cavusgil, T.S. (1980) 'On the internationalisation process of firms', *European Research*, **8** (6), 273–281.

Cavusgil, T.S. (1984) 'Organisational characteristics associated with export activity', *Journal of Management Studies*, **21** (1), 3–50.

Clarke, I. and P. Rimmer (1997) 'The anatomy of retail internationalisation: Diamaru's decision to invest in Melbourne, Australia', *Service Industries Journal*, **17** (3), 361–382.

Davies, K. (1993) 'Trade barriers in East and South East Asia: the implications for retailers', *International Review of Retail Distribution and Consumer Research*, **13** (1), 345–365.

Davies, K. (1994) 'Foreign investment in the retail sector of the People's Republic of China', *Columbia Journal of World Business*, **29** (3), 56–69.

Davies, K. and F. Fergusson (1995) 'The international activities of Japanese retailers', *Service Industries Journal*, **15** (4), 97–117.

Davies, B. and P. Jones (1993) 'International activity of Japanese department stores', *Service Industries Journal*, **13** (1), 126–132.

Davies, R.L. (1989) *Retail Planning in the European Community*, Farnborough, Saxon House.

Davies, R.L. (1995) *Retail Planning Policies in Western Europe*, Routledge, London.

Dawson, J.A. (1982) *Commercial Distribution in Europe*, Croom Helm, London.

Dawson, J.A. (1993) 'The internationalisation of retailing', in *Retail Change: Contemporary Issues*, R.D.F. Bromley and C.J. Thomas (eds), UCL Press, London, pp. 15–40.

Dawson, J.A. (1994) 'Internationalisation of retailing operations', *Journal of Marketing Management*, **10**, 267–282.

Dawson, J.A. (2001) 'Strategy and opportunism in European retail internationalisation'. *British Journal of Management*, **12** (4), pp. 253–266.

Dawson, J.A and S. Burt (1998) 'European retailing: dynamics, restructuring and development issues', in *The New Europe*, D. Pinder (ed.), Wiley, London, pp. 157–176.

Dawson, J.A. and T. Sato (1983) ' Controls over the development of large stores in Japan', *Service Industries Journal*, **3** (2), 136–145.

Doherty, A.M. (2000) 'Factors influencing international retailers market entry mode strategy: qualitative evidence from the UK fashion sector', *Journal of Marketing Management*, **16** (1–3), 223–245.

Dunning, J.H. (1981) *International Production and the Multinational Enterprise*, Allen and Unwin, London,

Dunning, J.H. (1988) 'The eclectic paradigm of international production: a restatement and some possible extensions', *Journal of International Business Studies*, **19**, 1–31.

Dunning, J.H. (1993) *The Globalisation of Business*, Routledge, London.

Dupuis, M. and N. Prime (1996) 'Business distance and global retailing: a model for analysis of key success/failure factors', *International Journal of Retail & Distribution Management*, **24** (11), 30–38.

Fernie, J. (1995) 'International comparisons of supply chain management in grocery retailing', *Service Industries Journal*, **15** (4), 134–147.

Fernie, J and F.R. Pierrel (1996) 'Own branded in the UK and French grocery markets', *Journal of Product and Brand Management*, **5** (3), 48–59.

Fréry, F. (1997) 'The Benetton nebula', in *European Cases in Retailing*, M. Dupuis and J.A. Dawson (eds), Blackwell Business, Oxford.

Gadry, J. and F. Jany-Catrice (2000) ' The retail sector: why so many jobs in America and so few in France?', *Service Industries Journal*, **20** (4), 21–32.

GEA (1994) *Supplier-Retailer Collaboration in Supply Chain Management*, Coca-Cola Retailing Research Group, Europe, Project V.

Gielen, K. and M. G. Dekimpe (2001) 'Do international entry decisions of retail chains matter in the long run?', *International Journal of Research in Marketing*, **18** (3), 235–259.

Godley, A and S. Fletcher (2000) 'Foreign entrants into British retailing, 1850–1994', *International Marketing Review*, **17** (4/5), 392–400.

Goldman, A. (1981) 'Transfer of a retailing technology into the less developed countries: the supermarket case', *Journal of Retailing*, **57** (2), 5–29.

Goldman, A. (2001) 'The transfer of retail formats into developing economies: the example of China', *Journal of Retailing*, **77**, 221–241.

Hakansson, H. (1982) *International Marketing and Purchasing of Industrial Goods: An Interaction Approach*, Wiley, London.

Hamill, J. and J. Crosbie (1990) 'British retail acquisition in the US', *International Journal of Retail & Distribution Management*, **18** (5), 15–20.

Helfferich, E., M. Hinfelaar and H. Kasper (1997) 'Towards a clear terminology on international retailing', *International Review of Retail Distribution and Consumer Research*, **7** (3), 287–307.

Ho, S.C. and J.M. Sin (1987) 'International transfer of retail and technology: the successful case of convenience stores in Hong Kong', *International Journal of Retailing*, **2** (3), 36–48.

Hofstede, G. (1980) *Culture's Consequences: International Differences in Work-Related Values*, Sage, Beverly Hills, CA.

Hofstede, G. (1992) 'Motivation, leadership and organization: do American theories apply abroad?', in *International Management Behaviour*, H. Lane and J. Distefano (eds), PWS-Kent, Boston, MA, pp. 98–122.

Hollander, S.C. (1970) *Multinational Retailing*, MSU, East Lansing, MI.

Hughes, A. (1996) 'Retail restructuring and the strategic significance of food retailers own-labels: a UK–USA comparison', *Environment and Planning A*, **28**, 2201–2226.

IGD (2000) *Global Retailing: The Future*, Institute of Grocery Distribution, Watford.

IGD (2001a) *European Grocery Retailing 2001*, Institute of Grocery Distribution, Watford.

IGD (2001b) *International Retailer Profiles: Carrefour*, Institute of Grocery Distribution, Watford.

Jackson, G.I. (1976) *British Retailers' Expansion into Europe*, unpublished PhD thesis, UMIST, Manchester.

Jefferys, J.B. and D. Knee (1962) *Retailing in Europe: Present Structure and Future Trends*, Macmillan, London.

Johanson, J. and J.E. Vahlne (1977) 'The internationalisation process of the firm: a model of knowledge development and increasing foreign market commitment', *Journal of International Business Studies*, **8** (1), 23–32.

Johanson, J. and J.E. Vahlne (1990) 'The mechanism of internationalisation', *International Marketing Review*, **7** (4), 11–24.

Johanson, J. and P.F. Wiedersheim-Paul (1975) 'The internationalisation of the firm: four Swedish cases', *Journal of Management Studies*, **12** (3), 305–322.

Johnson, M. and B. Allen (1994) 'Taking the English "apple" to Spain: the Adams experience', *International Journal of Retail & Distribution Management*, **22** (7), 3–9.

Kacker, M. (1985) *Transatlantic Trends in Retailing*, Quorum, Westport, CT.

Kacker, M. (1988) 'International flow of retailing know-how. Bridging the technology gap in distribution', *Journal of Retailing*, **64** (1), 41–67.

Kaikati, J. (2000) 'The large-scale retail store law: one of the thorny issues in the Kodak-Fuji case', in *Japanese Distribution Strategy*, M.R. Czinkota and M. Kotabe (eds), Thompson, pp. 154–163.

Laaksonen, H. (1994) *Own Brands in Food Retailing across Europe*, Oxford, OXIRM.

Laulajainen, R. (1991a) 'International expansion of an apparel retailer—Hennes and Mauritz of Sweden', *Zeitschrift für Wirtschaftsgeographie*, **35** (1), 1–15.

Laulajainen, R. (1991b) 'Two retailers go global: the geographical dimension', *International Review of Retail, Distribution and Consumer Research*, **1** (5), 607–626.

Levitt, T. (1983) 'The globalisation of markets', *Harvard Business Review*, **61** (May–June), 92–102.

Liu, H. and P.J. McGoldrick (1996) 'International retail sourcing: trend, nature and process', *Journal of International Marketing*, **4** (4), 9–33.

Martenson, R. (1987) 'Is standardisation of marketing feasible in culture-bound industries? A European case study', *International Marketing Review*, Autumn, 7–17.

Martensen, R. (1992) *The Future Role of Brands in the European Grocery Market*, University of Gothenburg, Gothenburg.

McGoldrick, P. (1995) 'Introduction to international retailing', in *International Retailing: Trends and Strategies*, P.J. McGoldrick and G. Davies (eds), Pitman, London, pp. 1–14.

McGoldrick, P. (1998) 'Spatial and temporal shifts in international retail images', *Journal of Business Research*, **42**, 189–196.

McGoldrick, P.J. and D. Blair (1995) 'International market appraisal and positioning', in *International Retailing: Trends and Strategies*, P.J. McGoldrick and G. Davies (eds), Pitman, London, pp. 168–190.

McGoldrick, P. and S. L. Ho (1992) ' International positioning: Japanese department stores in Hong Kong', *European Journal of Marketing*, **26** (8/9), 65–83.

Moore, C. (1998) 'L'internationalisation du Prêt-à-porter: the case of Kookai and Morgan's entry into the UK fashion market', *Journal of Fashion Marketing and Management*, **2** (2), 153–158.

Moore, C., J. Fernie and S. Burt (2000) 'Brands without boundaries: the internationalisation of the designer retailer's brand', *European Journal of Marketing*, **34** (8), 919–937.

Muniz-Martinez, N. (1998) 'The internationalisation of European retailers in America : the US experience', *International Journal of Retail & Distribution Management*, **26** (1), 29–37.

O'Grady, S. and H. W. Lane (1997) 'Culture: an un-noticed barrier to Canadian retail performance in the USA', *Journal of Retailing and Consumer Services*, **4** (3), 159–170.

Paché, G. (1995) 'Speculative inventories in the food retailing industry: a comment on French practices', *International Journal of Retail and Distribution Management*, **23** (12), 36–42.

Pellegrini, L. (1994) 'Carrefour: development of the retailer brand', in *Cases in Retail Management*, P.J. McGoldrick (ed.), London, Pitman, pp. 248–258.

Peterson, B. and L.S. Welch (2000) 'International retailing operations: downstream entry and control via franchising', *International Business Review*, **9**, 479–496.

Porter, M.E. (1985) *Competitive Advantage: Creating and Sustaining Superior Performance*, Free Press, New York.

PricewaterhouseCoopers (2001) 'Food for thought', *PricewaterhouseCoopers Retail and Consumer Worlds*, **38** (2), special insert.

Quelch, J.A. and E.J. Hoff (1986) 'Customising global marketing', *Harvard Business Review*, 64 (May–June), 59–68.

Quinn, B. (1998) 'Towards a framework for the study of franchising as an operating mode for international retail companies', *International Review of Retail Distribution and Consumer Research*, **8** (4), 445–467.

Quinn, B. (1999) 'The temporal context of UK retailers' motives for international expansion', *Service Industries Journal*, **19** (2), 102–117.

Quinn, B. and A.M. Doherty (2000) 'Power and control in international retail franchising: evidence from theory and practice', *International Management Review*, **17** (4/5), 354–372.

Salmon, W.J. and A. Tordjman (1989) 'The internationalisation of retailing', *International Journal of Retailing*, **4** (2), 3–16.

Shackleton, R. (1996) 'Retailer internationalization: a culturally constructed phenomenon', in *Retailing, Consumption and Capital*, N. Wrigley and M. Lowe (eds), Longman Group, London, pp. 137–156.

Simpson, E.M. and D.I. Thorpe (1995) 'A conceptual model of strategic consideration for international retail expansion', *Service Industries Journal*, **15** (4), 16–24.

Simpson, E.M. and D.I. Thorpe (1999) 'A speciality stores perspective on retail internationalisation: a case study', *Journal of Retailing and Consumer Services*, **6**, 45–53.

Sorenson, R.Z. and E.U. Wiechmann (1975) 'How multinationals view marketing standardisation', *Harvard Business Review*, **53** (May–June), 38–54, 166–167.

Sparks, L. (1995) 'Reciprocal retail internationalisation : the Southland Corporation, Ito-Yokado and 7-Eleven convenience stores', *Service Industries Journal*, **15** (4), 57–96.

Sternquist, B. (1997) 'International expansion of US retailers', *International Journal of Retail Distribution Management*, **25** (8), 262–268.

Sternquist, B. (1998) *International Retailing*, Fairchild Publications, New York.

Tordjman, A.D. (1988) 'The French hypermarket: could it be developed in the States?', *Retail and Distribution Management*, **16** (4), 14–16.

Treadgold, A.D. (1988) 'Retailing without frontiers', *Retail and Distribution Management*, **16** (6), 8–12.

Treadgold, A.D. (1990) 'The emerging internationalisation of retailing: present status and future strategies', *Irish Marketing Review*, **5** (2), 11–27.

Treadgold, A.D. (1991), 'Dixons and Laura Ashley: different routes to international growth', *International Journal of Retail and Distribution Management*, **19** (4), 13–19.

Truitt, N.S. (1984) 'Mass merchandising and economic development: Sears, Roebuck and Co in Mexico and Peru', in *Service Industries and Economics Development*, R.K. Shelp, J.C. Stephenson, N.S. Truitt and B. Wasow (eds), New York, Praeger, pp. 49–113.

Vida, I. and A. Fairhurst (1998) 'International expansion of retail firms: a theoretical approach for future investigations', *Journal of Retail and Consumer Services*, **5** (2), 143–151.

Williams, D.E. (1991) 'Differential firm advantages and retailer internationalisation', *International Journal of Retail Distribution Management*, **19** (4), 3–12.

Williams, D.E. (1992) 'Motives for retailer internationalisation: their impact, structure and implications', *Journal of Marketing Management*, **8**, 269–285.

Wrigley, N. (1989) 'The lure of the USA: further reflections on the internationalisation of British grocery retailing capital', *Environment and Planning A*, **21**, 283–288.

Wrigley, N. (1997a) 'British food retailing capital in the USA: Part 1: Sainsbury and the Shaw's experience', *International Journal of Retail & Distribution Management*, **25** (1), 7–21.

Wrigley, N. (1997b) 'British food retail capital in the USA: Part 2: giant prospects?', *International Journal of Retail & Distribution Management*, **25** (2–3), 48–58.

Wrigley, N. (2000) 'Strategic market behaviour in the internationalisation of food retailing: interpreting the third wave of Sainsbury's diversification', *European Journal of Marketing*, **34** (8), 891–981.

Yoshino, M.Y. (1966) 'International opportunities for American retailers', *Journal of Retailing*, **42**, 1–10.

Fifteen

E-tail Marketing

INTRODUCTION Electronic commerce has been a long time coming. Commentators were predicting the arrival of electronic shopping as long as 35 years ago (according to Burke, 1997). In 1980, Rosenberg and Hirschman presented vivid scenarios of retailing without stores. However, there have been many false dawns for e-tailing; Davies and Reynolds (1988) listed a series of North American and European schemes that were withdrawn, having failed to meet expectations.

Between 1998 and 2000, electronic commerce moved from the back burner to the front as the dot-com boom appeared to blind both executives and investors alike to long-term business realities (Brache and Webb, 2000; de Kare-Silver, 2001). Indeed, the long-heralded new economy appeared to have been hijacked by those seeking short-term gain. John Doerr (2000) distinguishes between mercenaries and missionaries during that period:

> *Mercenaries focus on their competitors and financial statements; missionaries focus on their customers and value statements. Mercenaries are motivated by the lust for making money; missionaries, while recognizing the importance of money, are fundamentally driven by the desire to make meaning.*

The harsh adjustment that followed the re-evaluation of technology stocks from April 2000 prompted more sober reflections upon the opportunities and economics of e-tailing. Data from research into global retail performance (Fig. 15.1) highlights the precipitous decline of B2C e-commerce stocks from April 2000 to March 2001. However, what is also indicated is the recent (since April 2001) slow recovery of the remaining stocks, alongside bricks and mortar businesses and the world price index in general. Early statistics on the penetration of e-commerce in the USA and across Europe appeared to bear out the gloomiest interpretation of the facts. Business-to-consumer e-commerce in the USA amounted to only 1.01 per cent of retail sales in the fourth quarter of 2000, according to the US Department of Commerce, falling back to

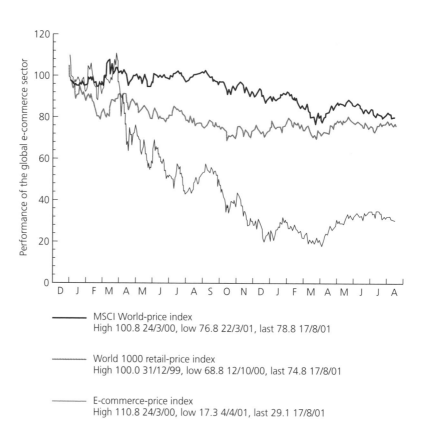

Figure 15.1
Performance of the
global e-commerce
sector, 1999–2001
Source: OXIRM (2001).

MSCI World-price index
High 100.8 24/3/00, low 76.8 22/3/01, last 78.8 17/8/01

World 1000 retail-price index
High 100.0 31/12/99, low 68.8 12/10/00, last 74.8 17/8/01

E-commerce-price index
High 110.8 24/3/00, low 17.3 4/4/01, last 29.1 17/8/01

0.91 per cent in the first quarter of 2001. However, this excluded ticket, travel and financial services sales. The NRF/Forrester Retail Index also showed January 2001 on-line sales little changed from January 2000 levels. UK National Statistics put the value of e-commerce in retail, travel and catering at £7.6 billion (0.27 per cent of sales) in 2000. Similar levels of penetration appear to prevail in France.

Certainly, much overclaim had been associated with the Internet, not least the inference that it brought interactivity to the marketing scene (Deighton, 1997). Personal selling has been offering interactivity in retail settings for centuries; call centres also offer interactions, without the requirement to access the Internet. Likewise, discussion of the 'attention economy' often overlooked the battles that have raged over many decades to win the attention of potential customers (Department of Trade and Industry, 2000a). Porter (2001) concludes that the 'new economy' is in fact the old economy, but with access to new technology. He maintains that, while a new way of conducting business has become available, the fundamentals of competition remain the same. Many commentators have abandoned the term 'new economy'; PricewaterhouseCoopers refer to the 'next economy' (Pricewater-houseCoopers, 2001)

So, as the hype subsides, the hard work gets underway. Gary Hamel (cited by Skapinker, 2000) remarks that:

E is over. That's not saying that electronic business is finished, or that the Internet is about to disappear; 'E' is only over in that we now understand it and need to get on with exploiting it.

The Internet does indeed provide the potential for lower-cost interactivity with customers; it can also deliver digital goods, such as entertainment and software. Most physical goods, however, must be picked, packed and delivered, expensive tasks that consumers have become accustomed to undertaking themselves. Given user-friendly and cheap ways to outsource these tasks, it is not surprising that many more consumers will be tempted. The challenge for the e-tailer is to construct a business model that can provide genuine value and convenience, as well as profitability.

This chapter starts with an overview of the driving forces in the development of e-tailing, notably the adoption of relevant technologies and competitive pressures, as well as some of the regulatory interventions that may affect the character and potential profitability of e-tail ventures. Some of the e-tailing essentials are then reviewed, including convenience, price, the product–service mix, trust and fulfilment. In conclusion, some forecasts and scenarios are examined, notably the convergence of 'clicks and bricks' working in complementary roles.

15.1 Development of B2C E-commerce

The term 'electronic commerce' is frequently used in an ambiguous and misleading way (Department of Trade and Industry, 2000b: de Kare-Silver, 2001) and has no widely accepted definition. This has particularly exercised national statistical offices and census agencies which seek to measure the scale and growth of the phenomenon, since dramatically different estimates of market size may result (OECD, 1998; Office for National Statistics, 2001). European governments are adopting a narrow OECD definition of e-commerce that makes it clear that it is the method by which an order is placed which makes it e-commerce, not the payment itself or the delivery channel employed. The US Bureau of the Census (2001) agrees, defining e-commerce as 'sales of goods and services over the Internet, an extranet, Electronic Data Interchange (EDI) or other online system. Payment may or may not be made online'. This definition nevertheless assumes that payment is made at some point and is focused upon measuring the direct effects of priced transactions, rather than, say, the free flow of information (which might lead indirectly to subsequent purchases on or off line).

It is therefore important to distinguish different forms of electronic commerce from other forms of electronic interaction. A wide spectrum of communications and transactions between individuals, businesses and governments can be mediated through electronic channels (Fig. 15.2): not all of them involve payment. Conventional wisdom has tended to distinguish between electronic commerce between businesses (B2B) and that between consumers and businesses (B2C) as the key components of e-commerce. Figure 15.2 makes it clear that not only governments, but

	Government	Business	Consumer
Government	G2G e.g. co-ordination	G2B e.g. information	G2C e.g. information
Business	B2G e.g. procurement	B2B e.g. e-commerce	B2C e.g. e-commerce
Consumer	C2G e.g. tax compliance	C2B e.g. price comparison	C2C e.g. auction markets

Figure 15.2
E-commerce and broader Internet applications
Source: OECD (2000).

consumers between each other (C2C) and consumers initiating contact with businesses (C2B) can also generate potential e-commerce niches. This chapter is especially concerned with the impact of electronic commerce in the shaded area of Fig. 15.2.

The largely pragmatic definition of the census agencies recognizes the difficulties of measurement and data-gathering from respondents trading in a rapidly changing technological environment: nevertheless, it neglects the potential impact on the conventional retail transaction process and retail market share of electronic commerce. Table 15.1 takes a more explicit marketing and operational stance, in distinguishing between the pre-purchase component of B2C e-commerce, where the focus is upon marketing, and the purchase stage, where the focus is primarily upon operational and logistics issues. In turn, this is distinct from the post-purchase experience, where marketing and logistics considerations once again become relevant. Intermediaries offering pre- and post-purchase information services are clearly in a position to influence consumers' search and evaluation strategies.

Table 15.1 B2C e-commerce and the impact on the conventional retail transaction process
Source: adapted from: Davies and Reynolds (1988).

Stage	Retailer focus	Consumer focus	Substitutions
Pre-purchase	Marketing	▶ Product promotion ▶ Pre-purchase evaluation by consumer ▶ Product availability	Complementing or substituting for conventional advertising and marketing media
Purchase	Operational and logistics	▶ Ordering ▶ Payment	Complementing or substituting for the conventional shopping trip and goods payment systems
Post-purchase	Marketing and logistics	▶ Delivery ▶ After-sales	Complementing or substituting for the retail store

The speed with which consumer markets may be transformed as a result of the introduction of electronic marketing channels, such as the Internet, digital television, mobile data services and convergent interactive media solutions, is heavily dependent upon the interaction of a broad series of forces, the chief of which are summarized in Table 15.2. Many commentators agree that a small number of key driving forces

Area	Selected factors	Elaboration
Consumer acceptance	Ease of access	Fall in price, extent of availability of technical means and reliability of access to electronic channels
	Time poverty	Extent of perceived time poverty among target consumer segments and consequent attractiveness of direct channels to market
	Fashionability	Extent to which electronic channels to market become a 'fashion accessory' among consumers
Technological progress	Convergence/ standardization	Speed of hardware and software standardization
	Interactivity	Extent to which software developments are able to increasingly mimic or enhance conventional retail experiences
	Capacity	Speed with which improvements in bandwidth and compression technology will enhance the speed and reliability of the on-line experience
Competition	Non-traditional competition	Ability of new entrants to stimulate consumer demand and prompt a competitive response by conventional retailers
	Global competition	Extent to which conventional retail internationalization will further complicate choices for conventional retailers seeking growth
	Internal competition	Extent to which e-commerce investment wins out internally in competition with other ways of allocating a company's resources to achieve growth
Legislative and institutional	Free trade	Extent to which harmonization between trade regions exists in respect of electronic commerce transactions
	Infrastructure	Speed of provision of competitive infrastructure, through telecoms deregulation, strategic alliances and partnerships, etc.
	Consumer protection	Existence of uncomplicated, but and trusted and effective pan-regional consumer protection legislation.

Table 15.2 Driving forces affecting the development of B2C e-commerce
Source: Reynolds (1999).

affect the pace of change in the adoption of B2C e-commerce (McGoldrick, 2000; Ody, 1998; OECD, 1998; 2000; Reynolds, 1999).

15.1.1 Technology Adoption

The growth in the availability and fall in the cost of technology has been a key driving force in the growth of e-commerce. 'While it has taken the world population just under 40 years to double in size, it has taken the Internet population just under a year in some countries' (NetValue, 2001). We should remember, nevertheless, that the Internet is still predominantly a phenomenon of the developed world (Fig. 15.3). Penetration levels in the Middle East, Africa, Asia and parts of Latin and South America are still low when compared with Europe, North America and Australasia. Furthermore, while these three economic regions have on average high penetration of Internet use, the variability of usage across Europe is much more of a patchwork quilt.

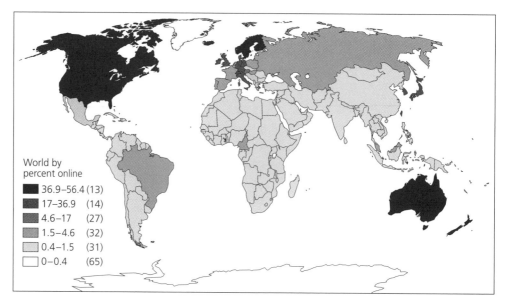

Figure 15.3 Global Internet penetration, December 2000

Source: Morgan Stanley Dean Witter (2001).

According to Internet intelligence business NetValue, Scandinavia continues to lead the rest of Europe and the USA for Internet penetration, with Sweden and Denmark taking first and second places. The USA was in third position, with nearly 52 per cent of households connected, and the UK was in fifth position. Table 15.3 makes it clear that other European countries were far less 'wired' at the end of 2000, for example, France and Spain. The Boston Consulting Group (2000a) found that the European on-line market was diverse but categorizes the participants as 'early adopters', 'awakening giants', 'middleweights' and 'small but connected'. More recently the gap appears to have closed even faster, with, for example, France experiencing a 76 per cent growth in numbers of households connected from December 1999 to December 2000, according to NetValue (2001).

The demographics of Internet connectivity reveal an evolutionary picture, in which the US market represents maturity, possessing the most representative mix of gender, age and occupation. Eighty per cent of US households have been on line for more than 12 months, for example. In Spain, the figure is less than 50 per cent. Less mature Internet markets around the world tend to be younger, with fewer women but more professionals and students, and this is reflected in the comparative demographics of on-line purchasers between Europe and the USA (Table 15.4).

It is this dynamic backdrop that provides the context for retailers' development of electronic commerce, but the rate of growth in e-commerce usage by on-line consumers itself appears to be moving even faster than Internet penetration, and in a somewhat different way. Early observations were that Europe as a whole was some 2–4 years behind US levels of electronic commerce activity, but was catching up fast. A comparison with the USA made by the Boston Consulting Group in

Country	USA	UK	Germany	France	Spain
Total households connected	53 488 000 (51.6% of population)	8 487 000 (35.9% of population)	9 976 000 (29.2% of population)	4 718 000 (19.6% of population)	2 031 000 (15.6% of population)
Less than 6 months	11.5%	20.8%	23.3%	24.3%	33.1%
Between 6 months and 1 year	8.3%	15.4%	20.8%	16.7%	17.6%
More than 1 year	79.0%	63.7%	55.6%	59.1%	49.4%
Gender breakdown:					
Men on line	50.6%	59.9%	59.2%	62.0%	68.7%
Women on line	49.4%	40.1%	40.8%	38.0%	31.3%
Men general population	48.9%	49.2%	48.9%	48.7%	49.0%
Women general population	51.1%	50.8%	51.1%	51.3%	51.0%
Age breakdown:					
14 and under	6.9%	5.1%	1.7%	3.3%	4.3%
15–24	17.6%	25.4%	24.9%	25.8%	35.3%
25–34	20.2%	19.0%	25.2%	24.2%	24.4%
35–49	30.8%	31.2%	31.0%	31.0%	28.5%
50–64	16.5%	13.2%	15.1%	12.3%	7.0%
65+	7.9%	6.1%	2.1%	3.4%	0.4%
Occupation:					
Students	17.2%	20.6%	25.8%	24.0%	37.4%
Managers and professionals	27.7%	30.6%	18.6%	35.5%	16.3%
Other non-manual employees	14.9%	16.3%	31.1%	18.1%	30.1%
Manual workers	9.3%	4.7%	5.7%	2.5%	2.6%
Non-working and retired	23.1%	19.1%	13.9%	18.0%	9.4%
Business proprietors	7.4%	8.4%	3.3%	1.6%	3.4%

Table 15.3 Comparative Internet demographics, selected countries, December 2000.
Source: NetValue (2001).

Table 15.4
Demographics of on-line purchasers
Source: adapted from: IGD (2001) based upon ProActive International 'Internet Monitor'.

		% ever purchased on line Europe	% ever purchased on line USA
Gender:			
	Male	14.3	35.9
	Female	6.7	31.2
Age:			
	15–24	13.0	35.8
	25–34	16.0	41.3
	35–44	13.6	42.1
	45–54	11.8	36.9
	55+	3.1	18.0
Income:			
	Low	4.0	13.2
	Middle	11.5	36.2
	High	23.1	60.6

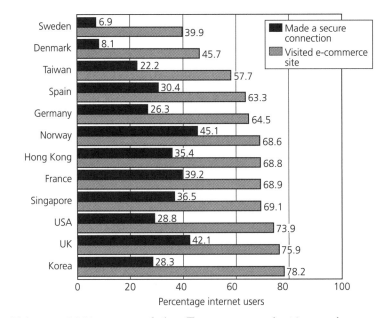

Figure 15.4 E-commerce by market, May 2001

Source: NetValue (2001).

February 2000 suggested that Europe was only 18 months to two years behind (Boston Consulting Group, 2000a). By the spring of 2001, accessing of secure sites (as a surrogate measure of making a purchase) showed some very different geographical patterns of patronage compared with the growth of the Internet infrastructure itself (Fig. 15.4), with the UK, Norway, France and Spain having higher conversion rates than the USA, but with Sweden and Denmark lagging behind. Cornet et al. (2000) are not surprised by this state of affairs:

> *The very idea of following in the footsteps of the United States was probably inaccurate anyway: for a variety of reasons, e-commerce in Europe was always likely to follow a different course. For one thing, the technological and cultural infrastructures are much more heterogeneous in Europe than they are in the United States. Moreover, European players have had the benefit of hindsight from seeing what has succeeded and failed in the United States. The later entry of European companies into e-commerce also gives them the advantage of applying technology that has advanced considerably over the past two years (Cornet et al., 2000).*

Technical platforms other than personal computers provide alternative routes to growth for retailers engaging in electronic commerce. A growing proportion of opinion over the last five years has seen television, or what television may become, as playing a potentially central role in delivering the Internet to the home (KPMG, 1997; Thompson and Rifredi, 1996). The Yankee Group, for example, predicts that 81.2 million European households will have interactive services via digital television by 2005, while 80.6 million households will have PC-based Internet access (Yankee Group, 2001). Strategy Analytics forecast that the global figure will be just 38 million homes (Strategy Analytics, 2001). Yankee Group call this segment the 'Third Wave Adopters', who may not be able to afford a PC, but have an interest in gaining access to the new basic interactive services available over interactive television, such as e-mail, banking, shopping, gambling and travel services.

Wade and McKechnie (1999) itemized a set of six factors that they believe are likely to affect the adoption of interactive digital television services (Table 15.5). It is interesting to note that, in the UK at least, a number of the factors with identifiably positive impacts have been successfully addressed at the time of writing: this observation would tend to support the optimistic forecasts of the analysts.

Factor	Implication for home shopping	Impact
Relative advantage (additional benefits compared with alternatives)	Convenience and accessibility of 24-hour shopping	Positive
Compatibility (with existing norms, values and behaviour)	Need for new equipment (set-top decoders) and product replacement rates for television equipment	Negative
	Changes in pre- and post-purchase information search (on prices and suppliers) but otherwise compatible with existing home shopping behaviour	Positive
Complexity (offset by ease of operation)	Lower perceived complexity than PC and similar to cable and satellite	Positive
Divisibility (trialability on a limited basis)	Local trials being conducted in the UK Possibility of subsidized set-top boxes	Positive
Communicability (ease of communicating benefits)	Much depends on way new technology is presented in press and by sales people to the general public.	Positive
Perceived risk (financial and social risk)	Concerns about security of on-line payments and of incompatible systems; trust in advertisers and vendors	Negative

Table 15.5 Factors affecting the rate of adoption of interactive digital television technology

Source: Wade and McKechnie, (1999); after Gatignon and Robertson (1985) and Rogers (1962).

Despite this optimistic assessment, however, use for e-shopping may be incompatible with existing motivations for watching the television. In addition to acquiring information and knowledge, Rubin (1984) identifies these motivations as relaxation, arousal, companionship and escape. Lin (1999) demonstrates that the motives for television viewing are not good predictors of on-line service adoption, at least in the USA. Lee and Lee (1995) also hypothesized that the social characteristics of television viewing is quite the opposite of the individualistic behaviour associated with PC use:

Television requires viewing from a distance and ... is usually a social activity. Interaction with TV is likely to involve some more advanced version of the remote control. The inherently interactive computer, on the other hand, is a keyboard-oriented appliance with a high resolution screen used by one person. We expect that each medium will take on some of the characteristics of the other but that the essential group-viewing-from-a-distance-with-a-remote-control versus one-person-up-close-with-a-keyboard difference will remain (Lee and Lee, 1995).

Nevertheless, Keeling et al. (2001a) illustrate that, although social factors may have negative effects on the use of the television for e-commerce in the short term, in effect, use is only postponed and motivated users 'find a time' to complete transactions. Technological developments, such as, split screen and 'screen in screen' capabilities that allow viewers to have two television channels displayed at the same time, are likely to further mitigate these effects.

Research undertaken on the UK market by Jupiter MMXI, while it agrees with other commentators on the likely exponential growth of interactive digital television (suggesting that over half of all UK households will use digital television by 2005), nevertheless cautions that retailers' revenues through the channel will be on average lower than those made by PC users. This is attributed to consumers purchasing higher-cost items like holidays, cars and electronics via their PCs while lower-cost impulse purchases for items like CDs and takeaway food, will tend to be made through interactive television (Jupiter MMXI, 2001). But it also remarks that, contrary to Lee and Lee's findings in the US, 20 per cent of UK interactive television households use e-mail via their keyboards regularly. Interactive digital television services at the moment look, though, rather different to PC-based platforms and provide correspondingly different commercial opportunities for retailers (Table 15.6).

Table 15.6 Interactive television capabilities

Source: Mayer et al. (2001).

Capability	Description
Electronic programme guide	Interactive application that enables user to review schedule of available video content
Enhanced broadcasting	Interactive, graphical content overlaid on regularly displayed video content
	Interactive content that may be synchronized with video (say, for an advertisement) or available on command
Internet on television	Internet content; adjusted for television's lower resolution and display capabilities; shown on television
Near video-on-demand	Video content with run times staggered at frequent intervals on multiple channels
Video-on-demand	Video content accessible at any time
Walled garden	Portal-like suite of Internet television applications that usually includes communications, gaming, commercial and customer-care applications
	Restriction of user to applications provided through operator

Convergence is therefore likely to be slow in coming:

> *the competitive dynamics—including the ways people use PCs and TVs when they are enabled for broadband, the extent of consumers' willingness to pay for added services, and the individual technologies—are so dissimilar that two dramatically different markets will coexist over the next few years (Mayer et al., 2001).*

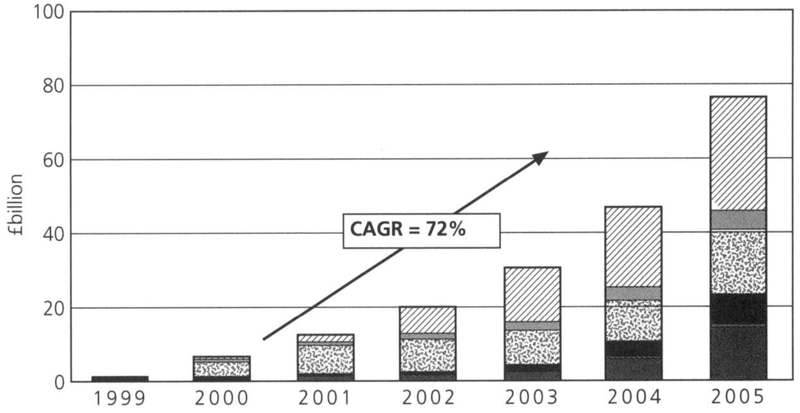

		1999	2000	2001	2002	2003	2004	2005	CAGR*
	Data traffic revenues	0.31	0.69	1.58	6.65	14.03	21.18	30.80	**115%**
	M-workforce revenues	0.07	0.23	0.63	1.25	1.78	3.08	5.10	**104%**
	M-CRM revenues	0.0	0.0	0.01	0.02	0.07	0.22	0.55	**172%**
	M-SCM revenues	0.0	0.0	0.0	0.01	0.03	0.12	0.35	**227%**
	M-communications revenues	2.15	4.38	7.90	8.91	9.30	11.05	16.12	**40%**
	M-transaction revenues	0.03	0.21	0.31	0.54	1.45	3.58	7.03	**148%**
	M-information	0.03	0.06	0.12	0.27	0.42	0.68	1.06	**81%**
	M-entertainment revenues	0.37	0.91	1.67	1.87	2.83	6.62	15.41	**86%**
	Total in £billion	**2.96**	**6.48**	**12.22**	**19.52**	**29.92**	**46.52**	**76.38**	

*Based on different base years

Figure 15.5 Mobile data revenues in Europe, split by revenue source
Source: Durlacher, (2000).

Finally, consumer adoption of mobile devices is of interest to those retailers able to identify value added content or data services relevant to mobile consumers. This is likely to be difficult; certainty here is even less apparent. While the rhetoric suggests that so-called 'third generation' mobile technology will enable new mobile transactional services, the network service providers not only labour under a millstone from the costs of their land-grabbing of operating licences, but are facing a plethora of technical standards from which to develop such services (Durlacher, 2000). There is no guarantee that retail transactions will be a 'killer application', it is just as likely to be betting or share-trading (Fig. 15.5). The phenomenal growth of mobile phone ownership, and the usage of phones in Europe and the Far East during the past two years for text messaging and crude data services, nevertheless serve to create an enormously attractive potential market.

Some commentators are optimistic about the commercial potential of these market segments, which is seen to be particularly attractive in Europe and Japan, with the US for once lagging behind:

> *for the consumer or worker on the move, the impact of mobile communications could be just as great. Consider this: by 2005 more people in the world will have mobile phones than TVs, let alone PCs, which means that mobile data phones could be the means by which most people discover the Internet and use interactive services (Kehoe, 2000).*

Research on the modelling of e-commerce use is very much in its early stages, but customer adoption or rejection of electronic shopping technology can be considered analogous to the adoption of other innovations. Those seeking to understand electronic shopping behaviour at an individual level have, therefore, frequently applied theoretical perspectives previously used in the study of technology adoption more generally. These include the Diffusion of Innovations (DOI) concept (e.g. Rogers, 1995), the Technology Acceptance Model (TAM) (e.g. Davis et al., 1989) and the Theory of Planned Behaviour (e.g. Ajzen, 1988).

The common core of these theories is that perceptions of the likely outcomes and complexity of the technology determine usage. The TAM is the most parsimonious, explaining technology adoption simply as a function the perceived usefulness and ease of use of a system. Features external to the model, such as system features or individual characteristics, are represented in their effects on user beliefs (see Fig. 15.6). The DOI literature (e.g. Rogers, 1995) identifies five key components influencing the acceptance of innovations. Two of these, relative advantage and complexity are comparable to usefulness and ease of use. The other three, compatibility, trialability and observability, introduce social components.

The TAM has been successfully applied to the use of Internet systems (Lederer et al., 2000; Lin and Lu, 1998; Moon and Kim, 2001). Perceived usefulness has repeatedly been shown to be the strongest influence on intentions and actual use of the Internet and e-commerce. Nevertheless, in the case of the adoption of electronic shopping and services, researchers have found more complex models helpful in providing extra clarification of usage. In particular, social and situational factors and prior behaviour have been found to have significant impact (e.g. Eastlick and Lotz, 1999; Keeling et al., 2001a; Vijayasarathy and Jones, 2000). These effects have been found to be important across e-commerce platforms: for example, in two studies of kiosk use incorporating the DOI attributes into the TAM, Keeling et al. (2001b) found that compatibility and normative influences significantly increased the explanation of intentions to use kiosks again.

Figure 15.6 A modified Technology Acceptance Model

Note: [1] additional to basic TAM.

Source: Keeling et al. (2001b).

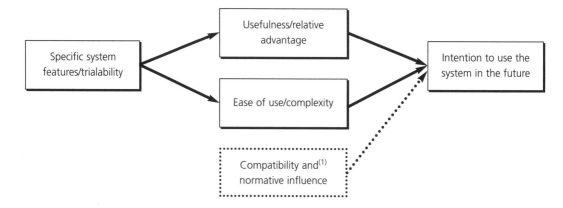

15.1.2 Competitive Pressures

Despite the potential of a range of technical routes to market, conventional retailers were initially slow to react to the threat that many perceived the Internet to hold to their traditional ways of doing business (de Kare-Silver, 2001; Morganosky, 1997; Reynolds, 1999). There were many other areas of potential retail investment competing internally for funds; these included conventional expansion, both domestically and internationally, and diversification into new formats or businesses. As a result, it has been suggested that European retailers in particular suffered from the early international expansion of US start-up on-line businesses. Research conducted by the Boston Consulting Group (2000a), for example, found that US companies concentrating solely on the business-to-consumer market already had a 20 per cent share of that market in Europe. The researchers were particularly critical of so-called 'legacy' (traditional off-line) businesses, which had focused on national markets for electronic commerce growth, while the new entrants had been able to develop increasingly pan-European businesses. As discussed above, most European and North American retail businesses are largely nationally oriented. Many internet-based US retailers still tend to think of Europe as a single undifferentiated market.

As electronic commerce moved up the retail chief executive officer's (CEO's) agenda, it reflected the threat perceived by conventional retailers both from start-up on-line businesses and more conventional competitors developing a web presence (Table 15.7). Nor were these conventional competitors always large retail businesses. Reynolds (1998) reported on the activity of independent Yorkshire, UK, butcher Jack Scaife, who was able to use a Euro 100 000 investment to generate up to 20 per cent of the business's sales on line, half of which was from overseas. Nor were they always retailers per se. Chircu and Kauffman (1999) suggested that a very wide range of new players had the potential to 'disintermediate' conventional value chains, notably ones within which retailers had been traditionally dominant.

Table 15.7 E-tailing and the retail CEO's agenda

Source: Higgins (2001).

Issue	Rank 2001	Rank 2000	Rank 1999	Rank 1998	Rank 1997
Retail internationalization	1	3	1	4	3
Customer loyalty and retention	2	1	2	2	2
B2B exchanges	3	–	–	–	–
Food safety	4	5	11	–	–
Efficient consumer response	5	4	3	1	1
Euro	6	9	6	6	–
E–tailing	7	2	9	7	6
Retailer as a brand	8	6	5	–	–
The store offer	9	7	4	10	–
Visibility/accountability	10	10	–	–	–

Truly international retailers, however, began to show a more aggressive approach to e-business, which is linked to their concerns over growth through consolidation and has already begun to affect their business structures (Reynolds, 2001)). By 2000, e-tailing ranked second on the CIES table of grocery CEOs' concerns after customer loyalty and retention, although not always for good strategic reasons, as Murphy's research confirmed (Murphy, 1998). 'There is an element of keeping up with the Joneses here. None of us wants to be left behind just in case the whole thing unexpectedly goes up like a rocket' (UK retailer quoted in KPMG, 1996). Following the crash in technology stocks and the demise of many overvalued start-up businesses, many established retailers breathed a sigh of relief and moved on to what they regarded as more tangible sources of profitability. The CIES rankings showed business-to-consumer e-commerce plunging to a poor seventh earlier in 2001.

Despite this return to the conventional agenda, the evidence is that the better off-line retailers have proved somewhat more proficient than other sectors at exploiting the opportunities of new electronic channels to market. Recent research undertaken for KPMG, for example, shows that e-business in the UK is not having a uniform impact and, in fact, has become somewhat polarized. The researchers distinguish generally between businesses that can be regarded as 'e-pioneers', 'e-followers' and 'e-laggards' (see Table 15.8) and remark that, while e-pioneers are to be found in all industry sectors, it is retailing which is characterized by an 'all-or-nothing' approach to e-business (Fig. 15.7).

Table 15.8 Stages of e-volution

Source: KPMG (2001).

E-group	Processes adopted
E-pioneers: 21% of UK business Advanced e-business	Knowledge management Customer relationship management Supply chain management and e-procurement
E-followers: 43% of UK business Basic e-business	Knowledge management E-mail and related IT Website creation and related IT
E-laggards: 36% of UK business Limited e-business	E-mail and related IT

Further, work commissioned by telecoms provider Energis commented, in a survey of the attitudes of European retailers to e-commerce in April 2001:

While the financial markets are showing volatility in relation to technology and internet stocks, it is clear that e-tailers remain confident of future growth and are focused on their business goals. For the vast majority, their main concern is getting the people and technology in place to enable them to compete effectively.

Figure 15.7 Degree of e-business involvement: retail v. all industry sectors
Source: KPMG (2001).

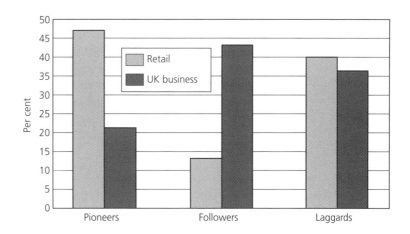

The Energis research, which interviewed some 250 e-commerce strategists at established retail businesses, as well as startup on-line retail brands across Europe, was similarly upbeat about short-term sales growth.

We need to remember, in our focus upon retailers, that retailers per se are not the only actors, nor indeed the most powerful actors, in the development of a global information infrastructure. Table 15.9 shows that a significant variety of new players, from conventional electronic hardware businesses, to telecommunications companies, to credit card operators, to content providers of all kinds, have stakes in the future development of the on-line medium. It is important to recognize that retailers may not have the loudest voice in the debate over the future form of electronic commerce.

Table 15.9 Seven layers of global information infrastructure
Source: adapted from KPMG (1996); Leer (1995).

Layer	Component	Interested parties (examples)
1	Global broadband network	AT&T, Cisco
2	Network security, performance and control	Visa
3	Standard operating systems	Microsoft, Sun
4	Consumer electronics	Philips, Sony, Nokia
5	Network service providers	AOL/Time Warner
6	Government and public services	France Telecom
7	Value-added information services	E.g. retailers

One result of this is the need to develop new kinds of networked organizational structures in the competition to deliver the complex package of on-line capability to consumers. As a consequence, retailers and retail marketers may find themselves partners in a joint effort to develop electronic commerce:

a new form of competition is spreading across global markets: group vs. group. Call them networks, clusters, constellations, or virtual corporations; these groups consist of companies joined together in a larger overarching relationship (Gomes-Casseres, 1994).

Finally, we should recall that competition works both ways. The strength of traditional retail intermediaries themselves should not be discounted. The characteristics of retailer buyer power that have prompted the referral of retailers to regulatory authorities in Europe and the US over the past few years (e.g. Competition Commission, 2000) is power that can also be seen to extend into the on-line channel.

> *The resistance which comes from interests threatened by an innovation in the productive process is not likely to die out as long as the capitalist order persists (Joseph Schumpeter, quoted in Atkinson, 2001).*

During periods of rapid technological change, political and corporate opposition to economic change can increase rapidly. The US Progressive Policy Institute argues that US consumers pay $15 billion more annually for goods and services as a result of e-commerce protectionism by intermediaries (Atkinson, 2001). The Institute cites examples of companies including Sony, Levi Strauss and Black and Decker who have not felt able to develop transactional websites because of retailer pressure, traditional auction houses forcing on-line auction sites to pass individual state licence examinations and on-line car-dealers being caught by state franchising laws. Attempts by manufacturers to use the Internet as a means to reach consumers directly by supporting indirectly 'pure play' business models have been largely unsuccessful. The Nestlé Le Shop trial in Switzerland has not proved greatly successful and Priceline's extension of its reverse bidding service into grocery goods lasted less than a year (Priluck, 2001).

15.1.3 Regulatory Issues

Governments have found it extraordinarily difficult to regulate the Internet. This can provide retailers with both obstacles but also opportunities. In particular, tax law continues to lag behind the development of e-tailing and the structure of the Internet destabilizes intellectual property rights and the present copyright system. While 'governments will still seek to raise revenue without distorting economic or technological choices' (Owens, 2000), in addition to greater cross-border activity through the trading of tangible products on line, trading of intangible, digitized products presents the tax authorities and intellectual rights agencies with significant challenges. Not least of these is that there is still disagreement over routes to harmonization between countries (Hardesty, 2001).

This suggests that there are still considerable opportunities for astute multinational e-retailers to reduce import duty and sales tax expenses through arbitraging different countries' income duty rates, tariff re-engineering (reclassifying a product to a lower-duty classification), reducing a product's dutiable value (unbundling dutiable costs) and monitoring the continuing discussions between tax authorities to determine the best short- and long-term stance on sales tax administration (Ernst & Young, 2001a).

Nevertheless, the regulatory authorities are catching up. While confirming that a distinction should be made between tariffs and taxes, such that e-commerce service should not be subject to tariffs, the 1998 Ottowa Taxation Conference began an international work programme in an attempt to harmonize policies in three broad areas:

 - consumption tax issues (developing further the notion of taxation in the place of consumption, for cross-border transactions)
 - international direct tax issues (how to treat business profits generated from different types of e-commerce transactions)
 - tax administration issues (including the use of the Internet to monitor transactions and levy taxes on consumers and businesses more fairly and comprehensively).

On income taxes, Organization for Economic Co-operation and Development (OECD) countries reached a broad consensus in 2001 on the interpretation of existing permanent establishment rules that are fundamental for deciding where profits on the conduct of e-commerce can be taxed. They are now working on clarifying the tax treaty treatment of various types of e-commerce payments (OECD, 2001). However, there is still some dispute between Europe and the USA in respect of consumption taxes. At present, the European Union does not charge a consumption tax on software, music and videos sold as digital downloads by non-EU companies. However, European retail companies selling the same items must collect the tax, and there is concern that this puts European retailers at a disadvantage. The UK is presently blocking the imposition of value added tax (VAT) on on-line sales, suggesting that this will hinder the development of electronic commerce and in any case is impractical to collect (Stafford, 2001).

Finally, the threat posed by peer-to-peer networking systems for undermining copyright in digitalized products, such as music and other forms of entertainment, creates challenges for retailers as much as it does for originating artists and their agents, the music and film producers. Retailers in susceptible categories trading on line have to invest resources to find legally acceptable mechanisms to protect intellectual property, while their own market share is threatened by the proliferation of unregulated (and arguably unregulable) transmission of samizdat digital material between individuals.

15.2 E-tailing Essentials

Christensen and Tedlow (2000) see retailing's core mission ('getting the right product in the right place at the right time') as unchanged within an electronic trading environment, but they argue that the way retailers might wish to fulfil this mission has changed, largely through what they call the effect of disruptive technologies. Why do shoppers go to websites? Underhill (2000) summarizes in his somewhat idiosyncratic way:

1 *Grab and go*: 'there's something in particular you're looking for, as a gift or for yourself, and you find it fast, buy it fast, and split'.

2 *Browse when you've got time to kill*: 'you may buy something or not, depending on what you find.'

3 *Search*: 'finding stuff we have no real-world access to'.

4 *Info-fuelling*: 'gathering specs and product reviews'.

5 *Contact the company* (pre- or post-purchase).

This section on e-tailing essentials seeks to understand how electronic channels to market might alter the way retailers bring goods and services to market. We review issues of convenience and accessibility, costs and pricing, considerations of branding and trust, the nature of the on-line product–service mix, and finally the practical challenges of distribution and fulfilment.

15.2.1 Convenience and Accessibility

Convenience is often suggested as being the most important 'order-winning' criterion for retailers (Hill, 1993; Wilson-Jeanselme, 2001). In bricks-and-mortar terms, this translates into the familiar adage of 'location, location, location'. The rhetoric suggests that e-tailing is generally considered to be a convenient way of shopping:

> *Shopping online can economise on time and effort by making it easy to locate merchants, find items and procure offerings. Consumers do not have to leave their home, nor travel to find and obtain merchandise online. They can also browse for items by category or online store. These time and browsing benefits of online shopping are likely to be manifested in more positive perceptions of convenience (Szymanski and Hise, 2000).*

> *You can shop at any time of day, on any day. You can get to any store in minutes flat. You never have to look for parking. You never have to wear a coat. You never have to wear anything (Underhill, 2000).*

What is the reality? Efficiency and effectiveness comprise the two keystones of good practice in e-commerce platform design. There appears to be a consensus that fast, uncluttered and easy to navigate sites both economize on shopping time, and reduce cognitive effort, thereby improving consumers' satisfaction with the on-line experience (Pastrick, 1997; Szymanski and Hise, 2000) and increasing the likelihood of sales and repeat purchases (Lohse and Spiller, 1998; Vassilopoulou et al., 2001). For example, Lohse and Spiller found that product list navigation features that reduce the time to purchase products on line accounted for 6 per cent of variance in monthly sales. Szymanski and Hise's own research found that convenience had the greatest impact on e-satisfaction levels. This is an unsurprising discovery, not least since the availability of bandwidth and the time-based cost of on-line access for the majority of consumers places a premium on timeliness.

Indeed, despite the rhetoric of price, convenience outranks price as a factor for many consumers in stimulating on-line behaviour. Morganosky and Cude (2000) reported that 70 per cent of US consumers surveyed at the end of 1999 cited convenience and saving time as their primary reason for buying groceries on line. Research undertaken among UK and European consumers (ECSoft, 2000; Forrester Research, 2000) suggests that price may be closing the gap. The initial importance of convenience may be a feature explained by the characteristics of early adopters of e-tailing, rather than by the mass market.

In addition to an efficient platform design, however, effectiveness is also important. In a discussion of on-line advertising effectiveness, Chen and Wells (1999) confirm, using empirical evidence, the common sense conclusion that a good website is one that delivers relevant and well-organized information in an engaging manner. They develop evaluative tools to assess dimensions of, and attitudes towards, effectiveness: and three explanatory dimensions that they propose explain the attitudes of consumers towards websites (Table 15.10).

Table 15.10 Factors affecting consumers' evaluations of websites

Source: Chen and Wells (1999).

Factor	Component	Variance explained	Factor score	Factor score	Factor score
1 Entertainment		36%			
	Fun		.87		
	Exciting		.82		
	Cool		.81		
	Imaginative		.78		
	Entertaining		.78		
	Flashy		.77		
2 Informativeness		13%			
	Informative			.85	
	Intelligent			.84	
	Knowledgeable			.81	
	Resourceful			.78	
	Useful			.77	
	Helpful			.75	
3 Organization		5%			
	Messy				–.78
	Cumbersome				–.78
	Confusing				–.76
	Irritating				–.74

Factors which reduce accessibility significantly affect the quality of the consumer's on-line experience. A survey by the UK Consumers' Association, for example, found that the main complaint affecting the on-line grocery experience was the time it took to place an order. Twenty orders took over an hour and a half to complete and almost a third took over two hours to order just 35 items. However, familiarity with a site may affect this finding: one regular Tesco shopper subsequently reported that she could do her weekly shop in just half an hour (Consumers' Association, 2001). Wilson-Jeanselme (2001) suggests that, in the case of on-line grocery retailing, the greater convenience benefits afforded by the on-line experience can 'leak away' as a result of four sets of ineffective or inefficient operational practices, including:

- a poor Internet interface (from slow response times to inefficient site design)
- ineffective management of customer demand information (from redundancy in the handling of information to poor use of information in the picking and packing of orders)
- badly planned warehouse/store operations (from poorly motivated staff to ineffective picking techniques)
- poor physical flow of product from warehouse/store (from limited delivery capacity to unreliable delivery slots).

Such poor consumer experiences, she suggests, serve to erode the genuine net benefit that consumer obtain from greater convenience on line.

Hoque and Lohse (1999) suggest that information-processing models provide a useful theoretical basis for predicting the ways in which electronic marketing channels influence consumer information processing and for generating more effective marketing interventions, although they believe that models of human–computer interaction are still in their infancy. For example, Moorthy et al. (1997) explore the effect of prior brand perceptions on information search. Shugan (1980) regards the cognitive cost of decision-making as a measure of the potential difficulty of a consumer's decision. Hoque and Lohse's own investigation of the choices made by consumers in consulting off-line and on-line telephone directories produced preliminary recommendations, including streamlined product list navigation and the avoidance of on-line advertising with extensive graphics.

Web usage also appears to generate somewhat different patterns of site patronage than conventional shopping activity, which will perhaps require substantially different approaches to building consumer awareness and encouraging repeat visits by e-tailers. Novak with Hoffman (1996; 1997; and Novak, 2000) have introduced the idea of 'flow' as a key construct in exploratory web browsing behaviour.

> *You've managed to get the kids into bed by 9 p.m. Instead of settling in for an evening of TV, you go online and begin navigating through cyberspace. Following one link to another, you begin to lose yourself … After what seems like minutes you glance at the clock. It's 2 a.m. The time warp you've fallen into is 'flow,' a psychological state of high involvement, skill and playfulness (Geirland and Sonesh-Kedar, 1998).*

Flow is a consequence of the intense concentration characteristic of an individual within an Internet session and its measurement has significant practical implications; if you help people search and browse a site in ways that fit this behavioural model, then they will be much more likely to buy. Similarly, Jarvenpaa and Todd (1997) identify the personal and emotional rewards the consumer feels after using a website contribute towards satisfaction and purchase intentions.

These results support Lohse and Spiller's (1998) argument that the customer's evaluation of an on-line store incorporates many of the same characteristics as 'bricks and mortar' shopping and so can be considered analogous to their evaluation of a physical store. They adopt the store attributes identified by Lindquist (1974), categorized into four groups: convenience, merchandise, service and promotions. They then demonstrate the linkage between these features, as applied to retail websites, and the number of visits and the amount of sales achieved.

Vassilopoulou et al. (2001) confirmed the importance of these attributes but also added a further variable identified by Lindquist but omitted by Lohse and Spiller, store atmosphere, to account for social, entertainment and flow aspects for Internet shopping. They found this factor to be one of the most influential in predicting purchasing and revisit intentions.

15.2.2 Costs and Pricing

The rhetoric of the new economy has suggested that retailers' transaction and other costs can be significantly reduced by trading on line; further, the Internet should allow prices to be more competitive on line than off, partly by reducing consumers' search costs, and that this in turn will create competitive pressure that will tend to drive price levels down. Kuttner (1998) observed: 'The Internet is a nearly perfect market. The result is fierce price competition, dwindling product differentiation and vanishing brand loyalty.'

Alba et al. (1997) suggested a scenario in which the consumer had the following capabilities:

- faithful reproduction of descriptive and experiential product information
- a greatly expanded universe of offerings relative to what can be accessed now through local or catalogue shopping
- an efficient means of screening the offerings to find the most appealing options for more detailed consideration
- unimpeded search across stores and brands
- memory for past selections, which simplifies information search and purchase decisions.

> *Therefore, the introduction of the IHS [interactive home shopping] channel will intensify the competitive environment, but this need not shift the emphasis from quality to price. By providing more information to consumers with minimal search cost, manufacturers and retailers with differentiated offerings will have a greater opportunity to educate consumers about the unique benefits they offer, and consumers will find it easier to access and compare the offerings of firms competing on price (Alba et al., 1997).*

The threat of price transparency on-line to retailers is, in principle, very considerable. According to Sinha (2000), the consequences can include:

- the erosion of the consumer's risk premium
- the enabling of more efficient searches
- the rendering of the price floor more easily visible (e.g. reverse auctions)

> the encouragement of highly rational shopping
> challenges to segmented pricing strategies
> changes in the consumer's perceptions of cost.

In order to understand the ways in which the Internet affects both consumers' perceptions of price and retailers' strategies towards price, we need to answer four specific questions (Table 15.11).

Table 15.11 The dimensions of Internet market efficiency

Source: Smith et al. (1999).

Dimension	Research question
1. Price levels	Are the prices charged on the Internet lower?
2. Price elasticity	Are consumers more sensitive to small price changes on the Internet?
3. Menu costs	Do retailers adjust their prices more finely or more frequently on the Internet?
4. Price dispersion	Is there a smaller spread between the highest and lowest prices on the Internet?

Commentators are by no means agreed that price levels on line are always lower. Bailey (1998) examined the books, software and CD markets and determined that higher prices were charged on line than off line, within similar categories. More recent US research suggested that the on-line price of books were in the order of 9 per cent lower and those of CDs 16 per cent lower than identical items off line (Brynjolfsson and Smith, 2000). Degeratu, et al. (1998) discovered that price sensitivity was lower for on-line grocery shoppers than for shoppers in traditional grocery stores. Some specific Internet business models, predominantly consumer-to-business (C2B), have been developed that do focus on price above other factors. Sites such as Priceline.com have successfully positioned themselves as 'name your own price' services, where the consumer bids for spare capacity in hotel rooms or airline seats. During the second quarter of 2001, Priceline added 1.025 million new customers, bringing its total customer base to 10.9 million, selling 3 million units of travel products, including 1.4 million airline tickets (Priceline.com, 2001). Priluck (2001) reviews the now defunct WebHouse Club initiative developed by Priceline in 1999. WebHouse Club extended the 'name your own price' principle to grocery goods. His analysis concluded that, had Priceline been able to withstand the cash drain on the business of this high-volume, low-margin business, then it could have significantly altered the power structure of the grocery industry.

It has been suggested that search engines and price comparison services could compensate for the apparently undifferentiated complexity of the on-line environment and make consumers using them considerably more sensitive to price levels (Maes, 1998). Bakos (2001) observes that, by reducing search costs on both sides, buyers ought to be able to consider more product offerings and better identify products that meet their needs.

Shopbots outperform and out-inform humans by providing extensive product coverage in just a few seconds, far more than a patient, determined human shopper could achieve after hours of manual search (Kephart and Greenwald, 2001).

Most price comparison services presently only offer the capability of finding the best price for a given product. Even so, services such as shopsmart.com and kelkoo.com have, for example, become successful intermediaries in their own right. These are often different from and considerably simpler than so-called 'intelligent agents'. Agents can be characterized by their *autonomy, adaptiveness, collaborative behaviour* and *mobility* (Feldman and Yu, 1999).

However, Rowley (2000) proposes that information-seeking, a key stage in the consumer buying process, becomes more structured and constrained in an e-commerce environment. The ability to collect product information and make comparisons between the different product offerings from different providers can become one of the main challenges of e-tailing for consumers. The technology itself may also facilitate the limiting of price comparison information. Many on-line services, for example in the grocery products sector, encourage consumers to develop lists of favourites, from which they may browse, rather than investigating the main store price lists, which may run into 20 000 SKUs. Degeratu et al. (2000) hypothesize that features that reduce consumers' 'consideration sets' may, in fact, keep consumers' price sensitivity lower on line than off line.

Price comparison agents may also explain the more frequent price changes observed among on-line retailers within particular markets (Bailey, 1998). Brynjolfsson and Smith (2000) determined in their study of books and CD sales that Internet retailers' price adjustments were over 100 times smaller than those of conventional retailers, reflecting lower menu costs. The channel characteristics that allow retailers' menu costs to be significantly smaller on line than off line also make it easier, technically if not behaviourally, to collect incremental or micropayments for information. Smartcard technology provider Mondex International estimated in 2001 that £14 million per month could be generated by Internet businesses in the UK alone through incremental charging of customers for information. Mondex commissioned research among UK consumers to demonstrate surprisingly, given the perception of the Internet as a 'free' medium, that British consumers would pay small amounts (between 90p and 112p on average) for financial information, mobile airtime, Internet gaming, tailored travel advice and music downloads.

Finally, we might expect that prices are less likely to vary between on-line providers in conditions of greater consumer knowledge. Lower search costs should lead not only to lower but also to more homogeneous prices on line than off line. Recently, however, and counter to this prevailing wisdom, Brynjolfsson and Smith (2000) and Bailey (1998) demonstrated that at present at least, on-line price dispersion is comparable to conventional markets. Internet retailer prices varied by an average of 33 per cent for books and 25 per cent for CDs. Nor is the most expensive on-line retailer always the least patronized. They demonstrated that Amazon.com had an on-line market share of almost 80 per cent in books at the time of their research, yet the company charged a 10 per cent premium over the least expensive on-line retailer in the study. This, Brynjolfsson and Smith determined, was a consequence of what they called a 'heterogeneity of trust'.

What sort of pricing strategies should retailers adopt on line as a consequence of these findings? Baker et al. (2001) identify two pricing approaches adopted historically by retailers but neither is optimal. They suggest:

> *Many start-ups have offered untenably low prices in the rush to capture first-mover advantage. Many incumbents, by contrast, have simply transferred their off-line prices onto the Internet. In some cases, they believe their brand strength inoculates them from the need to price competitively; in other cases, they feel pressure to establish an on-line presence but aren't prepared for the complexities of multi-channel pricing (Baker et al., 2001).*

The second approach could also create significant problems for international businesses whose price levels vary market by market, even if for perfectly justifiable reasons, now that consumers are learning to shop more globally. Some 58 per cent of non-US consumers claim to have purchased goods from a company in a foreign country, 55 per cent for reasons of availability, 29 per cent for reasons of price (Ernst & Young, 2001b). This final figure rose to 50 per cent for UK consumers.

Intelligent agents also have the capability of allowing sellers better to understand consumer trends and search patterns (Ernst & Young, 2001b). Because retail companies can therefore examine consumers' attitudes to price on line just as easily as consumers can compare prices, the Internet, at least in principle, allows retailers to price much more precisely, consistent with their strategy and brand (Table 15.12).

The mechanisms and environment of price-setting and consumer attitudes towards price may not be inherently stable over the longer term (Bailey, 1998; Reynolds, 2000a) and present behaviours may not be representative of future market conditions. Nevertheless, Bakos argues that, while lower search and information costs should push markets towards a greater degree of price discrimination, the reality is that Internet technology provides a means for retailers to create differentiation for which price premiums can be charged (Bakos, 2001). Very few products, he observes, are truly homogeneous. These differences can be developed in terms of levels of customer awareness and trust. Brynjolfsson and Smith (2000) agree:

	Source of value from the Internet	Conditions for selection	B2C examples
Precision	Greater precision in setting optimal price Better understanding of zone of price indifference	Testing needs to be run on at least 200 transactions to be significant	Toys Books CDs
Adaptability	Speed of price change Ease of response to external shocks to the system (changes in costs of competitive moves, for example)	Inventory or capacity is perishable Demand fluctuates over time	Consumer electronics Luxury cars
Segmentation	Ability to choose creative, accurate segmentation dimensions Ease in identifying which segment a buyer belongs to Ability to create barriers between segments	Different customers value your products' benefits differently Customer profitability varies widely	Credit cards Mortgages Automobiles

Table 15.12 Three approaches to improving pricing

Source: adapted from Baker et al. (2001).

far from being a great equaliser of retailers and eliminating the need for branding as is so often claimed, the Internet may heighten the importance of differences amongst retailers in dimensions such as trust and branding.

As a result:

The much heralded shift in market power from producer to the consumer that many associate with electronic commerce may be premature, overstated or incorrect (Bailey, 1998).

15.2.3 Branding and Trust

As simplifiers of choice, retail brands off line play a significant role in encouraging trust and increased frequency of patronage among consumers. According to de Chernatony and McDonald (1998), the growing consolidation of bricks and mortar retailers has led to 'high quality retailer brands, backed by significant corporate promotional campaigns reinforcing clear personalities.' The trustworthiness of retailer brands has already led to consumers believing that retailers would be at least as effective as traditional providers in a wide range of other product or service sectors (Eagle et al., 2000). New channels to market provide an additional challenge to such retailers, introducing new competitors for market share, as well as creating potential uncertainties over how the basic marketing building blocks work on line, as well as of what constitutes an effective retail marketing intervention on line:

Branding on the internet is of interest because the dynamics of a brand in a computer-mediated environment may well turn out to be different to the dynamics of a brand in the physical world and, whilst there is intuitive support for such a proposition, there is yet to be any evidence that Internet branding follows currently accepted branding principles (Jevons and Gabbott, 2000).

Whittle (2000) also concludes that the important factors in off-line brands do not necessarily apply to on-line ones and new factors have to be considered, e.g. ease of use and content of a site. Further, David Day, director of analytics, A.C. Nielsen eRatings.com, warns that company websites have a maximum of 6 minutes to make a good impression of the company. Unfortunately, while Newman (1999) notes that information technology has increased the opportunities for business to contact the customer, Byrne (1999) believes there is a general failure to communicate a coherent brand message during such contacts. Nevertheless, there are potential opportunities for brand building, Hall (2000) identifies that one of the benefits offered by the Internet for retailers is the chance to provide a more direct brand experience for the customer.

It is possible to draw a number of interesting conclusions in respect of on-line brand awareness from Ernst and Young's pioneering on-line brand observatory (Table 15.13), driven by data from the kelkoo.com search agent (Ernst & Young, 2001c). First, although a significant proportion of consumers are brand indifferent (see television and digital camera choices above), the majority of searches for televisions, irrespective of country, are undertaken on a small portfolio of brands (two, or at the most, three), largely related to the market share of established brands in each county. In the case of digital cameras, a relatively new product with little brand preference established within consumers' minds, the searches are more extensive.

The filter of brand awareness reduces on-line candidates in which consumers can place their trust. Basu proposes that a trusted brand is a composite of experience (looking back) and expectation (looking forward) (Basu, 2000). If there is little prior experience, trust on line may be difficult to establish and to sustain as a consequence, even if other aspects of the retail offer are compelling. The evidence from our earlier discussion on pricing demonstrates that, despite the more transparent nature of price competition on line, a 'heterogeneity of trust' exists that means that the cheapest e-tailer is not always the most heavily patronized (Brynjolffson and Smith, 2000).

This is because, for all that the early adopters of electronic commerce are sophisticated consumers, we know that they are also suspicious and demanding (Reynolds, 2000a). There is evidence that retail brands on line will have to work harder than through conventional channels. For example, on-line consumers appear to demand equivalent or superior customer service to regular stores, according to research commissioned

Table 15.13 Selected brands searched for on kelkoo.com (percentage)

Source: Ernst & Young (2001b).

Television brands	UK	France	Sweden	Netherlands
Brand indifferent	38	38	23	27
Sony	22	16	42	18
Philips	8	15	20	34
JVC	3	—	1	7
Thomson	2	13	3	—
Panasonic	8	4	5	5
Toshiba	6	—	—	—
Grundig	—	—	—	5
Samsung	—	—	1	3
Hitachi	3	—	—	—
LG	—	3	1	—
Other	10	11	4	1
Digital camera brands	**UK**	**France**	**Sweden**	**Netherlands**
Brand indifferent	33	25	—	59
Fuji	15	16	—	4
Canon	13	14	—	7
Olympus	10	9	—	4
Sony	8	10	—	11
Kodak	7	10	—	6
Nikon	4	6	—	—
Others	10	10	—	9

by ECSoft (2000) The so-called 'brand edge' capable of being established by start-up Internet retailers has proved no guarantee of continued sales and patronage (Crawford, in Ernst & Young LLP, 1999). Research commissioned by the UK National Consumers' Council (2000) concludes that the lack of consumer trust in electronic commerce, and the cautious on-line consumer behaviour that has resulted, reduces the potential of electronic commerce to bring greater competition and consumer choice. The report believes consumers' continuing fear of fraud will continue to be a deterrent to on-line shopping:

> *consumers sense there is a lack of respect for their rights and their safety online. Consumers are asked to pay for goods before they have seen them, and to hand over personal and financial details up front in an environment that they hear all the time harbours shady characters (National Consumer Council, 2000).*

We might expect that this perception of the infrastructure of electronic commerce may favour established brands. But the potential for increased complexity of many purchases on line is also a factor, even for these brands. Chircu et al. (2000) showed that trust and expertise become more important in determining the adoption intention as transaction complexity increases.

Can we try to unpack what constitutes 'trust' in an on-line experience? Work undertaken by Cheskin Research (1999) disaggregates those components that appear to be positively correlated with trust, as table 15.14 illustrates.

Component	Description
Overall brand equity	Consumer awareness of what this company does for consumers outside of the Web
Web brand equity	How well the company's website fits with consumers' sense of what the company is about generally
Benefit clarity	How easy is it to determine what the site is promising to deliver on the first visit
Portal/aggregator affilliations	Mention of an affiliation to portals and aggregators such as Yahoo! Lycos, etc.
Co-op third party brands	Promotion of third party quality brands
Relationship marketing	Sending updates and other notices to consumers
Community-building	Facilitating interactions between individual shoppers
Depth of product offering on site	How many varieties of product the site contains
Breadth of product offering on site	How many types of products the site contains

Table 15.14
Components of trust within brand

Source: Cheskin Research (1999).

Keeling et al. (2001c) confirm that website attributes, such as community-building and depth and breadth of product offering, have a strong relationship with perceptions of brand personality and brand confidence. They also demonstrate that 'high-touch' and less complex sites with good customer service are associated with higher brand image and greater brand confidence. They conclude that there are real dangers of brand dilution from poorly conceived websites.

Bakos (2001) reports on the growth of specialized intermediaries that seek to provide reassurance to consumers over price competitiveness as well as service and delivery quality. For example, security logos could provide a sense of comfort for consumers, but only if they are relevant and familiar:

> *The problem is that you have 5 or 6 there. Which one is better than the other? Which one do you actually trust? ... Frankly, they could be made up by anybody (quoted in National Consumers' Council, 2000).*

Services such as bizrate.com and 2020shops.com attempt to compensate for consumers' initial lack of brand awareness on line; however, they themselves of course will have to struggle to establish their own credentials with a suspicious on-line consumer. Certainly, even the most apparently successful on-line start-up brands have had to work hard to establish consumer trust. The on-line auction site eBay is a case in point. In order to reassure consumers in what for many new users can be a novel shopping activity, eBay offers no less than five levels of safeguards (Fig. 15.8).

> ▸ **Instantly check the 'reputation' or business practices of anyone at eBay.** The *Feedback Forum* is a place where users leave comments about each other's buying and selling experiences at eBay. If you're a bidder, check your seller's Feedback Profile before you place a bid to learn about the other person's reputation with previous buyers. If you're a seller, do the same with your bidders.
>
> ▸ **Every eBay user is covered, at no additional cost, by the eBay Fraud Protection Program.** If you paid for an item and never received it (or if you received the item, but it's less than what was described), eBay will reimburse buyers up to $200, less the standard $25 deductible. Visit our *Fraud Protection Program* page for more details.
>
> ▸ **SafeHarbor, eBay's comprehensive safety resource, is here for your protection.** It doesn't happen often, but sometimes there is misuse on Bay. *SafeHarbor* springs into action and tries to resolve issues in many areas such as fraud, trading offenses, and illegally listed items.
>
> ▸ **An escrow service can give you added security whether you're a buyer or seller in transactions involving expensive items.** eBay's escrow partner, *Tradenable*, will hold your payment and send it off to the seller only after you've inspected your merchandise and given your approval. As a seller, you have the same opportunity to inspect and approve a returned item before the buyer gets refunded.
>
> ▸ **A dispute resolution service will work with buyers and sellers to help resolve disputes that may arise.** *SquareTrade*, eBay's preferred dispute resolution provider, helps eBay users resolve disputes quickly and fairly.

Figure 15.8 Reassuring the customer at eBay
Source: eBay (n.d.).

Such effort appears to be worth while, however. Trust leads to customer loyalty and we can establish that attention to aspects of customer retention has a significant correlation with e-tail company profitability, just as it does in the bricks and mortar world (Chapter 3). McKinsey tracked 650 million visitors to eight different kinds of websites, and found a strong association between measures taken to increase customer retention and loyalty, and profitability (Agrawal et al., 2001). The best-performing sites achieved a customer conversion rate of 12 per cent (against an average of 2.5 per cent) and a repeat-purchase rate of 60 per cent (against an average of 18 per cent), far better than poorer performers. The researchers explained this superior performance as a direct consequence of superior underlying operational skills in acquiring, converting, and retaining customers, skills very similar to those of the best bricks and mortar retailers. These included:

1 *Attraction skills*: gaining large numbers of new customers at the lowest cost, through partnership arrangements or improved targeting.
2 *Retention skills*: simplifying the repurchase process, offering reassurance on payment and remedies and through personalization of the returning customer experience.

15.2.4 The Product–Service Mix

There are enormous generic similarities worldwide in what consumer tend to buy on line (Table 15.15). So-called commodity products notably books, CDs, computer hardware and software are to be found in the top three categories for most countries surveyed by Ernst & Young (2001) For Underhill (2000), this says it all:

Country	1	2	3	4	5
USA	Books	Computers	CDs	Apparel	Tickets/res
Non-USA	Books	CDs	Computers	Tickets/res	Videos
Australia	Books	Computers	CDs	Tickets/res	Apparel
Brazil	CDs	Books	Computers	Electronic products	Videos
Canada	Computers	Books	CDs	Tickets/res	Apparel
France	Books	Computers	Tickets/res	CDs	Videos
Germany	Books	Computers	CDs	Tickets/res	Videos
Israel	Books	CDs	Electronic products	Computers	Household goods
The Netherlands	Books	CDs	Computers	Tickets/res	Electronic products
South Africa	Books	CDs	Computers	Tickets/res	Financial services
Spain	Books	Computers	CDs	Tickets/res	Electronic products
UK	CDs	Books	Computers	Tickets/res	Videos

Table 15.15 Top five on-line purchase categories by country, 2000

Source: Ernst & Young (2001b).

Let's get human. Can you smell a ripe peach online? Can you accidentally discover a shoe that feels so good you impulsively take three pairs? There are three big things that stores alone can offer shoppers:

—touch, trial, or any other sensory stimuli

—immediate gratification

—social interaction

Notice how these have not much to do with the orderly, planned acquisition of goods and everything to do with the sensual, experiential aspects of shopping—the worldly pleasures we love but that are slow in coming to the Internet.

But, contrary to the views of some over the inappropriateness of higher-value/higher-touch products for on-line selling, categories such as clothing and health and beauty care are also starting to feature in certain markets. Clothing, for example, ranks in the top five in the USA and Australia, with over 37 per cent of US on-line consumers likely to purchase the category. While because of the greater development in the category, food and drink accounts for 23 per cent of on-line purchases in the UK. Ernst & Young take the view that, as on-line penetration increases worldwide, so most countries will see a broadening array of product categories patronized.

However, the product–service mix preferred by different age, gender and lifestyle segments differs just as much on line as we would expect it to within traditional retail markets. The mix also evolves over time, as on-line consumers become more adventurous in their purchasing (Table 15.16). Analysts NetValue have created an 'affinity' ratio for different on-line consumer segments (NetValue, 2001). Affinity is determined by the reach of the overall Internet population against the reach for the indicated target. For example, there appear to be some common affinities shared by men and women worldwide: men have a high affinity to the adult sector and women have a high affinity to the astrology/horoscope sector. There are also differences, with women in the USA having a high affinity with the environmental category and women in Spain had a high affinity with e-cards; while men in France had the highest affinity to the use of streaming video sites and men in Germany had the highest affinity to the weather sector.

Table 15.16 Households buying on line by year of Internet purchasing

Source: Forrester Research, quoted in IGD (2001).

Product categories (% making category purchase in)	First year (newbies)	Second year (intermediates)	Third year (veterans)
Books, CDs, videos	21	34	51
Travel, PCs	11	16	31
Groceries, health and beauty	3	4	8

We should also note that a relatively small number of e-commerce sites account for the bulk of on-line activity (Table 15.17). Across Europe, for example, the activities of Amazon in France, the UK and Germany and in a range of categories, from books and CDs to electronics, help it to dominate the European rankings for May 2001. Both bahn.de and lastminute.com are both tickets and reservations services, confirming the dominance of this category in terms of on-line purchases.

Rank	Domain	Reach (%)	Unique visitors (000)	Average min/month
1	amazon.de	5.2	2567	10.8
2	bahn.de	3.8	1887	14.0
3	amazon.com	3.4	1672	6.7
4	amazon.co.uk	3.2	1588	11.8
5	bonzi.com	2.9	1432	3.3
6	apple.com	2.6	1274	6.3
7	register.com	2.3	1135	1.5
8	comdirect.de	2.3	1131	33.1
9	lastminute.com	2.2	1073	7.6
10	adobe.com	2.1	1025	3.8

Table 15.17 Top 10 European e-commerce domains, May 2001[1]

Note: 1 This ranking includes data from Denmark, France, Germany, Norway, Spain, Sweden and the UK.

Source: NetValue (2001).

Morganosky and Cude (2000) suggest that retailers have two possibilities of creating value within the on-line channel: first, by improving consumers' productivity (by increasing the number of tasks that can be completed or reducing the time required for their completion) or, second, by expanding product assortments, perhaps adding a variety of services to their offering. The degree of authority in product or service selection might be also expected to be positively associated with consumer confidence and satisfaction. (Szymanski and Hise, 2000). Merchandising authority can be achieved on line through wider product assortments (perhaps including ranges not available off line) and more extensive, higher-quality information on available products, which may tend to lead to better buying decisions by consumers as well as increased sales and website revisits (Peterson et al., 1997; Vassilopoulou et al., 2001).

Finally, more dynamic and relevant product–services mixes can be generated in other ways than via personal computer interfaces. For example, the Virgin Group's VShop concept contains in-store Internet kiosks that provide consumers not only with access to an extended range of VShop's core product range of CDs and DVDs, but also to other sites run by the Virgin Group, including wines, cars as well as financial, travel, energy, mobile phone and Internet services. The so-called 'walled gardens' of the interactive digital television service providers (such as NTL and Telewest in the UK) provide carefully chosen selections of on-line retail brands to reduce the confusion and uncertainty of brand choice for this segment of the on-line population, who are generally not early adopters.

15.2.5 Distribution and Fulfilment

Early comments from third party distributors towards the attractions of direct distribution of goods to the home were optimistic:

> *to drive costs down we need to select the right vehicle, ensure it travels with the maximum volume and weight it can carry and organise its journey to be as short as possible with the distance between the delivery points being as close as possible ... We need to guarantee a minimum volume of goods in the system ... [as a result] the operation will not be cost prohibitive. Indeed, by cutting out the expensive retail stores, and delivering via a well-designed transport operation, the final cost of the goods to the consumer may well be cheaper (CEO, TNT White Arrow Express, quoted in KPMG, 1997).*

These claims are reinforced by the all-time records continually posted by the express carriers, although they report difficulty in calculating the exact impact of e-commerce on their businesses. This is because some on-line sales are replacing conventional catalogue sales. Nevertheless, UPS reported some 325 million parcels shipped between Thanksgiving and Christmas 2000, with daily volume increasing to 19 million deliveries on the busiest day (UPS, 2000b). On 19 December 2000, the company received a record of 6.5 million on-line package tracking requests in a single day (UPS, 2000a). E-commerce merchants are heavily reliant upon contractual arrangements with such private sector carriers, particularly in the USA. Indeed, guaranteed next-day or two-day delivery has become an implicit part of US e-commerce culture.

This has not always been straightforward. Christmas 1999 in the USA was a particularly difficult period (Reynolds, 2000b). The pressure is put upon newly fledged on-line merchants' essentially fragile distribution and logistics systems, as well as upon established shippers.

Order processing departments, especially within those businesses offering telesales options for purchase, were also heavily pressured. Web servers were overloaded and response times poor. Such experiences were relatively typical. Nor are the shippers themselves (with the exception of the US Postal Service) entirely comfortable with a rapid increase in residential deliveries boosted by on-line sales. Such deliveries, particularly to remote residential locations, create significant extra costs and may require the company to return to the address several times if the addressee is not available for any reason (BBC News Online, 2001). Further, a continued growth in such sales is likely to cause significant pressure on the conventional package shippers' business model. These companies are much more enthusiastic about the merits of business-to-business opportunities.

This experience is helpful. It tells us that, despite the hype and the investment, not many on-line retailers had the kind of capacity and systems to cope with the sort of exponential growth in demand that was to be seen among US consumers during 2000. Further, although US retail businesses claim to have put the worst behind them in terms of distribution shortfalls for the holiday 2000 season in the USA, regular horror stories keep this particular concern in the mind of the consumer (e.g. Enos, 2001). It has become clear that concerns about and the inadequacies of physical distribution of products ordered on line has become a major issue with consumers (Fig. 15.9). How e-tailers deal with out-of-stock items has also become a concern (Which?, 2001). So 'distribution *does* matter' (Cooke, 2000) after all.

What sort of distribution strategies are available for retailers seeking to overcome the concerns of consumers about fulfilment? Sawnhey (1999) identifies five 'distribution approaches' (Table 15.18). Both the 'speed' and 'niching' strategies have potential for differentiation and,

Figure 15.9 Reasons for dissatisfaction with on-line shopping experiences, UK

Source: ECSoft (2000).

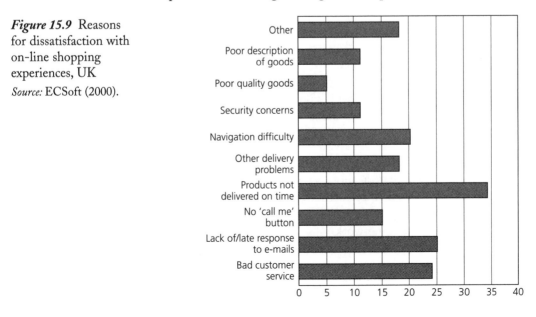

therefore, for retailers to command a price premium, provided there is market demand. This is not always the case: for example, of the plethora of 'emergency delivery' services on line in the USA and Europe during 1999–2000, very few have survived. Overbuild and portal strategies carry the possibility of generating profitability through economies of scope or of scale.

Table 15.18 Distribution approaches for e-tailers

Source: adapted from Sawhney, (1999).

Item	Portal	Overbuild	Caching	Speed	Niching
Strategy	Aggregate demand across categories within a household	Aggregate supply and demand across households	Reaggregate bulk by using collection points	Focus on time-sensitive and 'emergency' delivery solutions	Focus on specific categories or specific delivery solutions
Competitive advantage	Scope	Scale	Centralization	Speed	Specialization
Associated values	Customer intimacy	Operational excellence	Operational excellence, customer intimacy	Operational excellence	Product leadership
Key challenges	Delivery boxes (cost, reluctance); matching delivery cycles across categories	Capital intensity; high execution risk	Designing appropriate pickup locations; limited throughput	Maintaining delivery guarantee; small order sizes; low volumes	Narrow scope; limited scale; risk of being overcome by scale/scope players
Examples	Streamline.com	Webvan.com	Waitrose@Work	Pink.Dot.com	FurnitureFind.com EthnicGrocer.com

According to the research undertaken by the UK Foresight Retail Logistics Task Force (Department of Trade and Industry, 2000c), on-line grocers are presently using one of two models of distribution: store-based order-picking and e-fulfilment centres (Figs 15.10 and 15.11). While there are a number of other 'caching' strategies in operation (for example, work-based deliveries, such as Waitrose@Work, and the use of localized pick-up points, such as those offered by Consignia, Collectpoint and MBox in the UK), these are the two most popular routes to growth. The costs of e-fulfilment centres are in principle lower than for store-based operations, but a number of retailers find that the latter is attractive, for a number of reasons:

- Requires a low initial investment.
- Offers a short timescale between decision to provide services and their implementation.
- Is able to use spare capacity of human and physical resources within store network.
- Potentially reinforces store-based customer relationships.

The major challenge for store-based picking is the potential conflict that can arise between store-based customers and employees picking on

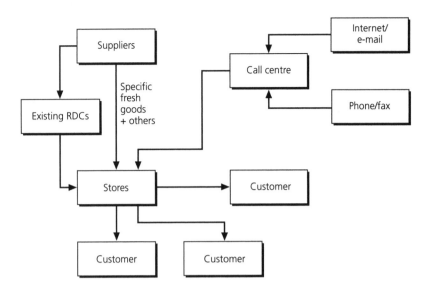

Figure 15.10 Logistics model for store-based picking of e-commerce orders

Source: Department of Trade and Industry (2000c).

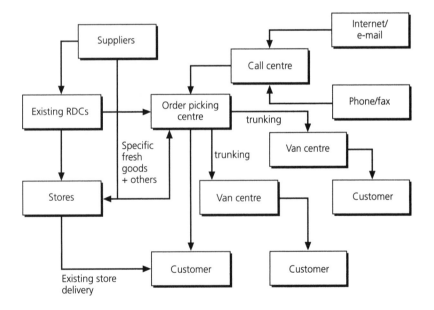

Figure 15.11 Logistics model for e-fulfilment centre picking of e-commerce orders

Source: Department of Trade and Industry (2000c).

behalf of remote customers; as a result, the store-based picking route has scaling limitations (Investec Henderson Crosthwaite, 2000).

An e-fulfilment centre, on the other hand, carries particular benefits of its own, including:

‣ centralized stock control and order fulfilment
‣ reduced overheads through economies of scale.

In addition to the requirement for home delivery, order picking itself can be extremely inefficient and expensive (Kämäräinen, et al., 2001):

Rather than simply investing in automation, the e-grocers also need to pay attention to the design principles of the distribution centre. Automation is a solution for achieving better picking efficiency in the e-grocery business. However ... if companies fail to consider automation from a capacity utilisation point of view, projected cost savings will not be realised.

The immediate attractions of an e-fulfilment centre strategy are somewhat diminished by the experience of Webvan, a start-up business in the USA. It sought to invest over $1.2 billion in an 'overbuild' distribution approach, by-passing the existing retail distribution system by constructing up to 26 fully-automated e-fulfilment centres. However, Webvan failed to recruit sufficient shoppers to realize its economies of scale (Helft, 2001). It reported sales in its San Francisco depot running at just under $17 million (2600 orders per day with an average size of $71) during the third quarter of 1999. The depot was designed to operate to cater for annualized sales of $290 million (8000 orders per day with an average size of $103) (Morgan Stanley Dean Witter, 2000). Further:

If Webvan had taken the time to work out the kinks with its first facility, it could have used what it learned to build smaller and more efficient facilities. Instead it had gone full force into building similarly gigantic, wasteful distribution centers in Atlanta, Dallas, Chicago, and other major cities ... the company needed the rigid efficiency of ... well, of grocery retailers (Alsop, 2001).

Despite reaching an active base of 750 000 customers from seven locations, Webvan filed for bankruptcy protection in the summer of 2001, having lost $700 million since its launch.

By comparison, Table 15.19 shows that the established UK food retailer Tesco was able to cut the direct cost of its e-commerce sales through its store-based Tesco Direct operation by an estimated two-thirds between 1997 and 1999, largely through switching to an Internet-only order capture system (abandoning manual telephone and fax orders) and designing a semi-automatic picking system in-store.

Table 15.19 Estimated costs and contribution of Tesco's e-commerce service, 1997–99

Source: Morgan Stanley Dean Witter (2000).

Sales = 100	Store shopper	Home shopper 1997	Home shopper 1999
Sales	100	100	100
Gross profit	26	28	29
Direct costs	—	22	7
Apportioned costs	17	15	15
Branch profit	9	−9	7
Delivery charge	—	5	5
Profit contribution	9	−4	12

Figure 15.12
Comparative
transportation costs
(indexed)

Source: Punakivi and
Saranen, (2001).

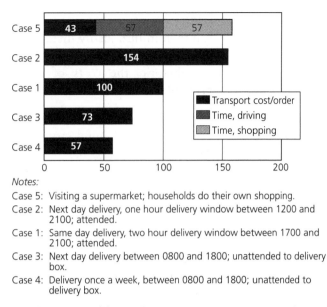

Notes:

Case 5: Visiting a supermarket; households do their own shopping.

Case 2: Next day delivery, one hour delivery window between 1200 and 2100; attended.

Case 1: Same day delivery, two hour delivery window between 1700 and 2100; attended.

Case 3: Next day delivery between 0800 and 1800; unattended to delivery box.

Case 4: Delivery once a week, between 0800 and 1800; unattended to delivery box.

It is suggested that the Tesco Direct service, operating through 250 outlets and taking some 60 000 orders per week with an average basket size of £85, is now breaking even after five years of operation with £250 million in sales. Ironically, a few weeks after the closure of Webvan, Tesco announced the acquisition for $22 million of a 35 per cent stake in the GroceryWorks on-line division of the US Safeway chain. The service will be operated from Safeway stores in the USA, rather than warehouses. One analyst suggests that Tesco will be able to squeeze between £1.4billion and £1.6 billion in sales from the store-based model in the UK alone using 400 stores, before having to migrate to e-fulfilment centres (which could, of course, be located in areas much more closely aligned to actual levels of consumer demand).

Logistics and distribution costs clearly require careful evaluation and monitoring. Tollington and Wachter (2001) observe that e-tailing is a niche market that works best when retail inventory 'throughput' is maximized. At the same time, it favours activity-based costing, because of the substantial fixed overhead costs incurred by retailers, for example, by many of the major supermarket companies, Punakivi and Saranen (2001) estimate that e-tailing of grocery goods can be as much as 43 per cent cheaper than conventional store visits by customers, if they properly account for the costs of using their own car and their spare time (Fig. 15.12).

Of course, this assumes that the consumer is conscious of and values the time he or she takes to shop the conventional grocery store. Punakivi and Saranen suggest that cost savings can be best achieved through the use of unattended delivery, by the use of a reception box such as that pioneered by the now-defunct Streamline in the USA or the Homeport box now being trialled in the USA, The Netherlands and the UK (Investec Henderson Crosthwaite, 2001). The Homeport is a secure, temperature-controlled box left outside the home. Kämäräinen et al.

(2001) agree that changing the service model in this way to level demand can then in turn justify investment in picking and packing automation. The example of grocery e-tailing nevertheless demonstrates that, despite the rhetoric, the costs of an Internet channel to market can be prohibitive for a retailer if not carefully understood and managed.

15.3 Prospects for B2C E-commerce

15.3.1 Forecasts and Scenarios

The development and diffusion of technology has been one of the principal forces behind structural change in economies and societies. The path of change has not always been clear, however. During the dot.com boom, many commentators were quick to forecast the demise of conventional retailing and its substitution with electronic transactions, as well as to make wildly optimistic forecasts. Dykema estimated in September 2000 that on-line retail sales of goods and services would grow from 1.5 per cent of retail sales in 2000 to 7.8 per cent in 2005. A further 10.8 per cent of retail sales made in 2005 would be influenced by the Internet as consumers used on-line information to determine their purchases of high-value goods and services. However, such forecasts also tended to be highly divergent and to some extent self-serving (Steckel, 2000). In early 2000, for example, research bringing together competitive forecasts, commissioned by the UK Department of Trade and Industry, reported the market for B2C e-commerce would grow to anything between £2.5 billion and £7 billion by 2003. By the middle of 2000, the most conservative estimates expected fivefold growth by 2003; the most optimistic, more than tenfold (Table 15.20).

Table 15.20 Consultant estimates of world-wide electronic commerce revenues

Note: Forrester's estimates include Internet-based EDI.

Source: Coppel, (2000).

Source	1999 $ billion	2003 $ billion	% average annual growth
e-Marketer	98.4	1244.0	89
IDC	111.4	1317.0	85
ActivMedia	95.0	1324.0	93
Forrester Low	70.0	1800.0	125
Forrester High	170.0	3200.0	108
Boston Consulting Group	1000.0	4600.0	46

With a now more uncertain future for e-tailing, it may be that scenario planning rather than forecasting represents a more realistic method for examining the prospects for B2C e-commerce. Scenarios are sketches of plausible or possible futures, which are intended to demonstrate threats and opportunities. They can be developed in many ways, from mathematical modelling to intuition. One of the most influential sets of such forecasts, those of Kahn (Kahn and Wiener, 1967), used the latter approach.

Comparing alternative scenarios can illustrate the range of contingencies that one should be prepared to consider. They can help pinpoint policies and strategies. They can cast light on the underlying processes which may

render one or other future more probable. Using different scenarios can be a way of expressing arguments about the drivers of social change, identifying opportunities for business innovation, differences in assumptions as to how the world operates, what influences are current (Department of Trade and Industry, 2000d).

Such exercises are not new. The Distributive Industries Training Board commissioned an environmental scanning study of the UK distribution industry in 1980. More recently, there have been attempts to incorporate electronic commerce into a scenario framework. A number have used quite simple spectra (see Table 15.21; Steckel, 2000). Each of these has implications for the changing nature of consumer demand. Small changes in causal assumptions drive very different growth rates.

Table 15.21 1997 for 2010: scenarios for the US food industry

Source: Matthews (1997).

Scenario	Description
Aldi Knows Best	Average household income is lower than today; technology has failed to make inroads into the home; 'consumers' shopping options are as meagre as their budgets'
J. Gatsby Grocery	High household incomes; technology has failed to make inroads into the home; high-touch triumphs over high-tech
A tale of two cities	Household incomes are polarized; the rich shop on-line; the poor are disenfranchised
The Cyber 7-11	High household incomes; high penetration of technology into the home; triumph of one-to-one marketing

Governments have also sought to use scenarios to better understand economic and social futures mediated by technology. The UK Government Foresight programme produced a number of scenario planning exercises for retailing (Department of Trade and Industry, 1998; 2000b; 2000d). In an early 2000 study, the DTI's researchers developed four scenarios, 'Explosive', 'Dynamic', 'Active' and 'Sluggish', to reflect the rate of development of personal e-commerce and its social and economic impact (Table 15.22). This study was also one of the first to incorporate an explicit policy dimension in recognizing that the growth of e-retailing could be affected by the extent and nature of government intervention.

Unsurprisingly, a relatively simplistic division of opinion exists among the majority of analysts over one of the most important components in many scenario planning exercises: the impact of electronic commerce upon bricks-and-mortar retailing property and location. The prevailing view is that electronic commerce will have little impact:

Retailers trading out of stores have successfully met the challenge of previous high growth formats. Mail order companies, telephone sales and

Scenario	Description
Explosive	*Rapid growth in wide range of information society activities, including consumer e-commerce.* Policy measures promote considerable social experimentation with information and communications technologies facilitating uptake of related services with low levels of social exclusion
Dynamic	*High growth in the value of consumer e-commerce transactions.* Low levels of social exclusion from e-commerce. Many existing differences eroded, though some groups may defy the general trend
Active	*Relative high growth in the value of consumer e-commerce transactions.* High levels of social exclusion from e-commerce, current differences persist or are amplified, though some groups may defy the trend
Sluggish	*Relative low growth in the value of consumer e-commerce transactions.* Obstacles to development predominate in the UK (and elsewhere)

television shopping channels have all done little more than chip away at the market share of property-based retailers (Donaldsons, cited in Estates Gazette, 1999).

This view is unsurprising, not least because of the importance of confidence in maintaining and enhancing the value of retail real estate in the minds of all parties. There is, however, a counter-argument which suggests that economies favouring overly restrictive planning regulation give rise to congested and overtrading retail space which, in turn, commands artificially high rental levels. United States consumers have access to some eight times as much shopping space per capita than UK shoppers (Management Horizons Europe, 1999). Partly as a consequence, average rental per square foot of speciality retailing tends to be twice as high in the UK as compared to the USA. In addition, the climate favouring five-year upward-only rent reviews (rather than turnover rental arrangements) tends to accentuate an upward spiral in property costs.

Some have suggested that electronic commerce could derail this upward trend. Research commissioned by the British Council of Shopping Centres (BCSC, 2001) examined the impact of electronic commerce on sales and rental values of retailers to 2005. It forecast that the Internet will lead to lower rental growth, higher yields and lower capital values and returns. Rental growth, in particular, could slow by between 0.2 per cent and 0.5 per cent per annum between 2000 and 2005: 'the internet will tend to "cannibalize" retail sales away from store-based retailers, thereby reducing the underlying value of retail real estate' (Merrill Lynch, 1999). It may be that the truth lies somewhere in between, suggesting more opportunities, but equally more potential

Category	Factor
The impact on existing stores and centres	*The showroom effect* (Where consumers touch and feel the product in the store and then return home to purchase cheaper on line)
	Experience over functionality? (Developing leisure and entertainment retailing as an effective and affordable antidote to the blandness of on-line retailing)
	The shopping hierarchy (Will increasing lack of confidence further reinforce, for example, investments in the existing top 70 shopping centres in the UK?)
	The return point advantage (US experience shows, as in the case of Gap, that being able to use existing real estate for returns is a competitive advantage for established businesses over new on-line entrants)
Geographical differences	*Overcoming the urban–rural split* (Many on-line trials have tended to be focused in urban areas, 'creaming off' revenue from densely populated and easy-to-service markets)
	Rural exclusion (Conversely, in more physically extensive rural areas, how will on-line retailing manifest itself physically? What tangible resources will be required to maintain a profitable and cost-efficient distribution system?)
Product–service mix	*The conventional merchandise mix* (Will on-line trading's differential effect on product groups affect the space and locational requirements of existing retailers? Will department stores need to focus on fewer, higher margin, more tangible and experiential departments, for example?)
	The effects of 'dynamic trade' (Will the notion of 'dynamic trade', a 'just-in-time' principle for the consumer, have a knock-on effect upon other channels of distribution and, if so, what are the implications for the size of and split between retail selling and non-selling space within conventional stores?)
New property requirements	*New e-fulfilment centres* (The knee-jerk reaction of the property industry faced with the challenge of e-commerce is to indicate a greater need for distribution centres. FDPSavills estimated some 8 million square feet will be required in the UK alone by 2005)
	New store sizes and formats (Will 'showroom effects' affect store size or format? Will retailers be able to open in smaller towns previously uneconomic, because of a new 'extended market' and increased activity through returns?)

Table 15.23 Forecast risks and opportunities for conventional retail property
Source: adapted from Reynolds (2000c).

risks, for traditional retail property investments. We can categorize these risks and opportunities (Table 15.23)

15.3.2 Product–Service Migration

The extent and speed to which different categories of merchandise will migrate from conventional retail channels to electronic ones in the future is of course of particular interest to retailers (Cheeseborough and Teece, 1996; Rowley, 2000). The research conducted by the British Council of Shopping Centres (BCSC, 2001) suggests a risk spectrum for the conventional delivery of retail goods and services (Fig. 15.13) that puts

Figure 15.13 An electronic commerce risk spectrum for UK property (2000–2005) *Source:* BCSC (2001).

High risk	▶ Banks/financial services
	▶ Travel agents
Low–medium risk	▶ Secondary shops
	▶ Other shopping centres
	▶ Department/variety stores
	▶ Retail warehouses
	▶ Supermarkets
	▶ Neighbourhood/district centres
	▶ Large city-centre shopping centres
	▶ Out-of-town shopping centres
	▶ Prime shops

banks and travel agents most at risk and prime shops and out-of-town shopping centres least at risk. In a typical town, they report that some 16.5 per cent of space is in the threatened categories.

So how do retailers determine which of their products and services are likely to be most affected by the growth of electronic commerce? One way might be to take de Kare-Silver's 'ES Test' (ES = electronic shopping), which seeks to provide a three-step process for identifying sectors at risk (de Kare-Silver, 2001). The test takes into account:

1 *Product characteristics*: the requirement for a product or service to be touched or trialled prior to purchase, from the physical to the virtual.
2 *Familiarity and confidence*: the degree of consumer recognition and trust already present.
3 *Consumer attributes*: the extent to which the consumer might want to make the purchase electronically, even if the product or service passes the first two tests.

Each of these steps is developed in further detail, but a simple scoring system is proposed to synthesize the evaluation along a linear scale. Table 15.24 illustrates a notional distribution of points by category.

Taking this a stage further, McGoldrick et al. (2001) have developed a checklist from the characteristics and requirements of specific purchase situations to assist retailers to determine products and services most at risk from on-line migration. They observe that: 'The simple axiom of understanding and satisfying customer needs can be easily forgotten in technology driven innovations.' The checklist used 25 variables to represent the most significant issues related to the shopping decision process. These were generated from a literature review, from qualitative analysis and discussion with senior retail executives. The checklist was administered to 1200 respondents to create product 'profiles'. The example in Fig. 15.14 shows the scores produced by prospective purchasers of grocery goods, compared to a microwave. Clear differences emerge in respect to, for example, shape and the requirement for independent information.

Sample products	1. Product characteristics (0–10)	2. Familiarity and confidence (0–10)	3. Consumer attributes (0–30)	Total out of 50
Basic grocery (e.g. branded cereals)	4	8	15	27
Basic household (e.g. branded cleaners)	8	8	15	31
Basic clothing (e.g. socks)	4	7	8	19
Drinks (e.g. branded beers)	4	8	15	27
Car insurance	10	5	8	23
Standing orders	10	6	15	31
Mortgages	10	1	4	15
Travel (e.g. airline tickets)	10	6	15	31
Hotels	7	6	8	21
Books	8	7	23	38

Table 15.24 Products with likely high ES potential scoring

Source: de Kare-Silver (2001).

Although a wide variety of goods and services are capable of being offered via electronic channels, there is nevertheless also general agreement that revenue and profitability from some categories will grow faster than others. Woodham-Smith (2001) distinguishes four groupings of product categories, based upon scale of gross profit and availability of supply:

> *High gross profit, high supply categories, such as travel where airlines, cross-border firms, and local outfits compete in every country, will see fierce battles that will leave only the biggest firms standing. High gross*

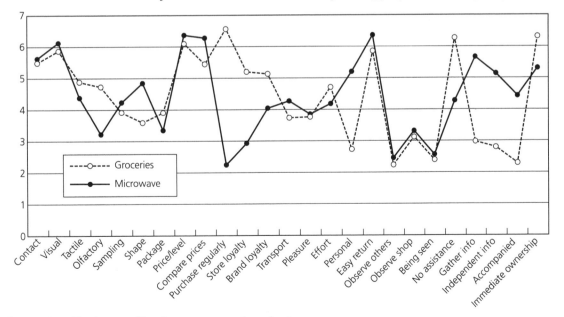

Figure 15.14 Product profiles for grocery goods and microwave ovens

Source: McGoldrick et al. (2001).

profit, low supply categories such as health and beauty contain Europe's unexploited opportunities, and the retrenchment of health and beauty pure plays has created a supply gap for multichannel retailers to grab 3 billion in gross profit through 2006. In the low gross profit, high supply segment—categories like music and books—too many retailers contend for too little gross profit, and continued consolidation and shifting business models will reign. Finally, categories such as jewelry in the low gross profit, low supply segment don't justify dedicated online stores. However, a dearth of competitors makes these categories prime range extensions for retailers (Woodham-Smith, 2001).

New opportunities clearly exist for retailers in capturing new revenue flows by exploiting the 'seamless' nature of the Internet medium. In the early days of the Internet, there was a proliferation of new entrants seeking to aggregate markets through the use of benefit, rather than geographical, segmentation. Mohanbir Sawhney called these businesses 'metamediaries' (Sawhney, 1999). His notion of the 'metamarket' took advantage of the Internet's more effective capability for linking and aggregating information and knowledge related to certain kinds of activities in a way that is not possible, or is more difficult, conventionally. We might see metamediary sites as specialized 'portals'.

Sawhney proposed that metamediaries:

▶ should offer a rich set of related activities that could be clustered together
▶ were important in terms of their demands on customers' time and their economic impact
▶ required customers to deal with many product and service providers across several industries
▶ were in markets containing integrated intermediaries who currently provide channel flows inefficiently and where the buying experience might be objectionable or uncomfortable.

We can think of plenty of examples of unpleasant or difficult buying experiences: car buying, or moving home spring to mind. But there are also some potentially new markets that can be created which satisfy Sawhney's criteria. These might include childbirth, weddings or holidays. In 2001, the UK Boots company launched its Wellbeing Network, a metasite seeking to cater for the needs of consumers in health care and products. Services ranged from 'Dr Foster', a medical advice service, through to digitally streamed programming. One assessment of the market for digital information goods opened up by the Internet foresaw such new potential sources of profitable growth for retailers. Bakos (2001) envisaged electronic channels creating new roles for content aggregating intermediaries bundling large numbers of information goods.

Sawhney's concepts of 'metamarkets' and 'metamediaries' are finally echoed in the more recent and more extensive analysis of futures for conventional retailing undertaken by Eagle et al. (2000):

Many retailers, building on their core merchandising and customer relations skills, may have the ability to pull all of these things together by offering a broad array of products and services to groups of customers defined by their common situation ... In effect, such companies are looking for new sources of profitable growth by shifting away from product lines and toward packages of inter-related products, services and information ... Ultimately, acting like a biological ecosystem that nourishes and supplies its denizens, retailers could fulfil the purchase needs of certain types of customers.

15.3.3 Hybrid Channel Marketing

The notion that the Web is going to replace bricks and mortar belongs in a fantasy novel. What the web may bring to retail is a more effective way to integrate distribution and marketing (Underhill, 2000).

Many contemporary commentators agree that the future is hybrid. Deloitte Consulting suggests struggling dot.coms have a significant amount of value 'in terms of information about consumers, their buying pattern, the technology and expertise', and that the traditional retailers can benefit from acquiring or building a partnership with the right dot.com (Deloitte Consulting, 2001). The data from webmergers.com (2001) is consistent with this view: conventional businesses, including retailers, are taking advantage of low dot.com valuations to acquire the information and customer assets of pure-play businesses. For example, the John Lewis Partnership acquired the UK operations of buy.com, one of the most prominent US e-tailers, in February 2001, for $4 million. The overall business had reported fourth-quarter losses of $27.4 million, had seen millions wiped off its share price and was forced to close its Australian operations. However, the UK operation had been adding new customers at the rate of 3000 per week. As a result, John Lewis will be able to get a much wider selection of its goods on line in a shorter space of time. At the beginning of this phase, Reynolds (2001) commented:

Established retailers are making efforts to become international multi-channel operators, partly by taking stakes in internet businesses. Such relationships are likely to proliferate as internet start-ups continue to stretch their resources. But are such moves overdue? Are they essentially defensive or offensive strategies? Investors' reactions suggest they will not be satisfied by rhetorical announcements. It is also clear that purely structural or organisational announcements in the absence of justifiable strategic objectives and milestones are likely to be viewed as inadequate. Taking a strategic approach to e-commerce is proving as problematic for the world's biggest retailers as for anyone else (Reynolds, 2001).

This kind of approach started to be referred to as 'bricks and clicks' by retailers and academics (Gulati and Garino, 2000). In terms of skills, no longer are surviving dot.com start-ups distinctive creatures which bear little relationship to their store-based ancestors. For example, Spector writes that Amazon.com threw away the business model that specified it needed no inventory to manage its book sales; it opened some of the world's biggest e-fulfilment centres and hired some of the best conventional logistics professionals, including some from Wal-Mart (Spector, 2000). In terms of branding, the most successful start-ups recognized the inherent power of established brands. For example, the UK's lastminute.com has used the partnership model to build relationships with established, mainstream brands such as British Airports Authority, Bass Hotels and Resorts and Sony Music.

Equally, no longer do conventional retailers disparage some of the tools and techniques of the new economy. Gulati and Garino cite the examples of Office Depot in integrating its website and physical stores to provide a 'seamless' retailing operation. Implicit in the hybrid marketing strategy of the UK Argos catalogue showroom retailer is that every product should be sold through every channel (Anon., 2001). Both Wal-Mart and Kmart, having experimented with spin-off websites managed out of Silicon Valley, have sought to bring these operations under their corporate wings and integrate some of the learning and skills into the core business. Many retailers from Europe, North America, Australia and the Far East have joined one of two major business-to-business electronic marketplaces (the worldwide retail exchange, WWRE, or GNX) which together constituted some $1.5 billion in buyer power. Much attention is beginning to focus upon organizational as well as marketing and business strategy. Reynolds (2000a) reported on the contrasting responses of investors and analysts to three particular examples: Kingfisher, Carrefour and Coles Myer. Moore (2000) believes that an integrated organizational model, while difficult, is increasingly a prerequisite of successful bricks-and-clicks operations.

Consumers, too, appreciate the seamless approach. A US National Retail Federation study based on some 5000 interviews in September 2000 found that 34 per cent of store shoppers surveyed looked for or purchased something in-store that they had seen on the retailers' website. Equally, some 27 per cent of store shoppers looked for or bought something on line that they had seen in the store (NRF, 2000).

The boundaries, therefore, between e-tailers and retailers are getting blurred from the point of view of all parties, not least consumers. As a result, it is not so much a matter of the new economy, or the old economy, but of the 'next economy' PricewaterhouseCoopers suggest that the next economy:

will be a synthesis of the operational excellence gleaned from the old economy, with the agility, transparency and speed of the new. The next economy will learn from the excesses of the past as companies are forced to focus, innovate and streamline their execution—in order to survive (PricewaterhouseCoopers, 2001).

SUMMARY

The growth of electronic channels to market in the form of electronic commerce will be a significant challenge to conventional forms of retailing, despite the collapse of investor interest in the so-called new economy. The pendulum has swung from rhetoric to disillusionment and is on its way back to a reality: it is possible for retailers, and others, to deliver value and convenience to consumers electronically, although perhaps not on the scale originally envisaged by the early commentators, at least in the short term.

Electronic commerce is a misleading and ambiguous term. Statisticians have developed relatively narrow definitions of what such activity entails but, in so doing, have ignored the many indirect effects of the Internet on retail sales through pre-purchase marketing and brand-building and post-purchase customer service, potentially leading to increased customer satisfaction and patronage. The interplay between a series of driving forces, technological, social, economic and regulatory, will determine the pace of change in the eventual adoption of e-commerce. Figure 15.15 offers a summary of driving forces, along with some areas of potential impact.

A key facilitator, the adoption of access technology, is still subject to much hyperbole, given that Internet penetration is still very much a phenomenon of the developed economies. Even across Europe, a 'patchwork quilt' of connectivity reduces the economies of scale in markets potentially available to retailers. Further, European e-commerce appears to be taking a different technical course from that in the USA, with broadband, interactive television and mobile platforms being much more evident in consumers' adoption patterns and some European consumers (notably from the UK) having a higher propensity to buy on line than a simplistic innovation-adoption curve would suggest.

Much of the early running in the development of electronic commerce was made by start-up businesses and conventional retailers were initially slow to react to the perceived competitive threat that such businesses posed. This has changed and, while there are always alternative routes to growth available to retailers, e-commerce is now more clearly on the agenda of the retail CEO. Indeed, there is some evidence to suggest that there are more e-commerce pioneers among retailers than in other sectors, but equally more e-commerce laggards, as companies make hard choices about investment.

Regulation can either help or hinder the growth of electronic commerce but, at present, retailers see regulation (particularly by European governments) as a potential obstacle to the growth of on-line revenues. Tariff, taxation and intellectual property policies lag Internet development, although the authorities are catching up. In the area of digitalized products: however, it remains to be seen to what extent legislative intervention can be effective in regulating peer-to-peer transmission of bootleg entertainment.

Retailing's mission in an electronic era remains fundamentally unchanged, despite these drivers, although who counts as a 'retailer' may well alter in the years ahead as a result. For example, it is clear that consumers shopping on line value convenience above price, just as they still do off line, so that 'location, location, location' has made an effortless transition into cyberspace. There is emerging agreement on

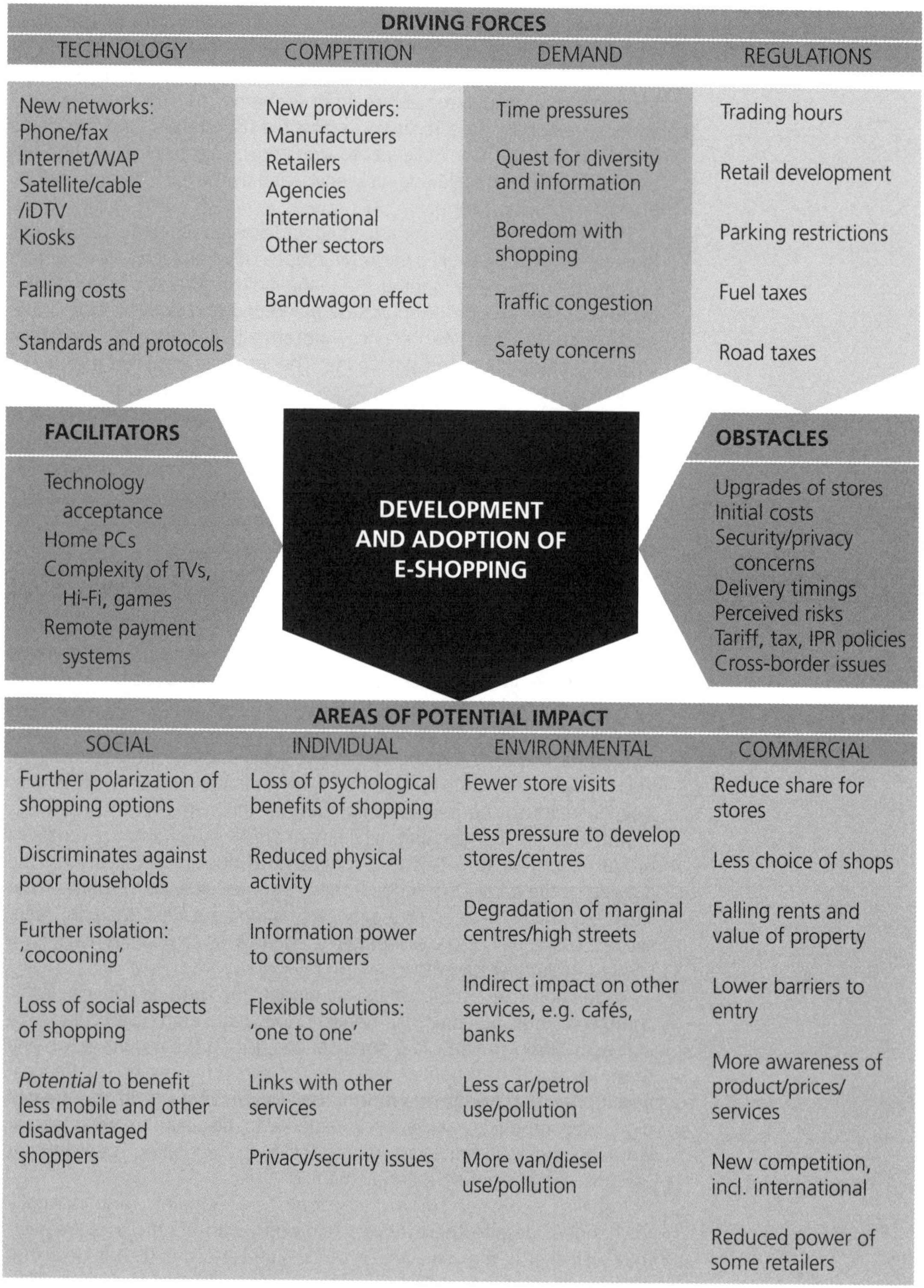

DRIVING FORCES			
TECHNOLOGY	COMPETITION	DEMAND	REGULATIONS
New networks: Phone/fax Internet/WAP Satellite/cable /iDTV Kiosks	New providers: Manufacturers Retailers Agencies International Other sectors	Time pressures Quest for diversity and information Boredom with shopping	Trading hours Retail development Parking restrictions
Falling costs	Bandwagon effect	Traffic congestion	Fuel taxes
Standards and protocols		Safety concerns	Road taxes

FACILITATORS		OBSTACLES
Technology acceptance Home PCs Complexity of TVs, Hi-Fi, games Remote payment systems	**DEVELOPMENT AND ADOPTION OF E-SHOPPING**	Upgrades of stores Initial costs Security/privacy concerns Delivery timings Perceived risks Tariff, tax, IPR policies Cross-border issues

AREAS OF POTENTIAL IMPACT			
SOCIAL	INDIVIDUAL	ENVIRONMENTAL	COMMERCIAL
Further polarization of shopping options	Loss of psychological benefits of shopping	Fewer store visits	Reduce share for stores
Discriminates against poor households	Reduced physical activity	Less pressure to develop stores/centres	Less choice of shops
Further isolation: 'cocooning'	Information power to consumers	Degradation of marginal centres/high streets	Falling rents and value of property
Loss of social aspects of shopping	Flexible solutions: 'one to one'	Indirect impact on other services, e.g. cafés, banks	Lower barriers to entry
Potential to benefit less mobile and other disadvantaged shoppers	Links with other services	Less car/petrol use/pollution	More awareness of product/prices/ services
	Privacy/security issues	More van/diesel use/pollution	New competition, incl. international
			Reduced power of some retailers

Figure 15.15 Driving forces and impacts of e-shopping
Source: adapted from McGoldrick (2000).

what makes for an efficient and effective site design to meet consumers' expectations in this respect. But new ways of thinking about the serendipitous behaviour of the on-line browser may be needed if retailers are to be able to more consistently attract the prospective shopper's attention.

The rhetoric of the efficient market and rational economic models of price as the ultimate determinant of consumer choice on line has been challenged, perhaps fatally so. In part, this may be a consequence of primitive and perhaps costly computer interfaces and early adopter motivations. But it is also a consequence of consumer irrationality and uncertainty. In an environment of greater choice, consumers plump for the brands they trust. The cheapest site does not always attract the most buyers. The most trusted site stands a better chance of attracting return visits and, ultimately, of becoming profitable, if it performs well. It may be easier for established brands to be trusted, but a transition for an established retail brand to an electronic channel is not always straightforward. Evidence shows that, in certain on-line categories, consumers hold even smaller brand portfolios in their heads than in conventional shopping activity.

Product-service mixes continue to evolve on line. The top-selling categories in most countries continue to be the 'obvious suspects', low-touch items, targets of purposive searches by consumers (books, software and entertainment). However, evidence is emerging of less obvious candidate categories, such as apparel, becoming popular in more mature on-line markets. A number of tools are available to help traditional retailers determine which categories are most at risk and to assist in the development of counter strategies. However, the boundaryless nature of the on-line medium makes it much easier for intermediaries (new or old) to develop gateways into aggregations of product and service, much more directly associated with consumer benefit segments than might be possible off line.

No other aspect of electronic commerce has been subject to more complaint by consumers than that of fulfilment. Early e-tailers neglected the distribution aspects of their businesses, to their cost. Contemporary debate centres around the identification of an appropriate operational design to deliver sustainable competitive advantage. There is now a much better understanding of the implication of different business models for distribution costs.

In examining e-tailing futures, we are challenged by the inadequacies of past forecasts and the inherent uncertainties of forecasting techniques. It may be that approaches centred on scenario planning techniques will yield more robust results. Most commentators agree that the future is hybrid; that the integration of bricks and mortar retailing and e-tailing is an inevitable consequence of consumer demand. Integration offers the opportunity to devise new marketing strategies which draw upon the strengths of all channels and platforms in reaching the consumer, while offsetting individual channel weaknesses. But while boundaries may be blurring and a future edition of this book may not need a separate e-tailing chapter as such, the roller-coaster ride of the last three years has thrown up exciting new opportunities for retail marketers.

REVIEW QUESTIONS

1 'Fast is good but smart is better' (Boston Consulting Group, 2000b). What were the main reasons for dot.com failure during 2000–01?

2 What are the key drivers of Internet growth? To what extent do they assist or obstruct the development of e-commerce?

3 Why is Internet penetration often described as a 'patchwork quilt'? What are the marketing implications of this?

4 Why do on-line consumers value convenience over price?

5 Do you agree with the assertion that Amazon.com is more like a traditional retailer than it claims to be?

6 Why does 'distribution matter'?

7 The economic rhetoric suggests that the Internet creates an efficient market. To what extent does observed consumer behaviour confound this rhetoric?

8 What do marketers really want to know about on-line consumers?

9 How might on-line businesses build consumer loyalty? To what extent might the strategies adopted differ from those practised off line?

10 What are the marketing implications of agent technology?

11 Why might conventional forecasting be inappropriate for examining e-commerce futures?

12 If the future is hybrid, does this mean that conventional retailers have 'won'?

REFERENCES

Agrawal, V., L.D. Arjona and R. Lemmens (2001) 'E-performance: the path to rational exuberance', *McKinsey Quarterly*, **1**, 30–43.

Ajzen, I. (1988) *Attitudes, Personality, and Behavior*, Dorsey Press, Chicago.

Alba, J., J. Lynch, B. Weitz, C. Janiszewski, R.Lutz, A. Sawer and S. Wood (1997) 'Interactive home shopping: consumer, retailer and manufacturer incentives to participate in electronic marketplaces', *Journal of Marketing*, **61** (3), 38–54.

Alsop, S. (2001) 'The tragedy of Webvan', *Fortune*, **144** (3), 52.

Anon. (2001) 'Argos cracks the multi-channel challenge', *Retail Automation*, **21** (3), 16–17.

Atkinson, R.D. (2001) 'Revenge of the disintermediated: how the middleman is fighting e-commerce and hurting consumers', *PPI Policy Report*, 26 January, Progressive Policy Institute, http://www.ppionline.org/documents/disintermediated.pdf

Bailey, J.P. (1998) *Electronic Commerce: Prices and Consumer Issues for Three Products: Books, Compact Discs and Software*, Internal Working Paper, OECD/GD(98)4, Paris.

Baker, W., M. Marn, and C. Zawada (2001) 'Price smarter on the net', *Harvard Business Review*, February, 122–127.

Bakos, Y. (2001) 'The emerging landscape for retail e-commerce', *Journal of Economic Perspectives*, **15** (1), 69–80.

Basu, K. (2000) 'E-branding or re-branding?', in *Moving to eBusiness*, L. Willcocks et al. (eds), Random House, London.

BBC News Online (2001) 'Online grocers fail to net rural pound', 7 August, http://news.bbc.co.uk/hi/english/uk/wales/newsid_1476000/1476669.stm

BCSC (2001) *Future Shock or E-Hype? The Impact of Online Shopping on UK Retail Property*, report prepared by the College of Estate Management, University of Reading, Reading.

Boston Consulting Group (2000a) *The Race for On-line Riches: eCommerce in Europe*, BCG, New York.

Boston Consulting Group (2000b) *Fast is Good, but Smart is Better*, BCG, New York.

Brache, A. and J. Webb (2000) 'The eight deadly assumptions of e-business', *Journal of Business Strategy*, **21** (3), 13–17.

Brynjolfsson, E. and M. Smith (2000) 'Frictionless commerce? A comparison of Internet and conventional retailers', *Management Science*, **46** (4), 563–585.

Burke, R.R. (1997) 'Do you see what I see? The future of virtual shopping', *Journal of the Academy of Marketing Science*, **25** (4), 352–360.

Byrne, S. (1999) Creating Internet-focused brand strategies. *Admap*, **34** (1), 36–38.

Cheeseborough, H. and D. Teece (1996) 'When is virtual virtuous?', *Harvard Business Review*, **74** (1), 65–72.

Chen, Q. and W.D. Wells (1999) 'Attitude toward the site', *Journal of Advertising Research*, **39** (5), 27–37.

Cheskin Research (1999) *eCommerce Trust Study*, Studio Archetype/Sapient, Cambridge, MA, January.

Chircu, A.M. and R.J. Kauffman (1999) 'Strategies for Internet middlemen in the intermediation disintermediation reintermediation cycle', *Electronic Markets*, **9** (2), 02/99, http://webfoot.csom.umn.edu/faculty/phds/achircu/ResearchWeb/ck_em_9_2_99.pdf#

Chircu, A.M., G.B. Davis and R. J. Kauffman (2000) 'Trust, expertise and e-commerce intermediary adoption', *Proceedings of the 2000 Americas Conference on Information Systems*, Long Beach, CA, 10–13 August.

Christensen, C.M. and R.S. Tedlow (2000) 'Patterns of disruption in retailing', *Harvard Business Review*, January–February, 42–45.

Competition Commission (2000) *Supermarkets. A Report on the Supply of Groceries from Multiple Stores in the United Kingdom*, Vols 1–3, Cm 4842, The Stationery Office, London.

Cooke, J.A. (2000) 'Clicks and mortar', *Logistics Management*, January, 39.

Consumers' Association (2001) 'E-tailers trailing behind', press release, http://www.which.net/whatsnew/pr/mar01/which/onlineshop.html

Coppel, J. (2000) 'E-commerce: impacts and policy challenges', *OECD Economics Department Working Papers 252*, ECO/WKP(2000)25, OECD, Paris.

Cornet, P., P. Milcent and P.-Y. Roussel (2000) 'From e-commerce to Euro-commerce', *McKinsey Quarterly*, **2** (Europe), 30–38.

Davies, R.L. and J. Reynolds (1988) *Teleshopping and Teleservices*, Longman, Harlow.

Davis, F.D., R.P. Bagozzi and P.R. Warshaw (1989) 'User acceptance of computer technology: a comparison of two theoretical models', *Management Science*, **35**, 982–1003.

De Chernatony, L. and M. McDonald (1998) *Creating Powerful Brands*, Butterworth-Heinemann, Oxford.

De Kare-Silver, M. (2001) *E-Shock: The New Rules*, Palgrave, Basingstoke.

Degeratu, A., A. Rangaswamy and J. Wu (1998) 'Consumer choice behaviour in online and regular stores: the effects of brand name, price and other search attributes', paper presented at Marketing Science and the Internet, INFORMS College on Marketing Mini-Conference. Cambridge, MA, 6–8 March.

Degeratu, A.M., A. Rangaswamy and J. Wu (2000) 'Consumer choice behaviour in online and traditional supermarkets: the effects of brand name, price and other search attributes', *International Journal of Research in Marketing*, **17** (1), 55–78.

Deighton, J. (1997) 'Commentary on "Exploring the implications of the Internet for consumer marketing"', *Journal of the Academy of Marketing Science*, **25** (4), 347–351.

Deloitte Consulting (2001) *The Dot.com Aftermarket: Where Does the Value Lie and How Can It Be Captured?*, Deloite Consulting, London, January.

Department of Trade and Industry (1998) *Future Consumer Needs*, Technology Foresight, Retail and Consumer Services Panel/Oxford Institute of Retail Management.

Department of Trade and Industry (2000a) *Information Relationships Report*, ICM Foresight Panel, DTI, London.

Department of Trade and Industry (2000b) *Clicks and Mortar: the new store fronts*, Technology Foresight, Retail & Consumer Services Panel, London.

Department of Trade and Industry (2000c) @ *Your Service. Future Models of Retail Logistics*, Foresight Retail Logistics Task Force Consultation Paper, DTI, London.

Department of Trade and Industry (2000d) 'E-tailing: a clockwork orange' in, *Retailing 2010*, Technology Foresight, Retail and Consumer Services Panel, London.

Distributive Industry Training Board (1980) *Political, Social, Economic and Technological Issues, their Probable Effects on the UK Distributive Industry 1980–1995 (Environmental Scan)*, DITB, Manchester.

Doerr, J. (2000) 'Mercenaries vs. missionaries: John Doerr sees two kinds of Internet entrepreneurs' Knowledge@Wharton, 13 April, http://knowledge.wharton.upenn.edu/articles.cfm?catid=12&articleid=170

Durlacher (2000) *Mobile Commerce Report*, July, Durlacher Research, http://www.durlacher.co.uk/fr-research-reps.htm

Dykema, E.B. (2000) Online Retail's Ripple Effect, *Forrester Research Report*, Forrester Research Inc., Cambridge, MA, September.

Eagle, J.S., E.E. Joseph and E.C. Lempres (2000) 'From products to ecosystems: retail 2010', *McKinsey Quarterly*, **4**, 108–115.

Eastlick, M.A., and S. Lotz, (1999) Profiling potential adopters and non-adopters of an interactive electronic shopping medium, *International Journal of Retail & Distribution Management*, **27** (6), 209–223.

eBay (n.d.) http://pages.ebay.com/community/aboutebay/overview/trust.html.

ECSoft (2000) 'UK consumer attitudes to eCommerce', unpublished study.

Enos, L. (2001) 'Internet flower sites fail Mother's Day test', *eCommerceTimes.com*, 15 May, http://www.ecommercetimes.com/perl/story/?id=9727.

Ernst & Young LLP. (1999) *The Second Ernst & Young Internet Shopping Study: The Digital Channel Continues to Gather Steam*, Ernst & Young LLP/National Retail Federation, New York.

Ernst & Young (2001a) 'Tax advantages in global online retailing', *Global Online Retailing Report*, Ernst & Young, New York.

Ernst & Young (2001b) *Global Online Retailing Report 2001*, Ernst & Young, New York.

Ernst & Young (2001c), 'Kelkoo and Ernst & Young launches Europe's first e-commerce "Brandometer"', press release, July, http://www.ey.com/GLOBAL/gcr.nsf/International/Brandometer_-_Release_-_Ernst_&_Young

Estates Gazette (1999) 'Agents' reports split over the Net's impact on retail', *Estates Gazette*, 12 June, 40.

Feldman, S. and E. Yu (1999) 'Intelligent agents: a primer', *Searcher*, **7** (9), October, http://www.infotoday.com/searcher/oct99/feldman+yu.htm

Forrester Research (2000) '*Getting consumers beyond the home page*', unpublished research.

Gatignon, H. and T.S. Robertson (1985) 'A prepositional inventory for new diffusion research', *Journal of Consumer Research*, **11**, 849–67.

Geirland, J. and E. Sonesh-Kedar (1998),'What is this thing called flow? Think nirvana on the Web', *Los Angeles Times*, 6 July.

Gomes-Casseres, B. (1994) 'Group versus group: how alliance networks compete', *Harvard Business Review*, **72** (July–August), 62.

Gulati, R. and J. Garino (2000) 'Get the right mix of bricks and clicks', *Harvard Business Review*, **78** (3), 107–114.

Hall, M. (2000) The nature of brands in the new era. *Admap*, **35** (4), 22 –26.

Hardesty, D. (2001) 'EU tries again for laws to tax downloads', *E-Commerce Tax News*, 24 June, http://www.ecommercetax.com/doc/062401.htm

Helft, M. (2001) 'Reality check, aisle 5', *The Industry Standard*, 30 April.

Higgins, K. (2001) 'Top of mind 2001', *Food Business News*, **22** (January), CIES.

Hill, T. (1993) *Manufacturing Strategy*, Macmillan, London.

Hoque, A.Y. and G.L. Lohse (1999) 'An information search cost perspective for designing interfaces for electronic commerce', *Journal of Marketing Research*, **36** (3), 387–94.

IGD (2001) *European Grocery Retailing*, Institute of Grocery Distribution, Watford.

Investec Henderson Crosthwaite (2000) 'Food retailers: can they deliver?', *Food and Drug Retailers Analyst Report*, 11 January.

Jarvenpaa, S.L. and P.A. Todd (1997) 'Consumer reactions to electronic shopping on the World Wide Web', *International Journal of Electronic Commerce*, **1** (2), 59–88.

Jevons, C. and M. Gabbott (2000) 'Trust, brand equity and brand reality in Internet business relationships: an interdisciplinary approach', *Journal of Marketing Management*, **16**, 619–634.

Jupiter MMXI (2001) *'By 2005, half of all UK households will be connected to the Internet from their TV'*, press release, 17 July, http://uk.jupitermmxi.com/press/releases/20010717.jsp

Kahn, H. and A.J. Wiener (1967) *The Year 2000. A Framework of Speculation on the Next Thirty-Three Years*, Macmillan, New York.

Kämäräinen, V., J. Småros, T. Jaakola and J. Holström (2001) 'Cost-effectiveness in the e-grocery business', *International Journal of Retail & Distribution Management*, **29** (1), 41–48.

Keeling, K., D. Fowler, P. McGoldrick and L. Macaulay (2001a) 'TV home banking and the technology acceptance model: intrinsic motivation and gender issues', *Proceedings of Interact '01; IFIP TC, 13th International Conference on Human-Computer Interaction*. July, Tokyo, 84–91.

Keeling, K., L Macaulay, D. Fowler, P. McGoldrick and K. Vassilopoulou (2001b) 'Electronic kiosk provision of public information: toward understanding and quantifying facilitators and barriers of use', *Proceedings of HCI 2001, 9th International Conference on Human–Computer Interaction*, August, New Orleans, 680–684.

Keeling, K., K. Vassilopoulou, L.A. Macaulay and P. McGoldrick (2001c) 'Innovation through e-commerce: building motivational websites: a brand too far?', *International Journal of New Product Development and Innovation Management*, **2** (4), 309–324.

Kehoe, C.F. (2000) 'M-commerce: advantage, Europe', *McKinsey Quarterly*, **2** (Europe), 43–45.

Kephart, J.O., and Greenwald, A.R. (2001) http://www.cs.brown.edu/people/amygreen/publications.html

KPMG (1996) *The Internet: Its Potential and Use by European Retailers*, KPMG/OXIRM, London/Oxford.

KPMG (1997) *Home Shopping across Europe: Experiences and Opportunities*, KPMG/OXIRM, London/Oxford.

KPMG (2001) *The Quiet Revolution. A Report on the State of E-business in the UK by the CBI and MPMG Consulting*, CBI/KPMG, London.

Kuttner, R. (1998) 'The net: a market too perfect for profits', *Business Week*, 11 May, 20.

Lederer, A.L., D.J. Maupin, M.P. Sena and Y. Zhuang (2000) 'The technology acceptance model and the World Wide Web', *Decision Support Systems*, **29** (3), 269–282.

Lee, B. and R.S. Lee (1995) 'How and why people watch TV: implications for the future of interactive television', *Journal of Advertising Research*, **35** (6), 9–18.

Leer, A. (1995) *It's a Wired World*, FT Pitman, London.

Lin, C.A. (1999) 'Online-service adoption likelihood', *Journal of Advertising Research*, March–April, 79–89.

Lin, J.C., and H. Lu (1998), 'Towards an understanding of the behavioural intention to use a web site', *International Journal of Information Management*, **20**, 197–208.

Lindquist, J.D. (1974) 'Meaning of image', *Journal of Retailing*, **50** (4), 29–38.

Lohse, G. and P. Spiller (1998) 'Quantifying the effect of user interface design features on cyberstore traffic and sales', in *CHI' 98 Conference Proceedings*, J. Coutaz and J. Karat (eds), ACM Press, Los Alamitos, CA.

Maes, P. (1998) 'Software agents and the future of electronic commerce', *Tutorial on Agents and Electronic Commerce*, MIT, Boston, MA, http://pattie.www.media.mit.edu/people/pattie/ECOM/

Management Horizons Europe (1999) *Comparative Retail Costs*, a report sponsored by the British Brands Group, MHE/Horizon Retail Design and Strategy, London.

Matthews, R. (1997) 'Food distribution 2010: four futures', *Progressive Grocer*, **76** (9), 24.

Mayer, M.D., W.A. Mohn and C. Zabbal (2001) 'PCs vs TVs', *McKinsey Quarterly*, **3**, 130–141.

McGoldrick, P. (2000) 'The driving forces and the impacts of e-tailing', in *Personnel Perspectives on 2010*, DTI (ed.), DTI Foresight, London, pp. 34–38.

McGoldrick, P.J., K.A. Keeling and A. Toelke (2001) 'Product migratability to electronic shopping channels', *Proceedings of World Marketing Congress*, Academy of Marketing Science, Cardiff.

Merrill Lynch (1999) 'Real estate. Minding the store: retailing will influence real estate', in *eCommerce*, Merrill Lynch & Co. (eds), Global Securities Research and Economics Group, Merrill Lynch & Co., New York.

Mondex International (2001) *'Internet businesses set to reap millions'*, press release, 18 May.

Moon, J.W. and Y.G. Kim, (2001) Extending the TAM for a World-Wide-Web context *Information and Management*, **38** (4), 217–230.

Moore, K. (2000) 'Organising for eBusiness', in *Moving to eBusiness*, C. Sauer and L. Willcocks (eds), Random House, London.

Moorthy, S., B.T. Ratchford, and D. Talukdar (1997) 'Consumer information search revisited: theory and empirical analysis', *Journal of Consumer Research*, **23** (4), 263–77.

Morgan Stanley Dean Witter (2000) *Tesco. Home Shopping: The E in Tesco*, Equity Research Europe, 23 February, MSDW, London.

Morgan Stanley Dean Witter (2001) 'A look at global TMT market status and internet user/usage propensity', *Internet: New Media and eCommerce and PC Software Industry Report*, Global Equity Research, 3 January, MSDW, New York, USA.

Morganosky, M. (1997) 'Research note. Retailing and the Internet: a perspective on the top 100 US retailers', *International Journal of Retail and Distribution Management*, **25** (11), 372–377.

Morganosky, M.A. and B.J. Cude (2000) 'Consumer response to online grocery shopping', *International Journal of Retail & Distribution Management*, **28** (1), 17–26.

Murphy, R. (1998) 'The Internet: a viable strategy for fashion retail marketing?', *Journal of Fashion Marketing and Management*, **2** (3), 209–216.

National Consumers' Council (2000) *E-commerce and consumer protection*, NCC, London.

NetValue (2001) 'NetValue study on US and European Internet usage', press release, 23 February, http://www.netvalue.com/corp/presse/index_frame.htm?fichier=cp0022.htm

Newman, A. (1999) 'The impact of information technology on branding in financial services', *Journal of Brand Management*, **6** (4), 225 –231.

Novak, T.P., and D.L. Hoffman (1996) 'Marketing in hypermedia computer-mediated environments: conceptual foundations', *Journal of Marketing*, **60** (3), 50–68.

Novak, T.P., and D.L. Hoffman (1997) 'A new marketing paradigm for electronic commerce', *The Information Society*, special issue on electronic commerce, 13 (January–March), 43–54.

Novak, T.P., D.L. Hoffman and Y.F. Yung (2000) 'Measuring the customer experience in online environments: a structural modeling approach', *Marketing Science*, **19** (1), 22–42.

NRF (2000) *Channel Surfing: Measuring Multi-Channel Shopping*, National Retail Federation, New York.

Ody, P. (1998) *Non-Store Retailing. Exploiting Interactive Media and Electronic Commerce*, FT Retail and Consumer, London.

OECD (1998) *The Economic and Social Impact of Electronic Commerce*, OECD, Paris.

OECD (2000) *E-Commerce: Impacts and Policy Challenges*, ECO/WKP(2000)25, OECD, Paris.

OECD (2001) 'OECD progresses towards achieving an international consensus on the tax treatment of e-commerce', press release, 12 February, http://www.oecd.int/media/release/nw01-15a.htm

Office for National Statistics (2001) *E-Commerce Inquiry into Business 2000*, http://www.statistics.gov.uk/themes/economy/Articles/downloads/E_Commerce_Inquiry_to_business_2000.pdf

Owens, J. (2000) *Taxation in the Wired World*, OECD, Paris.

OXIRM (Oxford Institute of Retail Management) (2001) Marketspace website, http://mww.temp.ox.ac.uk/marketspace/mcsi.htm.

Pastrick, G. (1997) 'Secrets of great site design', *Internet User*, Fall, 80–87.

Peterson, R.A., S. Balasubramanian and B.J. Bronnenberg (1997) 'Exploring the implications of the Internet for consumer marketing', *Journal of the Academy of Marketing Science*, **25** (Fall), 329–46.

Porter, M.E. (2001) 'Strategy and the Internet', *Harvard Business Review*, **79** (3), 63–78.

Priceline.com (2001) '*Priceline.com reports profitability and record revenue for 2nd quarter 2001*', press release, 31 July, http://www.corporate-ir.net/ireye/ir_site.zhtml?ticker=pcln&script=410&layout=-6&item_id=196457

PricewaterhouseCoopers (2001) 'The next economy', *Retail and Consumer Worlds*, **38** (July), 1.

Priluck, R. (2001) 'The effect of Priceline.com on the grocery industry', *International Journal of Retail and Distribution Management*, **29** (3), 127–134.

Punakivi, M. and J. Saranen (2001) 'Identifying the success factors in e-grocery home delivery', *International Journal of Retail & Distribution Management*, **28** (4), 156–163.

Reynolds, J. (1998) 'Opportunities for electronic commerce', *European Retail Digest*, **18** (June), 5–9.

Reynolds, J. (1999) 'Electronic commerce: a discussion paper', prepared for *Commerce 99: Seminar on Distributive Trades in Europe*, Eurostat and Enterprise DG, Brussels, 22–23 November.

Reynolds, J. (2000a) 'eCommerce: a critical review', *International Journal of Retail & Distribution Management*, special issue **28** (10), 417–444.

Reynolds, J. (2000b) 'Retailing on the Net: I'm dreaming of an e-Christmas', *International Journal of Retail & Distribution Management*, **28** (2/3), 107–108.

Reynolds, J. (2000c) 'Retailing on the Net: understanding the effects of eCommerce on retail property and location', *International Journal of Retail & Distribution Management*, **28** (1), 46–47.

Reynolds, J. (2001) 'Retailing wakes up late to global ambitions', *Mastering Management 2.0*, FT/Prentice-Hall, London.

Rogers, E.M. (1962) *Diffusion of Innovations*, The Free Press, New York.

Rogers, E. M. (1995) *Diffusion of Innovations*, 4th edn, The Free Press, New York.

Rosenberg, L.J. and E.C. Hirschman (1980) 'Retailing without stores', *Harvard Business Review*, **58** (4), 103–112.

Rowley, J. (2000) 'Product search in e-shopping: a review and research propositions', *Journal of Consumer Marketing*, **17** (1), 20–35.

Rubin, A.M. (1984) 'Ritualized and instrumental television viewing', *Journal of Communication*, **34** (3), 67–75.

Sawhney, M. (1999) 'The longest mile', *Business 2.0*, December, 235–244.

Shugan, S.M. (1980) 'The cost of thinking', *Journal of Consumer Research*, **7** (2), 99–111.

Sinha, I. (2000) 'The Net's real threat to prices and brands', *Harvard Business Review*, **78** (March–April), 43–48.

Skapinker, M. (2000) Inside track—California scheming—profile Gary Hamel, *Financial Times*, 24 April, 12.

Smith, M.D., J. Bailey and E. Brynjolfsson (1999) 'Understanding digital markets', in *Understanding the Digital Economy*, E. Brynjolfsson and B. Kahin (eds), MIT Press, Boston, MA.

Spector, R. (2000) *Amazon.com. Get Rich Fast*, Random House, London.

Stafford, N. (2001) 'Net taxes hit brick wall in Europe', *Newsbytes*, 7 June, http://www.newsbytes.com/news/01/166606.html

Steckel, J.H. (2000) 'On-line shopping: how many will come to the party? And when will they get there?', *Working Paper, Stern School of Business*, New York University, New York.

Strategy Analytics (2001) *Interactive Digital Television: Worldwide Market Forecasts*, Strategy Analytics, Boston, MA.

Szymanski, D.M. and R.T. Hise (2000) 'e-Satisfaction: an initial examination', *Journal of Retailing*, **76** (3), 309–322.

Thompson, M. and R. Rifredi (1996) 'Digital TV–Internet linkup faces obstacles', *Electronic Engineering Times*, 6 May, 40.

Tollington, T. and P. Wachter (2001) 'ABC/TA for internet retail shopping', *International Journal of Retail & Distribution Management*, **29** (4), 149–155.

Underhill, P. (2000) *Why We Buy: The Science of Shopping*, 2nd edn, Texere, New York.

UPS (2000a) 'UPS reaches online tracking milestone; UPS airlines ready for peak air day on Thursday', press release, http://pressroom.ups.com/pressreleases/0,1014,,00.html

UPS (2000b) 'Santa's UPS supply chain; year-round planning, technology and unmatched global network delivers more than 325 million holiday packages', November, 27, http://www.ups.com.

US Bureau of the Census (2001) 'Estimated quarterly retail e-commerce sales', *US Department of Commerce News*, 16 May, http://www.census.gov/mrts/www/current.html

Vassilopoulou, K., K. Keeling, L. Macaulay and P. McGoldrick (2001) 'Measuring purchasing intention for Internet retail sites against usability attributes', *Proceedings of Interact '01; IFIP TC, 13th International Conference on Human-Computer Interaction*, July, Tokyo, 76–83.

Vijayasarathy, L.R. and J.M. Jones (2000) 'Print and Internet catalog shopping: assessing attitudes and intentions'. *Internet Research*, **10** (3), 191–202.

Wade, N. and S.A. McKechnie (1999) 'The impact of digital television: will it change our shopping habits?', *Journal of Marketing Communications*, **5**, 71–84

Which? (2001) 'Meals on wheels', *Which?*, March, 46–48.

Whittle, S. (2000) 'Score with your Web site' *Computing*, **27**, 38–41.

Wilson-Jeanselme, M. (2001) 'Grocery retailing on the Internet: the leaky bucket theory', *European Retail Digest*, **30** (June), 9–12.

Woodham-Smith, J. (2001) *Europe's Online Retail Profits*, June, Forrester Research, Cambridge, MA.

www.webmergers.com (2001) Mid-Year M&A Report, http://www.webmergers.com/editorial/article.php?id=38

Yankee Group (2001) *Look Out Internet, Here Comes ITV*, Yankee Group, Boston, MA.

NAME **INDEX**

SUBJECT **INDEX**